W9-BUE-984

EIGHTH EDITION

Essentials of Human Communication

Joseph A. DeVito

Hunter College of the City University of New York

PEARSON

Boston   Columbus   Indianapolis   New York   San Francisco   Upper Saddle River
Amsterdam   Cape Town   Dubai   London   Madrid   Milan   Munich   Paris   Montreal   Toronto
Delhi   Mexico City   São Paulo   Sydney   Hong Kong   Seoul   Singapore   Taipei   Tokyo

Availability
This text is available in a variety of formats—digital and print. Check
your favorite digital provider for your etext, including CourseSmart,
MyCommunicationLab, Kindle, Nook, and more. To learn more
about our programs, pricing options and customization, visit

www.pearsonhighered.com

Editorial Director: Craig Campanella
Publisher: Karon Bowers
Senior Acquisitions Editor: Melissa Mashburn
Editorial Assistant: Megan Hermida
Director of Development: Sharon Geary
Senior Development Editor: Carol Alper
Director of Marketing: Brandy Dawson
Senior Marketing Manager: Blair Zoe Tuckman
Marketing Assistant: Cristina Liva
Marketing Coordinator: Theresa Graziano
Senior Managing Editor: Linda Mihatov Behrens
Project Manager: Raegan Keida Heerema
Senior Operations Supervisor: Mary Fischer

Operations Specialist: Mary Ann Gloriande
Cover Art Director: Anne Bonnano Nieglos
Cover Design: Nancy Sacks
Director of Digital Media: Brian Hyland
Senior Digital Editor: Paul DeLuca
Digital Media Editor: Lisa Dotson
Digital Media Project Manager: Michael Granger
Full-Service Project Management and Composition: Cenveo® Publishers Services
Printer/Binder: R R Donnelley-Jefferson City
Cover Printer: Lehigh-Phoenix Color/Hagerstown

Library of Congress Control Number: 2012954840

Credits and acknowledgments borrowed from other sources and reproduced, with permission, in this textbook appear on appropriate page within text (or on page 357).

10 9 8 7 6 5 4 3 2 1

Student Edition:
ISBN-13: 978-0-205-93066-1
ISBN-10: 0-205-93066-2

Instructor's Review Copy:
ISBN-13: 978-0-205-93072-2
ISBN-10: 0-205-93072-7

À la Carte:
ISBN-13: 978-0-205-93075-3
ISBN-10: 0-205-93075-1

www.pearsonhighered.com

BRIEF CONTENTS

PART ONE Foundations of Human Communication 1

PART TWO Interpersonal and Small Group Communication *119*

PART THREE Public Speaking *207*

The Interviewing Guidebook

A separate book focusing on informative and employment interviews is available for packaging with this book or for purchase separately.

CONTENTS

PART ONE   Foundations of Human Communication   *1*

1 The Essentials of Human Communication   *1*

2 Perception of Self and Others   *24*

PART TWO　Interpersonal And Small Group Communication　119

6
Interpersonal Communication
and Conversation　119

7
Interpersonal Relationships　136

PART THREE Public Speaking *207*

11 Public Speaking Preparation (Steps 1–6) *207*

12 Public Speaking Preparation (Steps 7–10) *236*

13 The Informative Speech 262

14 The Persuasive Speech 286

THE INTERVIEWING GUIDEBOOK

This separate book focuses on informative and employment interviews and is available to be packaged with the text or purchased separately.

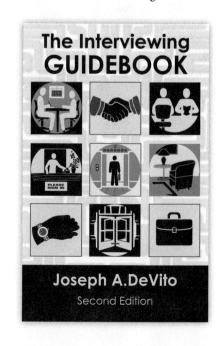

The Interviewing
GUIDEBOOK

Joseph A. DeVito
Second Edition

SPECIALIZED CONTENTS

SELF TESTS

These self-assessment tests will help you bring to awareness, analyze, and improve your communication patterns and strategies.

▶ VIDEO CHOICE POINT

These boxes provide suggestions for listening more effectively in a wide variety of communication situations. At the same time these discussions will remind you that communication can never occur without listening.

COMMUNICATING ETHICALLY

These sections examine ethical issues and dilemmas to illustrate the close connection between ethics and communication, to encourage you to think about the ethical implications of your messages, and to stimulate you to formulate your own code of ethical communication.

PUBLIC SPEAKING SAMPLE ASSISTANT

These sample speeches and outlines, along with their annotations, will assist you in preparing and outlining your own speeches.

SKILL DEVELOPMENT EXPERIENCES

These exercises are designed to help you work actively with the skills and applications discussed in the text and to help you make these skills a part of your everyday communication behavior.

WELCOME TO

Essentials of Human Communication

It's a pleasure to write a preface to this eighth edition of *Essentials of Human Communication*. This book continues to be responsive to the need for a brief, interesting, but serious text that emphasizes the *essential* skills of human communication, including interpersonal communication, small group communication, and public speaking. I continue to try my best to follow Einstein's directive that "things should be made as simple as possible, but not simpler." This new, eighth-edition remains true to that central purpose. The overriding theme and goal of this textbook is to help you build greater competence in interpersonal, group, and public communication. You should emerge from this course a more effective interpersonal communicator, group member and leader, and public speaker.

This eighth edition of *Essentials of Human Communication* is divided into three parts: Part One, Foundations of Human Communication, includes five chapters that cover the concepts and principles of human communication: the communication process, the self and perception, listening, verbal messages, and nonverbal messages. Part Two, Interpersonal and Small Group Communication, also includes five chapters; chapters 6, 7, and 8 cover the concepts and skills of interpersonal communication and conversation, interpersonal relationships, and managing interpersonal conflict and chapters 9 and 10 focus on small group interaction, the types of small groups, and the principles of effective group membership and leadership. Part Three, Public Speaking (Chapters 11–14), explains the nature of public speaking and the principles and skills for preparing and presenting effective informative and persuasive speeches.

What's New in the Eighth Edition?

NEW and ENHANCED CONTENT and THEMES reflect the latest research in human communication:

- New discussions throughout the book focus on how all communication forms incorporate the varied **social media** that are now an essential part of our everyday lives.
- Additional attention to the importance of effective **workplace** communication in all communication contexts includes a wide variety of examples.
- The newest research on the role of **culture** in communication in a world defined by cultural diversity is emphasized
- Because of the importance of **choice** throughout all your communication interactions, we've made the concept of choice a recurring theme in this new edition.
  [See page xviii to see how these themes fit into the book's organization as a whole.]

NEW LEARNING AIDS help you learn more efficiently and prepare for exams:

- **Learning objectives** now highlight the major concepts of the chapter through knowledge, application, and problem solving. At the end of each major section a series of **questions** ask you to test yourself to see if you can, in fact, accomplish the objectives for that section.

- **Messages in the Media** introduces each chapter with a photo from a television program that deals with the major topics of the chapter. **Messages in the Media: Wrap Up** at the end of each chapter invites you to reconsider that television program and similar programs in light of what you learned in the chapter.

- **ViewPoints** photos and captions ask you to consider a variety of communication issues, many of which are research based and/or focus on the themes of social media, the workplace, and culture.

- **Integrated Media** icons point you to a wealth of study tools, additional exercises including "Explore" activities, and video clips that are available on MyCommunicationLab (access code required).

- **QR (Quick Response) Codes** take you to specific posts on *The Communication Blog* where you can read more about a topic, read the comments of others, and post your own comments.

- New **examples** and four new **speeches** (two poorly constructed and two excellent) appear in each of the four public speaking chapters.

Additional details about the chapter-by-chapter changes we've made in this edition my be found in our e-Catalog at **www.pearsonhighered.com/communication.**

Understanding Essential Content and Themes

All communication forms—interpersonal, small group, and public—incorporate the varied **social media** that are now an essential part of our everyday lives. And so, to take just one example, the definition of listening—long defined as the reception of auditory signals—is redefined to include the reading of social media messages. The reasoning is simply that if posting on Facebook and Google+ are examples of communication (which they surely are) then the reading of these messages must also be part of communication and seems to fit most logically with listening. The QR (Quick Response) codes that appear throughout the text will take you to *The Communication Blog* where you can explore additional topics, read the comments of others, and comment on the posts yourself. This too is listening.

In *Essentials of Human Communication,* the crucial role that **culture** plays in our communication experiences is a recurring theme. You're living in a world defined by cultural diversity, where you interact with people differing in affectional orientation, socioeconomic position, race, religion, and nationality. Culture and cultural differences are always influential in communication. For this reason, this text fully integrates culture into every chapter. Topics covered include:

- culture and communication, the importance of culture, the dimensions of cultural differences, the aim of a cultural perspective, and ethnic identity and ethnocentrism (Chapter 1).

- cultural teachings in self-concept formation, increasing cultural sensitivity, stereotyping, and self-disclosure and culture (Chapter 2).

- the influences of culture and gender on listening (Chapter 3).

- gender and cultural differences in directness and politeness; cultural rules in verbal communication; sexism, heterosexism, racism, and ageism; and cultural identifiers (Chapter 4).

- cultural differences in nonverbal communication, most notably facial expressions, colors, touch, silence, and time orientation (Chapter 5).

- the role and influence of culture and gender in conversation (Chapter 6).

- cultural and gender differences in friendship, love, and family relationships (Chapter 7).

- gender and cultural influences on conflict and conflict management; cultural differences in face-enhancing and face-attacking strategies (Chapter 8).

- small group culture and the nature and importance of group and cultural norms in small group communication; high- and low-context cultures (Chapter 9).

- The role of culture in small group membership and leadership; cultural differences between individual and collective orientations and high- and low-power distances (Chapter 10).
- The role of culture in speech topics; guidelines to help public speakers avoid taboo topics when addressing culturally varied audiences; cultural factors in audience analysis (Chapter 11).
- cultural considerations in the language of public speaking, culture shock, and cultural sensitivity in speech criticism (Chapter 12).
- cultural sensitivity in selecting supporting materials (Chapter 13).
- Adapting to the culture (collectivist, high-power distance, uncertainty avoidance, and long-term orientation) of the audience; the impact of cultural differences on credibility appeals (Chapter 14).

In addition, many of the interior photos ViewPoints and the Communication Choice Points focus on culture.

VIEWPOINTS

Your Public Messages

Will knowing that some undergraduate and graduate admissions offices and potential employers may examine your postings on sites such as MySpace or Facebook influence what you write? For example, do you avoid posting opinions that might be viewed negatively by schools or employers? Do you deliberately post items that you want schools or employers to find?

Communication Choice Point

Misusing Cultural Identifiers

During a conversation a group of classmates all use negative self-reference terms. Trying to be one of the group, you too use these terms—but almost immediately realize that the linguistic privilege allowing insiders to use self-derogatory names does not apply to outsiders (i.e., you). You don't want anyone to think that you normally talk this way. *How can you try to reverse their impressions or at least minimize their negativity?*

Effective human communication is as important in the **workplace** as it is in any part of your life. Workplace material includes frequent examples, illustrations, and photo ViewPoints and discussions of a variety of clearly workplace related topics such as workplace messages, values in the workplace as seen by long- and short-term oriented executives, emotions at work, romantic relationships in the workplace, and workplace conflict.

A separate booklet, *The Interviewing Guidebook,* focusing on informative and employment interviews, is available for packaging with this book or for purchase separately.

Throughout your communication interactions, you'll need to make **choices** between saying one thing or another, between sending an e-mail or calling on the phone, between being supportive or critical, and so on. Because of the central importance of choice, Communication Choice Points (brief scenarios placed in the margins) invite you to analyze your choices for communicating.

In addition, a Video Choice Point box appears in each chapter inviting you to watch a video related to the chapter contents and to examine effective and ineffective choices that the actors use in a variety of communication situations.

Because the messages you use have effects on others, they also have ethical implications. As such, **ethics** receives focused attention throughout the text. Chapter 1

VIEWPOINTS

Group Norms

What norms govern your class in human communication? What norms govern your family? What norms govern your place of work? Do you have any difficulty with these norms?

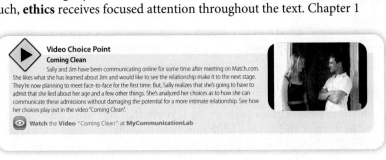

Video Choice Point

Coming Clean

Sally and Jim have been communicating online for some time after meeting on Match.com. She likes what he has learned about Jim and would like to see the relationship make it to the next stage. They're now planning to meet face-to-face for the first time. But, Sally realizes that she's going to have to admit that she lied about her age and a few other things. She's analyzed her choices as to how she can communicate these admissions without damaging the potential for a more intimate relationship. See how her choices play out in the video "Coming Clean".

Watch the **Video** "Coming Clean" at **MyCommunicationLab**

introduces ethics as a foundation concept in all forms of communication, an essential part of communication competence. In all remaining chapters, *Communicating Ethically* boxes highlight varied communication situations and ask you to apply ethical principles to various scenarios. For example, we'll consider the ethical issues that come into play in various communication situations: cultural practices, lying, and ways to engage in interpersonal conflict ethically. These boxes will serve as frequent reminders that ethical considerations are an integral part of all the communication choices/decisions you make. A list of these Communicating Ethically boxes appears in the Specialized Contents on page xi.

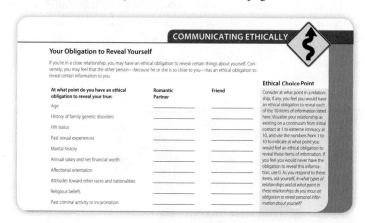

Learning and Mastering Essential Communication Skills

Learning objectives highlight the major concepts and skills of the chapter. The learning objectives system used here identify three major levels of thinking, each of which is included throughout the text (Bloom, 1956; Teacher & Educational Development, 2005; Eggen & Kauchak, 2013):

- **Knowledge** (recalling, remembering, and comprehending), introduced by such specific verbs as *define, paraphrase, describe,* and *differentiate.*
- **Application** (applying a concept to a new situation), introduced by such specific verbs as *diagram, illustrate, use,* and *give examples.*
- **Problem solving** (analyzing/breaking a concept into its parts, synthesizing/combining elements into a new whole, and evaluating/making value or appropriateness judgments), introduced by such specific verbs as *assess, construct, organize,* and *evaluate.*

At the end of each of the chapter's major sections, questions prompt students to test themselves to see if they can, in fact, accomplish the objectives.

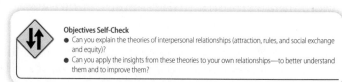

Skill Development Experiences throughout the text ask that you work actively with the concepts discussed in the text and cover a wide variety of essential communication skills. Completing these experiences will help you apply the material in the chapter to specific situations and thereby increase and perfect your own communication skills. Each chapter contains 2, or in some cases 3, skill development experiences to provide you with the opportunity to work actively with the concepts discussed in the text.

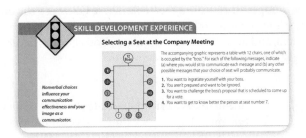

Essential terms in boldface, a vocabulary quiz, and a glossary at the end help you learn and review essential terms. The glossary also includes many skills discussed in the text.

The Public Speaking Sample Assistant boxes in each of the four public speaking chapters provide sample annotated speeches and outlines. New examples and four new speeches (two poorly constructed and two excellent) are included.

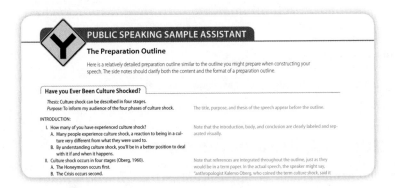

Learning through Interaction

Test Yourself sections throughout the text invite you to analyze your own patterns of communication and think about how you will alter your communication in the future. These tests will help you personalize the concepts and skills you'll read about in the text and improve your communication effectiveness. Additional self-tests are noted at the ends of the chapters and are available at MyCommunicationLab (www.mycommunicationlab.com) and on The Communication Blog (http://tcbdevito.blogspot.com).

TEST YOURSELF

What Kind of Group Member Are You?

For each statement below, respond with **T** if the statement is often true of your group behavior or **F** if the statement generally does not apply to your group behavior.

____ ❶ I present new ideas and suggest new strategies.

____ ❷ I ask for facts and opinions.

____ ❸ I stimulate the group.

____ ❹ I give examples and try to look for positive solutions.

____ ❺ I positively reinforce group members.

____ ❻ I try to reconcile differences.

____ ❼ I go along with the other members.

____ ❽ I offer compromises as ways of resolving conflict.

____ ❾ I express negative evaluation of the actions and feelings of the group members.

Messages in the Media, a new chapter opening photo program uses scenes from television shows as a useful laboratory for the study of communication. This feature is in two parts: (1) Messages in the Media introduces each chapter with a television program that deals with the major topics of the chapter and (2) Messages in the Media: Wrap Up (at the end of each chapter) invites you to reconsider the television program in light of what you read in the chapter.

Communication Choice Points appear throughout the text to encourage you to examine the choices you have available for communicating in actual real-life situations and to apply the information in the text to these situations.

Video Choice Point scenarios appear in each chapter and invite you to view a video of a communication interaction and then examine the available choices the characters in the scenario made (or could have made) for communicating effectively.

Viewpoints captions, accompanying all interior photos, pose questions (mostly based on communication research) designed to elicit discussion of a variety of different viewpoints.

Blog Posts

Quick Response Codes appear throughout the book. These QR codes will take you to specific posts on The Communication Blog where you can read more about a topic, read the comments of others, and post your own comments. You can also go directly to the blog: http://tcbdevito.blogspot.com.

Media Icons

Throughout the text, icons in the margins alert you to related media components (including videos, exercises, and audio segments) that you will find at MyCommunicationLab to enhance your learning:

Watch the **Video** at **MyCommunicationLab**

Listen to the **Audio Chapter** at **MyCommunicationLab**

Explore the **Exercise** at **MyCommunicationLab**

Study and **Review** the **Flashcards** at **MyCommunicationLab**

Instructor and Student Resources

Key instructor resources include an Instructor's Manual and Test Bank (ISBN 0205930689) and PowerPoint Presentation Package (ISBN 0205930735). These supplements are available at www.pearsonhighered.com/irc (instructor log in required). MyTest online test generating software (ISBN 0205930670) is available at www.pearsonmytest.com (instructor log in required).

For a complete listing of the instructor and student resources available with this text, please visit the Pearson Communication catalog at www.pearsonhighered.com/communication.

MyCommunicationLab™

MyCommunicationLab is an online homework, tutorial, and assessment program that truly engages students in learning. It helps students better prepare for class, quizzes, and exams—resulting in better performance in the course—and provides educators a dynamic set of tools for gauging individual and class progress. And, MyCommunicationLab comes from Pearson, your partner in providing the best digital learning experiences: www.mycommunicationlab.com

MyCommunicationLab Highlights:

- **MediaShare:** This comprehensive file upload tool allows students to post speeches, outlines, visual aids, video assignments, role plays, group projects, and more in a variety of file formats. Uploaded files are available for viewing, commenting, and grading by instructors and class members in face-to-face and online course settings. Integrated video capture functionality allows students to record video directly from a webcam and allows instructors to record videos via webcam, in class or in a lab, and attach them directly to a specific student and/or assignment. The MediaShare app is available via iTunes at no additional charge for those who have purchased MediaShare or MyCommunicationLab access.

- **The Pearson eText:** Identical in content and design to the printed text, the Pearson eText lets students access their textbook anytime, anywhere, and any way they want—including downloading to an iPad. Students can take notes and highlight, just like a traditional text.

- **Videos and Video Quizzes:** Videos provide students with the opportunity to watch and evaluate chapter-related multimedia. Many videos include automatically graded quiz questions.

- **PersonalityProfile:** PersonalityProfile is Pearson's online library for self-assessment and analysis. Online resources provide students with opportunities to evaluate their own and others' communication styles. Instructors can use these tools to show learning and growth over the duration of the course.

- **Study Tools:** A personalized study plan, chapter assessment, key term flashcards, an audio version of the text, and more provide a robust range of study tools to focus students on what they need to know, helping them succeed in the course and beyond.

- **Class Preparation Tool:** Finding, organizing, and presenting your instructor resources is fast and easy with Pearson's class preparation tool. This fully searchable database contains hundreds of resources such as lecture launchers, discussion topics, activities, assignments, and video clips. Instructors can search or browse by topic and sort the results by type. Personalized folders can be created to organize and store content or download resources, as well as upload your own content.

ACKNOWLEDGMENTS

I want to thank those who reviewed the text at the various stages of revision; they gave generously of their time and expertise and I am, as always, in their debt.

Lawrence Albert, Morehead State University; Pamela Ballow, Collin College; Laura Baxter, Collin College; Katie Delmore, Austin Community College; Susan Knott, Westminster College; Matthew Malloy, Caldwell Community College and Technical Institute; Donell C. Murray, Morehead State University.

I also want to thank the many people who worked so hard to turn a manuscript into this book. I'm especially grateful to the people at Pearson who make revisions so enjoyable, especially communication editor Melissa Mashburn for her good spirit and always helpful ideas, senior development editor Carol Alper who made valuable suggestions on just about every aspect of this revision, senior marketing manager Blair Zoe Tuckman who skillfully handled the marketing program, and Kate Cebik, who coordinated the ancillaries. Additional thank you's go to senior digital editor Paul DeLuca, digital editor Lisa Dotson, editorial assistant Megan Hermida, production manager Raegan Heerema, project manager Lois Lombardo and the staff at Cenveo, copyeditor Stephanie Magean, and Stefanie Ramsay for finding excellent photos that appear throughout this book.

Joseph A. DeVito
jadevito@earthlink.net
www.pearsonhighered.com/devito
http://tcbdevito.blogspot.com

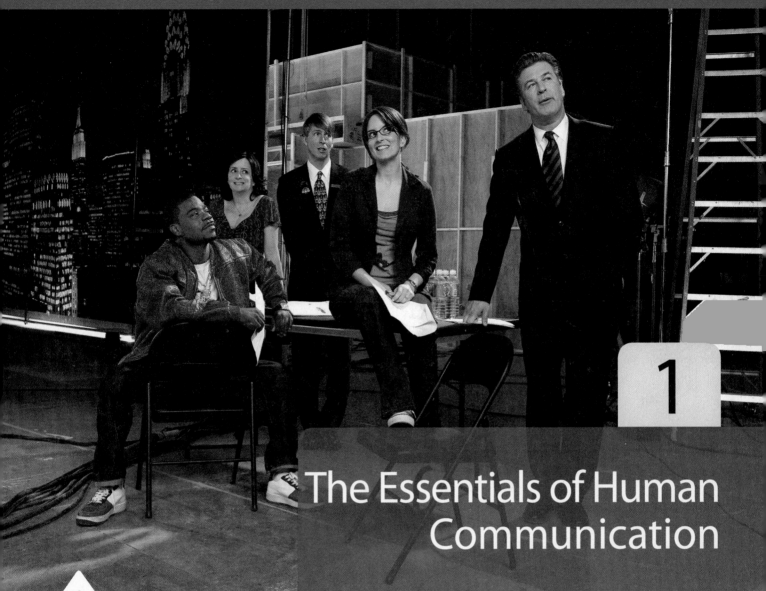

1

The Essentials of Human Communication

 Listen to the **Audio Chapter** in **MyCommunicationLab**

⚠ Messages in the Media

30 Rock is a situation comedy that revolves around characters who could all use a good course in human communication. In this chapter we introduce the basics of human communication, explaining what it is and how it works.

Objectives

After reading this chapter, you should be able to:

❶ Identify the myths, skills, and forms of human communication.

❷ Draw a model of communication that includes sources-receivers, messages, context, channel, noise, and effects; and define each of these elements.

❸ Paraphrase the major principles of human communication.

❹ Explain the role of culture in human communication, the seven ways in which cultures differ from one another, the aim of a cultural perspective; and define *ethnic identity* and *ethnocentrism*.

❺ Define *communication competence* and explain the four qualities identified as part of competence.

Of all the knowledge and skills you have, those concerning communication are among your most important and useful. Your communication ability will influence how effectively you live your personal and professional life; it will influence your effectiveness as a friend and lover. It will often make the difference between getting a job and not getting it. Your communication skills will determine your influence and effectiveness as a group member and your emergence as group leader. Your communication skills will increase your ability to communicate information and influence the attitudes and behaviors of others in a variety of public speaking situations.

This first section introduces human communication, beginning with the skills and forms of human communication and some of the popular but erroneous beliefs that can get in the way of effective communication.

Preliminaries to Human Communication

Human communication consists of the sending and receiving of verbal and nonverbal messages between two or more people. This seemingly simple (but in reality quite complex) process is the subject of this book, to which this chapter provides a foundation. Here we begin the study of human communication by looking first at the myths about communication (to get rid of them), the skills you'll learn, and the forms of communication discussed here.

Explore the **Exercise**
"I'd Prefer to Be" at
MyCommunicationLab

MYTHS ABOUT HUMAN COMMUNICATION

A good way to begin your study of human communication is to examine just a few of the popular but erroneous beliefs about communication, many of which are contradicted by research and theory. Understanding these myths and why they are false will help eliminate potential barriers and pave the way for more effective and efficient learning about communication.

- *The more you communicate, the better your communication will be.* Although this proposition seems logical—the same idea lies behind the popular belief that practice makes perfect—it actually is at the heart of much faulty learning. Practice may help make your communication perfect if you practice the right habits. But if you practice bad habits, you're likely to grow less, rather than more, effective. Consequently, it's important to learn and practice the principles of effectiveness.

  - *When two people are in a close relationship, neither person should have to communicate needs and wants explicitly; the other person should know what these are.* This assumption is at the heart of many interpersonal difficulties. People aren't mind readers, and to expect them to be sets up barriers to open and honest communication.

  - *Interpersonal or group conflict is a reliable sign that the relationship or group is in trouble.* Conflict is inevitable in relationships and in groups. If the conflict is managed effectively, it may actually benefit the individuals and the relationship.

  - *Like good communicators, leaders are born, not made.* Although some people are better suited to leadership than others, leadership, like communication and listening, is a learned skill. You'll develop leadership abilities as you learn the principles of human communication and those unique to group communication and group leadership.

- *Fear of speaking in public is detrimental and must be eliminated.* Most speakers are nervous—and, to be perfectly honest, you're probably not going to learn from this book or this course to eliminate what is commonly called stage fright or communication apprehension. But you can learn to *manage* your fear, making it work for you rather than against you; you can learn, and this is crucial, to become a more effective speaker regardless of your current level of anxiety.

Communication Choice Point

Choices and Human Communication

Throughout this book you'll find marginal items labelled Communication Choice Points. These items are designed to encourage you to apply the material discussed in the text to specific communication situations by first analyzing your available choices and then making a communication decision.

SKILLS OF HUMAN COMMUNICATION

Among the skills you'll learn through your study of human communication are these:

- **Self-presentation skills** enable you to present yourself as (and just for starters) a confident, likable, approachable, and credible person. It is also largely through your communication skills (or lack of them) that you display negative qualities.
- **Relationship skills** help you build friendships, enter into love relationships, work with colleagues, and interact with family members. These are the skills for initiating, maintaining, repairing, and sometimes dissolving relationships of all kinds.
- **Interviewing skills** enable you to interact to gain information, to successfully present yourself to get the job you want, and to participate effectively in a wide variety of other interview types. (This topic is covered in a separate supplement, The Interviewing Guidebook.)
- **Group interaction and leadership skills** help you participate effectively in relationship and task groups—informative, problem-solving, and brainstorming groups, at home or at work—as a member and as a leader.
- **Presentation or public speaking skills** will enable you to manage your fear and make it work for you, rather than against you. These skills will enable you to communicate information to small and large audiences and influence their attitudes and behaviors.

You'll learn these skills and reap the benefits as you develop facility in the varied forms of communication, to which we now turn.

VIEWPOINTS

Importance of Communication

Women often report that an essential quality—perhaps the most important quality—in a partner is the ability to communicate. And managers and employment interviewers routinely list communication skills among the most important job-related skills in a desirable employee. How important, compared to all the other factors you might take into consideration in choosing a partner or in succeeding at work, is the ability to communicate? What specific communication skills would you consider "extremely important" in a life partner?

FORMS OF HUMAN COMMUNICATION

You'll accomplish these objectives and acquire these skills as you engage in and master a variety of human communication forms. **Intrapersonal communication** is the communication you have with yourself—when you talk with, learn about, and judge yourself. You persuade yourself of this or that, reason about possible decisions to make, and rehearse messages that you plan to send to others. In intrapersonal communication you might, for example, wonder how you did in an interview and what you could have done differently. You might conclude you did a pretty good job but tell yourself you need to be more assertive when discussing salary.

Interpersonal communication occurs when you interact with a person with whom you have some kind of relationship; it can take place face-to-face as well as through electronic channels (e-mail or instant messaging, for example) or even in traditional letter writing. Perhaps you might e-mail your friends or family about your plans for the weekend, ask someone in class for a date, or confront a colleague's racist remarks at the water cooler. Through interpersonal communication you interact with others, learn about them and yourself, and reveal yourself to others. Whether with new acquaintances, old friends, lovers, family members, or colleagues at work, it's through interpersonal communication that you establish, maintain, sometimes destroy, and sometimes repair personal relationships.

Interviewing is a form of interpersonal communication that proceeds by question and answer. Through interviewing you learn about others and what they know, counsel or get counseling from others, and get or don't get the job you want. Today much interviewing (especially initial interviews) takes place through e-mail, phone conferencing, or video conferencing with Skype, for example.

"I'd like to see you do this online."

Small group communication or team communication is communication among groups of, say five to ten people and may take place face-to-face or, increasingly, in virtual space. Small group communication serves *relationship needs*—such as those for companionship, affection, or support—and *task needs*—such as balancing the family budget, electing a new chairperson, or designing a new ad campaign. Through small group communication you interact with others, solve problems, develop new ideas, and share knowledge and experiences.

Public communication is communication between a speaker and an audience. Audiences range in size from several people to hundreds, thousands, and even millions. Through public communication a speaker will inform and persuade you. And you, in turn, inform and persuade others—to act, to buy, or to think in a particular way. Much as you can address large audiences face-to-face, you also can address such audiences electronically. Through social networks, newsgroups, or blogs, for example, you can post your "speech" for anyone to read and then read their reactions to your message. In addition, with the help of the more traditional mass media of radio and television, you can address audiences in the hundreds of millions as they sit alone or in small groups all over the world.

Computer-mediated communication is a general term that includes all forms of communication between people that take place through some kind of computer, whether it's on your smartphone or via a standard Internet connection. Examples include e-mail, blogging, instant messaging, or posting or chatting on social network sites such as Facebook, Google+, or Twitter. Throughout this text, we'll make frequent reference to the similarities and differences between face-to-face and computer-mediated communication.

Mass communication refers to communication from one source to many receivers who may be scattered throughout the world. Newspapers, magazines, radio, television, and film are the major mass media. Recently *media literacy*—the skills and competencies needed to become a wiser, more critical consumer—has become central to the study of human communication. Accordingly, the coverage of mass communication here is limited to media literacy—a topic covered in the chapter-opening photos, in frequent examples, illustrations, and exercises, and the inclusion of a variety of Media Literacy boxes at **MyCommunicationLab**.

This text focuses on all these forms of communication—and on you as both message sender and message receiver. It has two major purposes:

Read the "Media Literacy boxes" at **MyCommunicationLab**

- *To explain the concepts and principles, the theory and research in human communication,* so that you'll have a firm understanding of what communication is and how it works.

- *To provide you with skills of human communication* that will help you increase your communication competence and effectiveness in your personal and professional lives.

Objectives Self-Check
- Can you identify the myths that can hinder the study of communication?
- Can you identify the wide variety of skills you'll learn as you progress through this course?
- Can you identify the forms of human communication to be covered here?

For some advice for beginning college students, see "To Beginning Students" at **tcbdevito.blogspot .com.** What additional advice would you want?

Communication Models and Concepts

In early **models** (representations) or theories, the communication process was thought to be linear. According to this *linear* view, the speaker spoke and the listener listened. Communication was seen as proceeding in a relatively straight line. Speaking and listening were seen as taking place at different times; when you spoke, you didn't listen, and when you listened, you didn't speak (Figure 1.1).

A more satisfying view, the one held currently, sees communication as a transactional process in which each person serves as both speaker and listener, sending and receiving messages (Watzlawick, Beavin, & Jackson, 1967; Watzlawick, 1977, 1978; Barnlund, 1970). In face-to-face communication, while you send messages you're also receiving messages from your own communications and from the reactions of the other person. This is also true in phone communication, in instant messaging, and in chatting. Other online communications, such as posting on Facebook or e-mail, more closely resemble the linear model of communication where sending and receiving occur at different times.

The transactional view also sees the elements of communication as interdependent (never independent). This means that each element exists in relation to the others. A change in any one element of the process produces changes in the other elements. For example, if you're having a meeting with a group of your coworkers and your boss enters the room, this change in "audience" will lead to other changes. Perhaps you'll change what you're saying or how you're saying it. Regardless of what change is introduced, other changes will occur as a result.

Communication occurs when you send or receive messages and when you assign meaning to another person's signals. All human communication occurs within a context, is transmitted via one or more channels, is distorted by noise, and has some effect. We can expand the basic transactional model of communication by adding these essential elements, as shown in Figure 1.2.

SOURCES–RECEIVERS

According to the transactional model, each person involved in communication is both a **source** (speaker) and a **receiver** (listener); hence the term *sources–receivers*. You send messages when you speak, write, gesture, or smile. You receive messages in listening, reading, seeing, smelling, and so on. At the same time that you send messages, you're also receiving messages: You're receiving your own messages (you hear yourself, feel your own movements, see many of your own gestures), and, at least in face-to-face communication, you're receiving the messages of the other person—visually, auditorily, or even through touch or smell. As you speak, you look at the person for responses—for approval, understanding, sympathy, agreement, and so on. As you decipher these nonverbal signals, you're performing receiver functions. When you write to or text someone with video; the situation is very similar to the face-to-face situation. Without video, you might visualize the responses you expect/want the person to give.

When you put your ideas into speech, you're putting them into a code; hence you're *encoding.* When you translate the sound waves (the speech signals) that impinge on your ears or read the words on a screen, into ideas, you take them out of the code they're in; hence you're *decoding.* Thus, speakers or writers are often referred to as **encoders,** and listeners or readers as **decoders.** The linked term *encoding–decoding* emphasizes the fact that you perform these functions simultaneously.

Usually, you encode an idea into a code that the other person understands—for example, English, Spanish, or Indonesian, depending on the shared knowledge that you and your listener possess. At times, however, you may want to exclude others by speaking in a language that only one of your listeners knows or by using jargon. The use of abbreviations and jargon in text messaging is another example of how people communicate in a code that only certain people will understand.

MESSAGES

Communication **messages** take many forms and are transmitted or received through one or more sensory organs or a combination of them. You communicate verbally (with words) and

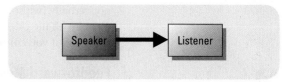

FIGURE 1.1

The Linear View of Human Communication
The speaker speaks and the listener listens.

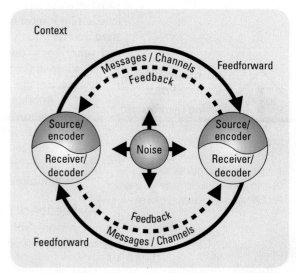

FIGURE 1.2

The Essentials of Human Communication

This is a general model of communication between two people and most accurately depicts communication as a transactional process. It puts into visual form the various elements of the communication process. How would you revise this model to depict small group interaction or public speaking?

Explore the **Exercise** "Comparing Human Communication" at **MyCommunicationLab**

nonverbally (without words). Your meanings or intentions are conveyed with words (Chapter 4) and with the clothes you wear, the way you walk, and the way you smile (Chapter 5). Everything about you communicates a message.

Feedforward Messages

Feedforward is information you provide before sending your primary messages (Richards, 1951). It reveals something about the messages to come and includes, for example, the preface or table of contents of a book, the opening paragraph of a chapter, movie previews, magazine covers, and introductions in public speeches.

Feedforward may be verbal ("Wait until you hear this one") or nonverbal (a prolonged pause or hands motioning for silence to signal that an important message is about to be spoken). Or, as is most often the case, it is some combination of verbal and nonverbal. Feedforward may refer to the content of the message to follow ("I'll tell you exactly what they said to each other") or to the form ("I won't spare you the gory details"). In e-mail, feedforward is given in the header, where the name of the sender, the date, and the subject of the message are identified. Caller ID is also an example of feedforward.

Another type of feedforward is **phatic communication**—"small talk" that opens the way for "big talk." It includes the "How are you?" and "Nice weather" greetings that are designed to maintain rapport and friendly relationships (Placencia, 2004; Burnard, 2003). Similarly, listeners' short comments that are unrelated to the content of the conversation but indicate interest and attention also may be considered phatic communication (McCarthy, 2003).

Feedback Messages

When you send a message—say, in speaking to another person—you also hear yourself. That is, you get **feedback** from your own messages; you hear what you say, you feel the way you move, you see what you write. In addition to this self-feedback, you also get feedback from others. This feedback can take many forms. A frown or a smile, a yea or a nay, a returned poke or a retweet, a pat on the back or a punch in the mouth are all types of feedback.

Feedback tells the speaker what effect he or she is having on listeners. On the basis of feedback, the speaker may adjust, modify, strengthen, deemphasize, or change the content or form of the messages. For example, if someone laughs at your joke (giving you positive feedback), it may encourage you to tell another one. If the feedback is negative—no laughing, just blank stares—then you may resist relaying another "humorous" story.

Metamessages

A **metamessage** is a message that refers to another message; it is communication about communication. For example, remarks such as "This statement is false" or "Do you understand what I am trying to tell you?" refer to communication and are therefore "metacommunicational."

Nonverbal behavior may also be metacommunicational. Obvious examples include crossing your fingers behind your back or winking when telling a lie. On a less obvious level, consider the blind date. As you say, "I had a really nice time," your nonverbal messages—the lack of a smile, failure to maintain eye contact—metacommunicate and contradict the verbal "really nice time," suggesting that you did not enjoy the evening. Nonverbal messages may also metacommunicate about other nonverbal messages. The individual who, on meeting a stranger, both smiles and extends a totally lifeless hand shows how one nonverbal behavior may contradict another.

Workplace Messages

In workplace organizations messages are often classified in terms of their direction.

Explore the **Exercise** "How to Give Feedforward" at **MyCommunicationLab**

Communication Choice Point

Giving Feedforward
The grades were just posted for a course, and you see that your dorm mate failed. You got an A. Your dorm mate asks you about the grades. You feel you want to preface your remarks. *What kind of feedforward might you give in this case?*

VIEWPOINTS

Feedback

Based on your own experiences, do you find that people who accurately read and respond to feedback are better liked than those who don't read feedback as accurately? In what ways might the ability to give effective feedback influence the growth or deterioration of a relationship? Is there a relationship between the ability to read feedback and the ability to communicate information or to persuade an audience?

- **Upward communication** consists of messages sent from the lower levels of a hierarchy to the upper levels—for example, from line worker to manager, or faculty member to dean. This type of communication usually is concerned with job-related activities and problems; ideas for change and suggestions for improvement; and feelings about the organization, work, other workers, or similar issues.

- **Downward communication** consists of messages sent from the higher levels to the lower levels of the hierarchy—for example, messages sent by managers to workers or by deans to faculty members. Common forms of downward communication include orders; explanations of procedures, goals, and changes; and appraisals of workers.

- **Lateral communication** refers to messages between equals—manager-to-manager, worker-to-worker. Such messages may move within the same subdivision or department of the organization or across divisions. Lateral communication, for example, is the kind of communication that takes place between two history professors at Illinois State University, between a psychologist at Ohio State and a communicologist at Kent State, or between a bond trader and an equities trader at a brokerage house.

- **Grapevine communication** messages don't follow any of the formal, hierarchical lines of communication established in an organization; rather, they seem to have a life of their own. **Grapevine** messages concern job-related issues that you want to discuss in a more interpersonal setting—for example, organizational issues that have not yet been made public, the real relationship among the regional managers, or possible changes that are being considered but not yet finalized.

VIEWPOINTS

Synchronous and Asynchronous Communication

In face-to-face and in much online communication, messages are exchanged with virtually no delay; communication is synchronous. In other forms of communication—for example, snail or e-mail and blog posts—the messages may be exchanged with considerable delay; communication here is asynchronous. What differences does this lead to in the way you communicate in these various forms?

COMMUNICATION CONTEXT

Communication exists in a context that determines, to a large extent, the meaning of any verbal or nonverbal message. The same words or behaviors may have totally different meanings when they occur in different contexts. For example, the greeting "How are you?" means "Hello" to someone you pass regularly on the street but "Is your health improving?" to a friend in the hospital. A wink to an attractive person on a bus means something completely different from a wink that signifies a put-on or a lie. Divorced from the context, it's impossible to tell what meaning was intended from just examining the signals.

The context will also influence what you say and how you say it. You communicate differently depending on the specific context you're in. Contexts have at least four aspects: physical, cultural, social-psychological, and temporal or time.

- The **physical context** is the tangible or concrete environment, the room, park, or auditorium; you don't talk the same way at a noisy football game as you do at a quiet funeral.

- The **cultural context** involves the lifestyles, beliefs, values, behavior, and communication of a group; it is the rules of a group of people for considering something right or wrong.

- The **social-psychological context** has to do with the status relationships among speakers, the formality of the situation, the norms of a group or organization; you don't talk the same way in the cafeteria as you would at a formal dinner at your boss's house.

Communication Choice Point

Message Overload

Several relatives have developed chain e-mail lists and send you virtually everything they come upon as they surf the Internet. You need to stop this e-mail overload. But, most of all, you don't want to insult your relatives or make them feel guilty. *What are some of the things you might say? What are the advantages and disadvantages of saying nothing?*

- The **temporal context** is a message's position within a sequence of events; you don't talk the same way after someone tells you about the death of a close relative as you do after someone reveals they've won the lottery.

These four contexts interact—each influences and is influenced by the others. For example, arriving late for a date (temporal context) may lead to changes in the degree of friendliness (social–psychological context), which would depend on the cultures of you and your date (cultural context), and may lead to changes in where you go on the date (physical context).

Communication Choice Point

Channels

You want to ask someone for a date and are considering how you might go about this. *What are your choices among channels? Which channel would be the most effective? Which channel would provoke the least anxiety?*

CHANNEL

The communication **channel** is the vehicle or medium through which messages pass. Communication rarely takes place over only one channel. Rather, two, three, or four channels may be used simultaneously. In face-to-face conversations, for example, you speak and listen (vocal channel), but you also gesture and receive signals visually (visual channel). You also emit and smell odors (olfactory channel) and often touch one another; this tactile channel, too, is communication.

Another way to classify channels is by the means of communication. Thus, face-to-face contact, telephones, e-mail, movies, television, smoke signals, and telegraph all are types of channels.

NOISE

Noise is anything that interferes with your receiving a message. At one extreme, noise may prevent a message from getting from source to receiver. A roaring noise or line static can prevent entire messages from getting through to your phone receiver. At the other extreme, with virtually no noise interference, the message of the source and the message received are almost identical. Most often, however, noise distorts some portion of the message a source sends as it travels to a receiver. Just as messages may be auditory or visual, noise comes in both auditory and visual forms. Four types of noise are especially relevant:

Noise of a somewhat different type is discussed in "The Chain Letter as Dysfunctional Communication" at tcbdevito.blogspot.com. What's your opinion of the chain letter? Are there some chain letters that you view more positively than others?

- **Physical noise** is interference that is external to both speaker and listener; it interferes with the physical transmission of the signal or message and would include the screeching of passing cars, the hum of a computer, sunglasses, blurred type or fonts that are too small or difficult to read, misspellings and poor grammar, and popup ads.
- **Physiological noise** is created by barriers within the sender or receiver and would include visual impairments, hearing loss, articulation problems, and memory loss.
- **Psychological noise** refers to mental interference in the speaker or listener and includes preconceived ideas, wandering thoughts, biases and prejudices, close-mindedness, and extreme emotionalism. You're likely to run into psychological noise when you talk with someone who is close-minded or who refuses to listen to anything he or she doesn't already believe.
- **Semantic noise** is interference that occurs when the speaker and listener have different meaning systems; it would include language or dialectical differences, the use of jargon or overly complex terms, and ambiguous or overly abstract terms whose meanings can be easily misinterpreted. You see this type of noise regularly in the medical doctor who uses "medicalese" without explanation or in the insurance salesperson who speaks in the jargon of the insurance industry.

As you can see from these examples, noise is anything that distorts your receiving the messages of others or their receiving your messages.

A useful concept in understanding noise and its importance in communication is **signal-to-noise ratio.** In this term the word *signal* refers to information that you'd find useful, and *noise* refers to information that is useless (to you). So, for example, a post or feed that contains lots of useful information is high on signal and low on noise; one that contains lots of useless information is high on noise and low on signal.

All communications contain noise. Noise can't be totally eliminated, but its effects can be reduced. Making your language more precise, sharpening your skills for sending and receiving nonverbal messages, adjusting your camera for greater clarity, and improving your listening and feedback skills are some ways to combat the influence of noise.

EFFECTS

Communication always has some **effect** on those involved in the communication act. For every communication act, there is some consequence. For example, you may gain knowledge or learn how to analyze, synthesize, or evaluate something. These are intellectual or cognitive effects. You may acquire new feelings, attitudes, or beliefs or change existing ones (affective effects). You may learn new bodily movements, such as how to throw a curve ball, paint a picture, give a compliment, or express surprise (psychomotor effects).

Communication Choice Point

Negative Communication Effects

You post a really negative remark on your friend's Facebook wall. The next day you realize you shouldn't have been so negative. You want to remain friends; you need to say something. *What are your options for communicating your feelings? What would you do?*

Video Choice Point

Ryan Asks for a Recommendation

Ryan, a communication major, needs a letter of recommendation for a summer internship. He wants to ask Professor Starck, a popular instructor who he previously had in class, for a recommendation. But, he isn't sure how to approach her. He considers the effect of the various elements of communication—including context, feedback, feedforward, noise, and channel–on the outcome as he contemplates composing an effective message. In this video you'll see Ryan try three different approaches with varying effects. See how his choices play out in the video, "Ryan Asks for a Recommendation".

👁 **Watch** the **Video** "Ryan Asks for a Recommendation" at **MyCommunicationLab**

Objectives Self-Check
- Can you draw/diagram a model of communication that contains the elements of source-receiver, messages, context, channel, noise, and effects and that illustrates how these are related to each other? Can you define each of these elements?

Principles of Communication

Several principles are essential to an understanding of human communication in all its forms. These principles, as you'll see throughout the text, also have numerous practical implications to help you increase your own communication effectiveness. A summary of these principles appears in Table 1.1.

Watch the **Video** "Going Up" at **MyCommunicationLab**

COMMUNICATION IS PURPOSEFUL

You communicate for a purpose; some motivation leads you to communicate. When you speak or write, you're trying to send some message and to accomplish some goal. Although different cultures emphasize different purposes and motives (Rubin, Fernandez-Collado, & Hernandez-Sampieri, 1992), five general purposes seem relatively common to most, if not all, forms of communication:

- **to learn:** to acquire knowledge of others, the world, and yourself
- **to relate:** to form relationships with others, to interact with others as individuals
- **to help:** to assist others by listening, offering solutions
- **to influence:** to strengthen or change the attitudes or behaviors of others
- **to play:** to enjoy the experience of the moment

TABLE 1.1   A Summary of Some Principles of Human Communication
Here, in brief, are the seven principles of human communication, their basic ideas and implications.

Principles	Basic Ideas	Skill Implications
Communication is purposeful.	Communication may serve a variety of purposes— for example, to learn, to relate, to help, to influence, to play.	Use your purposes to guide your verbal and nonverbal messages. Identify the purposes in the messages of others.
Communication involves choices.	In all communication situations you're confronted with choices as to what to say and how you say it. Communication training enlarges the number of choices.	Realize that you have choices in your communications and you don't have to say the first thing that comes into your head.
Communication is ambiguous.	All messages and all relationships are potentially ambiguous.	Use clear and specific terms, ask if you're being understood, and paraphrase complex ideas.
Communication involves content and relationship dimensions.	Messages may refer to the real world, to something external to both speaker and listener (the content) *and* to the relationships between the parties.	Distinguish between content and relationship messages and deal with relationship issues as relationship issues.
Communication has a power dimension.	Through verbal and nonverbal communication, you establish your power.	Follow the guidelines for effective ethical communication.
Communication is punctuated.	Communication events are continuous transactions, punctuated into causes and effects for convenience.	See alternative punctuations when trying to understand another's point of view.
Communication is inevitable, irreversible, and unrepeatable.	Messages are (almost) always being sent, can't be uncommunicated, and are always unique, one-time occurrences.	Be careful of what you say; you won't be able to take it back.

In research on the motivations/purposes for using social networking sites, it's the relationship purpose that dominates. One research study, for example, finds the following motivations/purposes, in order of frequency mentioned: Staying in touch with friends, staying in touch with family, connecting with friends with whom you've lost contact, connecting with those who share your interests, making new friends, reading comments by celebrities, and finding romantic partners (Smith, 2011). As you can see the reasons are mostly to relate but the other purposes are likely served in the process.

Popular belief and research findings both agree that men and women use communication for different purposes. Generally, men seem to communicate more for information and women more for relationship purposes (Gamble & Gamble, 2003; Stewart, Cooper, & Stewart, 2003; Helgeson, 2009). Gender differences also occur in electronic communication. For example, women chat more for relationship reasons; men chat more to play and to relax (Leung, 2001).

COMMUNICATION INVOLVES CHOICES

Throughout your communication life and in each communication interaction you're presented with **choice points**—moments when you have to make a choice as to whom you communicate with, what you say, what you don't say, how you phrase what you want to say, and so on. This course and this text aim to give you reasons (grounded in communication theory and research discussed throughout the text) for the varied choices you'll be called upon to make in your communication interactions. The course also aims to give you the skills you'll need to execute these well-reasoned choices.

You can look at the process of choice in terms of educational theorist John Dewey's (1910) steps in reflective thinking, a model used for explaining small group problem solving and conflict resolution. It can also be used to explain the notion of choice in five steps.

- **Step 1: The problem.** View a communication interaction as a problem to be resolved, as a situation to be addressed. Here you try to understand the nature of the communication situation and the elements involved. Let's say that your "problem" is that you said something you shouldn't have and it's created a problem between you and your friend, romantic partner, or family member. You need to resolve this problem.

- **Step 2: The criteria.** Ask yourself what your specific communication goal is. What do you want your message to accomplish? For example, you want to admit your mistake, apologize, and be forgiven.

- **Step 3: The possible solutions.** Ask yourself what are some of your communication choices. What are some of the messages you might communicate in your apology?

- **Step 4: The analysis.** Identify the advantages and disadvantages of each communication choice.

- **Step 5: The selection and execution.** Communicate your best choice, the one that you hope will resolve the problem and get you forgiveness.

As a student of communication, you would later reflect on this communication situation and identify what you learned, what you did well, and what you could have done more effectively.

COMMUNICATION IS AMBIGUOUS

Ambiguity is the condition in which something can be interpreted in more than one way. The first type, *language ambiguity,* is created by words that can be interpreted differently. Informal time terms offer good examples; *soon, right away, in a minute, early, late,* and similar terms can be understood differently by different people. The terms are ambiguous. A more interesting type of ambiguity is grammatical ambiguity. You can get a feel for this type of ambiguity by trying to paraphrase—rephrase in your own words—the following sentences:

- What has the cat in its paws?
- Flying planes can be dangerous.
- They are frying chickens.

Each of these ambiguous sentences can be interpreted and paraphrased in at least two different ways:

- What does the cat have in its paws? What monster has the cat in its paws?
- To fly planes is dangerous. Planes that fly can be dangerous.
- Those people are frying chickens. Those chickens are for frying.

Although these examples are particularly striking—and are the work of linguists who analyze language—some degree of ambiguity exists in all communication. When you express an idea, you never communicate your meaning exactly and totally; rather, you communicate your meaning with some reasonable accuracy—enough to give the other person a reasonably clear idea of what you mean.

The second type of ambiguity is *relationship ambiguity.* All relationships are ambiguous to some extent. Consider your own close relationships and ask yourself the following questions. Answer using a six-point scale on which 1 = completely or almost completely uncertain, and 6 = completely or almost completely certain. How certain are you about:

1. What can you say or not say to each other in this relationship?
2. Do you and your partner feel the same way about each other?
3. How would you and your partner describe this relationship?
4. How do you see the future of this relationship?

You probably were not able to respond with 6s for all four questions, and it is equally likely that your relationship partner would not respond with all 6s to these questions, adapted from a relationship uncertainty scale (Knobloch & Solomon, 1999).

As you think about making choices, take a look at "Satisficing: A Note on Making Choices" at tcbdevito.blogspot.com.

Communication Choice Point

Relationship Ambiguity

You've been dating Jessie on and off for the past six months. Today Jessie asks you to come to dinner and meet the parents. You're not sure what this means, what message Jessie's trying to send. *What options do you have for disambiguating this dinner invitation message? What would you say?*

You can look at the skills of human communication presented throughout this text as a means for appropriately reducing ambiguity and making the meanings you send and the meanings you receive as unambiguous as possible.

COMMUNICATION INVOLVES CONTENT AND RELATIONSHIP DIMENSIONS

Communication exists on at least two levels: a message referring to something external to both speaker and listener (e.g., the weather) or to the relationship between speaker and listener (e.g., who is in charge). These two aspects are referred to as **content and relationship dimensions** of communication (Watzlawick, Beavin, & Jackson, 1967). In the cartoon shown here, the father is explicitly teaching his son the difference between content and relationship messages. In real life this distinction is rarely discussed (outside of textbooks and counseling sessions).

"It's not about the story. It's about Daddy taking time out of his busy day to read you the story."

© Peter C. Vey/Condé Nast Publications/www.cartoonbank.com.

Some research shows that women send more **relationship messages** than men; they talk more about relationships in general and about the present relationship in particular. Men engage in more content talk; they talk more about things external to the relationship (Wood, 1994; Pearson, West, & Turner, 1995; Helgeson, 2009).

Problems often result from a failure to distinguish between the content and the relationship levels of communication. Consider a couple, Pat and Chris. Pat made plans to attend a rally with friends during the weekend without first asking Chris, and an argument has ensued. Both would probably have agreed that attending the rally was the right choice to make. Thus, the argument is not centered on the content level. The argument, instead, centers on the relationship level. Chris expected to be consulted about plans for the weekend. Pat, in not doing so, rejected this definition of the relationship.

COMMUNICATION HAS A POWER DIMENSION

Power refers to your ability to influence or control the behaviors of another person. Your power influences the way you communicate, and the way you communicate influences the power you wield. Research has identified six types of power: legitimate, referent, reward, coercive, expert, and information or persuasion (French & Raven, 1968; Raven, Centers, & Rodrigues, 1975). Before reading about these types of power, take the accompanying self-test; it will help personalize the material you'll read about.

SKILL DEVELOPMENT EXPERIENCE

Communicating Content and Relationship Messages

How would you communicate both the content and the relationship messages in the following situations?

Content and relationship messages serve different communication functions. Being able to distinguish between them is a prerequisite to using and responding to them effectively.

1. After a date that you didn't enjoy and don't want to repeat ever again, you want to express your sincere thanks; but you don't want to be misinterpreted as communicating any indication that you would go on another date with this person.
2. You're tutoring a high school freshman in algebra, but your tutee is really terrible and isn't paying attention or doing the homework you assign. You need to change this behavior and motivate a great change, yet at the same time you don't want to discourage or demoralize the young student.
3. You're interested in dating a friend on Facebook who also attends the college you do and with whom you've been chatting for a few weeks. But you don't know if the feeling is mutual. You want to ask for the date but to do so in a way that, if you're turned down, you won't be horribly embarrassed.

TEST YOURSELF

How Powerful Are You?

For each statement, indicate which of the following descriptions is most appropriate, using the scale below.

1 = true of 20 percent or fewer of the people I know; **2** = true of about 21 to 40 percent of the people I know; **3** = true of about 41 to 60 percent of the people I know; **4** = true of about 61 to 80 percent of the people I know; and **5** = true of 81 percent or more of the people I know.

❶   My position is such that I often have to tell others what to do. For example, a mother's position demands that she tell her children what to do, a manager's position demands that he or she tell employees what to do, and so on.

❷   People wish to be like me or identified with me. For example, high school football players may admire the former professional football player who is now their coach and want to be like him.

❸   People see me as having the ability to give them what they want. For example, employers have the ability to give their employees increased pay, longer vacations, or improved working conditions.

❹   People see me as having the ability to administer punishment or to withhold things they want. For example, employers have the ability to reduce voluntary overtime, shorten vacation time, or fail to improve working conditions.

❺   Other people realize that I have expertise in certain areas of knowledge. For example, a doctor has expertise in medicine and so others turn to the doctor to tell them what to do. Someone knowledgeable about computers similarly possesses expertise.

❻   Other people realize that I possess the communication ability to present an argument logically and persuasively.

HOW DID YOU DO?   These statements refer to the six major types of power, as described in the text. Low scores (1s and 2s) indicate your belief that you possess little of these particular types of power, and high scores (4s and 5s) indicate your belief that you possess a great deal of these particular types of power.

WHAT WILL YOU DO?   How satisfied are you with your level of power? If you're not satisfied, what might you do about it? A good starting place, of course, is to learn the skills of communication—interpersonal, small group, and public speaking—discussed in this text. Consider the kinds of communication patterns that would help you communicate power and exert influence in group situations.

- You hold **legitimate power** when others believe you have a right—by virtue of your position—to influence or control others' behaviors. For example, as an employer, judge, manager, or police officer, you'd have legitimate power by virtue of your role.

- You have **referent power** when others wish to be like you. Referent power holders often are attractive, have considerable prestige, and are well liked and well respected. For example, you may have referent power over a younger brother because he wants to be like you.

- You have **reward power** when you control the rewards that others want. Rewards may be material (money, promotion, jewelry) or social (love, friendship, respect). For example, teachers have reward power over students because they control grades, letters of recommendation, and social approval.

- You have **coercive power** when you have the ability to administer punishments to or remove rewards from others if they do not do as you wish. Usually, people who have reward power also have coercive power. For example, teachers may give poor grades or withhold recommendations. But be careful: Coercive power may reduce your other power bases. It can have a negative impact when used, for example, by supervisors on subordinates in business (Richmond et al., 1984).

- You have **expert power** when others see you as having expertise or special knowledge. Your expert power increases when you're perceived as being unbiased and as having nothing personally to gain from exerting this power. For example, judges have expert power in legal matters and doctors have expert power in medical matters.

Communication Choice Point

Unwanted Talk

Your supervisor at work continually talks about sex. You fear your lack of reaction has been interpreted as a sign of approval. You need to change that but at the same time not alienate the person who can fire you. *What are some of things you might do to stop this unwanted talk?*

● You have **information power**—also called "persuasion power"—when others see you as having the ability to communicate logically and persuasively. For example, researchers and scientists may acquire information power because people perceive them as informed and critical thinkers.

> **Communication Choice Point**
>
> **Establishing Power**
>
> As a new teacher, you want to establish your power as soon as possible. *What options do you have for communicating your power? What are some of the things you would say if you were a fourth-grade teacher? If you were a college professor?*

The power you wield is not static; it can be increased or decreased depending on what you do and don't do. For example, you might increase your reward power by gaining wealth and using it to exert influence, or you might increase your persuasive power by mastering the principles of public speaking.

You can also decrease or lose power. Probably the most common way to lose power is by unsuccessfully trying to control another person's behavior. For example, if you threaten someone with punishment and then fail to carry out your threat, you'll most likely lose power. Another way to lose power is to allow others to control you or to take unfair advantage of you. When you don't confront these power tactics of others, you lose power.

COMMUNICATION IS PUNCTUATED

Communication events are continuous transactions that have no clear-cut beginning or ending. As a participant in or an observer of communication, you divide this continuous, circular process into causes and effects, or stimuli and responses. The **punctuation of communication** is the segmenting of the continuous stream of communication into smaller pieces (Watzlawick, Beavin, & Jackson, 1967). Some of these pieces you label causes (or stimuli) and others effects (or responses).

Consider this example: The manager of a local supermarket lacks interest in the employees, seldom offering any suggestions for improvement or any praise for jobs well done. The employees are apathetic and morale is low. Each action (the manager's lack of involvement and the employees' low morale) stimulates the other. Each serves as the stimulus for the other but there is no identifiable initial starting point. Each event may be seen as a stimulus or as a response.

To understand what the other person in an interaction means from his or her point of view, try to see the sequence of events as punctuated by the other person. The manager, for example, needs to see the problem from the point of view of the employees; and the employees need to see it from the viewpoint of the manager. Further, recognize that neither person's punctuation reflects what exists in reality. Rather, it reflects the subjective and fallible perception of each individual (the other person as well as you).

SKILL DEVELOPMENT EXPERIENCE

Writing Your Social Network Profile

Examine your own social network profile (or that of a friend) in terms of the principles of communication discussed in this chapter:

1. What purposes does your profile serve? In what ways might it serve the five purposes of communication identified here (to learn, relate, influence, play, and help)?
2. In what way is your profile page a package of signals? In what ways do the varied words and pictures combine to communicate meaning?
3. Can you identify and distinguish between content from relational messages?
4. In what ways, if any, have you adjusted your profile as a response to the ways in which others have fashioned their profiles?
5. In what ways does your profile exhibit power? In what ways, if any, have you incorporated into your profile the six types of power discussed in this chapter (legitimate, referent, reward, coercive, expert, or information)?
6. What messages on your profile are ambiguous? Bumper stickers and photos should provide a useful starting point.
7. What are the implications of inevitability, irreversibility, and unrepeatability for publishing a profile on and communicating via social network sites?

Heightened awareness of how messages help create meanings should increase your awareness of the varied choices you have for communicating and ultimately your own communication effectiveness.

COMMUNICATION IS INEVITABLE, IRREVERSIBLE, AND UNREPEATABLE

Inevitability   Communication is inevitable; that is, in interactional situations it is always taking place, even when a person may not intend or want to communicate. To understand the **inevitability** of communication, think about a student sitting in the back of a classroom with an expressionless face, perhaps staring out the window. Although the student might claim not to be communicating with the instructor, the instructor may derive a variety of messages from this behavior. Perhaps the instructor assumes that the student lacks interest, is bored, or is worried about something. In any event, the teacher is receiving messages even though the student may not intentionally be sending any (Watzlawick, Beavin, & Jackson, 1967; Motley, 1990a, 1990b; Bavelas, 1990). This does not mean that all behavior is communication. For instance, if the student looked out the window and the teacher didn't notice, no communication would have taken place. The two people must be in an interactional situation and the behavior must be perceived for the principle of inevitability to operate.

Notice, too, that when you're in an interactional situation, you cannot *not* respond to the messages of others. For example, if you notice someone winking at you, you must respond in some way. Even if you don't respond actively or openly, your lack of response is itself a response: It communicates.

Irreversibility   Another all-important attribute of communication is its **irreversibility.** Once you say something or click "send" on your e-mail, you cannot uncommunicate the message. You can, of course, try to reduce its effects. You can say, for example, "I really didn't mean what I said." But regardless of how hard you try to negate or reduce the effects of a message, the message itself, once it has been received, cannot be taken back. In a public speaking situation in which the speech is recorded or broadcast, inappropriate messages may have national or even international effects. Here, attempts to reverse what someone has said (e.g., efforts to offer clarification) often have the effect of further publicizing the original statement.

In face-to-face communication, the actual signals (nonverbal messages and sound waves in the air) are evanescent; they fade almost as they are uttered. Some written messages, especially computer-mediated messages (such as those sent through e-mail or posted on social network sites) are unerasable. E-mails among employees in large corporations or even at colleges are often stored on disk or tape and may not be considered private by managers and administrators (Sethna, Barnes, Brust, & Kaye, 1999). Much litigation has involved evidence of racist or sexist e-mails that senders thought had been erased but were not. E-mails and entire hard drives are finding their way into divorce proceedings. As a result of the permanency of computer-mediated communication, you may wish to be especially cautious in these messages.

In all forms of communication, because of irreversibility (and unerasability), be careful not to say things you may be sorry for later, especially in conflict situations, when tempers run high. Commitment messages—"I love you" messages and their variants—also need to be monitored. Messages that you considered private but that might be interpreted as sexist, racist, or homophobic may later be retrieved by others and create all sorts of problems for you and your organization. Interestingly enough, only 55 percent of online teens say they do not post content that might reflect negatively on them in the future (Lenhart, Madden, Smith, Purcell, Cickuhr, & Rainie, 2011). In group and public communication situations, when the messages are received by many people, it's especially crucial to recognize the irreversibility of communication.

Unrepeatability   Finally, communication is unrepeatable. A communication act can never be duplicated. The reason is simple: Everyone and everything is constantly changing. As a result, you can never recapture the exact same situation, frame of mind, or relationship dynamics that defined a previous communication act. For example, you can never repeat meeting someone for the first time, comforting a grieving friend, leading a small group for the first time, or giving a public speech. You can never replace an initial impression; you can only try to counteract this initial (and perhaps negative) impression by making subsequent impressions more positive.

See "social media warnings" and "Social Networking and Getting a Job" at **tcbdevito.blogspot.com** for some added insights into the dangers of posting inappropriate photos and messages on your social media site. Do you think this concern is warranted? Overblown?

Communication Choice Point

The Irreversibility of Communication

You refer to your best friend's current romantic partner with the name of an ex-partner. From both their expressions you can tell your friend never mentioned the ex. You need to get your friend out of the trouble you just created. *What are some of the things you might say? What would you be sure not to say?*

For an application of some of these principles to a letter to Dear Abby, see "It's about communication, Abby" at **tcbdevito .blogspot.com**. How would you have answered this writer's letter?

Objectives Self-Check
- Can you paraphrase the seven principles of human communication and their implications for human interaction (it is purposeful; involves choices; is ambiguous; involves content and relationship dimensions; involves power; is punctuated; and is inevitable, irreversible, and unrepeatable)?

Explore the **Exercise**
"From Culture to Gender" at
MyCommunicationLab

Culture and Human Communication

Culture consists of the beliefs, ways of behaving, and artifacts of a group. By definition, culture is transmitted through communication and learning rather than through genes.

A walk through any large city, many small towns, or just about any college campus will convince you that the United States is a collection of many different cultures. These cultures coexist somewhat separately but all influence one another. This coexistence has led some researchers to refer to these cultures as *cocultures* (Shuter, 1990; Samovar & Porter, 1991; Jandt, 2010).

Gender is considered a cultural variable largely because cultures teach boys and girls different attitudes, beliefs, values, and ways of communicating and relating to one another. This means that you act like a man or a woman in part because of what your culture has taught you about how men and women should act. This is not to deny that biological differences also play a role in the differences between male and female behavior. In fact, research continues to uncover the biological roots of behavior we once thought was entirely learned—acting happy or shy, for example (McCroskey, 1997).

Yet we're living in a time of changing gender roles. Many men, for example, are doing more housekeeping chores and caring for their children. More obvious perhaps is that women are becoming more visible in career fields once occupied exclusively by men—politics, law enforcement, the military, and the clergy are just some examples. And, of course, women are increasingly present in the corporate executive ranks; the glass ceiling may not have disappeared, but it has cracked.

Because your communication is heavily influenced by the culture in which you were raised, culture is highly relevant to communication, and a cultural perspective serves numerous important purposes.

THE IMPORTANCE OF CULTURE

Culture is important for a variety of reasons. Here are a few:

- **Demographic changes**: Whereas at one time the United States was a country largely populated by Europeans, it's now greatly influenced by the enormous number of new citizens from Latin America, South America, Africa, and Asia. With these changes have come different customs and the need to understand and adapt to new ways of looking at communication.

- **Sensitivity to cultural differences**: As a people, we've become increasingly sensitive to cultural differences. U.S. society has moved from an *assimilationist perspective* (the idea that people should leave their native culture behind and adapt to their new culture) to a view that values *cultural diversity* (people should retain their native cultural ways). At the same time, the ability to interact effectively with members of other cultures often translates into financial gain and increased employment opportunities and advancement prospects.

- **Economic interdependence**: Today most countries are economically dependent on one another. Our economic lives depend on our ability to communicate effectively across cultures. Similarly, our political well-being depends in great part on that of other cultures. Political unrest or financial problems in any part of the world—Africa, Europe, or the Middle East, to take a few examples—affects our own security. Intercultural communication and understanding now seem more crucial than ever.

- **Communication technology**: Technology has made intercultural interaction easy, practical, and inevitable. It's common to have social network friends from different cultures, and these relationships require a new way of looking at communication and culture.

- **Culture-specific nature of communication**: Still another reason culture is so important is that communication competence is culture specific. As we'll see throughout this chapter, what proves effective in one culture may prove ineffective (even offensive) in another.

Explore the **Exercise**
"Cultural Beliefs" at
MyCommunicationLab

THE DIMENSIONS OF CULTURE

Because of its importance in all forms of human communication, culture is given a prominent place in this text; and theories and research findings that bear on culture and communication are discussed throughout. Prominent among these discussions are the seven major dimensions of culture, which we briefly preview here:

Watch the **Video**
"That's So Rude" at
MyCommunicationLab

- **Uncertainty avoidance**: The degree to which a culture values predictability. In high-uncertainty-avoidance cultures, predictability and order are extremely important; in low-uncertainty-avoidance cultures, risk-taking and ambiguity are tolerated more easily.

- **Masculinity–femininity**: The extent to which cultures embrace traditionally masculine characteristics, such as ambition and assertiveness, or embrace traditionally feminine characteristics, such as caring and nurturing others.

- **Power distance**: The way power is distributed throughout the society. In high-power-distance cultures, there is a great power difference between those in authority and others. In low-power-distance cultures, power is distributed more evenly.

- **Individualism–collectivism**: A culture's emphasis on the importance of the individual or of the group. Individualist cultures value qualities such as self-reliance, independence, and individual achievement; collectivist cultures emphasize social bonds, the primacy of the group, and conformity to the larger social group.

- **High and low context**: The extent to which information is seen as embedded in the context or tacitly known among members. In high-context cultures information is part of the context and does not have to be verbalized explicitly. In low-context cultures information is made explicit and little is taken for granted.

- **Indulgence and restraint**: The relative emphasis a culture places on the gratification of desires, on having fun, and enjoying life (indulgent cultures) as opposed to cultures which emphasize the curbing of these desires (restraint cultures).

- **Long- and short-term orientation**: The degree to which a culture teaches an orientation that promotes the importance of future rewards (long-term orientation) versus cultures that emphasize the importance of immediate rewards. These cultures also differ in their view of the workplace. Organizations in long-term-oriented cultures look to profits in the future. Managers or owners and workers in such cultures share the same values and work together to achieve a common good. Organizations in short-term-oriented cultures, on the other hand, look to more immediate rewards. Managers and workers are very different in their thinking and in their attitudes about work. Table 1.2 presents the differing values of the workplace selected by Asian and American executives.

TABLE 1.2   Values of the Workplace

Asian (long-term culture) and American (short-term culture) executives were asked to rank those values they considered most important in the workplace. The top six responses are presented here (in order of perceived importance) and show a dramatic difference between the two cultural groups (Hofstede, Hofstede, & Minkov, 2010). Notice that "hard work" makes both lists but in very different positions.

Values Selected by Asian (Long-Term Orientation) Executives	Values Selected by American (Short-Term Orientation) Executives
Hard work	Freedom of expression
Respect for learning	Personal freedom
Honesty	Self-reliance
Openness to new ideas	Individual rights
Accountability	Hard work
Self-discipline	Personal achievement

VIEWPOINTS

Campus Culture

How would you describe the culture of your campus? How would you describe the level of cultural awareness and cultural sensitivity on your campus?

Explore the **Exercise** "Cultural Identifiers" at **MyCommunicationLab**

THE AIM OF A CULTURAL PERSPECTIVE

Because culture permeates all forms of communication, and because what messages are effective in one culture may prove totally ineffective in another culture, it's necessary to understand cultural influences if you're to understand how communication works and master its skills. As illustrated throughout this text, culture influences communications of all types (Moon, 1996). It influences what you say to yourself and how you talk with friends, lovers, and family in everyday conversation. It influences how you interact in groups and how much importance you place on the group versus the individual. It influences the topics you talk about and the strategies you use in communicating information or in persuading.

Cultural differences exist across the communication spectrum—from the way you use eye contact to the way you develop or dissolve a relationship (Chang & Holt, 1996). But these differences should not blind you to the great number of similarities among even the most widely separated cultures. Close interpersonal relationships, for example, are common in all cultures, although they may be entered into for very different reasons by members of different cultures. Further, when reading about cultural differences, remember that they are usually matters of degree. For example, most cultures value honesty, but not all value it to the same extent. The advances in media and technology and the widespread use of the Internet, among other factors, are influencing cultures and cultural change and are perhaps homogenizing cultures, lessening intercultural differences, and increasing similarities. They're also Americanizing various cultures—because the dominant values and customs evidenced in the media and on the Internet are in large part American.

This text's emphasis on cultural understanding does not imply that you should accept all cultural practices or that all cultural practices must be evaluated as equally good (Hatfield & Rapson, 1996). For example, cockfighting, foxhunting, and bullfighting are parts of the cultures of some Latin American countries, England, and Spain, respectively; but you need not find these activities acceptable or equal to cultural practices in which animals are treated kindly. Similarly, you can reject your own culture's values and beliefs; its religion or political system; or its attitudes toward the homeless, the disabled, or the culturally different. Of course, going against your culture's traditions and values is often very difficult. Still, it's important to realize that culture *influences* but does not *determine* your values or behavior. Often, factors such as personality (your degree of assertiveness, extroversion, or optimism, for example) will prove more influential than culture (Hatfield & Rapson, 1996).

ETHNIC IDENTITY AND ETHNOCENTRISM

As you learn your culture's ways, you develop an **ethnic identity**—for example, you self-identity as a member of the group, you embrace (largely) the attitudes and beliefs of the group, and behave as a member of the group (perhaps celebrating ethnic holidays or preparing ethnic foods).

A healthy ethnic identity is generally regarded as a positive trait. It helps to preserve the ethnic culture, build group cohesiveness, and enable it to make its unique contributions to the culture as a whole. On the other hand, **ethnocentrism** is an extreme ethnic identity; it's the tendency to see others and their behaviors through your own cultural filters, often as distortions of your own behaviors. It's the tendency to evaluate the values, beliefs, and behaviors of your own culture as superior and as more positive, logical, and natural than those of other cultures. Although ethnocentrism may give you pride in your own culture and its achievements and encourage you to sacrifice for the culture, it also may lead you to see other cultures as inferior and may make you unwilling to profit from the contributions of other cultures. For example, there's a "substantial relationship" between ethnocentrism and homophobia (Wrench & McCroskey, 2003).

TABLE 1.3   The Ethnocentrism Continuum

This table summarizes some of the interconnections between ethnocentrism and communication. Five degrees of ethnocentrism are identified; in reality, there are as many degrees as there are people. The "communication distances" are general terms that highlight the attitude that dominates that level of ethnocentrism. Under "communications" are some of the major ways people might interact given their particular degree of ethnocentrism. Can you identify your own ethnocentrism in this table? For example, are there groups to which you have low ethnocentrism? Middle? High? What accounts for these differences? This table draws on the work of several intercultural researchers (Lukens, 1978; Gudykunst & Kim, 1992; Gudykunst, 1991).

Degree of Ethnocentrism	Communication Distance	Communications
Low	Equality	You treat others as equals; you view different customs and ways of behaving as equal to your own.
	Sensitivity	You want to decrease the distance between yourself and others.
	Indifference	You lack concern for others; you prefer to interact in a world of similar others.
	Avoidance	You avoid and limit interactions, especially intimate communication with interculturally different others.
High	Disparagement	You engage in hostile behavior and belittle others; you view different cultures and ways of behaving as inferior to your own.

Ethnocentrism exists on a continuum (Table 1.3). People are not either ethnocentric or non-ethnocentric; most are somewhere between these polar opposites. And, of course, your degree of ethnocentrism often varies depending on the group on which you focus. For example, if you're Greek American, you may have a low degree of ethnocentrism when dealing with Italian Americans but a high degree when dealing with Turkish Americans or Japanese Americans. Your degree of ethnocentrism will influence your communication in all its forms, as we'll see throughout this text.

Objectives Self-Check
- Can you explain the role of culture in human communication and the seven ways in which cultures different from one another (individualist-collectivist, high and low context, high and low power distance, masculine and feminine, high and low tolerance for ambiguity, long- and short-term orientation, and indulgence and restraint)?
- Can you define *ethnic identity* and *ethnocentrism*?

Communication Competence

Communication competence refers to (1) your knowledge and understanding of how communication works and (2) your ability to use communication effectively (Spitzberg & Cupach, 1989, 2002). Your understanding of communication would include a knowledge of the elements involved in communication, how these elements interact, and how each communication situation is both different from and similar to other situations. Your knowledge would also include an understanding of the choices you have for communicating in any given situation.

Using communication effectively would involve your ability to select and implement the best choices for communicating, and to read and adjust to the ongoing feedback that you receive from your own messages and that guide the choices you make in selecting future messages.

The more you know about communication, the more choices you'll have available for your day-to-day interactions. It's like learning vocabulary. The more vocabulary you know, the more choices you have to express yourself. In a similar way, the aim of this text is to increase your communicative competence and thus to give you a broad range of options to use in your own communications.

Let's spell out the nature of communication competence in more detail by discussing the major themes of competence that contemporary research and theory identify and that are highlighted in this text.

For a brief list of the characteristics of success, see "Communication and Success" at **tcbdevito .blogspot.com**.

THE COMPETENT COMMUNICATOR THINKS CRITICALLY AND MINDFULLY

An essential part of communication skill is the ability to think critically about the communication situations you face and the options for communicating that you have available; this is crucial to your success and effectiveness.

Without critical thinking there can be no competent exchange of ideas. Critical thinking is logical thinking; it's thinking that is well-reasoned, unbiased, and clear. It involves thinking intelligently, carefully, and with as much clarity as possible. And, not surprisingly, critical thinking is one of the stepping stones to effective management (Miller, 1997).

A special kind of critical thinking is **mindfulness**—a state of awareness in which you're conscious of your reasons for thinking or behaving. In its opposite, **mindlessness,** you lack conscious awareness of what or how you're thinking (Langer, 1989). To apply communication skills effectively in conversation, you need to be mindful of the unique communication situation you're in, of your available communication options, and of the reasons why one option is likely to be better than the others (Elmes & Gemmill, 1990; Burgoon, Berger, & Waldron, 2000).

As you progress through your study of human communication, actively increase your own mindfulness (Langer, 1989):

Communication Choice Point

Questionable Posts

Your friend has been posting some rather extreme socio-political statements that you think might turn out to be detrimental when searching for a graduate school or job. You've always been honest with each other but careful because you're both very sensitive to criticism. *What are some ways you can bring up this topic without seeming critical?*

- *Create and re-create categories.* Group things in different ways; remember that people are constantly changing, so the categories into which you may group them also should change. Learn to see objects, events, and people as belonging to a wide variety of categories. Try to see, for example, your prospective romantic partner in a variety of roles—child, parent, employee, neighbor, friend, financial contributor, and so on.

- *Be open to new information.* Be open even in listening to different points of view that may contradict your most firmly held beliefs. New information forces you to reconsider what might be outmoded ways of thinking and can help you challenge long-held, but now inappropriate, beliefs and attitudes.

- *Beware of relying too heavily on first impressions* (Chanowitz & Langer, 1981; Langer, 1989). Treat first impressions as tentative, as hypotheses that need further investigation. Be prepared to revise, reject, or accept these initial impressions.

- *Think before you act.* Especially in delicate situations such as anger or commitment messages, it's wise to pause and think over the situation mindfully (DeVito, 2003). In this way you'll stand a better chance of acting and reacting appropriately.

You'll find frequent opportunities to apply mindful, critical thinking throughout your reading of the text but perhaps especially in the Skill Development Experiences, in the Communication Choice Points, and in the Test Yourself quizzes.

THE COMPETENT COMMUNICATOR IS CULTURALLY SENSITIVE

Communication competence is culture-specific; that is, the principles of effective communication vary from one culture to another, and what proves effective in one culture may prove ineffective in another. For example, in American culture you would call a person you wish to date three or four days in advance. In certain Asian cultures, you might call the person's parents weeks or even months in advance. Thus, discussions of cultural implications accompany all of the major topics considered in this text.

Some examples include the major ways in which cultures differ and the implications these differences have for communication; cultural differences in politeness; cultural and gender differences in nonverbal messages such as facial expressions, colors, touch, silence, and time; cultural differences in approaches to small group communication and leadership; and cultural differences in varied aspects of public speaking such as language usage and approaches to proof and evidence.

THE COMPETENT COMMUNICATOR IS ETHICAL

Human communication also involves questions of **ethics,** the study of good and bad, of right and wrong, of moral and immoral. Ethics is concerned with actions, with behaviors; it's concerned with distinguishing between behaviors that are moral (ethical, good, right) and those that are immoral (unethical, bad, wrong). Not surprisingly, there's an ethical dimension to any communication act (Neher & Sandin, 2007; Bok, 1978).

In addition to this introductory discussion, ethical dimensions of human communication are presented in each of the remaining chapters in Communicating Ethically boxes. As a kind of preview, here are just a few of the ethical issues raised. As you read these questions, think about your own ethical beliefs and how they would influence the way you answered the questions.

- What are your ethical obligations as a listener? (Chapter 3, p. 55)
- When is it unethical to remain silent? (Chapter 5, p. 111)
- At what point in a relationship do you have an obligation to reveal intimate details of your life? (Chapter 6, p. 121)
- Are there ethical and unethical ways to engage in conflict and conflict resolution? (Chapter 8, p. 163)
- When is gossiping ethical and when is it unethical? (Chapter 9, p. 184)

For a brief self-test on what is ethical, see "ABCD: Ethics" at tcbdevito.blogspot.com. Add your own comments to the many that you'll find.

THE COMPETENT COMMUNICATOR IS AN EFFECTIVE LISTENER

Often we tend to think of competence in communication as "speaking effectiveness," paying little attention to listening. But listening is an integral part of communication; you cannot be a competent communicator if you're a poor listener.

If you measured importance by the time you spend on an activity, then—according to the research studies available—listening would be your most important communication activity. Studies conducted from 1929 to 1980 show that listening was the most often used form of communication. For example, in a study of college students conducted in 1980 (Barker, Edwards, Gaines, Gladney, & Holley), listening also occupied the most time: 53 percent compared to reading (17 percent), speaking (16 percent), and writing (14 percent). In a more recent survey, the figures for the four communication activities were listening (40%), talking (35%), reading (16%), and writing (9%) (Watkins, 2007). Again, listening is the most often used of all communication activities.

Because of the importance of listening, it is emphasized in this text in two major ways: (1) Chapter 3 is devoted exclusively to listening and covers the nature and importance of listening, the steps you go through in listening, the role of culture and gender in listening, and ways to increase your listening effectiveness. (2) In the remaining chapters, listening skills are integrated into the text discussions.

Objectives Self-Check
- Can you define *communication competence* and explain the four qualities identified as part of competence (mindful and critical thinking, cultural sensitivity, ethics, and effective listening)?

⚠ Messages in the Media *Wrap Up*

Situation comedies are replete with characters who have all types of communication problems. Watching your favorite sitcoms with the principles of communication discussed in this chapter in mind will help you see these concepts in operation in an imaginative variety of specific situations.

Summary of Concepts and Skills

 Listen to the **Audio Chapter Summary** at **MyCommunicationLab**

This chapter considered the nature of human communication, its major elements and principles, the role of culture in human communication, and communication competence.

Foundations of Human Communication

1. Communication is the act, by one or more persons, of sending and receiving messages that are distorted by noise, occur within a context, have some effect (and some ethical dimension), and provide some opportunity for feedback.
2. Communication is transactional. It is a process of inter-related parts in which a change in one element produces changes in other elements.

Communication Models and Concepts

3. The essentials of communication—the elements present in every communication act—are sources–receivers; messages (feedforward, feedback, and metamessages); context (physical, cultural, social–psychological, and temporal); channel; noise (physical, physiological, psychological, and semantic); and effects.

Principles of Communication

4. Communication is purposeful. Through communication, you learn, relate, help, influence, and play.
5. Communication involves choices and those choices will determine effectiveness or ineffectiveness.
6. Communication and relationships are always—in part—ambiguous.
7. Communication involves both content and relationship dimensions.
8. Communication and relationships invariably involve issues of power.
9. Communication sequences are punctuated for processing. Individuals divide the communication sequence into stimuli and responses in different ways.
10. In any interactional situation, communication is inevitable (you cannot not communicate, nor can you not respond to communication), irreversible (you cannot take back messages), and unrepeatable (you cannot exactly repeat messages).

Culture and Human Communication

11. Culture permeates all forms of communication, and intercultural communication is becoming more and more frequent as the United States becomes home to a variety of cultures and does business around the world.
12. Significant dimensions along which cultures may differ are uncertainty avoidance, masculinity–femininity, power

distance, individualism–collectivism, and high and low context.
13. Ethnocentrism, existing on a continuum, is the tendency to evaluate the beliefs, attitudes, and values of our own culture positively and those of other cultures negatively.

Communication Competence

14. Communication competence refers to your knowledge of how communication works and your ability to use communication effectively. Communication competence includes, for example, thinking critically and mindfully, being culturally sensitive, communicating ethically and listening effectively.

Several important communication skills emphasized in this chapter are presented here in summary form (as they are in every chapter). These skill checklists don't include all the skills covered in the chapter but rather are representative of the most important skills. Place a check mark next to those skills that you feel you need to work on most.

_____ 1. I'm sensitive to contexts of communication. I recognize that changes in physical, cultural, social–psychological, and temporal contexts will alter meaning.

_____ 2. I assess my channel options and evaluate whether my message will be more effective if delivered face-to-face, through e-mail, or by some third party, for example.

_____ 3. I look for meaning not only in words but also in nonverbal behaviors.

_____ 4. I am sensitive to the feedback and feedforward that I give to others and that others give to me.

_____ 5. I combat the effects of the various types of physical, psychological, and semantic noise that distort messages.

_____ 6. I listen not only to the more obvious content messages but also to the relational messages that I (and others) send, and I respond to the relational messages of others to increase meaningful interaction.

_____ 7. Instead of looking only at the punctuation patterns, I also look at the patterns that others might be using in order to understand better the meanings communicated.

_____ 8. Because communication is transactional, I recognize that all elements influence every other element in the communication process and that each person communicating is simultaneously a speaker/listener.

_____ 9. Because communication is purposeful, I look carefully at both the speaker's and the listener's purposes.

_____ 10. Because communication is inevitable, irreversible, and unrepeatable, I look carefully for hidden meanings, am cautious in communicating messages that I may later wish to withdraw, and am aware that any communication act occurs but once.

_____ 11. I am sensitive to cultural variation and differences, and I see my own culture's teachings and those of other cultures without undue bias.

 Key Word Quiz

The Essentials of Human Communication

Match the terms about human communication with their definitions. Record the number of the definition next to the appropriate term.

_____ a. intrapersonal communication (3)

_____ b. metamessages (6)

_____ c. encoding (5)

_____ d. communication competence (4)

_____ e. computer-mediated communication (4)

_____ f. feedback (6)

_____ g. power (13)

_____ h. transactional view of communication (5)

_____ i. ethnocentrism (18)

_____ j. ethnic identity (18)

1. Communication between two or more people through some electronic means

2. Knowledge of communication and the ability to apply that knowledge for effective communication

3. The view of communication that sees each person as taking both speaker and listener roles simultaneously

4. Communication with yourself

5. Commitment to the beliefs and values of your culture

6. The process of putting ideas into a code; for example, thinking of an idea and then describing it in words

7. The tendency to see others and their behaviors through your own cultural filters

8. The messages you get back from your own messages and from the responses of others to what you communicate

9. Messages that refer to other messages

10. The ability to influence the behaviors of others

These ten terms and additional terms used in this chapter can be found in the glossary.

Answers: a. 4; b. 9; c. 6; d. 2; e. 1; f. 8; g. 10; h. 3; i. 7; j. 5

 Study and **Review** the **Flashcards** in **MyCommunicationLab**

MyCommunicationLab

Throughout this chapter, there are icons in the margin that highlight media content for selected topics. Go to **MyCommunicationLab** for additional information on the essentials of human communication. Here you'll find flashcards to help you learn the jargon of communication, videos that illustrate a variety of concepts, additional exercises, and discussions to help you continue your study of human communication.

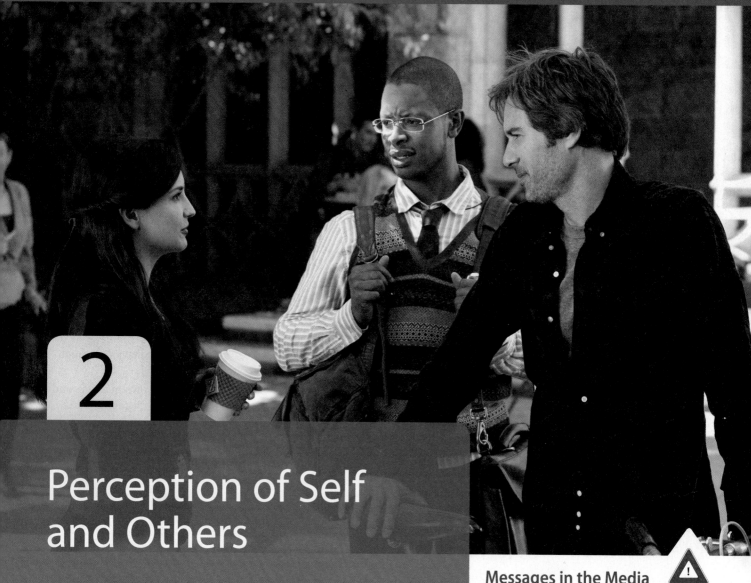

2

Perception of Self and Others

Objectives

 Listen to the **Audio Chapter**
at **MyCommunicationLab**

After reading this chapter, you should be able to:

❶ Define *self-concept*, *self-awareness*, and *self-esteem* and identify the ways in which self-awareness and self-esteem may be increased.

❷ Define *self-disclosure*, its rewards and dangers, and use the suggested guidelines in making, responding to, and resisting self-disclosure.

❸ Define *perception*, explain its five stages, and apply the suggestions to increase your own perceptual accuracy.

❹ Describe the nature of impression formation and the major factors that influence it.

❺ Explain and give examples of the strategies of impression management.

Messages in the Media

Perception is a dramatic series that revolves around the work of Professor Daniel Pierce, an unconventional neuroscientist who has the ability to perceive connections and relationships that others cannot see. Each episode provides a unique view into the importance of seeing what others do not, a topic explored in this chapter.

This chapter looks at the ways in which you perceive yourself, the ways others perceive you, and the ways you perceive others. First, we explore the nature of the self and a special form of communication known as self-disclosure and the nature of perception. With this as a background, we then explain how we perceive (form impressions of) others, how they perceive us, and how we manage the impressions that we communicate to others.

The Self in Human Communication

Who you are and how you see yourself influence not only the way you communicate but also how you respond to the communications of others. This first section explores the self: the self-concept and how it develops; self-awareness and ways to increase it; self-esteem and ways to enhance it; and self-disclosure, or communication that reveals who you are.

SELF-CONCEPT

Your **self-concept** is your image of who you are. It's how you perceive yourself: your feelings and thoughts about your strengths and weaknesses, your abilities and limitations. Self-concept develops from the image that others have of you, comparisons between yourself and others, your cultural experiences, and your evaluation of your own thoughts and behaviors (Figure 2.1).

Watch the **Video** "Sarah's Blog" at **MyCommunicationLab**

Others' Images of You   If you want to see how your hair looks, you'll probably look in a mirror. But what if you want to see how friendly or how assertive you are? According to the concept of the **looking-glass self** (Cooley, 1922), you'd look at the image of yourself that others reveal to you through the way they communicate with you.

Of course, you would not look to just anyone. Rather, you would look to those who are most significant in your life, such as your friends, family members, and romantic partners. If these significant persons think highly of you, you will see a positive self-image reflected in their behaviors; if they think little of you, you will see a more negative image.

Comparisons with Others   Another way you develop self-concept is by comparing yourself with others, most often with your peers (Festinger, 1954). For example, after an exam, you probably want to know how you performed relative to the other students in your class. This gives you a clearer idea of how effectively you performed. If you play on a baseball team, it's important to know your batting average in comparison to those of your teammates. You gain a different perspective when you see yourself in comparison to your peers.

For good or ill, social media have provided us with the tools (all very easy to use) to compare ourselves to others, perhaps to estimate our individual worth or make us feel superior. Here are just a half-dozen ways social media enables people to find out how they stand.

- **Search engine reports.** Type in your name on Google, Bing, or Yahoo, for example, and you'll see the number of websites on which your name (and others that are similarly named) appears. Type in a colleague's name and you get a number of websites on which his or her name appears which, you're hoping, is fewer than yours.

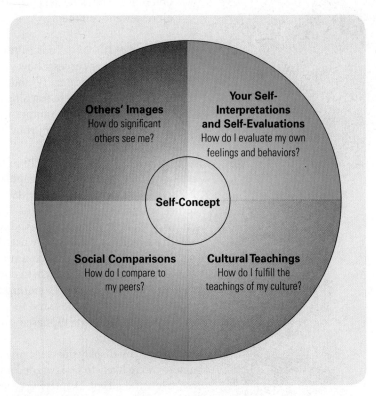

FIGURE 2.1

The Sources of Self-Concept

The four contributors to how you see yourself. As you read about self-concept, consider the influence of each factor throughout your life. Which factor influenced you most as a preteen? Which influences you most now? Which will influence you most in 25 or 30 years?

- **Network spread.** Your number of friends on Facebook or your contacts on LinkedIn or Plaxo is in some ways a measure of your potential influence. Look at a friend's profile and you have your comparison. Not surprisingly, there are websites that will surf the net to help you contact more social network friends.

- **Online influence.** Network sites such as Klout and PeerIndex provide you with a score (from 0-100) of your online influence. Your Klout score, for example, is a combination of your "true reach"—the number of people you influence, "amplification"—the degree to which you influence them, and "network"—the influence of your network. Postrank Analytics, on the other hand, provides you with a measure of engagement—the degree to which people interact with, pay attention to, read, or comment on what you write.

- **Twitter activities.** The number of times you tweet might be one point of comparison but, more important, is the number of times you are tweeted about or your tweets are repeated (retweets). Twitalyzer will provide you with a three-part score—an impact score, a Klout score, and a Peer Index score—and it will also enable you to search the "twitter elite" for the world as well as for any specific area (which you can search by zip code). Assuming your Twitter score is what you'd like it to be, a single click will enable you to post this score on your own Twitter page.

- **Blog presence.** Your blog presence is readily available from your "stats" tab where you can see how many people visited your blog since inception or over the past year, month, week, or day. And you'll also see a map of the world indicating where people who are visiting your blog come from.

- **References to written works.** Google Scholar, for example, will enable you to see how many other writers have cited your works (and how many cited the works of the person you're comparing) and the works in which you were cited. And, of course, Amazon and other online book dealers provide rankings of your books along with a star system based on reviewers' comments.

Explore the **Exercise**
"How Open Are You Culturally?"
at **MyCommunicationLab**

Cultural Teachings

Your culture instills in you a variety of beliefs, values, and attitudes about such things as success (how you define it and how you should achieve it); the relevance of religion, race, or nationality; and the ethical principles you should follow in business and in your personal life. These teachings provide benchmarks against which you can measure yourself. Your ability, for example, to achieve what your culture defines as success contributes to a positive self-concept; your failure to achieve what your culture values contributes to a negative self-concept.

Especially important in self-concept are cultural teachings about gender roles—how a man or woman should act. A popular classification of cultures is in terms of their masculinity and femininity (Hofstede, 1997). [Some intercultural theorists note that equivalent terms would be cultures based on "achievement" and "nurturance," but because research is conducted under the terms *masculine* and *feminine* and these are the terms you'd use to search electronic databases, we use them here (Lustig & Koester, 2013).] Masculine cultures socialize people to be assertive, ambitious, and competitive. For example, members of masculine cultures are more likely to confront conflicts directly and to fight out any differences; they're more likely to emphasize win—lose conflict strategies. Feminine cultures socialize people to be modest and to value close interpersonal relationships. For example, they are more likely to emphasize compromise and negotiation in resolving conflicts, win–win solutions.

When you display the traits prized by your culture—whether they be masculine or feminine—you're likely to be rewarded and complimented, and this feedback contributes to a positive self-concept. Displaying contrary traits is likely to result in criticism, which, in turn, will contribute to a more negative self-concept.

Explore the **Exercise**
"I'd Prefer to Be" at
MyCommunicationLab

Self-Interpretations and Self-Evaluations

Your self-interpretations (your reconstruction of your behavior in a given event and your understanding of it) and self-evaluations (the value—good or bad—that you place on that behavior) also contribute to your self-concept. For example, let's say you believe that lying is wrong. If you then lie and view what you said as a lie (rather than as, say, a polite way of avoiding an issue), you will probably evaluate this behavior in terms of your internalized beliefs about lying and will react negatively to your own behavior. You may, for example, experience guilt about violating your own beliefs. On the other hand, let's say that you pull someone out of a burning building at great personal risk. You will probably evaluate this behavior positively; you'll feel good about your behavior and, as a result, about yourself.

SELF-AWARENESS

Self-awareness is basic to all communication and is achieved when you examine several aspects of yourself as they might appear to others as well as to you. One commonly used tool for this examination is the **Johari window,** a metaphoric division of the self into four areas, as shown in Figure 2.2 (a).

Your Four Selves   The four areas or "panes" in the Johari window show different aspects or versions of the self: the open self, blind self, hidden self, and unknown self. These areas are not separate from one another: they are interdependent. As one dominates, the others recede to a greater or lesser degree; or, to stay with our metaphor, as one windowpane becomes larger, one or more others become smaller.

Communication Choice Point

Understanding Rejection

You've asked several different people at school for a date, but so far all you've received have been rejections. Something's wrong; you're not that bad. *What are some of the things you can do to gain insight into the possible reasons for these rejections? From whom might you seek suggestions?*

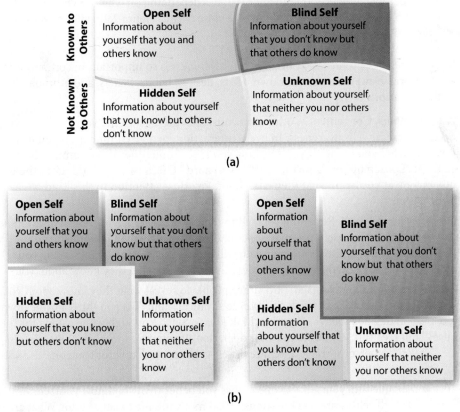

(a)

(b)

FIGURE 2.2

The Johari Window

The top window (a) presents a commonly used tool for examining what we know and don't know about ourselves. It can also help explain the nature of self-disclosure, covered later in this chapter. The window gets its name from its originators, *Joseph* Luft and *Harry* Ingham.

The two windows at the bottom (b) illustrate Johari windows of different structures. Notice that as one self grows, one or more of the other selves shrink. How would you describe the type of communication (especially self-disclosure) that might characterize the two people represented by these two windows.

- The **open self** represents all the information, behaviors, attitudes, and feelings about yourself that you, and also others, know. This could include your name, skin color, sex, age, religion, and political beliefs. The size of the open self varies according to your personality and the people to whom you're relating. For example, you may have a large open self about your romantic life with your friends (you tell them everything) but a very small open self about the same issues with, say, your parents.

- The **blind self** represents knowledge about you that others have but you don't. This might include your habit of finishing other people's sentences or your way of rubbing your nose when you become anxious. A large blind self indicates low self-awareness and interferes with accurate communication. To reduce your blind self, you can follow the suggestions offered below, in "Growing in Self-Awareness."

- The **unknown self** represents those parts of yourself that neither you nor others know. This is information buried in your subconscious. You may, for example, learn of your obsession with money, your fear of criticism, or the kind of lover you are through hypnosis, dreams, psychological tests, or psychotherapy.

- The **hidden self** represents all the knowledge you have of yourself but keep secret from others. This windowpane includes all your successfully kept secrets, such as your fantasies, embarrassing experiences, and any attitudes or beliefs you want to keep private.

Explore the **Exercise**
"Disclosing Your Hidden Self"
at **MyCommunicationLab**

Each person's Johari window will be different, and each individual's window will vary from one time to another and from one communication situation to another. You probably have a very different configuration of window panes depending on whether you're talking face to face with a parent or on Facebook with a close friend. Figure 2.2(b) illustrates two possible configurations.

Growing in Self-Awareness

Because self-awareness is so important in communication, try to increase awareness of your own needs, desires, habits, beliefs, and attitudes. You can do this in various ways.

- **Listen to others.** Conveniently, others are constantly giving you the very feedback you need to increase self-awareness. In every interaction, people comment on you in some way—on what you do, what you say, how you look. Sometimes these comments are explicit: "Loosen up" or "Don't take things so hard." Often they're "hidden" in the way others look at you or in what they talk about. Pay close attention to this kind of information.

- **Increase your open self.** Revealing yourself to others will help increase your self-awareness. As you talk about yourself, you may see connections that you had previously missed. With feedback from others, you may gain still more insight. Also, by increasing your open self, you increase the chances that others will reveal what they know about you.

- **Seek information about yourself.** Encourage people to reveal what they know about you. Use situations that arise every day to gain self-information: "Do you think I came down too hard on the kids today?" "Do you think I was assertive enough when asking for the raise?" But seek this self-awareness in moderation. If you do it too often, your friends may soon perceive you as insecure or self-centered and look for someone else with whom to talk.

- **Dialogue with yourself.** No one knows you better than you know yourself. Ask yourself self-awareness questions: What motivates me to act as I do? What are my short- and long-term goals? How do I plan to achieve them? What are my strengths and weaknesses?

SELF-ESTEEM

Self-esteem is a measure of how valuable you think you are. People with high self-esteem think very highly of themselves, whereas people with low self-esteem view themselves negatively. Before reading further about this topic, consider your own self-esteem by taking the accompanying self-test, How's Your Self-Esteem?

Communication Choice Point

Increasing Self-Awareness

You've asked several different people at school for a date, but so far all you've received are rejections. Something's wrong; you're not that bad. *What are some things you can do to increase your self-awareness of your dating techniques? To whom would you be most likely to speak? What would you say?*

TEST YOURSELF

How's Your Self-Esteem?

Respond to each of the following statements with **T** (for true) if the statement describes you at least a significant part of the time and **F** (for false) if the statement describes you rarely or never.

_____ **❶** Generally, I feel I have to be successful in all things.

_____ **❷** A number of my acquaintances are often critical or negative of what I do and how I think.

_____ **❸** I often tackle projects that I know are impossible to complete to my satisfaction.

_____ **❹** When I focus on the past, I more often focus on my failures than on my successes and on my negative rather than my positive qualities.

_____ **❺** I make little effort to improve my personal and social skills.

HOW DID YOU DO? "True" responses to the questions generally are seen as getting in the way of building positive self-esteem. "False" responses indicate that you think much like a self-esteem coach would want you to think.

WHAT WILL YOU DO? The discussion that follows here elaborates on these five issues and illustrates why each of them creates problems for the development of healthy self-esteem. So, this is a good starting place. You might also want to visit the National Association for Self-Esteem's website. There you'll find a variety of materials for examining and for bolstering self-esteem.

The basic idea behind self-esteem is that when you feel good about yourself—about who you are and what you're capable of doing—you will perform better. When you get up to give a speech and you visualize yourself as successful and effective, you're more likely to give a good speech. If, on the other hand, you think you're going to forget your speech, mispronounce words, or mix up your presentation aids, you are less likely to be successful. Increasing self-esteem will, therefore, help you to function more effectively in school, in interpersonal relationships, and in careers. Here are six suggestions for increasing self-esteem.

Attack Self-Destructive Beliefs

Challenge any beliefs you have about yourself that are unproductive or that make it more difficult for you to achieve your goals. Here are five beliefs that when taken to extremes are unrealistic and ultimately self-destructive. (Butler, 1981; Ellis & Dryden, 2007; Beck, 1988; Einhorn, 2006):

Watch the **Video**
"I'm Not Hungry" at
MyCommunicationLab

- **Perfect:** Do you believe that you have to perform at unrealistically high levels at work, school, and home, and that anything short of perfection is unacceptable?
- **Strong:** Do you believe that weakness and any of the more vulnerable emotions such as sadness, compassion, or loneliness are wrong?
- **Pleasing:** Do you believe you need the approval of others and that only if you gain it, will you be a worthy and deserving person?
- **Fast and complete:** Do you believe you have to do things quickly and take on more responsibilities than any one person might be expected to handle?
- **Doing more:** Do you believe you have to do more than anyone can reasonably do?

Do recognize that it's the extreme form of these beliefs that creates problems. Certainly, trying hard and being strong are not unhealthy when they're realistic. It's only when they become absolute—when you try to be everything to everyone—that they become impossible to achieve and create problems. Replace these self-destructive beliefs with more productive ideas.

Beware of the Impostor Phenomenon

The **impostor phenomenon** refers to the tendency to disregard outward signs of success and to consider yourself an "impostor," a

VIEWPOINTS

Self-Esteem

Popular wisdom emphasizes the importance of self-esteem. The self-esteem camp, however, has come under attack from critics (for example, Baumeister, Bushman, & Campbell, 2000; Bower, 2001). These critics argue that high self-esteem is not necessarily desirable: It does nothing to improve academic performance, it does not predict success, and it may even lead to antisocial (especially aggressive) behavior. On the other hand, it's difficult to imagine how a person would function successfully without positive self-feelings. What do you think about the benefits or liabilities of self-esteem?

Communication Choice Point

Self-Esteem

Your best friend has hit a new low in self-esteem—a long-term relationship failed, an expected promotion never materialized, a large investment went sour. You want to help your friend regain self-esteem. *What are your options? What's the first thing you would do or say?*

fake, a fraud, one who doesn't really deserve to be considered successful (Clance, 1985; Harvey & Katz, 1985). Even though others may believe you are a success, you "know" that they are wrong. One of the dangers of this belief is that it may prevent you from seeking advancement in your profession, believing you won't be up to the task. Becoming aware that such beliefs are not uncommon and that they are not necessarily permanent should help relieve some of these misperceptions. Another useful aid is to develop a relationship with an honest and knowledgeable mentor who will not only teach you the ropes but will let you know that you are successful.

Seek Out Nourishing People   Psychologist Carl Rogers (1970) drew a distinction between *noxious* and *nourishing* people. Noxious people criticize and find fault with just about everything. Nourishing people, on the other hand, are positive and optimistic, and make us feel good about ourselves. To enhance your self-esteem, seek out nourishing people and avoid noxious people. At the same time, seek to become more nourishing yourself so that you can build others' self-esteem while improving your own.

Work on Projects That Will Result in Success   Some people want to fail, or so it seems. Often they select projects that will result in failure simply because they are impossible to complete. Avoid this trap and choose projects that will result in success. Each success will help build self-esteem and make the next success a little easier. If a project does fail, recognize that this does not mean you're a failure. Everyone fails somewhere along the line. Failure is something that happens to you; it's not something you've created, and it's not something inside you.

Remind Yourself of Your Successes   Some people have a tendency to focus, sometimes too much, on their failures, their missed opportunities, their social mistakes. To counteract this tendency to dwell on failures, remind yourself of your successes. Recall these successes both intellectually and emotionally. Realize why they were successes, and relive the emotional experience when you sank the winning basket or helped your friend overcome personal problems.

Secure Affirmation   It's frequently recommended that you remind yourself of your successes with affirmations—that you focus on your good deeds; on your positive qualities, strengths, and virtues; and on your productive and meaningful relationships with friends, loved ones, and relatives (Aronson, Wilson, & Akert, 2013). The idea behind this advice is that the way you talk to yourself will influence what you think of yourself. If you *affirm* yourself—if you tell yourself that you're a success, that others like you, that you will succeed on the next test, and that you will be welcomed when asking for a date—you will soon come to feel more positive about yourself. Self-affirmations include statements like: "I'm a worthy person," "I'm responsible and can be depended upon," and "I'm capable of loving and being loved".

Some researchers argue, however, that such affirmations—although extremely popular in self-help books—may not be very helpful. These critics contend that if you have low self-esteem, you're not going to believe yourself (Paul, 2001). They propose that the alternative to self-affirmation is affirmation secured from others. You'd obtain this, for example, by becoming more competent in communication and interacting with more positive people. In this way you'd get more positive feedback from others—which, these researchers argue, is more helpful than self-talk in raising self-esteem.

Video Choice Point
My Brother's in Trouble

Marisol and her older brother Jose have always been close, choosing to spend time together and confiding in each other. Lately, Jose's self-esteem has hit a new low and he and Marisol have drifted apart. Jose's long-term relationships ended, an expected A turned into a C-, and a hoped-for job interview never materialized. Marisol wants to be able to help him get through this rough patch. She considers the topics covered in this chapter, especially self-esteem and the ways in which it may be enhanced, as she contemplates her communication choices. See how her choices play out in the video "My Brother's in Trouble."

👁 **Watch the Video** "My Brother's in Trouble" at **MyCommunicationLab**

Objectives Self-Check
- Can you define *self-concept*, *self-awareness*, and *self-esteem* and identify the ways in which self-awareness and self-esteem may be increased?

Self-Disclosure

Self-disclosure is a type of communication in which you reveal information about yourself (Jourard, 1968, 1971a, 1971b). You can look at self-disclosure as taking information from the hidden self and moving it to the open self. Overt statements about the self (e.g., "I'm getting fat"), slips of the tongue (e.g., using the name of your ex instead of your present lover's name), unconscious nonverbal movements (e.g., self-touching movements or eye avoidance), and public confessions (e.g., "Well, Jerry, it's like this …"), all can be considered forms of self-disclosure. A new and popular variation on self-disclosure is Twitter; when you send a tweet responding to the question, "What are you doing?" you're disclosing something about yourself, most often something you'd readily reveal to others. Usually, however, the term *self-disclosure* refers to the conscious revealing of information that you normally keep hidden.

Self-disclosure is "information"—something previously unknown by the receiver. This information may vary from the relatively commonplace ("I'm really afraid of that French exam") to the extremely significant ("I'm depressed; I feel like committing suicide"). For self-disclosure to occur, the communication must involve at least two people. You cannot self-disclose to yourself—the information must be received and understood by at least one other individual. The test below focuses on the influences of self-disclosure to be discussed next and will help you to personalize the discussion that follows.

"You'd know that about me if you followed me on Twitter."

TEST YOURSELF

How Willing to Self-Disclose Are You?

Respond to each of the following statements by indicating the likelihood that you would disclose such items of information to, say, other members of this class in a one-on-one face-to-face situation, on Facebook (either posting or commenting) and on the phone.

Use the following scale to fill in all three columns: **1** = would definitely self-disclose; **2** = would probably self-disclose; **3** = don't know; **4** = would probably not self-disclose; and **5** = would definitely not self-disclose.

Information	Face-to-Face Communication	On a Social Media Site	On the Phone
My attitudes toward other religions, nationalities, and races	_____	_____	_____
My financial status: how much money I earn, how much I owe, how much I have saved	_____	_____	_____
My feelings about my parents	_____	_____	_____
My sexual fantasies	_____	_____	_____
My physical and mental health	_____	_____	_____
My ideal romantic partner	_____	_____	_____
My drinking and/or drug behavior	_____	_____	_____
My most embarrassing moment	_____	_____	_____
My unfulfilled desires	_____	_____	_____
My self-concept	_____	_____	_____

HOW DID YOU DO? There are, of course, no right or wrong answers to this self-test. The higher your scores, the more apt to disclose you are in this channel. Generally, people will self-disclose most in interpersonal communication situations, least in public communication situations, and somewhere in-between in online communication.

WHAT WILL YOU DO? Taking this test, and ideally discussing it with others who also complete it, should get you started thinking about your own self-disclosing behavior and especially the factors that influence it. How does your personality influence your self-disclosure behavior? Are there certain topics on which you are less willing to disclose than others? Are you more likely to disclose positive secrets than negative ones? Are there topics about which you wish you had the opportunity to self-disclose but somehow can't find the right situation?

VIEWPOINTS

Self-Disclosure and Culture

Different cultures view self-disclosure differently. Some cultures view disclosing inner feelings as weakness. Among some groups, for example, it would be considered "out of place" for a man to cry at a happy occasion such as a wedding, whereas in some Latin cultures that same display of emotion would go unnoticed. Similarly, it's considered undesirable in Japan for workplace colleagues to reveal personal information, whereas in much of the United States it's expected (Barnlund, 1989; Hall & Hall, 1987). How would you describe your own culture's unwritten rules for appropriate self-disclosure?

Self-disclosure often brings rewards, but it can also create problems. Whether or not you self-disclose will depend on your assessment of the possible rewards and dangers.

SELF-DISCLOSURE REWARDS

There are many rewards related to self-disclosure :

- **Self-knowledge.** Self-disclosure helps you gain a new perspective on yourself and a deeper understanding of your own behavior. As you talk about yourself and listen to the reactions of others, you're likely to learn a great deal about yourself.

- **Improved coping abilities.** Self-disclosure may help you deal with a variety of problems. By verbalizing any problem or perceived failure, you'll likely see it more objectively and dispassionately. And, assuming you receive support rather than rejection from the other person, you'll likely be better able to cope with these and future problems or failures.

- **Communication enhancement.** Self-disclosure often improves communication. You understand the messages of others largely to the extent that you understand the individuals. You can tell what certain nuances mean, whether a person is serious or joking, and whether the person is being sarcastic out of fear or resentment.

- **More meaningful relationships.** By self-disclosing you tell others that you trust, respect, and care enough about them and your relationship to reveal yourself. This, in turn, is likely to lead the other individual to self-disclose and forms at least the start of a relationship that is honest and open and allows for more complete communication.

SELF-DISCLOSURE DANGERS

There are some dangers related to self-disclosure :

- **Personal risks.** The more you reveal about yourself to others, the more areas of your life you expose to possible attack. Especially in the competitive context of work (or even romance), the more that others know about you, the more they'll be able to use against you.
- **Relationship risks.** Even in close and long-lasting relationships, self-disclosure can cause problems. Parents, normally the most supportive people in most individuals' lives, frequently reject children who self-disclose their homosexuality, their plans to marry someone of a different race, or their belief in another faith. Your best friends—your closest intimates—may reject you for similar self-disclosures.
- **Professional risks.** Sometimes self-disclosure may result in professional or material losses. Politicians who disclose that they have been in therapy may lose the support of their own political party and find that voters are unwilling to vote for them. Students who disclose their alcohol or drug behavior in Facebook photos or posts may discover that jobs are more difficult to find or they may even be fired from an existing position.

Remember that self-disclosure, like any other communication, is irreversible. You cannot self-disclose and then take it back. Nor can you erase the inferences listeners make on the basis of your disclosures. Remember, too, to examine the rewards and dangers of self-disclosure in light of cultural rules. As with all cultural rules, following rules about self-disclosure brings approval, and violating them brings disapproval.

For a discussion of the factors influencing self-disclosure, see "Self-Disclosure Influences" at tcbdevito.blogspot.com. What other factors do you see influencing your own self-disclosures?

Communication Choice Point

Regulating Self-Disclosure

You're currently engaged to Kerry, but over the past few months you've been seeing someone else and have fallen in love. Now you want to break off your engagement and disclose this new relationship. But you don't want to hurt Kerry. *What are some of your choices? What would you say? Through what channel?*

GUIDELINES FOR MAKING SELF-DISCLOSURES

In addition to weighing the potential rewards and dangers of self-disclosure, consider the following suggestions, which should help you raise the right questions before you make what must be your own decision. Additional suggestions that apply especially to the workplace are identified in Table 2.1.

- **Consider the motivation for the self-disclosure.** Self-disclosure should be motivated by a concern for the relationship, for the others involved, and for yourself. Self-disclosure should serve a useful and productive function for all persons involved. Self-disclosing past indiscretions because you want to clear the air and be honest may be worthwhile; disclosing the same indiscretions to hurt your partner, however, is likely to damage the relationship.

TABLE 2.1 Self-Disclosure Cautions in the Workplace

Self-disclosure in the workplace involves somewhat different considerations from face-to-face disclosure with a friend, for example. Here are a few suggested cautions and comments.

Cautions	Comments
Assume that your disclosure will be repeated.	Although it may not be, assuming it will be, will give you a useful "what if" perspective.
Realize that your disclosure may be used against you.	This seems especially true if you're in a highly competitive organization; includes the relatively innocent office joking to the more serious issues of promotion and bonuses.
Realize that disclosure very often leads to a loss of power.	Assess whether you're willing to give up some of the power you have when people are not quite sure about you.
Understand that disclosure of a disability is your decision.	Whether or not you disclose a disability is entirely your decision, according to the U.S. Department of Labor's Office of Disability Employment Policy.
Realize that one colleague's disclosure does not obligate you to disclose.	Although reciprocating is a natural tendency, you are not required to also self-disclose—but you may be missing a great opportunity to connect with a colleague.

Explore the **Exercise** "The Timing of Self Disclosures" at **MyCommunicationLab**

- **Consider the appropriateness of the self-disclosure.** Self-disclosure should be appropriate to the context and to the relationship between you and your listener. Before making any significant self-disclosure, ask whether this is the right time (Do you both have the time to discuss this at the length it requires?) and place (Is the place free of distractions? Is it private?). Ask, too, whether this self-disclosure is appropriate to the relationship. Generally, the more intimate the disclosure, the closer the relationship should be. It's probably best to resist making intimate disclosures (especially negative ones) with nonintimates or with casual acquaintances, or in the early stages of a relationship.

  - **Consider the disclosures of the other person.** During your disclosures, give the other person a chance to reciprocate with his or her own disclosures. If the other person does not reciprocate, reassess your own self-disclosures. It may be that for this person at this time and in this context, your disclosures are not welcome or appropriate. For example, if you reveal your romantic mistakes to a friend and your friend says nothing or reveals only the most minor details, it may be a cue to stop disclosing. Generally, it's best to disclose gradually and in small increments so you can monitor your listener's responses and retreat if they're not positive enough.

  - **Consider the possible burdens self-disclosure might entail.** Carefully weigh the potential problems that you may incur as a result of your disclosure. Can you afford to lose your job if you disclose your prison record? Are you willing to risk relational difficulties if you disclose your infidelities? Are you willing to post on Facebook those images of you partying that a graduate school admissions officer or a prospective employer is likely to see?

Communication Choice Point

Corrective Self-Disclosure

When you met your current partner—with whom you want to spend the rest of your life—you minimized the extent of your romantic history. You now want to come clean and disclose your "sordid" past and need to preface this in some way. *What kinds of feedforward might you use? Through what channels? What would you say?*

GUIDELINES FOR FACILITATING AND RESPONDING TO OTHERS' DISCLOSURES

When someone discloses to you in person or through a social media site, it's usually a sign of trust and affection. In carrying out this most important receiver function, keep the following guidelines in mind:

Watch the **Video** "Friends" at **MyCommunicationLab**

- **Support and reinforce the discloser.** Express support for the person during and after the disclosures. Make your supportiveness clear through your verbal and nonverbal responses: Maintain eye contact, lean toward the speaker, ask relevant questions, and echo the speaker's thoughts and feelings. Try to refrain from judgment. Concentrate on understanding and empathizing with the discloser.

- **Be willing to reciprocate (generally).** When you make relevant and appropriate disclosures of your own in response to another's disclosures, you're demonstrating your understanding of that person's meanings and at the same time your willingness to communicate on a meaningful level—although you have no obligation to do so.

- **Keep the disclosures confidential.** If you reveal confidential disclosures, negative effects are inevitable. But most important, betraying a confidence is unfair; it debases what could be and should be a meaningful experience. Generally, the netiquette rule to not pass on e-mails to a third party without permission is a useful one for self-disclosure generally.

  - **Don't use the disclosures against the person.** Many self-disclosures expose some kind of vulnerability. If you later turn around and use a disclosure against someone, you betray the confidence and trust invested in you. Regardless of how angry you may get, resist the temptation to use the disclosures of others as weapons.

GUIDELINES FOR RESISTING PRESSURE TO SELF-DISCLOSE

You may, on occasion, find yourself in a position in which a friend, colleague, or romantic partner pressures you to self-disclose. In such situations, you may wish to weigh the pros and cons of self-disclosure and make your own decision as to whether and what you'll disclose. If your decision is not to disclose and you're still being pressured, then you need to say something. Don't be pushed. Although there

Communication Choice Point

Disclosure Encouragement

You're dating a wonderful person who is, unfortunately, extremely secretive. You wish to encourage greater disclosure but don't want to seem pushy or nosy. *What are some of the things you might say to encourage your dating partner to disclose?*

may be specific legal or ethical reasons for disclosing certain information under certain circumstances, generally you don't have to disclose if you don't want to. Recognize that you're in control of what you reveal and of when and to whom you reveal it. Should you decide to not disclose, here are two suggestions:

● **Be indirect and move to another topic.** Avoid the question that asks you to disclose and change the subject. If someone presses you to disclose your past financial problems, move the conversation to financial problems in general or nationally, or change the topic altogether. This is a polite way of saying, "I'm not talking about this," and may be the preferred choice in certain situations and with certain people. Most often people will get the hint.

● **Be assertive in your refusal to disclose.** If necessary, say very directly, "I'd rather not talk about that now," or "Now is not the time for this type of discussion."

With an understanding of the self in human communication, we can explore perception—the processes by which you come to understand yourself and others and, of course, the processes by which others come to understand you.

Communication Choice Point

Disclosure Pressure

You're dating a wonderful person who self-discloses easily and fully and who is now putting pressure on you to reveal more about yourself. You just aren't ready. *What are some of the things you can say to satisfy your partner's need for you to disclose and your own need to not reveal more about yourself right now?*

Objective Self-Check
● Can you define *self-disclosure*, its potential rewards and dangers, and the guidelines for making, responding to, and resisting the pressure for self-disclosure?
● Can you apply these guidelines in your own disclosure experiences?

Perception

Perception is your way of understanding the world; it helps you make sense of what psychologist William James called the "booming buzzing confusion." More technically, perception is the process by which you become aware of objects, events, and especially people through your senses of sight, smell, taste, touch, and hearing. Your perceptions result both from what exists in the outside world *and* from your own experiences, desires, needs and wants, loves and hatreds. Perception is important in communication because it influences your communication choices. The messages you send and listen to, the photos and messages you post and view will depend on how you see the world, how you see yourself, how you size up a specific situation, or what you think of the people with whom you interact.

Perception is a continuous series of processes that blend into one another. For convenience of discussion we can separate these processes into five stages (which may occur in a split second): (1) You sense or pick up some kind of stimulation; (2) you organize the stimuli in some way; (3) you interpret and evaluate what you perceive; (4) you store your perception in memory; and (5) you retrieve it when needed.

STIMULATION (STAGE 1)

At the first stage of perception, your sense organs are *stimulated*—you hear a new CD, you see a friend, you read someone's blog, you smell someone's perfume, you taste an orange, you feel another's sweaty palm. Naturally, you don't perceive everything; rather, you engage in **selective perception,** which includes selective attention and selective exposure.

● In **selective attention** you attend to those things that you anticipate will fulfill your needs or will prove enjoyable. For instance, when daydreaming in class, you don't hear what the instructor is saying until he or she calls your name. Your selective attention mechanism focuses your senses on the sound of your name.

● In **selective exposure** you tend to expose yourself to information that will confirm your existing beliefs, will contribute to your objectives, or will prove satisfying in some way. At the same time, you'd avoid information that would tell you that you made the wrong decision.

 Explore the **Exercise** "How Might You Perceive Other's Perceptions" at **MyCommunicationLab**

For an interesting application of perception research and theory, see "Perceiving Nonverbal Cues" at tcbdevito.blogspot.com. In what other fields would a knowledge of nonverbal behavior prove useful?

You're also more likely to perceive stimuli that are greater in intensity than surrounding stimuli. For example, television commercials normally play at a greater intensity than regular programming to ensure that you take special notice. And you're more likely to perceive stimuli that have novelty value; for example, you're more likely to notice the coworker who dresses in a unique way than the one who dresses like everyone else.

ORGANIZATION (STAGE 2)

At the second stage, you organize the information your senses pick up. One of the major ways you organize information is by rules. One frequently used rule of perception is that of **proximity,** or physical closeness: Things that are physically close to each other are perceived as a unit. Thus, using this rule, you would perceive people who are often together, or messages spoken one immediately after the other, as units, as belonging together.

Another rule is **similarity:** Things that are physically similar (they look alike) are perceived to belong together and to form a unit. This principle of similarity would lead you to see people who dress alike as belonging together. Similarly, you might assume that people who work at the same jobs, who are of the same religion, who live in the same building, or who talk with the same accent belong together.

The rule of **contrast** is the opposite of similarity: When items (people or messages, for example) are very different from each other, you conclude that they don't belong together; they're too different from each other to be part of the same unit. If you're the only one who shows up at an informal gathering in a tuxedo, you'd be seen as not belonging to the group because you contrast too much with other group members.

INTERPRETATION–EVALUATION (STAGE 3)

The third stage involves interpretation–evaluation (a combined term because the two processes cannot be separated)— and it is greatly influenced by your experiences, needs, wants, values, beliefs about the way things are or should be, expectations, physical and emotional state, and so on. Your interpretation–evaluation will be influenced by your gender; for example, women have been found to view others more positively than men (Winquist, Mohr, & Kenny, 1998).

Judgments about members of other cultures are often ethnocentric; because of your stereotypes, you can easily (but inappropriately) apply these to members of other cultures. And so it's easy to infer that when members of other cultures do things that conform to your ways of doing things, they're right, and when they do things that contradict your ways, they're wrong—a classic example of ethnocentric thinking. This tendency can easily contribute to intercultural misunderstandings.

MEMORY (STAGE 4)

Your perceptions and their interpretations—evaluations are put into memory; they're stored so that you may ultimately retrieve them at some later time. For example, you have in memory your stereotype for college athletes and the fact that Ben Williams is a football player. Ben Williams is then stored in memory with "cognitive tags" that tell you that he's strong, ambitious, academically weak, and egocentric. Despite the fact that you've not witnessed Ben's strength or ambitions and have no idea of his academic record or his psychological profile, you still may store your memory of Ben along with the qualities that make up your stereotype for college athletes.

RECALL (STAGE 5)

At some later date, you may want to recall or access the information you have stored in memory. Let's say you want to retrieve your information about Ben because he's the topic of discussion among you and a few friends. As we'll see in our discussion of listening in the next

For ways of organizing perceptions by schemata and scripts, see "Perceptual Organization" at tcbdevito.blogspot.com. How useful are these concepts to understanding your own perceptions?

Watch the **Video** "Art Appreciation" at **MyCommunicationLab**

For a brief example of the role of expectations, see "Expectations" at tcbdevito.blogspot.com. Have you ever perceived what you expected rather than what you actually sensed?

chapter, memory isn't reproductive; you don't simply reproduce what you've heard or seen. Rather, you reconstruct what you've heard or seen into a whole that is meaningful to you. It's this reconstruction that you store in memory. When you want to retrieve this information, you may recall it with a variety of inaccuracies.

Objective Self-Check
- Can you define *perception* and explain its five stages (stimulation, organization, interpretation-evaluation, memory, and recall)?
- Can you apply the skills for increasing your own perceptual accuracy?

Impression Formation

With an understanding of the self and how perception works, we can look at the ways they are intimately connected: first in **impression formation** and then in **impression management**—academic terms for what you do every day.

Impression formation (sometimes referred to as *person perception*) refers to the processes you go through in forming an impression of another person. Here, we look at a variety of impression management processes, each of which has pitfalls and potential dangers; and then we focus on some of the ways we can increase accuracy in impression formation.

IMPRESSION FORMATION PROCESSES

How you perceive another person and ultimately come to some kind of evaluation or interpretation of him or her is influenced by a variety of processes. Here, we consider some of the more significant: the self-fulfilling prophecy, primacy—recency, stereotyping, and attribution.

Watch the **Video** "Tonya" at **MyCommunicationLab**

Self-Fulfilling Prophecy A **self-fulfilling prophecy** is a prediction that comes true because you act on it as if it were true. Self-fulfilling prophecies occur in such widely different situations as parent–child relationships, educational settings, and business (Merton, 1957; Rosenthal, 2002; Madon, Guyll, & Spoth, 2004; Tierney & Farmer, 2004). There are four basic steps in the self-fulfilling prophecy:

1. You make a prediction or formulate a belief about a person or a situation. For example, you predict that Pat is friendly in social situations.

2. You act toward that person or situation as if such a prediction or belief were true. For example, you act as if Pat were a friendly person.

3. Because you act as if the belief were true, it becomes true. For example, because of the way you act, Pat becomes comfortable and friendly.

4. You observe your effect on the person or the resulting situation, and what you see strengthens your beliefs. For example, you observe Pat's friendliness, and this reinforces your belief that Pat is, in fact, friendly.

The self-fulfilling prophecy also can be seen when you make predictions about yourself and fulfill them. For example, suppose you enter a group situation convinced that the other members will dislike you. Almost invariably you'll be proved right; to you, the other members will appear to dislike you. What you may be doing is acting in a way that encourages the group to respond to you negatively. In this way, you fulfill your prophecies about yourself.

VIEWPOINTS

Your Public Messages

Will knowing that some undergraduate and graduate admissions offices and potential employers may examine your postings on sites such as MySpace or Facebook influence what you write? For example, do you avoid posting opinions that might be viewed negatively by schools or employers? Do you deliberately post items that you want schools or employers to find?

A widely known example of the self-fulfilling prophecy is the **Pygmalion effect** (Rosenthal & Jacobson, 1992). In this classic research study, experimenters told teachers that certain pupils were expected to do exceptionally well—that they were late bloomers). And although the experimenters selected the "late bloomers" at random, the students who were labeled "late bloomers" performed at higher levels than their classmates. These students became what their teachers thought they were. The expectations of the teachers may have caused them to pay extra attention to the students, and this may have positively affected the students' performance. The Pygmalion effect has also been studied in such varied contexts as the courtroom, the clinic, the work cubicle, management and leadership practices, athletic coaching, and stepfamilies (Eden, 1992; Solomon et al., 1996; Einstein, 1995; McNatt, 2001; Rosenthal, 2002).

Primacy–Recency   Assume for a moment that you're enrolled in a course in which half the classes are extremely dull and half extremely exciting. At the end of the semester, you evaluate the course and the instructor. Would your evaluation be more favorable if the dull classes occurred in the first half of the semester and the exciting classes in the second? Or would it be more favorable if the order were reversed? If what comes first exerts the most influence, you have a **primacy effect.** If what comes last (or most recently) exerts the most influence, you have a **recency effect.**

In the classic study on the effects of **primacy–recency** in perception, college students perceived a person who was described as "intelligent, industrious, impulsive, critical, stubborn, and envious" more positively than a person described as "envious, stubborn, critical, impulsive, industrious, and intelligent" (Asch, 1946). Notice that the descriptions are identical; only the order was changed. Clearly, there's a tendency to use early information to get a general idea about a person and to use later information to make this impression more specific.

For example, if you form a picture of a potential date solely on the basis of an introductory video, you may filter future information about this person through this picture/image/impression. So, if your initial impression was that the individual was supportive, friendly, and warm, you may interpret future behaviors of this person as confirming your initial assessment. Often, of course, first impressions are incorrect. For example, if you judged a job applicant as generally nervous and ill-at-ease when he or she may simply be showing normal nervousness in an interview for a much-needed job, you will have misperceived this individual. Similarly, this tendency can lead you to distort subsequent perceptions so as not to upset your original impression. For example, you may fail to see signs of deceit in someone you like because of your early impressions that this person is a good and honest individual.

Stereotyping   One of the most common shortcuts in perception is stereotyping. A **stereotype** is a fixed impression of a group of people. We all have attitudinal stereotypes—of national, religious, sexual, or racial groups, or perhaps of criminals, prostitutes, teachers, or plumbers. If you have these fixed impressions, you will, on meeting a member of a particular group, often see that person primarily as a member of that group and apply to him or her all the characteristics you assign to the group. If you meet someone who is a prostitute, for example, there are a host of characteristics for prostitutes that you may apply to this one person. To complicate matters further, you will often "see" in this person's behavior the manifestation of characteristics that you would not "see" if you didn't know what the person did for a living. Stereotypes can easily distort accurate perception and prevent you from seeing an individual purely as an individual. Stereotypes can be especially prevalent in online communication; because there are few visual and auditory cues, it's not surprising that people often rely heavily on stereotypes in forming impressions of online partners (Jacobson, 1999).

The tendency to group people and to respond to individuals primarily as members of groups can lead you to perceive an individual as possessing those qualities (usually negative) that you believe characterize his or her group (e.g., "All Mexicans are . . ."). As a result, you may fail to appreciate the multifaceted nature of all individuals and groups. Stereotyping also can lead you to ignore each person's unique characteristics so that you fail to benefit from the special contributions each individual might bring to an encounter.

Communication Choice Point

First Impression Correction

You made a bad impression at work—you drank too much at an office party and played the clown. This is an impression you want to change fast. Although you can't erase such an impression, you need to counteract it in some way. *What might you say and do to help lessen the negative effects?*

Watch the **Video** "She Can Stay" at **MyCommunicationLab**

Attribution of Control   Another way in which you form impressions is through the **attribution** of control, a process by which you focus on explaining why someone behaved as he or she did. For example, suppose you invite your friend Desmond to dinner at 7 p.m. and he arrives at 9. Consider how you would respond to each of these reasons:

Reason 1: "I just couldn't tear myself away from the beach. I really wanted to get a great tan."

Reason 2: "I was driving here when I saw some guys mugging an old couple. I broke it up and took the couple home. They were so frightened that I had to stay with them until their children arrived. The storm knocked out all the cell towers and electricity, so I had no way of calling to tell you I'd be late."

Reason 3: "I got in a car accident and was taken to the hospital."

Depending on the reason, you would probably attribute very different motives to Desmond's behavior. With reasons 1 and 2, you'd conclude that Desmond was in control of his behavior; with reason 3, that he was not. Further, you would probably respond negatively to reason 1 (Desmond was selfish and inconsiderate) and positively to reason 2 (Desmond was a good Samaritan). Because Desmond was not in control of his behavior in reason 3, you would probably not attribute either positive or negative motivation to it. Instead, you would probably feel sorry that he got into an accident.

In perceiving and especially in evaluating other people's behavior, you frequently ask if they were in control of their behavior. Generally, research shows that if you feel a person was in control of negative behaviors, you'll come to dislike him or her. If you believe the person was not in control of negative behaviors, you'll come to feel sorry for, and not blame, him or her.

In your attribution of controllability—or in attributing motives on the basis of any other reasons (e.g., hearsay or observations of the person's behavior), beware of three potential errors:

- **Self-serving bias.** You commit the **self-serving bias** when you take credit for the positive and deny responsibility for the negative. For example, you're more likely to attribute your positive outcomes (say, you get an A on an exam) to internal and controllable factors—to your personality, intelligence, or hard work. And you're more likely to attribute your negative outcomes (say, you get a D) to external and uncontrollable factors—to the exam's being exceptionally difficult or to your roommate's party the night before (Bernstein, Stephan, & Davis, 1979; Duval & Silva, 2002).

- **Overattribution.** The tendency to single out one or two obvious characteristics of a person and attribute everything that person does to these characteristics is known as **overattribution.** For example, if a person is blind or was born into great wealth, there's often a tendency to attribute everything that person does to such factors. So you might say, "Alex overeats because he's blind," or "Lillian is irresponsible because she never has had to work for her money." To prevent overattribution, recognize that most behaviors and personality characteristics result from many factors. You almost always make a mistake when you select one factor and attribute everything to it.

- **Fundamental attribution error.** The **fundamental attribution error** occurs when you overvalue the contribution of internal factors (e.g., your supervisor's personality) and undervalue the influence of external factors (e.g., the context or situation the person is in). This type of error leads you to conclude that people do what they do because that's how they are, not because of the situation they're in. When Pat is late for an appointment, you're more likely to conclude that Pat is inconsiderate or irresponsible than to attribute the lateness to a possible bus breakdown or traffic accident.

Communication Choice Point
Overattribution
Your friends overattribute your behavior, attitudes, values, and just about everything you do to your racial origins. *What communication choices do you have for explaining the illogical nature of this overattribution without insulting your friends? What would you say?*

INCREASING ACCURACY IN IMPRESSION FORMATION

Successful communication depends largely on the accuracy of the impressions you form of others. We've already identified the potential barriers that can arise with each of the perceptual processes—for example, the self-serving bias or overattribution. In addition to avoiding these barriers, here are other ways to increase your accuracy in impression formation.

Analyze Impressions   Subject your perceptions to logical analysis, to critical thinking. Here are three suggestions:

- **Recognize your own role in perception.** Your emotional and physiological state will influence the meaning you give to your perceptions. A movie may seem hysterically funny when you're in a good mood but just plain stupid when you're in a bad mood. Understand your own biases. For example, do you tend to perceive only the positive in people you like and only the negative in people you don't like?

- **Avoid early conclusions.** On the basis of your observations of behaviors, formulate hypotheses to test against additional information and evidence; avoid drawing conclusions that you then look to confirm. Look for a variety of cues pointing in the same direction. The more cues point to the same conclusion, the more likely your conclusion will be correct. Be especially alert to contradictory cues that seem to refute your initial hypotheses. At the same time, seek validation from others. Do others see things the same way you do? If not, ask yourself if your perceptions may be distorted in some way.

- **Beware of the just world hypothesis.** Many people believe that the world is just: Good things happen to good people (because they're good) and bad things happen to bad people (because they're bad) (Aronson, Wilson, & Akert, 2013; Hunt, 2000). Even when you mindfully dismiss this assumption, you may use it mindlessly when perceiving and evaluating other people. Consider a particularly vivid example: If a woman is raped in certain cultures (e.g., in Bangladesh or Yemen), she is considered by many in that culture (certainly not all) to have disgraced her family and to be deserving of severe punishment—in some cases, death. And although you may claim that this is unfair (and it surely is), much research shows that even in the United States many people do blame the rape victim, especially if the victim is male (Adams-Price, Dalton, & Sumrall, 2004; Anderson, 2004).

Check Perceptions   The process of **perception checking** is another way to reduce uncertainty and to ensure that your initial impressions are more accurate. The goal of perception checking is to further explore the thoughts and feelings of the other person, not to prove that your initial perception is correct. With this simple technique, you lessen your chances of misinterpreting another's feelings. At the same time, you give the other person an opportunity to elaborate on his or her thoughts and feelings. Let's take an example: Dolly and Jane have been Facebook friends for several years and have been very supportive of each other. Recently however, Dolly's messages have become more critical, often negative. Jane wonders if she did something wrong that offended Dolly or if something is wrong with Dolly. In using perception checking, Jane would seek to clarify the reasons for Dolly's behavior, rather than simply assume that her initial impression was correct. In its most basic form, perception checking consists of two parts:

- **Description/interpretation.** The first step is to describe what you see or hear or read and how you interpret the behavior. The descriptive part of this is that Jane sees that Dolly's messages have been unnecessarily negative. The interpretation part of this is that Jane's initial impressions are that she did something to offend Dolly or that something is wrong with Dolly.

- **Clarification.** At this second step Jane would seek clarification. Jane would ask Dolly, in one form or another, what's going on. For example, Jane may simply say "What's up? Your posts seem different" or "You didn't seem to like my last ten photos; did I do something wrong?" The objective here is simply to find out what was going on with Dolly. Be careful that your request for clarification does not sound as though you already know the answer.

Another way of checking your perceptions is to use "Galileo and the Ghosts," a technique for seeing how a particular group of people perceives a problem, person, or situation (DeVito, 1996). It involves two steps:

- **Set up a mental "ghost-thinking team,"** *much as corporations and research institutes maintain think-tanks.* Select a team of four to eight people. These can be people you admire and know or historical figures such as Galileo or Steve Jobs, fictional figures such as

Wonder Woman or Sherlock Holmes, public figures such as Hillary Clinton or Ralph Nader, or persons from other cultures or of a different sex or affectional orientation.

● **Pose a question or problem** *and then listen to how this team of ghosts perceives your problem.* Of course, you're really listening to yourself, but you are putting your perspectives aside and attempting to think like these other people. The technique forces you to step outside your normal role and to consider the perceptions of someone totally different from you.

Reduce Uncertainty   In every communication situation, there is some degree of ambiguity. A variety of strategies can help reduce uncertainty about another person (Berger & Bradac, 1982; Gudykunst, 1993; Brashers, 2007).

● **Observe.** Observing another person while he or she is engaged in an active task—preferably interacting with others in an informal social situation—will often reveal a great deal about the person, as people are less apt to monitor their behaviors and more likely to reveal their true selves in informal situations.

● **Construct situations.** You can sometimes manipulate situations so as to observe the person in more specific and revealing contexts. Employment interviews, theatrical auditions, and student teaching are good examples of situations arranged to give you an accurate view of the person in action.

● **Lurk.** When you log on to an Internet group and lurk, reading the exchanges between the other group members before saying anything yourself, you're learning about the people in the group and about the group itself, thus reducing uncertainty. When uncertainty is reduced, you're more likely to make contributions that will be appropriate to the group and less likely to violate the group's norms.

Communication Choice Point

Relationship Uncertainty
You've been dating someone casually over the past six months. You want to move to a more exclusive relationship in which you date only each other, but you've been getting mixed signals. *In what ways might you go about discovering how your partner feels?*

SKILL DEVELOPMENT EXPERIENCE

Checking Your Perceptions

Complete the table below by providing a description of how you perceive the incident and how you'd go about seeking confirmation. If you have several possible explanations for the incident, describe each of these in the second column. In the third column indicate the ways you might go about seeking clarification of your initial impressions—what your choices are for seeking clarification.

Incident	Describe What You Perceive and the Possible Interpretations or Meanings	Seek Clarification
You've extended an invitation to a classmate to be a Facebook friend but have heard nothing back.	_____	_____
Your manager at work seems to spend a lot of time with your peers but very little time with you. You're concerned about the impression you're making.	_____	_____
The person you've been dating for the last several months has stopped calling for a date. The messages have become fewer and less personal.	_____	_____

Perception checking is best thought of as a state of mind to seek clarification before forming conclusions.

VIEWPOINTS

Predictability and Uncertainty

As you and another person develop a closer and more intimate relationship, you generally reduce your uncertainty about each other; you become more predictable to each other. What level of predictability do you want in a romantic partner? Are there certain things about your partner (best friend, lover, or family member) that you'd simply rather not know?

- **Ask.** Learn about a person through asking others. You might inquire of a colleague if a third person finds you interesting and might like to have dinner with you.
- **Interact.** Interacting with the individual will of course give you considerable information. For example, you can ask questions: "Do you enjoy sports?" "What would you do if you got fired?" You also gain knowledge of another by disclosing information about yourself. These disclosures help to create an environment that encourages disclosures from the person about whom you wish to learn more.

Increase Cultural Sensitivity Recognizing and being sensitive to cultural differences will help increase your accuracy in perception. For example, Russian or Chinese artists, such as ballet dancers, will often applaud their audience by clapping. Americans seeing this may easily interpret it as egotistical. Similarly, a German man will enter a restaurant before a woman in order to see if the place is respectable enough for the woman to enter. This simple custom can easily be interpreted as rude by people from cultures in which it's considered courteous for the woman to enter first (Axtell, 2007).

Cultural sensitivity will help counteract the difficulty many people have in understanding the nonverbal messages of people from other cultures. For example, it's easier to interpret the facial expressions of members of your own culture than those of another culture (Weathers, Frank, & Spell, 2002). This "in-group advantage" will assist your perceptual accuracy for members of your own culture but will often hinder your accuracy for members of other cultures (Elfenbein & Ambady, 2002).

Within every cultural group there are wide and important differences. As all Americans are not alike, neither are all Indonesians, Greeks, or Mexicans. When you make assumptions that all people of a certain culture are alike, you're thinking in stereotypes. Recognizing differences between another culture and your own, and among members of the same culture, will help you perceive people and situations more accurately.

Objectives Self-Check
- Can you describe the nature of impression formation and the factors that influence perception: self-fulfilling prophecy, perceptual accentuation, primary-recency, and the attribution of control?
- Can you apply the skills for increasing your accuracy in impression formation?

Impression Management: Goals and Strategies

Communication Choice Point

Mutual Attraction Testing

You've become attracted to another student in your class but don't know if it's mutual. *In what ways might you use the suggestions discussed here for increasing your own accuracy in perceiving whether or not the attraction is mutual?*

Impression management (some writers use the term *self-presentation* or *identity management*) refers to the processes you go through to communicate the impression you want other people to have of you.

Impression management is largely the result of the messages communicated. In the same way that you form impressions of others largely on the basis of how they communicate, verbally and nonverbally, they also form impressions of you based on what you say (your verbal messages) and how you act and dress (your nonverbal messages). Communication messages, however, are not the only means for impression formation and management. For example, you also communicate your self-image and judge others by the people with whom they associate; if you associate with VIPs, then surely you must be a VIP yourself, the conventional wisdom goes. Or you might form an impression of someone on the basis of that person's age or gender or ethnic origin. Or you might rely on what others have said about the person and form impressions that are consistent with these comments. And, of course, they might well do the same in forming impressions of you.

Part of the art and skill of communication is to understand and be able to manage the impressions you give to others. Mastering the art of impression management will enable you to present yourself as you want others to see you, at least to some extent.

The strategies you use to achieve this desired impression will depend on your specific goal. The sections that follow focus on seven major communication goals and strategies. Note that although they may help you communicate the impression you want to convey, each of these strategies may also backfire and communicate exactly the opposite of your intended purpose.

"Any healthy relationship requires fundamental acting skills."

TO BE LIKED: AFFINITY-SEEKING AND POLITENESS STRATEGIES

If you're new at school or on the job and you want to be well-liked, included in the activities of others, and thought of highly, you'd likely use **affinity-seeking strategies** and **politeness strategies.** Another set of strategies often used to increase likability is *immediacy strategies* (discussed in Chapter 6, pp. 126-127).

Affinity-Seeking Strategies   Using the affinity-seeking strategies outlined here will probably increase your chances of being liked (Bell & Daly, 1984). Such strategies are especially important in initial interactions, and their use by teachers has even been found to increase student motivation (Martin & Rubin, 1998; Myers & Zhong, 2004; Wrench, McCroskey, & Richmond, 2008).

- Appear active, enthusiastic, and dynamic.
- Follow the cultural rules for polite, cooperative, respectful conversation.
- Communicate interest in the other person and include him or her in your social activities and groupings.
- Present yourself as comfortable and relaxed.
- Stimulate and encourage the other person to talk about him- or herself; reinforce his or her disclosures and contributions. Self-disclose yourself.
- Appear optimistic and positive rather than pessimistic and negative.
- Appear honest, reliable, and interesting.
- Arrange circumstances so that you and the other person come into frequent contact.
- Communicate warmth, supportiveness, and empathy.
- Demonstrate that you share significant attitudes and values with the other person.

Although this research was conducted before the advent of social media, you can easily see how the same strategies could be used in online communication. For example, you can post photos to show that you're active and enthusiastic; you can follow the rules for polite interaction by giving "likes" and "+1s" to others; and you can communicate interest in the other person by inviting him or her to hang out, by joining a group, by commenting on a post, or by retweeting. Not surprisingly, plain old flattery also goes a long way toward improving your likability. Flattery can increase your chances for success in a job interview, the tip a customer is likely to leave, and even your credibility (Varma, Toh, & Pichler, 2006; Seiter, 2007; Vonk, 2002).

Communication Choice Point

Face to Face

You've been communicating with Pat over the Internet for the past seven months and you finally have decided to meet for coffee. You really want Pat to like you. *What are some impression-management strategies you might use to get Pat to like you? What messages would you be sure not to communicate?*

Communication Choice Point

Online Dating

You've decided to join an online dating service. *How might you present yourself as likable? What types of information would you want to include and exclude in your profile?*

For a discussion of the functions of politeness, see "The Communication Functions of Politeness" at tcbdevito.blogspot.com. What function do you think is most important? Are there other functions that should be added here?

For three rules of politeness derived from letters to Dear Abby, see "Dear Abby and Politeness" at tcbdevito.blogspot.com. What one rule of politeness do you wish others would follow more often?

There is, however, a potential negative effect that can result from affinity-seeking strategies. Using them too often or in ways that might appear insincere may lead people to see you as attempting to ingratiate yourself for your own advantage and not really meaning "to be nice."

Politeness Strategies   Politeness strategies, another set of strategies people often use to appear likable, may be viewed in terms of negative and positive face (Goffman, 1967; Brown & Levinson, 1987; Holmes 1995; Goldsmith, 2007). Both are responsive to two needs that each individual has:

● **Positive face:** the desire to be viewed positively by others, to be thought of favorably.
● **Negative face:** the desire to be autonomous, to have the right to do as you wish.

Politeness in communication, then, refers to behavior that allows others to maintain both positive and negative face; and impoliteness refers to behaviors that attack either positive face (e.g., you criticize someone) or negative face (e.g., you make demands on someone).

To help another person maintain *positive face*, you speak respectfully to and about that person, you give him or her your full attention, you say "excuse me" when appropriate. In short you treat the person as you would want to be treated. In this way you allow the person to maintain positive face through what is called *positive politeness*. You *attack* the person's positive face when you speak disrespectfully about that individual, ignore the person or his or her comments, and fail to use the appropriate expressions of politeness such as *thank you* and *please*.

To help another person maintain *negative face,* you respect the person's right to be autonomous and so you request rather than demand that he or she do something; you say, "Would you mind opening a window" rather than "Open that window, damn it!" You might also give the person an "out" when making a request, allowing the person to reject your request if that is not what he or she wants. So you say, "If this is a bad time, please tell me, but I'm really strapped and could use a loan of $100" rather than "Loan me a $100" or "You have to lend me $100." If you want a recommendation, you might ask, "Would it be possible for you to write me a recommendation for graduate school?" rather than say, "You have to write me a recommendation for graduate school." In this way you enable the person to maintain negative face through what is called *negative politeness*.

Of course, we do this almost automatically and asking for a favor without any consideration for a person's negative face needs would seem totally insensitive. In most situations, however, this type of attack on negative face often appears in more subtle forms. For example, your mother saying "Are you going to wear that?"—to use Deborah Tannen's (2006) example—attacks negative face by criticizing or challenging your autonomy. This comment also attacks positive face by questioning your ability to dress properly.

As with all the strategies discussed here, politeness, too, may have negative consequences. Overpoliteness, for example, is likely to be seen as phony and be resented. Overpoliteness will also be resented if it's seen as a persuasive strategy.

TO BE BELIEVED: CREDIBILITY STRATEGIES

If you were a politician and wanted people to vote for you, at least part of your strategy would involve attempts to establish your **credibility,** a perception by others of your competence, character, and charisma. For example, to establish your competence, you might mention your great educational background or the courses you took that qualify you as an expert. Or you can post a photo with a Harvard diploma on the wall. To establish that you're of good character, you might mention how fair and honest you are, the causes you support, or your concern for those less fortunate. And to establish your charisma—your take-charge, positive personality—you might demonstrate this quality in your face-to-face interactions as well as in your posts and in your photos, and by being enthusiastic and emphatic, and by focusing on the positive while minimizing the negative.

Communication Choice Point

Impressions

You've just joined a social networking site. *How might you write your profile and use the many features of the site to make yourself appear credible and a perfect future employee? What would you be sure not to do?*

If you stress your competence, character, and charisma too much, however, you risk being seen as someone who lacks the very qualities that you seem too eager to present to others. Generally, people who are truly competent need say little directly about their own competence; their actions and their success will reveal it.

TO EXCUSE FAILURE: SELF-HANDICAPPING STRATEGIES

If you were about to tackle a difficult task and were concerned that you might fail, you might use what are called **self-handicapping strategies.** In the more extreme form of this strategy, you actually set up barriers or obstacles to make the task impossible. That way, when you fail, you won't be blamed or thought ineffective—after all, the task was impossible. Let's say you aren't prepared for your human communication exam and you believe you're going to fail. Using this self-handicapping strategy, you might stay out late at a party the night before so that when you do poorly on the exam, you can blame it on the party rather than on your intelligence or knowledge. In a less extreme form, you might manufacture excuses for failure and have them ready if you do fail. For example, you might prepare to blame a poorly cooked dinner on your defective stove.

On the negative side, using self-handicapping strategies too often may lead people to see you as generally incompetent or foolish. After all, a person who parties the night before an exam for which he or she is already unprepared is clearly demonstrating poor judgment.

TO SECURE HELP: SELF-DEPRECATING STRATEGIES

If you want to be taken care of and protected, or if you simply want someone to come to your aid, you might use **self-deprecating strategies.** Confessions of incompetence and inability often bring assistance from others. And so you might say, "I just can't fix that drain and it drives me crazy; I just don't know anything about plumbing" with the hope that another person will offer to help.

But be careful: Your self-deprecating strategies may convince people that you are, in fact, just as incompetent as you say you are. Or people may see you as someone who doesn't want to do something and so pretends to be incompetent to get others to do it. This strategy is not likely to benefit you in the long run.

TO HIDE FAULTS: SELF-MONITORING STRATEGIES

Much impression management is devoted not merely to presenting a positive image, but to suppressing the negative, to **self-monitoring strategies.** Here, you carefully monitor (self-censor) what you say or do. You avoid your normal slang to make your colleagues think more highly of you; you avoid chewing gum so you don't look juvenile or unprofessional; you avoid posting the photos from the last party. While you readily disclose favorable parts of your experience, you actively hide the unfavorable parts.

But if you self-monitor too often or too obviously, you risk being seen as someone unwilling to reveal himself or herself, and perhaps not trusting enough of others. In more extreme cases, you may be viewed as dishonest, as hiding your true self or trying to fool other people.

TO BE FOLLOWED: INFLUENCING STRATEGIES

In many instances you'll want to get people to see you as a leader. Here, you can use a variety of **influencing strategies.** One set of such strategies are those normally grouped under power—your knowledge (information power), your expertise (expert power), your right to

SKILL DEVELOPMENT EXPERIENCE

Using Impression Management Strategies

Try formulating impression management strategies for each of the following situations. In your responses focus on one or two things you would say or do to achieve the stated goals.

- **To be liked:** You're new at work and want your colleagues to like you.
- **To be believed:** You're giving a speech on something you feel deeply about; you want others to believe you.
- **To excuse failure:** You know you're going to fail that midterm and you need a good excuse.
- **To secure help:** You need help doing something on your computer that would take you hours to do on your own; you can't bear doing it alone.
- **To hide faults:** You don't have as many computer skills as your résumé might suggest and you need to appear to know a great deal.
- **To be followed:** You want members of the group to see you as the leader and, in fact, to elect you group leader.
- **To confirm self-image:** You want your colleagues to see you as a fun (but dedicated) worker.

Practicing with these strategies will help you understand the ways in which people (including yourself) manage the impressions they give to others.

lead by virtue of your position as, say, a doctor, judge, or accountant (legitimate power). You might also use leadership strategies that stress your prior experience, broad knowledge, or previous successes.

Influencing strategies can also backfire. If you try to influence someone and fail, you'll be perceived as having less power than before your unsuccessful attempt. And, of course, if you're seen as someone who is influencing others for self-gain, your attempts to influence might be resented or rejected.

TO CONFIRM SELF-IMAGE: IMAGE-CONFIRMING STRATEGIES

You may sometimes use **image-confirming strategies** to reinforce your positive perceptions about yourself. If you see yourself as the life of the party, you'll tell jokes, post photos in which you are in fact the life of the party, and just try to amuse people. This behavior confirms your own self-image and also lets others know that this is who you are and how you want to be seen. At the same time that you reveal aspects of yourself that confirm your desired image, you actively suppress other aspects of yourself that would disconfirm this image. Unfavorable wall postings, for example, are quickly removed.

If you use image-confirming strategies too frequently, you risk being seen as too perfect to be genuine. If you try to project an exclusively positive image, it's likely to turn others off—people want to see their friends and associates as real with some faults and imperfections. Also recognize that image-confirming strategies invariably involve your focusing on yourself, and with that comes the risk of appearing self-absorbed.

A knowledge of these impression management strategies and the ways in which they are effective and ineffective will give you a greater number of choices for achieving such widely diverse goals as being liked, being believed, excusing failure, securing help, hiding faults, being followed, and confirming your self-image.

Objectives Self-Check
- Can you explain and cite examples of the various strategies of impression management: to be liked, to be believed, to excuse failure, to secure help, to hide faults, to be followed, and to confirm your self-image?
- Can you apply the skills for effective (and ethical) impression management?

COMMUNICATING ETHICALLY

The Ethics of Impression Management

Impression management strategies may sometimes be used unethically and for less than noble purposes. For example, people may use affinity-seeking strategies to get you to like them so that they can then extract favors from you. Politicians frequently portray themselves as credible in order to win votes. The same could be said of the stereotypical used-car salesperson or insurance agent trying to make a sale. Some people use self-handicapping or self-deprecating strategies to get you to see their behavior from a perspective that benefits them rather than you. Self-monitoring strategies are often deceptive, designed to present a more polished image than what might surface without self-monitoring. And, of course, influencing strategies have been used throughout history in deception as well as in truth. Even image-confirming strategies can be used to deceive, as when people exaggerate their positive qualities (or make them up) and hide their negative ones.

Ethical Choice Point

You're ready to join one (perhaps several) of the online dating services. You need to write your profile and are wondering if everyone (or nearly everyone) exaggerates, you shouldn't also. Specifically, you're considering saying that you earn a very good salary (actually, it's not so great but you're hoping for a promotion), that you're twenty pounds lighter (actually, you intend to lose weight), and that you own a condo (actually, that's a goal once you get the promotion and save a down payment). If you don't exaggerate, you reason, you'll disadvantage yourself and not meet the people you want to meet. Also, you figure that people expect you to exaggerate and assume that you're probably a lot less ideal than your profile would indicate. Would this be ethical?

⚠ Messages in the Media   *Wrap Up*

Probably all television crime shows involve some character seeing what others miss. Watching such shows with a view toward seeing relationships and connections will help you see the principles of perception in operation.

⬇⬆ Summary of Concepts and Skills

✔ **Study** and **Review** materials for this chapter are at **MyCommunicationLab**

 Listen to the **Audio Chapter Summary** at **MyCommunicationLab**

This chapter explored the self—the ways you perceive yourself, and perception—the way you perceive others and others perceive you.

The Self in Human Communication

1. Self-concept, the image that you have of yourself, is composed of feelings and thoughts about both your abilities and your limitations. Self-concept develops from the image that others have of you, the comparisons you make between yourself and others, the teachings of your culture, and your own interpretations and evaluations of your thoughts and behaviors.

2. The Johari window model of the self is one way to view self-awareness. In this model there are four major areas: the open self, the blind self, the hidden self, and the unknown self. To increase self-awareness, analyze yourself, listen to others to see yourself as they do, actively seek information from others about yourself, see yourself from different perspectives, and increase your open self.

3. Self-esteem is the value you place on yourself and may be enhanced by attacking self-destructive beliefs, seeking out nourishing others, working on projects that will result in success, and securing affirmation.

Self-Disclosure

4. Self-disclosure is a form of communication in which information about the self that is normally kept hidden is communicated to one or more others.

5. Self-disclosure is more likely to occur when the potential discloser (a) feels competent, is sociable and extroverted, and is not apprehensive about communication; (b) comes from a culture that encourages self-disclosure; (c) is a woman; (d) is talking to supportive listeners who also disclose; and (e) talks about impersonal rather than personal topics and reveals positive rather than negative information.

6. The rewards of self-disclosure include increased self-knowledge, the ability to cope with difficult situations and guilt, communication efficiency, and chances for more meaningful relationships. The dangers of self-disclosure include personal and social rejection and material loss.

7. Before self-disclosing, consider the motivation for the self-disclosure, the possible burdens you might impose on your listener or yourself, the appropriateness of the self-disclosure, and the disclosures of the other person.

8. When listening to others' disclosures, try to understand what the discloser is feeling, support the discloser, be willing to reciprocate, keep the disclosures confidential, and don't use the disclosures against the person.

9. When you don't want to disclose, try being firm, being indirect and changing the topic, or assertively stating your unwillingness to disclose.

Perception

10. Perception is the process by which you become aware of the many stimuli impinging on your senses. It occurs in five stages: (a) sensory stimulation, (b) organization, (c) interpretation–evaluation, (d) memory, and (e) recall.

Impression Formation

11. Four important processes influence the way you form impressions: self-fulfilling prophecies, primacy–recency, stereotyping, and attributions of controllability.

12. To increase your accuracy in impression formation, analyze your impressions and recognize your role in perception; check your impressions; reduce uncertainty; and become culturally sensitive by recognizing the differences between you and others and also the differences among people from other cultures.

Impression Management: Goals and Strategies

13. Impression management includes these goals and strategies: to be liked (affinity-seeking and politeness strategies); to be believed (credibility strategies that establish your competence, character, and charisma); to excuse failure (self-handicapping strategies); to secure help (self-deprecating strategies); to hide faults (self-monitoring strategies); to be followed (influencing strategies); and to confirm one's self-image (image-confirming strategies).

14. Each of these impression management strategies can backfire and give others negative impressions of you. And each of these strategies may be used to reveal your true self or to present a false self and deceive others in the process.

Throughout this discussion of the self and perception, a variety of skills were identified. Place a check mark next to those skills that you feel you need to work on most.

_____ 1. I seek to understand my self-concept and to be realistic about my strengths and weaknesses.

_____ 2. I actively seek to increase self-awareness by talking with myself, listening to others, reducing my blind self, seeing myself from different perspectives, and increasing my open self.

_____ 3. I seek to enhance my self-esteem by attacking self-destructive beliefs, seeking out nourishing others, working on projects that will result in success, and securing affirmation.

_____ 4. I regulate my disclosures on the basis of the unique communication situation.

_____ 5. When deciding whether or not to self-disclose, I take into consideration my motivation, the possible burdens on my listener and on me, the disclosure's appropriateness to the other person and its context, and the other person's disclosures.

_____ 6. I respond to the disclosures of others by trying to feel what the other person is feeling, using effective and active listening skills, expressing supportiveness, refraining from criticism and evaluation, and keeping the disclosures confidential.

_____ 7. I resist disclosing when I don't want to by being firm, by trying indirectness and changing the topic, and/or by stating assertively my refusal to disclose.

_____ 8. I think mindfully when I use perceptual shortcuts so that they don't mislead me and result in inaccurate perceptions.

_____ 9. I guard against ethnocentric thinking by regarding the behavior and customs of others from a multicultural viewpoint rather than from just my cultural perspective.

_____ 10. To guard against the self-fulfilling prophecy, I take a second look at my perceptions when they conform too closely to my expectations.

_____ 11. Recognizing how primacy–recency works, I actively guard against first impressions that might prevent accurate perceptions of future events; I formulate hypotheses rather than conclusions.

_____ 12. I recognize stereotyping in the messages of others and avoid it in my own.

_____ 13. I am aware of and careful to avoid the self-serving bias, overattribution, and the fundamental attribution error when trying to account for another person's behavior.

_____ 14. I think critically about perception, analyzing my perceptions, checking my perceptions for

accuracy, using uncertainty reduction strategies, and acting with cultural sensitivity.

_____ 15. I can use the strategies of impression management (to be liked, to be believed, to excuse failure, to secure help, to hide faults, to be followed, and to confirm my self-image) effectively and ethically.

Key Word Quiz

The Language of the Self and Perception

Match the terms about the self and perception with their definitions. Record the number of the definition next to the appropriate term.

_____ a. stereotype (38)

_____ b. attribution (39)

_____ c. self-fulfilling prophecy (37)

_____ d. credibility strategies (44)

_____ e. social comparison (25)

_____ f. selective perception (35)

_____ g. self-concept (25)

_____ h. self-esteem (28)

_____ i. self-disclosure (31)

_____ j. self-serving bias (39)

1. Techniques to make yourself seem competent, of high character, and charismatic

2. The tendency to attend to and expose yourself to information that is confirming

3. The process by which you compare yourself to others, most often your peers

4. Your image of who you are

5. A measure of how valuable you think you are

6. The process of talking to others about yourself, of revealing things that you normally keep hidden

7. The tendency to take credit for positive outcomes and to deny responsibility for negative outcomes

8. The process by which you try to explain the motivation for another person's behavior

9. The process of making a prediction that comes true because you made the prediction and acted as if it were true

10. A fixed impression of a group of people

These ten terms and additional terms used in this chapter can be found in the glossary.

Answers: a. 10; b. 8; c. 9; d. 1; e. 3; f. 2; g. 4; h. 5; i. 6; j. 7

 Study and **Review** the **Flashcards** at **MyCommunicationLab**

MyCommunicationLab

Throughout this chapter, there are icons in the margin to highlight media content for selected topics. Go to **MyCommunicationLab** for additional information on the self and perception in human communication. Here you'll find flashcards to help you learn the jargon of communication, videos that illustrate a variety of concepts, additional exercises, and discussions to help you continue your study of these fundamental communication concepts.

3

Listening in Human Communication

Objectives

 Listen to the Audio Chapter at MyCommunicationLab

After reading this chapter, you should be able to:

❶ Define *listening* and its five stages and apply the suggestions for increasing accuracy at each of these stages.

❷ Describe the four major barriers to effective listening and apply the suggestions for effectiveness in your own listening behavior.

❸ Identify the five styles of listening and listen in the appropriate style for the specific situation.

❹ Explain the major cultural and gender differences found in listening and assess their influence on your own communication/listening.

Messages in the Media ⚠️

The strength of talk show hosts such as Wendy Williams, pictured here, rests on their ability to listen to their guests and to show the audience that they are listening.

In light of Facebook, Twitter, wikis, and blogs, we need to expand the traditional definition of listening as the receiving and processing of auditory signals. If posting messages on social media sites is part of human communication (which it surely is), then reading these messages must also be part of human communication and most logically a part of listening. **Listening**, then, may now be defined as the process of receiving, understanding, remembering, evaluating, and responding to verbal and/or nonverbal messages.

The skills of listening will prove crucial to you in both your professional and personal lives (Brownell, 2010; Worthington & Fitch-Hauser, 2011). In today's workplace listening is regarded as a crucial skill. Employees' communication skills are especially significant in this era of technological transformation; workers' advancement will depend on their ability to speak and write effectively, to display proper etiquette, and *to listen attentively*. In a survey of 40 CEOs of Asian and Western multinational companies, respondents cited a lack of listening skills as *the major shortcoming* of top executives (Witcher, 1999).

There can be little doubt that listening skills play a crucial role in developing and maintaining a variety of interpersonal relationships (Brownell, 2010). When asked what they want in a partner, women overwhelmingly reply, "a partner who listens." And most men would agree that they too want a partner who listens. Among friends, listening skills rank consistently high; in fact, it would be hard to think of a person as a friend if that person were not a good listener.

The effective listener is more likely to emerge as group leader and a more effective salesperson, healthcare worker, and manager (Johnson & Bechler, 1998; Lauer, 2003; Stein & Bowen, 2003; Levine, 2004; Pelham & Kravitz, 2008; Brownell, 2010). Medical educators, claiming that doctors are not trained to listen to their patients, have introduced what they call "narrative medicine" to teach doctors how to listen to their patients and to recognize how their perceptions of their patients are influenced by their own emotions.

Here we look at the importance of listening, the nature of the listening process, the major barriers to listening effectiveness, varied styles of listening for different situations, and some cultural and gender differences in listening.

For a brief discussion of the importance of listening in health care, see "Listening Doctors" at **tcbdevito**.blogspot.com. In what other areas would you like to see people listening more effectively?

"This requires both ears."

Stages of Listening

According to our contemporary definition, listening is a collection of skills involving (1) attention and concentration (*receiving*), (2) learning (*understanding*), (3) memory (*remembering*), (4) critical thinking (*evaluation*), and (5) feedback (*responding*). You can enhance your listening ability by strengthening these skills, which make up the five steps of the listening process (Figure 3.1).

Note that the process of listening is circular: The response of person A stimulates a response from person B, which stimulates a response from person A, and so on. All five stages overlap. When you listen, you're performing all five processes at essentially the same time. For example, when listening in conversation, you're not only paying attention to what other people are saying but also critically evaluating what they just said and perhaps giving feedback. Let's take a look at each stage separately.

RECEIVING

Hearing (which is not the same as *listening*), begins and ends with the first stage of the listening process, receiving. Hearing happens when you get within range of some auditory stimulus. Listening, on the other hand, begins only when the messages the speaker sends are received, or heard.

At the *receiving* stage, you note not only what is said (verbally and nonverbally) but also what is omitted. For example, you receive not only the politician's

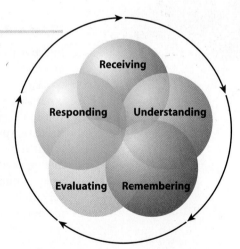

FIGURE 3.1

A Five-Stage Model of the Listening Process
This model, which depicts the various stages involved in listening, draws on a variety of previous models that listening researchers have developed (e.g., Alessandra, 1986; Barker, 1990; Brownell, 2010; Steil, Barker, & Watson, 1983). In what other ways might you visualize the listening process?

summary of accomplishments in education but also his or her omission of failures in health care or pollution control. This receiving stage of listening can be made more effective if you follow these suggestions:

● **Focus attention** on the speaker's verbal and nonverbal messages, on what is said and what is not said—not on what you'll say next.

● **Maintain your role** as listener by not interrupting the speaker.

● **Avoid assuming you understand** what the speaker is going to say before he or she actually says it.

In this brief discussion of receiving, and in fact throughout this chapter on listening, the unstated assumption is that both individuals can receive auditory signals without difficulty. But for many people who have hearing impairments, listening presents a variety of problems. Table 3.1 provides tips for communication between people with and people without hearing loss.

UNDERSTANDING

Understanding occurs when you decode the speaker's signals, when you learn what the speaker means. *Understanding* means grasping both the thoughts that are expressed and the emotional tone that accompanies them—for example, the urgency, joy, or sorrow expressed in the message. The understanding phase of listening can be made more effective if you follow these suggestions:

● **Relate** the speaker's new information to what you already know.

● **See the speaker's messages from the speaker's point of view,** in part by not judging the message until it's fully understood as the speaker intended it.

● **Rephrase/paraphrase** the speaker's ideas, a simple process that's especially important when listening to complicated instructions.

REMEMBERING

Effective listening depends on *remembering*. When Joe says his mother is ill, the effective listener remembers this and inquires about her health later in the week.

Perhaps the most important point to understand about memory is that what you remember is not what was said but what you remember was said. Memory for speech is not reproductive; you don't simply reproduce in your memory what the speaker said. Rather, memory is reconstructive; you actually reconstruct the messages you hear into a system that makes sense to you.

If you want to remember what someone says or the names of various people, this information needs to pass from your **short-term memory** (the memory you use, say, to remember a phone number just long enough to dial it) into **long-term memory.** Short-term memory is very limited in capacity—you can hold only a small amount of information there. Long-term memory is unlimited. Here are FOUR suggestions for facilitating the passage of information from short-term to long-term memory:

● **Focus** your attention on the central ideas. Even in the most casual of conversations, there are central ideas. Fix these in your mind. Repeat these ideas to yourself as you continue to listen. Avoid focusing on minor details that often lead to detours in listening and in conversation.

● **Organize** what you hear; summarize the message in a more easily retained form, but take care not to ignore crucial details or qualifications. If you chunk the material into categories, you'll be able to remember more information. For example, if you want to remember 15 or 20 items to buy in the supermarket, you'll remember more if you group them into chunks—say, produce, canned goods, and meats.

TABLE 3.1 Communication Tips

Between People With and Without Hearing Difficulties

People with hearing loss differ greatly in their hearing ability: Some are totally deaf and can hear nothing, others have some hearing loss and can hear some sounds, and still others have impaired hearing but can hear most speech. Although people with profound hearing loss can speak, their speech may appear labored and may be less clear than the speech of those with unimpaired hearing. Here are some suggestions for more effective communication between people who hear well and those who have hearing problems.

If you have unimpaired hearing:	
Generally	**Specifically**
Set up a comfortable context.	Reduce the distance between yourself and the person with a hearing impairment; reduce background noise; make sure the lighting is adequate.
Avoid interference.	Make sure the visual cues from your speech are clearly observable; face the person squarely and avoid smoking, chewing gum, or holding your hand over your mouth.
Speak at an adequate volume.	But avoid shouting, which can distort your speech and may insult the person; be careful to avoid reducing volume at the ends of your sentences.
Phrase ideas in different ways.	Because some words are easier to lip-read than others, it often helps if you can rephrase your ideas in different words.
Avoid overlapping speech.	In group situations only one person should speak at a time; similarly, direct your comments to the person with hearing loss himself or herself; don't talk to the person through a third party.
Ask for additional information.	Ask the person if there is anything you can do to make it easier for him or her to understand you.
Don't avoid common terms.	Use terms like *hear, listen, music,* or *deaf* when they're relevant to the conversation. Trying to avoid these common terms will make your speech sound artificial.
Use nonverbal cues.	Nonverbals can help communicate your meaning; gestures indicating size or location and facial expressions indicating feelings are often helpful.

If you have impaired hearing:	
Do your best to eliminate background noise.	Reduce the distance between yourself and the speaker; reduce background noise; make sure the lighting is adequate.
Move closer to the speaker if this helps you hear better.	Alert the speaker that this closer distance will help you hear better.
Ask for adjustments.	If you feel the speaker can make adjustments, ask the speaker to repeat a message, to speak more slowly, or to increase volume.
Position yourself for best reception.	If you hear better in one ear than another, position yourself accordingly and, if necessary, clue the speaker in to this fact.
Ask for additional cues.	If necessary, ask the speaker to write down certain information, such as phone numbers or website addresses. Carrying a pad and pencil will prove helpful for this and in the event that you wish to write something down for others.

Sources: These suggestions were drawn from a variety of sources including the Rochester Institute of Technology, the National Technical Institute for the Deaf, and the Division of Public Affairs, and Department of Labor websites.

- **Unite** the new with the old; relate new information to what you already know. Avoid treating new information as totally apart from all else you know. There's probably some relationship and if you identify it, you're more like to remember the new material.
- **Repeat** names and key concepts to yourself or, if appropriate, aloud. By repeating the names or key concepts, you in effect rehearse these names and concepts, and as a result they'll be easier to learn and remember. If you're introduced to Alice, you'll stand a better chance of remembering her name if you say, "Hi, Alice" than if you say just "Hi."

EVALUATING

Evaluating consists of judging the messages you hear. At times you may try to evaluate the speaker's underlying intent, often without much conscious awareness. For example, Elaine tells you she is up for a promotion and is really excited about it. You may then try to judge her intention. Does she want you to use your influence with the company president? Is she preoccupied with the possible promotion and therefore telling everyone? Is she looking for a pat on the back? Generally, if you know a person well, you will be able to identify his or her intention and respond appropriately.

In other situations, your evaluation may be more like critical analysis. For example, in a business meeting on upgrading office equipment, you would evaluate the office manager's proposals while listening to them. As you listen, you'd be asking yourself, "Are the proposals practical? Will they increase productivity? What is the evidence? Are there more practical alternatives?" Follow these three steps to make the evaluation stage of listening more effective:

- **Resist evaluating** until you fully understand the speaker's point of view.
- **Assume that the speaker is a person of goodwill** and give the speaker the benefit of any doubt by asking for clarification on issues you object to (e.g., are there any other reasons for accepting this new proposal?).
- **Distinguish facts from opinions** and personal interpretations and identify any biases, self-interests, or prejudices that may lead the speaker to slant unfairly what is presented.

RESPONDING

Responding occurs in two forms: (1) responses you make while the speaker is talking and (2) responses you make after the speaker has stopped talking. Responses made while the speaker is talking should be supportive and should acknowledge that you're listening. These responses are called **backchanneling cues**—messages (words and gestures) that let the speaker know you're paying attention, as when you nod in agreement or say, "I see" or "Uh-huh."

Responses after the speaker has stopped talking are generally more elaborate and might include empathy ("I know how you must feel"); requests for clarification ("Do you mean this new health plan will replace the old plan, or will it only be a supplement?"); challenges ("I think your evidence is weak"); and/or agreement ("You're absolutely right, and I'll support your proposal when it comes up for a vote"). You can improve this responding phase of listening by following these suggestions:

- **Express support** and understanding for the speaker throughout the conversation.
- **Use varied backchanneling cues** (for example, nodding, using appropriate facial expressions, or saying "I see") that tell the speaker that you're listening.
- **Own your own responses;** that is, state your thoughts and feelings as your own, using **I-messages**—for example, saying, "I don't agree" rather than "No one will agree with that."
- **Avoid the common problem-causing listening responses,** such as being static or overly expressive, giving feedback that is monotonous and not responsive to the messages, avoiding eye contact, or appearing preoccupied with, say, a cell phone.

Take a look at "e-mail responding" at tcbdevito.blogspot.com for a list of reasons people may not respond to an email—even though you expect one.

Communication Choice Point

Listening Cues

Friends have told you that people don't address comments directly to you because you don't give listening cues to let the other person know that you're listening and interested. *What are some of the things you can do to help change this perception?*

COMMUNICATING ETHICALLY

Ethical Listening

As a listener you have at least two ethical obligations (generally):

- You owe the other person an honest hearing, without prejudgment, putting aside prejudices and preconceptions as best you can. At the same time, you owe the person your best effort at understanding emotionally as well as intellectually what he or she means. This does not mean, however, that there are not situations when you don't owe the speaker a fair hearing.

- You owe the other person honest responses. Just as you should be honest with the listener when speaking, you should be honest with the speaker when listening. This means giving open and honest feedback and also reflecting honestly on the questions that the speaker raises. Again, this does not mean that there are not situations in which you would not owe the speaker an honest response.

These obligations, as you might have guessed, will vary with the relationship between yourself and the other person. If this "other person" is a life partner, then your obligations are considerable. If this "other person" is a stranger, your obligations are less. Generally, as the intimacy of a relationship increases, so do your obligations to serve as a supportive and honest listener.

Ethical Choice Point

Your partner of ten years has decided to come clean about a sordid past, essentially the ten years before you met. You really don't want to hear this (it just depresses you) but your partner insists on self-disclosing. What is your ethical obligation to both your partner and to yourself?

Objectives Self-Check
- Can you define *listening* and its five stages (receiving, understanding, remembering, evaluating, and responding)?
- Can you apply the skills for more effective listening recommended for each of these stages?

Listening Barriers

In addition to practicing the various skills for each stage of listening, consider some of the common barriers to listening. Here are four such barriers and some suggestions for dealing with them as both listener and speaker, because both speaker and listener are responsible for effective listening. As you read this, consider the barriers that arise in listening in the classroom, a topic also discussed in Table 3.2.

DISTRACTIONS: PHYSICAL AND MENTAL

Physical barriers might include hearing impairment, a noisy environment, or loud music. Multitasking(for example, trying to watch TV and listen to someone at the same time) with the aim of being supportive simply doesn't work. As both listener and speaker, try to remove whatever physical barriers can be removed; for those that you can't remove, adjust your listening and speaking to lessen the effects as much as possible. As a listener, focus on the speaker; you can attend to the room and the other people later.

Mental distractions too get in the way of focused listening. These barriers may take the form of thinking about your upcoming Saturday night date or becoming too emotional to think (and listen) clearly. When listening, recognize that you can think about your date or other distracting thoughts later. In speaking, make what you say compelling and relevant to the listener.

BIASES AND PREJUDICES

In biased and prejudiced listening, you hear what the speaker is saying through stereotypes. This type of listening occurs when you listen differently to a person because of his or her race, affectional orientation, age, or gender when these characteristics are irrelevant to the message.

Explore the Exercise
"Your Listening Barriers"
at **MyCommunicationLab**

Explore the Exercise
"Sequential Listening"
at **MyCommunicationLab**

Communication Choice Point

Hate Speech
Your work colleagues in neighboring cubicles regularly use derogatory racial terms. You really don't want to listen to this and want to protest this kind of talk. At the same time, however, you don't want to alienate people you're going to have to work with for some time. *What are some of the things you can say to register your protest (cooperatively)?*

TABLE 3.2 **Listening in the Classroom**

In addition to following the general guidelines for listening noted throughout this chapter, here are a few additional suggestions for making your listening for understanding in the classroom more effective.

General Suggestions	Specifically
Prepare yourself to listen.	Sit up front where you can see your instructor and any visual aids clearly and comfortably. Remember that you listen with your eyes as well as your ears.
Avoid distractions.	Avoid mental daydreaming, and put away physical distractions like your laptop, smartphone, or newspaper.
Pay special attention to the introduction.	Listen for orienting remarks and for key words and phrases (often written on the board or on PowerPoint slides), such as "another reason," "three major causes," and "first." Using these cues will help you outline the lecture.
Take notes in outline form.	Avoid writing in paragraph form. Listen for headings and then use these as major headings in your outline. When the instructor says, for example, "there are four kinds of noise," you have your heading and you will have a numbered list of four kinds of noise.
Assume relevance.	A piece of information may eventually prove irrelevant (unfortunately), but if you listen with the assumption of irrelevancy, you'll never hear anything relevant.
Listen for understanding.	Avoid taking issue with what is said until you understand fully and then, of course, take issue if you wish. But, generally, don't rehearse in your own mind your arguments against a particular position. When you do this, you run the risk of missing additional explanation or qualification.

Do you notice bias in your instructors? See "Teacher Bias?" at tcbdevito.blogspot.com. How might this type of research help instructors and students alike?

Such listening can occur in a wide variety of situations. For example, when you dismiss a valid argument or attribute validity to an invalid argument because the speaker is of a particular race, affectional orientation, age, or gender, you're listening with prejudice.

However, there are many instances in which these characteristics are pertinent to your evaluation of the message. For example, the sex of a speaker talking about pregnancy, fathering a child, birth control, or surrogate motherhood probably is, most would agree, relevant to the message. So, in these cases it is not sexist listening to take the gender of the speaker into consideration. It is, however, sexist listening to assume that only one gender can be an authority on a particular topic or that one gender's opinions are without value. The same is true when listening through the filter of a person's race, affectional orientation, or age.

LACK OF APPROPRIATE FOCUS

Focusing on what a person is saying is necessary for effective listening—yet there are many influences that can lead you astray. For example, listeners often get lost because they focus on irrelevancies, such as an especially vivid example that conjures up old memories. Try not to get detoured from the main idea. Try to repeat the idea to yourself and see the details in relation to this main concept. As a speaker, try to avoid language or examples that may divert attention from your main idea.

Another misplaced focus is often on the responses a listener is going to make while the speaker is still speaking. Anticipating how you're going to respond or what you're going to say (and even interrupting the speaker) prevents you from hearing the message in full. Instead, make a mental note of something and then get back to listening. As a speaker, when you feel someone is preparing to argue with you, ask him or her to hear you out: "I know you disagree with this, but let me finish and we'll get back to that."

PREMATURE JUDGMENT

Perhaps the most obvious form of premature judgment is assuming you know what the speaker is going to say and that there's no need to really listen. Let the speaker say what he or she is going to say before you decide that you already know it. As a speaker, it's often wise to assume that listeners will do exactly this, so make clear that what you're saying will be unexpected.

Watch the **Video** "Fast Food" at **MyCommunicationLab**

Video Choice Point
A Bad Day at Work

Sue and Harry are a romantic couple. Harry is visibly upset, but Sue doesn't know why. Sue considers the elements of the listening process and the various barriers that can interfere with effective listening as she contemplates her communication choices. This video looks at how Sue's listening choices will affect the outcome of this interaction and potentially help Harry better cope with his issues. See how Sue's choices play out in the video, "A Bad Day at Work", and respond to the questions posed.

Watch the **Video** "A Bad Day at Work" at **MyCommunicationLab**

A common listener reaction is to draw conclusions or judgments on incomplete evidence. Sometimes, listeners will stop listening after hearing, for example, an attitude they disagree with or some sexist or culturally insensitive remark. Instead, this is a situation that calls for especially concentrated listening so that you don't rush to judgment. Wait for the evidence or argument; avoid making judgments before you gather all the information. Listen first, judge second. As a speaker, be aware of this tendency and, when you feel this is happening, ask for a suspension of judgment. A simple "Hear me out" is often sufficient.

 Objectives Self-Check
- Can you describe the four major barriers to effective listening (physical and mental distractions, biases and prejudices, lack of appropriate focus, and premature judgment)?
- Can you effectively avoid and combat these barriers as they appear?

Styles of Effective Listening

Before reading about the styles of effective listening, examine your own listening habits and tendencies by taking the self-test, "How Do You Listen?"

Explore the **Concept**
"Listening" at
MyCommunicationLab

TEST YOURSELF

How Do You Listen?

Respond to each statement using the following scale:

1 = always, **2** = frequently, **3** = sometimes, **4** = seldom, and **5** = never.

_____ ❶ I listen actively, communicate acceptance of the speaker, and prompt the speaker to further explore his or her thoughts.

_____ ❷ I listen to what the speaker is saying and feeling; I try to feel what the speaker feels.

_____ ❸ I listen without judging the speaker.

_____ ❹ I listen to the literal meanings that a speaker communicates; I don't look too deeply into hidden meanings.

_____ ❺ I listen without active involvement; I generally remain silent and take in what the other person is saying.

_____ ❻ I listen objectively; I focus on the logic of the ideas rather than on the emotional meaning of the message.

_____ ❼ I listen critically, evaluating the speaker and what the speaker is saying.

_____ ❽ I look for the hidden meanings, the meanings that are revealed by subtle verbal or nonverbal cues.

HOW DID YOU DO? These statements focus on the ways of listening discussed in this chapter. All of these ways are appropriate at some times but not at other times. It depends. So the only responses that are really inappropriate are "always" and "never." Effective listening is listening that is tailored to the specific communication situation.

WHAT WILL YOU DO? Consider how you might use these statements to begin to improve your listening effectiveness. A good way to begin doing this is to review these statements, trying to identify situations in which each statement would be appropriate and inappropriate.

TABLE 3.3 **Listening to Emotions (Ten Ways)**

Listening to the emotions of others is difficult but essential. Here are a few guidelines for making it a little easier and a lot more effective.

Generally...	Specifically...
Confirm the other person and his or her emotions.	A simple "You must be worried about finding another position" confirms the feelings of a person who has just lost a job.
Show interest by encouraging the person to explore his or her feelings.	Use simple encouragers like "I see" or "I understand." Or ask questions to let the speaker know that you're listening/interested.
Give the person permission to express feelings.	Let the person know that it's acceptable and okay with you if she or he expresses feelings in the ways that feel most comfortable—for example, by crying or talking about old times.
Don't try to force the person to talk about experiences or feelings she or he may not be willing to share.	A simple "Would you like to talk about it?" will cue the person that you're listening but not forcing him or her to talk.
Be especially sensitive to leave-taking cues. Don't overstay your welcome.	Notice especially comments like "It's getting late" or a glance at the clock, or a polite yawn.
Empathize.	See the situation from the point of view of the speaker. Avoid comments such as "Don't cry; it wasn't worth it," which can be interpreted as a rejection of the person's feelings.
Focus on the other person; don't refocus the conversation on yourself.	Instead, provide a supportive atmosphere that encourages the person to express her or his feelings.
Don't try to solve the other person's problems.	Listening to another's emotions comes first; offer solutions only when asked.
Avoid trying to focus on the bright side.	Avoid expressions such as "You're lucky you have some vision left" or "It is better this way; Pat was suffering so much."
Avoid interrupting.	Emotional expression frequently involves extra-long pauses, so wait before jumping in.

As stressed throughout this chapter, effective listening is **situational listening**—appropriate listening that will vary with the situation, each set of circumstances calling for a different combination of listening styles. The art of effective listening is in making appropriate choices along the following five dimensions: (1) empathic and objective listening, (2) nonjudgmental and critical listening, (3) surface and depth listening, (4) polite and impolite listening, and (5) active and inactive listening. These dimensions exist on a continuum with, say, extremely empathic at one end and extremely objective at the other end. Most, if not all, listening exists somewhere between these extremes. Yet, there will be an emphasis toward one side or the other depending on the specifics of the communication situation. A case in point is in listening to the emotions of others, a topic discussed in Table 3.3.

EMPATHIC AND OBJECTIVE LISTENING

To understand what a person means and what a person is feeling, you need to listen with some degree of **empathy** (Rogers, 1970; Rogers & Farson, 1981). To empathize with others is to feel with them: to see the world as they see it and to feel what they feel. **Empathic listening** will also help you enhance your relationships (Barrett & Godfrey, 1988; Snyder, 1992).

To express empathy, it's often helpful to do so in two ways, corresponding to the two parts of true empathy: thinking empathy and feeling

"Empathy? Yeah, I can see how that could be useful."

empathy (Bellafiore, 2005). In *thinking empathy* you express an understanding of what the person means. For example, when you paraphrase someone's comment, showing that you understand the meaning the person is trying to communicate, you're demonstrating thinking empathy. The second part of empathy is *feeling empathy*; here you express your ability to feel what the other person is feeling. For example, if a friend tells you of problems at home, you might respond by saying, "Your problems at home do seem to be getting worse. I can imagine how you feel so angry at times."

Although for most communication situations empathic listening is the preferred mode of responding, there are times when you need to go beyond it and to measure the speaker's meanings and feelings against some objective reality. It's important to listen as Peter tells you how the entire world hates him and to understand how he feels and why he feels this way (empathic listening). But then you need to look a bit more objectively at the situation and perhaps see Peter's paranoia or self-hatred (objective listening). Sometimes you have to put your empathic responses aside and listen with objectivity and detachment. In adjusting your empathic and objective listening focus, keep the following recommendations in mind:

- **Punctuate from the speaker's point of view.** That is, see the sequence of events as the speaker does and try to figure out how this perspective can influence what the speaker says and does.

- **Engage in equal, two-way conversation.** To encourage openness and empathy, try to eliminate any physical or psychological barriers to equality; for example, step from behind the large desk separating you from your employees. Avoid interrupting the speaker—a sure sign that you think what you have to say is more important.

- **Seek to understand both thoughts and feelings.** Don't consider your listening task finished until you've understood what the speaker is feeling as well as thinking.

- **Avoid "offensive listening"**—the tendency to listen to bits and pieces of information that will enable you to attack the speaker or find fault with something the speaker has said.

- **Strive to be objective** when listening to friends and foes alike. Guard against "expectancy hearing," in which you fail to hear what the speaker is really saying and instead hear what you expect.

VIEWPOINTS

Negative Empathy

Although empathy is almost universally considered positive, there is some evidence to show that it also can have a negative side. For example, people are most empathic with those who are similar—racially and ethnically as well as in appearance and social status. The more empathy you feel toward your own group, the less empathy—possibly even the more hostility—you feel toward other groups. The same empathy that increases your understanding of your own group decreases your understanding of other groups. So although empathy may encourage group cohesiveness and identification, it also can create dividing lines between your group and "them" (Angier, 1995b). Have you ever experienced or witnessed these negative effects of empathy?

 Watch the **Video** "Listening with Empathy" at **MyCommunicationLab**

SKILL DEVELOPMENT EXPERIENCE

Expressing Empathy

For either one or two of the following situations, indicate in one sentence (or more) how you'd respond to the speaker with *thinking empathy* and in one sentence (or more) how you'd respond with *feeling empathy*. Assume that all three people are your peers.

1. "I've never felt so alone in my life. Chris left last night and said it was all over. We were together for three years and now—after a 10-minute argument—everything is lost."
2. "I just got $20,000 from my aunt's estate. She left it to me! Twenty thousand! Now I can get that car and buy some new clothes!"
3. "A Camry! My parents bought me a Camry for graduation. What a bummer. They promised me a Lexus."

Expressing empathy is crucial to meaningful communication, but it is not an easily acquired skill; it takes practice.

Communication Choice Point

Empathic Listening

Your neighbors, who've avoided work all their lives and lived off unfairly obtained government disability payments, have just won the lottery for $36 million. They want you to share their joy and invite you over for a champagne toast. *What are some of the things you can do to strengthen your ability to empathize with these people? What might you say to show empathic listening?*

NONJUDGMENTAL AND CRITICAL LISTENING

Effective listening includes both nonjudgmental and critical responses. You need to listen nonjudgmentally—with an open mind and with a view toward understanding. But you also need to listen critically—with a view toward making some kind of evaluation or judgment. Clearly, it's important to listen first for understanding while suspending judgment. Only after you've fully understood the relevant messages should you evaluate or judge.

Supplement open-minded listening with critical listening. Listening with an open mind will help you understand the messages better; listening with a critical mind will help you analyze and evaluate the messages. In adjusting your nonjudgmental and critical listening, focus on the following guidelines:

- **Avoid filtering out or oversimplifying difficult or complex messages.** Similarly, avoid filtering out undesirable messages. Clearly, you don't want to hear that something you believe is untrue or that ideals you hold are self-destructive. Yet it's important that you reexamine your beliefs by listening to these messages.

- **Recognize your own biases.** These may interfere with accurate listening and cause you to distort message reception through a process of **assimilation**—the tendency to integrate and adapt what you hear or think you hear to your own biases, prejudices, and expectations.

- **Combat the tendency to sharpen**—to highlight, emphasize, and perhaps embellish one or two aspects of a message. See the message as a whole.

Table 3.4 presents a few fallacies of language that you need to identify and combat in your critical thinking.

TABLE 3.4 Listening to Fallacies of Language

Here are four language fallacies that often get in the way of meaningful communication and need to be identified in critical listening. Often they're used to fool you; these are ways in which language can be used to serve less-than-noble purposes, to convince or persuade you without giving you valid reasons. After reviewing these fallacies, take a look at some of the commercial websites for clothing, books, music, or any product you're interested in, and try to find examples of these fallacies.

Fallacy	Example	Notes
Weasel words are those whose meanings are slippery and difficult to pin down (Hayakawa & Hayakawa, 1989).	A commercial claiming that medicine M works "better than Brand X" but doesn't specify how much better or in what respect Medicine M performs better. It's quite possible that it performs better in one respect but less effectively according to nine other measures.	Other weasel words are "help," "virtually," "as much as," "like" (as in "it will make you feel like new"), and "more economical." Ask yourself, "Exactly what is being claimed?" For example, "What does 'may reduce cholesterol' mean?"
Euphemisms make the negative and unpleasant appear positive and appealing.	An executive calls the firing of 200 workers "downsizing" or "reallocation of resources." Justin Timberlake's reference to the highly publicized act with Janet Jackson during the 2004 Super Bowl as a "wardrobe malfunction."	Often euphemisms take the form of inflated language designed to make the mundane seem extraordinary, the common seem exotic ("the vacation of a lifetime," "unsurpassed vistas"). Don't let words get in the way of accurate first-hand perception.
Jargon is the specialized language of a professional class.	The language of the computer hacker, the psychologist, and the advertiser.	When used to intimidate or impress, as with people who aren't members of the profession, it prevents meaningful communication. Don't be intimidated by jargon; ask questions when you don't understand.
Gobbledygook is overly complex language that overwhelms the listener instead of communicating meaning.	Extra-long sentences, complex grammatical constructions, and rare or unfamiliar words.	Some people normally speak in complex language. But, others use complexity to confuse and mislead. Ask for simplification when appropriate.

SURFACE AND DEPTH LISTENING

In most messages there's an obvious meaning that you can derive from a literal reading of the words and sentences. But in reality, most messages have more than one level of meaning. Sometimes the other level is the opposite of the literal meaning; at other times it seems totally unrelated. Consider some frequently heard types of messages. Carol asks you how you like her new haircut. On one level, the meaning is clear: Do you like the haircut? But there's also another and perhaps more important level: Carol is asking you to say something positive about her appearance. In the same way, the parent who complains about working hard at the office or in the home may, on a deeper level, be asking for an expression of appreciation.

To recognize these other meanings, you need to engage in depth listening. If you respond only to the surface-level communication (i.e., the literal meaning), you miss the opportunity to make meaningful contact with the other person's feelings and needs. If you say to the parent, "You're always complaining. I bet you really love working so hard," you fail to respond to this call for understanding and appreciation. In regulating your surface and depth listening, consider the following guidelines:

- **Focus on both verbal and nonverbal messages.** Recognize both consistent and inconsistent "packages" of messages and use these as guides for drawing inferences about the speaker's meaning. When in doubt, ask questions. Listen also to what is omitted: Speakers communicate by what they leave out as well as by what they include.

- **Listen for both content and relational messages.** The student who constantly challenges the teacher is, on one level, communicating disagreement over content. However, on another level—the relationship level—the student may be voicing objections to the instructor's authority or authoritarianism. The instructor needs to listen and respond to both types of messages.

- **Make special note of statements that refer back to the speaker.** Remember that people inevitably talk about themselves. Whatever a person says is, in part, a function of who that person is. Attend carefully to those personal, self-referential messages.

- **Don't disregard the literal meaning of messages.** Balance your listening between surface and underlying meanings. Respond to the different levels of meaning in the messages of others as you would like others to respond to yours—sensitively but not obsessively, readily but not over ambitiously.

POLITE AND IMPOLITE LISTENING

Politeness is often thought of as the exclusive function of the speaker, as solely an encoding or sending function. But, politeness (or impoliteness) may also be signaled through listening (Fukushima, 2004).

Of course, there are times when you would not want to listen politely (for example, to someone being verbally abusive or condescending or using racist or sexist language). In these cases you might want to show your disapproval by showing that you're not listening. But most often you'll want to listen politely, and you'll want to express this politeness through your listening behavior. Here are a few suggestions for demonstrating that you are in fact listening politely; these are strategies designed to be supportive of the speaker's positive and negative face needs:

- **Avoid interrupting the speaker.** Avoid trying to take over the speaker's turn. Avoid changing the topic. If you must respond and can't wait until the speaker finishes, then say it as briefly as possible and pass the turn back to the speaker.

- **Give supportive listening cues.** These might include nodding your head, giving minimal verbal responses, such as "I see" or "yes, it's true," or moving closer to the speaker. Listen in a way that demonstrates that what the speaker is saying is important. In some cultures, polite listening cues must be cues of agreement (Japanese culture is often used as an example); in other cultures, polite listening cues are attentiveness and support rather than cues of agreement (as in much of United States, for example).

Communication Choice Point

Relationship Listening

A young nephew tells you that he can't talk with his parents. No matter how hard he tries, they don't listen. "I tried to tell them that I can't play baseball and I don't want to play baseball," he confides. "But they ignore me and tell me that all I need is practice." *What are some of the things you can say or do that will show your nephew that you're listening.*

Communication Choice Point

Responding Politely

You're working as a manager at a restaurant, and a regular customer complains about the server: "I don't like the way she treated me, and I'm not coming back here." *What are some of the things you might say without losing the customer or your server (who is usually excellent)? Are there things you'd be sure not to say?*

● **Show empathy with the speaker.** Demonstrate that you understand and feel the speaker's thoughts and feelings by giving responses that show this level of understanding—smiling or cringing or otherwise echoing the feelings of the speaker. If you echo the speaker's nonverbal expressions, your behavior is likely to be seen as empathic.

● **Maintain eye contact.** In much of the United States this is perhaps the single most important rule. If you don't maintain eye contact when someone is talking to you, then you'll appear not to be listening, and definitely not listening politely. This rule, however, does not hold in all cultures. In some Latin and Asian cultures, polite listening would consist of looking down and avoiding direct eye contact when, for example, listening to a superior or much older person.

● **Give positive feedback.** Throughout the listening encounter, perhaps especially after the speaker's turn (when you continue the conversation as you respond to what the speaker has said), positive feedback will be seen as polite and negative feedback as impolite. If you must give negative feedback, then do so in a way that does not attack the person's negative face: For example, first mention areas of agreement and what you liked about what the person said and stress your good intentions. Then, when you give negative feedback, it is important to do it in private. Public criticism feels especially threatening, and the original speaker will surely see it as a personal attack.

A somewhat different slant on politeness and listening can be seen in "forcing" people to listen when they don't want to. Generally, the polite advice is to notice when the other person wants to leave and to allow the person to discontinue listening. Closely related to this is the "forced" listening that many cell phone users impose on others, a topic addressed in Table 3.5.

TABLE 3.5 Politeness and the Smartphone

The ubiquity of the smartphone has led to enormous increases in telephone communication and texting, but it has also created problems, many of which are problems of politeness. Because much smartphone use occurs in public spaces, people often are forced to hear conversations that don't involve them.

General Rule	Specifics	Adjustments
Avoid using cell phones where inappropriate.	Especially avoid calling in restaurants, hospitals, theaters, museums, commuter buses or trains, and in the classroom.	If you must make or take a call when in these various situations, try to move to a less public area.
Silence your cell.	Put your phone on vibrate mode, or let your voicemail answer and take a message when your call might interfere with others.	When you can't avoid taking a call, speak as quietly as possible and as briefly as possible.
Avoid unwanted photo-taking	Don't take pictures of people who aren't posing for you, and erase photos if the person you photographed requests it.	Of course, if you're involved in or are a witness to an accident or a robbery, you may want to photograph the events.
Avoid extended talking when your reception is weak.	Talking on your cell on a crowded street will probably result in poor reception, which is annoying to the other person.	In an emergency, caution trumps politeness.
Consider the other person.	It's easy to assume that when you have nothing better to do, the person you're calling also has nothing better to do.	As with any phone call, it's wise to ask if this is a good time to call—a strategy that helps maintain the autonomy (negative face) of the person you're calling.

ACTIVE AND INACTIVE LISTENING

One of the most important communication skills you can learn is that of **active listening.**
Consider the following interaction: You're disappointed that you have to redo your entire budget report, and you say, "I can't believe I have to redo this entire report. I really worked hard on
this project, and now I have to do it all over again." To this you get three different responses:

Ethan: That's not so bad; most people find they have to redo their first reports. That's the
norm here.

Aiden: You should be pleased that all you have to do is a simple rewrite. Peggy and Michael
both had to completely redo their entire projects.

Tyler: You have to rewrite that report you've worked on for the last three weeks? You sound
really angry and frustrated.

All three listeners are probably trying to make you feel better. But they go about it in very
different ways and, it appears, with very different results. Ethan tries to lessen the significance
of the rewrite. This type of well-intended and extremely common response does little to promote meaningful communication and understanding. Aiden tries to give the situation a positive spin. In their responses, however, both Ethan and Aiden also suggest that you should not
feel the way you do; they imply that your feelings are not legitimate and should be replaced
with more logical feelings.

Tyler's response, however, is different from the others. Tyler uses active listening. Active
listening owes its development to Thomas Gordon (1975), who made it a cornerstone of his
Parent Effectiveness Training (P.E.T.) technique; it is a process of sending back to the speaker
what you as a listener think the speaker meant—both in content and in feelings. Active listening, then, is not merely repeating the speaker's exact words but, rather, putting together into
some meaningful whole your understanding of the speaker's total message.

Active listening helps you check your perception of what the speaker said and, more
important, what he or she meant. Reflecting back perceived meanings to the speaker gives the
speaker an opportunity to offer clarification and correct any misunderstandings. Active
listening also lets the speaker know that you acknowledge and accept his or her feelings. In
this example, Tyler listened actively and reflected back what he thought you meant while
accepting what you were feeling. Note too that he also explicitly identified your emotions
("You sound angry and frustrated"), allowing you the opportunity to correct his interpretation. Still another function of active listening is that it stimulates the speaker to explore feelings and thoughts. Tyler's response encourages you to elaborate on your feelings and perhaps
to better understand them as you talk them through. When combined with empathic listening, active listening proves the most effective approach for successful sales transactions
(Comer & Drollinger, 1999).

Three simple techniques may help you succeed in active listening:

- **Paraphrase the speaker's meaning.** Stating in your own words what you think the speaker
means and feels will help ensure understanding and demonstrate your interest. When you
paraphrase what you think the speaker means, you give the speaker a chance to extend
what was originally said. However, remember to be objective; be especially careful not to
lead the speaker in the direction you think he or she should go. And don't overdo it; paraphrase when you feel there's a chance for misunderstanding or when you want to keep the
conversation going.

- **Ask questions.** Asking questions strengthens your own understanding of the speaker's
thoughts and feelings and elicits additional information ("How did you feel when you
read your job appraisal report?"). Ask questions to provide only enough stimulation and
support so the speaker will feel he or she can elaborate on these thoughts and feelings.

- **Express understanding of the speaker's feelings.** In addition to paraphrasing the content,
echo the feelings that the speaker expressed or implied ("You must have felt horrible"). This
expression of feelings will help you further check your perception of the speaker's feelings.
It also will allow the speaker to see his or her feelings more objectively—especially helpful
when they're feelings of anger, hurt, or depression—and to elaborate on these feelings.

Watch the **Video**
"Adapting to Serve a Client"
at **MyCommunicationLab**

Explore the **Exercise**
"Paraphrasing to Ensure
Understanding" at
MyCommunicationLab

But, of course, not all questions are
polite to ask. For a brief discussion
of impolite questions, see
"Impolite questions, what are
they?" at tcbdevito.blogspot
.com. Have you ever asked or
been asked an impolite question?

SKILL DEVELOPMENT EXPERIENCE

Using Active Listening Strategies

Here are three situations that might require active listening. For each situation compose an active listening response in which you (a) paraphrase the speaker's meaning, (b) express understanding of the speaker's meaning, and (c) ask questions to clarify any potential misunderstandings.

1. Your friend has just broken up a love affair and is telling you about it: *I can't seem to get Chris out of my head. All I do is think about what we used to do and all the fun we used to have.*
2. A young nephew tells you that he cannot talk with his parents. No matter how hard he tries, they just don't listen. *I tried to tell them that I can't play baseball and I don't want to play baseball. But they ignore me and tell me that all I need is practice.*
3. Your mother has been having a difficult time at work. She was recently passed up for a promotion and received one of the lowest merit raises given in the company. *I'm not sure what I did wrong. I do my work, mind my own business, don't take my sick days like everyone else. How could they give that promotion to Helen who's only been with the company for two years? Maybe I should just quit.*

Active listening allows you to connect with another person by demonstrating your understanding and support.

Communication Choice Point

Active Listening

Your life partner comes home from work visibly upset and clearly has a need to talk about what happened—but simply says, "Work sucks!" *What are some of the ways you can use active listening techniques?*

In communicating your understanding back to the speaker, be especially careful to avoid sending what are called "solution messages" (Gordon, 1975)—messages that tell the person how he or she *should* feel or what he or she *should* do. You'll want to avoid solution messages such as these:

- Ordering messages: "Do this." "Don't touch that."
- Warning and threatening messages: "If you don't do this, you'll . . ." "If you do that, you'll . . ."
- Preaching and moralizing messages: "People should all . . ." "You have responsibilities . . ."
- Advising messages: "Why don't you . . ." "I think you should . . ."

Objectives Self-Check
- Can you identify the five styles of listening?
- Can you select the appropriate listening style for the specific situation and regulate your listening for greatest effectiveness?

Listening Differences: Culture and Gender

Listening is difficult in part because of the inevitable differences in the communication systems between speakers and listeners. Because each person has had a unique set of experiences, each person's communication and meaning system is going to be unique. When speaker and listener come from different cultures or are of different genders, the differences and their effects are, naturally, much greater.

CULTURE AND LISTENING

In today's multicultural world, where people from very different cultures live and work together, it's especially important to understand the ways in which cultural differences can influence listening. Three of these cultural influences on listening are (1) language and speech, (2) nonverbal behaviors, and (3) feedback.

Language and Speech

Even when a speaker and a listener speak the same language, they speak it with different meanings and different accents. Speakers of the same language will, at the very least, have different meanings for the same terms because they have had different experiences. For example, the word "parents" to someone brought up in a series of foster homes will be drastically different from someone who grew up in a "traditional" family.

Speakers and listeners who have different native languages and who may have learned English as a second language will have even greater differences in meaning. If you learned your meaning for *house* in a culture in which everyone lives in his or her own house with lots of land around it, then communicating with someone whose meaning of house was learned in a neighborhood of high-rise tenements is going to be difficult. Although each of you will hear the word *house*, the meanings you'll develop will be drastically different. In adjusting your listening—especially in an intercultural setting—understand that the speaker's meanings may be very different from yours even though you're speaking the same language.

In many classrooms throughout the United States, there will be a wide range of accents. Those whose native language is tonal, such as Chinese (in which differences in pitch signal important meaning differences), may speak English with variations in pitch that may be puzzling to others. Those whose native language is Japanese may have trouble distinguishing *l* from *r,* because Japanese does not include this distinction. The native language acts as a filter and influences the accent given to the second language.

Nonverbal Behaviors

Speakers from different cultures have different *display rules,* cultural rules that govern which nonverbal behaviors are appropriate and which are inappropriate in a public setting. As you listen to other people, you also "listen" to their nonverbals. If nonverbal signals are drastically different from what you would expect on the basis of the verbal message, you may see them as a kind of noise or interference or even as a contradictory message. If a colleague at work, for example, consistently averts her eyes when talking with you, you may interpret this as an indication of shyness or dishonesty (which are often associated with averted eyes), but it may be merely a sign that your colleague's culture discourages direct eye contact. (Some, often collectivist, cultures consider direct eye contact overly forward, impolite, or inappropriate [Axtell, 2007]. Other, often individualist, cultures consider direct eye contact a sign of honesty and forthrightness.) To complicate matters further, different cultures often have very different meanings for the same nonverbal gesture. For example, the thumb and forefinger forming a circle means "OK" in most of the United States, but it means "money" in Japan, "zero" in some Mediterranean countries, and "I'll kill you" in Tunisia.

Feedback

Members of some cultures give very direct and very honest feedback. Speakers from these largely individualist cultures—the United States is a good example—expect feedback to be an honest reflection of what their listeners are feeling. In other largely collectivist cultures—Japan and Korea are good examples—it's more important to be positive (and to respect the other person's need for positive face) than to be truthful. As a result, people may respond with positive feedback (say, in commenting on a business colleague's proposal) even if it doesn't reflect their true opinion. Listen to feedback, as you would to all messages, with a full recognition that various cultures view feedback very differently.

GENDER AND LISTENING

Men and women learn different styles of listening, just as they learn different styles for using verbal and nonverbal messages. Not surprisingly, these different styles can create difficulties in opposite-sex communication.

Rapport and Report Talk

According to linguistic scholar and popular writer Deborah Tannen (1990) in her best-selling *You Just Don't Understand: Women and Men in Conversation*, women seek to share feelings, build rapport, and establish closer relationships, and they use listening to achieve these ends. Men, on the other hand, play up their expertise, emphasize it, and use it to dominate the interaction.

Watch the **Video**
"American Spoken Here"
at **MyCommunicationLab**

Explore the **Exercise**
"Typical Man, Typical Woman"
at **MyCommunicationLab**

Communication Choice Point

Support Not Solutions
You need to make some major decisions in your life, and you need to bounce your ideas off someone, just to clarify them in your own mind. Your romantic partner almost always tries to solve your problems rather than just be a supportive listener. *What are some of the things you might say to help secure support rather than the offering of solutions?*

VIEWPOINTS

Gender and Listening Differences

The popular belief is that men listen in the way they do to prove themselves superior and that women listen as they do to ingratiate themselves. Although there is no evidence to show that these images are valid, they persist in the assumptions that people make about the opposite sex. What do you believe accounts for the differences in the way men and women listen?

Their focus is on reporting information. Tannen argues that in conversation a woman seeks to be liked, so she expresses agreement. The goal of a man, on the other hand, is to be given respect, so he seeks to show his knowledge and expertise.

Listening Cues Men and women give different types of listening cues and, consequently, show that they're listening in different ways. In conversation, a woman is more apt to give lots of listening cues—interjecting "Yeah" or "Uh-huh," nodding in agreement, and smiling. A man is more likely to listen quietly, without giving lots of listening cues as feedback. Women also make more eye contact when listening than do men, who are more apt to look around and often away from the speaker (Brownell, 2010). As a result of these differences, women seem to be more engaged in listening than do men.

Amount and Purposes of Listening Tannen (1990, 1994a) argues that men listen less to women than women listen to men. The reason, says Tannen, is that listening places the person in an inferior position, but speaking places the person in a superior position. Men may seem to assume a more confrontational posture while listening and to ask questions that are argumentative or seek to puncture holes in the speaker's position as a way to play up their own expertise. Women are more likely than men to ask supportive questions and offer constructive criticism. Men and women act this way both to members of the same and of the opposite sex; their usual ways of speaking and listening don't seem to change depending on whether the person they're communicating with is male or female.

It's important to note that not all researchers agree that there is sufficient evidence to support the claims of Tannen and others about gender differences (Goldsmith & Fulfs, 1999). Gender differences are changing drastically and quickly; it's best to take generalizations about gender as starting points for investigation and not as airtight conclusions (Gamble & Gamble, 2003). Further, be mindful that, as you no doubt have observed from your own experiences, gender differences—although significant—are far outnumbered by similarities.

Objectives Self-Check
- Can you explain the major cultural and gender differences in listening?
- Can you take these into consideration in our own listening to make it more effective?

⚠️ **Messages in the Media** *Wrap Up*

Choose a representative sampling of talk show hosts to observe—whether Jerry Springer, Jay Leno, or Wendy Williams—and focus on their listening behaviors. Does the host listen with empathy and demonstrate active listening? You'll probably be able to see the strategies of effective listening and the pitfalls of ineffective listening in action.

Summary of Concepts and Skills

 Study and **Review** materials for this chapter are at **MyCommunicationLab**

Listen to the **Audio Chapter Summary** at **MyCommunicationLab**

This chapter discussed the ways you listen and how you can listen more effectively.

Stages of Listening

1. Listening is crucial to success in a wide range of professions and in personal relationships.
2. Listening may be defined as "the process of receiving, constructing meaning from, and responding to spoken and/or nonverbal messages."
3. Listening serves a variety of purposes: You listen to learn; to relate to others; to influence the attitudes, beliefs, and behaviors of others; to play; and to help. Listening is a five-step process consisting of receiving, understanding, remembering, evaluating, and responding.
4. Both listener and speaker share in the responsibility for effective listening.

Listening Barriers

5. Among the obstacles to effective listening are physical and mental distractions, biases and prejudices, lack of appropriate focus, and premature judgment.

Styles of Effective Listening

6. Effective listening involves a process of making adjustments—depending on the situation—along dimensions such as empathic and objective listening, nonjudgmental and critical listening, surface and depth listening, polite and impolite listening, and active and inactive listening.

Listening Differences: Culture and Gender

7. Culture influences listening in a variety of ways. Contributing to listening difficulties are cultural differences in language and speech, nonverbal behaviors, and feedback.
8. Men and women listen differently and perhaps for different reasons. For example, women give more messages that say, "I'm listening" than men. According to some theorists, women use listening to show empathy and to build rapport, and men minimize listening because it puts them in a subordinate position.

Throughout this discussion of listening, a variety of skills were identified. Place a check mark next to those skills that you feel you need to work on most.

_____ 1. I recognize that listening serves a variety of purposes, and I adjust my listening on the basis of my purposes: for example, to learn, relate, influence, play, or help.

_____ 2. I realize that listening is a multistage process, and I regulate my listening behavior as appropriate in receiving, understanding, remembering, evaluating, and responding.

_____ 3. When receiving messages I seek to increase my chances of effective listening by, for example, paying attention to the speaker's verbal and nonverbal messages; avoiding distractions; and focusing on what the speaker is saying, not on what I'm going to say next.

_____ 4. I facilitate understanding in listening by relating new information to what I already know and trying to see the messages from the speaker's point of view.

_____ 5. In remembering the speaker's messages, I try to identify the central ideas and the major supporting materials, summarize the main ideas, and repeat important concepts to etch them more firmly in my mind.

_____ 6. In evaluating messages, I first make sure I understand the speaker's point of view and seek to identify any sources of bias or self-interest.

_____ 7. In responding, I am supportive of the speaker and own my own thoughts and feelings.

_____ 8. I am mindful of the common listening obstacles (i.e., distractions, biases, lack of focus, and premature judgment) and try to reduce their effects.

_____ 9. I am especially careful to adjust my listening on the basis of the immediate situation between empathic and objective, nonjudgmental and critical, surface and depth, polite and impolite, and active and inactive listening.

_____ 10. I practice active listening when appropriate by paraphrasing the speaker's meaning, expressing my understanding of the speaker's feelings, and asking questions.

_____ 11. I recognize the influence of culture on listening and cultural differences in listening and take these into consideration when listening in intercultural situations.

_____ 12. I recognize gender differences in listening and take these into consideration when communicating with members of the opposite sex.

Key Word Quiz

The Language of Listening

Match the terms about listening with their definitions. Record the number of the definition next to the appropriate term.

_____ a. active listening (63)

_____ b. paraphrasing (63)

_____ c. situational listening (58)

_____ d. disclaiming (52)

_____ e. listening (51)

_____ f. assimilation (60)

_____ g. backchanneling cues (54)

_____ h. memory (52)

_____ i. I-messages (54)

_____ j. empathic listening (58)

1. The process of asking the listener to receive your message without prejudice, to give you a fair hearing.

2. A reconstructive rather than a reproductive process.

3. The tendency to integrate and interpret what you hear or think you hear in terms of your own expectations and biases.

4. A process of sending back to the speaker what you think the speaker meant.

5. Restating what another says but in your own words.

6. An approach to listening in which effective listening style depends on the specifics of the communication.

7. A five-step process consisting of receiving, understanding, remembering, evaluating, and responding.

8. Listening responses that let the speaker know that you're paying attention.

9. Listening to what a person is feeling as well as to what the person is thinking.

10. Messages in which you take responsibility for your thoughts and actions rather than attributing these to others.

These ten terms and additional terms used in this chapter can be found in the glossary.

Answers: a. 4 b. 5 c. 6 d. 1 e. 7 f. 3 g. 7 h. 2 i. 10 j. 9

 Study and **Review** the **Flashcards** at **MyCommunicationLab**

MyCommunicationLab

Throughout this chapter, there are icons in the margin that highlight media content for selected topics. Go to **MyCommunicationLab** for additional information on listening in human communication. Here you'll find flashcards to help you learn the jargon of communication, videos that illustrate a variety of concepts, additional exercises, and discussions to help you continue your study of the skills of effective listening.

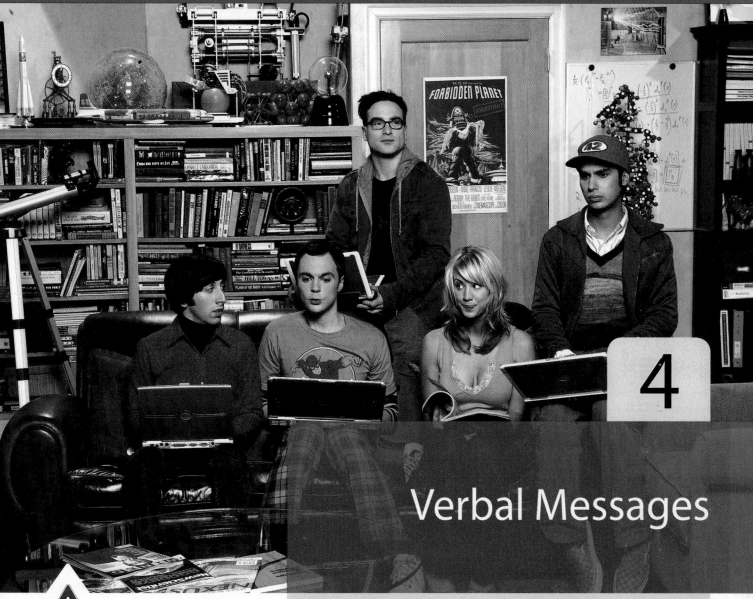

Verbal Messages

4

⚠ Messages in the Media

The television sitcom *The Big Bang Theory* provides humorous illustrations, as do many such shows, of the different ways in which people use language. Here we have an assortment of physicists and engineering types who have little ability to use language to communicate about feelings, relationships, and the practical issues of the day, topics we address in this chapter.

Objectives

 Listen to the Audio Chapter at MyCommunicationLab

After reading this chapter, you should be able to:

❶ Paraphrase the eight principles of verbal messages and use their skills components in your own communication.

❷ Define and distinguish between-*disconfirmation*-and-*confirmation*-and use appropriate cultural identifiers, without sexism, heterosexism, racism, and ageism.

❸ Explain the five ways in which language can distort thinking and apply the suggested guidelines for communicating more logically.

Your messages normally occur in "packages" consisting of both verbal and nonverbal signals (Pittenger, Hockett, & Danehy, 1960). Usually, verbal and nonverbal behaviors reinforce, or support, each other. For example, you don't usually express fear with words while the rest of your body relaxes. You don't normally express anger with your face while your words are warm and cheerful. Your entire being works as a whole—verbally and nonverbally—to express your thoughts and feelings. At other times, the verbal and nonverbal messages contradict each other; you say you enjoyed the meal but eat very little or you say you're happy to meet someone but avoid eye contact. Regardless of whether verbal and nonverbal messages support or contradict each other, they occur together.

This chapter focuses on the verbal message system: the system's key principles, the concepts of confirmation and disconfirmation, and the ways you can use verbal messages most effectively. The next chapter will examine the nonverbal message system.

Principles of Verbal Messages

Your verbal messages, of course, rely on the rules of grammar; you can't just make up sounds or words or string words together at random and expect to be understood. But following the rules of grammar is not enough to achieve effective communication. Here we look at eight principles to help you understand how verbal messages work.

MESSAGE MEANINGS ARE IN PEOPLE

To discover the meaning a person is trying to communicate, it's necessary to look into the person as well as the words. The word *cancer,* for example, will mean something very different to a mother whose child has just been diagnosed with cancer and to an oncologist.

Also recognize that, as you change, you also change the meanings you created out of past messages; although the message sent may not have changed, the meanings you created from it yesterday and the meanings you create today may be quite different. Yesterday, when a special someone said, "I love you," you created certain meanings. But today, when you learn that the same "I love you" was said to three other people, you drastically change the meaning you derive from those three words.

MESSAGES ARE DENOTATIVE AND CONNOTATIVE

When you speak, you use verbal messages both denotatively and connotatively. **Denotation** has to do with the objective meaning of a term, the meaning you would find in a dictionary. It's the meaning that people who share a common language assign to a word. **Connotation** is the subjective or emotional meaning that specific speakers or listeners give to a word. Take as an example the word *migrants* (used to designate Mexicans coming into the United States to better their economic condition) with the word *settlers* (meaning Europeans who came to the United States for the same reason) (Koppelman, 2005). Though both terms describe essentially the same activity (and are essentially the same denotatively), they differ widely in their connotations, with the former often negatively evaluated and the latter often positively valued.

Semanticist S. I. Hayakawa (Hayakawa & Hayakawa, 1989) coined the terms **snarl words** and **purr words** to clarify further the distinction between denotation and connotation. Snarl words are highly negative: "She's an idiot," "He's a pig," "They're a bunch of losers." Purr words are highly positive: "She's a real sweetheart," "He's a dream," "They're the greatest." Snarl and purr words, although they may sometimes seem to have denotative meaning and to refer to the "real world," are actually connotative in meaning. These terms do not describe objective realities but rather express the speaker's feelings about people or events.

Do women communicate different messages when they change their names to their husband's, when they hyphenate their birth name with their husband's, or when they retain their birth name? Check out "Names" at tcbdevito.blogspot .com. How do you feel about this topic? Do men and women view this similarly or differently?

Explore the **Concept**
"Verbal Communication" at **MyCommunicationLab**

FIRST DAY BACK TO VERBAL COMMUNICATION

MESSAGES VARY IN ABSTRACTION

Consider the following terms:

- Entertainment
- Film
- American film
- Class American films
- *Casablanca*

Explore the **Exercise**
"Using the Abstraction
Ladder as a Creative Tool" at
MyCommunicationLab

At the top is an **abstraction,** or general concept—*entertainment*. Note that *entertainment* includes all the other items on the list plus various other items—*television, novels, drama, comics,* and so on. *Film* is more specific and concrete. It includes all of the items below it as well as various other items such as *Indian film* or *Russian film*. It excludes, however, all entertainment that is not film. *American film* is again more specific than *film* and excludes all films that are not American. *Classic American films* further limits *American film* to those considered to be timeless. *Casablanca* specifies concretely the one item to which reference is made.

A verbal message that uses the most general term—in this case, entertainment—will conjure up many different images in listeners' minds. One person may focus on television, another on music, another on comic books, and still another on radio. To some listeners, the word *film* may bring to mind the early silent films; to others it may connote high-tech special effects; to still others it will recall Disney's animated cartoons. *Casablanca* guides listeners still further—in this case, to one film. So, as you get more specific—less abstract—you more effectively guide the images that come to your listeners' minds.

Effective verbal messages include words that range widely in abstractness. At times a general term may suit your needs best; at other times a more specific term may serve better. The widely accepted recommendation for effective communication is to use abstractions sparingly and to express your meanings explicitly with words that are low in abstraction.

MESSAGES CAN DECEIVE

Although we operate on the assumption that people tell the truth, it should come as no surprise to learn that some people do lie. Lying also begets more lying; when one person lies, the likelihood of the other person lying increases (Tyler, Feldman, & Reichert, 2006). **Lying** refers to the act of sending messages with the intention of giving another person information you believe to be false.

Explore the **Exercise**
"Must Lie Situations" at
MyCommunicationLab

Large cultural differences exist in the way lying is defined and in the way lying is treated. For example, as children get older, Chinese and Taiwanese (but not Canadians) see lying about the good deeds that they do as positive (as you'd expect for cultures that emphasize modesty), and taking credit for these same good deeds is seen negatively (Lee et al., 2002). Some cultures consider lying to be more important than others—in one study, for example, European Americans viewed lies less negatively than did Ecuadorians. Both, however, felt that lying to an out-group member was more acceptable than lying to an in-group member (Mealy, Stephan, & Urrutia, 2007).

Types of Lies

Lies vary greatly in type; each lie seems a bit different from every other lie. Here is one useful system that classifies lies into four types (McGinley, 2000).

Watch the **Video**
"Please Don't Lie to Me" at
MyCommunicationLab

- **Pro-Social Deception: To Achieve Some Good** These are lies that are designed to benefit the person lied to or lied about— for example, praising a person's effort to give him or her more confidence.

- **Self-Enhancement Deception: To Make Yourself Look Good** Presenting yourself as younger or as having a better job, in your social networking profile is a common example.

- **Selfish Deception: To Protect Yourself** These lies protect you, for example, not answering the phone because you want to do something else.

- **Anti-Social Deception: To Harm Someone** These lies are designed to hurt another person,—for example, spreading false rumors about someone or falsely accusing an opposing candidate of some wrongdoing.

Here's a somewhat different take on deception detection—this one in the area of real estate—at tcbdevito.blogspot.com.

Communication Choice Point

Confronting a Lie

You ask about the previous night's whereabouts of your romantic partner of two years and are told something you're almost certain is false. You don't want to break up the relationship over this, but you do want the truth and an opportunity to resolve the problems that contributed to this situation. *What are some of the things you might say? What are some things you'd definitely avoid saying?*

The Behavior of Liars   One of the more interesting questions about lying is how liars behave. Do they act differently from those telling the truth? And, if they do act differently, how can we tell when someone is lying? These questions are not easy to answer, and we are far from having complete answers to them. But we have learned a great deal.

For example, after an examination of 120 research studies, the following behaviors were found to most often accompany lying (DePaulo, et al., 2003; Knapp, 2008):

- **Liars hold back.** They speak more slowly (perhaps to monitor what they're saying), take longer to respond to questions (again, perhaps monitoring their messages), and generally give less information and elaboration.
- **Liars make less sense.** Liars' messages contain more discrepancies, more inconsistencies.
  - **Liars give a more negative impression.** Generally, liars are seen as less willing to be cooperative, smile less than truth-tellers, and are more defensive.
  - **Liars are tense.** The tension may be revealed by their higher pitched voices and their excessive body movements.

It is very difficult to detect when a person is lying and when a person is telling the truth. The hundreds of research studies conducted on this topic find that in most instances people judge lying accurately in less than 60 percent of the cases, only slightly better than chance (Knapp, 2008).

Lie detection is even more difficult (that is, less accurate) in long-standing romantic relationships—the very relationships in which the most significant lying occurs (Guerrero, Andersen, & Afifi, 2007). One important reason for this is the **truth bias:** we assume that the person is telling the truth. This truth bias is especially strong in long-term relationships where it's simply expected that each person tells the truth (Knapp, 2008).

MESSAGES VARY IN POLITENESS

It will come as no surprise that messages vary greatly in politeness. Polite messages (such as compliments or pats on the back reflect positively on the other person (contributing to positive face). They also respect the other person's right to be independent and autonomous, as when you ask permission or acknowledge the person's right to refuse (contributing to negative face needs). Impolite messages (criticism or negative facial expressions) attack our needs to be seen positively and to be autonomous.

Politeness and Directness   Direct messages are usually less polite than indirect messages: "Write me a recommendation," "Lend me $100." Indirectness—"Do you think you could write a recommendation for me?" "Would it be possible to lend me $100?"—is often more polite because it allows the person to maintain autonomy and provides an acceptable way for the person to refuse your request.

Indirect messages allow you to express a desire without insulting or offending anyone; they allow you to observe the rules of polite interaction. So instead of saying, "I'm bored with this group," you say, "It's getting late and I have to get up early tomorrow." Instead of saying, "This food tastes like cardboard," you say, "I just started my diet." In each instance you're stating a preference but are saying it indirectly so as to avoid offending someone.

The differences between direct and indirect messages may easily create misunderstandings. For example, a person who uses an indirect style of speech may be doing so to be polite and may have been taught this style by his or her culture. If you assume, instead, that the person is using indirectness to be manipulative, because your culture regards it so, then miscommunication is inevitable.

Communication Choice Point

Rejecting Directly

A colleague at work continues to ask you for a date, but you're just not interested. You've used every polite excuse in the book and now feel you have to be more direct and more assertive. *What can you do to stop these requests but not insult your colleague?*

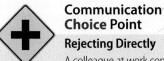

Politeness and Gender   There are considerable gender differences in politeness (Tannen, 1994b, Holmes, 1995; Kapoor, Hughes, Baldwin, & Blue, 2003; Dindia & Canary, 2006). Among the research findings are, for example, that women are more

COMMUNICATING ETHICALLY

Lying

Lying occurs when you try to make others believe something is true that you believe is untrue (Ekman, 2009; Knapp, 2007; Burgoon & Hoobler, 2002). You can lie by commission (i.e., by making explicitly false statements) or by omission (i.e., by omitting relevant information, thus allowing others to draw incorrect inferences). Similarly, you can lie verbally (e.g., in speech or writing) or nonverbally (e.g., wearing an innocent facial expression instead of acknowledging the commission of some wrong, or nodding knowingly instead of expressing honest ignorance) (O'Hair, Cody, & McLaughlin, 1981). Lies range from "white lies" and truth stretching to lies that form the basis of relationship infidelity, libel, and perjury. Not surprisingly, lies have ethical implications.

Some lies may be considered *ethical lies,* lies that are commonly accepted by society as harmless, right, and even as having some good effects (e.g., lying to a child to protect a fantasy belief in Santa Claus or the tooth fairy, or publicly agreeing with someone to enable the person to save face). Some ethical lies may even be considered to be required (e.g., lying to protect someone from harm or telling the proud parents that their child is beautiful). Other lies are clearly *unethical,* for example, lying to defraud investors, to falsely accuse someone of a crime, or to slander someone.

Ethical Choice Point

Of course, not all lies are easy to classify as ethical or unethical. For example, what would you do in each of these situations?

- Would it be ethical for you to lie to get what you deserve but couldn't get any other way? For example, would it be ethical to lie to get a well-earned promotion or a raise?

- Would it be ethical for you to lie to your relationship partner to avoid a conflict and, perhaps, splitting up? Would it make a difference if the issue was a minor one (e.g., you were late for an appointment because you wanted to see the end of the football game) or a major one (e.g., continued infidelity)?

- Would it be ethical for you to lie to get yourself out of an unpleasant situation? For example, would it be ethical to lie to get out of an unpleasant date, an extra office chore, or a boring conversation?

▶ Video Choice Point

Homecoming Party

Margo and Luis have been good friends for several years. Recently, Luis asked Margo to go with him to the homecoming party at their school. Margo isn't sure what this invitation means—are they going as friends, is this a date, does Luis want to change their relationship from friendship to romance? Margo wants to resolve this ambiguity and uncertainty and find out Luis's intentions without jeopardizing their friendship. She considers the topics covered in this chapter as she contemplates her communication choices. See how her choices play out in the video "Homecoming Party".

👁 **Watch** the **Video** "Homecoming Party" at **MyCommunicationLab**

polite and more indirect in giving orders than are men; they are more likely to say, for example, "it would be great if these letters could go out today" than "Have these letters out by three." Men are more likely to be indirect when they express weakness, reveal a problem, or admit an error. Generally, men will speak indirectly when expressing meanings that violate the masculine stereotype (e.g., messages of weakness or doubt or incompetence). Women's greater politeness is also seen in the finding that women express empathy, sympathy, and supportiveness more than men. Women also apologize more than men, and both women and men make most of their apologies to women.

Politeness Online   Internet communication has very specific rules for politeness, called **netiquette** (Kallos, 2005). Much as the rules of etiquette provide guidance in communicating in social situations, the rules of netiquette provide guidance in communicating online, and they concern everyone using computer-mediated communication (CMC). These rules are helpful for making Internet communication more pleasant and easier and also for achieving greater personal efficiency. As you review these guidelines think of how you might apply them to specific online communication, say, e-mailing your instructor or inquiring about a job:

- **Familiarize yourself with the site or rules for communicating before contributing.** Before asking questions about the system, read the Frequently Asked Questions (FAQs). "Lurk" before speaking. Lurking (which, in CMC, is good) will help you learn the rules.

- **Be brief.** Communicate only the information that is needed clearly, briefly, and in an organized way.

- **Don't shout.** WRITING IN CAPS IS PERCEIVED AS SHOUTING. It's okay to use capital letters occasionally to achieve emphasis. If you wish to give emphasis, however, it's better to highlight like _this_ or *this*.

- **Don't spam or "flame."** Don't send unsolicited mail, repeatedly send the same mail, or post the same message (or irrelevant messages) to lots of people or groups. As in face-to-face conflicts, don't make personal attacks on other users.

- **Avoid offensive language.** Refrain from expressions that would be considered offensive to others, such as sexist or racist terms.

- **Be polite.** Follow the same rules of behavior online that you would in a face-to-face encounter.

A special case of online politeness concerns the ever popular social networking sites, which have developed their own rules of netiquette, some of which are noted in Table 4.1.

MESSAGES CAN BE ONYMOUS OR ANONYMOUS

Some messages are **onymous messages** or "signed"; that is, the author of the message is clearly identified, as it is in your textbooks, news-related editorials, feature articles, and of course when you communicate face-to-face and, usually, by phone or chat. In many cases, you have the opportunity to respond directly to the speaker/writer and voice your opinions, your agreement or disagreement, for example. Other messages are anonymous: the author is not identified.

VIEWPOINTS

Gender Speech Patterns

When asked what they would like to change about the communication patterns of the opposite sex, men said they wanted women to be more direct, and women said they wanted men to stop interrupting and offering advice (Noble, 1994). What one change would you like to see in the communication system of the opposite sex? Of your own sex?

TABLE 4.1 Social Networking Politeness

The social networking sites such as Facebook and MySpace have developed their own rules of politeness. Here are five such rules.

Rules of Politeness	The Rule in Operation
Engage in networking feedforward before requesting friendship.	Sending a message complimenting the person's latest post provides some background and eases the way for a friendship request.
Avoid negativity.	Avoid writing negative or embarrassing messages or posting unflattering photos that may generate conflict.
Keep networking information confidential.	It's considered inappropriate and impolite to relay information on Facebook, for example, to those who are not themselves friends.
Be gentle in refusals.	Refuse any request for friendship gently or, if you wish, ignore it. If you're refused, don't ask for reasons; it's considered impolite.
Avoid making potentially embarrassing requests.	Avoid asking to be friends with someone who you suspect may have reasons for not wanting to admit you. For example, your work associate may not want you to see her or his profile.

For example, on faculty evaluation questionnaires and on online ratings websites, the ratings and the comments are published anonymously.

The Internet has made anonymity extremely easy and there are currently a variety of websites that offer to send your e-mails to your boss, your ex-partner, your secret crush, your noisy neighbors, or your inadequate lawyer—all anonymously. Thus, your message gets sent but you are not identified with it. For good or ill, you don't have to deal with the consequences of your message.

One obvious advantage of anonymity is that it allows people to voice opinions that may be unpopular and may thus encourage greater honesty. In the case of ratings websites, for example, anonymity ensures that the student writing negative comments about an instructor will not be penalized. An anonymous e-mail to a sexual partner informing him or her about your having an STD and suggesting testing and treatment might never get said in a face-to-face or phone conversation. The presumption is that anonymity encourages honesty and openness.

Anonymity also enables people to disclose their inner feelings, fears, hopes, and dreams with a depth of feeling that they may be otherwise reluctant to do. A variety of websites which enable you to maintain anonymity are available for these purposes. And in these cases, not only are you anonymous but the people who read your messages are also anonymous, a situation that is likely to encourage a greater willingness to disclosure and to make disclosures at a deeper level than otherwise.

An obvious disadvantage is that anonymity might encourage people to go to extremes—since there are no consequences to the message—to voice opinions that are outrageous. This in turn can easily spark conflict that is likely to prove largely unproductive. With anonymous messages, you can't evaluate the credibility of the source. Advice on depression, for example, may come from someone who knows nothing about depression and may make useless recommendations.

MESSAGES VARY IN ASSERTIVENESS

Assertiveness refers to a willingness to stand up for your rights but with respect for the rights of others. Before reading any further take the accompanying self-test, How Assertive Are Your Messages? Assertive people operate with an "I win, you win" philosophy; they assume that both parties can gain something from an interaction, even from a confrontation. Assertive people are more positive and score lower on measures of hopelessness than do nonassertive people (Velting, 1999). Assertive people are willing to assert their own rights, but unlike their aggressive counterparts, they don't hurt others in the process. Assertive people speak their minds and welcome others' doing likewise.

Watch the **Video** "Hey Roomie" at **MyCommunicationLab**

SKILL DEVELOPMENT EXPERIENCE

Using Assertiveness Strategies

For any one of the following situations, compose (a) an aggressive, (b) a nonassertive, and (c) an assertive response. Then, in one sentence, explain why your message of assertiveness will be more effective than the aggressive or nonassertive message.

1. You've just redecorated your apartment, making it exactly as you want it. A good friend of yours brings you a house gift—the ugliest poster you've ever seen—and insists that you hang it over your fireplace, the focal point of your living room.
2. Your friend borrows $30 and promises to pay you back tomorrow. But tomorrow passes, as do 20 subsequent tomorrows. You know that your friend has not forgotten about the debt, and you also know that your friend has more than enough money to pay you back.
3. Your next-door neighbor repeatedly asks you to take care of her four-year-old while she runs some errand or another. You don't mind helping out in an emergency, but this occurs almost every day.

Assertiveness is the most direct and honest response in situations such as these. Usually it's also the most effective.

TEST YOURSELF

How Assertive Are Your Messages?

Indicate how true each of the following statements is about your own communication. Respond instinctively rather than in the way you feel you should respond.

Use a scale on which **5** = always or almost always true; **4** = usually true; **3** = sometimes true, sometimes false; **2** = usually false; and **1** = always or almost always false.

_____ **①** I would express my opinion in a group even if it contradicted the opinions of others.

_____ **②** When asked to do something that I really don't want to do, I can say no without feeling guilty.

_____ **③** I can express my opinion to my superiors on the job.

_____ **④** I can start up a conversation with a stranger on a bus or at a business gathering without fear.

_____ **⑤** I voice objection to people's behavior if I feel it infringes on my rights.

HOW DID YOU DO? All five items in this test identify characteristics of assertive communication. So high scores (say about 20 and above) would indicate a high level of assertiveness. Low scores (say about 10 and below) would indicate a low level of assertiveness.

WHAT WILL YOU DO? The remaining discussion in this section clarifies the nature of assertive communication and offers guidelines for increasing your own assertiveness. These suggestions can help you not only to increase your assertiveness but also, when appropriate, to reduce your aggressive tendencies.

Realize that, as with many other aspects of communication, there will be wide cultural differences when it comes to assertiveness. For example, the values of assertiveness are more likely to be extolled in individualist cultures than in collectivist cultures. Assertiveness will be valued more by those cultures that stress competition, individual success, and independence. It will be valued much less by those cultures that stress cooperation, group success, and interdependence of all members. U.S. students, for example, are found to be significantly more assertive than Japanese and Korean students (Thompson, Klopf, & Ishii, 1991; Thompson & Klopf, 1991). Thus, for a given situation, assertiveness may be an effective strategy in one culture but would create problems in another. Assertiveness with an elder in many Asian and Hispanic cultures may be seen as insulting and disrespectful.

Most people are nonassertive in particular situations. If you're one of these people, and if you wish to modify your behavior, here are some suggestions for communicating assertiveness (Windy & Constantinou, 2005; Bower & Bower, 2005). (If you are always nonassertive and are unhappy about this, then you may need to work with a therapist to change your behavior.)

- **Describe the problem;** don't evaluate or judge it. *We're all working on this advertising project together. You're missing half our meetings and you still haven't produced your first report.* Be sure to use I-messages and to avoid messages that accuse or blame the other person.

- **State how this problem affects you;** tell the person how you feel. *My job depends on the success of this project, and I don't think it's fair that I have to do extra work to make up for what you're not doing.*

- **Propose solutions that are workable and that allow the person to save face.** Describe or visualize the situation if your solution were put into effect. *If you can get your report to the group by Tuesday, we'll still be able to meet our deadline. I could give you a call on Monday to remind you.*

- **Confirm understanding.** *It's clear that we can't produce this project if you're not going to pull your own weight. Will you have the report to us by Tuesday?*

Communication Choice Point

Criticizing

You're supervising a group of five interns who have been doing just about nothing. You don't want to discourage them or criticize them too harshly, but at the same time you have to get them to do some work. *What are some of the things you can say to help turn this group around? What are some of the things you should probably avoid saying?*

Keep in mind that assertiveness is not always the most desirable response. Effectively assertive people are assertive when they want to be, but they can back down if the situation calls for it—for example, when they risk emotionally hurting another person. Let's say that an older relative wishes you to do something for her or him. You could assert your rights and say no, but because this would probably hurt this person's feelings, it might be better simply to do as asked.

A note of caution should be added to this discussion. It's easy to visualize a situation such as this one: People are talking behind you in a movie theater, and you—drawing from your newfound enthusiasm for assertiveness—tell them to be quiet. It's also easy to see yourself getting smashed in the teeth as a result. In applying the principles of assertive communication, be careful that you don't go beyond what you can handle effectively.

Communication Choice Point

Acting Assertively

The person you've been dating for the last few months is wonderful and you're looking forward to continuing this relationship. The only problem is that your partner uses language more vulgar than you can stand. You've expressed your displeasure about this, but nothing has changed. You need to be more assertive. *What options do you have for communicating more assertively?*

MESSAGES ARE INFLUENCED BY CULTURE AND GENDER

Your verbal messages are influenced in large part by your culture and gender. Let's look first at some of the cultural influences.

Cultural Influences   Your culture teaches you that certain ways of using verbal messages are acceptable and certain ways are not. When you follow these **cultural rules,** or cultural principles, in communicating, you're seen as a properly functioning member of the culture. When you violate the principles, you risk being seen as deviant or perhaps as offensive. Here are a variety of such principles:

- **Principle of cooperation.** In any communication interaction, both parties will hope for **cooperation**—that they will make an effort to help each other to understand each other (Grice, 1975). That is, we assume cooperation, for example, that the other person will tell the truth, talk about what is relevant, and be as clear and as informative as possible.

- **Principle of peaceful relations.** This principle holds that when you communicate, your primary goal is to maintain peaceful relationships. This means that you would never insult anyone; in fact, when communicating according to this principle, you may even express agreement with someone when you really disagree, which violates the principle of cooperation (Midooka, 1990).

- **Principle of self-denigration.** This principle advises you to avoid taking credit for accomplishments and to minimize your abilities or talents in conversation (Gu, 1997). At the same time, through self-denigration you raise the image of the people with whom you're talking.

- **Principle of directness.** As explained earlier, directness and indirectness communicate different impressions. Levels of directness also vary greatly from culture to culture and between men and women. In most of the United States, directness is the preferred style. "Be up front" and "Tell it like it is" are commonly heard communication guidelines. Contrast these with the following two principles of indirectness found in the Japanese language (Tannen, 1994a):

- *Omoiyari,* close in meaning to *empathy,* says that listeners need to understand the speaker without the speaker's being specific or direct. This style places a much greater demand on the listener than would a direct speaking style.

- *Sassuru* advises listeners to anticipate a speaker's meanings and to use subtle cues from the speaker to infer his or her total meaning.

VIEWPOINTS

Culture and Vocabulary

A widely held assumption in anthropology, linguistics, and communication is that the importance of a concept to a culture can be measured by the number of words the language has for talking about the concept. So, for example, in English there are many words for money, transportation, and communication—all crucial to the English-speaking world. With this principle in mind, consider the findings of Julia Stanley, for example. Stanley researched English-language terms indicating sexual promiscuity and found 220 terms referring to a sexually promiscuous woman but only 22 terms for a sexually promiscuous man (Thorne, Kramarae, & Henley, 1983). What does this finding suggest about our culture's attitudes and beliefs about promiscuity in men and women?

Communication Choice Point

Cultural Maxims

In introducing yourself to your class, you mention your high grades, success in sports, and plans to transfer to Harvard. The students following you, however, all appear very modest. You quickly realize that you misunderstood the culture of this classroom. *What are some things you can say to counteract the snob image you inadvertently communicated?*

For a brief discussion of some gender differences, see "Gender Differences" at **tcbdevito.blogspot .com**. What gender differences do you observe?

Cultural differences often can create misunderstandings. For example, a person from a culture that values an indirect style of speech may be speaking indirectly to be polite. If, however, you're from a culture that values a more direct style of speech, you may assume that the person is using indirectness to be manipulative, which may be how your culture regards indirectness.

Gender Influences   Verbal messages reflect considerable gender influences also. For example, studies from various different cultures show that women's speech is more polite than men's speech, even on the telephone (Brown, 1980; Wetzel, 1988; Holmes, 1995; Smoreda & Licoppe, 2000). Women seek areas of agreement in conversation and in conflict situations more often than men do. Similarly, young girls are more apt to try to modify expressions of disagreement, whereas young boys are apt to express more "bald disagreements" (Holmes, 1995). Women also use more polite speech when seeking to gain another person's compliance than men do (Baxter, 1984).

Objectives Self-Check
- This section focused on the eight basic principles of verbal messages: (1) meanings are in people, (2) messages are denotative and connotative, (3) messages vary in abstraction, (4) messages can deceive, (5) messages vary in politeness, (6) messages can be onymous or anonymous, (7) messages vary in assertiveness, and (8) messages are influenced by culture and gender.
- Can you paraphrase and then apply the skills component of these principles? For example, can you vary your level of abstraction to communicate your meanings more precisely?
- Can you act assertively in the proper circumstances?

Disconfirmation and Confirmation

The terms *confirmation* and *disconfirmation* refer to the extent to which you acknowledge another person. Consider this situation. You've been living with someone for the last six months and you arrive home late one night. Your partner, let's say Pat, is angry and complains about your being so late. Which of the following is most likely to be your response?

1. Stop screaming. I'm not interested in what you're babbling about. I'll do what I want, when I want. I'm going to bed.

2. What are you so angry about? Didn't you get in three hours late last Thursday when you went to that office party? So knock it off.

3. I don't blame you for being angry. I should have called to tell you I was going to be late, but I got involved in an argument at work, and I couldn't leave until it was resolved.

In response 1, you dismiss Pat's anger and even indicate dismissal of Pat as a person. In response 2, you reject the validity of Pat's reasons for being angry but do not dismiss either Pat's feelings of anger or Pat as a person. In response 3, you acknowledge Pat's anger and the reasons for it. In addition, you provide some kind of explanation and, in doing so, show that both Pat's feelings and Pat as a person are important and that Pat has the right to know what happened. The first response is an example of disconfirmation, the second of rejection, and the third of confirmation.

Disconfirmation is a communication pattern in which we ignore someone's presence as well as that person's communications. We say, in effect, that this person and what this person has to say are not worth serious attention or effort. The Amish community practices an extreme form of disconfirmation called "shunning," in which the community members totally ignore a person who has violated one or more of their rules. The specific aim of shunning is to get the person to repent and to reenter the community of the faithful. All cultures practice some form of exclusion for those who violate important cultural rules.

Explore the **Exercise** "Recognizing Gender Differences" at **MyCommunicationLab**

Communication Choice Point

Discouraging Disconfirmation

For the last several months you've noticed how disconfirming your neighbors are toward their preteen children; it seems the children can never do anything to the parents' satisfaction. *What are some of the things you might say (if you do decide to get involved) to make your neighbors more aware of their communication patterns and the possible negative effects these patterns might have?*

SKILL DEVELOPMENT EXPERIENCE

Constructing Confirming, Rejecting, and Disconfirming Responses

For each situation below (a) write a confirming, a rejecting, and a disconfirming response, and (b) indicate what effects each type of response is likely to generate.

1. Angel receives this semester's grades in the mail; they're a lot better than previous semesters' grades but are still not great. After opening the letter, Angel says: *I really tried hard to get my grades up this semester.* Angel's parents respond:

   With confirmation: _____
   With rejection: _____
   With disconfirmation: _____

2. Carrie's boyfriend of seven years left her and married another woman. Carrie confides this to Samantha, who responds:

   With confirmation: _____
   With rejection: _____
   With disconfirmation: _____

Although each type of response serves a different purpose, confirming responses seem most likely to promote communication satisfaction.

Note that **rejection** is not the same as disconfirmation. In rejection, you disagree with the person; you indicate your unwillingness to accept something the other person says or does. However, you do not deny that person's significance.

Confirmation is the opposite of disconfirmation. In confirmation you not only acknowledge the presence of the other person but also indicate your acceptance of this person, of this person's self-definition, and of your relationship as defined or viewed by this other person. Disconfirmation and confirmation may be communicated in a wide variety of ways. Table 4.2 shows a few examples.

TABLE 4.2 Confirmation and Disconfirmation

This table identifies some specific confirming and disconfirming messages. As you review this information, try to imagine a specific illustration for each of the ways you might communicate disconfirmation and confirmation (Pearson, 1993; Galvin, Bylund, & Brommel, 2012).

Disconfirmation	Confirmation
Ignore the presence or contributions of the other person; express indifference to what the other person says.	**Acknowledge** the presence and the contributions of the other person by interacting with what he or she says.
Make no nonverbal contact; avoid direct eye contact; avoid touching and general nonverbal closeness.	**Make nonverbal contact** by maintaining direct eye contact and, when appropriate, touching, hugging, kissing, and otherwise demonstrating acknowledgment of the other person.
Monologue; engage in communication in which one person speaks and one person listens; there is no real interaction; there is no real concern or respect for each other.	**Dialogue**; engage in communication in which both persons are speakers and listeners; both are involved; both are concerned with and have respect for each other.
Jump to interpretation or evaluation rather than working at understanding what the other person means.	**Demonstrate understanding** of what the other person says and means and reflect your understanding in what you say, or when in doubt ask questions.
Discourage, interrupt or otherwise make it difficult for the other person to express himself or herself.	**Encourage** the other person to express his or her thoughts and feelings by showing interest and asking questions.
Avoid responding, or respond tangentially by acknowledging the other person's comment but shifting the focus of the message in another direction.	**Respond directly** and exclusively to what the other person says.

For an application of this concept of confirmation, see "Because I said so" at tcbdevito.blogspot.com. How do you see confirmation denied?

Watch the **Video** "You Shouldn't Have to Deal with That" at **MyCommunicationLab**

You can gain insight into a wide variety of offensive language practices by viewing them as types of disconfirmation—as language that alienates and separates. Four obvious disconfirming practices are racism, heterosexism, ageism, and sexism; we'll look at these practices next.

Another "-ism" is **ableism**—discrimination against people with disabilities. This particular practice is handled throughout this text in a series of tables offering tips for communicating with people with and without a variety of communication disabilities:

- between people with and without hearing problems (Chapter 3)
- between people with and without visual problems (Chapter 5)
- between people with and without speech and language disorders (Chapter 6)

RACIST SPEECH

Racist speech is speech that puts down, minimizes, and marginalizes a person or group because of their race. Not only does racist speech express racist attitudes, it also contributes to the development of racist attitudes in those who use or hear the language. Even when racism is subtle, unintentional, or even unconscious, its effects are systematically damaging (Dovidio, Gaertner, Kawakami, & Hodson, 2002).

Racism exists on both individual and institutional levels (Koppelman, 2005). *Individual racism* takes the form of negative attitudes and beliefs held about specific races. Assumptions that certain races are intellectually inferior to others or incapable of particular types of achievements are clear examples of individual racism. Prejudices against American Indians, African Americans, Hispanics, and Arabs, in particular, have been with us throughout U.S. history and are still a part of many people's lives today. Such racism can be seen, for example, in the negative terminology that some people use to refer to members of other races and to disparage their customs and accomplishments.

Institutional racism takes forms such as communities' de facto school segregation, companies' reluctance to hire members of minority groups, and banks' unwillingness to extend loans to members of some ethnic groups or readiness to charge these groups higher interest rates. Here are some "obvious" suggestions for avoiding racist speech:

- Avoid using derogatory terms for members of a particular race.
- Avoid basing your interactions with members of other races on stereotypes perpetuated by the media.
- Avoid mentioning race when it's irrelevant, as in references to "the African American surgeon" or "the Asian athlete."
- Avoid attributing individuals' economic or social problems to the race of the individuals rather than to their actual sources: for example, institutionalized racism or general economic problems that affect everyone

HETEROSEXIST SPEECH

Heterosexist speech also exists on both individual and institutional levels. *Individual heterosexism* refers to attitudes, behaviors, and language that disparage gay men and lesbians and includes the belief that all sexual behavior that is not heterosexual is unnatural and deserving of criticism and condemnation. Such beliefs are at the heart of antigay violence and "gay bashing." Individual heterosexism also includes the idea that homosexuals are more likely than heterosexuals to commit crimes (actually, they are neither more nor less likely) or to molest children (actually, child molesters are overwhelmingly heterosexual married men) (Abel & Harlow, 2001; Koppelman, 2005). It also includes the belief that homosexuals cannot maintain stable relationships or effectively raise children, a belief that contradicts research evidence (Fitzpatrick, Jandt, Myrick, & Edgar, 1994; Johnson & O'Connor, 2002).

Institutional heterosexism is easy to identify. The ban on gay marriage in many states and the fact that at this time only a handful of states allow gay marriage is a good example of institutional heterosexism. In some cultures homosexual relations are illegal (for example, in Pakistan, Yemen, and Iran, with sentences that can range from years in prison to death).

Explore the **Exercise** "Identifying the Barriers to Communication" at **MyCommunicationLab**

And, interestingly enough, in some cultures homosexual relationships are illegal for men but legal for women (for example, in Palau, Cook Islands, Tonga, and Guyana).

Heterosexist speech includes derogatory terms used for lesbians and gay men. For example, surveys in the military showed that 80 percent of those surveyed had heard "offensive speech, derogatory names, jokes or remarks about gays" and that 85 percent believed that such derogatory speech was "tolerated" (*New York Times,* March 25, 2000, p. A12). You also see heterosexism in more subtle forms of language usage; for example, someone who qualifies a person's profession with "gay" or "lesbian"—as in "gay athlete" or "lesbian doctor"—says in effect that athletes and doctors are not normally gay or lesbian.

Still another instance of heterosexism is the presumption of heterosexuality. Usually, people assume the person they're talking to or about is heterosexual. And usually they're correct, because most people are heterosexual. At the same time, however, this presumption denies the legitimacy of a lesbian or gay identity. This practice is very similar to the social presumptions of whiteness and maleness that we have taken significant steps toward eliminating. Here are a few additional suggestions for avoiding heterosexist (or what some call *homophobic*) speech:

- Avoid offensive nonverbal mannerisms that parody stereotypes when talking about gay men and lesbians. Avoid the "startle eyeblink" with which some people react to gay couples (Mahaffey, Bryan, & Hutchison, 2005).

- Avoid "complimenting" gay men and lesbians by saying that they "don't look it." This is not a compliment.

- Avoid making the assumption that every gay or lesbian knows what every other gay or lesbian is thinking. It's very similar to asking a Japanese person why Sony is investing heavily in the United States or, as one comic put it, asking an African American, "What do you think Jesse Jackson meant by that last speech?"

- Avoid denying individual differences. Comments such as "Lesbians are so loyal" or "Gay men are so open with their feelings" ignore the reality of wide differences within any group and are potentially insulting to all groups.

- Avoid overattribution—the tendency to attribute almost everything a person does, says, and believes to the fact that the person is gay or lesbian. This tendency helps to activate and perpetuate stereotypes.

- Remember that relationship milestones are important to all people. Ignoring anniversaries or, say, the birthday of a relative's partner is bound to cause resentment.

Communication Choice Point

Homophobia

You're bringing your college roommate home for the holidays. She's an outspoken lesbian, but your family is rather homophobic. You want to prepare your family and your roommate for their holiday get-together. *What are some things you might say to prepare your roommate and your family for what probably will be a bumpy weekend?*

AGEIST SPEECH

Although used mainly to refer to prejudice against older people, the term **ageism** can refer to prejudice against people of other age groups also. For example, if you describe all teenagers as selfish and undependable, you're discriminating against a group purely because of their age and thus are ageist in your statements. In some cultures—some Asian and African cultures, for example—the old are revered and respected. Younger people seek out elders for advice on economic, ethical, and relationship issues.

Individual ageism can be seen, for example, in the general disrespect many people exhibit toward older people and in negative age-based stereotypes. *Institutional ageism* can be seen in mandatory retirement laws and age restrictions in certain occupations (rather than restrictions based on demonstrated competence). In less obvious forms ageism emerges in the media's portrayal of old people as incompetent, complaining, and, as evidenced perhaps most clearly in both television and films, lacking romantic feelings. Rarely, for example, do television shows or films show older people working productively, being cooperative and pleasant, and engaging in romantic and sexual relationships.

Communication Choice Point

Ageism

One of your instructors is extremely sensitive in talking about women, different races, and different affectional orientations but consistently speaks of old people using stereotypical and insulting language. *What are some of the things you can say (you're in your early twenties and your instructor is at least 65) to voice your objection to this type of talk?*

Popular language is replete with examples of linguistic ageism; expressions such as "little old lady," "old hag," "old-timer," "over the hill," "old coot," and "old fogy" are some examples. As with sexism, qualifying a description of someone in terms of his or her age demonstrates ageism. For example, if you refer to "a quick-witted 75-year-old" or "an agile 65-year-old" or "a responsible teenager," you're implying that these qualities are unusual in people of these ages and thus need special mention. One of the problems with this kind of stereotyping is that it's simply wrong. There are, for example, many 75-year-olds who are extremely quick-witted (and, for that matter, many 30-year-olds who aren't).

One useful way to avoid ageism is to recognize and avoid the illogical stereotypes that ageist language is based on:

● Avoid talking down to a person because he or she is older. Most older people remain mentally alert.

● Don't assume that older people don't know pop culture or technology.

● Refrain from refreshing an older person's memory each time you see the person. Assume that older people remember things.

● Avoid implying that relationships are no longer important. Older people continue to be interested in relationships.

● Speak at a normal volume and maintain a normal physical distance. Being older does not necessarily mean being hard of hearing or being unable to see.

● Engage older people in conversation as you would wish to be engaged. Older people are interested in the world around them.

Explore the **Concept**
"Sexist Language" at
MyCommunicationLab

For an article on sexual equality in different countries, see "Gender Gap" at tcbdevito.blogspot.com. Do you see "gender gaps"? Where are they most prevalent?

SEXIST SPEECH

Sexist speech also exists on both an individual and an institutional level. *Individual sexism* involves prejudicial attitudes about men or women based on rigid beliefs about gender roles. These beliefs may include, for example, the notion that all women should be caretakers, should be sensitive at all times, and should acquiesce to men's decisions concerning political or financial matters. Other sexist beliefs imply that all men are insensitive, interested only in sex, and incapable of communicating feelings.

Institutional sexism involved customs and practices that discriminate against people because of their gender. Clear examples come from the world of business: the widespread practice of paying women less than men for the same job and the frequent discrimination against women in the upper levels of management. Another clear example of institutionalized sexism is the divorce courts' practice of automatically, or almost automatically, granting child custody to the mother rather than the father.

Of particular interest here is **sexist language**—language that disparages someone because of his or her gender (but usually language derogatory toward women). The National Council of Teachers of English (NCTE) has proposed guidelines for nonsexist (gender-free, gender-neutral, or sex-fair) language. These guidelines concern the use of the generic word *man,* the use of generic *he* and *his,* and sex role stereotyping (Penfield, 1987):

● Avoid using *man* generically. Using the term to refer to both men and women emphasizes maleness at the expense of femaleness. Gender-neutral terms can easily be substituted. Instead of "mankind," say "humanity," "people," or "human beings." Similarly, the use of terms such as *policeman* or *fireman* and other terms that presume maleness as the norm—and femaleness as a deviation from this norm—are clear and common examples of sexist language.

● Avoid using *he* and *his* as generic. Instead, you can alternate pronouns or restructure your sentences to eliminate any reference to gender. For example, the NCTE guidelines (Penfield, 1987) suggest that instead of saying, "The average student is worried about his grades," you say, "The average student is worried about grades."

- Avoid sex role stereotyping. When you make the hypothetical elementary school teacher female and the college professor male or refer to doctors as male and nurses as female, you're sex role stereotyping, as you are when you mention the sex of a professional in terms such as "female doctor" or "male nurse."

CULTURAL IDENTIFIERS

One way to develop nonracist, nonheterosexist, nonageist, and nonsexist speech is to examine the preferred cultural identifiers to use in talking to and about members of different groups. Keep in mind, however, that preferred terms frequently change over time, so keep in touch with the most current preferences (Schwartz & Task Force, 1995; Faigley, 2009).

One general guideline is to *include* rather than *exclude*; excluding is a form of talk in which you use the terms of your own cultural group as universal, as applying to everyone. For example, *church* refers to the place of worship for some religions, not all religions. Similarly, *Bible* refers to the Christian religious scriptures and is not a general term for religious scriptures. Nor does the *Judeo-Christian tradition* include the religious traditions of everyone. Similarly, the terms *marriage, husband,* and *wife* refer to some heterosexual relationships and exclude others; in most of the world they also exclude gay and lesbian relationships.

Consider the vast array of alternative terms that are inclusive rather than exclusive. For example, the Association of American University Presses (Schwartz & Task Force, 1995) recommends using *place of worship* instead of *church* when you wish to include the religious houses of worship of all people. Similarly, *committed relationship* is more inclusive than *marriage, couples therapy* is more inclusive than *marriage counseling,* and *life partner* is more inclusive than *husband* or *wife. Religious scriptures* is more inclusive than *Bible*. Of course, if you're referring to, say, a specific Baptist church or married heterosexual couples, then the terms *church* and *marriage* are perfectly appropriate.

Race and Nationality   Some research finds that the term African American is preferred over black in referring to Americans of African descent (Hecht, Jackson, & Ribeau, 2003). Other research, however, concludes that "a majority of blacks in America today do not have a preference (Newport, 2007). Black is often used with white, as well as in a variety of other contexts (for example, Department of Black and Puerto Rican Studies, the *Journal of Black Studies,* and Black History Month)." The American Psychological Association recommends that both terms—White and Black—be capitalized, but *The Chicago Manual of Style* recommends using lowercase. The terms *Negro* and *colored,* although used in the names of some organizations (e.g., the United Negro College Fund and the National Association for the Advancement of Colored People), are not used outside these contexts.

White is generally used to refer to those whose roots are in European cultures and usually does not include Hispanics. Analogous to *African American* (which itself is based on a long tradition of terms such as *Irish American* and *Italian American*) is the phrase *European American.* Few European Americans, however, call themselves that; most prefer to emphasize their national origins, as in, for example, *German American* or *Greek American. People of color*— a more literary-sounding term appropriate perhaps to public speaking but may sound awkward in many conversations—is preferred to *nonwhite,* which implies that whiteness is the norm and nonwhiteness is a deviation from that norm. The same is true of the term *non-Christian*: It implies that people who have other beliefs deviate from the norm.

Generally, *Hispanic* refers to anyone who identifies himself or herself as belonging to a Spanish-speaking culture. *Latina* (female) and *Latino* (male) refer to persons whose roots are in one of the Latin American countries, such as Haiti or Guatemala. *Hispanic American* refers to U.S. residents whose ancestry is in a Spanish culture; the term includes Mexican, Caribbean, and Central and South Americans. In emphasizing Spanish heritage, however, the term is really inaccurate; it leaves out the large numbers of people in the

VIEWPOINTS

-Isms on Campus

How would you rate the state of racist, heterosexist, ageist, and sexist language on your campus, using a 10 point scale with 1 being "totally absent" to 10 "used very frequently."

Communication Choice Point

Objecting to Disconfirmation

A supervisor at work persists in using sexist, heterosexist, and racist language. You want to object to this type of talk. *What options do you have for voicing your objections? To whom would you address these objections? What would you say?*

Communication Choice Point

Misusing Cultural Identifiers

During a conversation a group of classmates all use negative self-reference terms. Trying to be one of the group, you too use these terms—but almost immediately realize that the linguistic privilege allowing insiders to use self-derogatory names does not apply to outsiders (i.e., you). You don't want anyone to think that you normally talk this way. *How can you try to reverse their impressions or at least minimize their negativity?*

Caribbean and in South America whose origins are African, Native American, French, or Portuguese. *Chicana* (female) and *Chicano* (male) refer to persons with roots in Mexico, although it often connotes a nationalist attitude (Jandt, 2010). *Mexican American* is generally preferred.

Inuk (plural, *Inuit*), also spelled with two *n*'s (*Innuk* and *Innuit*), is preferred to *Eskimo* (a term the U.S. Census Bureau uses), a term applied to the indigenous peoples of Alaska and Canada by Europeans and that literally means "raw meat eaters."

The word *Indian* technically refers only to someone from India, not to members of other Asian countries or to the indigenous peoples of North America. *American Indian* or *Native American* is preferred, even though many Native Americans do refer to themselves as Indians and Indian people. The word *squaw*, used to refer to a Native American woman and still used in some U.S. place names and textbooks, is clearly a term to be avoided; its usage is almost always negative and insulting.

In Canada indigenous people are called *first people* or *first nations*. The term *native American* (with a lowercase *n*) is most often used to refer to persons born in the United States. Although technically the term could refer to anyone born in North or South America, people outside the United States generally prefer more specific designations such as *Argentinean*, *Cuban*, or *Canadian*. The term *native* describes an indigenous inhabitant; it is not used to indicate "someone having a less developed culture."

Muslim (rather than the older *Moslem*) is the preferred form to refer to a person who adheres to the religious teachings of Islam. *Quran* (rather than *Koran*) is the preferred term for the scriptures of Islam. *Jewish people* is often preferred to *Jews*, and *Jewess* (a Jewish female) is considered derogatory.

When English-language history books were being written exclusively from a European perspective, Europe was taken as the focal point and the rest of the world was defined in terms of its location relative to that continent. Thus, Asia became "the East" or "the Orient," and Asians became "Orientals"—a term that is today considered inappropriate or "Eurocentric." It is preferable simply to refer to people from Asia as *Asians*, just as people from Africa are *Africans* and people from Europe are *Europeans*.

Affectional Orientation Generally, *gay* is the preferred term to refer to a man who has an affectional preference for other men, and *lesbian* is the preferred term for a woman who has an affectional preference for other women. (*Lesbian* means "homosexual woman," so the term *lesbian woman* is redundant.) *Homosexual* refers to both gays and lesbians, but more often to a sexual orientation to members of one's own sex. *Gay* and *lesbian* refer to a gay and lesbian identification and not only to sexual behavior. *Gay* as a noun, although widely used, may prove offensive in some contexts, as in "We have gays in our office." Because most scientific thinking holds that sexuality is largely biologically determined, the terms *sexual orientation* and *affectional orientation* are preferred to *sexual preference* or *sexual status* (which also is vague). In the case of same-sex marriages—there are two husbands or two wives. In a male-male marriage, each person is referred to as *husband* and in the case of female-female marriage, each person is referred to as *wife*. Some same-sex couples—especially those who are not married—prefer the term "partner" or "lover".

Age *Older person* is generally preferred to *elder*, *elderly*, *senior*, or *senior citizen* (which technically refers to someone older than 65). Terms designating age are rarely necessary. There are times, of course, when you need to refer to a person's age group, but most of the time you don't—in much the same way that gender, race, and affectional orientation terms are usually irrelevant.

Sex Generally, the term *girl* should be used only to refer to very young females and is equivalent to *boy*. Neither term should be used for people older than 13 or 14. *Girl* is never used to refer to a grown woman, nor is *boy* used to refer to people in blue-collar positions, as it once was. *Lady* is negatively evaluated by many because it connotes the stereotype of the prim and proper woman. *Woman* or *young woman* is preferred.

The term *ma'am*, originally an honorific used to show respect, is probably best avoided since today it's often used as a verbal tag to comment (indirectly) on the woman's age or marital status (Angier, 2010).

Transgendered people (people who identify themselves as members of the sex opposite to the one they were assigned at birth and who may be gay or straight, male or female) are addressed according to their self-identified sex. Thus, if the person identifies herself as a woman, then the feminine name and pronouns are used—regardless of the person's biological sex. If the person identifies himself as a man, then the masculine name and pronouns are used.

Transvestites (people who prefer at times to dress in the clothing of the sex other than the one they were assigned at birth and who may be gay or straight, male or female) are addressed on the basis of their clothing. If the person is dressed as a woman—regardless of the birth-assigned sex—she is referred to and addressed with feminine pronouns and feminine name. If the person is dressed as a man—regardless of the birth-assigned sex—he is referred to and addressed with masculine pronouns and masculine name.

Objectives Self-Check
- Can you define and distinguish between *confirmation* and *disconfirmation*?
- Can you communicate with appropriate cultural identifiers and without racist, heterosexist, ageist, and sexist talk?

Principles for Using Verbal Messages Effectively

Watch the **Video** "Interpersonal Communication" at **MyCommunicationLab**

The principles governing the verbal messages system suggest a variety of practices for using language more effectively. Here are six additional guidelines for making your verbal messages more effective and a more accurate reflection of the world in which we live: (1) extensionalize—avoid intensional orientation, (2) see the individual—avoid allness, (3) distinguish between facts and inferences—avoid fact-inference confusion, (4) discriminate among—avoid indiscrimination, (5) talk about the middle—avoid polarization, and (6) update messages—avoid static evaluation.

EXTENSIONALIZE: AVOID INTENSIONAL ORIENTATION

Intensional orientation refers to the tendency to view people, objects, and events in terms of how they're talked about or labeled rather than in terms of how they actually exist. **Extensional orientation** is the opposite: the tendency to look first at the actual people, objects, and events and then at the labels—to be guided by what you see happening rather than by the way something or someone is talked about.

Intensional orientation occurs when you act as if the words and labels were more important than the things they represent—as if the map were more important than the territory. In its extreme form, intensional orientation is seen in the person who is afraid of dogs and who begins to sweat when shown a picture of a dog or when hearing people talk about dogs. Here the person is responding to a label as if it were the actual thing. In its more common form, intensional orientation occurs when you see people through your schemata instead of on the basis of their specific behaviors. For example, it occurs when you think of a professor as an unworldly egghead before getting to know the specific professor.

The corrective to intensional orientation is to focus first on the specific object, person, or event and then on the way in which the object, person, or event is talked about. Labels are certainly helpful guides, but don't allow them to obscure what they're meant to symbolize.

SEE THE INDIVIDUAL: AVOID ALLNESS

The world is infinitely complex, and because of this you can never say all there is to say about anything—at least not logically. This is particularly true when you are dealing with people. You may think you know all there is to know about certain individuals or about why they do what they do, but you don't know everything.

You may, for example, go on a first date with someone who, at least during the first hour or so, turns out to be less interesting than you would have liked. Because of this initial impression you may infer that this person is generally dull. Yet, it could be that this person is simply ill-at-ease or shy during first meetings. The problem is that you run the risk of judging a person on the basis of a very short acquaintanceship. Further, if you then define this person as dull, you're likely to treat the person as dull and create a self-fulfilling prophecy.

A useful extensional device that can help you avoid allness is to end each statement, sometimes verbally but always mentally, with an *et cetera* (etc.)—a reminder that there is more to learn, know, and say; that every statement is inevitably incomplete. To be sure, some people overuse "et cetera." They use it as a substitute for being specific, which defeats its purpose. Instead, it should be used to mentally remind yourself that there is more to know and more to say.

DISTINGUISH BETWEEN FACTS AND INFERENCES: AVOID FACT-INFERENCE CONFUSION

Language enables you to form statements of facts and inferences without making any linguistic distinction between the two. Similarly, when you listen to such statements you often don't make a clear distinction between statements of facts and statements of inference. Yet there are great differences between the two. Barriers to clear thinking can result when inferences are treated as facts, a tendency called **fact-inference confusion.**

For example, you can make statements about things that you observe, and you can make statements about things that you have not observed. In form or structure these statements are similar; they cannot be distinguished from each other by any grammatical analysis. You can say, "She is wearing a blue jacket" as well as "She is harboring an illogical hatred." If you were to diagram these sentences, they would yield identical structures, and yet you know that they're different types of statements. In the first sentence, you can observe the jacket and the blue color; the sentence constitutes a factual statement. But how do you observe "illogical hatred"? This is an inferential rather than a descriptive statement, made not on the basis solely of what you observe but on the basis this plus your own conclusions.

Making inferential statements is necessary if you're to talk about much that is meaningful. However, a problem arises when you act as though those inferential statements are factual statements. You may wish to test your ability to distinguish facts from inferences by taking the accompanying self-test "Can You Distinguish Facts from Inferences?"

TEST YOURSELF

Can You Distinguish Facts from Inferences?

Carefully read the following report and the observations based on it, modeled on a test developed by William Haney (1973). Write **T** if the observation is definitely true, **F** if the observation is definitely false, and **?** if the observation may be either true or false. Judge each observation in order. Do not reread the observations after you have indicated your judgment, and do not change any of your answers.

A well-liked college teacher had just completed making up the final examinations and had turned off the lights in the office. Just then a tall, broad figure with dark glasses appeared and demanded the examination. The professor opened the drawer. Everything in the drawer was picked up and the individual ran down the corridor. The dean was notified immediately.

_____ **1** The thief was tall, broad, and wore dark glasses.

_____ **2** The professor turned off the lights.

_____ **3** A tall figure demanded the examination.

_____ **4** The examination was picked up by someone.

_____ **5** The examination was picked up by the professor.

_____ ⑥ A tall, broad figure appeared after the professor turned off the lights in the office.

_____ ⑦ The man who opened the drawer was the professor.

_____ ⑧ The professor ran down the corridor.

_____ ⑨ The drawer was never actually opened.

_____ ⑩ Three persons are referred to in this report.

HOW DID YOU DO? After you respond to all the statements, form small groups of five or six and discuss your answers. Look at each statement from each member's point of view. For each statement, ask yourself, "How can you be absolutely certain that the statement is true or false?" You should find that only one statement can be clearly identified as true and only one as false; eight should be marked "?".

WHAT WILL YOU DO? Think about this exercise and try to formulate specific guidelines that will help you distinguish facts from inferences.

Distinguishing between these two types of statements does not imply that one type is better than the other. Both types of statements are useful and important. The problem arises when you treat an inferential statement as if it were fact. Phrase your inferential statements as tentative. Recognize that such statements may be wrong. Leave open the possibility of other alternatives.

DISCRIMINATE AMONG: AVOID INDISCRIMINATION

Everything is unique. Language, however, provides common nouns, such as teacher, student, friend, enemy, war, politician, liberal, and the like, that may lead you to focus on similarities within the group rather than individuals' differences.

Indiscrimination, a form of stereotyping, can be seen in such statements as these:

- He's just like the rest of them: lazy, stupid, a real slob.
- I really don't want another ethnic on the board of directors. One is enough for me.
- Read a romance novel? I read one when I was 16. That was enough to convince me.

A useful antidote to indiscrimination is the extensional device called the **index,** a spoken or mental subscript that identifies each individual in a group as an individual even though all members of the group may be covered by the same label. For example, when you think and talk of an individual politician as only a "politician," you may fail to see the uniqueness in this politician and the differences between this particular politician and other politicians. However, when you think with the index—when you think not of politician but of $politician_1$ or $politician_2$ or $politician_3$—you're less likely to fall into the trap of indiscrimination and more likely to focus on the differences among politicians. The same is true with members of cultural, national, or religious groups; when you think and even talk of $Iraqi_1$ and $Iraqi_2$, you'll be reminded that not all Iraqis are the same. The more you discriminate among individuals covered by the same label, the less likely you are to discriminate against any group.

These guidelines are derived from the work of general semanticists. For a look at this area of study concerned with the relationships among language, thought, and behavior, see "General Semantics" at tcbdevito.blogspot.com. Which of these principles/ guidelines do you see violated most often?

TALK ABOUT THE MIDDLE: AVOID POLARIZATION

Polarization, often referred to as the fallacy of "either/or," is the tendency to look at the world and to describe it in terms of extremes—good or bad, positive or negative, healthy or sick, brilliant or stupid, rich or poor, and so on. Polarized statements come in many forms. Here are some examples:

- After listening to the evidence, I'm still not clear who the good guys are and who the bad guys are.
- Well, are you for us or against us?
- College had better get me a good job. Otherwise, this has been a big waste of time.

Most people and situations exist somewhere between the extremes of good and bad, healthy and sick, brilliant and stupid, rich and poor. Yet there seems to be a strong tendency to view only the extremes and to categorize people, objects, and events in terms of these polar opposites (Gamson, 1998).

You can easily demonstrate this tendency by filling in the opposites for each of the following words:

		Opposite
tall	__:__:__:__:__:__:	_____
heavy	__:__:__:__:__:__:	_____
strong	__:__:__:__:__:__:	_____
happy	__:__:__:__:__:__:	_____
legal	__:__:__:__:__:__:	

Filling in the opposites should have been relatively easy and quick. The words should also have been fairly short. Even if various people were to supply their own opposites, there would be a high degree of agreement among them.

Now try to fill in the middle positions with words meaning, for example, "midway between tall and short," "midway between heavy and light," and so on. Do this before continuing to read.

These midway responses (compared to the opposites) were probably more difficult to think of and took you more time. The responses should also have been long words or phrases of several words. In addition, different people would probably agree less on these midway responses than on the opposites.

This exercise illustrates the ease with which you can think and talk in opposites and the difficulty you have in thinking and talking about the middle. But recognize that the vast majority of cases exist between extremes. Don't allow the ready availability of extreme terms to obscure the reality of what lies in between (Read, 2004).

In some cases, of course, it's legitimate to talk in terms of two values. For example, this thing you're holding either is or is not a book. Clearly, the classes "book" and "not-book" include all possibilities. There is no problem with this kind of statement. Similarly, you may say that a student either will pass this course or will not, as these two categories include all the possibilities.

You create problems when you use this either/or form in situations in which it's inappropriate: for example, "The supervisor is either for us or against us." The two choices simply don't include all possibilities: The supervisor may be for us in some things and against us in others, or he or she may be neutral. Right now there is a tendency to group people into categories of pro- and antiwar; similarly, you see examples of polarization in opinions about the Middle East, with some people entirely and totally supportive of one side and others entirely and totally supportive of the other side. However, polarizing categories are created for almost every important political or social issue: "pro" and "anti" positions on abortion and taxes, for example. These extremes do not include all possibilities and prevent us from entertaining the vast middle ground that exists on all such issues and in most people's minds.

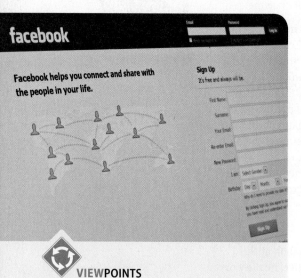

VIEWPOINTS

Social Networks and Language

How would you describe intensional orientation, allness, fact-inference distinction, indiscrimination, polarization, and static evaluation in social networking sites? Can you provide examples of problems created when the guidelines suggested here are violated?

UPDATE MESSAGES: AVOID STATIC EVALUATION

Language changes very slowly, especially when compared to the rapid pace at which people and things change. When you retain a judgment of a person, despite the inevitable changes in the person, you're engaging in **static evaluation.**

Although you would probably agree that everything is in a constant state of flux, the relevant question is whether you *act* as if you know this. Do you treat your little sister as if she were 10 years old, or do you treat her like the 20-year-old woman she has become? Your evaluations of yourself and others need to keep pace with the rapidly changing real world. Otherwise you'll be left with attitudes and beliefs—static evaluations—about a world that no longer exists.

To guard against static evaluation, use a device called the **date,** a mental subscript that enables you to look at your statement in the context of time. Dating your statement is especially important when your statements are evaluative. Remember that Gerry Smith$_{2002}$ is not Gerry Smith$_{2010}$, that academic abilities$_{2006}$ are not academic abilities$_{2010}$.

At the same time, recognize that each of these six guidelines can be used to deceive you. For example, when people treat individuals as they're labeled or influence you to respond to people in terms of their labels (often racist, sexist, or homophobic), they are using intensional orientation unethically. Similarly, when people present themselves as knowing everything about something (gossip is often a good example), they are exploiting the natural tendency for people to think in allness terms to achieve their own ends. When people present inferences as if they are facts (again, gossip provides a good example) to secure your belief or when they stereotype, they are relying on your tendency to confuse facts and inferences and to fail to discriminate. And, when people talk in terms of opposites (polarize) or as if things and people don't change (static evaluation) in order to influence you, they are again assuming you won't talk about the middle ground or ask for updated information.

Objectives Self-Check
- Can you explain the six ways in which language can distort thinking (intensional orientation, allness, the distinction between facts and inferences, indiscrimination, polarization, and static evaluation)?
- Can you use verbal messages that avoid such misevaluations?
- Can you identify these misevaluations in the messages of others?

 ## Messages in the Media *Wrap Up*

Television sitcoms provide great examples of effective as well as ineffective use of language. As you watch a sitcom, focus on the language used by different characters. and ask yourself how the choices they made could have been more effective?

 ## Summary of Concepts and Skills

✓ **Study** and **Review** materials for this chapter are at **MyCommunicationLab**

((**Listen** to the **Audio Chapter Summary** at **MyCommunicationLab**

Focusing on verbal messages, this chapter first looked at the nature of language and identified several major ways in which language works. The next section examined disconfirmation and confirmation and the related topics of racist, heterosexist, ageist, and sexist speech. The final section presented ways to make verbal communication more accurate and effective.

1. Communication is a package of verbal and nonverbal signals.

Principles of Verbal Messages

2. Message meanings are in people.

3. Messages are denotative (i.e., objective and generally easily agreed on) and connotative (i.e., subjective and generally highly individual in meaning).

4. Messages vary in abstraction; they can range from extremely general to extremely specific.

5. Messages can deceive.

6. Messages vary in politeness.

7. Messages can be onymous or anonymous.

8. Messages vary in assertiveness.

9. Messages are influenced by culture and gender.

Disconfirmation and Confirmation

10. Disconfirmation is the process of ignoring the presence and the communications of others. Confirmation means accepting, supporting, and acknowledging the importance of other people.

11. Racist, heterosexist, ageist, and sexist language disconfirms, puts down, and negatively evaluates various groups.

Principles for Using Verbal Messages Effectively

12. Avoid intensional orientation; remember that language symbolizes reality and is not the reality itself.

13. Avoid allness; you can never know all or say all about anything.

14. Avoid confusing facts with inferences; remember that language doesn't indicate this distinction grammatically;

15. Avoid indiscrimination; everything is unique.

16. Avoid polarization; avoid focusing solely on extremes.

17. Avoid static evaluation; language tends to be static, whereas people and events are forever changing.

The study of verbal messages and of how meaning is communicated from one person to another has important implications for the skills of effective communication. Place a check mark next to those skills that you feel you need to work on most.

_____ 1. Because communication is a package of signals, I ensure my verbal and nonverbal messages reinforce rather than contradict each other.

_____ 2. I try to understand not only objective, denotative meanings but also the speaker's subjective, connotative meanings.

_____ 3. I recognize that snarl and purr words describe the speaker's feelings and not objective reality.

_____ 4. I use terms varying in abstraction to best communicate my meanings.

_____ 5. I vary my directness depending on the situation and my communication goal.

_____ 6. I take special care to make spoken messages clear and unambiguous, especially when using terms for which people will have very different connotative meanings.

_____ 7. I recognize cultural and gender differences in the use of verbal messages and avoid assuming that my principles are followed by members of other cultures.

_____ 8. I focus attention not only on words but also on the person communicating, recognizing that meanings are largely in the person.

_____ 9. I avoid disconfirmation and instead use messages that confirm the other person.

_____ 10. I avoid racist, heterosexist, ageist, and sexist language and, in general, language that puts down other groups.

_____ 11. I use the cultural identifiers that facilitate communication and avoid those that set up barriers to effective interaction.

_____ 12. I avoid responding intensionally to labels as if they are objects; instead, I respond extensionally and look first at the reality and then at the words.

_____ 13. To avoid allness, I end my statements with an implicit "et cetera" in recognition that there is always more to be known or said.

_____ 14. I distinguish facts from inferences and respond to inferences with tentativeness.

_____ 15. I avoid indiscrimination by viewing the uniqueness in each person and situation.

_____ 16. I avoid polarization by using "middle ground" terms and qualifiers in describing the world, especially people.

_____ 17. I mentally date my statements and thus avoid static evaluation.

 **Key Word Quiz**

The Language of Verbal Messages

Match the terms about verbal messages with their definitions. Record the number of the definition next to the appropriate term.

_____ a. static evaluation (88)

_____ b. confirmation (79)

_____ c. intensional orientation (85)

_____ d. direct messages (73)

_____ e. ableism (80)

_____ f. denotation (70)

_____ g. disconfirmation (78)

_____ h. polarization (87)

_____ i. connotation (70)

_____ j. ageist speech (81)

1. The objective meaning of a term; the meaning you'd find in a dictionary.
2. Messages that are often considered impolite.
3. Speech that puts down a person because of age.
4. A communication pattern in which you ignore someone's presence as well as that person's communication.
5. The failure to recognize the influence of change.

6. The subjective or emotional meaning that specific speakers give a word.
7. A communication pattern in which you indicate your acceptance of the other person's self-definition.
8. The tendency to view people, objects, and events in the way they're talked about or labeled.
9. The tendency to talk and think in terms of extremes or opposites.
10. Discrimination against people with disabilities.

These ten terms and additional terms used in this chapter can be found in the glossary.

Answers: a.5 b.7 c.8 d.2 e.10 f.1 g.4 h.9 i.6 j.3

 Study and **Review** the **Flashcards** at **MyCommunicationLab**

MyCommunicationLab

Throughout this chapter, there are icons in the margin that highlight media content for selected topics. Go to **MyCommunicationLab** for a wealth of additional information on verbal messages. Here you'll find flashcards to help you learn the jargon of communication, videos that illustrate a variety of concepts, additional exercises, and discussions to help you continue your study of verbal messages and the corresponding skills for effective communication.

ADRIAN
STARTING WEIGHT
370
CURRENT WEIGHT

DIFFERENCE

5

Nonverbal Messages

Objectives

 Listen to the **Audio Chapter** at **MyCommunicationLab**

After reading this chapter, you should be able to:

❶ Explain the six principles that identify the ways in which nonverbal communication functions.

❷ Describe the channels of nonverbal messages and give examples of messages in each channel.

❸ Apply the encoding and decoding suggestions for effectiveness in your own nonverbal interactions

Messages in the Media

The Biggest Loser is a reality television show that focuses on overweight contestants who compete with each other to lose weight and get into shape. As we'll see in this chapter, our bodies—in all their shapes and sizes—communicate a great deal and are one of the nonverbal channels through which we share meaning with each other.

Nonverbal communication is communication without words. You communicate nonverbally when you gesture, smile or frown, widen your eyes, move your chair closer to someone else's, wear jewelry, touch someone, raise your vocal volume, or even say nothing. The crucial aspect is that the message you send is in some way received by one or more other people. If you gesture while you are alone in your room and no one is there to see you, then, most theorists would argue, communication has not taken place.

The ability to use nonverbal communication effectively can yield two major benefits (Burgoon & Hoobler, 2002; Burgoon, Guerrero, & Floyd, 2010). First, the greater your ability to send and receive nonverbal signals, the higher your popularity and psychosocial well-being are likely to be. Second, the greater your nonverbal skills, the more successful you're likely to be at influencing others. Skilled nonverbal communicators are highly persuasive.

Perhaps the best way to begin the study of nonverbal communication is to look at your own beliefs. Which of the following statements do you think are true?

1. Nonverbal communication conveys more meaning than verbal communication.

2. Liars avoid eye contact.

3. Studying nonverbal communication will enable you to detect lying.

4. Unlike verbal communication, nonverbal communication is universal throughout the world.

5. When verbal and nonverbal messages contradict each other, it's wise to believe the nonverbal.

Actually, all of these statements are popular myths about nonverbal communication. Briefly, (1) in some instances, nonverbal messages may communicate more meaning than verbal messages, but, in most cases, it depends on the situation. You won't get very far discussing science and mathematics nonverbally, for example. (2) This is an impossible task; you may get ideas about what someone is thinking but you really can't be certain on the basis of nonverbal behaviors alone. (3) Lie detection is a far more difficult process than any chapter or even series of courses could accomplish. (4) Although some nonverbal behaviors may be universal in meaning, many signals communicate different meanings in different cultures. (5) People can be deceptive verbally as well as nonverbally; it's best to look at the entire group of signals before making a judgment.

Principles of Nonverbal Communication

Let's begin our study of nonverbal communication by examining several principles which, as you'll see, also identify the different functions that nonverbal messages serve (Burgoon & Hoobler, 2002; Burgoon & Bacue, 2003; Afifi, 2007).

NONVERBAL MESSAGES INTERACT WITH VERBAL MESSAGES

Verbal and nonverbal messages interact with each other in six major ways: to accent, to complement, to contradict, to control, to repeat, and to substitute for each other.

- **Accent.** Nonverbal communication is often used to accent or emphasize some part of the verbal message. You might, for example, raise your voice to underscore a particular word or phrase, bang your fist on the desk to stress your commitment, or look longingly into someone's eyes when saying "I love you."

- **Complement.** Nonverbal communication may be used to complement, to add nuances of meaning not communicated by your verbal message. Thus, you might smile when telling a story (to suggest that you find it humorous) or frown and shake your head when recounting someone's deceit (to suggest your disapproval).

- **Contradict.** You may deliberately contradict your verbal messages with nonverbal movements; for example, by crossing your fingers or winking to indicate that you're lying.

Watch the **Video**
"Judy Burgoon Discusses Nonverbal Communication" at **MyCommunicationLab**

Explore the **Exercise**
"Recognizing Verbal and Nonverbal Message Functions" at **MyCommunicationLab**

Communication Choice Point

Smiling

Sally smiles almost all the time. Even when she reprimands a subordinate, she ends with a smile and this dilutes the strength of her message. As Sally's supervisor, you need her to realize what she's doing and to change her nonverbals. *What can you say to Sally that would not encourage defensiveness or resistance? What would be the best place to say what you want to say? What would you say?*

Watch the **Video** "Louder Than Words" at **MyCommunicationLab**

- **Control.** Nonverbal movements may be used to control, or to indicate your desire to control, the flow of verbal messages, as when you purse your lips, lean forward, or make hand movements to indicate that you want to speak. You might also put up your hand or vocalize your pauses (for example, with "um") to indicate that you have not finished and aren't ready to relinquish the floor to the next speaker.

- **Repeat.** You can repeat or restate the verbal message nonverbally. You can, for example, follow your verbal "Is that all right?" with raised eyebrows and a questioning look, or you can motion with your head or hand to repeat your verbal "Let's go."

- **Substitute.** You may also use nonverbal communication to substitute for verbal messages. You can, for example, signal "OK" with a hand gesture. You can nod your head to indicate yes or shake your head to indicate no.

When you communicate electronically, of course, your message is **transmitted** by means of typed letters without facial expressions or gestures that normally accompany face-to-face communication and without the changes in rate and volume that are a part of normal telephone communication. To compensate for this lack of nonverbal behavior, the **emoticon** was created (see Table 5.1). Sometimes called a "smiley," the emoticon is a typed symbol that communicates through a keyboard the nuances of the message normally conveyed by nonverbal expression. The absence of the nonverbal channel through which you can clarify your message—for example, smiling or winking to communicate sarcasm or humor—make such typed symbols extremely helpful. And of course you can post photos, book and music album covers, for example, to further communicate your emotional meaning.

NONVERBAL MESSAGES HELP MANAGE IMPRESSIONS

It is largely through the nonverbal communications of others that you form impressions of them. Based on a person's body size, skin color, and dress, as well as on the way the person smiles, maintains eye contact, and expresses himself or herself facially, you form impressions—you judge who the person is and what the person is like.

And, at the same time that you form impressions of others, you are also managing the impressions they form of you. As explained in the discussion of impression management in Chapter 2 (pp. 42–47), you use different strategies to achieve different impressions. And of course many of these strategies involve nonverbal messages. Here are some examples:

- **To be liked,** you might smile, pat another on the back, and shake hands warmly. See Table 5.2 for some additional ways in which nonverbal communication may make you seem more attractive and more likeable.

TABLE 5.1 Some Popular Emoticons

These are some of the emoticons used in computer communication. The first six are widely used in the United States; the last three are popular in Japan and illustrate how culture influences such symbols. Because Japanese culture considers it impolite for women to show their teeth when smiling, the emoticon for a woman's smile shows a dot signifying a closed mouth. Depending on your computer, these typed symbols are often on auto correct (as in the first two examples) and change into the graphic smileys. Additional emoticons, acronyms, and abbreviations—in varied cultures—are plentiful on the Internet.

Emoticon	Meaning	Emoticon	Meaning
:-) ☺	Smile: I'm kidding	{*****}	Hugs and kisses
:-(☹	Frown: I'm feeling down	^.^	Woman's smile
;-)	Wink	^_^	Man's smile
*	Kiss	^0^	Happy
{ }	Hug		

TABLE 5.2 Ten Nonverbal Messages and Attractiveness

Here are ten nonverbal messages that help communicate your attractiveness and ten that will probably do the opposite (Andersen, 2004; Riggio & Feldman, 2005).

Do	But Don't
Gesture to show liveliness and animation in ways that are appropriate to the situation and to the message.	Gesture for the sake of gesturing or gesture in ways that may prove offensive to members of other cultures.
Nod and lean forward to signal that you're listening and are interested.	Go on automatic pilot, nodding without any coordination with what is being said or lean so forward that you intrude on the other's space.
Smile and otherwise show your interest, attention, and positiveness facially.	Overdo it; inappropriate smiling is likely to be perceived negatively.
Make eye contact in moderation.	Stare, ogle, glare, or otherwise make the person feel that he or she is under scrutiny.
Touch in moderation when appropriate.	Touch excessively or too intimately. When in doubt, avoid touching.
Use vocal variation in rate, rhythm, pitch, and volume to communicate your enthusiasm and involvement in what you're saying.	Fall into the pattern in which, for example, your voice goes up and down, up and down, up and down without any relationship to what you're saying.
Use silence to listen at least the same amount of time as you speak. Show that you're listening with appropriate facial reactions, posture, and back-channeling cues, for example.	Listen motionlessly or in ways that suggest you're only listening half-heartedly.
Stand reasonably close to show connectedness.	Exceed the other person's comfort zone.
Present a pleasant smell and be careful to camouflage the onions, garlic, or smoke that you may be so used to you don't notice.	Overdo the cologne or perfume.
Dress appropriately to the situation.	Wear clothing that is uncomfortable or that calls attention to itself and hence away from your message.

- **To be believed,** you might use focused eye contact, a firm stance, and open gestures.
- **To excuse failure,** you might look sad, cover your face with your hands, and shake your head.
- **To secure help by indicating helplessness,** you might use open hand gestures, a puzzled look, and inept movements.
- **To hide faults,** you might wear flattering clothing or makeup.
- **To be followed,** you might dress the part of a leader or display your diploma or awards where others can see them.
- **To confirm self-image and to communicate it to others,** you might dress in certain ways or decorate your apartment with things that reflect your personality.

NONVERBAL MESSAGES HELP FORM RELATIONSHIPS

Much of your relationship life is lived nonverbally. You communicate affection, support, and love, in part at least, nonverbally (Floyd & Mikkelson, 2005). At the same time, you also communicate displeasure, anger, and animosity through nonverbal signals.

You also use nonverbal signals to communicate the nature of your relationship to another person, and you and that person communicate nonverbally with each other. These signals that communicate your relationship status are known as "tie signs": They indicate the ways in which

SKILL DEVELOPMENT EXPERIENCE

Messages are a combination of verbal and nonverbal signals; even subtle variations in, say, eye movements or intonation can drastically change the impression communicated.

Using Nonverbal Impression Management Strategies

Now that you've read about how nonverbal messages may help you manage impressions, consider how you would manage yourself nonverbally in the following situations. For each of these situations, indicate (a) the impressions you'd want to create (e.g., an image as a hardworking self-starter); (b) the nonverbal cues you'd use to create these impressions; and (c) the nonverbal cues you'd be especially careful to avoid.

1. You want a job at a conservative, prestigious law firm and are meeting your prospective boss for your first face-to-face interview.
2. You want a part in a movie in which you'd play a homeless drug addict.
3. You're single and you're applying to adopt a child.
4. You want to ask another student to go out with you.
5. You want to convince your romantic partner that you did not see your ex last night; you were working.

Communication Choice Point
Communicating Closeness

How would you go about increasing the intimacy of a relationship nonverbally in face-to-face communication? *Lacking nonverbal signals, how would you do it on a social network site such as MySpace or Facebook?*

your relationship is tied together (Goffman, 1967; Afifi & Johnson, 2005; Knapp & Hall, 2009). Tie signs are also used to confirm the level of the relationship; for example, you might hold hands to see if this is responded to positively. And of course tie signs are often used to let others know that the two of you are tied together.

Tie signs vary in intimacy and may extend from the relatively informal handshake through more intimate forms, such as hand holding and arm linking, to very intimate contact, such as full mouth kissing (Andersen, 2004).

NONVERBAL MESSAGES STRUCTURE CONVERSATION

When you're in conversation, you give and receive cues—signals that you're ready to speak, to listen, to comment on what the speaker just said. These cues regulate and structure the interaction. These **turn-taking cues** may be verbal (as when you say, "What do you think?" and thereby give the speaking turn over to the listener). Most often, however, they're nonverbal; a nod of the head in the direction of someone else, for example, signals that you're ready to give up your speaking turn and want this other person to say something. You also show that you're listening and that you want the conversation to continue (or that you're not listening and want the conversation to end) largely through nonverbal signals of posture and eye contact (or the lack thereof).

NONVERBAL MESSAGES CAN INFLUENCE AND DECEIVE

You can influence others not only through what you say but also through your nonverbal signals. A focused glance that says you're committed; gestures that further explain what you're saying; appropriate dress that says, "I'll easily fit in with this organization"—these are just a few examples of ways in which you can exert nonverbal influence.

And with the ability to influence, of course, comes the ability to deceive—to mislead another person into thinking something is true when it's false or that something is false when it's true. One common example of nonverbal deception is using your eyes and facial expressions to communicate a liking for other people when you're really interested only in gaining their support in some endeavor. Not surprisingly, you also use nonverbal signals to detect deception in others. For example, you may well suspect a person of lying if he or she avoids eye contact, fidgets, and conveys inconsistent verbal and nonverbal messages.

But be careful. Research shows that it is much more difficult to tell when someone is lying than you probably think it is. So, use caution in judging deception (Knapp, 2008).

For additional reasons why identifying lying is so difficult, see "Deception Detection" at tcbdevito.blogspot.com. Based on your own deception detection experiences, do you agree/disagree with what is said here?

NONVERBAL MESSAGES ARE CRUCIAL FOR EXPRESSING EMOTIONS

Although people often explain and reveal emotions verbally, nonverbal signals communicate a great part of their emotional experience. For example, you reveal your level of happiness or sadness or confusion largely through facial expressions. Of course, you also reveal your feelings by posture (for example, whether tense or relaxed), gestures, eye movements, and even the dilation of your pupils. Nonverbal messages often help people communicate unpleasant messages that they might feel uncomfortable putting into words (Infante, Rancer, & Womack, 2003). For example, you might avoid eye contact and maintain large distances between yourself and someone with whom you didn't want to interact or with whom you wanted to decrease the intensity of your relationship.

At the same time, you also use nonverbal messages to hide your emotions. You might, for example, smile even though you feel sad so as not to dampen the party spirit. Or you might laugh at someone's joke even though you think it silly.

Explore the **Exercise** "Communicating Emotions Nonverbally" at **MyCommunicationLab**

Objectives Self-Check
- Can you explain the six principles that identify the ways in which nonverbal communication functions? (Keep in mind that nonverbal messages interact with verbal messages, that they help manage impressions, that they help form relationships, that they structure conversation, that they can influence and deceive, and that they are crucial to emotional expression.)
- Can you identify instances in which your own nonverbal messages illustrated each of these principles?

The Channels of Nonverbal Communication

You communicate nonverbally through a wide range of channels: the body, the face, the eyes, space, artifacts, touch, paralanguage, silence, and time.

BODY COMMUNICATION

The body communicates with movements and gestures and just by its general appearance, an area of nonverbal communication referred to as **kinesics**.

Body Gestures   Nonverbal researchers identify five major types of kinesics: emblems, illustrators, affect displays, regulators, and adaptors (Ekman & Friesen, 1969; Knapp & Hall, 2006).

Emblems are body gestures that translate directly into words or phrases: for example, the OK sign, the thumbs-up for "good job," and the V for "victory." You use these consciously and purposely to communicate the same meaning as the words. But emblems are culture specific, so be careful when using your culture's emblems in other cultures.

As shown in Figure 5.1, there is much variation in gestures and their meanings among different cultures (Axtell, 1993). Consider a few common gestures that you might use without thinking but that could get you into trouble if you were to use them in another culture:

Explore the **Concept** "Nonverbal Communication" at **MyCommunicationLab**

- Folding your arms over your chest would be considered disrespectful in Fiji.
- Waving your hand would be insulting in Nigeria and Greece.
- Gesturing the "thumbs up" would be rude in Australia.
- Tapping your two index fingers together would be considered an invitation to sleep together in Egypt.
- Pointing with your index finger would be impolite in many Middle Eastern countries.
- Bowing to a lesser degree than your host would be considered a statement of your superiority in Japan.
- Inserting your thumb between your index and middle finger in a clenched fist would be viewed in certain African countries as a wish that evil befall someone.
- Resting your feet on a table or chair would be insulting in some Middle Eastern cultures.

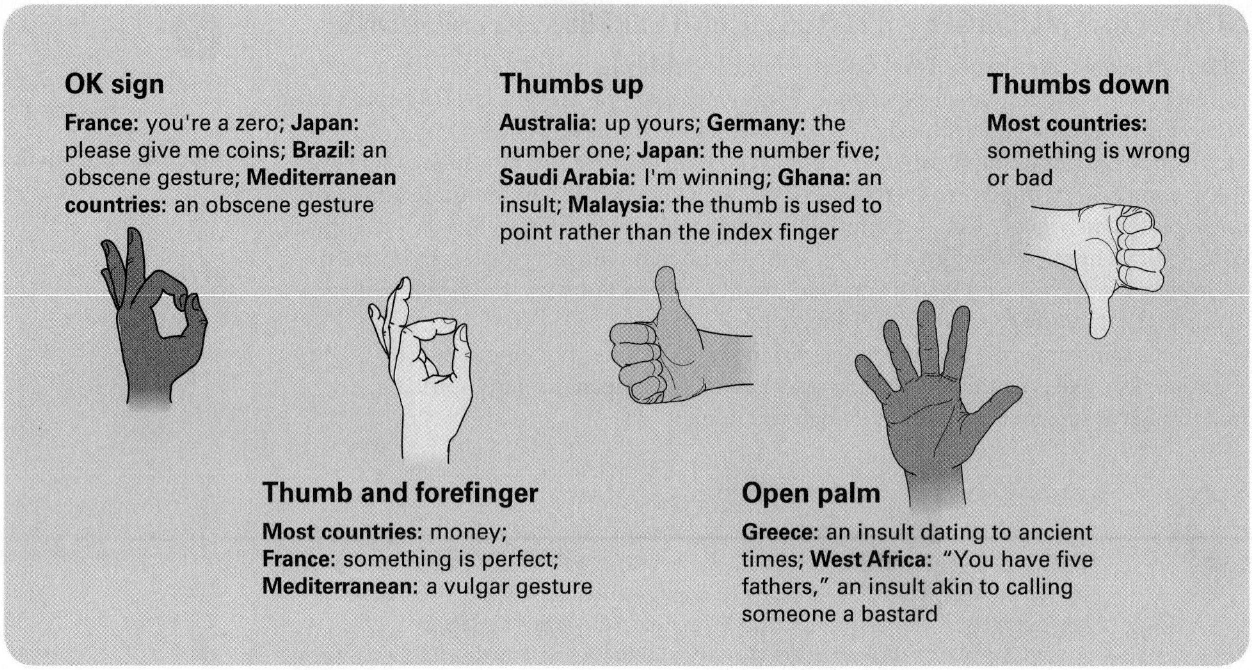

OK sign

France: you're a zero; **Japan:** please give me coins; **Brazil:** an obscene gesture; **Mediterranean countries:** an obscene gesture

Thumbs up

Australia: up yours; **Germany:** the number one; **Japan:** the number five; **Saudi Arabia:** I'm winning; **Ghana:** an insult; **Malaysia:** the thumb is used to point rather than the index finger

Thumbs down

Most countries: something is wrong or bad

Thumb and forefinger

Most countries: money; **France:** something is perfect; **Mediterranean:** a vulgar gesture

Open palm

Greece: an insult dating to ancient times; **West Africa:** "You have five fathers," an insult akin to calling someone a bastard

FIGURE 5.1

Some Cultural Meanings of Gestures

Cultural differences in the meanings of nonverbal gestures are often significant. The over-the-head clasped hands that signify victory to an American may signify friendship to a Russian. To a North American, holding up two fingers to make a V signifies victory or peace. To certain South Americans, however, it is an obscene gesture that corresponds to an extended middle finger in the United States. This figure highlights some additional nonverbal differences. Can you identify others?

Illustrators enhance (literally "illustrate") the verbal messages they accompany. For example, when referring to something to the left, you might gesture toward the left. Most often you illustrate with your hands, but you can also illustrate with head and general body movements. You might, for example, turn your head or your entire body toward the left. You might also use illustrators to communicate the shape or size of objects you're talking about. Recent research points to an interesting advantage of illustrators—namely, that they increase your ability to remember. In this research people who illustrated their verbal messages with gestures remembered 20 percent more than those who didn't gesture (Goldin-Meadow, Nusbaum, Kelly, & Wagner, 2001).

Affect displays are movements of the face (smiling or frowning, for example) but also of the hands and general body (body tenseness or relaxed posture, for example) that communicate emotional meaning. You use affect displays to accompany and reinforce your verbal messages and also as substitutes for words. For example, you might smile while saying how happy you are to see your friend, or you might simply smile. (Affect displays, being primarily centered in the facial area, are covered in more detail in the next section.)

Regulators are behaviors that monitor, control, coordinate, or maintain the speech of another individual. When you nod your head, for example, you tell the speaker to keep on speaking; when you lean forward and open your mouth, you tell the speaker that you would like to say something.

Adaptors are gestures that satisfy some personal need, such as scratching to relieve an itch or moving your hair out of your eyes. **Self-adaptors** are self-touching movements (e.g., rubbing your nose). **Alter-adaptors** are movements directed at the person with whom you're speaking: for example, removing lint from a person's jacket or straightening his or her tie, or folding your arms in front of you to keep others at a comfortable distance. **Object-adaptors** are gestures focused on objects (e.g., doodling on or shredding a Styrofoam coffee cup.) Table 5.3 summarizes these five types of body movements.

TABLE 5.3 Five Body Movements

What other examples can you think of for these five movements?

	Name and Function	Examples
	EMBLEMS directly translate words or phrases; they are especially culture specific.	"OK" sign, "come here" wave, hitchhiker's sign
	ILLUSTRATORS accompany and literally "illustrate" verbal messages.	Circular hand movements when talking of a circle; hands far apart when talking of something large
	AFFECT DISPLAYS communicate emotional meaning.	Expressions of happiness, surprise, fear, anger, sadness, disgust/contempt
	REGULATORS monitor, maintain, or control the speech of another.	Facial expressions and hand gestures indicating "keep going," "slow down," or "what else happened?"
	ADAPTORS satisfy some need.	Scratching your head

Body Appearance Your general body appearance also communicates. Height, for example, has been shown to be significant in a wide variety of situations. Tall presidential candidates have a much better record of winning elections than do their shorter opponents. Tall people seem to be paid more and are favored by personnel interviewers over shorter job applicants (Keyes, 1980; Knapp & Hall, 2009). Taller people also have higher self-esteem and greater career success than do shorter people (Judge & Cable, 2004).

Your body also reveals your race, through skin color and tone, and may even give clues as to your nationality. Your weight in proportion to your height also will communicate messages to others, as will the length, color, and style of your hair.

Your general **attractiveness,** which includes both visual appeal and pleasantness of personality, is also a part of body communication. Attractive people have the advantage in just about every activity you can name. They get better grades in school, are more valued as friends and lovers, and are preferred as coworkers (Burgoon, Guerrero, & Floyd, 2010). Not surprisingly, positive facial expressions contribute to the perception of attractiveness for both men and women (Koscriski, 2007).

FACIAL COMMUNICATION

Throughout your communication interactions, your face communicates many things, especially your emotions. In fact, facial movements alone seem to communicate the degree of pleasantness, agreement, and sympathy felt; the rest of the body doesn't provide any additional information in those realms. But for other aspects—for example, the intensity with which an emotion is felt—both facial and bodily cues enter in (Graham, Bitti, & Argyle, 1975; Graham & Argyle, 1975). These cues are so important in communicating your full meaning that graphic representations are now commonly used in electronic communication. On the Internet, emoticon buttons to help you encode your emotions graphically are now common. (See again Table 5.1, which identified some of the more common emoticons.)

Some nonverbal research claims that facial movements may communicate at least the following eight emotions: happiness, surprise, fear, anger, sadness, disgust, contempt, and interest (Ekman, Friesen, & Ellsworth, 1972). Try to communicate surprise using only facial movements. Do this in front of a mirror and try to describe in

VIEWPOINTS

The Importance of Appearance

On a 10-point scale, with 1 indicating "not at all important" and 10 indicating "extremely important," how important is body appearance to your own romantic interest in another person? Do the men and women you know conform to the stereotypes that say males are more concerned with the physical and females more concerned with personality?

as much detail as possible the specific movements of the face that make up a look of surprise. If you signal surprise like most people, you probably use raised and curved eyebrows, horizontal forehead wrinkles, wide-open eyes, a dropped-open mouth, and lips parted with no tension.

Explore the **Exercise** "Facial Expressions" at **MyCommunicationLab**

Facial Management
As you grew up, you learned your culture's system of nonverbal communication. You also learned certain **facial management techniques** that enable you to express feelings while achieving certain desired effects—for example, to hide certain emotions and to emphasize others. Consider your own use of such facial management techniques. As you do so, think about the types of situations in which you would use facial management techniques for each of the following purposes (Malandro, Barker, & Barker, 1989; Metts & Planalp, 2002):

- **to intensify**—for example, to exaggerate your astonishment at a surprise party to make your friends feel better.
- **to deintensify**—for example, to cover up your own joy about good news in the presence of a friend who didn't receive any such news.
- **to neutralize**—for example, to cover up your sadness so as not to depress others.
- **to mask**—for example, to express happiness in order to cover up your disappointment at the set of luggage you received, rather than the car you expected.
- **to simulate**—to express an emotion you don't feel.

Facial management techniques help you display emotions in socially acceptable ways. For example, if someone gets bad news in which you secretly take pleasure, the social display rule dictates that you frown and otherwise nonverbally signal sorrow. If you place first in a race and your best friend barely finishes, the display rule requires that you minimize your expression of happiness—and certainly avoid any signs of gloating. If you violate these display rules, you'll appear insensitive. So, although facial management techniques may be deceptive, they're expected and even required by the rules for polite interaction.

Facial Feedback
The **facial feedback hypothesis** claims that your facial expressions influence physiological arousal (Cappella, 1993). In one study, for example, participants held a pen in their teeth to simulate a sad expression and then rated a series of photographs. Results showed that mimicking sad expressions actually increased the degree of sadness the subjects reported feeling when viewing the photographs (Larsen, Kasimatis, & Frey, 1992). Generally, research finds that facial expressions can produce or heighten feelings of sadness, fear, disgust, and anger. But this effect does not occur with all emotions; smiling, for example, doesn't seem to make us feel happier. Further, it has not been demonstrated that facial expressions can eliminate one feeling and replace it with another. So if you're feeling sad, smiling will not eliminate the sadness and replace it with gladness. A reasonable conclusion seems to be that your facial expressions can influence some feelings, but not all (Burgoon, Guerrero, & Floyd, 2010).

Culture and Facial Expression
The wide variations in facial communication that we observe in different cultures seem to reflect which reactions are publicly permissible, rather than a difference in the way emotions are facially expressed. For example, when Japanese and American students watched a film of a surgical operation (Ekman, 1985), they were video-taped both while being interviewed about the film and alone while watching the film. When alone, the students showed very similar reactions. In the interview, however, the American students displayed facial expressions indicating displeasure, whereas the Japanese students did not show any great emotion.

Similarly, cultural differences exist in decoding the meaning of a facial expression. In one study, for example, American and Japanese students judged the meaning of a smiling and a neutral facial expression. The Americans rated the smiling face as more attractive, more intelligent, and more sociable than the neutral face. The Japanese, however, rated the smiling face as more sociable but not as more attractive—and they rated the neutral face as more intelligent (Matsumoto & Kudoh, 1993).

EYE COMMUNICATION

Research on communication via the eyes (a study known technically as **oculesics**) shows that the duration, direction, and quality of the eye movements communicate different messages. For example, in every culture there are strict, though unstated, rules for the proper duration for eye contact. In our culture, the average length of gaze is 2.95 seconds. The average length of mutual gaze (two persons gazing at each other) is 1.18 seconds (Argyle & Ingham, 1972; Argyle, 1988). When eye contact falls short of this duration, you may think the person is uninterested, shy, or preoccupied. When the appropriate amount of time is exceeded, you may perceive the person as showing unusually high interest.

The direction of the eye glance also communicates. In much of the United States, you're expected to glance alternately at the other person's face, then away, then again at the face, and so on. The rule for the public speaker is to scan the entire audience, not focusing for too long on or ignoring any one area of the audience. When you break these directional rules, you communicate different meanings—abnormally high or low interest, self-consciousness, nervousness over the interaction, and so on. The quality of eye behavior—how wide or how narrow your eyes get during interaction—also communicates meaning, especially interest level and emotions such as surprise, fear, and disgust.

Eye Avoidance   The eyes are "great intruders," observed sociologist Erving Goffman (1967). When you avoid eye contact or avert your glance, you help others to maintain their privacy. You may do this when you see a couple arguing in public: You turn your eyes away (though your eyes may be wide open) as if to say, "I don't mean to intrude; I respect your privacy." Goffman refers to this behavior as **civil inattention.**

Eye avoidance can also signal lack of interest—in a person, a conversation, or some visual stimulus. At times you may hide your eyes to block off unpleasant stimuli (a particularly gory or violent scene in a movie, for example) or close your eyes to block out visual stimuli and thus heighten other senses. For example, you may listen to music with your eyes closed. Lovers often close their eyes while kissing, and many prefer to make love in a dark or dimly lit room.

Culture, Gender, and Eye Messages   Not surprisingly, eye messages vary with both culture and gender. Americans, for example, consider direct eye contact an expression of honesty and forthrightness, but the Japanese often view this as a lack of respect. A Japanese person will glance at the other person's face rarely, and then only for very short periods (Axtell, 1990). Interpreting another's eye contact messages with your own cultural rules is a risky undertaking; eye movements that you may interpret as insulting may have been intended to show respect.

Women make eye contact more and maintain it longer (both in speaking and in listening) than men. This holds true whether women are interacting with other women or with men. This difference in eye behavior may result from women's greater tendency to display their emotions (Wood, 1994). When women interact with other women, they display affiliative and supportive eye contact, whereas when men interact with other men, they avert their gaze (Gamble & Gamble, 2003).

In some cases, the visual channel may be damaged and adjustments have to be made. Table 5.4 (p. 102) gives you an idea of how such adjustments between people with visual impairments and those without such impairments can make communication more effective.

SPATIAL COMMUNICATION

Space is an especially important factor in nonverbal communication, although we seldom think about it. Edward T. Hall (1959, 1963, 1966), who pioneered the study of spatial communication, called this study **proxemics.** We can sample this broad area by looking at proxemic distances and territoriality.

Proxemic Distances   Hall (1959, 1966) distinguishes four types of proxemic distances that define types of relationships between people: (1) intimate distance, (2) personal distance, (3) social distance, and (4) public distance. Each distance communicates specific kinds of messages.

Another type of eye movement is the eye roll. Take a look at "The Eye Roll" at tcbdevito.blogspot.com. Do you use the eye roll? What messages would you be most likely to communicate with the eye roll?

Explore the **Exercise** "Eye Contact" at **MyCommunicationLab**

For a brief note on something you may have encountered in a restaurant or similar place, take a look at "Eye Contact" at tcbdevito .blogspot.com. What's been your experience in situations like this?

Explore the **Exercise** "Interpersonal Interactions and Space" at **MyCommunicationLab**

TABLE 5.4 Communication Tips

Between People with and People without Visual Impairments

People vary greatly in their visual abilities; some are totally blind, some are partially sighted, and some have unimpaired vision. Ninety percent of people who are "legally blind" have some vision. All people, however, have the same need for communication and information. Here are some tips for making communication better between those who have visual impairments and those without such difficulties.

If you're the person without visual impairment and are talking with a visually impaired person:	
Generally	**Specifically**
Identify yourself.	Don't assume the visually impaired person will recognize your voice.
Face your listener; you'll be easier to hear.	Don't shout. Most people who are visually impaired are not hearing impaired. Speak at your normal volume.
Encode into speech all the meanings you wish to communicate.	Remember that your gestures, eye movements, and facial expressions cannot be seen by the visually impaired.
Use audible turn-taking cues.	When you pass the role of speaker to a person who is visually impaired, don't rely on nonverbal cues; instead, say something like, "Do you agree with that, Joe?"
Use normal vocabulary and discuss topics that you would discuss with sighted people.	Don't avoid terms like "see" or "look" or even "blind." Don't avoid discussing a television show or the way your new car looks; these are normal topics for all people.

If you are a person with visual impairment and are talking with a person without visual impairment:	
Help the sighted person meet your special communication needs.	If you want your surroundings described, ask. If you want the person to read the road signs, ask.
Be patient with the sighted person.	Many people are nervous talking with people who are visually impaired for fear of offending. Put them at ease in a way that also makes you more comfortable.
Demonstrate your comfort.	When appropriate, let the other person know that you're comfortable with the interaction, verbally or nonverbally.

Sources: These suggestions were drawn from a variety of sources, including the websites of the Cincinnati Association for the Blind and Visually Impaired, the Association for the Blind of WA, the National Federation of the Blind, and the American Foundation for the Blind, all accessed May 9, 2012.

Communication Choice Point

Proxemics

Like the close-talker in an episode of *Seinfeld,* one of your team members at work maintains an extremely close distance when talking. Coupled with the fact that this person is a heavy smoker and reeks of smoke, you need to say something. *In what ways might you deal with this issue? What would you say (if anything)? Through what channel?*

Watch the **Video** "Personal Space" at **MyCommunicationLab**

At an **intimate distance,** ranging from touching to 18 inches apart, the presence of the other individual is unmistakable. Each person experiences the sound, smell, and feel of the other's breath. You use intimate distance for lovemaking and wrestling, for comforting and protecting. This distance is so short that most people do not consider it proper in public.

Personal distance constitutes the protective "bubble" that defines your personal space, which measures from 18 inches to 4 feet. This imaginary bubble keeps you protected and untouched by others. You can still hold or grasp another person at this distance—but only by extending your arms—allowing you to take certain individuals such as loved ones into your protective bubble. At the outer limit of personal distance, you can touch another person only if both of you extend your arms.

At a **social distance,** ranging from 4 to 12 feet, you lose the visual detail you have at personal distance. You conduct impersonal business and interact at a social gathering at this social distance. The more distance you maintain in your interactions, the more formal they appear. Many people in executive and management positions place their desks so that they are assured of at least this distance from employees.

Public distance, measuring from 12 to 25 feet or more, protects you. At this distance you could take defensive action if threatened. On a public bus or train, for example, you might

TABLE 5.5   Relationships and Proxemic Distances

Note that the four proxemic distances can be further divided into close and far phases, and that the far phase of one level (say, the personal level) blends into the close phase of the next level (social). Do your relationships also blend into one another, or are your personal relationships totally separate from your social relationships?

Relationship	Distance		Relationship	Distance	
Intimate Relationship	**Intimate Distance** 0 ——————— 18 inches Close phase Far phase		Social Relationship	**Social Distance** 4 ——————— 12 feet Close phase Far phase	
Personal Relationship	**Personal Distance** 1½ ——————— 4 feet Close phase Far phase		Public Relationship	**Public Distance** 12 ——————— 25 feet Close phase Far phase	

keep at least this distance from a menacing or intoxicated fellow passenger. Although you lose fine details of the face and eyes at this distance, you are still close enough to see what is happening. These four distances are summarized in Table 5.5.

Territoriality

Another type of communication having to do with space is **territoriality**, a possessive reaction to an area or to particular objects. You interact basically in three types of territory (Altman, 1975):

- **Primary territories:** Areas that you might call your own; these areas are your exclusive preserve. Primary territories might include your room, your desk, or your office.

- **Secondary territories:** Areas that don't belong to you but that you have occupied and with which you're associated. They might include your usual table in the cafeteria, your regular seat in the classroom, or your neighborhood turf.

- **Public territories:** Areas that are open to all people; they may be owned by some person or organization, but they are used by everyone. They are places such as movie theaters, restaurants, and shopping malls.

When you operate in your own primary territory, you have an advantage, often called the **home field advantage.** In their own home or office, people take on a kind of leadership role: They initiate conversations, fill in silences, assume relaxed and comfortable postures, and maintain their positions with greater conviction. Because the territorial owner is dominant, you stand a better chance of getting your raise approved, your point accepted, or a contract resolved in your favor if you're in your own territory (e.g., your office or your home) rather than in someone else's (e.g., your supervisor's office) (Marsh, 1988).

Like many animals, humans mark both their primary and secondary territories to signal ownership. Humans use three types of **markers:** central, boundary, and earmarkers (Goffman, 1971). **Central markers** are items you place in a territory to reserve it for you—for example, a drink at the bar, books on your desk, or a sweater over a library chair. Some people, perhaps because they can't own territories, might use markers to indicate a kind of pseudo-ownership or to appropriate someone else's turf or a public territory for their own use (Childress, 2004). Examples include graffiti and the markings of gang boundaries.

Boundary markers serve to divide your territory from that of others. In the supermarket checkout line, the bar placed between your groceries and those of the person behind you is a boundary marker, as are fences, armrests that separate your seat from those on either side, and the contours of the molded plastic seats on a bus.

Communication Choice Point

Inviting and Discouraging Conversation

Sometimes you want to encourage people to come into your office and chat, and at other times you want to be left alone. *What might you do nonverbally to achieve each goal?*

Earmarkers—a term taken from the practice of branding animals on their ears—are identifying marks that indicate your possession of a territory or object. Trademarks, nameplates, and initials on a shirt or attaché case are all examples of earmarkers.

Markers are also important in giving you a feeling of belonging. For example, one study found that students who marked their college dorm rooms by displaying personal items stayed in school longer than did those who didn't personalize their spaces (Marsh, 1988).

ARTIFACTUAL COMMUNICATION

Artifactual messages are messages conveyed through objects or arrangements made by human hands. The colors you prefer, the clothing or jewelry you wear, the way you decorate your space, and even bodily scents communicate a wide variety of meanings.

Color Communication   There is some evidence that the colors with which people surround themselves affect them physiologically. For example, respiration rates increase in the presence of red light and decrease in the presence of blue light. Similarly, eye blinks increase in frequency when eyes are exposed to red light and decrease when exposed to blue. These findings seem consistent with our intuitive feelings that blue is more soothing and red more provocative. After the administration at one school changed the classroom walls from orange and white to blue, the students' blood pressure levels decreased and their academic performance improved (Ketcham, 1958; Malandro, Barker, & Barker, 1989).

Colors influence our perceptions and behaviors (Kanner, 1989). People's acceptance of a product, for example, is strongly influenced by its packaging. In one experiment consumers in the United States described the very same coffee taken from a yellow can as weak, from a dark brown can as too strong, from a red can as rich, and from a blue can as mild. Even our acceptance of a person may depend on the colors that person wears. Consider, for example, the comments of one color expert (Kanner, 1989, p. 23): "If you have to pick the wardrobe for your defense lawyer heading into court and choose anything but blue, you deserve to lose the case. . . ." Black is so powerful that it can work against the lawyer with the jury. Brown lacks sufficient authority.

VIEWPOINTS

Status Signals

One signal of status is an unwritten "law" granting the right of invasion. Higher-status individuals have more of a right to invade the territory of others than vice versa. The boss, for example, can invade the territory of junior executives by barging into their offices, but the reverse would be unacceptable. In what ways do you notice this "right" of territorial invasion in your workplace (or your dorm room)?

SKILL DEVELOPMENT EXPERIENCE

Selecting a Seat at the Company Meeting

Nonverbal choices influence your communication effectiveness and your image as a communicator.

The accompanying graphic represents a table with 12 chairs, one of which is occupied by the "boss." For each of the following messages, indicate (a) where you would sit to communicate each message and (b) any other possible messages that your choice of seat will probably communicate.

1. You want to ingratiate yourself with your boss.
2. You aren't prepared and want to be ignored.
3. You want to challenge the boss's proposal that is scheduled to come up for a vote.
4. You want to get to know better the person at seat number 7.

Green will probably elicit a negative response; it's likely to be seen as too different from the expected and acceptable norm for lawyers.

Colors vary greatly in their meanings from one culture to another. To illustrate this cultural variation, here are some of the many meanings that popular colors communicate in a variety of different cultures (Dreyfuss, 1971; Hoft, 1995; Dresser, 1996; Singh & Pereira, 2005). As you read this section, you may want to consider your own meanings for these colors and where your meanings came from.

- **Red.** In China red signifies prosperity and rebirth and is used for festive and joyous occasions; in France and the United Kingdom it indicates masculinity; in many African countries, blasphemy or death; and in Japan, anger and danger. Red ink, especially among Korean Buddhists, is used only to write a person's name at the time of death or on the anniversary of the person's death; this can create problems when U.S. teachers use red ink to mark homework.

- **Green.** In the United States green signifies capitalism, go ahead, and envy; in Ireland, patriotism; among some Native American cultures, femininity; to the Egyptians, fertility and strength; and to the Japanese, youth and energy.

- **Black.** In Thailand black signifies old age; in parts of Malaysia, courage; and in much of Europe, death.

- **White.** In Thailand white signifies purity; in many Muslim and Hindu cultures, purity and peace; and in Japan and other Asian countries, death and mourning.

- **Blue.** In Iran blue signifies something negative; in Ghana, joy; among the Cherokee it signifies defeat; for the Egyptian, virtue and truth; and for the Greek, national pride.

- **Yellow.** In China yellow signifies wealth and authority; in the United States, caution and cowardice; in Egypt, happiness and prosperity; and in many countries throughout the world, femininity.

- **Purple.** In Latin America purple signifies death; in Europe, royalty; in Egypt, virtue and faith; in Japan, grace and nobility; in China, barbarism; and in the United States, nobility and bravery.

Clothing and Body Adornment   People make inferences about who you are partly on the basis of how you dress. Whether accurate or not, these inferences will affect what people think of you and how they react to you. Your social class, your seriousness, your attitudes, your concern for convention, your sense of style, and perhaps even your creativity will all be judged—in part at least—by the way you dress. In the business world, what you wear may communicate your position within the hierarchy and your willingness and desire to conform to the clothing norms of the organization. It also may communicate your level of professionalism, which seems to be the reason some organizations favor dress codes (Smith, 2003).

Your jewelry also communicates messages about you. Wedding and engagement rings are obvious examples. If you wear a Rolex watch or large precious stones, others are likely to infer that you are rich. Men who wear earrings will be judged differently from men who do not.

The way you wear your hair says something about who you are—from a concern about being up to date to a desire to shock to, perhaps, a lack of interest in appearances. Men with long hair, to take only one example, will generally be judged as less conservative than those with shorter hair. And in a study of male baldness, participants rated a man with a full head of hair as younger and more dominant, masculine, and dynamic than the same man without hair (Butler, Pryor, & Grieder, 1998).

Body piercings and tattoos communicate too. Although people wearing, for example, nose rings or belly button jewelry may wish to communicate positive meanings, those interpreting the messages of body piercings seem to infer that wearers are communicating an unwillingness to conform to social norms and a willingness to take greater risks than those without such piercings (Forbes, 2001). In a study of employers' perceptions, employers rated and ranked job applicants with eyebrow piercings significantly lower than those without such piercings (Acor, 2001).

See "The Nonverbal Message of Red" at **tcbdevito.blogspot.com** for a brief note on the color red. Would you have responded similarly?

Explore the **Exercise** "Color Meaning" at **MyCommunicationLab**

Communication Choice Point

Clothing Communication

One of your friends has been passed over for promotion several times. You think you know the reason—your friend dresses inappropriately. *What are some things you might say to help, knowing that your friend is extremely sensitive to criticism?*

For another function of rings, see "The Divorce Ring" at **tcbdevito .blogspot.com**. If you were divorced, would you wear a divorce ring?

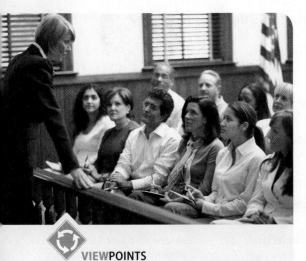

VIEWPOINTS

Blaming Clothing

A popular defense tactic in sex crimes against women, gay men, and lesbians is to blame the victim by referring to the way the victim was dressed and implying that the victim, by wearing certain clothing, provoked the attack. What do you think of this tactic? Is it likely to be effective? Is it ethical?

Take a look at "Nonverbal Communication: Scent" at **tcbdevito** **.blogspot.com** for a brief discussion of the connection between scent and memory. Have you ever experienced this?

Nose-pierced job candidates received lower scores on measures of credibility, such as ratings of character and trustworthiness, as well as on sociability and hirability (Seiter & Sandry, 2003).

Tattoos—whether temporary or permanent—likewise communicate a variety of messages, often the name of a loved one or some symbol of allegiance or affiliation. Tattoos also communicate to the wearers themselves. For example, tattooed students see themselves (and perhaps others do as well) as more adventurous, creative, individualistic, and risk prone than those without tattoos (Drews, Allison, & Probst, 2000). Tattoos and piercings on health care professionals have been found to communicate such undesirable traits as impulsiveness, unpredictability, and a tendency toward being reckless or violent (Rapsa & Cusack, 1990; Smith, 2003).

Space Decoration   The decoration of your workplace tells a lot about you. The office with the mahogany desk and bookcase and oriental rugs communicates importance and status within an organization, just as a metal desk and bare floor indicate an entry-level employee much farther down in the company hierarchy.

Similarly, people will make inferences about you based on the way you decorate your home. The expensiveness of the furnishings may communicate your status and wealth; their coordination, your sense of style. The magazines on your coffee table may reflect your interests, and the arrangement of chairs around a television set may reveal how important watching television is to you. The contents of bookcases lining the walls reveal the importance of reading in your life. In fact, there is probably little in your home that does not send messages from which others will make inferences about you. At the same time, the lack of certain items will communicate something about you. Consider what messages you would get from a home where no television, phone, or books could be seen.

People also will make judgments about your personality on the basis of room decorations—for example, your openness to new experiences (distinctive decorating usually communicates openness, as would travel souvenirs), conscientiousness, emotional stability, degree of extroversion, and agreeableness.

Smell Communication   Smell, or **olfactory communication,** is extremely important in a wide variety of situations and is now big business. There is some evidence (though it is clearly not very conclusive) that the smell of lemon contributes to a perception of health; the smells of lavender and eucalyptus seem to increase alertness; and the smell of rose oil seems to reduce blood pressure. The smell of chocolate seems to reduce theta brain waves and thus produces a sense of relaxation and a reduced level of attention (Martin, 1998). Findings such as these have contributed to the growth of aromatherapy and to a new profession of aromatherapists. Because humans possess so many scent glands, it has been argued that it only remains for us to discover how we use scent to communicate a wide variety of messages (Furlow, 1996, p. 41). Two particularly important messages that scent communicates are those of attraction and identification.

Attraction Messages.   People use perfumes, colognes, aftershave lotions, powders, and the like in an effort to enhance attractiveness. You also use scents to make yourself feel better. When you smell pleasant, you feel better about yourself; when you smell unpleasant, you feel less good about yourself—and probably shower and perhaps put on some cologne.

Identification Messages.   Smell is often used to create an image or an identity for a product (Spence, 2008). Advertisers and manufacturers spend millions of dollars each year creating scents for cleaning products and toothpastes, for example, which have nothing to do with products' cleaning power; instead, they function solely to create an image for the products. There is also evidence that we can identify specific significant others by smell. For example, young children were able to identify the T-shirts of their brothers and sisters solely by smell (Porter & Moore, 1981).

TOUCH COMMUNICATION

Touch communication, or tactile communication, is perhaps the most primitive form of nonverbal communication (Montagu, 1971). Touch develops before the other senses; a child is stimulated by touch even in the womb. Soon after birth, the child is fondled, caressed, patted, and stroked. In turn, the child explores its world through touch and quickly learns to communicate a variety of meanings through touch.

Touching varies greatly from one culture to another. For example, African Americans touch each other more than European Americans; and touching declines from kindergarten to the sixth grade for European Americans but not for African American children (Burgoon, Guerrero, & Floyd, 2010). Japanese people touch each other much less than Anglo-Saxons, who in turn touch much less than southern Europeans (Morris, 1977; Burgoon, Guerrero, & Floyd, 2010).

Not surprisingly, touch also varies with your relationship stage. In the early stages of acquaintance, you touch little; in intermediate stages of relationship development (i.e., involvement and intimacy), you touch a great deal; and at stable or deteriorating stages of a relationship, you again touch little (Guerrero & Andersen, 1991).

The Meanings of Touch

Researchers in the field of **haptics,** or the study of touch communication, have identified the major meanings of touch (Jones, 2005; Jones & Yarbrough, 1985). Here are five of the most important:

- **Touch may communicate positive emotions,** such as support, appreciation, inclusion, sexual interest or intent, and affection.
- **Touch often communicates playfulness,** either affectionately or aggressively.
- **Touch may also control or direct the behaviors, attitudes, or feelings of another person.** To get attention, for example, you may touch a person as if to say, "Look at me" or "Look over here."
- **Ritual touching centers on greetings and departures,** as in shaking hands to say hello or good-bye, or hugging, kissing, or putting your arm around another's shoulder when greeting or saying farewell.
- **Task-related touching occurs while you are performing some function**—for example, removing a speck of dust from another person's face or helping someone out of a car.

As you can imagine, touching may also get you into trouble. For example, touching that is too positive (or too intimate) too early in a relationship may send the wrong signals. Similarly playing that is too rough or holding someone's arm to control their movements may be resented. Using ritualistic touching incorrectly or in ways that may be culturally insensitive may likewise get you into difficulty.

Touch Avoidance

Much as we have a tendency to touch and be touched, we also have a tendency to avoid touch from certain people or in certain circumstances. Researchers in nonverbal communication have found some interesting relationships between **touch avoidance** and other significant communication variables (Andersen & Leibowitz, 1978).

Touch avoidance is positively related to communication apprehension: Those who fear oral communication also score high on touch avoidance. Touch avoidance is also high in those who self-disclose little. Both touch and self-disclosure are intimate forms of communication; people who are reluctant to get close to another person by self-disclosing also seem reluctant to get close by touching.

Communication Choice Point

Smell

Your colleague in the next cubicle wears extremely strong cologne that you find horrendous. You can't continue smelling this horrible scent any longer. *What choices do you have to changing this colleague's use of cologne? What might you say? What channel would you use?*

Explore the **Exercise**
"Do You Avoid Touch?"
at **MyCommunicationLab**

Communication Choice Point

Touch Boundaries

A colleague at work continually touches you in passing—your arm, your shoulder, your waist. These touches are becoming more frequent and more intimate. You want this touching to stop. *What are some of your options for stopping this behavior? To whom would you speak/write? What would you say?*

Touch avoidance is also affected by age and gender (Guerrero & Andersen, 1994; Crawford, 1994). Older people have higher touch-avoidance scores for opposite-sex persons than do younger people. Males score higher on same-sex touch avoidance than do females, which matches our stereotypes (Martin & Anderson, 1993). That is, men avoid touching other men, but women may and do touch other women. On the other hand, women have higher touch-avoidance scores for opposite-sex touching than do men (Andersen, Andersen, & Lustig, 1987).

Touch and Culture   The functions and examples of touching discussed earlier were based on studies in North America; in other cultures these functions are not served in the same way. In some cultures, for example, some task-related touching is viewed negatively and is to be avoided. Among Koreans, it is considered disrespectful for a store owner to touch a customer in, say, handing back change; doing so is considered too intimate a gesture. Members of other cultures who are used to such touching may consider the Koreans' behavior cold and aloof. Muslim children in many countries are socialized to refrain from touching members of the opposite sex, a practice that can easily be interpreted as unfriendly by American children, who are used to touching one another (Dresser, 1996).

Students from the United States reported being touched twice as much as did the Japanese students. In Japan there is a strong taboo against strangers' touching, and the Japanese are therefore especially careful to maintain sufficient distance (Barnlund, 1975).

Some cultures, such as those of southern Europe and the Middle East, are contact cultures. Others, such as those of northern Europe and Japan, are noncontact cultures. Members of contact cultures maintain close distances, touch each other in conversation, face each other more directly, and maintain longer and more focused eye contact. Members of noncontact cultures maintain greater distance in their interactions, touch each other rarely if at all, avoid facing each other directly, and maintain much less direct eye contact. As a result, northern Europeans and Japanese may be perceived as cold, distant, and uninvolved by southern Europeans—who may in turn be perceived as pushy, aggressive, and inappropriately intimate.

PARALANGUAGE AND SILENCE

Paralanguage is the vocal but nonverbal dimension of speech. It has to do with *how* you say something rather than what you say. **Silence,** on the other hand, is the absence of sound but not of communication.

Paralanguage   An old exercise that teachers used to increase students' ability to express different emotions, feelings, and attitudes was to have the students repeat a sentence while accenting or stressing different words each time. Placing the stress on different words easily communicates significant differences in meaning. Consider the following variations of the sentence "Is this the face that launched a thousand ships?"

1. *Is* this the face that launched a thousand ships?
2. Is *this* the face that launched a thousand ships?
3. Is this the *face* that launched a thousand ships?
4. Is this the face that *launched* a thousand ships?
5. Is this the face that launched *a thousand ships?*

Each sentence communicates something different—in fact, each asks a different question, even though the words are the same. All that varies among the sentences is which words are stressed, one aspect of paralanguage.

In addition to stress, paralanguage includes such vocal characteristics as rate, volume, and rhythm. It also includes the vocalizations you make when crying, whispering, moaning, belching, yawning, and yelling (Trager, 1958, 1961; Argyle, 1988). A variation in any of these vocal features communicates. When you speak quickly, for example, you communicate something different from when you speak slowly. Even though the words are the same, if the speed (or volume, rhythm, or pitch) differs, the meanings people receive also differ.

Judgments About People.   Many people make judgments about people's personalities on the basis of their paralinguistic cues. For example, they might conclude that your colleague who speaks softly when presenting ideas at a meeting isn't sure of the ideas' usefulness and believes that no one really wants to listen to them. Or they might assume that people who speak loudly have overinflated egos, or those who speak in a monotone are uninterested in what they are saying and perhaps in life in general. All such judgments are based on little evidence, yet they persist in much popular talk.

Research has found that people can accurately judge the socioeconomic status (whether high, middle, or low) of speakers from 60-second voice samples (Davitz, 1964). Participants also rated people whom they judged to be of high status as more credible than speakers judged to be of middle and low status.

Listeners also can accurately judge the emotional states of speakers from vocal expression alone. In these studies, speakers recite the alphabet or numbers while expressing emotions. Some emotions are easier to identify than others; it is easy to distinguish between hate and sympathy but more difficult to distinguish between fear and anxiety (Scherer, 1986).

Judgments About Communication Effectiveness.   Speech rate is an important component of paralanguage. In one-way communication (when one person is doing all or most of the speaking and the other person is doing all or most of the listening), those who talk fast (about 50 percent faster than normal) are more persuasive. That is, people agree more with a fast speaker than with a slow speaker and find the fast speaker more intelligent and objective (MacLachlan, 1979).

Although, generally, research finds that a faster-than-normal speech rate lowers listener comprehension, a rapid rate may still have the advantage in communicating information (MacLachlan, 1979; Jones, Berry, & Stevens, 2007). For example, when speaking rate increases by 50 percent, comprehension level drops by only 5 percent. When the rate doubles, the comprehension level drops only 10 percent. If, however, the speeds are more than twice that of normal speech, comprehension level falls dramatically.

Exercise caution in applying this research to all forms of communication (MacLachlan, 1979). While the speaker is speaking, the listener is generating, or framing, a reply. If the speaker talks too rapidly, the listener may not have enough time to compose a reply and may become resentful. Furthermore, the increased rate may seem so unnatural that the listener may focus on the speed rather than on the message being communicated.

Paralanguage and Culture.   Cultural differences need to be taken into consideration also in evaluating the results of studies on speech rate. In one study, for example, Korean male speakers who spoke rapidly were given unfavorable credibility ratings, in contrast to the positive ratings received by Americans who spoke rapidly (Lee & Boster, 1992). Researchers have suggested that in individualistic societies a rapid-rate speaker is seen as more competent than a slow-rate speaker, but in collectivist cultures a speaker who uses a slower rate is judged more competent.

Silence   Just as words and gestures communicate meaning, so does silence. (see Jaworski, 1993). Here we look at some functions of silence and at a theory of silence that has important implications for society as a whole.

Functions of Silence.   Silence allows the speaker and the listener *time to think,* time to formulate and organize the meaning of the message. For example, a lawyer may have many sophisticated points to make

VIEWPOINTS

Gender Differences and Nonverbal Communication

Here is a brief summary of findings from research on gender differences in nonverbal expression (Burgoon, Guerrero, & Floyd, 2010; Guerrero & Hecht, 2006; Pearson, West, & Turner, 1995): (1) Women smile more than men; (2) women stand closer to one another than do men and are generally approached more closely than men; (3) both men and women, when speaking, look at men more than at women; (4) women both touch and are touched more than men; (5) men extend their bodies, taking up greater areas of space, more than women. What problems might these differences create when men and women communicate with each other?

during closing arguments to the jury. A skilled lawyer will use silence, not only to give herself or himself time to present these issues in an organized way, but also to give the jury time to digest the information presented.

Silence may also signal *the importance or solemnity of the message*. Before and after messages of intense conflict or those confessing undying love, there is often silence. Similarly, there would be silence during a prayer or flag-raising service. Similarly, you might use silence to communicate your interest and respect for what someone is saying.

Some people use silence as a *weapon* to hurt others. We often speak of giving someone "the silent treatment." After a conflict, for example, one or both individuals may remain silent as a kind of punishment. Silence used to hurt others may also take the form of refusal to acknowledge the presence of another person, as in disconfirmation (see Chapter 4); in this case, silence is a dramatic demonstration of the total indifference one person feels toward the other.

People sometimes use silence because of *personal anxiety* or shyness, or in response to threats. You may feel anxious or shy among new people and prefer to remain silent. By remaining silent you preclude the chance of rejection. Only when you break your silence and attempt to communicate with another person do you risk rejection.

Like the eyes, face, or hands, silence can also *communicates emotional responses* (Ehrenhaus, 1988). Sometimes silence communicates a determination to be uncooperative or defiant: By refusing to engage in verbal communication, you defy the authority or the legitimacy of the other person's position. Silence often communicates annoyance; in this case, it is usually accompanied by a pouting expression, arms crossed in front of the chest, and flared nostrils. Silence also may express affection or love, especially when coupled with longing gazes into another's eyes.

Of course, you also may use silence when you simply have *nothing to say*, when nothing occurs to you or you do not want to say anything.

Not all cultures view silence in the same way (Vainiomaki, 2004). In the United States, for example, silence is often interpreted negatively. At a business meeting or even in informal social groups, the silent member may be seen as not listening or as having nothing interesting to add, not understanding the issues, being insensitive, or being too self-absorbed to focus on the messages of others. Other cultures, however, view silence more positively. In many situations in Japan, for example, silence is a response that is considered more appropriate than speech (Haga, 1988).

The traditional Apache, to take another example, regard silence very differently than do European Americans (Basso, 1972). Among the Apache, mutual friends do not feel the need to introduce strangers who may be working in the same area or on the same project. The strangers may remain silent for several days. This period enables them to observe and evaluate each other. Once this assessment is made, the individuals talk. When courting, especially during the initial stages, the Apache remain silent for hours; if they do talk, they generally talk very little. Only after a couple has been dating for several months will they have lengthy conversations. These periods of silence are often erroneously attributed to shyness or self-consciousness. But the use of silence is explicitly taught to Apache women, who are especially discouraged from engaging in long discussions with their dates. Silence during courtship is a sign of modesty to many Apache.

Communication Choice Point

Remaining Silent

Your college roommate is selling term papers and uses your jointly owned computer to store them. You're becoming increasingly uncomfortable about the situation and want to distance yourself from this unethical behavior. *How might you distance yourself or sever yourself entirely from this operation, without creating too much trouble in the same dorm room you'll have to continue sharing for the rest of the year? What would you say? How would you say it?*

The Spiral of Silence. The "spiral of silence" theory offers a somewhat different perspective on silence. This theory, originally developed to explain the media's influence on opinion, argues that you're more likely to voice agreement than disagreement (Noelle-Neumann, 1991; Severin & Tankard, 2001; Scheufele & Moy, 2000). The theory claims that when a controversial issue arises, you estimate the opinions of others and figure out which views are popular and which are not. You also estimate the rewards and the punishments you'd probably get from expressing popular or unpopular positions. You then use these estimates to determine which opinions you'll express and which you won't.

COMMUNICATING ETHICALLY

Communication Silence

In the U.S. legal system, although people have the right to remain silent so as not to incriminate themselves, they are obliged to reveal information about, for example, the criminal activities of others that they may have witnessed. However, rightly or wrongly (and this in itself is an ethical issue), psychiatrists, lawyers, and some clergy are often exempt from this general rule. Similarly, a wife can't be forced to testify against her husband, nor a husband against his wife.

Unlike the legal system, however, most day-by-day communication situations lack written rules, so it's not always clear whether or when silence is ethical. For example, most people (though not all) would agree that you have the right to withhold information that has no bearing on the matter at hand. Consider, for example, in what situations would it be ethical to remain silent about your previous relationship history, affectional orientation, or religion, and in what situations silence would be unethical.

Ethical Choice Point

With all this discussion of ethics in communication, you now wonder if you should come clean to your steady dating partner of two years about previous relationships and a brief incarceration for robbery. Would it be ethical to remain silent about these past behaviors?

Generally, you're more likely to voice your opinions when you agree with the majority than when you disagree. You may do this to avoid being isolated from the majority or for fear of being proved wrong or being disliked. Or you may simply assume that the majority, because they're a majority, must be right.

As people with minority views remain silent, the majority position gets stronger (because those who agree with it are the only ones speaking); so, as the majority position becomes stronger and the minority position becomes weaker, the silence becomes an ever-widening spiral. The Internet (blogs and social network sites, especially) may in some ways act as a counteragent to the spiral of silence, because it provides so many opportunities to express minority viewpoints (anonymously if you wish) and to quickly find like-minded others (McDevitt, Kiousis, & Wahl-Jorgenen, 2003).

TIME COMMUNICATION

The study of **temporal communication,** known technically as **chronemics,** concerns the use of time—how you organize it, react to it, and communicate messages through it (Bruneau, 1985, 1990, 2010). Time is important in both face-to-face and computer-mediated communication. The time you take to poke someone back on Facebook, or the time you take to respond to an e-mail request for a favor, or the delay in returning a phone call will all communicate varied messages. Often, as you have probably already discovered, the meanings that the sender intends to communicate are not the same as the meanings the receiver constructs.

Time Orientation   Before reading further about time, take a look at your own time orientation by taking the accompanying self-test.

TEST YOURSELF

What's Your Time?

For each statement indicate whether the statement is true (**T**) or false (**F**) of your general attitude and behavior.

_____ ❶ I work hard today basically because of tomorrow's expected rewards.

_____ ❷ I enjoy life as it comes.

_____ ❸ I enjoy planning for tomorrow and the future generally.

_____ ❹ I avoid looking too far ahead.

_____ ⑤ I'm willing to endure difficulties if there's a payoff/reward at the end.

_____ ⑥ I frequently put off work to enjoy the moment.

_____ ⑦ I prepare "to do" lists fairly regularly.

_____ ⑧ I'm late with assignments at least 25% of the time.

_____ ⑨ I'm very disappointed with myself when I'm late with assignments.

_____ ⑩ I look for immediate payoffs/rewards.

HOW DID YOU DO? These questions were designed to raise the issue of present and future time orientation, whether you focus more on the present or more on the future. Future-oriented individuals would respond with T to odd-numbered statements (1, 3, 5, 7, 9) and F to even-numbered questions (2, 4, 6, 8, 10). Present-oriented individuals would respond in reverse: F for odd-numbered statements and T for even-numbered statements.

WHAT WILL YOU DO? As you read more about time and nonverbal communication generally, consider how these time orientations work for or against you? For example, will your time orientation help you achieve your social and professional goals? If not, what might you do about changing these attitudes and behaviors?

An especially important aspect of temporal communication is **psychological time:** the relative importance people place on the past, present, or future. With a *past* orientation, you have a particular reverence for the past. You relive old times and regard the old methods as the best. You see events as circular and recurring and find that the wisdom of yesterday is applicable also to today and tomorrow. With a *present* orientation, you live in the present—for now—without planning for tomorrow. With a *future* orientation, you look toward to and live for the future; we save today, work hard in college, and deny yourself luxuries because you are preparing for the future.

Consider some of the findings on these time orientations (Gonzalez & Zimbardo, 1985). Future income is positively related to future orientation; the more future oriented you are, the greater your income is likely to be. Present orientation is strongest among lowest-income males and also among those with high emotional distress and hopelessness (Zaleski, Cycon, & Kurc, 2001).

The time orientation you develop depends largely on your socioeconomic class and your personal experiences (Gonzalez & Zimbardo, 1985). For example, parents in unskilled and semiskilled occupations are likely to teach their children a present-oriented fatalism and a belief that enjoying yourself is more important than planning for the future. Parents who are teachers or managers, for example, teach their children the importance of planning and preparing for the future along with strategies for success.

Different time perspectives also account for much intercultural misunderstanding, because different cultures often teach their members drastically different time orientations. For example, members of some Latin cultures would rather be late for an appointment than end a conversation abruptly. The Latin person sees the lateness as politeness toward the person with whom he or she is conversing, but people of another culture may see it as impolite to the person with whom he or she had the appointment (Hall & Hall, 1987).

Time and Culture   Culture influences time communication in a variety of ways. Here we look at three of them: (1) time orientation, (2) monochronism and polychronism, and (3) social clocks.

Time Orientation.   Not surprisingly, time orientation is heavily influenced by culture. Some cultures—individualistic cultures in particular—seem to emphasize a future orientation; members work hard today for a better future and without much regard for the past, for example. Collectivist cultures, on the other hand, have greater respect for the past; the past is often looked to for guidance for the present.

According to some intercultural researchers, many Asian cultures (e.g., Japanese and Chinese) place great value on the past; Latinos and Native Americans place more emphasis on the present; and European Americans emphasize the future (Lustig & Koester, 2013).

Attitudes toward the importance of time vary from one culture to another. For example, one study measured the accuracy of clocks in six cultures—Japan, Indonesia, Italy, England, Taiwan, and the United States. Japan had the most accurate and Indonesia the least accurate clocks. The researchers also measured the speed at which people in these six cultures walked; results showed that the Japanese walked the fastest, the Indonesians the slowest (LeVine & Bartlett, 1984).

Another type of time is Interpersonal Time explained at **tcbdevito** .blogspot.com. What's your experience with any of these dimensions of interpersonal time?

Monochronism and Polychronism   Another important cultural distinction exists between **monochromic time orientation** and **polychronic time orientation** (Hall, 1959, 1976; Hall & Hall, 1987). Monochronic peoples or cultures, such as those of the United States, Germany, Scandinavia, and Switzerland, schedule one thing at a time. These cultures compartmentalize time and set sequential times for different activities. Polychronic peoples or cultures, such as those of Latin America, the Mediterranean, and the Arab world, on the other hand, schedule multiple things at the same time. Eating, conducting business with several different people, and taking care of family matters may all go on at once. No culture is entirely monochronic or polychronic; rather, these are general or preponderant tendencies. Some cultures combine both time orientations; in Japan and in parts of American culture, for example, both orientations can be found.

Social Clocks   Your culture maintains a social clock—a time schedule for the right time to do various important things, such as starting to date, finishing college, buying your own home, or having a child. The social clock tells you whether you're keeping pace with your peers, are ahead of them, or are falling behind (Neugarten, 1979; Greene, 2003). On the basis of this social clock, which you learned as you grew up, you evaluate your own social and professional development. If you're keeping pace with the rest of your peers (e.g., you started dating at the "appropriate" age or you're finishing college at the "appropriate" age), you'll feel well adjusted, competent, and a part of the group. If you're late, you'll probably experience feelings of dissatisfaction. Although today the social clock is becoming more flexible and more tolerant of deviations from the acceptable time table, it still exerts pressure on each of us to keep pace with our peers (Peterson, 1996).

Objectives Self-Check
- Can you describe and give examples of the channels through which you send and receive nonverbal messages (body communication, facial communication, eye communication, spatial communication, artifactual communication, touch communication, paralanguage, silence, and time communication)?

Some Nonverbal Communication Skills

Throughout the discussion of nonverbal communication, you've probably deduced a number of suggestions for improving your own nonverbal communication. Here, we bring together some suggestions for both receiving and sending nonverbal messages.

Perhaps the most general skill that applies to both receiving and sending is to become mindful of nonverbal messages—those of others as well as your own. Observe those whose nonverbal behavior you find particularly effective and those you find ineffective and try to identify exactly what makes one effective and one ineffective. Consider this chapter a brief introduction to a lifelong study.

In addition to mindfulness, general suggestions can be offered under two headings: decoding (or interpreting) nonverbal messages and encoding (or sending) nonverbal messages.

DECODING SKILLS

When you make judgments or draw conclusions about another person on the basis of her or his nonverbal messages, consider these suggestions:

- **Be tentative.** Resist the temptation to draw conclusions from nonverbal behaviors. Instead, develop hypotheses (educated guesses) about what is going on, and test the validity of your hypotheses on the basis of other evidence.

- **When making judgments, mindfully seek alternative judgments.** Your first judgment may be in error, and one good way to test it is to consider alternative judgments. When your romantic partner creates a greater than normal distance in relation to you, it may signal an annoyance with you; but it can also signal that your partner needs some space to think something out.

- **Notice that messages come from many different channels** and that reasonably accurate judgments can only be made when multiple channels are taken into consideration. Although textbooks (like this one) must present the areas of nonverbal communication separately, the various elements all work together in actual communication situations.

- **Consider the possibility that you are incorrect,** even after you've explored the different channels. This is especially true when you make a judgment that another person is lying, based on, say, eye avoidance or long pauses. These nonverbal signals may mean many things (as well as the possibility of lying).

  - **Interpret your judgments and conclusions against a cultural context.** For example, think about whether you are interpreting the nonverbal behavior of someone through its meaning only in your own culture. So, if you interpret someone's "overly close" talking distance as intrusive or pushy because that's your culture's interpretation, you may miss the possibility that this distance is simply standard in the other person's culture; or it's a way of signaling closeness and friendliness.

  - **Consider the multitude of factors that can influence the way a person behaves nonverbally;** for example, a person's physical condition, personality, or particular situation may all influence a person's nonverbal communication. An upset stomach may be more influential in unpleasant expressions than any communication factor. A low grade in an exam may make your normally pleasant roommate scowl and grumble. Without knowing these factors, it's difficult to make an accurate judgment.

**Communication
Choice Point**
**Demonstrating
Credibility**
    At work people don't attribute any credibility to you, although you're probably as competent as anyone else. You need to increase the nonverbal credibility cues you give off. *What nonverbal cues can you use to communicate your competence and ability? How might you begin to integrate these into your everyday interactions?*

ENCODING SKILLS

When using nonverbal messages to express your meanings, consider these suggestions:

- **Think about your choices for your nonverbal communication just as you do for your verbal messages.** Identify and think mindfully about the choices you have available for communicating what you want to communicate.

- **Keep your nonverbal messages consistent with your verbal messages;** avoid sending verbal messages that say one thing and nonverbal messages that say something else—at least not when you want to be believed.

- **Monitor your own nonverbal messages with the same care that you monitor your verbal messages.** If it's not appropriate to say "this meal is terrible," then it's not appropriate to have a negative expression when you're asked if you want seconds.

- **Avoid extremes and monotony.** Too little nonverbal communication or too much are likely to be responded to negatively. Similarly, always giving the same nonverbal message—say, continually smiling and nodding your head when listening to a friend's long story—is likely to be seen as insincere.

Watch the **Video**
"Go for It" at
MyCommunicationLab

- **Take the situation into consideration.** Effective nonverbal communication is situational; to be effective adapt your nonverbal messages to the specific situation. Nonverbal behavior appropriate to one situation may be totally inappropriate in another.

- **Maintain eye contact with the speaker**—whether at a meeting, in the hallway, or on an elevator; it communicates politeness and says that you are giving the person the consideration of your full attention. Eye contact that is too focused and too prolonged is likely to be seen as invasive and impolite.

- **Avoid using certain adaptors in public**—for example, combing your hair, picking your teeth, or putting your pinky in your ear; these will be seen as impolite. And, not surprisingly, the greater the formality of the situation, the greater the perception of impoliteness is likely to be. So, for example, combing your hair while sitting with two or three friends would probably not be considered impolite (or perhaps only mildly so); but in a classroom or at a company meeting, it would be considered inappropriate.

- **Avoid strong cologne or perfume.** While you may enjoy the scent, those around you may find it unpleasant and intrusive. Much like others do not want to hear your cell messages, they probably don't want to have their sense of smell invaded either.

- **Be careful with touching;** it may or may not be considered appropriate or polite depending on the relationship you have with the other person and on the context in which you find yourselves. The best advice to give here is to avoid touching unless it's part of the culture of the group or organization.

Video **Choice Point**

Inviting or Discouraging Conversation

Kendra is sitting alone intently studying and not having time for her roommate, Lori. While Kendra is working on her laptop, Lori comes into the room and Kendra lets Lori know that she'd rather be left alone. Later on, however, she welcomes the interruption. See the video "Inviting or Discouraging Conversation" to see how, in both cases, body language, eye contact, and other nonverbal cues communicate messages that encourage or discourage interaction.

👁 **Watch** the **Video** "Inviting or Discouraging Conversation" at **MyCommunicationLab**

Objectives Self-Check

- Can you apply these encoding and decoding suggestions to your own nonverbal communication?

⚠ Messages in the Media   *Wrap Up*

Television programs are extremely body conscious and often focus on people and characters who are at the extremes—for example, Mike and Molly or the Housewives shows. Think about how we all often form impressions of people on the basis of the way they look as you watch just about any television show. Doing this will help you become more aware of the nonverbal cues that we communicate.

Summary of Concepts and Skills

Listen to the **Audio Chapter Summary** at MyCommunicationLab

This chapter explored nonverbal communication—communication without words—and looked at the functions nonverbal messages serve, the channels of nonverbal communication, and some of the cultural and gender-related influences on and differences in nonverbal communication.

Principles of Nonverbal Communication

1. Nonverbal messages often interact with verbal messages to accent, complement, contradict, regulate, repeat, or substitute.

2. Nonverbal messages help manage impressions. We present ourselves nonverbally to give people the desired impression.

3. Nonverbal messages help form relationships.

4. Nonverbal messages structure conversation.

5. Nonverbal messages can influence and deceive.

6. Nonverbal messages are crucial for expressing emotions.

The Channels of Nonverbal Communication

7. Body gestures are classified into five categories: emblems (which rather directly translate words or phrases); illustrators (which accompany and literally "illustrate" verbal messages); affect displays (which communicate emotional meaning); regulators (which coordinate, monitor, maintain, or control the speaking of another individual); and adaptors (which usually are unconscious and serve some kind of need, as in scratching an itch).

8. Body appearance (for example, height and general attractiveness) communicates a variety of messages.

9. Facial movements may communicate a variety of emotions. The most frequently studied are happiness, surprise, fear, anger, sadness, and disgust/contempt. Facial management techniques enable you to control your facial expression of emotions. The facial feedback hypothesis claims that facial display of an emotion can lead to physiological and psychological changes.

10. Eye movements may seek feedback, invite others to speak, signal the nature of a relationship, or compensate for physical distance.

11. The study of proxemics investigates the communicative functions of space and spatial relationships. Four major proxemic distances are: (1) intimate distance, ranging from actual touching to 18 inches; (2) personal distance, ranging from 18 inches to 4 feet; (3) social distance, ranging from 4 to 12 feet; and (4) public distance, ranging from 12 to 25

or more feet. Your treatment of space is influenced by such factors as status, culture, context, subject matter, sex, age, and positive or negative evaluation of the other person. Territoriality involves people's possessive reactions to particular spaces or objects.

12. Artifactual communication consists of messages conveyed by objects or arrangements created by humans; for example, by the use of color, clothing, body adornment, or space decoration.

13. Touch communication, or haptics, may communicate a variety of meanings, the most important being positive affect, playfulness, control, ritual, and task-relatedness. Touch avoidance is the desire to avoid touching and being touched by others.

14. Paralanguage has to do with the vocal but nonverbal dimension of speech. It includes rate, pitch, volume, resonance, and vocal quality as well as pauses and hesitations. Based on paralanguage, we make judgments about people, sense conversational turns, and assess believability.

15. Silence communicates a variety of meanings, from anger (as in the "silent treatment") to deep emotional responses.

16. Time communication, or chronemics, consists of messages communicated by our treatment of time.

17. Smell can communicate messages of attraction, taste, memory, and identification.

18. Cultural variations in nonverbal communication are great. Different cultures, for example, assign different meanings to gestures, facial expressions, and colors; have different spatial rules; and treat time very differently.

Some Nonverbal Communication Skills

19. Encoding skills (maintaining eye contact, avoiding intrusive touching) will enable you to communicate more effectively with nonverbal messages.

2.. Decoding skills (being conscious of the several nonverbal channels sending messages simultaneously, interpreting messages in a cultural context) will enable you to more effectively understand the meanings being communicated with nonverbal signals.

This chapter has covered a wide variety of nonverbal communication skills. Place a check mark next to those skills that you feel you want to work on most.

 1. I recognize the varied functions that nonverbal messages (my own and those of others) serve: for example, to form and manage impressions, to define relationships, and to structure conversations.

✓ 2. I use body and gesture messages to help communicate my desired meanings, and I recognize these messages in others.

✓ 3. I use my eyes to seek feedback, to inform others to speak, to signal the nature of my relationship with others, and to compensate for physical distance.

✓ 4. I give others the space they need: for example, I give extra space to those who are angry or disturbed.

5. I am sensitive to the markers (i.e., central, boundary, and earmarkers) of others and use these markers to define my own territories.

6. I use artifacts thoughtfully to communicate desired messages.

✓ 7. I am sensitive to the touching behaviors of others and distinguish among touches that communicate positive emotion, playfulness, control, and ritual or task-related messages.

✓ 8. I recognize and respect each person's touch-avoidance tendency. I am especially sensitive to cultural and gender differences in touching preferences and in touch-avoidance tendencies.

✓ 9. I vary paralinguistic features (e.g., rate, emphasis, pauses, tempo, volume) to communicate my intended meanings.

✓ 10. I use silence to communicate varied meanings (e.g., for example, disappointment or the need for time to think), and I examine the silence of others for meanings just as I would eye movements or body gestures.

✓ 11. I interpret time cues with an awareness of the cultural perspective of the person with whom I am interacting.

✓ 12. I balance my time orientation and don't ignore the past, present, or future.

✓ 13. In decoding nonverbal messages, I draw conclusions tentatively, consider alternative judgments, take into consideration the varied nonverbal channels, consider the possibility of being incorrect, interpret the judgments in a cultural context, and consider influences from other factors.

✓ 14. In encoding my own nonverbal messages, I aim for consistency between verbal and nonverbal messages, monitor my nonverbal messages, avoid extremes, and take the situation into consideration.

Key Word Quiz

The Language of Nonverbal Messages

Match the terms about nonverbal messages with their definitions. Record the number of the definition next to the appropriate term.

_____ a. facial feedback hypothesis (100)
_____ b. artifactual communication (104)
_____ c. civil inattention (101)
_____ d. secondary territory (103)
_____ e. adaptors (98)
_____ f. paralanguage (108)
_____ g. facial management techniques (100)
_____ h. haptics (107)
_____ i. central markers (103)
_____ j. emblems (97)

1. Body gestures that directly translate into words or phrases.
2. Gestures that satisfy some personal need, such as scratching.
3. Strategies that enable you to express feelings nonverbally so as to achieve your desired purpose.
4. Eye movements that respect another's privacy and avoid looking at something that might cause embarrassment.
5. The assumption that your facial expressions influence the way you feel.
6. Items you place in a territory to reserve it for yourself or someone else.
7. The study of touch communication.
8. The vocal but nonverbal dimension of speech; includes, for example, vocal volume and stress.
9. Messages that are communicated through objects and their arrangements.
10. An area that doesn't belong to you but that you have occupied and with which you're associated.

These ten terms and additional terms used in this chapter can be found in the glossary.

Answers: a. 5, b. 9, c. 4, d. 10, e. 2, f. 8, g. 3, h. 7, i. 6, j. 1

 Study and **Review** the **Flashcards** at **MyCommunicationLab**

MyCommunicationLab

Throughout this chapter, there are icons in the margin that highlight media content for selected topics. Go to **MyCommunicationLab** for additional information on nonverbal communication. Here you'll find flashcards to help you learn the jargon of communication, videos that illustrate a variety of concepts, additional exercises, and discussions to help you continue your study of nonverbal communication.

6

Interpersonal Communication and Conversation

⚠ **Messages in the Media**

Sports discussion shows—in which sports writers, commentators, reporters and players offer their opinions on sports events and interact with each other—provide good examples of the topics discussed in this chapter.

Objectives

Listen to the **Audio Chapter** at **MyCommunicationLab**

After reading this chapter, you should be able to:

❶ Explain the stages of conversation, the role and types of turn-taking in conversation and its dialogic nature; and define *immediacy, flexibility,* and *politeness* in conversation.

❷ Communicate effectively in making small talk, apologies, and complimenting.

Interpersonal communication is communication that occurs between two people who have a relationship and who are thus influenced by each other's communication messages. It includes what takes place between a server and a customer, a son and his father, two people in an interview, and so on. This definition makes it almost impossible for communication between two people not to be considered interpersonal—inevitably, some relationship exists. Even a stranger asking directions from a local resident has established a clearly defined relationship as soon as the first message is sent. Sometimes this relational, or "dyadic," definition of interpersonal communication is extended to include small groups of people, such as family members, groups of three or four friends, or work colleagues.

Social media have somewhat blurred this distinction. For example, when you write on someone's Facebook wall, it is interpersonal because it's between you and a friend but it is also sent to others in the group (making it small group communication). And in many ways it's public since the audience can be extremely large—not only is the wall message available to those with access to your page, but it's available to anyone who is sent the posting by others in your group.

Another way to look at interpersonal communication is along a continuum ranging from relatively impersonal to highly personal (Miller, 1978, 1990). At the impersonal end of the spectrum there is simple conversation between people who really don't know each other: the server and the customer, for example. At the highly personal end is the communication that takes place between people who are intimately interconnected, such as a father and son (see Figure 6.1).

A few characteristics distinguish these two extremes. First, in the impersonal example, the individuals are likely to respond to each other according to the roles they are currently playing: The server treats the customer not as a unique individual but as one of many customers; and the customer, in turn, acts toward the server not as if he or she were a unique individual but as he or she would act toward any server. The father and the son, however, react to each other as unique individuals.

Notice too that the server and the customer interact according to the rules of society governing the server–customer interaction. The father and the son, on the other hand, interact on the basis of personally established rules. The way they address each other, their touching behavior, and their degree of physical closeness, for example, are unique to them and are established by them rather than by society.

Still another difference is that the messages that the server and customer exchange are themselves impersonal; there is little self-disclosure and little emotional content, for example. In the father–son example, the messages may run the entire range and may at times be highly personal with considerable disclosure and emotion.

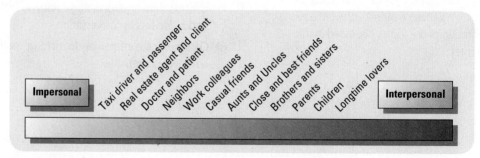

FIGURE 6.1

An Interpersonal Continuum

Here is one possible interpersonal continuum. Other people would position the relationships differently. You may want to try constructing an interpersonal continuum of your own relationships.

COMMUNICATING ETHICALLY

Your Obligation to Reveal Yourself

If you're in a close relationship, you may have an ethical obligation to reveal certain things about yourself. Conversely, you may feel that the other person—because he or she is so close to you—has an ethical obligation to reveal certain information to you.

At what point do you have an ethical obligation to reveal your true:	Romantic Partner	Friend
Age	_____	_____
History of family genetic disorders	_____	_____
HIV status	_____	_____
Past sexual experiences	_____	_____
Marital history	_____	_____
Annual salary and net financial worth	_____	_____
Affectional orientation	_____	_____
Attitudes toward other races and nationalities	_____	_____
Religious beliefs	_____	_____
Past criminal activity or incarceration	_____	_____

Ethical Choice Point

Consider at what point in a relationship, if any, you feel you would have an ethical obligation to reveal each of the 10 items of information listed here. Visualize your relationship as existing on a continuum from initial contact at 1 to extreme intimacy at 10, and use the numbers from 1 to 10 to indicate at what point you would feel an ethical obligation to reveal these items of information. If you feel you would never have the obligation to reveal this information, use 0. As you respond to these items, ask yourself, *In what types of relationships and at what point in these relationships do you incur an obligation to reveal personal information about yourself?*

There are, of course, many gradations between these extremes. Some friendships, for example, are casual; others are highly intimate. Romantic pairs vary in their levels of intimacy, and so do families.

This chapter introduces interpersonal communication, explains the process of conversation and some of its essential principles, and tackles some everyday conversation situations.

The Principles of Conversation

Although conversation is an everyday process and one we seldom think about, it is, like most forms of communication, governed by several principles. Especially important are the principles of (1) process, (2) turn-taking, (3) dialogue, (4) immediacy, (5) flexibility, and (6) politeness.

THE PRINCIPLE OF PROCESS: CONVERSATION IS A DEVELOPMENTAL PROCESS

Conversation is best viewed as a process rather than as an act. It's convenient to divide up this process into chunks or stages and to view each stage as requiring a choice as to what you'll say and how you'll say it. Here we divide the sequence into five steps: (1) opening, (2) feedforward, (3) business, (4) feedback, and (5) closing (see Figure 6.2). These stages and the way people follow them will vary depending on the personalities of the communicators, their culture,

Explore the **Concept**
"Talkaholic Scale"
at **MyCommunicationLab**

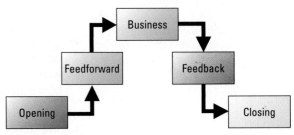

FIGURE 6.2

A Five-Stage Model of Conversation

This model of the stages of conversation is best seen as a way of talking about conversation and not as a hard-and-fast depiction of stages all conversations follow. As you review the model, consider how accurately it depicts conversation as you experience it. Can you develop a more accurate and more revealing model?

TABLE 6.1 **Six Steps to an Effective Handshake**

Here are six steps that, in the culture of much of the United States, go into an effective handshake.

Dos	Don'ts
• Make eye contact at the beginning and maintain it throughout the handshake.	• Look away from the person or down at the floor or at your hand that is being shaken.
• Smile and otherwise signal positiveness.	• Appear static or negative.
• Extend your entire right hand.	• Extend only your fingers or your left hand.
• Grasp the other person's hand firmly but without so much pressure that it would be uncomfortable.	• Grasp the other person's fingers as if you really don't want to shake hands but you're making a gesture to be polite.
• Pump 3 times; a handshake in the United States lasts about 3 to 4 seconds. In other cultures, it might be shorter or, more often, longer.	• Give the person a "dead fish": Be careful that the other person's pumping doesn't lead you to withdraw your own pumping. Avoid pumping much more than 3 times.
• Release your grasp while still maintaining eye contact.	• Hold your grasp for an overly long time or release too early.

For a more extended discussion of phatic communication (also and originally called phatic communion), see "ABCD: Phatic Communion" at **tcbdevito** .blogspot.com. In what ways do you use phatic communication/ communion?

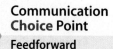

Communication Choice Point

Feedforward

You want to break up your relationship with someone you've been dating rather steadily over the last eight months. You want to remain friends but end the romance, something your partner has no idea about. *What might you say as a preface (as feedforward) to your breakup speech?*

the context in which the conversation occurs, the purpose of the conversation, and the entire host of factors considered throughout this text.

- **Opening.** The first step is to open the conversation, usually with some kind of greeting: "Hi. How are you?" "Hello, this is Joe." The greeting is a good example of phatic communication— a message that establishes a connection between two people and opens up the channels for more meaningful interaction. Openings, of course, may be nonverbal as well as verbal. A smile or kiss may be as clear an opening as "Hello." Greetings are so common that they often go unnoticed. But when they're omitted—as when a doctor begins a conversation by saying, "What's wrong?"—you may feel uncomfortable and thrown off guard. Of course, the most common greeting, socially and especially in business, is the handshake, which is the focus of Table 6.1.

- **Feedforward.** At the second step, you (usually) provide some kind of **feedforward**, which gives the other person a general idea of the conversation's focus: "I've got to tell you about Jack," "Did you hear what happened in class yesterday?" or "We need to talk about our vacation plans." Feedforward also may identify the tone of the conversation ("I'm really depressed and need to talk with you") or the time required ("This will just take a minute") (Frentz, 1976; Reardon, 1987). Conversational awkwardness often occurs when feedforwards are used inappropriately— for example, using overly long feedforwards or omitting feedforward before a truly shocking message.

- **Business.** The third step is the "business," the substance or focus of the conversation. The term *business* is used to emphasize that most conversations are goal directed. That is, you converse to fulfill one or several of the general purposes of interpersonal communication: to learn, relate, influence, play, or help (see Chapter 1). The term is also sufficiently general to incorporate all kinds of interactions. In general, the business is conducted through an exchange of speaker and listener roles. Brief, rather than long, speaking turns characterize most satisfying conversations. In the business stage, you talk about Jack, what happened in class, or your vacation plans. This is obviously the longest part of the conversation and the reason for the opening and the feedforward.

- **Feedback.** The fourth step is **feedback,** the reverse of the second step. Here you (usually) reflect back on the conversation to signal that, as far as you're concerned, the business is completed: "So you want to send Jack a get-well card," "Wasn't that the craziest class you ever heard of?" or "OK, so I'll call for reservations, and you'll shop for what we need."

SKILL DEVELOPMENT EXPERIENCE

Opening and Closing a Conversation

Effectively opening and closing conversations often can be challenging. Consider, first, a few situations in which you might want to open a conversation. For each situation develop a possible opening message in which you seek to accomplish one or more of the following: (a) telling others that you're accessible and open to communication, (b) showing that you're friendly, or (c) showing that you like the other person.

1. You're one of the first guests to arrive at a friend's party and are now there with several other people to whom you've only just been introduced. Your friend, the host, is busy with other matters.
2. In surfing through your Facebook photos you decide that you want to get to know better someone for a possible romantic relationship. This friend-of-a-friend-of-a-friend who friended you a while back and to whom you paid no attention, now seems just the right potential partner. You've never communicated directly before.

Here are two situations in which you might want to bring a conversation to a close. For each situation, develop a possible closing message in which you seek to accomplish one or more of the following: (a) end the conversation without much more talk, (b) leave the other person with a favorable impression of you, or (c) keep the channels of communication open for future interaction.

1. You and a friend have been talking on the phone for the past hour, but not much new is being said. You have a great deal of work to do and want to wrap it up. Your friend just doesn't seem to hear your subtle cues.
2. You're at a party and are anxious to meet a person with whom you've exchanged eye contact for the past ten minutes. The problem is that a friendly and talkative older relative of yours is demanding all your attention. You don't want to insult your relative, but at the same time you want to make contact with this other person.

Opening and closing conversations are often difficult; your handling of these steps is going to help create an impression that's likely to be long-lasting and highly resistant to change.

● **Closing.** The fifth and last step, the opposite of the first step, is the closing, the goodbye, which often reveals how satisfied the persons were with the conversation: "I hope you'll call soon" or "Don't call us, we'll call you." The closing also may be used to schedule future conversations: "Give me a call tomorrow night" or "Let's meet for lunch at 12." When closings are indefinite or vague, conversation often becomes awkward; you're not quite sure if you should say goodbye or if you should wait for something else to be said.

THE PRINCIPLE OF TURN-TAKING

Throughout the speaking–listening process, both speaker and listener exchange cues for what are called **conversational turns** (Burgoon, Buller, & Woodall, 1996; Duncan, 1972; Pearson & Spitzberg, 1990). These cues enable the speaker and listener to communicate about the communication in which they're currently engaged; that is, a form of **metacommunication** takes place through the exchange of these often subtle cues. The use of turn-taking cues—like almost every aspect of human communication—will naturally vary from one culture to another. The description that follows here is valid largely for the United States and many Western cultures (Iizuka, 1993; Lee, 1984; Grossin, 1987; Ng, Loong, He, Liu, & Weatherall, 2000). As you read the following discussion, take a look at Figure 6.3 (p. 124); it provides a visual guide to the various turn signals.

Speaker Cues   Speakers regulate the conversation through two major types of cues: turn-maintaining cues and turn-yielding cues. Using these cues effectively not only ensures communication efficiency but also increases likeability (Place & Becker, 1991; Heap, 1992).

VIEWPOINTS

Gender Stereotypes

One of the stereotypes about gender differences in communication and widely reported in the popular writings on gender is that women talk more than men. But a recent study of 396 college students finds that women and men talk about the same number of words per day, about 16,000; more precisely women spoke an average of 16,215 words while men spoke an average of 15,669 words, a difference that was statistically insignificant (Mehl, Vazire, Ramirez-Esparza, Slatcher, & Pennebaker, 2007). Do your own experiences support these research findings?

Conversational Wants

	To speak	To listen
Speaker	1 Turn-maintaining cues	2 Turn-yielding cues
Listener	3 Turn-requesting cues	4 Turn-denying cues

FIGURE 6.3

Turn-Taking and Conversational Wants

Quadrant 1 represents the speaker who wants to speak (continue to speak) and uses turn-maintaining cues; quadrant 2, the speaker who wants to listen and uses turn-yielding cues; quadrant 3, the listener who wants to speak and uses turn-requesting cues; and quadrant 4, the listener who wants to listen (i.e., continue listening) and uses turn-denying cues. Back-channeling cues would appear in quadrant 4, because they are cues that listeners use while they continue to listen.

Watch the **Video**
"Talk, Talk, Talk" at
MyCommunicationLab

Explore the **Exercise**
"Conversational Turns" at
MyCommunicationLab

Turn-Maintaining Cues.   Through **turn-maintaining cues** you can communicate your wish to maintain the role of speaker in a variety of ways:

- Audibly inhale breath to show that you have more to say.
- Continue a gesture or series of gestures to show that you've not yet completed your thought.
- Avoid eye contact with the listener in order to indicate that you are not passing along your speaking turn.
- Vocalize pauses ("er," "umm") to prevent the listener from speaking and to show that you're still talking.

In most conversations we expect the speaker to maintain relatively brief speaking turns and to turn over the speaking role to the listener willingly (when so signaled by the listener). People who don't follow those unwritten rules are likely to be evaluated negatively.

Turn-Yielding Cues.   **Turn-yielding cues** tell the listener that the speaker is finished and wishes to exchange the role of speaker for the role of listener. They tell the listener (if in a group, such cues may be addressed to a specific listener or to just any listener) to take over the role of speaker. For example, at the end of a statement you may add some cue such as "okay?" or "right?" to ask one of the listeners to assume the role of speaker. You also can indicate that you've finished speaking by dropping your intonation or pausing at length (Wennerstrom & Siegel, 2003), by making direct eye contact with a listener, by asking a question, or by nodding in the direction of a particular listener.

Listener Cues   As a listener you can regulate the conversation by using three types of cues: turn-requesting cues, turn-denying cues, and back-channeling cues and interruptions.

Turn-Requesting Cues.   **Turn-requesting cues** let the speaker know that you would like to say something and take a turn as speaker. Sometimes you can do this simply by saying, "I'd like to say something," but often it's done more subtly through some vocalized "er" or "um" that tells the speaker that you would like to speak. The request to speak is also often made with facial and mouth gestures. Frequently a listener will indicate a desire to speak by opening his or her eyes and mouth wide as if to say something, by beginning to gesture with a hand, or by leaning forward.

Turn-Denying Cues.   You can use **turn-denying cues** to indicate your reluctance to assume the role of speaker— for example, by intoning a slurred "I don't know" or by giving some brief grunt that signals you have nothing to say. Often people accomplish turn-denying by avoiding eye contact with the speaker (who wishes them now to take on the role of speaker) or by engaging in some behavior that is incompatible with speaking, such as coughing or blowing their nose.

Back-Channeling Cues and Interruptions.   **Back-channeling cues** are used to communicate various types of information back to the speaker without assuming the role of speaker. Some researchers call brief utterances—such as "mm-hm," "uh-huh," and "yeah"—that tell the speaker you're listening *acknowledgment tokens* (Schegloff, 1982; Drummond & Hopper, 1993). Other researchers call them *overlaps* to distinguish them from those interruptions that are aimed at taking over the speaker's turn (Tannen, 1994 a, b). Back-channeling cues are generally supportive and confirming and show that you're listening and are involved in the interaction (Kennedy & Camden, 1988), but you can communicate a variety of messages with these back-channeling cues (Burgoon, Buller, & Woodall, 1996; Pearson & Spitzberg, 1990):

- **To indicate agreement or disagreement.** A smile, nod of approval, brief comments such as "right" and "of course," or a vocalization like "uh-huh" signals agreement. Frowning, shaking your head, or making comments such as "no" and "never" signal disagreement.

- **To indicate degree of involvement.** An attentive posture, forward leaning, and focused eye contact tell the speaker that you're involved in the conversation. An inattentive posture, backward leaning, and avoidance of eye contact communicate a lack of involvement.

- **To pace the speaker.** Ask the speaker to slow down by raising your hand near your ear and leaning forward or to speed up by continued nodding of your head. Cue the speaker verbally by asking the speaker to slow down or to speed up.

- **To ask for clarification.** Puzzled facial expressions—perhaps coupled with a forward lean or direct interjection of "Who?" "When?" or "Where?"—signal your need for clarification.

Interruptions, in contrast to back-channeling cues, are attempts to take over the role of the speaker. These are not supportive and are often disconfirming. Interruptions are often interpreted as attempts to change the topic to one that the person knows more about or to emphasize one's authority. Interruptions may also be seen as attempts to assert power and to maintain control. Not surprisingly, research finds that superiors (bosses and supervisors) and those in positions of authority (police officers and interviewers) interrupt those in inferior positions more than the other way around (Carroll, 1994; Ashcraft, 1998).

Numerous studies have focused on gender differences in interruption behavior. Research finds that the popular belief that men interrupt more than women is basically accurate. Men interrupt other men and women more than women interrupt. For example, one analysis of 43 published studies on interruptions and gender differences showed that men interrupted significantly more than women (Anderson, 1998). In addition, the more male-like the person's gender identity—regardless of the person's biological sex—the more likely the person will interrupt (Drass, 1986). Fathers interrupt their children more than mothers do (Greif, 1980). Some research, however, finds no differences (Stratford, 1998; Crown & Cummins, 1998; Smith-Lovin & Brody, 1989; Donaldson, 1992).

Whatever gender differences do exist, however, seem small. More important than gender in determining who interrupts whom is the specific type of situation; some situations, such as task-oriented situations, may call for many interruptions; and others, such as relationship discussions, may call for numerous back-channeling cues (Anderson, 1998):

Communication Choice Point
Dealing with Interruptions
One of your friends repeatedly interrupts you and others and takes the conversation off onto a totally different topic. *What are some of the things you might say or do to stop this annoying behavior but not insult your friend? What would be the ideal situation in which to bring this up? What channel of communication would you use?*

THE PRINCIPLE OF DIALOGUE

Often the term *dialogue* is used as a synonym for *conversation*. But dialogue is more than simple conversation; it's conversation in which there is genuine two-way interaction (Buber, 1958; Yau-fair Ho, Chan, Peng, & Ng, 2001; McNamee & Gergen, 1999). It's useful to distinguish the ideal dialogic communicator from his or her opposite, the totally monologic communicator. Of course, no one engages in dialogue at all times, and no one is totally monologic. These descriptions represent extremes, intended only to clarify the differences between these types of communication.

During a **dialogue** each person is both speaker and listener, sender and receiver. It's conversation in which there is deep concern for the other person and for the relationship between the two. The objective of dialogue is mutual understanding and empathy. There is respect for the other person, not because of what this person can do or give but simply because this person is a human being and therefore deserves to be treated honestly and sincerely.

For a somewhat different take on achieving conversational effectiveness and satisfaction, see "Conversational Coolers and Warmers" at tcbdevito.blogspot .com. What is the single most annoying conversational habit you can think of? What is the single most pleasant conversational habit?

In a dialogic interaction you respect the other person enough to allow that person the right to make his or her own choices without coercion, without the threat of punishment, without fear or social pressure. A dialogic communicator believes that other people can make decisions that are right for them and implicitly or explicitly lets them know that, whatever choices they make, they will still be respected.

The dialogic communicator avoids negative criticism and negative personal judgments and instead practices using positive criticism ("I liked those first two explanations best; they were really well reasoned"). This person avoids dysfunctional communication patterns and keeps the channels of communication open by displaying a willingness to listen. While listening, this person indicates involvement by giving cues (e.g., nonverbal nods, brief verbal expressions of agreement, paraphrasing) that show he or she is paying attention. When in doubt the dialogic communicator asks for clarification—asks for your point of view, your perspective—and thus signals a real interest in you and in what you have to say. This person does not manipulate the conversation so as to get positive comments.

Monologic communication—the **monologue**— is the opposite: One person speaks and the other listens, and there is no real interaction between participants. The monologic communicator is focused only on his or her own goals and has no real concern for the listener's feelings or attitudes; this speaker is interested in the other person only insofar as that person can serve his or her purposes.

The monologic communicator frequently uses negative criticism ("I didn't like that explanation") and negative judgments ("You're not a very good listener, are you?"). This communicator also often uses dysfunctional communication patterns, such as expressing an unwillingness to talk or to listen to what the other person has to say. The monologic communicator rarely demonstrates that he or she understands you; this person gives no cues that he or she is listening (cues such as paraphrasing or expressing agreement with what you say). Nor would this person request clarification of your ideas, because he or she is less interested in you than in representing himself or herself. Still another characteristic of the monologic communicator is a tendency to request that you say positive things about him or her ("How did you like the way I handled that?").

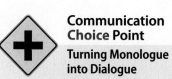

Communication Choice Point

Turning Monologue into Dialogue

You're dating a wonderful person, your ideal in every way except one, which is that your conversations together are a series of monologues; there is little dialogue. *What are some of the things you might do to change this situation and to encourage more dialogue?*

THE PRINCIPLE OF IMMEDIACY

Of all the characteristics of effective communication, the one that most clearly defines effective conversation is **immediacy**—the creation of closeness, a sense of togetherness, of oneness, between speaker and listener. When you communicate immediacy you convey a sense of interest and attention, a liking for and an attraction to the other person. As noted in our discussion of impression management strategies in Chapter 2 (pp. 42–47), immediacy strategies are often used to make someone like us.

Not surprisingly, people respond to communication that is immediate more favorably than to communication that is not. You can increase your interpersonal attractiveness—the degree to which others like you and respond positively toward you—by using immediacy behaviors. In addition there is considerable evidence to show that immediacy behaviors are effective in teaching and in health care (Richmond, Smith, Heisel, & McCroskey, 2001; Richmond, McCroskey, & Hickson, 2008).

You can communicate immediacy with both verbal and nonverbal messages (Mottet & Richmond, 1998; Richmond, McCroskey, & Hickson, 2008):

- Self-disclose: reveal something significant about yourself.
- Refer to the other person's good qualities, say, dependability, intelligence, character: for example, "You're always so reliable."
- Express your positive view of the other person and of your relationship: for example, "I'm sure glad you're my roommate; you know everyone."
- Talk about commonalities, things you and the other person have done together or share.
- Demonstrate your responsiveness by giving feedback cues that indicate you want to listen more and that you're interested: for example, "And what else happened?"

- Express psychological closeness and openness by, for example, maintaining physical closeness and arranging your body to exclude third parties.

- Maintain appropriate eye contact and limit looking around at others.

- Smile and express your interest in the other person.

- Focus on the other person's remarks. Make the speaker know that you heard and understood what was said, and give the speaker appropriate verbal and nonverbal feedback.

At the same time that you'll want to demonstrate these immediacy messages, try also to avoid nonimmediacy messages such as interrupting the other person, avoiding small talk, making potentially offensive or condescending comments, closing off the channels of communication ("I don't have the time to chat"), or talking about things for which the other person has no reference or experience. Nonverbally, avoid speaking in a monotone, looking away from the person you're talking to, frowning while talking, having a tense body posture, and avoiding gestures (Richmond, McCroskey, & Hickson, 2008).

Not all cultures or all people respond in the same way to immediacy messages. For example, in the United States (and in individualist and low-power-distance cultures generally), immediacy behaviors are seen as friendly and appropriate. In other cultures (e.g., many collectivist and high-power-distance cultures), however, the same immediacy behaviors may be viewed as overly familiar—as presuming that a relationship is close when it is only an acquaintanceship (Axtell, 2007).

In addition, recognize that some people may interpret immediacy behaviors as indicating a desire for increased intimacy in the relationship. So, if you're trying to signal a friendly closeness, the other person may perceive a romantic invitation. Recognize too that because immediacy behaviors prolong and encourage in-depth communication, they may not be responded to favorably by persons who are fearful about communication and who want to get the interaction over with as soon as possible (Richmond, McCroskey, & Hickson, 2008).

THE PRINCIPLE OF FLEXIBILITY

Because conversations vary depending on the people involved, the topic being talked about, the context in which it takes place, and a host of other factors discussed throughout this text, the effective conversationalist needs to be flexible. You can increase your communication flexibility by following a few simple steps:

- **Analyze the specific conversational situation** by asking yourself what is unique or different about this specific situation and applying the concepts and principles discussed throughout the text.

- **Mindfully consider your available choices** for any given conversational situation, a suggestion offered throughout this text.

- **Estimate the potential advantages and disadvantages** of each potential choice, using the theories and research evidence discussed throughout the text.

- **Competently communicate your choice,** using the skills discussed throughout this text.

THE PRINCIPLE OF POLITENESS: CONVERSATION IS (USUALLY) POLITE

Not surprisingly, conversation is expected (at least in many cases) to follow the principle of politeness. Six maxims/fundamental principles/general rules/accepted truths of politeness have been identified by linguist Geoffrey Leech (1983) and seem to encompass a great deal of what we commonly think of as conversational politeness. Before reading about these maxims, take the self-test on p.128 to help you personalize the material that follows.

Communication Choice Point

Immediacy

You've become interested in one of the other students in your class and would really like to date this person. You want to appear friendly and interested but not overly pushy. *How might you use immediacy to make yourself appear likeable, friendly, and interesting? In what context would you attempt this? Through what channel?*

Explore the Exercise "How Flexible Is Your Communication?" at **MyCommunicationLab**

VIEWPOINTS

Shake Hands or Kiss?

It's sometimes difficult to tell when you should shake hands and when you should hug or air kiss or actually kiss the other person. How do you tell which form of greeting will be most appropriate?

TEST YOURSELF

How Polite Are You?

Try estimating your own level of politeness. For each of the statements below, indicate how closely they describe your typical communication. Avoid giving responses that you feel might be considered "socially acceptable"; instead, give responses that accurately represent your typical communication behavior. Use a 10-point scale, with 10 being "very accurate description of my typical conversation" and 1 being "very inaccurate description of my typical conversation."

_____ **①** I tend not to ask others to do something or to otherwise impose on others.

_____ **②** I tend to put others first, before myself.

_____ **③** I maximize the expression of approval of others and minimize any disapproval.

_____ **④** I seldom praise myself but often praise others.

_____ **⑤** I maximize the expression of agreement and minimize disagreement.

_____ **⑥** I maximize my sympathy for another and minimize any feelings of antipathy.

HOW DID YOU DO? All six statements would characterize politeness, so high numbers, say 8–10, would indicate politeness whereas low numbers, say 1–4, would indicate impoliteness.

WHAT WILL YOU DO? As you read this material, personalize it with examples from your own interpersonal interactions, and try to identify specific examples and situations in which increased politeness might have been more effective.

For a self-test that itemizes the factors that account for workplace politeness, see "Politeness in the Workplace: Self-Test" at **tcbdevito** **.blogspot.com**.

Explore the **Exercise** "How Polite Is Your Conversation?" at **MyCommunicationLab**

The *maxim of tact* (statement 1 in the self-test) helps to maintain the other person's autonomy (what we referred to earlier as negative face, p. 44). Tact in your conversation would mean that you do not impose on others or challenge their right to do as they wish. For example, if you wanted to ask someone a favor, using the maxim of tact, you might say something like, "I know you're very busy but . . . " or "I don't mean to impose, but . . ." Not using the maxim of tact, you might say something like, "You have to lend me your car this weekend" or "I'm going to use your ATM card."

The *maxim of generosity* (statement 2) helps to confirm the other person's importance—for example, the importance of the person's time, insight, or talent. Using the maxim of generosity, you might say, "I'll walk the dog; I see you're busy." Violating the maxim, you might say, "I'm really busy, why don't you walk the dog since you're not doing anything important."

The *maxim of approbation* (statement 3) refers to praising someone or complimenting the person in some way (for example, "I was really moved by your poem") and minimizing any expression of criticism or disapproval (for example, "For a first effort, that poem wasn't half bad").

The *maxim of modesty* (statement 4) minimizes any praise or compliments *you* might receive. At the same time, you might praise and compliment the other person. For example, using this maxim you might say something like, "Well, thank you, but I couldn't have done this without your input; that was the crucial element." Violating this maxim, you might say, "Yes, thank you, it was one of my best efforts, I have to admit."

The *maxim of agreement* (statement 5) refers to your seeking out areas of agreement and expressing them ("That color you selected was just right; it makes the room exciting") and at the same time avoiding and not expressing (or at least minimizing) disagreements ("It's an interesting choice, very different"). Violating this maxim, you might say "That color—how can you stand it?"

The *maxim of sympathy* (statement 6) refers to the expression of understanding, sympathy, empathy, supportiveness, and the like for the other person. Using this maxim, you might say, "I understand your feelings; I'm so sorry." Violating this maxim, you might say, "You're making a fuss over nothing" or "You get upset over the least little thing. What is it this time?"

Video Choice Point
First Day of Class

Tim would like to initiate a conversation with his classmate Emad, but feels awkward. Tim considers some of the principles of conversation that you will read about in this chapter as he makes both effective and ineffective communication choices. See how his choices play out in the video "First Day of Class" and respond to the questions posed.

Watch the **Video** "First Day of Class" at **MyCommunicationLab**

Objectives Self-Check
● Can you explain the principles of conversation—process, turn-taking, dialogue, immediacy, flexibility, and politeness?
● Can you apply the skills suggested in these principles in your own conversations?

Take a look at "Interpersonal Communication Exercise, Discourse Analysis" at **tcbdevito.blogspot .com** for an opportunity to apply the content of this chapter (and other chapters) to a short dialogue.

Everyday Conversations

Having covered the basic principles of conversation, we can now explore a variety of everyday conversation situations: making small talk, apologizing, and complimenting. In reviewing the everyday conversations included here, do realize that not everyone speaks with the fluency and ease that textbooks often assume. Speech and language disorders, for example, can seriously disrupt the conversation process if some elementary guidelines aren't followed. Table 6.2 (p. 130) offers suggestions for making such conversations run more smoothly.

SMALL TALK

Before reading about small talk, examine your own small talk behavior by taking the accompanying self-test.

TEST YOURSELF

How Do You Small Talk?

Examine your small talk communication by responding to the following questions.

_____ ❶ On an elevator with three or four strangers, I'd be most likely to
    a. try to avoid interacting.
    b. respond to another but not initiate interaction.
    c. be the first to talk.

_____ ❷ When I'm talking with someone and I meet a friend who doesn't know the person I'm with, I'd most apt to
    a. avoid introducing them.
    b. wait until they introduce each other.
    c. introduce them to each other.

_____ ❸ At a party with people I've never met before, I'd be most likely to
    a. wait for someone to talk to me.
    b. nonverbally indicate that I'm receptive to someone interacting with me.
    c. initiate interaction with others nonverbally and verbally.

Another "everyday conversation" concerns the giving and receiving of advice. For an introduction to this topic, see "Advice Giving" at tcbdevito.blogspot.com.

_____ ❹ When confronted with someone who doesn't want to end the conversation, I'd be most apt to
    a. just stick it out and listen.
    b. tune out the person and hope time goes by quickly.
    c. end it firmly myself.

_____ ❺ When the other person monologues, I'd be most apt to
    a. listen politely.
    b. try to change the focus.
    c. exit as quickly as possible.

HOW DID YOU DO? A majority of *a* responses would indicate some level of dissatisfaction and discomfort with the experience of small talk; *b* responses indicate that you probably experience both satisfaction and dissatisfaction with small talk; *c* responses indicate comfort and satisfaction with small talk. Put in terms of assertiveness, discussed in Chapter 4 (pp. 75–77), the *a* responses are unassertive, the *b* responses are indirect (not totally unassertive but not assertive either), and the *c* responses are direct and assertive.

WHAT WILL YOU DO? If your small talk experiences are not satisfying to you, read on. You will learn about the value of small talk, as well as guidelines for more successfully engaging in small talk.

TABLE 6.2 Communication Tips

Between People With and Without Speech and Language Disorders

Speech and language disorders vary widely—from fluency problems such as stuttering, to indistinct articulation, to difficulty in finding the right word (aphasia). Following a few simple guidelines can facilitate communication between people with and without speech and language disorders.

If you're the person without a speech or language disorder:	
Generally	**Specifically**
Avoid finishing another person's sentences.	Finishing the person's sentences may communicate the idea that you're impatient and don't want to spend the extra time necessary to interact effectively.
Avoid giving directions to the person with a speech disorder.	Saying "slow down" or "relax" will often seem insulting and will make further communication more difficult.
Maintain eye contact.	Show interest and at the same time avoid showing any signs of impatience or embarrassment.
Ask for clarification as needed.	If you don't understand what the person said, ask him or her to repeat it. Don't pretend that you understand when you don't.
Don't treat people who have language problems like children.	A person with aphasia, say, who has difficulty with names or nouns generally, is in no way childlike. Similarly, a person who stutters is not a slow thinker; in fact, stutterers differ from non-stutterers only in their oral fluency.
If you're the person with a speech or language disorder:	
Let the other person know what your special needs are.	If you stutter, you might tell others that you have difficulty with certain sounds and so they need to be patient.
Demonstrate your own comfort.	Show that you have a positive attitude toward the interpersonal situation. If you appear comfortable and positive, others will also.
Be patient.	For example, have patience with those who try to finish your sentences; they're probably just trying to be helpful.

Sources: These suggestions were drawn from a variety of sources, including the websites of the National Stuttering Association, the National Aphasia Association, the U.S. Department of Labor, and the American Speech and Hearing Association, all accessed May 9, 2012.

All of us engage in small talk, whether it occurs on an elevator, in a hallway, on Twitter, or on some other social media site. Sometimes, we use it as a preface to big talk. For example, before a conference with your boss or even a job interview, you're likely to engage in some preliminary small talk. "How are you doing?" "I'm pleased this weather has finally cleared up." The purpose here is to ease into the major topic, or the "big talk."

Sometimes, small talk is a politeness strategy and a more extensive way of saying hello as you pass someone in the hallway or meet a neighbor at the post office. You might say, "Good seeing you, Jack. You're looking ready for the big meeting," or "See you in Geology at 1."

Sometimes, your relationship with another person revolves totally around small talk, perhaps with your barber or hairdresser, a colleague at work, your next-door neighbor, or a fellow student you sit next to in class. In these relationships, neither person makes an effort to deepen the relationship, and it remains on a small talk level.

Despite its name, small talk serves important purposes. One is simply to pass the time more pleasantly than you might in silence. Small talk also demonstrates that the normal rules of politeness are operating. In the United States, for example, you would be expected to smile and at least say hello to people in an elevator in your apartment building, and perhaps at your place of work. Furthermore, small talk confirms to others that all is well with you. Should you scowl and avoid eye contact with someone in your apartment building elevator, you'd signal that something is wrong.

> **⬦ Communication Choice Point**
>
> **Making Small Talk**
>
> You're on an elevator with three other people from your office building. The elevator gets stuck without any indication of when power will go back on. You figure now is the time for small talk. *What are some things you might say to make the situation more comfortable?*

Topics and Contexts of Small Talk   Small talk topics must be noncontroversial in the sense that they are something about which you and the other person are unlikely to disagree. If a topic is likely to arouse deep emotions or different points of view, then it is probably not a suitable topic for small talk.

Small talk is also relatively short in duration. The context in which small talk occurs allows for only a brief interaction. Waiting in line to get into a movie, riding in an elevator, or stopping briefly in the hallway of a school on the way to class are the kinds of occasions that create small talk opportunities. The cocktail party, at which guests are meant to mingle and exchange pleasantries, is perhaps the classic example.

Another popular occasion, which is an exception to this short duration characteristic, is sitting next to someone on a long plane flight. Here, the small talk—assuming you keep it to small talk—can last for hours. Sometimes, as explained in the discussion of self-disclosure in Chapter 2 (pp. 31–35), this situation produces a kind of "in-flight intimacy" in which you engage in significant self-disclosure, revealing secrets you normally keep hidden, largely because you know you'll never see this person again.

"It's definitely true. Inane conversation is better with masks."

© Steve Duenes/Condé Nast Publications/www.cartoonbank.com

Guidelines for Effective Small Talk   Although "small," this talk still requires the application of the communication skills for "big" talk. As already noted, remember that the best topics are noncontroversial and that most small talk is relatively brief. Here are a few additional guidelines for more effective small talk.

- **Be positive.** No one likes a negative doomsayer. So, comment on the weather when it's nice; move to another topic when it isn't.

- **Be sensitive to leavetaking cues.** Small talk is necessarily brief, but at times one person may want it to be a preliminary to big talk and another person may see it as the sum of the interaction.

- **Stress similarities rather than differences.** This is a good way to ensure that the small talk stays noncontroversial.

 VIEWPOINTS

Social Media Apologizing

What kinds of apologies do you see on social media sites? In what ways are apologies online different from face-to-face apologies?

- **Answer questions with enough elaboration to give the other person information to use to interact with you.** The more elaborate answer also signals your willingness to engage in small talk, whereas the simple "yes" response can be interpreted as indicating you don't want to interact.

- **Avoid monologuing.** Listen and be responsive to the other person. Even small talk is two-way and requires each person to talk and each person to listen. Remember the principles of turn-taking and dialogue.

- **Remember that you will be associated with the topics you frequently select to talk about.** If all your small talk concerns the marriage of Justin Timberlake and Jessica Biel, the feud between Christina Aguilera and Simon Cowell, or Lindsay Lohan's financial difficulties, then you might become defined as someone who is only interested in shallow celebrity gossip.

APOLOGIES

Despite your best efforts, there are times when you'll say or do the wrong thing and it may be necessary to offer an **apology**—an expression of regret or sorrow for having done what you did or for what happened, a statement that says you're sorry. And so, the most basic of all apologies is simply to say "I'm sorry." In popular usage, the apology includes some admission of wrongdoing on the part of the person making the apology. Sometimes the wrongdoing is acknowledged explicitly ("I'm sorry I lied") and sometimes only by implication ("I'm sorry you're so upset"). In many cases the apology also includes a request for forgiveness ("Please excuse me for being late") and some assurance that this won't happen again ("Please forgive my lateness; it won't happen again").

An effective apology must be crafted for the specific situation. An effective apology to a longtime lover, to a parent, or to a new supervisor are likely to be very different because the individuals are different and your relationships are different. And so the first rule of an effective apology is to take into consideration the uniqueness of the situation—the people, the context, the cultural rules, the relationship, the specific wrongdoing—for which you might want to apologize. Each situation will call for a somewhat different message of apology. Nevertheless, we can offer some general recommendations.

Watch the **Video** "I Didn't Do It" at **MyCommunicationLab**

- **Admit wrongdoing** (if indeed wrongdoing occurred). Accept responsibility. Take ownership of your actions; don't try to pass them off as the work of someone else. Instead of "Smith drives so slow, it's a wonder I'm only 30 minutes late," say "I should have taken traffic into consideration."

- **Be apologetic.** Say (and mean) the words *I'm sorry*. Don't justify your behavior by mentioning that everyone does it. For example, don't say "Everyone leaves work early on Friday." And don't justify your behavior by saying that the other person has done something equally wrong: "So I play poker; you play the lottery."

- **Be specific.** State, in specific rather than general terms, what you've done. Instead of "I'm sorry for what I did" say "I'm sorry for flirting at the party."

- **Empathize.** Express understanding of how the other person feels and acknowledge the legitimacy of these feelings: "You have every right to be angry; I should have called." Express your regret that this has created a problem for the other person: "I'm sorry I made you miss your appointment." Don't minimize the problem that this may have caused. Avoid comments such as "So the figures arrived a little late. What's the big deal?"

- **Give assurance that this will not happen again.** Say, quite simply, "It won't happen again" or, better and more specifically, "I won't be late again." And, whenever possible, offer to correct the problem: "I'm sorry I didn't clean up the mess I made; I'll do it now."

- **Avoid excuses.** Be wary of including excuses with your apology: "I'm sorry the figures are late, but I had so much other work to do." An excuse often takes back the apology and says, in effect, I'm really not sorry because there was good reason for what I did, but I'm saying "I'm sorry" to cover all my bases and to make this uncomfortable situation go away.

Communication Choice Point

Apologizing

You borrowed a friend's car and got into an accident—and, to make matters worse, it was totally your fault. *What are some of the things you might say that would help you explain the situation, alleviate any anxiety your friend will have over the accident, and pave the way for a request to borrow the car again next week for the most important date of your life? What would be your first sentence?*

SKILL DEVELOPMENT EXPERIENCE

Formulating Apologies

Apologies are often helpful in lessening the possible negative effects of a mishap. Here are several situations in which you might want to offer an apology. For each of the following situations, formulate one apology that you think will prove effective.

1. Your boss confronts you with your office telephone log. The log shows that you've been making numerous long-distance personal phone calls, a practice that is explicitly forbidden.
2. In talking with your supervisor, you tell a joke that puts down lesbians and gay men. Your supervisor tells you she finds the joke homophobic and offensive; she adds that she has a gay son and is proud of it. This supervisor's approval is essential to your retention.
3. You're caught in a lie. You told your romantic partner that you were going to visit your parents but were discovered to have visited a former lover. You don't want to break up your relationship over this.

> *Apologies will not reverse your errors, but they may help repair—at least to some extent—conversational or relationship damage.*

- **Choose the appropriate channel.** Don't take the easy way out and apologize through e-mail (unless the wrongdoing was committed in e-mail or if e-mail is your only or main form of communication). Generally, it's more effective to use a more personal mode of communication—face-to-face or phone, for example. It's harder but it's more effective.

Introducing people often creates uncertainty and awkwardness. For some help with this everyday conversation, see "Introducing People" at tcbdevito.blogspot.com.

COMPLIMENTS

A **compliment** is a message of praise, flattery, or congratulations. It can be expressed in face-to-face interaction or on social media sites when, for example, you retweet someone's post or indicate "like" or "+1" or when you comment on a blog post. The compliment functions like a kind of interpersonal glue; it's a way of relating to another person with positiveness and immediacy. It's also a conversation starter: "I like your watch; may I ask where you got it?" Another purpose the compliment serves is to encourage the other person to compliment you—even if not immediately (which often seems inappropriate).

Compliments can be unqualified or qualified. The unqualified compliment is a message that is purely positive: "Your paper was just great, an A." The qualified message is not entirely positive: "Your paper was great, an A; if not for a few problems, it would have been an A+." You might also give a qualified compliment by qualifying your own competence: "That song you wrote sounded great, but I really don't know anything about music."

Compliments are sometimes difficult to give and even more difficult to respond to without discomfort or embarrassment. Here are some guidelines.

Giving a Compliment   Here are a few suggestions for giving a compliment:

- **Be real and honest.** Say what you mean and refrain from giving compliments you don't believe in. They'll probably sound insincere.

- **Compliment in moderation.** A compliment that is too extreme (for example, "That's the best decorated apartment I've ever seen in my life") may be viewed as dishonest. Similarly, don't compliment at every possible occasion; if you do, your compliments will seem too easy to win and not really meaningful.

- **Be totally complimentary; avoid qualifying your compliments.** If you hear yourself giving a compliment and then adding *but* or *however*, stop and rethink what you are going to say. Many people will remember the qualification rather than the compliment, and it will instead feel like a criticism.

VIEWPOINTS

What Do You Compliment?

Some interpersonal watchers recommend that you compliment people for their accomplishments rather than for who they are or for things over which they have no control. With this recommendation in mind, what are some of the things that might be appropriately complimented in the home? In the workplace? What would be some of the things that would be inappropriate to compliment at home or at the workplace?

- **Be specific.** Direct your compliment at something specific rather than something general. Instead of saying, "I liked your story," you might say, "I liked your story—it made me realize something I had forgotten. . . ."

- **Be personal in your own feelings**—"Your song really moved me; it made me recall so many good times." But don't be personal about the other person: "Your hair looks so natural; is that a weave or a toupee?"

Receiving a Compliment   In receiving a compliment, people generally take either one of two options: denial or acceptance. Many people deny the compliment ("It's nice of you to say, but I know I was terrible"), minimize it ("It isn't like I wrote the great American novel; it was just an article that no one will read"), change the subject ("So, where should we go for dinner?"), or say nothing. Each of these responses denies the legitimacy of the compliment. Accepting the compliment is a much better alternative. An acceptance might be communicated in three ways: (1) just smile, with eye contact—avoid looking at the floor, (2) simply say "thank you," and(3) offer a personal reflection in which you explain (very briefly) why the compliment is important to you ("I really appreciate your comments; I worked hard on the project and it's great to hear it was effective").

Objectives Self-Check
- Can you make effective small talk?
- Can you formulate effective apologies?
- Can you give and receive compliments comfortably?

Messages in the Media *Wrap Up*

As you watch shows revolving around sports commentators, consider the principles of conversation discussed in this chapter. Very probably, those interviewers and interviewees who follow the suggestions offered here are going to present an interesting show; those that violate the rules are likely to bore the audience. Analyzing why and how this happens will help you learn the principles of conversation.

Summary of Concepts and Skills

 Study and **Review** materials for this chapter are at **MyCommunicationLab**

 Listen to the **Audio Chapter Summary** at **MyCommunicationLab**

This chapter explored interpersonal communication and the principles of conversation and some common everyday conversations.

The Principles of Conversation

1. The process of conversation consists of five general stages: opening, feedforward, business, feedback, and closing.

2. Throughout the speaking–listening process, both speaker and listener exchange cues for *conversational turns;* these cues enable the speaker and listener to communicate *about* the communication in which they're engaged.

3. Speakers regulate the conversation through two major types of cues: turn-maintaining cues and turn-yielding cues. Listeners regulate the conversation by using three types of cues: turn-requesting cues, turn-denying cues, and back-channeling cues and interruptions.

4. Dialogue is conversation in which there is genuine two-way interaction; each person is both speaker and listener, sender and receiver. Monologue communication is the opposite: One person speaks and the other listens—there's no real interaction between participants.

5. Immediacy is the creation of closeness, a sense of togetherness, between speaker and listener.

Everyday Conversations

6. Small talk is pervasive, noncontroversial, and often serves as a polite way of introducing yourself or a topic.

7. Apologies are expressions of regret or sorrow for having done what you did or for what happened.

8. A compliment is a message of praise, flattery, or congratulations and often enables you to interact with positiveness and immediacy.

Consider your competence in using the skills of effective interpersonal communication and conversation. Place a check mark next to those skills you want to work on most.

_____ 1. I understand that conversation occurs in stages and that each stage serves a different function.

_____ 2. I follow the principles of turn-taking in conversation, giving appropriate speaker and listener cues and responding to the cues of others.

_____ 3. I engage in dialogic rather than monologic conversation.

_____ 4. I adjust my immediacy cues as appropriate to the conversation and the relationship.

_____ 5. I can engage in small talk in a variety of situations with comfort and ease.

_____ 6. I can formulate effective apologies and can use them appropriately in interpersonal interactions.

_____ 7. I can extend and receive a compliment graciously.

 Key Word Quiz

The Language of Interpersonal Communication and Conversation

Match the terms about interpersonal communication and conversation with their definitions. Record the number of the definition next to the appropriate term.

_____ a. phatic communication (122)

_____ b. turn-maintaining cues (124)

_____ c. dialogue (125)

_____ d. immediacy (126)

_____ e. apology (132)

_____ f. turn-denying cues (124)

_____ g. monologue (126)

_____ h. compliment (133)

_____ i. small talk (131)

_____ j. back-channeling cues (124)

1. Genuine two-way interaction.
2. Expression of regret
3. Signals indicating your reluctance to assume the role of speaker.
4. A form of flattery, an expression of positiveness.
5. A type of listener cue that says "I'm listening."
6. Communication in which one person speaks and the other listens.
7. Defined most clearly by its noncontroversial nature.
8. Signals that indicate that the speaker wishes to continue speaking.
9. The quality of togetherness, of oneness, that joins speaker and listener.
10. Messages that open the channels of communication.

These ten terms and additional terms used in this chapter can be found in the glossary.

 Study and **Review** the **Flashcards** at **MyCommunicationLab**

Answers: a. 10; b. 3; c. 1; d. 9; e. 2; f. 8; g. 6; h. 4; i. 7; j. 5

MyCommunicationLab

Throughout this chapter, there are icons in the margin that highlight media content for selected topics. Go to **MyCommunicationLab** for additional information on conversation. Here you'll find flashcards to help you learn the jargon of communication, videos that illustrate a variety of concepts, additional exercises, and discussions to help you continue your study of interpersonal communication and especially conversation.

7

Interpersonal Relationships

Objectives

 Listen to the **Audio Chapter** at **MyCommunicationLab**

After reading this chapter, you should be able to:

❶ Describe the advantages and disadvantages of interpersonal relationships and assess your own relationships in light of these advantages and disadvantages.

❷ Explain the stages of interpersonal relationships and provide examples of the types of messages that occur at each stage.

❸ Define *friendship, love, family, workplace,* and *online-only relationships.*

❹ Explain the theories of interpersonal relationships and apply the insights to your own relationships.

Messages in the Media

The television series *Dallas* centers on the complicated interactions of a large family, as do many other dramas and sitcoms, and illustrates in clear terms, some of the ways family members communicate with one another, admittedly in an extreme form. Both effective and ineffective interactions are regularly dramatized in the words and gestures of a wide array of characters.

Contact with other human beings is so important that when you're deprived of it for long periods, depression sets in, self-doubt surfaces, and you may find it difficult to manage even the basics of daily life. Research shows clearly that the most important contributor to happiness—outranking money, job, and sex—is a close relationship with one other person (Freedman, 1978; Laroche & deGrace, 1997; Lu & Shih, 1997). The desire for relationships is universal; interpersonal relationships are important to men and to women, to homosexuals and to heterosexuals, to young and to old (Huston & Schwartz, 1995). Not surprisingly, this seems the principle motivation for much of social media communication.

This chapter looks at some of the advantages and disadvantages of interpersonal relationships, the stages of relationships, the varied types of relationships, theories that explain why we enter and exit relationships, and the influence of culture, technology, and work on our relationships.

Advantages and Disadvantages of Interpersonal Relationships

A good way to begin the study of interpersonal relationships is to examine your own relationships (past, present, or those you look forward to) by asking yourself what your relationships do for you. What are the advantages and the disadvantages? Visualize a 10-point scale on which 1 indicates that your relationship(s) never serves this function, 10 indicates that your relationship(s) always serves this function, and the numbers in between indicate levels between these extremes. You may wish to do this twice—once for your face-to-face relationships and once for your online relationships.

_____ 1. My relationships help to lessen my loneliness.

_____ 2. My relationships help me gain in self-knowledge and in self-esteem.

_____ 3. My relationships help enhance my physical and emotional health.

_____ 4. My relationships maximize my pleasures and minimize my pains.

_____ 5. My relationships help me to secure stimulation (intellectual, physical, and emotional).

Let's elaborate just a bit on each of these commonly accepted advantages of interpersonal communication:

1. One of the major benefits of relationships is that they help to lessen loneliness (Rokach, 1998; Rokach & Brock, 1995). They make you feel that someone cares, that someone likes you, that someone will protect you, that someone ultimately will love you.

2. Through contact with others you learn about yourself and see yourself from different perspectives and in different roles, as a child or parent, as a coworker, as a manager, as a best friend. Healthy interpersonal relationships help enhance self-esteem and self-worth. Simply having a friend or romantic partner (at least most of the time) makes you feel desirable and worthy.

3. Research consistently shows that interpersonal relationships contribute significantly to physical and emotional health (Goleman, 1995; Pennebacker, 1991; Rosen, 1998; Rosengren, 1993) and to personal happiness (Berscheid & Reis, 1998). Without close interpersonal relationships you're more likely to become depressed—and this depression, in turn, contributes significantly to physical illness. Isolation, in fact, contributes as much to mortality as high blood pressure, high cholesterol, obesity, smoking, or lack of physical exercise (Goleman 1995).

4. The most general function served by interpersonal relationships, and the function that encompasses all the others, is that of maximizing pleasure and minimizing pain. Your good friends, for example, will make you feel even better about your good fortune and less hurt when you're confronted with hardships.

VIEWPOINTS

Parasocial Relationships

Parasocial relationships are relationships that audience members perceive themselves to have with media personalities (Rubin & McHugh, 1987; Giles, 2001; Giles & Maltby, 2004). At times viewers develop these relationships with real media personalities—Wendy Williams, Anderson Cooper, or Ellen DeGeneres, for example—and at other times the relationship is with a fictional character—an investigator on *CSI*, a scientist on *Bones*, or a doctor on a soap opera. What's your view of parasocial relationships? Are there advantages to these relationships? Disadvantages? What's your experience with parasocial relationships?

5. As plants are heliotropic and orient themselves to light, humans are stimulotropic and orient themselves to sources of stimulation (Davis, 1973). Human contact is one of the best ways to secure this stimulation—intellectual, physical, and emotional. Even an imagined relationship seems better than none.

Now, respond to these sentences as you did to the above.

_____ 6. My relationships put uncomfortable pressure on me to expose my vulnerabilities.

_____ 7. My relationships increase my obligations.

_____ 8. My relationships prevent me from developing other relationships.

_____ 9. My relationships scare me because they may be difficult to dissolve.

_____ 10. My relationships hurt me.

These statements express what most people would consider disadvantages of interpersonal relationships.

6. Close relationships put pressure on you to reveal yourself and to expose your vulnerabilities. Although this is generally worthwhile in the context of a supporting and caring relationship, it may backfire if the relationship deteriorates and these weaknesses are used against you.

7. Close relationships increase your obligations to other people, sometimes to a great extent. Your time is no longer entirely your own. And although you enter relationships to spend more time with these special people, you also incur time (and perhaps financial) obligations with which you may not be happy.

8. Close relationships can lead you to abandon other relationships. Sometimes the other relationship involves someone you like, but your partner can't stand. More often, however, it's simply a matter of time and energy; relationships take a lot of both and you have less to give to these other and less intimate relationships.

9. The closer your relationships, the more emotionally difficult they are to dissolve, a feeling which may be uncomfortable for some people. If a relationship is deteriorating, you may feel distress or depression. In some cultures, for example, religious pressures may prevent married couples from separating. And if considerable money is involved, dissolving a relationship can often mean giving up the fortune you've spent your life accumulating.

10. And, of course, your partner may break your heart. Your partner may leave you—against all your pleading and promises. Your hurt will be in proportion to how much you care and need your partner. If you care a great deal, you're likely to experience great hurt; if you care less, the hurt will be less—it's one of life's little ironies.

Objectives Self-Check
● Can you describe the advantages and disadvantages of interpersonal relationships?
● Can you assess your own relationships in light of these advantages and disadvantages?

Explore the **Concept**
"Relationships" at
MyCommunicationLab

The Stages of Interpersonal Relationships

As a preface to this discussion, realize that different cultures will view relationships very differently. What is presented here is generally derived from research conducted in the United States, and so, for example, the assumption made is that you voluntarily choose your relationship partners—that you consciously choose to pursue certain relationships and not others. In some cultures, however, your parents choose your romantic partner for you. In some cases your husband or wife is chosen to unite two families or to bring some financial advantage to your family or village.

In the United States, researchers study and textbook authors write about dissolving relationships and how to survive relationship breakups. It's generally assumed that you have the right to exit an undesirable relationship. However, in some cultures you simply cannot dissolve a relationship once it has been formed or once there are children. More important to such cultures may be issues such as how to maintain a relationship that has problems, what to do to survive in an unpleasant relationship, and how to repair a troubled relationship (Moghaddam, Taylor, & Wright, 1993).

You and another person don't become intimate friends immediately on meeting. Rather, you build an intimate relationship gradually, through a series of steps or stages. The same is true of most relationships.

The model in Figure 7.1 describes the six main stages in relationships: contact, involvement, intimacy, deterioration, repair, and dissolution, each of which has an early and a late

Explore the **Exercise**
"Analyzing Stage Talk" at
MyCommunicationLab

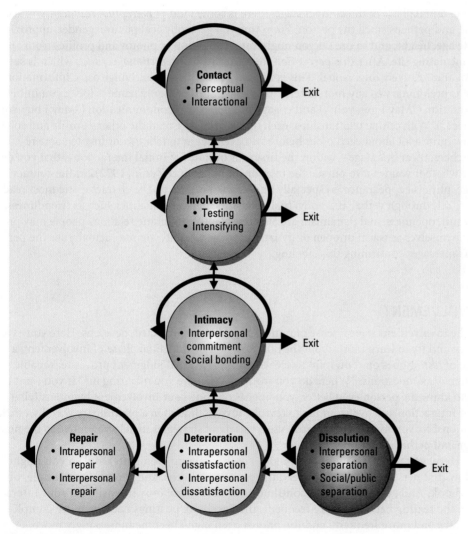

FIGURE 7.1

The Six Stages of Relationships

Because relationships differ so widely, it's best to think of this or any relationship model as a tool for talking about relationships rather than as a specific map that indicates how you move from one relationship position to another. Can you identify other steps or stages that would further explain what goes on in relationship development? What happens when the two people in a relationship experience the stages differently? Can you provide an example from literature or from your own experience?

Communication Choice Point

Relationship Stage

Your partner gives you a gift that contradicts your perception of your relationship stage. The gift is much too intimate and too expensive for the casual nature of what you believe your relationship is. You need to refuse the gift. *What can you say? What channel would you use?*

phase. These stages describe relationships as they are; they don't evaluate or prescribe how relationships should be. For a particular relationship, you might wish to modify the basic model, but as a general description the stages seem fairly standard. They are also applicable generally to face-to-face as well as to online relationships. As you read about these stages, keep in mind that both partners may not perceive their relationship in the same way; one person, for example, may see the relationship as having reached the intimate stage and the other may not.

Social network sites seem to recognize this stage nature of relationships by enabling you to treat your online "friends" differently. For example, the circles on Google+ and the "friends lists" on Facebook enable you to group people on the basis of the information that you want them to be able to access. This makes it very easy to distinguish acquaintances from intimate friends, for example, as well as family from friends from workplace colleagues.

CONTACT

At the initial phase of the **contact** stage, there is some kind of *perceptual contact*—you see, hear, and perhaps smell the person. From this you get a physical picture: gender, approximate age, height, and so on. Or you might browse a group of photos and profiles from an online dating site. After this perception there is usually *interactional contact*, which is superficial and relatively impersonal. This is the stage at which you exchange basic information that is preliminary to any more intense involvement ("Hello, my name is Joe"); you initiate interaction ("May I join you?") and engage in invitational communication ("May I buy you coffee?"). With online relationships, each of you will have read the other's profile and so will know quite a lot about each other before you even begin to talk. According to some researchers, it's at this stage—within the first four minutes of initial interaction—that you decide whether you want to pursue the relationship (Zunin & Zunin, 1972). At the contact stage, physical appearance is especially important, because it's the characteristic most readily seen. Yet, through verbal and nonverbal behaviors, personal qualities such as friendliness, warmth, openness, and dynamism are also revealed. With online relations people may profile themselves as warm or open or dynamic and, as a result, you may actually see the person's messages confirming this labeling.

For cyberflirting see, "Cyberflirting etc." at tcbdevito.blogspot.com. How do you see cyberflirting? What cyberflirting techniques do you find most interesting?

For an interesting article on moving from involvement to intimacy, see "From Dating to Mating" at tcbdevito.blogspot.com. Any further suggestions?

INVOLVEMENT

At the **involvement** stage a sense of mutuality, of being connected, develops. Here you experiment and try to learn more about the other person. At the initial phase of involvement, a kind of *testing* goes on. You want to see whether your initial judgment proves reasonable. You may ask questions: "Where do you work?" "What are you majoring in?" If you want to get to know the person even better, you might continue your involvement by intensifying your interaction and by beginning to reveal yourself, though in a preliminary way. In a dating relationship, you might, for example, use a variety of strategies to help you move to the next stage and perhaps to intimacy.

Here, you're committed to getting to know someone even better and so you might follow that person on Twitter or read the postings, photos, and causes, for example, on Facebook. And at this stage you continue your involvement by intensifying your interaction; the texting becomes more frequent, the Facebook postings become more complimentary and more frequent, and the photos exchanged become increasingly more personal and revealing.

For example, you might increase contact with your partner; give your partner tokens of affection, such as gifts, cards, or flowers; write affectionate messages on a person's Facebook wall, increase your own personal attractiveness; do things that suggest intensifying the relationship, such as flirting or making your partner jealous; and become more physically intimate (Tolhuizen, 1989).

INTIMACY

The contact and involvement stages make up **relationship development**—a movement toward intimacy. At the **intimacy** stage you commit yourself still further to the other person and establish a relationship in which this individual becomes your best or closest friend, lover, or companion. Because intimacy is essentially an emotional/communication connection, it can occur in face-to-face and in online relationships equally. You also come to share each other's social networks, a practice followed by members of widely different cultures (Gao & Gudykunst, 1995). This is seen most clearly on social network sites where the site itself identifies people with whom you might want to become "friends" based on mutual friends or interests. Both the quantity and the quality of your interpersonal exchanges increase (Emmers-Sommer, 2004), and of course you also talk more and in greater detail about the relationship (Knobloch, Haunani, & Theiss, 2006). Not surprisingly, your relationship satisfaction also increases with the move to this stage (Siavelis & Lamke, 1992). One research study defined intimacy as the feeling that you can be honest and open when talking about yourself, sharing thoughts and feelings that you don't reveal in other relationships (Mackey, Diemer, & O'Brien, 2000).

The intimacy stage usually divides itself into two phases. In the *interpersonal commitment phase*, the two people commit themselves to each other in a private way. In the *social bonding phase*, the commitment is made public—perhaps to family and friends, perhaps to the public at large, perhaps with a simple "married to" on Facebook. Here you and your partner become a unit, an identifiable pair.

Communication Choice Point

Relationship Résumé

Although you've been mostly honest in your two-month Internet relationship, you have padded your relationship résumé—lopped off a few years and pounds and made your temporary job seem like the executive fast track. You now want to come clean. *What might you do in preface to this revelation? What would you say? What channel would you use?*

DETERIORATION

The relationship deterioration stage is characterized by a weakening of the bonds between the friends or lovers. The first phase of **deterioration** is usually *intrapersonal dissatisfaction:* You begin to experience personal dissatisfaction with everyday interactions and begin to view the future with your partner more negatively. If this dissatisfaction grows, you pass to the second phase, *interpersonal deterioration.* You withdraw and grow further and further apart. You share less of your free time. You exchange fewer messages. When you're together, there are awkward silences, fewer disclosures, less physical contact, and a lack of psychological closeness. Conflicts become more common and their resolution more difficult.

Relationship deterioration involves unique communication patterns. During the deterioration stage you may, for example, increase withdrawal, communicate less, respond to Facebook pokes and requests for "likes" less often; texting becomes infrequent, and face-to-face meetings are fewer. In communication, each person reduces his or her level of self-disclosure. These patterns are in part a response to the deterioration; you communicate the way you do because you feel that your relationship is in trouble. However, these patterns are also causative: The communication patterns you use largely determine the fate of your relationship.

Explore the **Exercise** "Learning to Hear Stage Talk" at **MyCommunicationLab**

Video Choice Point

Coming Clean

Sally and Jim have been communicating online for some time after meeting on Match.com. She likes what she has learned about Jim and would like to see the relationship make it to the next stage. They're now planning to meet face-to-face for the first time. But, Sally realizes that she's going to have to admit that she lied about her age and a few other things. She's analyzed her choices as to how she can communicate these admissions without damaging the potential for a more intimate relationship. See how her choices play out in the video "Coming Clean".

 Watch the **Video** "Coming Clean" at **MyCommunicationLab**

SKILL DEVELOPMENT EXPERIENCE

Exchanging Cherishing Messages

Cherishing behaviors are an especially insightful way to affirm another person and to increase favor exchange, a concept that comes from the work of William Lederer (1984). **Cherishing behaviors** are those small gestures you enjoy receiving from your partner (e.g., a smile, a wink, a squeeze, a kiss, a phone call, an "I love you").

Prepare a list of ten cherishing behaviors that you would like to receive from your real or imagined relationship partner. Identify these cherishing behaviors according to the following categories:

1. Specific and positive—nothing overly general or negative
2. Focused on the present and future rather than on issues about which you've argued in the past
3. Capable of being performed daily
4. Easily executed—nothing that you have to go out of your way to accomplish

Lists of cherishing behaviors will also give you insight into your own relationship needs and the kind of communicating partner you want.

If you have a relationship partner, ask him or her also to prepare a list, and exchange lists, and begin exchanging cherishing behaviors. Ideally, you and your partner will begin to perform these cherishing behaviors for one another. In time these behaviors should become a normal part of your interaction, which is exactly what you'd hope to achieve.

Explore the **Exercise** "Giving Repair Advice" at **MyCommunicationLab**

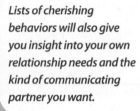

Communication Choice Point

Relationship Dissolution

You realize that your six-month relationship is going nowhere, and you want to break it off. It's just not exciting and not taking you where you want to go. You want to avoid making a scene. *What would you say? Where would you say it? What kinds of feedforward would you use before breaking the news?*

"We broke up, Stuart—don't you read your e-mail?"

REPAIR

At this stage of a relationship, some partners may pause during deterioration and try to seek **repair.** Others, however, may progress without stopping to dissolution.

At the first repair phase, *intrapersonal repair,* you analyze what went wrong and consider ways of solving your relational difficulties. You might at this stage consider changing your behaviors or perhaps changing your expectations of your partner. You might also evaluate the rewards of your relationship as it is now and the rewards to be gained if your relationship ended.

Should you decide that you want to repair your relationship, you might move to the *interpersonal repair phase*—you might discuss with your partner the problems in the relationship, the changes you want to see, and perhaps what you'd be willing to do and what you'd want your partner to do. This is the stage of negotiating new agreements and new behaviors. You and your partner might try to repair your relationship by yourselves, or you might seek the advice of friends, family, or relationship therapists.

Fortunately, social media sites offer considerable help in making relationship repair by providing ready access to cards and virtual gifts, for example, to help you express your desire to repair the relationship.

DISSOLUTION

Dissolution—the last stage in the relationship model—involves cutting the bonds that tie you together. In the beginning it usually takes the form of *interpersonal separation*: If it's an online friendship, you might de-friend or uncircle or perhaps, most often, just cut off communication. You might move into your own apartments and begin to lead separate lives. If the separation works better than the original relationship, you enter the phase of *social* or *public separation*. Avoidance of each other and a return to a "single" status are among the primary characteristics of the dissolution of a relationship.

Objectives Self-Check
- Can you explain the varied stages of interpersonal relationships (contact, involvement, intimacy, deterioration, dissolution, and repair)?
- Can you provide examples of the types of messages that occur at each of these stages?

For a brief discussion of gay-straight friendships, their problems and advantages, see "Friendship, Gay and Straight" at **tcbdevito.blogspot.com**. How do you see such friendships?

Interpersonal Relationship Types

Each relationship, whether friendship or love, for example, is unique. Yet there are general types that research has identified—and these categories will offer considerable insight into your own interpersonal relationships. Here we consider friendship, love, family, work, and online-only relationships.

FRIENDSHIP

One theory of **friendship** identifies three major types that we can easily see in our own face-to-face and online relationships: (1) friendship of reciprocity, (2) friendship of receptivity, and (3) friendship of association (Reisman, 1979, 1981).

- The **friendship of reciprocity,** the ideal type, is characterized by loyalty, self-sacrifice, mutual affection, and generosity. This type of friendship is based on equality, where each individual shares equally in giving and receiving the benefits and rewards of the relationship.

- In the **friendship of receptivity,** in contrast, there is an imbalance in giving and receiving; one person is the primary giver and the other the primary receiver. This is a positive imbalance, however, because each person gains something from the relationship. The different needs of both the person who receives affection and the person who gives it are satisfied. This is the friendship that may develop between a teacher and a student or between a doctor and a patient. In fact, a difference in status is essential for the friendship of receptivity to develop.

- The **friendship of association** is transitory; it might be described as a friendly relationship rather than a true friendship. Associative friendships are the kind you have with classmates, neighbors, or coworkers. There is no great loyalty, no great trust, no great giving or receiving. The association is cordial but not intense.

LOVE

Like friendships, romantic partnerships come in different styles as well. Six primary love styles have been identified (Lee, 1976; Hendrick & Hendrick, 1990):

- **Eros love** seeks beauty and sensuality and focuses on physical attractiveness, sometimes to the exclusion of qualities others might consider more important and more lasting. The erotic lover has an idealized image of beauty that is unattainable in reality. Consequently, the erotic lover often feels unfulfilled.

- **Ludic love** seeks entertainment and excitement and sees love as fun, a game. To the ludic lover, love is not to be taken too seriously; emotions are to be held in check lest they get out of hand and make trouble. The ludic lover retains a partner only so long as the partner is interesting and amusing. When the partner is no longer interesting enough, it's time to change.

Communication Choice Point

Moving Through Relationship Stages

Your current romantic partner seems to be moving too fast for your liking. You want to take things a lot slower, yet you don't want to turn this person off; this may be The One. *What might you say (and where might you say it) to get your partner to proceed more slowly?*

VIEWPOINTS

Online Dissolution

As more relationships are established and maintained online, more of them are also dissolved online. How would you describe the "rules" for breaking up online versus face-to-face? What are the major differences?

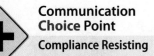

Communication Choice Point

Compliance Resisting

Your friend asks you for a loan of $150 to pay off some bills. Unfortunately, you've never been paid back when you've lent money in the past, so you don't want to do it again. Yet you don't want to lose this otherwise good friend. *What would you say?*

Explore the **Exercise** "What Type of Relationship Do You Prefer?" at **MyCommunicationLab**

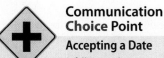

Communication Choice Point

Accepting a Date

A fellow student in one of your classes asks you for a date. You're really very excited and have been waiting for this all semester. *What are your options for communicating a clear yes, but without appearing overly eager?*

- **Storge love** is a peaceful and tranquil love. Like ludic love, storge lacks passion and intensity. Storgic lovers set out not to find a lover but to establish a companionable relationship with someone they know and with whom they can share interests and activities. Storgic love is a gradual process of unfolding thoughts and feelings and is sometimes difficult to distinguish from friendship.

- **Pragma love** is practical and traditional and seeks compatibility and a relationship in which important needs and desires will be satisfied. The pragma lover is concerned with the social qualifications of a potential mate even more than with personal qualities; family and background are extremely important to the pragma lover, who relies not so much on feelings as on logic.

- **Manic love** is an obsessive love that needs to give and receive constant attention and affection. When attention and affection are not constant, or when an expression of increased commitment is not returned, reactions such as depression, jealousy, and self-doubt can lead to extreme lows.

- **Agapic love** is compassionate and selfless. The agapic lover loves both the stranger on the road and the annoying neighbor. Jesus, Buddha, and Gandhi practiced and preached this unqualified spiritual love—a love that is offered without concern for personal reward or gain and without any expectation that the love will be reciprocated.

Men and women differ in the types of love they prefer (Hendrick, Hendrick, Foote, & Slapion-Foote, 1984). For example, men indicate a preference for erotic and ludic love, whereas women indicate a preference for manic, pragmatic, and storgic love. No difference was found for agapic love. Women and men seem to experience love to a similar degree (Rubin, 1973). However, women indicate greater love than men do for their same-sex friends. This may reflect a real difference between the sexes, or it may be a function of the greater social restrictions on men. A man is not supposed to admit his love for another man, but women are permitted to communicate their love for other women.

FAMILY RELATIONSHIPS

Families are central to contemporary life. It will come as no surprise to note that families come in various configurations and are undergoing major changes. Table 7.1 provides a few findings from the U.S. Census to illustrate some of the major changes.

The communication principles that apply to the traditional nuclear family (i.e., the mother-father-child family) also apply to all family configurations. In the discussion that follows, the term *primary relationship* denotes the relationship between two principal parties—husband

TABLE 7.1 **The American Family**

Here are several findings on the American family from the United States Census. For each finding, indicate what you think the reasons for these changes might be and the possible trends they indicate. In one sentence of not more than 140 characters, summarize the changes you see happening in the American family.

- The percentage of one-person households increased from 25% in 1990 to 27% in 2010.
- The percentage of multigenerational households increased from 14% in 1990 to 16% in 2010.
- The percentage of births by unmarried women increased from 26% in 1990 to 41% in 2010.
- Fifty percent of women who marry did so at 24 in 1990; in 2010 50% married at 26.
- In 2000 (the first year the U.S. Census Bureau allowed people to indicate more than one race), 1.6% indicated mixed race; in 2010 it was 2%.
- In 2005, 53% of men and 46% of women between the ages of 18 and 24 lived with their parents; in 2011 59% of men and 50% of women did.
- In 2000, 57% of all adults were married; in 2010, 51% were married.
- In 2000, the average size of the family was 2.62; in 2010, it was 2.59.

and wife, husband-husband, wife-wife, lovers, or domestic partners, for example—and the term *family* may denote a broader constellation that includes children, relatives, and assorted significant others.

A **primary relationship** is a relationship between two people that the partners see as their most important interpersonal relationship. An interesting typology of primary relationships (based on more than 1,000 couples' responses to questions concerning their degree of sharing, their space needs, their conflicts, and the time they spend together) identifies three basic types: traditionals, independents, and separates (Fitzpatrick, 1983, 1988, 1991; Noller & Fitzpatrick, 1993).

- **Traditional couples** share a basic belief system and philosophy of life. They see themselves as a blending of two persons into a single couple rather than as two separate individuals. They're interdependent and believe that each individual's independence must be sacrificed for the good of the relationship. In their communications, traditionals are highly responsive to each other. They lean toward each other, smile, talk a lot, interrupt each other, and finish each other's sentences.

- **Independents** stress their individuality. The relationship is important, but never more important than each person's individual identity. Although independents spend a great deal of time together, they don't ritualize it, for example, with schedules. Each individual spends time with outside friends. The communication between independents is responsive. They engage in conflict openly and without fear. Their disclosures are quite extensive and include high-risk and negative disclosures that are typically absent among traditionals.

- **Separates** live together, but they view their relationship more as a matter of convenience than a result of their mutual love or closeness. They seem to have little desire to be together and, in fact, usually are together only at ritual occasions such as mealtime or holiday get-togethers. It's important to these separates that each has his or her own physical as well as psychological space. The most significant characteristic of this type is that each person sees himself or herself as a separate individual and not as a part of a "we."

Like couples, families can also be classified in any number of ways—for example, according to the number of people in the family, their affectional orientation, the presence or absence of children or of extended family members. In a communication-oriented typology (Koerner & Fitzpatrick, 1997, 2004; Galvin, Bylund, & Brommel, 2012; Arnold, 2008), family types are looked at in terms of conformity and conversation.

Conformity-orientation refers to the degree to which family members express similar or dissimilar attitudes, values, and beliefs. So, we can speak of high-conformity families as those who express highly similar attitudes, beliefs, and values and try to avoid conflict, and low-conformity families as those whose members express highly divergent attitudes, beliefs, and values and may frequently engage in conflict interactions. As you can appreciate, families high in conformity are likely to be harmonious with children who are expected to obey their parents, largely without question. Families low in conformity are likely to be less harmonious with children who are given greater freedom to say or do as they wish.

Conversation-orientation refers to the degree to which family members can speak their mind. A family high on conversation orientation encourages members to discuss a variety of issues and the voicing of members' opinions. A family low on conversation orientation discourages discussion and the voicing of opinions.

With these two dimensions in mind, we can identify four types of families:

- **Consensual families:** high in conversation and high in conformity. These families encourage open communication and agreement.

- **Protective families:** high in conformity and low in conversation. These families stress agreement and strive to avoid conflict but with little communication.

- **Pluralistic families:** low in conformity and high in conversation. These family members are encouraged to express different attitudes and points of view and to engage in open communication while being supportive of each other.

Communication Choice Point

Verbal Abuse

On your way to work, you witness a father verbally abusing his three-year-old child. You worry that he might psychologically harm the child, and your first impulse is to speak up and tell this man that verbal abuse can have lasting effects on the child and often leads to physical abuse. At the same time, you don't want to interfere with his right to speak to his child, and you certainly don't want to make him angrier. *What are some things you might say or do in this difficult situation?*

For a brief discussion of how the media *might* influence self-esteem, see "Relationship and Work Esteem" at **tcbdevito.blogspot .com**. Have the media influenced your image of yourself?

● **Laissez-faire families:** low in confirmation and low in conversation. These families avoid interaction and communication, encourage privacy, and a "do what you want" attitude.

These family types are simply descriptions and are not meant to be evaluation; no assumption is made that one family type is better or more productive than another. What works for some people will not work for others.

WORK RELATIONSHIPS

Workplace relationships come in a variety of types. Here we'll consider just four: we'll begin with the more positive relationships (networking, mentoring, and romance) and conclude with the negative bullying.

Networking Relationships

Networking can be viewed as a process of using other people to help you solve your problems, or at least to offer insights that bear on any number of problems or decisions you need to make. The most popular image that probably comes to mind is networking for a possible job. But networking is much broader and would include, for example, how to set up a blog, where to look for low-cost auto insurance, how to find an affordable apartment, or how to politely refuse an invitation to become a friend on Facebook. The great value of networking, of course, is that it provides you with access to a wealth of specialized information. At the same time, it often makes accessing that information a lot easier than if you had to find it all by yourself.

In networking it's often recommended that you try to establish relationships that are mutually beneficial. After all, much as others are useful sources of information for you, you're likely to be a useful source of information for others. If you can provide others with helpful information, it's more likely that they will provide helpful information for you. In this way, a mutually satisfying and productive network is established.

Mentoring Relationships

Mentoring is a partnership in which an experienced individual (the mentor) helps someone who is less experienced (the protégé) learn how to achieve his or her goals (Mullen, 2005; Caproni, 2012). Having a mentor, some organizational experts argue, is crucial for rising in a hierarchy and for developing your skills (Dahle, 2004). An accomplished teacher, for example, might mentor a younger teacher who has newly arrived or who has never taught before (Nelson, Pearson, & Kurylo, 2008). The mentor guides the new person through the organizational maze, teaches the strategies and techniques for success, and otherwise communicates his or her accumulated knowledge and experience to the protégé.

Not surprisingly, mentoring is frequently conducted online. One great advantage of e-mentoring is the flexibility it allows for communication. E-mail messages, for example, can be sent and received at times that are convenient for the individuals involved (Stewart, 2006). Further, because the individuals may be separated geographically, it's possible to have mentor-protégé relationships with people in foreign countries and in widely differing cultures—relationships that would be impossible without online communication. Still another advantage is that persons with disabilities (whether mentor or protégé) who cannot easily travel can still enjoy and profit from e-mentoring relationships (Burgstahler, 2007).

Social networking sites, designed originally as places where people could make new friends and stay in touch with old ones, are increasingly being used for both mentoring and networking. Some sites are "by invitation only" and have been compared to gated communities or exclusive country clubs. These sites seem designed not for friendships but solely for mentoring and networking (MacMillan & Lehman, 2007). For example, Reuters Space is a private online community specifically for hedge fund managers to network, and INmobile is designed for executives in the wireless industry.

Workplace Romance

Opinions vary widely concerning workplace romances. On the positive side, the work environment seems a perfect place to meet a potential romantic partner. After all, by virtue of the fact that you're working in the

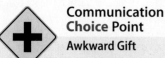

Communication Choice Point

Awkward Gift

A coworker with whom you're becoming friendly gives you a very intimate gift, much too intimate for the relationship as you see it. *What are some things you might say to refuse the gift but not close off the possibility of dating?*

same office, you're probably both interested in the same field, have similar training and ambitions, and spend considerable time together—all factors that foster the development of a successful interpersonal relationship. Another advantage is that office romances can lead to greater work satisfaction. If you're romantically attracted to another worker, it can make going to work, working together, and even working added hours more enjoyable and more satisfying.

Office relationships, however, may cause problems for management when, for example, a promotion is to be made or relocation decisions are necessary. When an office romance goes bad or when it's one-sided, it can be especially difficult. One obvious problem is that it can be stressful for the former partners to see each other regularly and to continue to work together. Other workers may feel they have to take sides, being supportive of one partner and critical of the other, which can cause friction throughout the organization. Another, perhaps more serious, issue is the potential for charges of sexual harassment, especially if the romance was between a supervisor and a worker.

The generally negative attitude of management (as well as explicit policies, rules, and regulations) toward workplace relationships and the problems inherent in dealing with the normal stresses of both work and romance seem to outweigh the positive benefits that may be derived from such relationships. Therefore, workers are generally advised not to romance their colleagues. Friendship seems the much safer course.

Bullying   Bullying, especially prominent in the workplace (but also occurs in close relationships, the playground, or even the family) consists of abusive acts repeatedly committed by one person (or a group) against another. Bullying is behavior that has become a pattern; it's repeated frequently rather than being an isolated instance. On the playground, bullying often involves physical abuse; in the workplace (at least in most civilized countries), bullying is generally verbal. Bullying may take a variety of forms: gossiping about other employees, making them the butt of jokes, treating them as inferior—for example, frequently interrupting them or otherwise not giving their ideas due attention—excluding someone from social functions, verbal insults, name calling, negative facial expressions, sneering, avoiding eye contact, excessive blaming, being supervised (watched, monitored) more closely than others, being unnecessarily criticized, often with shouting and in public. From an ethical point of view, bullying destroys a person's right to personal dignity and a workplace free from intimidation and is therefore unethical. And yet, bullying is not illegal in the United States, unless it involves harassment based on a person's gender or race, for example.

A special type of bullying is cyberbullying, which can take place through any electronic communication system—Facebook, Twitter, e-mail, instant messages, blog posts—and can take the form of sending threatening messages or images, posting negative comments, revealing secrets, or lying about another person. Among the reasons why cyberbullying is so important is that it can occur at any time; the messages, photos, and videos can be distributed quickly and widely; the bully can hide behind false names or anonymity; and attacks—because they occur electronically—are often more cruel than those made in face-to-face attacks (Hinduja & Patchin, 2008).

ONLINE-ONLY RELATIONSHIPS

In addition to the friendships, romantic, family, and workplace relationships—which will probably involve both face-to-face and online experiences—there is another group of what might be called "online-only" relationships. These are the relationships that exist between a Tweeter and a

For another perspective on office romance, see "Romance in the Workplace" at **tcbdevito** **.blogspot.com**. What are your feelings about office romance?

Watch the **Video** "Power Moment" at **MyCommunicationLab**

VIEWPOINTS
Cyberbullying

According to the StopBullying website for the U.S. Department of Health and Human Service, a 2009 survey of 13- to 18-year-olds reported that 15% of respondents said they had been cyberbullyied; in another study of 12- to 17-year-olds, 33% said they were threatened or embarrassed by things said about them online. What has been your experience with cyberbullying? In what ways might it be discouraged?

follower, a blogger and a reader, a friend or contact on Facebook or LinkedIn, for example. The suggestions for more effective relationships are the same as are the suggestions for more effective communication. In all of these relationships, it is dialogue (rather than monologue) that is emphasized. In fact, the defining characteristics of Web 2.0 is to move the online experience from monologue (for example, reading newspapers online) to dialogue (where commenting/reviewing/liking/+1ing) are essential parts of the communication experience.

Tweeting Unlike other social network sites, people can follow you on Twitter whether you like it or not. But, assuming that you want some kind of relationships between yourself and those who follow you, consider these suggestions. In all of these lists of suggestions, the recommendations are generally applicable to all social networks and yet some seem more logically placed with one medium rather than another.

- Leave room for retweets (if you want retweets). Keep your tweet to 120 characters.
- Avoid "fast following" tools. These will likely create problems for you.
- Tweet items of interest to yourself but also keep in mind your readers.
- Treat criticism as the start of a dialogue rather than a personal attack.
- Tweet in moderation. Not everything that happens deserves a tweet.
- Tweet positively; avoid angry tweets.
- Create a complete profile; revealing what you want and keeping hidden what you don't want revealed.
- Limit promotional materials; Twitter is personal.
- Retweet if you wish to be retweeted.

Blogging Although many people view blogs as monologic, they are best viewed as dialogic. Their great value is in creating dialogue and so a blog post, at least for the traditional blog, is ideally one that provides information with a personal slant for a specific audience that creates some measure of discussion. Assuming that this is your aim or close to it, here are a few suggestions for making this a more effective interaction.

- Offer syndication. RSS feeds will greatly help in spreading the word.
- Be both informational and personal; blog posts are more personal in nature than are articles or websites that are more purely informational.
- Be consistent in style and format. It will help brand your blog as unique—not unlike McDonald's; readers will know what to expect.
- Build your blog and your posts around a theme. Posts unrelated to the theme are generally perceived as noise and are likely to lose you readers.
- Reply to comments. Dialogue.
- Track statistics so you can get insight into the posts that are read often and those that aren't.
- Create attractive titles and relevant identifying labels. Make it as easy as possible for others to retrieve your materials.

Social/Workplace Networking Perhaps the social media that comes first to mind is Facebook, by far the largest of the social networking sites. But, Google+ and Myspace serve similar purposes as do numerous others. LinkedIn and Plaxo, on the other hand, serve mainly business purposes—for example, getting a job or promotion, finding likely candidates for a job, networking, or mentoring. Despite these differences, some similar suggestions govern effective relationships and communication in these types of sites.

- Be careful of uploading photos that will reflect on you negatively, especially with alcohol or drugs. Interesting enough, one research student found that 85% of 225 profiles examined (average age 19.9 years) make alcohol references (Egan & Moreno, 2011).

- Be positive about your current position. Complaining about your job online for all to see is likely to make management less positive toward you and also to lead prospective employers to see you as a complainer and someone who would be critical of the new organization as well.

- Avoid revealing any negative work habits or discussing inappropriate workplace behavior—even if (especially if) you think it's funny.

- Use the Friends List or the Google+ Circles to distinguish the people you want to see certain information and those you wouldn't. But, remember, again, that anyone who receives your message can post it to anyone, even those you'd rather not see it.

- Give your social network profile even more attention than you give to dressing up for a long-anticipated face-to-face date. After all, a lot more people are going to see your online profile than the way you dressed for a date.

- Keep your posts (at least on Facebook and Google+) personal and informative. Avoid promoting any commercial enterprise.

- Poke and tag in moderation. Learn first the norms of the group with which you're communicating.

- Avoid asking to be friends with anyone you think may have difficulty with your seeing their more personal side.

Objectives Self-Check
- Can you define *friendship, love, family, workplace,* and *online-only* relationships?
- Can you explain their varied types?

Theories of Interpersonal Communication and Relationships

Several theories offer insight into why and how people develop and dissolve relationships. Here we'll examine three such theories: attraction, relationship rules, and social exchange and equity.

ATTRACTION THEORY

Attraction theory holds that people form relationships on the basis of **attraction.** You are no doubt drawn, or attracted, to some people and not attracted to others. In a similar way, some people are attracted to you and some are not. If you're like most people, you're attracted to others on the basis of five major factors:

- **Physical attractiveness and personality:** It's easily appreciated that people like physically attractive people more than they like physically unattractive people. What isn't so obvious is that we also feel a greater sense of familiarity with more attractive people than with less attractive people; that is, we're more likely to think we've met a person before if that person is attractive (Monin, 2003). Additionally, you probably tend to like people who have a pleasant rather than an unpleasant personality, although people differ on what is an attractive personality to them and what isn't. The fact that different people find different personality characteristics attractive, that there does seem to be someone for everyone, may be a comforting thought.

- **Similarity:** According to the principle of **similarity,** if you could construct your mate, it's likely that your mate would look, act, and think very much like you (Burleson, Samter, & Luccetti, 1992; Burleson, Kunkel, & Birch, 1994). Generally, people like those who are similar to them in nationality, race, abilities, physical characteristics, intelligence, and attitudes (Pornpitakpan, 2003). Sometimes people are attracted to their opposites, in a pattern

For a seldom discussed view on attraction, see "Facial Attraction" at tcbdevito.blogspot.com. Does this all seem logical?

Explore the **Exercise** "Mate Preferences: I Prefer Someone Who . . ." at **MyCommunicationLab**

VIEWPOINTS

Online Relationships

Among the advantages of online relationships is that they reduce the importance of physical characteristics and instead emphasize such factors as rapport, similarity, and self-disclosure and in the process promote relationships that are based on emotional intimacy rather than physical attraction (Cooper & Sportolari, 1997). What do you see as the main advantages of online relationships?

called **complementarity:** For example, a dominant person might be attracted to someone who is more submissive. Generally, however, people prefer those who are similar.

● **Proximity:** If you look around at people you find attractive, you will probably find that they are the people who live or work close to you. People who become friends are the people who have had the greatest opportunity to interact with each other.

● **Reinforcement:** You're attracted to people who give rewards or reinforcements, which can range from a simple compliment to an expensive cruise. You're also attracted to people you reward (Jecker & Landy, 1969; Aronson, Wilson, & Akert, 2013). That is, you come to like people for whom you do favors.

● **Reciprocity of liking:** You tend to be attracted to people you think are attracted to you; you come to like those who you think like you. We initiate potential friendships and romantic relationships with people who we think like us, certainly not with those we think dislike us. There is even evidence to show that people like "likers"—people who like others generally—more than they like people who don't express such liking (Eastwick & Finkel, 2009).

RELATIONSHIP RULES THEORY

You can gain an interesting perspective on interpersonal relationships by looking at them in terms of the rules that govern them (Shimanoff, 1980). The general assumption of **rules theory** is that relationships—friendship, love, family, and work—are held together by adherence to certain rules. When those rules are broken, the relationship may deteriorate and even dissolve.

Relationship rules theory helps to clarify several aspects of relationships. First, these rules help you identify successful versus destructive relationship behavior. By looking at the rules of a relationship, you can better identify the reasons a relationship is in trouble (i.e., what rules were broken) and how it may be repaired (i.e., what rules need to be reinforced and honored). Second, if you know what the rules are, you will be better able to master the social skills involved in developing and maintaining relationships.

Watch the **Video** "Juggling Act" at **MyCommunicationLab**

"Are you growing that mustache to make me break up with you?"

Friendship Rules   According to friendship rules theory, maintaining a friendship depends on your knowing the rules and having the ability to apply the appropriate interpersonal skills that friendships require (Trower, 1981; Blieszner & Adams, 1992). Friendship rules include such behaviors as standing up for your friend in his or her absence, sharing information and feelings about successes, demonstrating emotional support for your friend, trusting and offering to help your friend when in need, and trying to make your friend happy when you're together (Argyle & Henderson, 1984; Argyle, 1986). When these and other rules are followed, the friendship is strong and mutually satisfying. When the rules are broken, the friendship suffers and may die.

Romantic Rules   Romantic relationships may also be viewed from a rules perspective. For example, one research study identified some of the rules that romantic relationships establish and follow (Baxter, 1986). These rules keep the relationship together—or, when broken, lead to deterioration and eventually dissolution. The general

COMMUNICATING ETHICALLY

Relationship Ethics

A starting place for considering the ethical issues and guidelines that operate within a friendship or romantic, family, or workplace relationship can be identified with the acronym ETHICS: empathy (Cheney & Tompkins, 1987), talk (rather than force), honesty (Krebs, 1989), interaction management, confidentiality, and supportiveness (Johannesen, 2001).

- **Empathy:** People in relationships have an ethical obligation to empathize with their relationship partners.
- **Talk:** Decisions in a relationship should be arrived at by talk rather than by force—by persuasion, not coercion.
- **Honesty:** Relationship communication should be honest and truthful.
- **Interaction management:** Relationship communication should be satisfying and comfortable and is the responsibility of all individuals.
- **Confidentiality:** People have a right to expect that what they say in close relationships will not be revealed to others.
- **Supportiveness:** A supportive and cooperative climate should characterize the interpersonal interactions of people in relationships.

Ethical Choice Point

A neighbor, with whom you're generally friendly, repeatedly wants you to listen to everything she did during the day—a kind of Twitter monologue. You just don't want to do this anymore. What is your ethical obligation in this case—to your neighbor as well as to yourself?

assumption here is that if people are in a close romantic relationship then they should follow these rules:

- acknowledge each other's individual identities and lives beyond the relationship.
- express similar attitudes, beliefs, values, and interests.
- enhance each other's self-worth and self-esteem.
- be open, genuine, and authentic with each other.
- remain loyal and faithful to each other.
- have substantial shared time together.
- reap rewards commensurate with their investments relative to the other party.
- experience a mysterious and inexplicable "magic" in each other's presence.

Communication Choice Point

Virtual Infidelity
Although in a monogamous relationship for the past 15 years, you have established romantic relationships online and you suspect your partner has as well. Now, it's causing you anxiety and you want to come clean but not give up these online affairs. *In your ideal world, what are some of the rules you would like to see you and your partner establish for online relationships?*

Watch the Video
"Please Don't Lie to Me" at
MyCommunicationLab

Family Rules   Family communication research also points to the importance of rules in defining and maintaining the family (Galvin, Bylund, & Brommel, 2007). Like the rules of friends and lovers, family rules tell you which behaviors will be rewarded (and therefore what you should do) and which will be punished (what you should not do). Rules also provide a kind of structure that defines the family as a cohesive unit and that distinguishes it from other similar families. Family rules encompass three main interpersonal communication issues (Satir, 1983):

- What can you talk about? Can you talk about the family finances? Grandpa's drinking? Your sister's lifestyle?
- How can you talk about something? Can you joke about your brother's disability? Can you address directly questions of family history and family skeletons?
- To whom can you talk? Can you talk openly to extended family members such as cousins and aunts and uncles? Can you talk to close neighbors about family health issues?

Workplace Rules   Rules also govern your workplace relationships. These rules are usually a part of the corporate culture that an employee would learn from observing other employees (especially those who move up the hierarchy) as well as from official memos on dress, sexual

For a discussion of politeness as a relationship theory, see "Politeness as an Interpersonal Relationship Theory" at tcbdevito.blogspot .com. What role does politeness play in your own relationships?

harassment, and the like. Of course, each organization will have different rules, so it's important to see what rules are operating in any given situation. These are among the rules that you might find:

- Work very hard.
- Be cooperative in teams; the good of the company comes first.
- Don't reveal company policies and plans to workers at competing firms.
- Don't form romantic relationships with other workers.
- Avoid even the hint of sexual harassment.

SOCIAL EXCHANGE AND EQUITY THEORY

Social exchange theory claims that you develop relationships that will enable you to maximize your profits (Thibaut & Kelley, 1986; Stafford, 2008)—a theory based on an economic model of profits and losses. And, although the theory was formulated before social media, you'll see that it applies equally well to Facebook and Google+ relationships, for example. The theory begins with a simple equation: Profits = Rewards – Costs. Rewards are anything that you would incur costs to obtain. Research has identified six types of rewards in a relationship: money, status, love, information, goods, and services (Baron, Branscombe, & Byrne, 2009). For example, to get the reward of money, you might have to work rather than play. To earn (the status of) an A in an interpersonal communication course, you might have to write a term paper or study more than you want to.

Costs are things that you normally try to avoid, that you consider unpleasant or difficult. Examples might include working overtime, washing dishes and ironing clothes, watching your partner's favorite television show that you find boring, or doing favors for those you dislike.

Equity theory uses the ideas of social exchange but goes a step farther and claims that you develop and maintain relationships in which the ratio of your rewards relative to your costs is approximately equal to your partner's (Walster, Walster, & Berscheid, 1978; Messick & Cook, 1983; Stafford, 2008). For example, if you and a friend start a business and you put up two-thirds of the money and your friend puts up one-third, equity would demand that you get two-thirds of the profits and your friend get one-third. An equitable relationship, then, is simply one in which each party derives rewards that are proportional to their costs. If you contribute more to the relationship than your partner, then equity requires that you should get greater rewards. If you both work equally hard, then equity demands that you

SKILL DEVELOPMENT EXPERIENCE

Analyzing Interpersonal Relationships in the Media

Becoming mindful of what the media teach and how they do it will help you to avoid internalizing relationship values before examining them critically.

Interpersonal relationships, as they're expressed in the popular media, provide an interesting perspective on the ways in which our culture views relationships and on the principles of relationship communication it teaches. Think of all the media you're exposed to throughout an average day and consider the messages you are receiving about relationships. Look at the media in any form—television (in dramas, sitcoms, commercials, talk shows, reality shows), newspapers, magazines, blogs, websites, music, and film—and try to identify the values and attitudes they communicate about interpersonal relationships. Think about these examples:

- Do the popular media approve of certain types of relationships and not others?
- How do the media "define" friendship, love, and family?
- What do the media say about the rules for relationships?
- How do the media deal with the dark side of interpersonal relationships, such as relationship violence and spousal abuse?

should get approximately equal rewards. You also see the demand for equity in on-line relationships; if you indicate "like" or "+1" to a friend's photos or posts, you expect reciprocity; you expect equity. In fact social media have rather strict, though unwritten, equity expectations.

Equity theory puts into clear focus the sources of relational dissatisfaction seen every day. For example, in a relationship both partners may have full-time jobs, but one partner may also be expected to do the major share of the household chores. Thus, although both may be deriving equal rewards—they have equally good cars, they live in the same three-bedroom house, and so on—one partner is paying more of the costs. According to equity theory, this partner will be dissatisfied.

Equity theory claims that you will develop, maintain, and be satisfied with relationships that are equitable. You will not develop, will be dissatisfied with, and will eventually terminate relationships that are inequitable. The greater the inequity, the greater the dissatisfaction and the greater the likelihood that the relationship will end.

Communication Choice Point

Negotiating Equity
You feel your romantic relationship of the last three months has become inequitable—you seem to do more of the work but get few benefits, while your partner does less work but gets more benefits. You want to correct this imbalance before the relationship goes any further. *What are some options you have for negotiating greater equity? What are some of the things you might say?*

Objectives Self-Check
- Can you explain the theories of interpersonal relationships (attraction, rules, and social exchange and equity)?
- Can you apply the insights from these theories to your own relationships—to better understand them and to improve them?

 Messages in the Media   *Wrap Up*

Television dramas and sitcoms are perfect laboratories for studying communication patterns in relationships of all kinds. Watching these shows with a view to the ways in which the characters define themselves and communicate with each other will provide a useful follow-up to this chapter.

Summary of Concepts and Skills

 Study and **Review** materials for this chapter are at **MyCommunicationLab**

Listen to the **Audio Chapter Summary** at **MyCommunicationLab**

This chapter explored interpersonal relationships—their stages and types; the reasons they are formed; and the influence of culture, technology, and work on relationships.

Advantages and Disadvantages of Interpersonal Relationships

1. Among the advantages are that relationships lessen loneliness and raise self-esteem.

2. Among the disadvantages are that relationships put pressure on you to expose weakness and increase your obligations.

The Stages of Interpersonal Relationships

3. Relationships may be viewed in terms of six stages: contact, involvement, intimacy, deterioration, repair, and dissolution. Each of these stages can be further broken down into an early and a late phase.

4. Among the major causes of relationship deterioration are a lessening of the reasons for establishing the relationship, changes in the people involved, sexual difficulties, and work and financial problems.

Interpersonal Relationship Types

5. Friendships may be classified as those of reciprocity, receptivity, and association.

6. Six primary love styles have been identified: eros, ludus, storge, pragma, mania, and agape.

7. Primary relationships may be classified into traditionals, independents, and separates; families as consensual, protective, pluralistic, and laissez-faire.

8. Work relationships can be productive (networking and mentoring), destructive (bullying), and both positive and negative (office romance).

9. Online-only relationships have their own sets of rules to promote more effective interaction.

Theories of Interpersonal Communication and Relationships

10. Attraction depends on such factors as physical and personality attractiveness, similarity (especially attitudinal), reinforcement, proximity, and reciprocity of liking.

11. The relationship rules theory views relationships as held together through adherence to an agreed on set of rules.

12. Social exchange theory holds that you develop relationships that yield the greatest profits. You seek relationships in which the rewards exceed the costs and are likely to dissolve relationships when the costs exceed the rewards.

13. Equity theory claims that you develop and maintain relationships in which the rewards are distributed in proportion to costs. When your share of the rewards is less than would be demanded by equity, you are likely to experience dissatisfaction and exit the relationship.

Throughout this discussion of interpersonal relationships, a variety of relationship skills were discussed. Place a check mark next to those skills that you feel you want to work on most.

_____ 1. I adjust my communication patterns on the basis of the relationship's intimacy.

_____ 2. I can identify changes in communication patterns that may signal deterioration.

_____ 3. I can use the accepted repair strategies to heal an ailing relationship: for example, reversing negative communication patterns, using cherishing behaviors, and adopting a positive action program.

_____ 4. I can deal with relationship dissolution and apply such skills as breaking the loneliness-depression cycle, bolstering self-esteem, and seeking support.

_____ 5. I understand the different types of friendships and can identify the goals that each type serves.

_____ 6. I understand the different types of love and can appreciate the varied ways in which people can love.

_____ 7. I understand the varied types of primary relationships and families and can see the similarities and differences among them.

_____ 8. I can communicate effectively in the workplace.

_____ 9. I follow the rules for effective communication in online communication.

_____ 10. I can effectively manage physical proximity, reinforcement, and emphasizing similarities as ways to increase interpersonal attractiveness.

_____ 11. I can apply the rules of friendship, romantic relationships, family relationships, and work relationships as appropriate.

_____ 12. I can identify, and to some extent control, the rewards and costs of my relationships.

_____ 13. I can appreciate the other person's perception of relationship equity and can modify my own behavior to make the relationship more productive and satisfying.

_____ 14. I understand the differences between face-to-face and online relationships and can modify my behavior accordingly.

_____ 15. I take into consideration the advantages and disadvantages of workplace romantic relationships.

 Key Word Quiz

The Language of Interpersonal Communication, Conversation, and Relationships

Match the terms about interpersonal communication/relationships with their definitions. Record the number of the definition next to the appropriate term.

_____ a. cherishing behaviors (142)

_____ b. deterioration (141)

_____ c. reciprocity (143)

_____ d. family types (145)

_____ e. agapic love (144)

_____ f. social exchange theory (152)

_____ g. equity theory (152)

_____ h. online-only relationships (147)

_____ i. storge love (144)

_____ j. involvement (144)

1. A friendship of loyalty and mutual affection.

2. An important stage between contact and intimacy.

3. A theory claiming that you experience relational satisfaction when there is an equal distribution of

rewards and costs between the two persons in the relationship.

4. Connections between, say, tweeter and Twitter follower.

5. A love that is peaceful and tranquil.

6. Small gestures people enjoy receiving.

7. A love that is compassionate and selfless.

8. The stage at which the bonds between people are weakened.

9. Characterized by three types: traditional, independents, and separates.

10. A theory based on the expectation of fairness.

These ten terms and additional terms used in this chapter can be found in the glossary.

Answers: a. 6 b. 8 c. 1 d. 9 e. 7 f. 10 g. 3 h. 4 i. 5 j. 2

 Study and **Review** the **Flashcards** at **MyCommunicationLab**

MyCommunicationLab

Throughout this chapter, there are icons in the margin that highlight media content for selected topics. Go to **MyCommunicationLab** for additional materials on interpersonal relationships. Here you'll find flashcards to help you learn the jargon of communication, videos that illustrate a variety of concepts, additional exercises, and discussions to help you continue your study of interpersonal relationships.

8

Managing Interpersonal Conflict

Objectives

 Listen to the **Audio Chapter** at **MyCommunicationLab**

After reading this chapter, you should be able to:

❶ Define *interpersonal conflict* and the major conflict issues, and explain the myths about interpersonal conflict.

❷ Explain the three principles of conflict and give examples of how conflict can be negative or positive, how it is influenced by culture and gender, and what the consequences of your chosen conflict style are.

❸ Describe and distinguish between the conflict management strategies of avoiding and fighting actively, force and talk, defensiveness and supportiveness, face-attacking and face-enhancing, silences and facilitating open expression, gunnysacking and present focus, and verbal aggressiveness and argumentativeness; and explain how to use these strategies constructively in your own interpersonal conflicts.

Messages in the Media

Most sporting events are, in essence, conflict episodes—zero sum games in which one team or one player must win and one must lose. Interpersonal conflict, in contrast, is not a zero sum game—both individuals can win, both can lose, or one can win and one can lose. The task of achieving a situation in which both can win is the subject of this chapter.

Of all your interpersonal interactions, those involving conflict are among your most important. Interpersonal conflict often creates ill will, anxiety, and problems for relationships. But as you'll soon see, conflict can also create opportunities for improving and strengthening relationships.

Preliminaries to Interpersonal Conflict

Listen to the **audio clip** "Managing Conflict" at **MyCommunicationLab**

Before considering the stages and strategies of conflict management, it is necessary to define exactly what is meant by *interpersonal conflict,* the issues around which interpersonal conflict often centers, and some of the myths surrounding conflict.

DEFINITION OF INTERPERSONAL CONFLICT

You want to go to the movies with your partner. Your partner wants to stay home. Your insisting on going to the movies interferes with your partner's staying home, and your partner's determination to stay home interferes with your going to the movies. You can't both achieve your goals, so there will be conflict.

As this example illustrates, **interpersonal conflict** is disagreement between or among connected individuals (e.g., close friends, lovers, family members) who perceive their goals as incompatible (Hocker & Wilmot, 2007; Folger, Poole, & Stutman, 2013; Cahn & Abigail, 2007). More specifically, conflict occurs when people:

- **are interdependent** (they're connected in some significant way); what one person does has an impact or an effect on the other person.

- **are mutually aware that their goals are incompatible;** if one person's goal is achieved, then the other person's goal cannot be achieved. For example, if one person wants to buy a new car and the other person wants to pay down the mortgage, and there is not enough money to do both, there is conflict.

- **perceive each other as interfering** with the attainment of their own goals. For example, you may want to study but your roommate may want to party; the attainment of either goal would interfere with the attainment of the other goal.

An important implication of this concept of interdependency is that, the greater the interdependency, the greater (1) the number of issues around which conflict can center and (2) the impact of the conflict and the conflict management interaction on the individuals and on the relationship (see Figure 8.1). Looked at in this way, it's easy to appreciate the importance to your relationships of understanding interpersonal conflict and learning strategies for effective conflict management.

INTERPERSONAL CONFLICT ISSUES

Interpersonal conflicts cover a wide range of issues and have been categorized differently by different researchers. One system, for example, classifies conflicts into four categories (Canary, 2003): (1) goals to be pursued (e.g., disagreement between parent and child on what college to attend or what romantic partner to get involved with); (2) the allocation of resources, such as money or time (e.g., partners' differing on how to spend their money); (3) decisions to be made (e.g., whether to save or splurge the recent bonus); and (4) behaviors that are considered appropriate or desirable by one person but inappropriate

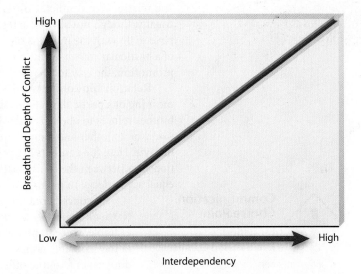

FIGURE 8.1

Conflict and Interdependency

This figure illustrates that, as interdependency increases, so do the potential for and the importance of conflict. Does this diagram effectively depict the likelihood and the significance of your own interpersonal conflicts?

VIEWPOINTS

Conflict Issues

What issues do television characters fight about? Are the issues fought over in situation comedies different from those in real life?

Explore the **Concept** "Conflict" at **MyCommunicationLab**

or undesirable by the other (e.g., disagreement over one person's flirting or drinking or not working as hard on the relationship).

Another approach, based on surveys of gay, lesbian, and heterosexual couples, found six major issues that virtually all couples share (Kurdek, 1994). These issues are arranged here in order, with the first being the most commonly cited. As you read this list, ask yourself how many of these issues you argue about.

- Intimacy issues, such as affection and sex
- Power issues, where one person makes excessive demands on the other or makes decisions unilaterally concerning mutual friends or how you'll spend your leisure time
- Personal flaws involving, for example, drinking or smoking, personal grooming, and driving style
- Personal distance issues, such as frequent absence and heavy school or job commitments
- Social issues, such as politics and social policies, parents, and personal values
- Distrust involving, for example, previous lovers and lying

In the workplace, conflicts are especially important because of their potential negative effects, such as personnel leaving the job (necessitating new recruitment and retraining), low morale, and a lessening desire to perform at top efficiency. Workplace conflicts, according to one study (Psychometrics, 2010), center on such issues as these :

- Personality differences and resulting clashes, 86%
- Ineffective leadership, 73%
- Lack of openness, 67%
- Physical and emotional stress, 64%
- Differences in values and resulting clashes, 59%

Using concepts developed in Chapter 1, you can distinguish between content conflict and relationship conflict. **Content conflict** centers on objects, events, and persons that are usually, though not always, external to the parties involved in the conflict. Content conflicts have to do with the millions of issues that people argue and fight about every day: the merit of a particular movie, what to watch on television, the fairness of the last examination or job promotion, the way to spend accumulated savings.

Relationship conflicts are equally numerous and are those that center on the nature and meaning of a particular relationship. Examples include clashes that arise when a younger brother refuses to obey his older brother, two partners both want their say in making vacation plans, or a mother and daughter each want to have the final word concerning the daughter's lifestyle. Here the conflicts are concerned not so much with external objects as with the relationships between the individuals—with issues such as who is in charge, whether there is equal say in decision making, and who has the right to set down rules of behavior.

Of course, content and relationship dimensions are always easier to separate in a textbook than they are in real life, where many conflicts contain elements of both. For example, you can probably imagine both content and relationship dimensions in each of the "content" issues mentioned. Yet certain issues seem oriented more toward one dimension than the other. For example, disagreements on political and social issues are largely content focused, whereas intimacy and power issues are largely relational.

MYTHS ABOUT INTERPERSONAL CONFLICT

Many people have problems dealing with conflict because they hold false assumptions about what conflict is and what it means. Think about your own assumptions

Communication Choice Point

Escalating to Relationship Conflict

Your own interpersonal conflicts often start out as content conflicts but quickly degenerate into relationship conflicts, and that's when things get ugly. *What types of things might you say or do to keep conflicts and their resolution focused on content and not on the relationship?*

about interpersonal and small group conflict, which were probably shaped by the communications you witnessed in your family and in your social interactions. For example, do you think the following statements are true or false?

- Conflict is best avoided. Time will solve the problem; it will all blow over.
- If two people experience relationship conflict, it means their relationship is in trouble.
- Conflict damages an interpersonal relationship.
- Conflict is destructive because it reveals our negative selves—our pettiness, our need to be in control, our unreasonable expectations.
- In any conflict, there has to be a winner and a loser. Because goals are incompatible, someone has to win and someone has to lose.
- These are myths and, as we'll see in this chapter, they can interfere with your ability to deal with conflict effectively.

"I can't remember what we're arguing about, either. Let's keep yelling, and maybe it will come back to us."

© David Sipress/Condé Nast Publications/www.cartoonbank.com.

Objectives Self-Check
- Can you define *interpersonal conflict*?
- Can you identify the major conflict issues and the popular myths about conflict?

Principles of Interpersonal Conflict

You can increase your understanding of interpersonal conflict by looking at some general principles: (1) conflict can be positive or negative, (2) conflict is influenced by culture and gender, and (3) conflict styles have consequences.

CONFLICT CAN BE NEGATIVE OR POSITIVE

Although interpersonal conflict is always stressful, it's important to recognize that it has both negative and positive aspects.

Negative Aspects   Conflict often leads to increased negative regard for the opponent. One reason for this is that many conflicts involve unfair fighting methods (which we'll examine shortly) and are focused largely on hurting the other person. When one person hurts the other, increased negative feelings are inevitable; even the strongest relationship has limits.

At times, conflict may lead you to close yourself off from the other person. When you hide your true self from an intimate, you prevent meaningful communication from taking place. Because the need for intimacy is so strong, one or both parties may then seek intimacy elsewhere. This often leads to further conflict, mutual hurt, and resentment—qualities that add heavily to the costs carried by the relationship. Meanwhile, rewards may become difficult to exchange. In this situation, the overall costs increase and the rewards decrease, which often leads to relationship deterioration and eventual dissolution.

Positive Aspects   The major value of interpersonal conflict is that it forces you to examine a problem and work toward a potential solution. If both you and your opponent use productive conflict strategies (which will be described in this chapter), the relationship may well emerge from the encounter stronger, healthier, and more satisfying than before. And you may emerge stronger, more confident, and better able to stand up for yourself (Bedford, 1996).

See "Relationships and Relationship Conflict" at **tcbdevito.blogspot .com** for a discussion of the relationship between health and effective conflict management. What other advantages do you see for effective conflict management?

Through conflict and its resolution, you also can stop resentment from increasing and let your needs be known. For example, suppose your partner needs lots of attention after coming home from work but you need to review and get closure on the day's work. If you both can appreciate the legitimacy of these needs, then you can find solutions. Perhaps you can make your important phone call after your partner's attention needs are met, or perhaps your partner can delay the need for attention until you get closure about work. Or perhaps together you can find a way for your closure needs and your partner's attention needs to be met simultaneously through, for example, talking while cuddling at the end of the day. This situation would be considered a *win–win*.

Consider, too, that when you try to resolve conflict within an interpersonal relationship, you're saying in effect that the relationship is worth the effort. Usually, confronting a conflict indicates commitment and a desire to preserve the relationship.

CONFLICT IS INFLUENCED BY CULTURE AND GENDER

As in other areas of interpersonal communication, it helps to consider conflict in light of the influences of culture and gender. Both exert powerful influences on how people view and resolve conflicts.

Conflict and Culture Culture influences both the issues that people fight about and the ways of dealing with conflict that people consider appropriate and inappropriate. Cohabiting teens, for example, are more likely to experience conflict with their parents about their living style if they live in the United States than if they live in Sweden, where cohabitation is more accepted and more prevalent. Similarly, male infidelity is more likely to cause conflict between U.S. spouses than in cultures in which such behavior is more common. Students from the United States are more likely to engage in conflict with another U.S. student than with someone from another culture; Chinese students, on the other hand, are more likely to engage in a conflict with a non-Chinese student than with another Chinese (Leung, 1988).

The types of interpersonal conflicts that tend to arise depend on the cultural orientation of the individuals involved. For example, in **collectivist cultures,** (such as those of Ecuador, Indonesia, and Korea), conflicts most often involve violations of larger group norms and values, such as failing in your role, for example, as family provider or overstepping your social status by publicly disagreeing with a superior. Conversely, in **individualistic cultures** (such as those of the United States, Canada, and Western Europe), conflicts are more likely to occur when people violate expected norms—for example, not defending a position in the face of disagreement (Ting-Toomey, 1985).

VIEWPOINTS

Conflict and Culture

What does your own culture teach about conflict and its management? For example: What strategies does it prohibit? Are some strategies prohibited in conflicts with certain people (say, your parents) but not in conflicts with others (say, your friends)? Does your culture prescribe certain ways of dealing with conflict? Does it have different expectations for men and for women? Do these teachings influence your actual conflict behaviors?

Conflict and Gender Do men and women engage in interpersonal conflict differently? One of the few stereotypes that are supported by research is that of the withdrawing and sometimes aggressive male. Men are more apt to withdraw from a conflict situation than are women. It has been argued that this may happen because men become more psychologically and physiologically aroused during conflict (and retain this heightened level of arousal much longer than do women) and so may try to distance themselves and withdraw from the conflict to prevent further arousal. Another explanation for the male tendency to withdraw is that the culture has taught men to avoid conflict. Still another explanation is that withdrawal is an expression of power (Gottman & Carrere, 1994; Canary, Cupach, & Messman, 1995; Goleman, 1995; Noller, 1993).

Women, on the other hand, want to get closer to the conflict; they want to talk about it and resolve it. Even adolescents reveal these differences; in a study of boys and girls aged 11 to 17, boys withdrew more than girls but were more aggressive when they didn't withdraw

(Lindeman, Harakka, & Keltikangas-Jarvinen, 1997). Similarly, a study of offensive language found that girls were more easily offended by language than boys, but boys were more apt to fight when they were offended by the words used (Heasley, Babbitt, & Burbach, 1995a, 1995b). Another study showed that young girls used more prosocial strategies (i.e., behaviors designed to help others rather than oneself) than boys (Rose & Asher, 1999).

It should be mentioned that some research fails to support these gender differences in conflict style—the differences that cartoons, situation comedies, and films portray so readily and so clearly. For example, several studies dealing with both college students and men and women in business found no significant differences in the ways men and women engage in conflict (Wilkins & Andersen, 1991; Canary & Hause, 1993; Gottman & Levenson, 1999).

CONFLICT STYLES HAVE CONSEQUENCES

Watch the **Video** "Time Troubles" at **MyCommunicationLab**

The way in which you engage in conflict has consequences for who wins and who loses, if and when the conflict is resolved, and ultimately for the relationship as a whole. As you read through these styles (Blake & Mouton, 1984), try to identify your own conflict style as well as the styles of those with whom you have close relationships. A summary of these five styles appears in Table 8.1.

Competing: I Win, You Lose   The competitive style involves great concern for your own needs and desires and little for those of others. As long as your needs are met, you think the conflict has been dealt with successfully. In conflict motivated by competitiveness, you'd be likely to be verbally aggressive and to blame the other person.

This style represents an "I win, you lose" philosophy. This is the conflict style of a person who simply imposes his or her will on the other: "I make the money, and we'll vacation at the beach or not at all." But this philosophy often leads to resentment on the part of the person who loses, which can cause additional conflicts. Further, the fact that you win and the other person loses probably means that the conflict hasn't really been resolved but has only concluded (for now).

Avoiding: I Lose, You Lose   Conflict avoiders are relatively unconcerned with their own or with their opponents' needs or desires. They avoid any real communication about the problem, change topics when the problem is brought up, and generally withdraw both psychologically and physically.

TABLE 8.1 Five Conflict Styles and Their Consequences

Here are the five conflict styles and their likely consequences or outcomes (Blake & Mouton (1984). Do you have a general conflict style or does your conflict style vary with your relationship to the other person? For example, are you likely to engage in conflict differently depending on the other person, whether friend, romantic partner, work colleague, and so on?

	You	Other
Competing: great concern for your needs; little concern for other's	Win ☺	Lose ☺
Avoiding: little concern for your own or other's needs	Lose ☺	Lose ☺
Compromising: some concern for your own and other's needs	Win and lose ☺ ☺	Win and lose ☺ ☺
Accommodating: great concern for other's needs; little concern for your own	Lose ☺	Win ☺
Collaborating: great concern for your own and other's needs	Win ☺	Win ☺

As you can appreciate, the avoiding style does little to resolve any conflicts and may be viewed as an "I lose, you lose" philosophy. If a couple can't agree about where to spend their vacation, but each person refuses to negotiate a resolution to the disagreement, the pair may not take any vacation at all; both sides lose. Interpersonal problems rarely go away of their own accord; rather, if they exist, they need to be faced and dealt with effectively. Avoidance merely allows the conflict to fester and probably grow, only to resurface in another guise.

Compromising: I Win and Lose, You Win and Lose

Compromise is the kind of strategy you might refer to as "meeting each other halfway," "horse trading," or "give and take." There's some concern for your own needs and some concern for the other's needs. This strategy is likely to result in maintaining peace, but there will be a residue of dissatisfaction over the inevitable losses that each side has to endure.

Compromise represents an "I win and lose, you win and lose" philosophy. So, if you and your partner can't vacation at both the beach and the mountains, then you might settle for weekend trips or use the money to have a hot tub installed instead. These may not be your first choices, but they're not bad and may satisfy (to some degree at least) each of your vacation wants.

Accommodating: I Lose, You Win

When **accommodation** takes place, you sacrifice your own needs for the needs of the other person(s). Your primary goal is to maintain harmony and peace in the relationship or group. This style may help maintain peace and may satisfy the opposition, but it does little to meet your own needs, which are unlikely to go away.

Accommodation represents an "I lose, you win" philosophy. If your partner wants to vacation in the mountains and you want to vacation at the beach, and you, instead of negotiating an agreement acceptable to both, give in and accommodate, then you lose and your partner wins. Although this style may make your partner happy (at least on this occasion), it's not likely to provide a lasting resolution to an interpersonal conflict. You'll eventually sense unfairness and inequality and may easily come to resent your partner, and perhaps even yourself.

Collaborating: I Win, You Win

In **collaboration** you address both your own and the other person's needs. This style, often considered the ideal, takes time and a willingness to communicate—especially to listen to the perspectives and needs of the other person.

Collaboration enables each person's needs to be met, an "I win, you win" situation. For example, you might both agree to split the vacation—one week in the mountains and one week at the beach. Or you might agree to spend this year's vacation at the beach and next year's in the mountains. This is obviously the style that, in an ideal world, most people would choose for interpersonal conflict.

SKILL DEVELOPMENT EXPERIENCE

Generating Win–Win Solutions

For any one of the situations listed, (a) generate as many win-lose solutions as you can—solutions in which one person wins and the other loses; (b) generate as many possible win-win solutions as you feel the individuals involved in the conflict could reasonably accept; and (c) explain in one sentence the difference between win-lose and win-win solutions

Win-win solutions exist for most interpersonal conflict situations if the people involved are willing to put in a little effort to find them.

1. Jessie and Johnnie have decided to get a pet. Jessie wants a cat; Johnnie wants a dog.
2. Casey, who has been in a 12-year relationship with Devon, recently received a $10,000 bonus and has already used the whole amount for a down payment on a new car. Devon was expecting to share the bonus.
3. Pat smokes and stinks up the apartment. Chris hates this, and they argue about it almost daily.

Objectives Self-Check
● Can you explain and give examples of how conflict can be negative or positive?
● Can you explain how conflict and conflict management may be influenced by culture and gender?
● Can you explain the varied conflict styles (competing, avoiding, compromising, accommodating, and collaborating)?

Explore the **Exercise**
"Analyzing a Conflict Episode"
at **MyCommunicationLab**

Conflict Management Strategies

When managing conflict, you can choose from a variety of productive or unproductive strategies, which we'll investigate here. Realize that the strategies you choose will be influenced by numerous factors. Understanding these factors may help you select more appropriate and more effective conflict strategies (Koerner & Fitzpatrick, 2002).

● **The goals (short-term and long-term) you wish to achieve.** If you only want to salvage today's date, you may want to simply "give in" and ignore the difficulty. If you want to build a long-term relationship, on the other hand, you may want to fully analyze the cause of the problem and look for strategies that will enable both parties to win.

● **Your emotional state.** You're unlikely to select the same strategies when you're sad as when you're angry. You will tend to use different strategies if you're seeking to apologize than if you're looking for revenge.

● **Your cognitive assessment of the situation.** For example, your attitudes and beliefs about what is fair and equitable will influence your readiness to acknowledge the fairness in the other person's position. Your own assessment of who (if anyone) is the cause of the problem will also influence your conflict style. You may also assess the likely effects of various possible strategies. For example, do you risk alienating your teenager if you use force?

● **Your personality and communication competence.** For example, if you're shy and unassertive, you may tend to avoid conflict rather than fight actively. If you're extroverted and have a strong desire to state your position, then you may be more likely to fight actively and to argue forcefully.

● **Your family history.** If, for example, your parents argued aggressively about religious differences, you might tend to be aggressive when your partner expresses different religious beliefs. If you haven't *un*learned family conflict patterns, you're likely to repeat them.

Before examining these various strategies, take the self-test on conflict management strategies included here, and examine your own patterns of conflict management.

COMMUNICATING ETHICALLY

Ethical Listening

Because communication strategies also have an ethical dimension, it's important to look at the ethical implications of conflict management strategies. Here are a few questions to consider as you reflect on the conflict strategies discussed in this chapter:

● Does conflict avoidance have an ethical dimension? For example, is it unethical for one relationship partner to refuse to discuss disagreements or to walk out of an argument?

● Can the use of physical force to influence another person ever be ethical? Can you identify a situation in which it would be appropriate for someone with greater physical strength to overpower another person to compel that person to accept his or her point of view?

● Are face-attacking strategies inherently unethical, or might it be appropriate to use them in certain situations? Can you identify such situations?

● Is verbal aggressiveness necessarily unethical?

Ethical Choice Point

Mary spent the night gambling (and losing a considerable amount of money), but she knows that revealing this will cause conflict and hurt her partner. Would it be ethical for Mary to say she had to work late to avoid the conflict and hurt?

Take a look at "Conflict Management" at **tcbdevito.blogspot.com** for some additional suggestions. What management strategies do you find especially effective?

TEST YOURSELF

Conflict Management Strategies

The following statements refer to ways in which people engage in interpersonal conflict.

Respond to each statement with **True** if this is a generally accurate description of your interpersonal conflict behavior and **False** if the statement is a generally inaccurate description of your behavior.

_____ **1** I strive to seek solutions that will benefit both of us.

_____ **2** I look for solutions that will give me what I want.

_____ **3** I confront conflict situations as they arrive.

_____ **4** I avoid conflict situations as best I can.

_____ **5** My messages are basically descriptive of the events leading up to the conflict.

_____ **6** My messages are often judgmental.

_____ **7** I take into consideration the face needs of the other person.

_____ **8** I advance the strongest arguments I can find even if these attack the other person.

_____ **9** I center my arguments on issues rather than on personalities.

_____ **10** I use messages that may attack a person's self-image if this will help me win the argument.

HOW DID YOU DO? This test on conflict management strategies was designed to make you sensitive to some of the conflict strategies discussed in this section of the chapter. It is not intended to give you a specific score. Generally, however, you'd be following the general principles of effective interpersonal conflict management if you answered True to the odd-numbered statements (1, 3, 5, 7, and 9) and False to the even-numbered statements (2, 4, 6, 8, and 10).

WHAT WILL YOU DO? As you think about your responses and read the text discussion, ask yourself what you can do to improve your own conflict management skills.

AVOIDANCE AND FIGHTING ACTIVELY

Conflict **avoidance** may involve actual physical flight. You may leave the scene of the conflict (e.g., walk out of the apartment or go to another part of the office), fall asleep, or blast the stereo to drown out all conversation. Avoidance also may take the form of emotional or intellectual avoidance, in which you may leave the conflict psychologically by not dealing with any of the arguments or problems raised.

Sometimes avoidance is a response to demands—a conflict pattern known as *demand-withdrawal*. Here one person makes demands (e.g., *You* will *go out again tonight*) and the other person, unwilling to accede to the demands, withdraws from the interaction (Canary, Cupach, & Messman, 1995; Sagrestano, Heavey, & Christensen, 2006; Guerrero, Andersen, Afifi, 2007). This pattern is obviously unproductive, but it can be easily broken by either individual—either by not making demands or by not withdrawing and instead participating actively in the conflict management.

Nonnegotiation is a special type of avoidance. Here you refuse to discuss the conflict or to listen to the other person's argument. At times nonnegotiation takes the form of hammering away at your own point of view until the other person gives in—a technique known as "steamrolling."

Instead of avoiding the issues, take an active role in your interpersonal conflicts:

- **Involve yourself on both sides of the communication exchange.** Be an active participant; voice your own feelings and listen carefully to your opponent's feelings. This is not to say that periodic moratoriums are not helpful; sometimes they are. But in general, be willing to communicate.

- **Take ownership of your thoughts and feelings.** When you disagree with your partner or find fault with her or his behavior, take responsibility for these feelings. Say, for example, "I disagree with . . . " or "I don't like it when you. . . . " Avoid statements that deny your responsibility: "Everybody thinks you're wrong about . . . " or "Chris thinks you shouldn't. . . . "

- **Focus on the present.** Concentrate your attention on the here and now, rather than on issues that occurred two months ago. Similarly, focus your conflict on the person with whom you're fighting, not on the person's parents, child, or friends.

- **Listen carefully.** Act and think as a listener. Turn off the television, stereo, or computer; face the other person. Devote your total attention to the other person. Make sure you understand what the person is saying and feeling. Use perception checking (Chapter 2) and active listening techniques (Chapter 3). And, get ready to listen to the other person's responses to your statements.

Communication Choice Point

Avoiding Conflict
Your work team members all seem to have the same conflict style: avoidance. When there is disagreement, they refuse to argue for one alternative or the other or even to participate in the discussion. You need spirited discussion and honest debate if your team is going to come up with appropriate solutions. *What options do you have for dealing with this problem? What would you say?*

FORCE AND TALK

When confronted with conflict, many people prefer to force their position on the other person, not to deal with the issues. **Force** is an unproductive conflict strategy that may be emotional or physical. In either case, however, the issues are avoided and the "winner" is the combatant who exerts the most force. This is the technique of warring nations, quarreling children, and even some normally sensible and mature adults.

In one study more than 50 percent of both single people and married couples reported that they had experienced physical violence in their relationships. If symbolic violence was included (e.g., threatening to hit the other person or throwing something), the percentages rose above 60 percent for singles and above 70 percent for married couples (Marshall & Rose, 1987). In another study, 47 percent of a sample of 410 college students reported some experience with violence in a dating relationship (Deal & Wampler, 1986). In most cases the violence was reciprocal—each person in the relationship used violence. In cases in which only one person was violent, the research results are conflicting. For example, some surveys (Deal & Wampler, 1986; Cate, Henton, Koval, Christopher, & Lloyd, 1982) have found that in such cases the aggressor was significantly more often the female partner. Other research, however, has tended to confirm the widespread view that men are more likely to use force than women (DeTurck, 1987).

Instead of resorting to force, consider the value of talking and listening:

- Explain what you think the problem is about and listen to what the other person says about the problem.

- Talk about what you want and listen to what the other person wants.

- Talk over possible solutions and listen to the proposed solutions of the other person.

- Talk the conflict through a logical sequence from understanding the problem through evaluating a solution. (Take a look at the Problem-Solving Sequence discussed in Chapter 9, pp. 184–186.)

DEFENSIVENESS AND SUPPORTIVENESS

Although talking is preferred to using force, not all talk is equally productive in conflict resolution. One of the best ways to look at destructive versus productive talk is to look at how the style of your communications can create unproductive **defensiveness** or a productive sense of **supportiveness**, a system developed by Jack Gibb (1961). The type of talk that generally proves destructive and sets up defensive reactions in the listener is talk that is evaluative, controlling, strategic, indifferent or neutral, superior, and certain.

Evaluation   When you evaluate or judge another person or what that person has done, that person is likely to become resentful and defensive and perhaps at the same time to

SKILL DEVELOPMENT EXPERIENCE

Generally and perhaps especially in conflict situations, I-messages are less likely to aggravate conflict than are you-messages.

Constructing I-Messages

Recognizing a conflict starter early—some incident that signals that this is the beginning of an interpersonal conflict— can often diffuse a later and more extensive conflict. Here, for example, are accusatory comments using you-messages. Turn each of these into an I-message. What do you see as the major differences between you-messages and I-messages?

1. You're late again. You're always late. Your lateness is so inconsiderate!
2. All you do is sit home and watch cartoons; you never do anything useful.
3. Well, there goes another anniversary that you forgot.
4. You think I'm fat, don't you?
5. You never want to do what I want. We always have to do what you want.

become equally evaluative and judgmental. In contrast, when you describe what happened or what you want, it creates no such defensiveness and is generally seen as supportive. The distinction between evaluation and description can be seen in the differences between **you-messages** and **I-messages**.

Evaluative You-Messages	Descriptive I-Messages
You never reveal your feelings.	I sure would like hearing how you feel about this.
You just don't plan ahead.	I need to know what our schedule for the next few days will be.
You never call me.	I'd enjoy hearing from you more often.

If you put yourself in the role of the listener hearing these statements, you probably can feel the resentment or defensiveness that the evaluative messages (you-messages) would create and the supportiveness from the descriptive messages (I-messages).

Control   When you try to control the behavior of another person, when you order that person to do this or that, or when you make decisions without mutual discussion and agreement, defensiveness is a likely response. Control messages deny the legitimacy of the person's contributions and in fact deny his or her importance. On the other hand, when you focus on the problem at hand—not on controlling the situation or getting your own way—defensiveness is much less likely. This problem orientation invites mutual participation and recognizes the significance of each person's contributions.

Strategy   When you use strategy and try to get around other people or situations through **manipulation**—especially when you conceal your true purposes—others are likely to resent it and to respond defensively. But when you act openly and with **spontaneity,** you're more likely to create an atmosphere that is equal and honest.

Neutrality   When you demonstrate **neutrality**—in the sense of indifference or a lack of caring for the other person—it's likely to create defensiveness. Neutrality seems to show a lack of empathy or interest in the thoughts and feelings of the other person; it is especially damaging when intimates are in conflict. This kind of talk says, in effect, "You're not important or deserving of attention and caring." When, on the other hand, you demonstrate empathy, defensiveness is unlikely to occur. Although it can be especially difficult in conflict situations, try to show that you can understand what the other person is going through and that you accept these feelings.

Communication Choice Point

Empathy

   Your roommate just made the dean's list (as did you) and as a reward received a new Mercedes from a rich uncle. Your roommate is ecstatic and runs to you to share the news. You want to demonstrate empathy, but in all honesty you're annoyed that some people just seem to get everything. *What are some things you can say that would demonstrate empathy? Would you express your true feelings? If so, what would you say?*

Superiority   When you present yourself as superior to another person, you put the other person in an inferior position, and this is likely to be resented. Such superiority messages say in effect that the other person is inadequate or somehow second class. A superior attitude is a violation of the implicit equality contract that people in a close relationship have. The other person may then begin to attack your superiority; the conflict can quickly degenerate into a conflict over who's the boss, with personal attacks being the mode of interaction.

Certainty   The person who reflects an attitude of **certainty**—who appears to know it all—is likely to be resented and often sets up a defensive climate. After all, there is little room for negotiation or mutual problem solving when one person already has the answer. An attitude of **provisionalism**—"Let's explore this issue together and try to find a solution"—is likely to be much more productive than an attitude of **closed-mindedness.**

The following suggestions will help you foster supportiveness rather than defensiveness:

- Talk descriptively rather than evaluatively.
- Focus on the problem rather than on personalities.
- Act and react honestly and spontaneously, rather than strategically.
- Empathize with the other person.
- Approach the conflict resolution process as an equal and treat the other person as an equal.
- Be provisional; suggest rather than demand.

Take a look at "Interpersonal Communication and . . ." at **tcbdevito.blogspot.com** for a discussion of interpersonal conflict training. Would interpersonal conflict training be useful to people in the profession you're in or hope to enter?

FACE-ATTACKING AND FACE-ENHANCING STRATEGIES

In the discussion of politeness in Chapter 2 (p. 44), the concepts of face and face-threatening acts were introduced. The concepts of face and face-threatening acts have special relevance to interpersonal conflict. **Face-attacking conflict strategies** are strategies that attack a person's positive face (e.g., making comments that criticize the person's contribution to a relationship or the person's ability) or a person's negative face (e.g., making demands on a person's time or resources that attack the person's autonomy). **Face-enhancing conflict strategies,** on the other hand, are those that support and confirm a person's positive face (e.g., praise, a pat on the back, a sincere smile) or negative face (e.g., giving the person space and asking rather than demanding).

One popular but destructive face-attacking strategy is **beltlining** (Bach & Wyden, 1968). Much like fighters in a ring, each of us has an emotional "beltline." When you hit below it, you can inflict serious injury. When you hit above the belt, however, the person is able to absorb the blow. With most interpersonal relationships, especially those of long standing, you know where the beltline is. You know, for example, that to hit Pat with the inability to have children is to hit below the belt. You know that to hit Chris with the failure to get a permanent job is to hit below the belt. This type of face-attacking strategy doesn't help move a conflict toward resolution, and often has the opposite effect of intensifying it. Keep blows to areas your opponent can absorb and handle.

Another such face-attacking strategy is **blame.** Instead of focusing on a solution to a problem, some people try to affix blame to the other person. Whether true or not, blaming is generally unproductive for at least two reasons. First, it diverts attention away from the problem and from its potential solution. Second, it creates resentment that is likely to be responded to with resentment. The conflict then spirals into personal attacks, leaving the individuals and the relationship worse off than before the conflict was ever addressed.

VIEWPOINTS

Online Conflict

One study found that, generally at least, people are more positive in dealing with conflict in face-to-face situations than in computer-mediated communication (Zornoza, Ripoll, & Peiro, 2002). Do you notice this in your own interactions? If so, why do you think it's true? In what ways might you make your own online conflicts more positive?

Communication Choice Point

Resolving Differences

You've just moved into a new apartment. Unfortunately, your next-door neighbors play their stereo loudly and long into the night. You need to say something but just aren't sure how to go about it. *What options do you have for dealing with this situation? To whom might you speak? Through what channel? What would you say?*

Strategies that enhance positive face involve helping the other person to maintain a positive image, an image as competent and trustworthy, able and good. Even when you get what you want, say by bargaining, it's wise to help the other person retain positive face; this makes it less likely that future conflicts will arise and increases the likelihood that the relationship can be repaired (Donahue, 1992).

Instead of using face-attacking strategies, consider face-saving strategies:

- Confirm the other person's self-image.
- Listen supportively and actively. Express your support or empathy: *I can understand how you feel. I can appreciate that my handling the checkbook could create a feeling of inequality.*
- Use I-messages that avoid blaming the other person.
- Use excuses and apologies as appropriate. (See Chapter 6, pp. 132–133.)
- Respect the other person's negative face needs by making few (if any) demands; also respect the other person's time, space (especially in times of stress), and point of view.

SILENCERS AND FACILITATING OPEN EXPRESSION

Silencers are a wide variety of unproductive fighting techniques that literally silence another person. One frequently used silencer is crying. When a person is unable to deal with a conflict or when winning seems unlikely, the person may cry, and thus silence the other person.

Another silencer is to feign extreme emotionalism—to yell and scream and pretend to be losing control. Still another is to develop some "physical" reaction—headaches and shortness of breath are probably the most popular. One of the major problems with such silencers is that as an opponent you can never be certain that they are mere tactics; they may be real physical reactions that you should pay attention to. Regardless of what you do, the conflict remains unexamined and unresolved.

In addition to avoiding silencers, avoid power tactics (e.g., raising your voice or threatening physical force) that suppress or inhibit freedom of expression. Such tactics are designed to put the other person down and to subvert real interpersonal equality.

Instead of using silencers, try to facilitate open expression:

- Listen actively and give appropriate and positive feedback.
- Verbalize your appreciation for how the other person sees the conflict (say, by punctuating the conflict episode differently).
- Create or increase **immediacy**—a sense of interest in and liking for the other person in an interchange (discussed in Chapter 6).
- Give the other person permission to express himself or herself openly and honestly.

GUNNYSACKING AND PRESENT FOCUS

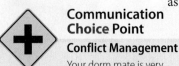

Communication Choice Point

Conflict Management

Your dorm mate is very popular and has an open-door policy. Throughout the day and evening, friends drop by to chat, borrow a book, check their e-mail, and do a range of things—all of which prevents you from studying. You need to resolve this problem. *What can you say to your roommate to begin to change this situation? What channel would you use?*

The process of **gunnysacking** is the unproductive conflict strategy of storing up grievances—as if in a gunnysack—and then unloading them when an argument arises (Bach & Wyden, 1968). The immediate occasion for unloading stored-up grievances may be relatively simple (or so it may seem at first); for example, say you come home late one night without calling. Instead of arguing about this, the gunnysacker pours out a mass of unrelated past grievances. As you probably know from experience, gunnysacking does nothing to help resolve conflict and often begets further gunnysacking. Frequently, the trigger problem never gets addressed. Instead, resentment and hostility escalate.

Instead of gunnysacking, focus on the present:

- Concentrate on the here and now, rather than on issues that occurred two months ago.
- Focus your conflict on the person with whom you're fighting, not on the person's mother, child, or friends.

VERBAL AGGRESSIVENESS AND ARGUMENTATIVENESS

An especially interesting perspective on conflict has emerged from work on verbal aggressiveness and argumentativeness, concepts that were isolated by communication researchers but quickly interested people in other disciplines such as psychology, education, and management, among others (Infante, 1988; Rancer, 1998; Wigley, 1998; Rancer & Avtgis, 2006). Understanding these two concepts will help you understand some of the reasons why things go wrong and some of the ways in which you can use conflict to improve rather than damage your relationships (see Table 8.2).

Verbal aggressiveness is a method of winning an argument by inflicting psychological pain, by attacking the other person's self-concept. The technique is a type of disconfirmation in that it seeks to discredit the individual's view of self. **Argumentativeness,** a quality to be cultivated rather than avoided, refers to your willingness to argue for a point of view, your tendency to speak your mind on significant issues. It's the mode of dealing with disagreements that is the preferable alternative to verbal aggressiveness (Infante & Rancer, 1996).

Argumentativeness differs greatly from verbal aggressiveness (Rancer & Avtgis, 2006). Argumentativeness is constructive in a variety of communication situations and leads to relationship satisfaction. In organizations, it enhances relationships between subordinates and supervisors. Verbal aggressiveness is destructive and leads to relationship dissatisfaction. In organizations, it demoralizes workers.

Argumentative individuals are generally seen as having greater credibility; they're seen as more trustworthy, committed, and dynamic than their aggressive counterparts. In addition, argumentativeness is likely to increase your power of persuasion and will also increase the likelihood that you'll be seen as a leader. Aggressiveness tactics, on the other hand, decrease your power and your likelihood of being seen as a leader.

VIEWPOINTS

Your Conflict Style

How would you describe your conflict style in your own close relationships in terms of competing-avoiding-compromising-accommodating- collaborating? Is it the same at work?

Watch the **Video** "Jim and Jack Joust" at **MyCommunicationLab**

TABLE 8.2 Differences Between Verbal Aggressiveness and Argumentativeness

Here are just a few differences between being verbally aggressive and arguing (Atvgis & Rancer, 2010; Infante & Rancer, 1996; Rancer & Atvgis, 2006). As you read this table consider your own conflict tendencies.

Verbal Aggressiveness	Argumentativeness
Is **destructive;** the outcomes are negative in a variety of communication situations.	Is **constructive;** the outcomes are positive in a variety of communication situations.
Leads to relationship **dissatisfaction,** not surprising for a strategy that aims to attack another's self-concept.	Leads to relationship **satisfaction.**
May lead to **relationship violence.**	May **prevent relationship violence,** especially in domestic relationships.
Damages organizational life and demoralizes workers on varied levels.	**Enhances organizational life;** for example, subordinates prefer supervisors who encourage argumentativeness.
Prevents meaningful parent-child communication and makes corporal punishment more likely.	**Enhances parent-child communication** and enables parents to gain greater compliance.
Decreases the user's credibility, in part because it's seen as a tactic to discredit the person rather than address the argument.	**Increases the user's credibility;** argumentatives are seen as trustworthy, committed, and dynamic.
Decreases the user's power of persuasion.	**Increases the user's power of persuasion;** argumentatives are more likely to be seen as leaders.

Communication Choice Point

Verbal Aggressiveness

Your partner engages in verbal aggression whenever you have an argument. Regardless of what the conflict is about, you feel that your self-concept is attacked. *What are some of the things you might say or do to stop these attacks? What channel(s) would you use?*

Instead of being verbally aggressive, try to practice argumentativeness (Infante, 1988; Rancer & Avtgis, 2006):

- **Treat disagreements as objectively as possible.** Avoid assuming that, because someone takes issue with your position or your interpretation, they're attacking you as a person.

- **Center your arguments on issues rather than personalities.** Avoid attacking a person (rather than a person's arguments), even if this would give you a tactical advantage—it will probably backfire at some later time and make your relationship or group participation more difficult.

- **Reaffirm the other person's sense of competence.** Compliment the other person as appropriate.

- **Allow the other person to state her or his position fully.** Do this before you respond and, of course, avoid interrupting.

- **Stress equality.** Stress the similarities that you have with the other person or persons; stress your areas of agreement before attacking with disagreements.

- **Express interest in the other person's position, attitude, and point of view.**

- **Avoid getting overemotional.** Avoid using an overly loud voice or interjecting vulgar expressions that will prove offensive and eventually ineffective.

- **Allow people to save face.** Never humiliate another person.

Video Choice Point

Conflict Strategies

Pat and Andi, a dating couple, just won the top prize in their Fantasy Football league. They have enjoyed working together to build a winning team, but now that they've won, they cannot agree on what to do with the money. As demonstrated in this chapter, they have a variety of conflict resolution strategies to deal with this problem. See how their conflict resolution choices play out in the video "Conflict Strategies".

👁 **Watch** the **Video** "Conflict Strategies" at **MyCommunicationLab**

Objectives Self-Check

- Can you describe and distinguish between the popular conflict management strategies (avoidance and fighting actively, force and talk, defensiveness and supportiveness, face-attacking and face-enhancing strategies, silencers and facilitating open expression, gunnysacking and present focus, and verbal aggressiveness and argumentativeness)?

- Can you use the more effective strategies in your own conflict management interactions?

⚠ **Messages in the Media** *Wrap Up*

In addition to sports, all varieties of television shows—from talk shows to sitcoms and dramas—provide vivid examples of conflict and the varied ways in which characters or contestants can deal with it. You will most likely see the principles and pitfalls discussed here echoed in the conflict resolution strategies depicted in these programs.

Summary of Concepts and Skills

Study and **Review** materials for this chapter are at **MyCommunicationLab**

Listen to the **Audio Chapter** Summary at **MyCommunicationLab**

This chapter looked at the nature of interpersonal conflict and at how best to manage conflict.

Preliminaries to Interpersonal Conflict

1. Interpersonal conflict (in face-to-face situations and in cyberspace) is a disagreement between or among connected individuals whose positions are to some degree both interrelated and incompatible.

2. Conflict can be content or relationship oriented but is usually a combination of both.

Principles of Interpersonal Conflict

3. Conflict can have both negative and positive effects.

4. Conflict is heavily influenced by both culture and gender, and any effective management of conflict needs to consider these influences.

5. Conflict styles (competing or win-lose, avoiding or lose-lose, accommodating or lose-win, collaborating or win-win, and compromising or win-lose/win-lose) have consequences.

Conflict Management Strategies

6. Conflict management strategies are influenced by the goals you seek, your emotional state, your cognitive assessment of the situation, your personality and communication competence, and your family history.

7. Conflict management strategies include making decisions between avoidance and active fighting, force and talk, defensiveness and supportiveness, face-attacking and face-enhancing strategies, silencers and facilitating open expression, gunnysacking and present focus, and verbal aggressiveness and argumentativeness.

The skills covered in this chapter are vital to managing interpersonal conflict. Place a check mark next to those skills you want to work on most.

_____ 1. I seek to derive positive benefits from interpersonal conflict and to avoid conflict's possible negative outcomes.

_____ 2. I engage in conflict with an understanding of the cultural and gender influences present.

_____ 3. I understand the consequences of different conflict styles and adjust my style of conflict depending on the specific circumstances.

_____ 4. I look for win-win rather than win-lose strategies.

_____ 5. I engage in conflict actively rather than avoid the problem.

_____ 6. I talk conflict differences through rather than try to force my way of thinking on the other person.

_____ 7. I express support rather than encourage defensiveness.

_____ 8. I use I-messages (rather than you-messages) and assume responsibility for my thoughts and feelings.

_____ 9. I use face-enhancing rather than face-attacking tactics.

_____ 10. I express empathy rather than try to blame the other person.

_____ 11. I facilitate open expression rather than try to silence the other person.

_____ 12. I focus on the present rather than gunnysack.

_____ 13. I use the skills of argumentativeness rather than verbal aggressiveness.

Key Word Quiz

The Language of Conflict Management

Match the terms about interpersonal conflict management with their definitions. Record the number of the definition next to the appropriate term.

_____ a. interpersonal conflict (157)

_____ b. accommodating style (167)

_____ c. face-attacking strategies (167)

_____ d. gunnysacking (168)

_____ e. beltlining (167)

_____ f. collaborating style (167)

_____ g. verbal aggressiveness (169)

_____ h. neutrality (166)

_____ i. content conflict (158)

_____ j. argumentativeness (169)

1. An "I win, you win" approach to conflict management.
2. The willingness to argue for a point of view and to speak your mind without attacking the other person.
3. A kind of indifference that is likely to create defensiveness.
4. Disagreement between connected individuals.
5. Conflict strategies that attack the other person's self-image.
6. A conflict strategy in which stored-up prior grievances are introduced into the present conflict.
7. A conflict strategy in which one person attacks the other with criticisms that are difficult to absorb.
8. Disagreement that addresses issues external to the relationship and that does not challenge the agreed-on interpersonal relationship between the conflicting parties.
9. A method of trying to win an argument by inflicting psychological pain or distress.
10. An approach to conflict in which you sacrifice your own needs for the needs of the other person.

These ten terms and additional terms used in this chapter can be found in the glossary.

Answers: a. 4 b. 10 c. 5 d. 6 e. 7 f. 1 g. 9 h. 3 i. 8 j. 2

 Study and **Review** the **Flashcards** at **MyCommunicationLab**

MyCommunicationLab

Throughout this chapter, there are icons in the margin that highlight media content for selected topics. Go to **MyCommunicationLab** for additional information on interpersonal conflict management. Here you'll find flashcards to help you learn the jargon of communication, videos that illustrate a variety of concepts, additional exercises, and discussions to help you continue your study and understanding of interpersonal conflict and especially its effective management.

9

Small Group Communication

 Messages in the Media

Political talk show *Morning Joe,* like any talk show, provides vivid examples of small group communication, the topic of this chapter. Think about these types of shows as we explore here the nature of the small group and the team, the varied types of groups, and the ways to promote effective group communication.

Objectives

Listen to the **Audio Chapter** at **MyCommunicationLab**

After reading this chapter, you should be able to:

❶ Define *small group* and *team,* the stages of small group communication, small group formats, small group apprehension, and small group culture.

❷ Define *brainstorming* and its four rules, and use this technique for generating ideas.

❸ Define the *educational or learning group* and the *focus group,* and participate effectively in these for information sharing.

❹ Define the *encounter group,* the *assertiveness training group,* the *consciousness raising group,* and the *intervention.*

❺ Describe the problem-solving sequence and decision-making methods; and define *nominal, Delphi,* and *quality circle* groups.

Consider the number of groups to which you belong. Your family is the most obvious example, but you might also be a member of a team, a class, a club, an organization, a sorority or fraternity, a collection of friends on Facebook or MySpace, a work group at your job, professional groups on LinkedIn, or perhaps a band or theater group. Some of your most important and satisfying communications probably take place in small groups and teams like these.

Mastering the skills of small group communication and leadership will enable you to function more productively and creatively in groups, enjoy group interaction more, and lead groups more comfortably and effectively. Your ability to function in a group—as a member and as a leader—is an essential job skill in today's workplace (Morreale & Pearson, 2008).

In this introduction to small group communication, the chapter will first cover the essential concepts and principles of the small group, look at culture and the group, and then focus on the various types of groups.

Essentials of Small Groups and Teams

Let's begin with some basic definitions.

THE SMALL GROUP

A **small group** is (1) a collection of individuals who (2) are connected to one another by some common purpose, (3) are interdependent, (4) have some degree of organization among them, and (5) see themselves as a group.

Collection of Individuals   Generally, a small group consists of approximately 3 to 12 people. The collection of individuals must be few enough in number that all members may communicate with relative ease as both senders and receivers. In face-to-face situations, there are also limits that the available space imposes; in online groups, no such spatial barrier exists. If the group gets much larger than 12, however, even online group communication becomes difficult. On Facebook and similar social networking sites, the number of individuals in a group may number in the hundreds of friends. These would not be a small groups—communicating via these sites is more akin to public speaking—but the subgroups that form would likely fall into the small group category.

Common Purpose   The members of a group must be connected to one another through some common purpose. People on a bus normally do not constitute a group, because they're not working toward a common goal. However, if the bus were to get stuck in a ditch, the riders may quickly become a group and work together to get the bus back on the road. This does not mean that all members of a group must have exactly the same purpose, but generally there must be some similarity in the individuals' reasons for interacting. Social media sites provide easy ways of connecting with others who have similar purposes. Social media groups—whether professional as on LinkedIn or more purely social (although there are now apps to establish more professional groups) such as Facebook or a mixture as on Google+—enable you to form groups on just about any topic you'd like. If you're interested in something, there are probably others out there who are interested in the same thing and who would like to get together in virtual space. By joining a social media site group you can, depending on which one you join, receive e-mails from group members about group activities, network for a variety of reasons, discuss topics of mutual interest, plan events or hangouts, or solve problems—the very same purposes that face-to-face groups serve.

VIEWPOINTS

Uses and Gratifications

One study identified seven gratifications you derive from online communication: being in a virtual community, seeking information, aesthetic experience, financial compensation, diversion, personal status, and maintaining relationships (Song, LaRose, Eastin, & Lin, 2004). How would you describe the gratifications you receive from online groups? Which are the most important?

Interdependence   In a small group, members are interdependent, meaning that the behavior of one member is significant to and has an impact on all other members. When one member attacks or supports the ideas of another member, that behavior influences the other members and the group as a whole. When one member proposes a great idea or posts a clever quotation or photo, that behavior has an effect on all group members.

Organizing Rules   Members of small groups must be connected by some organizing rules, or structure. At times the structure is rigid, as in groups operating under parliamentary procedure, in which each comment must follow prescribed rules. At other times, as in a social gathering, especially online groups, the structure is very loose; however, there's some organization and some structure—for example, comments or questions by one member are responded to by others rather than ignored, and so on.

Self-Perception as a Group   Members of small groups feel they are, in fact, members of a larger whole. This doesn't mean that individuality is ignored or that members do not see themselves as individuals; it simply means that each member thinks, feels, and acts as a part of the group. The more members see themselves as part of the group, the greater the group cohesion (or sense of "groupness"); the more they see themselves as individuals, separate from the group, the less the group cohesion. Members in highly cohesive groups are usually more satisfied and more productive than members of low-cohesiveness groups.

THE TEAM

A **team is** a particular kind of small group. As such it possesses all of the characteristics of the small group, as well as some additional qualities. Drawing on a number of small group researchers in communication and organizational theory, the team can be defined as a small group (1) constructed for a specific task, (2) whose members have clearly defined roles and (3) are committed to achieving the same goal, and (4) which is content focused (Beebe & Masterson, 2012; Kelly, 2006; Hofstrand, 2006).

Specific Purpose   A team is often constructed for a specific purpose or task. After it is completed the members of the task group may be assigned to other teams or go their separate ways. Players on a baseball team, for example, come together for practice and for the actual game; but after the game, they each go their separate ways. After the book is published, members of the book team may go on to work on different books with different team members.

Clearly Defined Roles   In a team, member's roles are rather clearly defined. A sports team is a good example. Each player has a unique function: the shortstop's functions are very different from the pitcher's or the catcher's, for example. In a business setting, the team that is responsible for publishing a book, say, would also consist of people with clearly defined roles, including the editor, the designer, the marketing manager, the sales manager, the photo researcher, the author, and so on. Each brings a unique perspective to the task and each is an authority in a specific area.

Goal Directed   In a team all members are committed to achieving the same, clearly identified goal. Again, a sports team is a good example: All members are committed to winning the game. In the publishing business example, all members of the team are committed to producing a successful book.

Content Focused   Teams are generally content focused. In terms of the distinction between content and relationship messages introduced in Chapter 1 (p. 12), teams communicate largely through the exchange of content messages—on winning the game or creating the book—and much less through messages about the interpersonal relationships of its members.

Watch the **Video** "Politics of Sociology" at **MyCommunicationLab**

"If I put mustaches on all of us, we look more like a team."

VIRTUAL GROUPS AND TEAMS

Small groups and teams use a wide variety of channels. Often, interactions take place face-to-face; this is the channel that probably comes to mind when you think of groups. But, a great deal of small group and team interaction takes place online, among geographically separated members who communicate as a group via computer or phone connections—with Skype, LinkedIn, or Facebook, for example . These *virtual groups and teams* serve both relationship and social purposes on the one hand (these are best thought of as small groups) and business and professional purposes on the other (these are best thought of as teams).

Perhaps the best example of virtual groups serving relationship purposes are social networking sites, where friends interact in groups but may be separated by classrooms or by oceans. And, increasingly, these social networking sites are being used to perform business tasks as well—for finding jobs, conducting business, solving organizational problems, and conducting just about any kind of function that a face-to-face group would serve.

Business and professional purposes often are served by virtual teams. Some of these team members may be working at home; but increasingly, virtual teams consist of people who are in different work spaces, perhaps in different parts of an office building, perhaps in different countries.

The same principles of effective group communication apply to all kinds of groups and teams, whether social or business, face-to-face or virtual (we'll use the most inclusive term "small group" to refer to all types of groups). Whether you're working on a team project with colleagues in different countries, communicating with new friends on Facebook, or interacting face-to-face with your extended family, the principles discussed here will prove useful.

SMALL GROUP STAGES

With knowledge of the various kinds of small groups, we can now look at how groups interact in the real world. Small group interaction develops in much the same way as a conversation. As in conversation (see Chapter 6), there are five stages: opening, feedforward, business, feedback, and closing.

- **Opening.** The opening period is usually a getting-acquainted time during which members introduce themselves and engage in small talk (e.g., "How was your weekend?" "Does anyone want coffee?"). Your objective here is to get comfortable with the group members.

- **Feedforward.** After this preliminary get-together, there is usually some feedforward—some attempt to identify what needs to be done, who will do it, and so on. In a more formal group, the agenda (which is a perfect example of feedforward) may be reviewed and the tasks of the group identified. This is much like making a "to do" list.

- **Business.** The business portion is the actual discussion of the tasks—the problem solving, the sharing of information, or whatever else the group needs to achieve.

- **Feedback.** At the feedback stage, the group may reflect on what it has done and perhaps on what remains to be done. Some groups may even evaluate their performance at this stage: for example, *We need to focus more on the financial aspects* or *We need to consider additional alternatives.*

- **Closing.** At the closing stage, the group members return to their focus on individuals and will perhaps exchange closing comments ("Good seeing you again," "See you next time").

Note that the group focus shifts from members to task and then back again to members. A typical pattern would look like Figure 9.1. Different groups will naturally follow different patterns. For example, a work group that has gathered to solve a problem is likely to spend a great deal more time focused on the task than on each other; whereas an informal social group, say two or three couples who get together for dinner, will spend most of their time focused on the concerns of individuals. Similarly, the amount of time spent on the opening or closing, for example, will vary with the type and purpose of the group.

SMALL GROUP FORMATS

Small groups serve their functions in a variety of formats. Among the most popular small group formats for relatively formal functions are the round table, the panel, the symposium, and the symposium-forum (Figure 9.2).

- In the **roundtable,** group members arrange themselves physically (usually in chairs) in a circular or semicircular pattern. They share information or solve a problem without any set pattern of who speaks when. Group interaction is informal, and members contribute as they see fit. A leader or moderator may be present; he or she may, for example, try to keep the discussion on the topic or encourage more reticent members to speak up.

- In the **panel,** group members are "experts" but participate informally and without any set pattern of who speaks when, as in a roundtable. The difference is that they are sitting, often side-by-side, in front of an audience, whose members may interject comments or ask questions.

- In the **symposium,** each member delivers a prepared presentation much like a public speech. All speeches address different aspects of a single topic. A symposium leader introduces the speakers, provides transitions from one speaker to another, and may provide periodic summaries.

- The symposium-forum consists of two parts: a symposium with prepared speeches (as explained above) and a **forum,** a period of questions from the audience and responses by the speakers. The leader introduces the speakers and moderates the question-and-answer session.

These four formats are *general* patterns that describe a wide variety of groups. Within each type, there will naturally be variation. For example, in the symposium-forum, there is no set pattern for how much time will be spent on the symposium part and how much on the forum part. Combinations may also be used. Thus, for example, group members may each present a position paper (basically a symposium) and then participate in a roundtable discussion.

SMALL GROUP APPREHENSION

Just as you may have apprehension about public speaking (a topic to be discussed in Chapter 11), you probably experience apprehension to some degree in group discussions. Because small groups vary so widely, you're likely to experience different degrees of apprehension depending on the nature of the specific group. Work groups, for example, may cause greater apprehension than groups of friends. And interacting with superiors is likely to generate greater anxiety than meeting with peers or subordinates. Similarly, the degree of familiarity you have with the group members and the extent to which you see yourself as a part of the group (as opposed to an

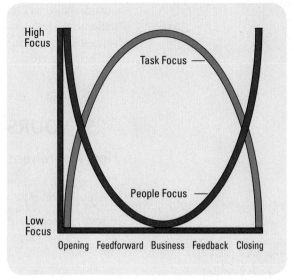

FIGURE 9.1

Small Group Stages and the Focus on Task and People
Do the groups to which you belong follow these five stages when interacting? How do these groups divide their focus between people and task?

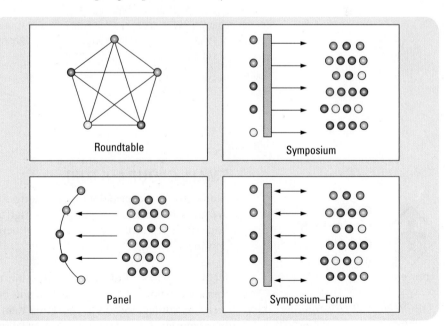

FIGURE 9.2

Small Group Formats
With how many of these group formats have you had experience?

outsider) also will influence your level of apprehension. If you are apprehensive in group situations (the self-test included here will help you determine this), you may want to review the suggestions for reducing your apprehension in public speaking; they are the same skills that will help you reduce apprehension in groups and meetings (see pp. 209–210).

TEST YOURSELF

How Apprehensive Are You in Group Discussions?

This brief test is designed to measure your apprehension in small group communication situations. The questionnaire consists of six statements concerning your feelings about participating in group discussions.

Indicate the degree to which each statement applies to you by marking whether you **1** = strongly agree, **2** = agree, **3** = are undecided, **4** = disagree, or **5** = strongly disagree. (Each of these answers then becomes the "score" for each item.) There are no right or wrong answers. Do not be concerned that some of the statements are similar. Work quickly; just record your first impression.

_____ **1** I dislike participating in group discussions.

_____ **2** Generally, I am comfortable while participating in group discussions.

_____ **3** I am tense and nervous while participating in group discussions.

_____ **4** I like to get involved in group discussions.

_____ **5** Engaging in a group discussion with new people makes me tense and nervous.

_____ **6** I am calm and relaxed while participating in group discussions.

HOW DID YOU DO? To obtain your score, use the following formula:

Start with 18; add the scores for items 2, 4, and 6; then subtract the scores for items 1, 3, and 5. A score of over 18 shows some degree of apprehension.

WHAT WILL YOU DO? Think about the kinds of groups that generate the most anxiety for you. Can you identify the major characteristics of these high-apprehension groups? How do these differ from groups generating little apprehension? What other factors might influence your small group apprehension? When you read suggestions for reducing public speaking anxiety given in Chapter 10, consider how you might use them in the various types of groups in which you participate.

Source: From James C. McCroskey, *An Introduction to Rhetorical Communication*, 9/e. Copyright © 2005 by Allyn & Bacon. Printed and electronically reproduced by permission of Pearson Education, Inc., Englewood Cliffs, New Jersey.

SMALL GROUP CULTURE

Many groups—especially those of long standing—develop cultural norms and are greatly influenced by their own high-context or low-context orientation. Each of these cultural dimensions influences the group, its members, and its communication.

Group Norms Rules or standards, known as **group norms,** identify which behaviors are considered appropriate (such as being willing to take on added tasks or directing conflict toward issues rather than toward people) and which are considered inappropriate (such as arriving late or failing to contribute actively). These rules for appropriate behavior are sometimes explicitly stated in a company contract or policy: *All members must attend department meetings.* Sometimes they are unstated: *Group members should be well groomed.*

Communication Choice Point

Group Norms

The first 20 minutes of just about every meeting at work invariably revolves around personal talk. You really don't enjoy this interaction; you want to participate in the work part of the meeting but not in the interpersonal part. *What are some of your options in this situation? Which option do you think will most likely advance your career?*

Online groups vary a great deal in terms of norms and, as with all groups, it's wise to familiarize yourself with the norms of the group before actively participating. For example, social media groups will vary greatly in their tolerance for self-promotion and commercializing. LinkedIn groups and other sites frown upon self-promotion and may ostracize you for doing so. And even if you don't get thrown off Facebook, you're likely to incur considerable negative reaction. On the other hand, other groups—for example, the listserv for communication professionals, called Crtnet—frequently includes posts in which individual members will advertise their own books. Sometimes, a group will tolerate self-promotion officially while individual members may look on the posts very negatively.

Norms may apply to individual members as well as to the group as a whole and, of course, will differ from one cultural group to another (Axtell, 1990, 1993). For example, although business associates from the United States might prefer to get right down to business, those from Japan might prefer rather elaborate socializing before addressing the business at hand. In the United States, men and women in business are expected to interact when making business decisions as well as when socializing. In Muslim and Buddhist societies, however, religious restrictions prevent mixing between the sexes. In some cultures (e.g., those of the United States, Bangladesh, Australia, Germany, Finland, and Hong Kong), punctuality for business meetings is very important. But in others (e.g., those of Morocco, Italy, Brazil, Zambia, Ireland, and Panama), punctuality is less important; being late is no great insult and in some situations is even expected. In the United States and in much of Asia and Europe, meetings are held between two parties. In many Persian Gulf states, however, a business executive is likely to conduct meetings with several different groups—sometimes dealing with totally different issues—at the same time. In the United States very little interpersonal touching goes on during business meetings, but in Arab countries touching such as hand holding is common and is a gesture of friendship.

VIEWPOINTS

Group Norms

What norms govern your class in human communication? What norms govern your family? What norms govern your place of work? Do you have any difficulty with these norms?

Communication Choice Point

Group Culture

You're new to an organization and want to learn, as quickly as possible, its operating cultural rules, which you don't want to violate. *What choices do you have for seeking out this information?*

High-Context and Low-Context Cultures

A cultural distinction that has special relevance to small group communication is that between high-context and low-context cultures (Hall, 1976; Singh & Pereira, 2005). In a **high-context culture** (for example, Japan, China, Korea, Malaysia, and Indonesia) much of the information conveyed is communicated by the context, or in the person, rather than explicitly coded in verbal messages. In such cultures, individuals have a great deal of information in common, and this shared knowledge does not have to be made explicit. In a **low-context culture** (for example, Denmark, Germany, the United States, Canada, Australia, and New Zealand), most information is communicated through explicitly stated verbal messages. In such cultures, people do not assume that they share certain information and so must make all crucial details explicit.

Members of high-context cultures spend a lot of time getting to know each other before engaging in any small group interaction. Because of this prior personal knowledge, a great deal of information is already shared and therefore does not have to be explicitly stated. Members of low-context cultures, on the other hand, spend less time getting to know each other and therefore do not have that shared knowledge. As a result everything has to be stated explicitly. When this simple difference is not taken into account, misunderstandings can result. For example, the directness and explicitness characteristic of the low-context culture may prove insulting, insensitive, or unnecessary to members of a high-context culture. Conversely, to someone from a low-context culture, members from a high-context culture may appear vague, underhanded, and even dishonest in their reluctance to be explicit or to engage in what a low-context culture would consider to be open and direct communication.

"Honey, please don't talk to Daddy when he's in a chat room."

© Jack Ziegler/Condé Nast Publications/www.cartoonbank.com

Video Choice Point
First Impressions

Angie, an accounting major, worked hard in college and has landed a good first job with a large accounting firm. She has been assigned to join a team of four others to work on new accounting procedures for a major client. As the newest member of the team, she wants to be perceived as both like-able and competent. She is eager to make a good impression with her new colleagues. She considers the topics covered in this chapter as she contemplates her communication choices. See how her choices play out in the video "First Impressions".

 Watch the **Video** "First Impressions" at **MyCommunicationLab**

Objectives Self-Check
- Can you define *small group* and *team?*
- Can you explain the stages and the formats of small group communication?
- Can you explain the nature of small group apprehension and the influence of culture?

Brainstorming Groups

Many small groups exist solely to generate ideas through **brainstorming**—a technique for analyzing a problem by presenting as many ideas as possible (Osborn, 1957; Beebe & Masterson, 2012). Although brainstorming also can be useful when you're trying to come up with ideas by yourself—ideas for speeches or term papers, ideas for a fun vacation, or ways to make money—it is more typical in small group settings. Organizations have come to embrace brainstorming, because it lessens group members' inhibitions and encourages all participants to exercise their creativity. It also fosters cooperative teamwork; members soon learn that their own ideas and creativity are sparked by the contributions of others. The technique builds member pride and ownership in the final solution (or product or service), because all members contribute to it.

Brainstorming occurs in two phases: (1) the brainstorming period itself and (2) the evaluation period. The procedures are simple. First, a problem is selected. The "problem" may be almost anything that is amenable to many possible solutions or ideas—for example, how to recruit new members to the organization or how to market a new product. Before the actual session, group members are informed of the problem so they can think about the topic. When the group meets, each person contributes as many ideas as he or she can think of. Companies often use chalkboards, whiteboards, or easels to record all the ideas. A brainstorming group may appoint one person to be the scribe; that person keys the group's notes into a laptop for instant circulation via e-mail to other group members after the group has concluded its business. During the initial idea-generating session, members follow four rules:

- **Rule 1: No evaluations are permitted at this stage.** All ideas are recorded for the group to see (or hear later). Prohibiting both verbal and nonverbal evaluation encourages group members to participate freely.

    This first rule is perhaps the most difficult for members to follow, so you might want to practice responding to what are called "idea killers." For example, what might you say if someone were to criticize an idea with the following comments?

We tried it before and it didn't work.	It would cost too much.
No one would vote for it.	We don't have the facilities.
It's too complex.	What we have is good enough.
It's too simple.	It just doesn't fit us.
It would take too long.	It's not possible.

SKILL DEVELOPMENT EXPERIENCE

Using Brainstorming Techniques

Together with a small group or with the class as a whole, sit in a circle and brainstorm on one of the topics identified later in this chapter in the Skill Development Experience "Solving Problems in Groups" on page 187. Be sure to appoint someone to write down all the contributions, or record the discussion. After this brainstorming session, consider these questions:

1. Did any members give negative criticism (even nonverbally)?
2. Did any members hesitate to contribute really wild ideas? Why?
3. Was it necessary to re-stimulate the group members at any point? Did this help?
4. Did possible solutions emerge that would not have been thought of without the group stimulation?

Brainstorming is useful even if you do it by yourself. Follow the same rules.

- **Rule 2: Quantity of ideas is the goal.** The more ideas generated, the more likely it is that a useful solution will be found.
- **Rule 3: Combinations and extensions of ideas are encouraged.** Although members may not criticize a particular idea, they may extend or combine it. The value of a particular idea may be that it stimulates another idea.
- **Rule 4: Freewheeling (i.e., developing as wild an idea as possible) is desirable.** A wild idea can be tempered easily, but it's not so easy to elaborate on a simple or conservative idea.

After all the ideas are generated—a period that lasts about 15 or 20 minutes—the group evaluates the entire list. Unworkable ideas are crossed off the list; those showing promise are retained and evaluated. During this phase, criticism is allowed.

Objectives Self-Check
- Can you define *brainstorming?*
- Can you paraphrase the four major rules of brainstorming?
- Can you effectively apply these rules in an idea-generating group?

Information-Sharing Groups

The purpose of information-sharing groups is to acquire new information or skills by sharing knowledge. In most of these groups, all members have something to teach and something to learn; a good example is a group of students sharing information to prepare for an exam. In others, the group interaction takes place because some members have information and some do not. An example is a discussion between a patient and a health care professional.

EDUCATIONAL OR LEARNING GROUPS

Members of educational or learning groups may follow a variety of discussion patterns. For example, a historical topic, such as the development of free speech or equal rights, might be explored chronologically, with the discussion progressing from the past into the present and, perhaps, into predictions of the future. Issues in developmental psychology, such as a child's language development or physical maturity, might also be discussed chronologically. Other topics lend themselves to spatial development. For example, the development of the United States might take a spatial pattern—from east to west—or a chronological pattern—from 1776 to the present. Other suitable patterns, depending on the topic and the group's needs, might be cause and effect, problem and solution, or structure and function.

Perhaps the most popular discussion pattern is the topical pattern. A group might discuss the legal profession by itemizing and discussing each of the profession's major functions. Another might consider a corporation's structure in terms of its major divisions. Groups could further systematize each of these topics by, say, listing the legal profession's functions in order of importance or complexity, or ordering the corporation's major structures in terms of decision-making power.

FOCUS GROUPS

A different type of information sharing group is the **focus group,** a small group that is assembled and subjected to a kind of in-depth interview, often for market research. The aim of conducting a focus group is to discover through a sample of individuals what it is that people in general think about an issue or product; for example, what do men between 18 and 25 think of a particular brand of aftershave lotion and its packaging? In the focus group, a leader/interviewer tries to discover the members' beliefs, attitudes, thoughts, and feelings to use as a guide for decisions on, for example, changing the scent or redesigning the packaging. It is the leader's task to prod members of the focus group to analyze their thoughts and feelings on a deeper level and to use the thoughts of one member to stimulate the thoughts of others.

Communication Choice Point

Stimulating Contributions

You're in charge of a focus group in which members will discuss what they like and dislike about the websites they visit. The problem you anticipate, based on past experience, is that a few members will do all the talking and the rest will hardly talk at all. *What are some of the ways you can confront this problem?*

Generally, a focus group leader, who is usually a professional facilitator rather than a member of the hosting organization itself, assembles approximately 12 people who represent the general population. The leader explains the process, the time limits, and the general goal of the group—let's say, to discover why these 12 individuals requested information on the XYZ health plan but purchased a plan from another company. The leader then asks a variety of questions. In our example the questions might be, "How did you hear about the XYZ health plan? What other health plans did you consider before making your actual purchase? What influenced you to buy the plan you eventually bought? Were any other people influential in helping you make your decision?" Through the exploration of these and similar questions, the facilitator and the relevant organizational members (who may be seated behind a one-way mirror, watching the discussion) may put together a more effective health plan or more effective advertising strategies.

Objectives Self-Check
- Can you define the *educational* or *learning group* and the *focus group?*
- Can you participate effectively in these information-sharing groups?

Personal Growth Groups

Some **personal growth groups,** sometimes referred to as *support groups,* aim to help members cope with particular difficulties—such as drug addiction, not being assertive enough, being an ex-convict, or dealing with an alcoholic parent, a hyperactive child, or a promiscuous spouse. Other groups are more clearly therapeutic and are designed to change significant aspects of an individual's personality or behavior. Still other groups are devoted to making healthy individuals function even more effectively.

Because personal growth groups vary widely in their procedures, it's not possible to provide a standard pattern that all such groups follow (as is the case with brainstorming groups, discussed above, or with problem-solving groups, discussed later in this chapter). But let's look briefly at four well-known types of personal growth groups: (1) the encounter group, (2) the assertiveness training group, (3) the consciousness-raising group, and (4) the intervention group.

A word of caution should be injected here: Personal growth groups are highly personal and ego-involving; and although they will all seem easy and reasonable to set up and participate in, they are actually very complex and difficult. They are discussed here (briefly) to give you an idea of the types of personal growth groups available rather than to provide a set of guidelines for using these groups.

THE ENCOUNTER GROUP

The **encounter group,** also known as the "sensitivity group" or "T [Training]-group," constitutes a form of psychotherapy; these groups try to facilitate members' personal growth and foster their ability to deal effectively with other people (Hirsch, Kett, & Trefil, 2002; Rogers, 1970). One of the encounter group's assumptions is that the members will be more effective, both psychologically and interpersonally, if they get to know and like themselves better. Consequently, members are encouraged to look at themselves and their relationships honestly and in depth and to react to others in the group openly and honestly. Members are encouraged to express their inner thoughts, fears, and doubts in the encounter group, in which interactions are always characterized by total acceptance and support.

THE ASSERTIVENESS TRAINING GROUP

The **assertiveness training group** aims to increase the willingness of its members to stand up for their rights and to act more assertively in a wide variety of situations (Adler, 1977; Bishop, 2006). Distinctions are made between being assertive (which is good and effective); being non-assertive (which is ineffective, because your own wants and needs are unlikely to be met); and being aggressive (which also is ineffective, because it contributes to escalating the conflict and causing resentment). The group aims to increase the assertiveness skills of its members, who are likely to be individuals who feel they are not assertive enough. The skill of assertiveness is covered in more detail in the discussion of verbal messages in Chapter 4.

VIEWPOINTS

Chatting

In research of online messages, it was found that people were more likely to comment on a message when that message was negative than when it was positive (Rollman, Krug, & Parente, 2000). Do you find this to be true in your social network messages? If so, why do you think this occurs? Would it be fair to say, from your own experience, that the reverse would be true in face-to-face communication?

THE CONSCIOUSNESS-RAISING GROUP

The **consciousness-raising group** aims to help people cope with the problems society confronts them with. The members of this type of group all have one characteristic in common (for example, they may all be women, unwed mothers, gay fathers, or recently unemployed executives). It's this commonality that leads the members to join together and help one another. In the consciousness-raising group the assumption is that similar people are best equipped to assist one another's personal growth. The procedures generally followed are simple: A topic is selected, and each member speaks on the topic as it relates to the general group topic. For example, if the group consists of unwed mothers, then whatever the topic (taxes, children, school, prejudice), the members address it in the context of the group's focus on unwed motherhood. No interruptions are allowed. After each member has finished, the other group members may ask questions of clarification. The feedback from other members is to be totally supportive. After the last member has spoken, a general discussion follows. This procedure is designed to help raise members' consciousness by giving them an opportunity to formulate and verbalize their thoughts on a particular topic, hear how others feel and think about the same topic, and formulate and answer questions of clarification.

COMMUNICATING ETHICALLY

The Ethics of Gossip

Gossip is social talk that involves making evaluations about persons who are not present during the conversation; and it can occur between only two people or in a small group, as in office gossip at the cafeteria, for example (Eder & Enke, 1991; Wert & Salovey, 2004). One study estimates that approximately two-thirds of people's conversation time is devoted to social topics, and that most of these topics can be considered gossip (Dunbar, 2004). Gossip bonds people together and solidifies their relationship; it creates a sense of camaraderie (Greengard, 2001; Hafen, 2004). At the same time, of course, it helps to create an in-group (i.e., those doing the gossiping) and an out-group (i.e., those being gossiped about).

As you might expect, in many instances gossip would be considered unethical. Some instances generally identified as unethical include the following (Bok, 1983):

Ethical Choice Point

You're supervising a new group of interns and you're wondering if you should tell them about the supervisor who has made romantic overtures to several former interns? Would this just be unethical gossip or would it be ethical and well within your mission to warn them?

- When gossip is used to unfairly hurt another person—for example, spreading gossip about an office romance or an instructor's past indiscretions
- When you know that what you're saying is not true—for example, lying to make another person look bad or spreading false rumors
- When no one has the right to such personal information—for example, revealing the income of neighbors to others or revealing another student's poor grades to your friends
- When you've promised secrecy—for example, revealing something that you promised not to repeat to others

THE INTERVENTION GROUP

In the **intervention group** participants gather to help one of their members overcome some problem. For example, family members may join together to confront an alcoholic parent or sibling. Other commonly confronted issues are drug, gambling, and sex addiction and eating disorders. Usually a leader is designated (sometimes a professional intervention leader and sometimes a group member). Under the leader's guidance the group members express their support and love for the person with the problem behavior, explain the impact of this member's behavior on all connected others, and offer to help the person. As you can imagine, the skills of empathy, supportiveness, and immediacy are especially important in the intervention.

Objectives Self-Check
- Can you define and distinguish among the *encounter group*, the *assertiveness training group*, the *consciousness-raising group*, and the *intervention*?

Watch the **Video** "Helping Annie" at **MyCommunicationLab**

For a brief discussion of the skills of small group, see "Small Group Advice" at http://tcbdevito .blogspot.com. What other advice would you give?

Problem-Solving Groups

A **problem-solving group** meets to solve a particular problem or to reach a decision on some issue. In a sense, this is the most demanding kind of group. It requires not only a knowledge of small group communication techniques but also a thorough knowledge of the particular problem on the part of all group members. Also, for the most successful outcome, it usually demands faithful adherence to a set of procedural rules.

THE PROBLEM-SOLVING SEQUENCE

The **problem-solving sequence** identifies six steps and owes its formulation to philosopher John Dewey's insights into how people think (see Figure 9.3). These steps are designed to make problem solving more efficient and effective.

Step 1: Define and Analyze the Problem   In some instances, the nature of the problem is clearly specified. For example, a work team might discuss how to package new tablets or smart phones Valentine's Day. In other instances, however, the problem may be vague, and it may be up to the group to define it—for example, the general topic of poor campus communications. In this case, the topic has to be more clearly defined and limited—for example, how the college website can be improved. Define the problem as an open-ended question ("How can we improve the college website?") rather than as a statement ("The website needs to be improved") or as a yes/no question ("Does the website need improvement?").

Step 2: Establish Criteria for Evaluating Solutions   Decide how you'll evaluate the solutions before proposing them. Identify the standards or criteria you'll use in evaluating solutions or in preferring one solution over another. For example, you might decide that a solution must lead to a 10 percent increase in website visits, that the solutions must not increase the budget, that the website information must not violate anyone's right to privacy, or that the website must provide a forum for all members of the college community. Set up criteria that are realistic and that can, in fact, be attained; otherwise, no solution is going to prove acceptable.

Step 3: Identify Possible Solutions   Identify as many solutions as possible. Focus on quantity rather than quality. Brainstorming may be particularly useful at this point. Solutions to the website improvement problem might include incorporating reviews of faculty publications, student evaluations of specific courses, reviews of restaurants in the campus area, outlines for new courses, and employment information.

Step 4: Evaluate Solutions   After all solutions have been proposed, evaluate each one. For example, does incorporating reviews of area restaurants meet the criteria? Would it increase the budget, for example? Would posting grades violate students' rights to privacy? Each potential solution should be matched against the evaluating criteria.

Step 5: Select the Best Solution(s)   Select the best solution and put it into operation. Let's assume that reviews of faculty publications and outlines for new courses best meet the evaluating criteria for solutions. The group might then incorporate these two new items into the website.

Groups use different decision-making methods when deciding, for example, which solution to accept. The method to be used should, naturally, be stated at the outset of the group discussion. Three main decision-making methods can be followed:

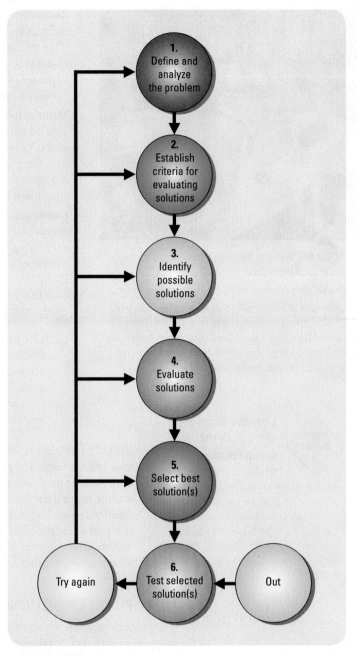

FIGURE 9.3

The Problem-Solving Sequence

Although most small group theorists would advise you to follow the problem-solving pattern as presented here, others would alter it somewhat. For example, some would advise you to reverse steps 2 and 3: to identify possible solutions first and then consider the criteria for evaluating them. The advantage of this approach is that you're likely to generate more creative solutions, because you will not be restricted by standards of evaluation. The disadvantage is that you may spend a great deal of time generating impractical solutions that will never meet the standards you will eventually propose.

VIEWPOINTS

Developing Criteria

What type of criteria would an advertising agency use in evaluating a campaign to sell soap? A university, in evaluating a new multicultural curriculum? Parents, in evaluating a preschool for their children? A group of people creating a sign for protest?

Communication Choice Point

Group Pressure

All of your colleagues at your new job pad their expense accounts. You don't want to go along with this, but if you don't, everyone else will be found out. You don't want to make waves, yet you don't want to do something unethical. *What are some of the options you have for dealing with this issue?*

For an interesting article on the importance of communication, see "The Importance of Communication in the Workplace" at **tcbdevito .blogspot.com**. How will communication figure into your own anticipated or current workplace?

- **Authority:** In decision making by authority, group members voice their feelings and opinions, but the leader or boss makes the final decision. This method has the advantages of being efficient and of giving greater importance to the suggestions of more experienced members. The disadvantage is that members may feel that their contributions have too little influence and therefore may not participate with real enthusiasm.

- **Majority rule:** The group agrees to abide by the majority decision and may vote on various issues as the group searches to solve its problem. Like decision by authority, this method is efficient. A disadvantage is that it may lead the group to limit discussion by calling for a vote once a majority has agreed. Also, members not voting with the majority may feel disenfranchised and left out.

- **Consensus:** In small group decision making, consensus means reaching agreement. The agreement does not have to be unanimous; it is, rather, something that the group members can live with; they agree that they can do whatever the group's solution requires (Kelly, 1994). It does not imply that each individual group member agrees with the solution, but only that members agree that at this time (for this situation, for this group) this solution should be adopted and followed:

  > Consensus is the most time-consuming of the decision-making methods. However, it is also the method that best secures the cooperation and participation of all members in implementing the group's decisions. If you want members of the group to be satisfied with and committed to the decision, consensus seems to be the best way to arrive at a solution (Beebe & Masterson, 2012).

Step 6: Test Selected Solutions   After putting solutions into operation, test their effectiveness. The group might, for example, poll the students or college employees about the new website. Or the group might analyze the number of visits to the website to see if the number of visits increases by the desired 10 percent. If the selected solutions prove ineffective, the group will need to return to a previous stage and repeat that part of the process. This often involves selecting other solutions to test. But it also may mean going even farther back in the process—to a reanalysis of the problem, an identification of other solutions, or a restatement of criteria, for example.

PROBLEM-SOLVING GROUPS AT WORK

The problem-solving sequence discussed here is used widely in a variety of different types of business groups. Let's examine three popular approaches that rely largely on the problem-solving techniques just discussed: (1) the nominal group technique, (2) the Delphi method, and (3) quality circles.

As you read these discussions, realize that the available technology will dictate some of the ways in which these groups operate. If the members only have a whiteboard, then much will be recorded on the board. If all members have computers connected to the company website, then much of the record keeping will go onto the website and at the same time into each laptop or tablet.

The Nominal Group Technique   The **nominal group** technique is a method of problem solving that uses limited discussion and confidential voting to obtain a group decision. It's especially helpful when some members may be reluctant to voice their opinions in a regular problem-solving group or when the issue is controversial or sensitive. The nominal group technique can be divided into eight steps (Kelly, 1994):

1. The problem is defined and clarified for all members.

2. Each member writes down (without discussion or consultation with others) his or her ideas on or possible solutions to the problem.

SKILL DEVELOPMENT EXPERIENCE

Solving Problems in Groups

Together with four, five, or six other group members—online or face-to-face—problem-solve one of the following questions:

a. What should we do about the homeless?
b. What should we do to improve the college's website?
c. What should we do to better prepare ourselves for the job market?
d. How can social networking sites be used more effectively?
e. How can we improve student-faculty communication?

Before beginning discussion of the topic, prepare a discussion outline, answering the following questions:

1. What is the problem? What are its causes? What are its effects?
2. What criteria should a solution have to satisfy?
3. What are some possible solutions?
4. What are the advantages and disadvantages of each of these solutions?
5. What solution seems best (in light of the advantages and disadvantages)?
6. How might this solution be tested?

Following patterns like this helps you move a discussion along without unnecessary detours, and it ensures that you'll cover all essential steps.

3. Each member—in sequence—states one idea from his or her list, which is recorded on a board or flip chart so everyone can see it. This process is repeated until all suggestions are stated and recorded.

4. Each suggestion is clarified (without debate). Ideally, each suggestion is given equal time.

5. Each member rank-orders the suggestions in writing.

6. The rankings of the members are combined to get a group ranking, which is then written on the board.

7. Clarification, discussion, and possible reordering may follow.

8. The highest-ranking or several high-ranking solutions may then be put into operation and tested.

The Delphi Method

In the **Delphi method** a group of "experts" is established, but there's no interaction among them; instead, they communicate by repeatedly responding to questionnaires (Kelly, 1994; Tersine & Riggs, 1980). The Delphi method is especially useful when you want to involve people who are geographically distant from one another, when you want all members to become part of the solution and to uphold it, or when you want to minimize the effects of dominant members or even of peer pressure. The method is best explained as a series of eight steps (Kelly, 1994):

1. The problem is defined (for example, "We need to improve intradepartmental communication"). What each member is expected to do is specified (for example, each member should contribute five ideas on this specific question).

2. Each member then anonymously contributes five ideas in writing.

3. The ideas of all members are combined, written up, and distributed to all members.

4. Members then select the three or four best ideas from this composite list and submit these.

5. From these responses another list is produced and distributed to all members.

6. Members then select the one or two best ideas from the new list and submit these.

7. From these responses another list is produced and distributed to all members. The process may be repeated any number of times, but usually three rounds are sufficient for achieving a fair degree of agreement.

8. The "final" solutions are identified and are communicated to all members.

Communication Choice Point

Critical Thinking

You're on a team (all equal in your organizational position) charged with designing the packaging for a new cell phone, and you need to establish how a decision will be made. *What are some of your decision-making options? What are the advantages and disadvantages of each decision-making option?*

Quality Circles   A **quality circle** is a group of employees (usually about 6 to 12) whose task it is to investigate and make recommendations for improving the quality of some organizational function. The members are drawn from the workers whose area is being studied; for example, if the problem were how to improve advertising on the Internet, then the quality circle membership would be drawn from the advertising and technology departments. The basic assumption is that people who work on similar tasks will be best able to improve their departments or jobs by pooling their insights and working through problems they share.

Quality circle members investigate problems using any method they feel might be helpful; for example, they may form face-to-face problem-solving groups or use nominal groups or Delphi methods. The group then reports its findings and suggestions to those who can implement the proposals.

Objectives Self-Check
- Can you describe the problem-solving sequence?
- Can you use this sequence in group problem solving?
- Can you describe and use appropriate methods of decision making?
- Can you define *nominal, Delphi,* and *quality circle* groups?

⚠ Messages in the Media *Wrap Up*

Most television talk shows, you'll find, demonstrate the effective use of small group communication techniques. Analyzing these shows for the principles of small group communication that they follow will help you see the principles discussed here in concrete operation.

⇅ Summary of Concepts and Skills

✓ **Study** and **Review** materials for this chapter are at **MyCommunicationLab**

Listen to the **Audio Chapter** Summary at **MyCommunicationLab**

This chapter provided an overview of the four major types of small groups (brainstorming, information sharing, personal growth, and problem solving) and how they work, and the popular small group formats.

Essentials of Small Groups and Teams

1. A small group is a collection of individuals who share a common purpose, are interdependent, operate with organizing rules, and see themselves as a group. A team is also a small group, but it is usually established for a specific task in which the members' roles are specifically defined; members are committed to accomplishing the task; and their messages are largely content focused.

2. Virtual groups and teams are increasing dramatically in businesses and social networking.

3. Small group interactions generally follow the five stages of conversation: opening, feedforward, business, feedback, closing.

4. Four popular small group formats are the roundtable, the panel, the symposium, and the symposium-forum.

5. Small group apprehension can be managed by using the same techniques for managing fear of public speaking.

6. Small groups develop norms (i.e., rules or standards of behavior) and are heavily influenced by the larger culture of which the groups are a part.

Brainstorming Groups

7. The brainstorming group attempts to generate as many ideas as possible by avoiding critical evaluation and

encouraging quantity of ideas, combinations and extensions of ideas, and freewheeling.

Information-Sharing Groups

8. Information-sharing groups (e.g., learning groups and focus groups) attempt to acquire new information or skill through a mutual sharing of knowledge or insight.

Personal Growth Groups

9. The personal growth group helps members to deal with personal problems and to function more effectively. Popular types of personal growth groups are the encounter group, the assertiveness training group, the consciousness-raising group, and the intervention group.

Problem-Solving Groups

10. The problem-solving group attempts to solve a particular problem, or at least to reach a decision that may be a preface to solving the problem, and may do so through decision by authority, majority rule, or consensus.

11. The steps in the problem-solving approach are (1) define and analyze the problem, (2) establish criteria for evaluating solutions, (3) identify possible solutions, (4) evaluate solutions, (5) select the best solution(s), and (6) test selected solution(s).

12. Small group approaches that are widely used in business today include the nominal group, the Delphi method, and quality circles.

The skills covered in this chapter focus on your ability to function effectively in a variety of small groups. Place a check mark next to those skills you want to work on most.

_____ 1. I actively seek to discover the norms of the groups in which I function and take these norms into consideration when interacting in the group.

_____ 2. I can communicate in virtual groups, such as social networking groups.

_____ 3. I can adjust my messages and listening in light of differences between high-context and low-context cultures.

_____ 4. I follow the general rules when brainstorming: I avoid negative criticism, strive for quantity, combine and extend the contributions of others, and contribute as wild an idea as I can.

_____ 5. I appropriately re-stimulate a brainstorming group that has lost its steam.

_____ 6. I employ organizational structure in educational or learning groups.

_____ 7. I interact responsibly in personal growth groups.

_____ 8. I follow the six steps when in group problem-solving situations: Define and analyze the problem, establish the criteria for evaluating solutions, identify possible solutions, evaluate solutions, select the best solution(s), and test selected solution(s).

_____ 9. I can make use of techniques such as the nominal group, Delphi method, and quality circles.

Key Word Quiz

The Language of Small Group Communication

Match the terms about small group communication with their definitions. Record the number of the definition next to the appropriate term.

_____ a. interdependence (175)

_____ b. group norms (178)

_____ c. quality circles (188)

_____ d. brainstorming (180)

_____ e. team (175)

_____ f. high-context culture (179)

_____ g. symposium (177)

_____ h. consensus (186)

_____ i. nominal group (186)

_____ j. focus group (182)

1. A group of employees charged with identifying ways to improve the organization.

2. A series of prepared presentations introduced and coordinated by a leader.

3. A kind of in-depth interview of a small group.

4. Rules or standards identifying which behaviors are considered appropriate and which are considered inappropriate in a group.

5. A type of agreement in which group members all agree that a solution is acceptable.

6. That relationship in which one person's behavior significantly impacts on the other person.

7. A culture in which much of the information in communication is not explicitly coded in verbal messages but is considered common knowledge to all participants.

8. A problem-solving technique in which there is little discussion and confidential voting.

9. A small group constructed for a specific purpose.

10. A small group process for generating ideas.

These ten terms and additional terms used in this chapter can be found in the glossary.

Answers: a. 6 b. 4 c. 1 d. 10 e. 9 f. 7 g. 2 h. 5 i. 8 j. 3

 Study and **Review** the **Flashcards** at **MyCommunicationLab**

MyCommunicationLab

Throughout this chapter, there are icons in the margin that highlight media content for selected topics. Go to **MyCommunicationLab** for additional materials on the small group. Here you'll find flashcards to help you learn the jargon of communication, videos that illustrate a variety of concepts, additional exercises, and discussions to help you continue your study of small group communication.

THE VIEW

10

Members and Leaders in Small Group Communication

Objectives

 Listen to the **Audio Chapter** at **MyCommunicationLab**

After reading this chapter, you should be able to:

❶ Explain the role of culture in small group communication and define and distinguish between individual and collective orientations and high- and low-power distances.

❷ Describe and distinguish among group task roles, group building/maintenance roles, and individual roles, and serve (or avoid) these roles for effective member participation.

❸ Define *leadership,* explain its myths, the approaches to leadership, and the general styles of leadership; and apply the skills for effective small group leadership.

As you saw in Chapter 9, you're a part of many different groups, and you serve a wide variety of roles and functions in these groups. This chapter focuses on both membership and leadership in small groups. By gaining insight into these roles and functions, you'll increase your own effectiveness as a group member and leader. A good way to begin is to look at how both membership and leadership are viewed differently in different cultures.

Membership, Leadership, and Culture

Because most of the research (and also the resulting theory) concerning small group communication, membership, and leadership has been conducted in universities in the United States and reflects U.S. culture, it's important that we look at both membership and leadership from the point of view of different cultures.

All cultures maintain their own belief systems, which influence group members' behavior. Members of many Asian cultures, influenced by Confucian principles, believe that "the protruding nail gets pounded down" and are therefore not likely to voice disagreement with the majority of the group. Members of U.S. culture, on the other hand, influenced by the axiom that "the squeaky wheel gets the grease," are likely to voice disagreement or to act in ways different from other group members in order to get what they want (Hofstede, Hofstede, & Minkov, 2010).

All cultures also have their own rules of preferred and expected leadership style. In the United States, the general and expected style for a group leader is democratic. Our political leaders are elected by a democratic process; similarly, company directors are elected by the shareholders of their corporations. In other situations, of course, leaders are chosen by those in authority. The president of a company will normally decide who will supervise and who will be supervised. Even in this situation, however, the supervisor is expected to behave democratically: to listen to the ideas of the employees; to take their views into consideration when decisions are to be made; to keep them informed of corporate developments; and not to discriminate on the basis of sex, race, or affectional orientation. In the United States people expect that organizational and other group leaders will be changed fairly regularly, much as we change political leaders on a regular basis. In some other cultures, leaders get their positions by right of birth. They are not elected, nor are they expected to behave democratically.

INDIVIDUAL AND COLLECTIVE ORIENTATIONS

Small group cultures and cultures in general differ in the extent to which they promote individualistic values (e.g., power, achievement, hedonism, and stimulation) versus collectivist values (e.g., benevolence, tradition, and conformity).

One of the major differences between an **individual orientation** and a **collective orientation** is in the extent to which an individual's goals or the group's goals are given precedence. Individual and collective tendencies are, of course, not mutually exclusive; this is not an all-or-none orientation, but rather one of emphasis. You probably have both tendencies. Thus, you may, for example, compete with other members of your basketball team to make the most baskets; but in a game, you'd likely act in a way that will benefit the entire team (and thus emphasize group goals). In practice, both individual and collective tendencies will help both you and your team achieve your goals. Still, most people and most cultures have a dominant orientation.

In an *individualist culture* you're responsible to your own conscience; responsibility is largely an individual matter. Examples of individualist cultures include those of the United States, Australia, United Kingdom, Netherlands, Canada, New Zealand, Italy, Belgium, Denmark, and Sweden (Hofstede, Hofstede, & Minkov, 2010; Singh & Pereira, 2005). In a *collectivist culture* you're responsible to the rules of the social group; all members share responsibility for accomplishments as well as for failures. Examples include the cultures of Guatemala, Ecuador, Panama, Venezuela, Colombia, Indonesia, Pakistan, China, Costa Rica, and Peru (Hofstede, Hofstede, & Minkov, 2010). Individualistic cultures foster competition, whereas collectivist cultures promote cooperation.

Communication Choice Point

Asserting Yourself in a Group

In your meetings at work, the supervisor consistently ignores your cues that you want to say something—and when you do manage to say something, no one reacts. You're determined to change this situation. *What are some of your options for addressing this situation?*

One obvious consequence of this difference in orientation can be seen in how individualistic and collectivist groups treat members who commit serious errors. A group governed by individualistic norms is likely to single out, reprimand, and perhaps fire an errant member. Further, the leader or supervisor is likely to distance himself or herself from this group member for fear that the error will reflect negatively on his or her leadership. In a more collectivist culture, the error is more likely to be seen as a group mistake. The group is unlikely to single out the member—especially not in public—and the leader is likely to bear part of the blame. The same is true when one member comes up with a great idea. In individualist cultures that person is likely to be singled out for praise and rewards, even though the effort was to benefit the group. In collectivist cultures the group is recognized and rewarded for the idea.

HIGH AND LOW POWER DISTANCES

In **high-power-distance cultures,** power is concentrated in the hands of a few, and there is a great difference between the power held by these people and the power held by the ordinary citizen; examples include the cultures of Malaysia, Panama, Guatemala, Philippines, Venezuela, Mexico, China, the Arab world, Indonesia, and Ecuador (Hofstede, Hofstede, & Minkov, 2010; Singh & Pereira, 2005). In **low-power-distance cultures,** power is more evenly distributed throughout the citizenry; examples include Austria, Israel, Denmark, New Zealand, Ireland, Norway, Sweden, Finland, Switzerland, and Costa Rica (Hofstede, Hofstede, & Minkov, 2010).

The power distance between groups will influence the group of friends you develop, as well as whom you might date (Andersen, 1991). For example, in India (which is high-power distance) your group of friends is expected to be chosen from those within your cultural class (as are your dating partners). In Sweden (which is low-power distance), a person is expected to form friendships (and romances) on the basis not of class or culture but of individual factors such as personality, appearance, and the like.

In high-power-distance cultures, you're taught to have great respect for authority; people in these cultures see authority as desirable and beneficial and generally do not welcome challenges to authority (Westwood, Tang, & Kirkbride, 1992; Bochner & Hesketh, 1994). In low-power-distance cultures, there's a certain distrust of authority; it's seen as a kind of necessary evil that should be limited as much as possible. This difference in attitudes toward authority can be seen in the classroom. In high-power-distance cultures, there's a great power distance between students and teachers; students are expected to be modest, polite, and totally respectful. In low-power-distance cultures, students are expected to demonstrate their knowledge and command of the subject matter, participate in discussions with the teacher, and even challenge the teacher—something many members of high-power-distance cultures wouldn't think of doing.

High-power-distance cultures rely on symbols of power. For example, titles (e.g., Dr., Professor, Chef, Inspector) are more important in high-power-distance cultures. Failure to include these honorifics in forms of address is a serious breach of etiquette. Low-power-distance cultures rely less on symbols of power, so there is less of a problem if you fail to use a respectful title (Victor, 1992). Regardless, you still may create problems if, for example, you address a medical doctor, police captain, military officer, or professor with "Ms." or "Mr."

The groups in which you'll participate as a member or a leader will vary in power distance; some will be high-power-distance groups and others will be low. You need to recognize which is which, to follow the cultural rules generally, and to break the rules only after you've thought through the consequences.

VIEWPOINTS

Power Distances

In low-power-distance cultures, there is a general feeling of equality, which is consistent with acting assertively; so you're expected to confront a friend, partner, or supervisor assertively (Borden, 1991). In high-power-distance cultures, direct confrontation and assertiveness may be viewed negatively, especially if directed at a superior. How would you describe the cultures of the group in which you participate—face-to-face and online?

For politeness in the workplace, see the self-test on this topic at http://tcbdevito.blogspot.com. How did you do? What will you do?

Objectives Self-Check
- Can you explain the role of culture in small group communication?
- Can you define and distinguish between individual and collective orientations and between high-power and low-power distances?

Members in Small Group Communication

Each of us serves many **roles,** patterns of behaviors that we customarily perform and that we're expected by others to perform. Javier, for example, is a part-time college student, father, bookkeeper, bowling team captain, and sometime poet. That is, he acts as a student—attends class, reads textbooks, takes exams, and does the things we expect of college students. He also performs those behaviors associated with fathers, bookkeepers, and so on. In a similar way, you develop relevant ways of behaving when participating in small groups. Before reading about these roles, take the accompanying self-test, "What Kind of Group Member Are You?"

TEST YOURSELF

What Kind of Group Member Are You?

For each statement below, respond with **T** if the statement is often true of your group behavior or **F** if the statement generally does not apply to your group behavior.

_____ ❶ I present new ideas and suggest new strategies.

_____ ❷ I ask for facts and opinions.

_____ ❸ I stimulate the group.

_____ ❹ I give examples and try to look for positive solutions.

_____ ❺ I positively reinforce group members.

_____ ❻ I try to reconcile differences.

_____ ❼ I go along with the other members.

_____ ❽ I offer compromises as ways of resolving conflict.

_____ ❾ I express negative evaluation of the actions and feelings of the group members.

_____ ❿ I try to run the group.

_____ ⓫ I express personal perspectives and feelings.

_____ ⓬ I express confusion or deprecate myself.

HOW DID YOU DO? As you'll see as you read further, these behaviors are characteristic of the three general types of group member roles. The first four statements refer to your taking on group task roles, and the next four refer to your taking on group building and maintenance roles. Both of these types of roles are productive. The final four refer to your taking an individual rather than a group focus; these are the behaviors that often work against the group achieving its goals.

WHAT WILL YOU DO? As you read the sections in the text on member roles, try to relate these roles to your own behavior or to group behavior you've witnessed. Then ask yourself what worked and what didn't work. Which roles were productive, and which ones were unproductive?

MEMBER ROLES

Group member roles fall into three general classes—group task roles, group building and maintenance roles, and individual roles—a classification introduced in early research (Benne & Sheats, 1948) and still widely used today (Lumsden & Lumsden, 1996; Beebe & Masterson, 2012). These roles are frequently served by leaders as well.

Watch the **Video**
"Planning a Playground" at
MyCommunicationLab

Group Task Roles
Group task roles help the group focus on achieving its goals. Effective group members serve several roles. Some people lock into a few specific roles, but this single focus is usually counterproductive—it's better for the roles to be spread more evenly among the members and for the roles to be alternated frequently. Here are some examples of group task roles.

- **The information seeker or giver or the opinion seeker or giver** asks for or gives facts or opinions, seeks clarification of issues being discussed, and presents facts or opinions to group members: "Sales for May were up 10 percent. Do we have the sales figures for June?"
- **The initiator-contributor** presents new ideas or new perspectives on old ideas, suggests new goals, or proposes new procedures or organizational strategies: "We need to also look at the amount of time visitors spend on our new site."
- **The elaborator** gives examples and tries to work out possible solutions, trying to build on what others have said: "That three-part division worked at ABC and should work here as well."
- **The evaluator-critic** evaluates the group's decisions, questions the logic or practicality of the suggestions, and provides the group with both positive and negative feedback: "That's a great idea, but it sounds expensive."
- **The procedural technician** or recorder takes care of various mechanical duties, such as distributing group materials and arranging the seating; writing down the group's activities, suggestions, and decisions; and/or serving as the group's memory: "We have another meeting scheduled to discuss just this issue, so perhaps we can skip it for today."

Group Building and Maintenance Roles
No group can be task oriented at all times. Group members have varied interpersonal relationships, and these need to be nourished if the group is to function effectively. Group members need to be satisfied if they are to be productive. Group building and maintenance roles serve these relationship needs. Here are some examples of these roles.

- **The encourager or harmonizer** provides members with positive reinforcement through social approval or praise for their ideas and mediates the various differences between group members: "Pat, another great idea."
- **The compromiser** tries to resolve conflict between his or her ideas and those of others and offers compromises: "This looks like it could work if each department cut back at least 10 percent."
- **The gatekeeper-expediter** keeps the channels of communication open by reinforcing the efforts of others: "Those were really good ideas; we're on a roll."
- **The standard setter** proposes standards for the functions of the group or for its solutions: "We need to be able to increase the number of visits by several thousand a day."
- **The follower** goes along with members, passively accepts the ideas of others, and functions more as an audience than as an active member: "If you all agree, that's fine with me."

VIEWPOINTS

Group Roles in Interpersonal Relationships

Can you identify roles that you habitually or frequently serve in certain groups? Do you serve these roles in your close interpersonal relationships as you do in your workplace relationships?

Individual Roles
Whereas group task and group building and maintenance roles are productive and help the group achieve its goal, **individual roles** involve behavior that is counterproductive. They hinder

SKILL DEVELOPMENT EXPERIENCE

Responding to Individual Roles

For each of the five individual roles, compose a response or two that you as a leader might make in order to deal with this dysfunctional role playing. Be careful that your responses don't alienate the individual or the group.

One major value of small group interaction is that everyone profits from the insights of everyone else; individual roles can get in the way.

Individual, Dysfunctional Roles	Responding to Individual Roles
The aggressor	_____
The recognition seeker or self-confessor	_____
The blocker	_____
The special interest pleader	_____
The dominator	_____

Communication Choice Point

Individual Roles

In a group of workers, one member consistently plays the role of blocker, objecting to everything anyone says. Another member plays the role of self-confessor, revealing feelings no one wants to hear. *What are some of the options that members have for dealing with individual role players like these?*

the group from achieving its goal and are individual rather than group oriented. Such roles, often termed dysfunctional, hinder the group's effectiveness in terms of both productivity and personal satisfaction. Here are some examples of individual roles:

- **The aggressor** expresses negative evaluation of members and attacks the group: "That's a terrible idea. It doesn't make any sense."

- **The recognition seekers and self-confessors** try to focus attention on themselves, boast about their accomplishments rather than the task at hand, and express their own feelings rather than focus on the group: "The system I devised at B&B was a great success; everyone loved it. We should just go with that."

- **The blocker** provides negative feedback, is disagreeable, and opposes other members or suggestions regardless of their merit: "You're dreaming if you think that will work."

- **The special interest pleader** disregards the goals of the group and pleads the case of some special group: "This solution isn't adequate; it doesn't address the needs of XYZ."

- **The dominator** tries to run the group or members by pulling rank, flattering members, or acting the role of boss: "I've been here the longest; I know what works and what doesn't work."

A popular individual role born on the Internet is *trolling,* the practice of posting messages that you know are false or outrageous just so you can watch the group members correct you or get emotionally upset by your message. As in any group, behavior such as trolling or flaming wastes time and energy and diverts the group from its primary objective.

MEMBER PARTICIPATION AND SKILLS

Here are several guidelines to help make your participation in small group communication more effective and enjoyable.

Watch the **Video** "Group Project" at **MyCommunicationLab**

Be Group Oriented   When participating in a small group, you serve as a member of a team. You share common goals with the other group members, and your participation is valuable to the extent that it advances this shared goal. In a team situation, you need to pool your talents, knowledge, and insights to promote the best possible solution for the group. Although a group orientation calls for the participation and cooperation of all group members, this guideline does not suggest that you abandon your individuality, personal values, or beliefs for the group's sake. Individuality *with* a group orientation is most effective. And because the most effective and the most creative solutions often emerge from a combination of ideas, approach small group situations with flexibility; come to the group with ideas and information but without firmly formulated conclusions. The importance of a group orientation is also seen in one of the rules of netiquette, which holds that you should not protest the subject of, say, a mailing list or a chat group. If you don't wish to be group oriented and discuss what the group is discussing, you're expected to unsubscribe from the mailing list or withdraw from the group.

Center Conflict on Issues   Conflict in small group situations is inevitable; it's a natural part of the give and take of ideas and often promotes a better outcome. To manage conflict effectively, however, center it on issues rather than on personalities. When you disagree, make it clear that your disagreement is with the ideas expressed, not with the person who expressed them. For example, if you think that a colleague's ideas to raise funds for your social service agency are impractical and shortsighted, concentrate your criticisms on your colleague's proposed plan and suggest ways that the plan could be improved rather than attacking your colleague personally. Similarly, when someone disagrees with you, try not to take it personally or react emotionally. Rather, view the disagreement as an opportunity to discuss issues from an alternative point of view. In the language of the Internet, don't flame—don't attack the person. And don't contribute to flame wars by flame baiting, or saying things that will further incite the personal attacks.

Be Critically Open-Minded   When members join a group with their minds already made up, the small group process degenerates into a series of debates in which each person argues for his or her position—a clear example of members' taking on individual and dysfunctional roles. Group goals are neglected and the group process breaks down.

Let's say you have spent several hours developing what you think is the best, most effective advertising campaign to combat your company's low sales numbers. At the group meeting, however, members' reactions are extremely critical. Instead of becoming defensive, listen to their criticisms and try to think of ways that your plan could be modified to be as effective as possible for the company. To avoid this situation in the future, try to come to the group with ideas rather than conclusions; with suggestions rather than final decisions; and, of course, with information that will contribute to the discussion and the group goal. Be willing to accept other people's suggestions as well as to revise your own in light of the discussion. Listen openly but critically to comments of all members (including your own).

Beware of Social Loafing   Visualize yourself in a rope pulling contest—you need to successfully pull the other side into the pond or they will pull you. With this vision in mind, consider whether you would exert more effort if you were alone or if you were part of a group of five or six. The concept of **social loafing**—the theory that you exert less effort when you're part of a group than when alone—resulted from experiments such as this that measured the amount of effort people actually exerted alone versus in groups (Latané, Williams, & Harkins, 2006). Being aware of this tendency is a useful first step in combating it. It's often an unproductive group tendency that leads to less productive group interactions and decisions. And it is probably noticed by others and so hurts you professionally. Some of the factors that influence social loafing and corresponding correctives are identified in Table 10.1 (p. 198).

Ensure Understanding   Make sure all participants understand your ideas and information. If something is worth saying, it's worth making clear. When in doubt, ask questions: "Is that clear?" "Did I explain that clearly?" Make sure, too, that you fully understand other members'

Communication Choice Point

Small Group Conflicts

You're leading a group of graduate and undergraduate students, charged with evaluating the core curriculum. The problem is that neither the graduate students nor the undergraduates want to listen fairly to each other. *Thinking back to the discussion of listening (Chapter 3), what are some of the things you might say to promote more effective group listening?*

VIEWPOINTS

Social Facilitation

The opposite of social loafing is social facilitation, which holds that in a group you exert more effort than you would if you were alone. You might feel this way if you felt you were being watched and evaluated, for example. Under what conditions are you likely to perform below your normal level? Under what conditions are you likely to perform above your normal level?

TABLE 10.1 Social Loafing

Here are a few factors that influence the likelihood that social loafing will occur and some correctives (Kenrick, Neuberg, & Cialdini, 2007).

When Social Loafing Is More Likely to Occur	Corrective
An individual group member's contributions cannot be easily identified.	Make contributions easily identifiable and make members aware of this.
The punishment for or cost of poor performance is insignificant.	Reward excellent performance and/or punish poor performance.
The group lacks cohesion.	Stress the importance of being part of a group or team; following the suggestions for group membership and leadership will help here.
The task has little personal importance.	Stress the personal connection between the members of the group and the task.

contributions, especially before you disagree with them. In fact, it's often wise to preface any expression of disagreement with some kind of paraphrase to ensure you really are in disagreement. For example, you might say, "If I understand you correctly, you feel that marketing should bear sole responsibility for updating the product database." After waiting for the response, you would state your thoughts.

Communication Choice Point

Groupthink

Your work group is displaying all the symptoms of groupthink you've read about. You want to get the group's members to re-evaluate their decision-making processes. *What are some of the things you might say to effect this change?*

Explore the Concept
"Enhancing Groups" at
MyCommunicationLab

Beware of Groupthink In some groups, agreement among members becomes so important that it takes the form of **groupthink**—a tendency that shuts out realistic and logical analysis of a problem and of possible alternatives (Janis, 1983; Mullen, Tara, Salas, & Driskell, 1994). Such agreement is meant to signal the "deterioration of mental efficiency, reality testing, and moral judgment that results from in-group pressures" (Janis, 1983, p. 9).

In groupthink, members are extremely selective about the information they consider. They tend to ignore facts and opinions contrary to the group's position, and they readily and uncritically accept those that support the group's position. When you recognize that groupthinking is occurring, try the following:

- When too-simple solutions are offered to problems, try to illustrate (with specific examples, if possible) for the group members how the complexity of the problem is not going to yield to the solutions offered.

- When you feel that members are not expressing their doubts about the group's decisions, encourage them to voice disagreement, to play devil's advocate, to test the adequacy of the solution. If you feel there is unexpressed disagreement, ask specifically if anyone disagrees.

- To combat the group pressure toward agreement, reward members who do voice disagreement or doubt. Say, for example, "That's a good argument; we need to hear more about the potential problems of this proposal. Does anyone else see any problems?"

Video Choice Point

Leading in Service Learning

Charles has joined an ongoing service learning group with three other students and wants to make a worthwhile contribution. But the other members, who have already been working together for a week, consistently ignore his cues when he wants to say something. And when he does manage to say something, no one reacts. He's determined to change this situation as he considers the topics covered in this chapter—for example, the functional and dysfunctional roles of group members, the importance of group norms, and the skills of group members and leaders, and considers his various communication choices and their potential effects. See how his choices play out in the video "Leading in Service Learning".

 Watch the Video "Leading in Service Learning" at **MyCommunicationLab**

Leaders in Small Group Communication

Leadership is defined in two very different ways in research and theory:

- Leadership is the process of influencing the thoughts, feelings, and behaviors of group members and establishing the direction that others follow; leadership and influence are parts of the same skill.
- Leadership is the process of empowering others; the leader is the person who helps others to maximize their potential and to take control of their lives.

These two definitions are not mutually exclusive; in fact, most effective leaders do both: they influence and they empower. As you read about leadership, keep these two definitions or functions of power and empowerment in mind.

In many small groups one person serves as leader; in other groups leadership may be shared by several persons. In some cases a person may be appointed the leader or may serve as leader because of her or his position within the company or hierarchy. In other cases the leader may emerge as the group proceeds in fulfilling its functions or instead may be elected by the group members. Two significant factors exert considerable influence on who emerges as group leader. One is the extent of active participation: The person who talks the most is more likely to emerge as leader (Mullen, Salas, & Driskell, 1989; Shaw & Gouran, 1990). The second factor is effective listening: Members who listen effectively will emerge as leaders more often than those who do not (Johnson & Bechler, 1998; Bechler & Johnson, 1995).

MYTHS ABOUT LEADERSHIP

Many common beliefs about leadership are erroneous. The following are three examples of myths about leadership paraphrased from small group theorists (Bennis & Nanus, 2003):

- **Myth: The skills of leadership are rare.** Actually, all of us have the potential for leadership. There are millions of people throughout the world who are serving leadership functions in government, business, education, and countless other fields.
- **Myth: Leaders are born.** Actually, the major leadership skills can be learned by just about everyone. No specific genetic endowment is necessary. We all can improve our leadership abilities.
- **Myth: Leaders are all charismatic.** Actually, only some leaders are. According to one survey of leaders they were of all heights, varied in articulateness, and dressed both well and poorly (Bennis & Nanus, 2003, p. 208).

APPROACHES TO LEADERSHIP

Not surprisingly, leadership has been the focus of considerable research attention. Researchers have identified several views of leadership, called *approaches*. Looking at a few of these approaches will give you a better idea of the varied ways in which leadership may be viewed and a better grasp of what leadership is and how it may be achieved.

The Traits Approach This approach views the leader as the one who possesses those characteristics or skills that contribute to leadership. The traits approach is valuable for stressing the characteristics that often (but not always) distinguish leaders from nonleaders. For example, some of the world's leading corporations seek technology project managers and leaders by looking for people who have technological skills, group building skills, and

For an interesting article on styles of leadership, see "Leadership Styles" at **http://tcbdevito** **.blogspot.com**. What style would you be most comfortable with?

interpersonal skills (Crowley, 1999). Research has found that the traits most frequently associated with leadership include intelligence, self-confidence, determination, integrity, and sociability (Northouse, 1997).

A shortcoming of the traits approach is that these qualities often vary according to the situations in which the leader functions, such as the group type, the personalities and roles of the other members, and the group's cultural context. Thus, for some groups (e.g., a new computer game company), a youthful, energetic, humorous leader might be most effective; for other groups (e.g., a medical diagnosis team), an older, more experienced and serious leader might be most effective.

The Functional Approach

This approach to leadership focuses on what the leader should do in a given situation. We've already encountered some of these functions in the discussion of group roles. Other functions associated with leadership are setting group goals, giving the group members direction, and summarizing the group's progress (Schultz, 1996). Additional functions are identified in the section entitled "Leadership Skills" later in this chapter.

The Transformational Approach

This approach describes a "transformational" (also called visionary or charismatic) leader who elevates the group's members, enabling them not only to accomplish the group task but also to emerge as more empowered individuals (Hersey, Blanchard, & Johnson, 2001). At the center of the transformational approach is the concept of charisma, that quality of an individual that makes us believe or want to follow him or her. Gandhi, Martin Luther King, Jr., and John F. Kennedy are often cited as examples of transformational leaders. These leaders were role models, were seen as extremely competent and able, and articulated moral goals (Northouse, 1997). We'll return to this concept of charisma and its qualities when we examine credibility in Chapter 14.

The Situational Approach

This approach holds that the effective leader shifts his or her emphasis between task accomplishment (i.e., identifying and focusing on the specific problem that the group must solve) and member satisfaction (i.e., providing for the psychological and interpersonal needs of the group members) on the basis of the specific group situation. This twofold function, you'll notice, rests on essentially the same distinction between relationship and task groups that we considered in Chapter 9. Some groups call for a high focus on task issues and need little people encouragement; this might be the case, for example, with a group of experienced scientists researching a cure for AIDS. In contrast, a group of recovering alcoholics might require leadership that stresses the members' emotional needs. The general idea of situational leadership is that there is no one style of leadership that fits all situations; each situation will call for a different ratio of emphasis on task and on member satisfaction (Fielder, 1967).

Effective leadership, according to this approach, depends on the leader's assessment of the group's ability to do the task and their willingness and commitment to do it. This theory identifies four leadership styles:

- **Telling style:** The leader provides high levels of task guidance and *tells* the group members what to do, when and where to do it, and how to do it. This style is most appropriate for a group that lacks knowledge of the issues involved and needs direct guidance on how to complete the task.

- **Selling style:** The leader gives the group high levels of both task guidance and relationship support. This leader not only tells people what to do but also tells them why they should do it; the leader wants to get the members' psychological support (i.e., to get them to "buy into" the task at hand).

- **Participating style:** The leader gives the group high levels of relationship support but little in the way of task direction. This leadership style is appropriate for a group that knows what to do (hence little task direction is needed) but that seems to have lost the motivation or willingness to accomplish the task.

- **Delegating style:** The leader gives little task direction and little emotional support. This leadership style is most appropriate for a group that knows what to do and how to do it and also has the confidence, commitment, and motivation to accomplish the task. The leader merely needs to delegate tasks for the group's goals to be accomplished.

Communication Choice Point

Situational Leadership

You're a member of an introductory Internet Design team whose leader uses a delegating style that isn't working. Group members are all new to this business and need more direction and guidance. The group members have elected you to clue the leader into appropriate and inappropriate styles. *What are some options for dealing with this problem?*

At this point you should find it interesting to analyze your own leadership qualities by taking the self-test, "What Kind of Leader Are You?" It will help personalize the preceding discussion on the four approaches to leadership.

TEST YOURSELF

What Kind of Leader Are You?

This self-test will help you think about yourself in the role of leader. Respond to each of the following statements with **T** if you feel the statement is often or always true of your leadership behavior or **F** if you feel the statement often or always does not apply to your leadership behavior.

_____ ❶ Popular with group members

_____ ❷ Knowledgeable about the topics discussed

_____ ❸ Dependable

_____ ❹ Effective in establishing group goals

_____ ❺ Competent in giving directions

_____ ❻ Capable of energizing group members

_____ ❼ Charismatic (i.e., dynamic, engaging, powerful)

_____ ❽ Empowering of group members

_____ ❾ Moral and honest

_____ ❿ Skilled in satisfying both task and relationship needs

_____ ⓫ Flexible in adjusting leadership style on the basis of the situation

_____ ⓬ Able to delegate responsibility

HOW DID YOU DO? This test was designed to encourage you to look at yourself in terms of the four approaches to leadership discussed in this chapter. Perceptions 1–3 refer to the *traits approach* to leadership, which defines a leader as someone who possesses certain qualities. If you answered T for these statements, you have the qualities normally associated with the trait theory of leadership. F responses would indicate that you don't see yourself possessing these traits. Perceptions 4–6 refer to the *functional approach,* which defines a leader as someone who performs certain functions. T responses indicate that you serve the functions normally viewed as the province of a leader. Perceptions 7–9 refer to the *transformational approach,* which defines a leader as someone who enables the group members to become the best they can be. T responses indicate your leadership is transformational. Perceptions 10–12 refer to the *situational approach,* which defines a leader as someone who can adjust his or her style to balance the needs of the specific situation. T responses indicate your flexibility to adjust to changing circumstances.

WHAT WILL YOU DO? As you read the remainder of this chapter, try to identify specific skills and competencies you might learn that would enable you to respond with T to all 12 statements.

GENERAL STYLES OF LEADERSHIP

In addition to the styles identified in the situational approach to leadership, small group theorists also distinguish among laissez-faire, democratic, and authoritarian leaders (Bennis & Nanus, 2003; Hackman & Johnson, 1991). As you'll see, these three styles represent a different way of looking at leadership and leadership style.

The **laissez-faire leader** takes no initiative in directing or suggesting alternative courses of action. Rather, this leader allows the group to develop and progress on its own, even allowing it to make its own mistakes. The laissez-faire leader answers questions and provides information only when specifically asked. During the interaction, this leader neither compliments nor criticizes group members or the group's progress.

Communication Choice Point

Leadership Styles

The leader of your work group (and the group members' supervisor) is extremely authoritarian, and the entire group has asked you to confront the leader to change to a more democratic style. *What are some options you have for communicating this to the leader?*

Explore the **Concept**
"Teams: Leadership Style" at
MyCommunicationLab

The **democratic leader** provides direction but allows the group to develop and progress the way its members wish; this form of leadership is similar to the "participating style" in the situational approach. The democratic leader encourages group members to determine their own goals and procedures and aims to stimulate self-direction and self-actualization of the group members.

The **authoritarian leader** is the opposite of the laissez-faire leader. As in the "telling style" of leadership in the situational approach, this leader determines group policies and makes decisions without consulting or securing agreement from the other members of the group. The authoritarian leader discourages member-to-member communication. This person is concerned with getting the group to accept his or her decisions rather than making its own.

LEADERSHIP SKILLS

Keeping the various views of leadership in mind, especially the situational theory with its concern for both task and people, we can look at some of the major functions leaders serve and their corresponding skills, the skills of leadership. These functions/skills are not exclusively the leader's; they are often shared or served wholly by group members. But when there's a specific leader, she or he is expected to perform these functions and exhibit the skills for accomplishing these goals.

VIEWPOINTS

The Emergent Leader

Early research found that the member with the highest rate of participation is the one most likely to be chosen group leader (Mullen, Salas, & Driskell, 1989). How well would this finding transfer to online communication? Are group leaders and generally those with the most influence the ones who post the most? Why do you suppose this relationship exists (or exists in face-to-face but not in online communication)?

Prepare Members and Start Interaction
Groups form gradually and often need to be eased into meaningful discussion. As the leader, you need to prepare members for the small group interaction as well as for the discussion of a specific issue or problem. Don't expect diverse members to work together cohesively to solve a problem without first becoming familiar with one another. Similarly, if members are to discuss a specific problem, a proper briefing may be necessary. If materials need to be distributed before the actual discussion, consider e-mailing them to members. Or perhaps members need to view a particular film or television show. Whatever the preparations, you need to organize and coordinate them. Once the group is assembled, you may need to stimulate the members to interact.

Build Group Cohesiveness
Groups vary greatly in **cohesiveness**—the members' closeness to and liking for each other. In general, cohesiveness is a positive quality, and cohesive groups seem to be more effective. For example, cohesive group members enjoy the interaction more and consequently come to meetings on time and stay until the end. They are more likely to be satisfied with the time spent in the group and to develop a "we-ness," seeing the group as a unit. Because members are comfortable with one another, they will be more willing to offer suggestions and ideas that may at first seem impossible, which may help the group eventually find a workable solution.

In a group that is excessively cohesive, however, members may be less apt to disagree with one another, which may hinder the group's critical analysis of any proposed idea. Still, a cohesive group is more likely to be successful. Cohesiveness is built by leaders who stress the positives, reward members frequently, and make the entire group experience as pleasant and personally rewarding as possible. Simple compliments and expressions of fondness will help build a cohesive group. Group accomplishments also build cohesiveness.

"Sage nodding got me where I am today."

Maintain Effective Interaction
Even after the group has begun to interact, you'll need to monitor the members' effective interaction. When the discussion begins to drag, you may need to step in and motivate the group: "Do we have any additional comments on the proposal to eliminate required courses?" "What do you, as members of the college curriculum committee, think about the proposal?" You'll also want to ensure that all members have an opportunity to express themselves.

COMMUNICATING ETHICALLY

The Leader's Ethical Responsibilities

In addition to mastering the skills of effective and efficient leadership, as a leader you also need to consider the ethical issues involved in leading a group. Because the leader is often called a "chair," CHAIR seems an appropriate acronym to help identify at least some of the characteristics of the ethical leader. As you reflect on these qualities, you'll probably think of other ethical qualities that a leader should possess.

- **C**oncern for the welfare of group members: Leaders who are more concerned with their own personal interests, rather than with the group task or the interpersonal needs of the members, are acting unethically.
- **H**onesty: Leaders should be honest with the group members by, for example, revealing any hidden agendas and presenting information fairly.
- **A**ccountability: Leaders should take responsibility for their actions and decisions, admit making mistakes, and take corrective action when necessary.
- **I**ntegrity: Leaders have integrity; they take the high road. They don't lie or deceive. And they avoid actions that would violate the rights of others.
- **R**esponsiveness: The leader must be responsive to all members of the group.

Ethical Choice Point

You're leading a discussion among a group of high school freshmen whom you're mentoring. The topic turns to marijuana, and the students ask you directly if you smoke pot. The truth is that on occasion you do—but it's a very controlled use, and you feel that it would only destroy your credibility and lead the students to experiment with or continue smoking pot if they knew you did (something you do not want to do). At the same time, you wonder if you can ethically lie to them and tell them that you do not smoke. What is your ethical obligation in this situation? What would you do?

Guide Members Through the Agreed-on Agenda   As the leader, you need to keep the discussion on track by asking relevant questions, summarizing the group discussions periodically, or offering a transition from one issue to the next. This involves following the list of tasks to be accomplished by the group as outlined in the meeting agenda and efficiently managing the amount of time allotted for each event.

Ensure Member Satisfaction   Members have different psychological needs and wants, and many people enter groups because of them. Even though a group may, for example, deal with political issues, members may have come together for psychological as well as for political reasons. If a group is to be effective, it must achieve the group goal (in this case, a political one) without denying the psychological purposes or goals that motivate many of the members to come together. One way to meet these needs is for you as leader to allow digressions and personal comments, assuming they are not too frequent or overly long. Another way is to be supportive and reinforcing.

Empower Group Members   An important function of a leader is to empower other group members—to help them gain increased power over themselves and their environment. Empowerment will occur when you follow these guidelines as a leader:

- Raise members' self-esteem; compliment, reinforce; resist fault finding.
- Share skills and decision-making power and authority.
- Be constructively critical. Be willing to offer your perspective and to react honestly to suggestions from all group members, not only those in high positions.
- Listen willingly and eagerly. Acknowledge your understanding by appropriately nodding or using such minimal responses as *I see* or *I understand*, ask questions if something isn't clear, maintain eye contact, and lean forward as appropriate.
- Avoid interrupting to change the topic or to shift the focus to something else. When you interrupt, you say, in effect, that what the other group member is saying is less important than what you're saying.
- React supportively. Let other group members know that you appreciate what they are saying.

Communication Choice Point

Leader Guidance

Members of your group are not participating equally. Of the eight members, three monopolize the discussion; the other five say as little as possible. *What are some of the things you might say to get the group into better balance?*

Watch the **Video** "Director's Cut" at **MyCommunicationLab**

For a discussion of self-esteem in the workplace, see "Relationship and Work Esteem" at http://tcbdevito.blogspot.com. How is your own work esteem?

SKILL DEVELOPMENT EXPERIENCE

Empowering Group Members

For each situation, indicate what you might say to help empower the other person, using such strategies as (a) raising the other person's self-esteem; (b) listening actively and supportively; (c) being open, positive, and empathic; and (d) avoiding verbal aggressiveness or any unfair conflict strategies.

1. A team member is having many difficulties: He recently lost his job, received poor grades in a night class, and is gaining a lot of weight. At the same time, you're doing extremely well. You want to give your team member back his confidence.

2. You're managing four college interns, three men and one woman, who are working on redesigning your company's website. The men are extremely supportive of one another and regularly contribute ideas. Although equally competent, the woman doesn't contribute; she seems to lack confidence. Because the objective of this redesign is to increase the number of female visitors, you really need the woman intern's input and want to empower her.

3. You're a third-grade teacher. Most of the students are from the same ethnic-religious group; three, however, are from a different group. The problem is that these three have not been included in the social groupings of the students; they're treated as outsiders. As a result, these children stumble when they have to read in front of the class and make a lot of mistakes at the chalkboard (though they consistently do well in private). You want to empower these students.

Power is not a zero-sum game; empowering others often adds to, rather than subtracts from, your own power.

Watch the **Video**
"The Interns" at
MyCommunicationLab

Encourage Ongoing Evaluation and Improvement   All groups encounter obstacles as they try to solve a problem, reach a decision, or generate ideas. No group is totally effective. All groups have room for improvement. To improve, the group must focus on itself. Along with trying to solve some external problem, it must try to solve its own internal problems—for example, personal conflicts, failure of members to meet on time, or members who come unprepared. When you notice some serious group failing, address it, perhaps suggesting that a particular issue (say, member tardiness) is a problem to be solved.

Manage Conflict   As in interpersonal relationships, conflict is a part of small group interaction. And it's a leader's responsibility to deal with it effectively. The conflict management techniques that are useful in small groups are the same techniques discussed in the context of interpersonal communication (see Chapter 8). You may wish to think of them as small group conflict management strategies.

Mentor   Another function of leadership that is especially applicable to the small group but is used extensively in the workplace and in business and personal relationships generally is that of **mentoring**—a process that occurs when an experienced individual helps to train less experienced group members. An accomplished teacher, for example, might mentor younger teachers who are newly arrived or who have never taught before. A group leader might be the group members' supervisor and may mentor those supervised. The mentor guides new people through the ropes, teaches strategies and techniques for success, and otherwise communicates his or her accumulated knowledge and experience to the "mentee" or protégé. At the same time, the mentor benefits from clarifying his or her thoughts, from seeing the job from the perspective of a newcomer, and from considering and formulating answers to a variety of questions. Just as a member learns from the leader, the leader learns from the members.

Objectives Self-Check
- Can you define *leadership* and explain its myths?
- Can you explain the approaches to leadership and the general styles of leadership?
- Can you effectively apply the skills of leadership: preparing members, building cohesiveness, maintaining effective interaction, guiding discussion through the agenda, ensuring member satisfaction, empowering group members, encouraging ongoing evaluation, managing conflict, and mentoring?

 Messages in the Media *Wrap Up*

Talk shows are excellent laboratories for studying small group interaction, especially membership and leadership. In an hour of television you should be able to see many of the membership roles discussed here as well as varied leadership styles.

 **Summary of Concepts and Skills**   ✓ **Study** and **Review** materials for this chapter are at **MyCommunicationLab**

 Listen to the **Audio Chapter** Summary at **MyCommunicationLab**

This chapter looked at membership and leadership in the small group. It examined the roles of members—some productive and some counterproductive—and considered leadership theories, leadership styles, leadership functions, and cultural factors in small groups.

Membership, Leadership, and Culture

1. Group membership and leadership attitudes and behaviors are likely to be heavily influenced by culture, especially by the individual and collective orientations and high- and low-power distances.

Members in Small Group Communication

2. A popular classification of small group member roles divides them into three types: group task roles, group building and maintenance roles, and individual roles.

3. Among the group task roles are those of information seeker or giver, opinion seeker or giver, evaluator-critic, and procedural technician or recorder. Among the group building and maintenance roles are the encourager/harmonizer, compromiser, gatekeeper-expediter, standard setter, and follower. Among the individual (dysfunctional) roles are the aggressor, recognition seeker/self-confessor, blocker, special interest pleader, and dominator.

4. Group members should be group-oriented, center conflict on issues, be critically open-minded, recognize social loafing, ensure understanding, and be wary of groupthink.

5. Groupthink is an excessive concern with securing agreement that discourages critical thinking and the exploration of alternative ways of doing things.

Leaders in Small Group Communication

6. Several theories of leadership help to clarify aspects of leadership. The traits approach identifies characteristics, such as intelligence and self-confidence, which contribute to leadership. The functional approach focuses on what the leaders should do. The transformational approach focuses on leaders as people who raise the performance of group members and empower them. The situational approach views leadership as varying its focus between accomplishing the task and serving the members' social and emotional needs, depending on the specific group and the unique situation.

7. An extension of the situational approach to leadership identifies four leadership styles: telling, selling, participating, and delegating. The appropriate style to use depends on the group's level of task and relationship maturity.

8. Three general leadership styles are discussed: laissez-faire, democratic, and authoritarian.

9. Among the leader's functions and requisite skills are to prepare members for and start the group interaction, build group cohesiveness, maintain effective interaction, guide members through the agreed-on agenda, ensure member satisfaction, empower members, encourage ongoing evaluation and improvement, and manage conflict.

10. *Mentoring* refers to a relationship in which an experienced and knowledgeable individual helps guide and train a less-experienced person.

The skills identified in this discussion center on increasing your ability to function more effectively as a small group member and leader. Place a check mark next to those skills you feel you should work on most.

_____ 1. I recognize and appreciate the cultural differences that people have toward group membership and leadership.

_____ 2. I avoid playing the popular but dysfunctional individual roles in a small group—those of aggressor, blocker, recognition seeker, self-confessor, and dominator.

_____ 3. When participating in a small group, I am group-rather than individual-oriented, center the conflict on issues rather than on personalities, am critically open-minded, and make sure that my meanings and the meanings of others are clearly understood.

_____ 4. I recognize the symptoms of groupthink and actively counter my own groupthink tendencies as well as those evidenced in the group.

_____ 5. I adjust my leadership style according to the task at hand and the needs of group members.

_____ 6. As a small group leader, I start group interaction, maintain effective interaction throughout the discussion, keep members on track, ensure member satisfaction, encourage ongoing evaluation and improvement, and prepare members for the discussion as necessary.

 # Key Word Quiz

The Language of Small Group Membership and Leadership

Match the terms about group membership and leadership with their definitions. Record the number of the definition next to the appropriate term.

_____ a. groupthink (198)

_____ b. collective orientation (192)

_____ c. individual roles (195)

_____ d. laissez-faire leader (201)

_____ e. transformational approach (200)

_____ f. group task roles (195)

_____ g. mentoring (204)

_____ h. group building and maintenance roles (195)

_____ i. low-power-distance culture (193)

_____ j. cohesiveness (203)

1. The process or relationship in which a more experienced member helps train a less experienced member.

2. Member roles that help the group focus on achieving its goals.

3. The tendency of a group to overvalue agreement and ignore differences.

4. A cultural view that holds that the group is more important than the individual.

5. Group roles of which encouraging, compromising, and following are examples.

6. A leader who takes no initiative in directing or suggesting alternative courses of action.

7. The closeness and liking for each other of group members.

8. A leadership style that elevates and empowers group members.

9. Group roles of which expressing aggressiveness, dominating, and seeking self-recognition are examples.

10. A culture in which there is a feeling of equality and in which there is little difference in power among members.

These ten terms and additional terms used in this chapter can be found in the glossary.

Answers: a. 3; b. 4; c. 9; d. 6; e. 8; f. 2; g. 1; h. 5; i. 10; j. 7

 Study and **Review** the **Flashcards** at **MyCommunicationLab**

MyCommunicationLab

Throughout this chapter, there are icons in the margin that highlight media content for selected topics. Go to **MyCommunicationLab** for additional information on small group membership and leadership. Here you'll find flashcards to help you learn the jargon of communication, videos that illustrate a variety of concepts, additional exercises, and discussions to help you continue your study of small group communication members and leaders.

11

Public Speaking Preparation (Steps 1–6)

⚠ Messages in the Media

Rachel Maddow, or other political talk show hosts, provides perfect examples of short persuasive speeches. Almost any question results in a two or three minute speech, the subject of this chapter. Here we consider some preliminaries to public speaking—speaker apprehension and the first steps in preparing an informative or persuasive speech.

Objectives

Listen to the **Audio Chapter** at **MyCommunicationLab**

After reading this chapter, you should be able to:

❶ Explain the nature of public speaking and communication apprehension; apply the suggestions for managing apprehension in public speaking and for overcoming procrastination.

❷ Select and narrow public speaking topics, purposes, and theses.

❸ Explain the sociological and psychological characteristics of an audience and use these characteristics in analyzing your own audiences.

❹ Identify the basic principles of and sources for researching your speech topic and the criteria for evaluating research; effectively evaluate, integrate, and cite this research in your speech.

❺ Explain the nature and types of supporting materials in informative and persuasive speeches.

❻ Generate main points for your speech from your thesis.

❼ Describe the major patterns of speech organization and organize your own speech into an appropriate pattern.

Before getting to the steps for preparing and presenting a public speech, we'll define public speaking and consider the benefits that will reward your public speaking efforts. In addition, we'll address what is probably your number one problem: the fear that so often accompanies giving speeches. As you read these four chapters dealing with public speaking, you'll find it useful to consult the public speaking sections of My Communication Lab.

The Nature of Public Speaking

Public speaking is a form of communication in which a speaker addresses a relatively large audience with a relatively continuous discourse, usually in a face-to-face situation. A student

FIGURE 11.1

Pearson's MyCommunicationLab/Public Speaking Website

delivering a report to a political science class, a teacher lecturing on the structure of DNA, a minister preaching a sermon, and a politician delivering a campaign speech are all examples of public speaking. In addition, delivering a speech to a television camera to be broadcast to an entire nation or over the radio to be heard by thousands or millions of people is similar in many ways to what is traditionally thought of as public speaking. One way in which it differs is in the nature of the audience feedback. In face-to-face public speaking, the audience gives the speaker immediate feedback largely through facial expressions, head nodding, and posture. In mediated public speaking, the feedback may come a while after the speech in the form of political commentary, for example. Increasingly, however, both remote and immediate audiences are communicating with both face-to-face and mediated public speaking through social media sites such as Twitter. While the speaker is speaking (and afterward as well), listeners are sending messages—communicating approval or disapproval or asking questions they hope the speaker will address—to the speaker as well as to other audience members. The simple hashtag has already brought about dramatic changes in public speaking and will surely continue to do so (Atkinson, 2010).

In addition to the speeches that you will give in this class and during your college career, you will also be called on to make formal and informal speeches throughout your life. For example, you may make a presentation about a new product at a sales meeting, present your company's rules and regulations to a group of new employees, explain the benefits of a new playground to members of your local PTA, or give a speech about your family genealogy at a family reunion. Regardless of the circumstances under which you give a speech, you will find the 10 steps to public speaking preparation discussed in this chapter and the next extremely practical.

Take a look at "A Preface to a Public Speaking Course" at **tcbdevito** .blogspot.com.

BENEFITS AND SKILLS OF PUBLIC SPEAKING

Public speaking draws together a wide variety of social, academic, and career skills. Although these skills are central to public speaking, they also enrich other competencies. Among these are your ability to present yourself to others with confidence and self-assurance, to conduct research efficiently and effectively, to understand human motivation, to analyze and evaluate the validity of persuasive appeals, and to use persuasion effectively.

Public speaking will also develop and refine your general communication abilities by helping you explain complex concepts; organize a variety of messages for clarity and persuasiveness; develop logical, emotional, and ethical appeals to support an argument; and improve your listening and delivery skills.

It's important to remember, however, that effective public speakers aren't born; they're made. Through instruction, exposure to different speeches, feedback, and individual learning experiences, you can become an effective speaker. Regardless of your present level of competence, you can improve your public speaking skills through proper training.

Now that you have a good idea of what public speaking is and what benefits you'll derive from studying it, we can focus on what is probably your major concern: communication apprehension/ stage fright/fear of speaking in public.

COMMUNICATION APPREHENSION

People experience **communication apprehension** in all types of situations (as illustrated throughout this text), but it is in the public speaking situation that apprehension is most common and most severe (Richmond & McCroskey, 1998; Wrench, McCroskey, & Richmond, 2008). To measure your own fear of speaking in public, take the apprehension self-test that follows.

TEST YOURSELF

How Apprehensive Are You About Public Speaking?

This questionnaire consists of six statements concerning your feelings about public speaking. Indicate the degree to which each statement applies to you by marking whether you **(1)** strongly agree, **(2)** agree, **(3)** are undecided, **(4)** disagree, or **(5)** strongly disagree with each statement. There are no right or wrong answers. Don't be concerned that some of the statements are similar to others. Work quickly; just record your first impression.

_____ **①** I have no fear of giving a speech.

_____ **②** Certain parts of my body feel very tense and rigid when I am giving a speech.

_____ **③** I feel relaxed while giving a speech.

_____ **④** My thoughts become confused and jumbled when I am giving a speech.

_____ **⑤** I face the prospect of giving a speech with confidence.

_____ **⑥** While giving a speech, I get so nervous that I forget facts I really know.

HOW DID YOU DO? To obtain your public speaking apprehension score, use the following formula: Start with 18 points; add the scores for items 1, 3, and 5; then subtract the scores for items 2, 4, and 6.

A score above 18 shows some degree of apprehension. Most people score above 18, so if you scored relatively high, you're among the vast majority of people. You may find it interesting to compare your apprehension scores from this test and from the test in Chapter 9. Most people would score higher on public speaking apprehension than on apprehension in group discussions.

WHAT WILL YOU DO? As you read the suggestions for reducing apprehension in the text, consider what you can do to incorporate these ideas into your own public speaking experiences. Consider too how these suggestions might be useful in reducing apprehension more generally—for example, in social situations and in small groups and meetings.

Source: Adaptation of "Test Yourself: How Apprehensive Are You about Public Speaking?" from _An Introduction to Rhetorical Communication_ by James C. McCroskey, 9th Ed. Copyright © 2006 by Pearson Education, Inc. Printed and Electronically reproduced by permission of Pearson Education, Inc. Upper Saddle River, New Jersey.

If you experience public speaking apprehension, the following 10 suggestions will help you reduce it, as well as any communication apprehension you might have in small group and interpersonal communication situations (Beatty, 1988; Wrench, McCroskey, & Richmond, 2008).

- **Gain experience.** New situations such as public speaking are likely to make you anxious, so try to reduce their newness. The best way to do this is to get as much public speaking experience as you can. With experience, your initial fears and anxieties will give way to feelings of control, comfort, and pleasure. Experience will show you that the feelings of accomplishment in public speaking are rewarding and will outweigh any initial anxiety.

- **Think positively.** When you see yourself as inferior—for example, when you feel that others are better speakers or that they know more than you do—anxiety increases. To gain greater confidence, think positive thoughts and be especially thorough in your preparation. Visualize success; dismiss thoughts of failure.

For additional insight into the terminology of apprehension, take a look at "ABCD: Communication Apprehension and Related Terms" at **tcbdevito.blogspot.com**.

Explore the **Profile** "Personal Report of Speaking Anxiety" at **MyCommunicationLab**

Explore the **Concept** "Overcoming Nervousness" at **MyCommunicationLab**

- **Be realistic.** Unrealistically high expectations are likely to create anxiety and make you more fearful of the public speaking situation (Ayres, 1986). You do not have to be perfect; you do not have to give the best speech in the class. View your goal as giving a speech that represents the best you can do. At the same time, avoid "catastrophizing," visualizing the very worst that can happen.

- **See public speaking as conversation.** When you're the center of attention, as you are in public speaking, you feel especially conspicuous; this often increases anxiety. It may help, therefore, to think of public speaking as another type of conversation (some theorists call it "enlarged conversation").

- **Focus on your listeners.** When you focus on your listeners, you'll be less fixated on your own performance and less apprehensive. Focus on informing them about your topic or persuading them to think differently or do something. The more attention you place on your audience, the less you'll have for worrying about your performance.

- **Stress similarity.** When you feel similar to (rather than different from) your audience, your anxiety should lessen. With all audiences, but especially with multicultural gatherings, stress similarities in experiences, attitudes, and values; it will make you feel more at one with your listeners.

- **Project confidence.** Stand tall, and maintain direct eye contact with your listeners. Behaving confidently is likely to feed back and lead you to feel confident. Acting confidently is also likely to increase the positive reactions from the audience, which will further help to put you at ease.

- **Prepare and practice thoroughly.** Much of the fear you experience is a fear of failure. Adequate and even extra preparation will lessen the possibility of failure and the accompanying apprehension. Because apprehension is greatest during the beginning of the speech, try memorizing the first few sentences of your talk. If there are complicated facts or figures, be sure to write these out and plan to read them; this will remove from your mind any worry about forgetting them.

- **Move about and breathe deeply.** Physical activity—gross bodily movements as well as the small movements of the hands, face, and head—lessens apprehension. Using a visual aid, for example, will temporarily divert attention from you and will allow you to get rid of your excess energy. If you breathe deeply a few times before getting up to speak, you'll sense your body relax. This will help you overcome your initial fear of walking to the front of the room.

- **Avoid chemicals as tension relievers.** Unless prescribed by a physician, avoid any chemical means for reducing apprehension. Alcohol does not lessen public speaking anxiety (Himle, Abelson, & Haghightgou, 1999); and tranquilizers, marijuana, and artificial stimulants are likely to create problems rather than reduce them. They're likely to impair your ability to remember the parts of your speech, to accurately read audience feedback, and to regulate the timing of your speech.

If, as a listener, you perceive that the speaker is apprehensive, you can help in a number of ways:

- **Positively reinforce the speaker.** A nod, a smile, an attentive appearance (especially maintaining eye contact) will help put the speaker at ease. Resist the temptation to check your text messages or talk with a friend.

- **Ask questions in a supportive manner.** If there's a question period, ask information-seeking questions rather than firing off critical challenges. And ask questions in a way that won't encourage defensiveness. Instead of saying, "Your criticism of heavy metal music is absurd," say, "Why do you find the lyrics of heavy metal harmful?"

- **Don't focus on errors.** If the speaker fumbles, don't put your head down, cover your eyes, or otherwise communicate your awareness of the fumble. Instead, continue listening to the content of the speech; let the speaker know that you're focused on what is being said.

STARTING EARLY

At the most obvious level, starting early provides you with the time needed to process the information you're going to talk about and to get used to the idea of preparing for the presentation of your speech. Starting early also provides you with the time to overcome the inevitable unanticipated roadblocks: a website that you thought would be helpful is

Communication Choice Point

Apprehension Management

This is your first experience with public speaking, and you're very nervous; you're afraid you'll forget your speech and stumble. So you're wondering if it would be a good idea to alert your audience to your nervousness. *If you decide to say something, what would you say? What good reasons can you give for saying nothing?*

now dead, the person you wanted to interview isn't available, or your neighbor's parties make the weekends useless for working on your speech. You will also have the time to rehearse your speech to ensure that your delivery will be effective and to help reduce any fear of public speaking you might have. Interesting enough, starting early may enable you to avoid health problems often associated with procrastination; for example, college students who procrastinate experience more colds and flu, more gastrointestinal problems, and more insomnia (Marano, 2003).

Here are several suggestions for overcoming this tendency to delay certain tasks. Supplement these with the excellent advice given on college websites (just search for "procrastination").

- **Make a commitment to starting early.** Create a computer file for your speech, collect information, and file it for easy retrieval.
- **Don't lie to yourself about the value of procrastination** (Marano, 2003). You don't do better under pressure, for example.
- **Beware of your tendency to seek out distractions.** You don't have to rearrange and organize your photos or redo your Facebook profile, for example. When you get the urge to do something else, become mindful of what you're really doing—making an excuse to delay the task at hand.
- **Avoid self-handicapping strategies** (Chapter 2, p. 45); these will only make it more difficult for you to prepare and present an effective speech.
- **Work in small steps.** Fortunately, this aid to overcoming procrastination is built into the 10-step public speaking system used here; each step is already a relatively small unit. Set aside 20 or 30 minutes (it's often best to start with small units of time) and see what you can do with step 1. Then, when you're farther along in the process, increase the time you spend on each step.

The rest of this chapter looks at the first six of the 10 steps for preparing an effective public speech, as summarized in Figure 11.2. The final four steps are covered in the next chapter.

For additional suggestions on reducing apprehension, see "Strategies for Apprehension Management" at **tcbdevito** .blogspot.com.

Communication Choice Point

Applying Listening Skills

You notice that the speaker approaching the front of the room to give a speech is visibly nervous. *What are some of the things you can do as a listener to help the speaker manage this apprehension and get through the speech?*

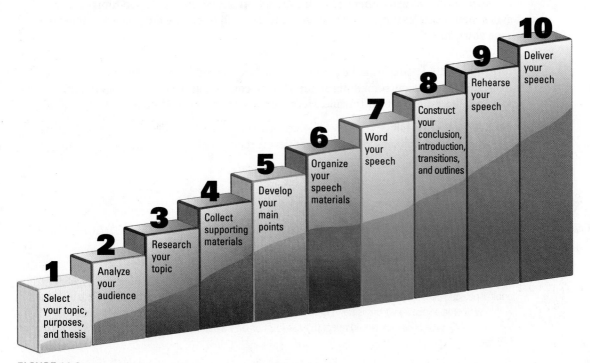

FIGURE 11.2

The Steps in Public Speaking Preparation and Delivery

Speakers differ in the order in which they follow these steps. Some speakers, for example, prefer to begin with audience analysis, asking themselves what the audience is interested in and then selecting the topic and purpose. Some speakers prefer to identify their main points before conducting extensive research; others prefer to allow the propositions to emerge from the research. The order presented here will prove useful to most speakers for most situations; however, vary the order when it serves your purposes. As long as you cover all the steps, you should be in good shape.

Objectives Self-Check
- Can you explain the nature of public speaking and its benefits?
- Can you explain the nature of communication apprehension and apply the suggestions for managing apprehension in public speaking?
- Can you explain the nature of procrastination and apply the suggestions for avoiding it?

Watch the **Video** "Martin Cox Discusses Tips on Developing a Topic for a Speech" at **MyCommunicationLab**

Explore the **Concept** "Topic" at **MyCommunicationLab**

Step 1: Select Your Topic, Purposes, and Thesis

The first step in preparing an effective public speech is to select the topic on which you'll speak, the general and specific purposes you hope to achieve, and your thesis or central idea.

YOUR TOPIC

Select a worthwhile topic that will be interesting to the audience. If your first speech is to be informative, select a topic about which your audience probably knows little but would be curious to learn more. If your first speech is persuasive, you might select a topic about which you and the audience agree, and aim to strengthen their attitudes. Or you might select a topic on which you and the audience disagree; your aim would be to persuade them to change their attitudes.

Not surprisingly, the appropriateness of a speech topic will vary with the culture of the audience. For example, each culture has its own topics that tend to cause conflict. Generally these subjects should be avoided, especially by visitors from other cultures. Although the topics that are taboo vary from one culture to another and from one time to another, generally it is best to avoid criticizing any deeply held belief, whether about religion or politics or child-rearing practices. If you're going to address an audience with members from cultures other than your own, find out what these taboo topics are and avoid them; or at least present them in a way that will not cause audience members to tune you out.

Finding Your Topic   Public speaking topics are all around you. Select a topic that you're interested in and know something about. And, of course, select a topic that your audience will find interesting and worthwhile. Here are a few ways you can find topics:

- **Keep yourself in mind.** What are you interested in? What news articles or blogs do you read, what feeds do you subscribe to? What titles of articles would interest you enough so that you

SKILL DEVELOPMENT EXPERIENCE

Using Cultural Beliefs as Assumptions

How effective would it be to use each of the following cultural beliefs as a basic assumption in a speech to your public speaking class? Use the following scale: **A** = the audience would favorably accept this assumption and would welcome a speaker with this point of view; **B** = some members would listen open-mindedly, but others wouldn't; or **C** = the audience would reject this assumption and would not welcome a speaker with this point of view.

Knowing your audience's beliefs will help you identify with your listeners, avoid offending them, and adapt your speech.

_____ 1. Religious differences are the main causes of war.

_____ 2. The group is more important than the individual.

_____ 3. The rich (countries, individuals) are morally obligated to give to the poor.

_____ 4. Men and women should each enter occupations for which they are biologically suited.

_____ 5. Pleasure is the only real goal in life.

would open them and read them? If you plan a speech on a topic that you're interested in, your enthusiasm for your topic is likely to make your delivery more exciting, less anxiety-provoking, and more engaging to the audience.

- **Try brainstorming.** You can use the small group technique of brainstorming to generate speech topics. Begin with your "problem"—what will I talk about?—and follow the four rules of brainstorming discussed in Chapter 9 (pp. 180-181). In just a few minutes, you should have a sizable list of potential topics.

- **Use topic lists.** For example, the interactive topic selector on MyCommunicationLab lists hundreds of appropriate topics for informative and persuasive speeches (see Figure 11.3). A variety of educational and commercial websites contain topic generators, similar to that on MyCommunicationLab, where you can view a wide variety of topics—for example, those provided by WritingFix and McMaster eBusiness Research Center. Just search for "public speaking topics + .edu".

- **Read surveys to see what your audience finds important.** Take a look at some of the national and regional polls concerned with the issues people feel are most significant. Search for polling sites with your favorite search engine or start with some of the more widely known,

VIEWPOINTS

Taboo

What is and what is not taboo will also vary with different audiences. Consider your own classroom. What public speaking topics would be considered taboo?

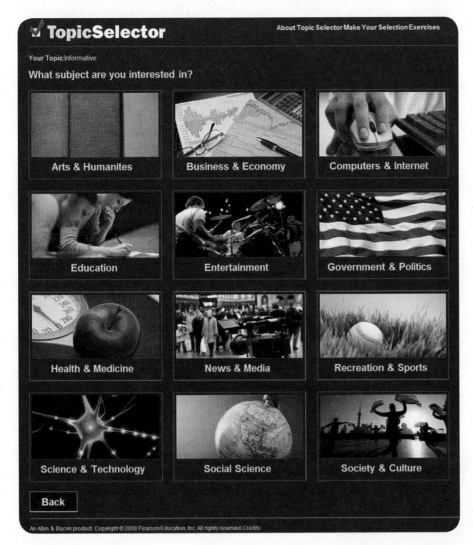

Explore the **Concept**
"Visual Brainstorming" at
MyCommunicationLab

FIGURE 11.3

MyCommunicationLab's Topic Selector

With this topic selector, you can find topics suitable for informative and persuasive speeches.

such as the Gallup Poll, the Marist Poll, or Pew Research Center. Or take a look at what people are talking about on social media sites. What are people tweeting about? What are they posting about? You can also conduct a survey yourself through a variety of social media sites or classroom management systems.

● **Check news sites.** A useful starting point is your online news page, which will provide you with important international, domestic, financial, and social issues all conveniently accessible from one screen. But, of course, news items also appear on Twitter and on blogs and a variety of social media sites.

Limiting Your Topic   Plan to cover a limited topic in depth, rather than a broad topic superficially. The limiting process is simple: Repeatedly divide the topic into its significant parts. First, divide your general topic into its component parts, then divide one of these parts into its component parts. Continue until you arrive at a topic that seems manageable—a topic that you can reasonably cover in some depth in the allotted time.

For example, if you were to take mass communication as a general topic area (see Figure 11.4), it would take you, without some limitation, a lifetime to cover adequately. But you could divide this general subject into subtopics, such as Internet, film, television, radio, and advertising. You could then select one of these topics and further subdivide it. For example, you could subdivide television into comedy, children's programs, educational programs, news, movies, soap operas, game shows, and sports. You might then take one of these topics, say comedy, and divide it into subtopics. You might consider comedy on a time basis and divide television comedy into its significant time periods: pre-1960, 1961–2000, and 2001 to the present. Or you might focus on situation comedies. Here you might examine a topic such as "Women in Television Comedy," "Race Relations in Situation Comedy," or "Families in Television Comedies." At this stage the topic is beginning to look manageable.

YOUR PURPOSES

In some cases you'll select your topic and purpose almost simultaneously. At other times you'll select your topic and later formulate your purpose. In preparing public speeches, you'll need to formulate both a general and a specific purpose.

Watch the **Video** "Martin Cox Discusses Tips on Developing the Purpose of a Speech" at **MyCommunicationLab**

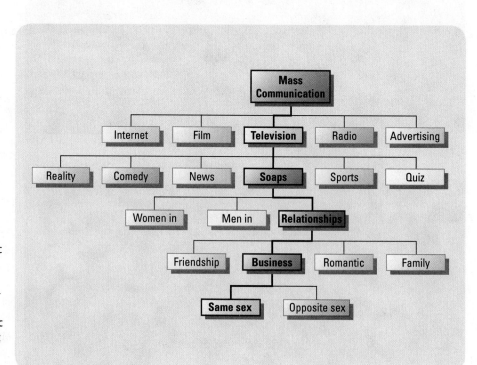

FIGURE 11.4

Tree Diagram for Limiting Speech Topics

Here is a tree diagram illustrating how a topic can be divided until it becomes manageable for a short speech: "Same-Sex Business Relationships in television Soaps." Construct a different tree diagram by selecting Internet, film, radio, Television, or advertising as a topic and subdividing it until you reach a level that would be appropriate for a 5- to 10-minute informative or persuasive speech.

SKILL DEVELOPMENT EXPERIENCE

Limiting Topics

Think about the overly general topics listed below. Using one of the methods discussed in this chapter (or any other method you're familiar with), limit one of these topics to a subject that would be reasonable for a 5- to 10-minute speech:

- Sports
- Male-female relationships
- Parole
- Surveillance on the Internet
- Children
- Student problems
- Morality
- Fitness
- Political corruption
- Violence

A limited topic makes your speech easier to construct and easier to understand and remember.

Your General Purpose   The two **general purposes** (major aims or objectives) of public speeches are to inform and to persuade. The **informative speech** creates understanding; it clarifies, enlightens, corrects misunderstandings, demonstrates how something works, or explains how something is structured (see Chapter 13). The **persuasive speech**, on the other hand, influences attitudes or behaviors. It may strengthen existing attitudes or change the audience's beliefs. Or it may move the audience to act in a particular way (see Chapter 14). Table 11.1 identifies some of the major differences between informative and persuasive speeches; keep these distinctions in mind as you read the next sections.

Your Specific Purpose   Your **specific purpose** identifies the information you want to communicate (in an informative speech) or the attitude or behavior you want to change (in a persuasive speech). For example, your specific purpose in an informative speech might be:

- to inform my audience of three ways to save time using the Internet for research;
- to inform my audience about how the new interoffice e-mail system works; or
- to inform my audience of the benefits of integrated work teams.

TABLE 11.1 Differences Between Informative and Persuasive Speeches
Here are some of the major differences between speeches that primarily aim to inform and those that aim to persuade.

Element of Speech	Informative Speeches	Persuasive Speeches
	Examples include classroom lectures, demonstrations of how things work	Examples include political speeches, religious sermons
Topic/subject	Significant but generally noncontroversial	Significant and controversial or debatable
Purpose	To communicate new information to listeners	To change the attitudes, beliefs, or behaviors of listeners
Thesis	States the central idea of the speech	States the debatable position to be argued
Support	Primarily examples, definitions, numerical data, and presentation aids	In addition to informative support, relies heavily on logical, emotional, and credibility support

VIEWPOINTS

Defining Purpose

Izzie is considering developing her 10-minute persuasive speech around one of the following purposes that will persuade her listeners (1) to vote for the pro-life candidate in the upcoming election, (2) to contribute $250 to the college's scholarship fund, or (3) to attend a religious ceremony of a religion other than the listeners' own. Assuming that the audience was your human communication class, what do you see as the advantages and disadvantages of each purpose?

Explore the Exercise
"How Are Cultural Beliefs and Theses Related?" at
MyCommunicationLab

See "Change and Audience Analysis" at **tcbdevito.blogspot.com** for an additional perspective on audience analysis.

Your specific purpose in a persuasive speech might be:

● to persuade my audience that all cigarette advertising should be abolished;

● to persuade my audience that the college should establish courses on the prevention of AIDS and other STDs; or

● to persuade my audience to contribute time to working with students with disabilities.

Whether you intend to inform or to persuade, limit your specific purpose so you'll be able to go into it in some depth. Your audience will benefit more from a speech that covers a small area in depth than one that covers a broad topic superficially.

YOUR THESIS

The **thesis** is the main idea that will be conveyed to an audience. In fact, terms such as "central idea" or "controlling idea" are often used instead of *thesis*. The thesis of Lincoln's Second Inaugural Address was that northerners and southerners should work together for the good of the entire country. The thesis of many science fiction movies is that working together, people—often from very different cultures and different walks of life—can repel any conquering force and achieve just about anything.

Let's say, for example, you're planning to present a persuasive speech in favor of the election of Senator Winters. Your thesis statement might be, "Winters is the best candidate." This is what you want your audience to believe, what you want your audience to remember even if they forget everything else. In an informative speech, on the other hand, the thesis statement focuses on what you want your audience to learn. For example, for a speech on jealousy, a suitable thesis might be: "Two main theories of jealousy exist."

The thesis and the purpose of a speech are similar in that they both guide you in selecting and organizing your materials. In two major ways, however, they are different:

● **Form of expression:** Thesis and purpose differ in how they are phrased. The thesis is phrased as a complete, declarative sentence. The purpose is phrased as an infinitive phrase ("to inform . . .," "to persuade . . .").

● **Focus:** The thesis focuses on the message; the purpose focuses on the audience. The thesis succinctly identifies the central idea of your speech. The purpose identifies the change you hope to bring about in your audience—for example, to learn information, to change attitudes, or to influence people to act in a certain way.

Objectives Self-Check
● Can you select and narrow an appropriate speech topic, phrase a general and specific purpose, and state your thesis or central idea as a simple declarative sentence?

Step 2: Analyze Your Audience

If you are going to inform or persuade an audience, you must know who they are. What are their beliefs, attitudes, and values? What are their interests? What do they already know? What would they want to know more about? Where do they stand on the issues you wish to address? We can group these various questions into two general categories: sociological and psychological characteristics. We'll then look at some of the things you can do during the speech to help you analyze and adapt to your audience.

AUDIENCE SOCIOLOGY

When analyzing an audience, be careful not to assume that people covered by the same label are necessarily all alike. As soon as you begin to use a sociological characteristic with an expressed or implied "all," consider the possibility that you may be stereotyping. Don't assume that all women or all older people or all highly educated people think or believe the same things. They don't. Nevertheless, there are characteristics that seem to be more common among one group than another, and it is these characteristics that you want to explore in analyzing your audience. Some of the most important factors are considered in Table 11.2.

AUDIENCE PSYCHOLOGY

Focus your psychological analysis of the audience on three questions: How willing is your audience? How knowledgeable is your audience? And how favorable is your audience?

How Willing Is Your Audience?
If you face an audience that is willing (even eager) to hear your speech, you'll have an easy time relating your speech to them. If, however, your audience is listening unwillingly, consider the following suggestions:

- Secure their attention as early in your speech as possible—and maintain their interest throughout—with supporting materials that will speak to their motives, interests, and concerns.

- Relate your topic and supporting materials directly to your audience's needs and wants; show them how what you are saying will help them achieve what they want.

Communication Choice Point

Unpopular Thesis
You've decided to tackle the hypocrisy you see in classmates who publicly support the values of racial equality but privately express racist attitudes. You're afraid, however, that your audience will walk out on you as soon as you state your thesis. *What are some of the things you can do to avoid any knee-jerk reaction from your listeners? What might you say (especially in your introduction) to make them listen to what essentially will be criticism?*

Take a look at "Religion and Religiousness" at **tcbdevito** .blogspot.com. How important is religion to members of your communication class?

TABLE 11.2 Audience Sociology

No list of audience characteristics can possibly be complete, and the list presented here is no exception. These, then, are some of the audience factors you may want to consider and some questions you may want to ask, depending on your specific thesis and audience.

Audience Characteristics	Questions to Ask
Cultural factors	Are the cultural beliefs and values of the audience relevant to your topic and purpose? Might the cultural memberships of this audience influence the way they see the topic?
Age	Will the ages of your audience members influence how your speech topic and purpose are viewed? Will they see what you're saying as relevant to the present and near future?
Gender	Will both genders find your topic and supporting materials interesting and relevant? Will men and women have different attitudes toward the topic or different experiences that will be relevant to your topic?
Religion and religiousness	Will the religion and religiousness of your listeners influence their responses to your speech? Might your topic or purpose be seen as an attack on the religious beliefs of any segment of your audience?
Educational levels	Does the educational level of your audience suggest any stylistic adjustment? Will technical terms have to be defined? Will the educational level suggest different persuasive strategies or supporting materials?
Occupation and income	Is your audience's level of job security and occupational pride related to your topic, purpose, or examples? Will people from different economic levels see your topic and purpose in different ways?
Relational status	Will singles be interested in hearing about the problems of selecting preschools? Will those in long-term relationships be interested in the depression many people who are not in close relationships feel?
Values	What do audience members value? What do they consider important to their current and future lives? What do they hold sacred? What do they consider profane?
Special interests	What special interests do the audience members have? What occupies their leisure time? How can you integrate these interests into your examples and illustrations or use them as you select quotations?
Political beliefs	Will audience members' political affiliations influence how they view your topic or purpose? Are they politically liberal? Conservative? Might this influence how you develop your speech?
Organizational memberships	Might audience members' affiliations give you cues as to their other beliefs and values? Might you use references to these organizations in your speech, perhaps as examples or illustrations?

VIEWpoints

Analyzing an Audience

Ted wants to give his speech on the values of atheism. If this speech were to be given to your class, what are some of the things Ted would need to know about his audience?

Explore the **Concept**
"Audience Analysis" at
MyCommunicationLab

Explore the **Exercise**
"Analyzing an Unknown
Audience" at
MyCommunicationLab

● Show the audience why they should listen to your speech by connecting your purpose to their purposes.

● Involve the audience directly in your speech by showing them that you understand their perspective, asking rhetorical questions, and referring to their experiences and interests.

How Knowledgeable Is Your Audience?

If your audience knows little about your topic, consider these suggestions:

● Don't talk down to audience members.

● Don't confuse a lack of knowledge with a lack of intelligence.

If your audience knows a great deal about your topic, consider these suggestions:

● Let the audience know that you are aware of their knowledge and expertise and that your speech will not simply repeat what they already know but will go beyond it.

● Emphasize your competence in this general subject area.

How Favorable Is Your Audience?

If you face an audience that has unfavorable attitudes toward your topic or your purpose, or even toward you, consider these suggestions:

● Build on commonalities; emphasize not the differences but the similarities between you and the audience.

● Build your speech from areas of agreement, through areas of slight disagreement, up to the major differences.

● Strive for small gains.

● Ask for a fair hearing.

ANALYSIS AND ADAPTATION DURING THE SPEECH

In your classroom speeches, you'll face a known audience, an audience you've already analyzed and for which you've made appropriate adaptations. At other times, however, you may face an audience that you've not been able to analyze beforehand or that differs greatly from what you expected. In these cases you'll have to analyze and adapt as you speak. Here are a few suggestions.

"I know you're angry at me—I'm angry at me, too!"

Focus on Listeners as Message Senders   As you're speaking, look at your listeners and make adjustments as necessary. For example, if your audience shows signs of boredom, increase your volume, move closer to them, or tell them how what you're going to say will be of value to them. If your audience shows signs of disagreement or hostility, stress a similarity you have with them. If your audience looks puzzled or confused, pause a moment and rephrase your ideas, provide necessary definitions, or insert an internal summary. If your audience seems impatient, say, for example, "my last argument" instead of your originally planned "my third argument."

Use Answers to Your "What If" Questions   The more preparation you put into your speech, the better prepared you'll be to make on-the-spot adjustments and adaptations. For example, let's say that you're to explain the opportunities available to the nontraditional student at your college. You've been told that your audience will consist mainly of working women in their 30s and 40s who are just beginning college. As you prepare your speech with this audience in mind, ask yourself "what if" questions. Keeping such questions in mind will force you to consider possible answers as you prepare your speech: What if the audience has a large number of men? What if the audience consists of women much older than 40? What if the audience members also come with their spouses or their children?

Address Audience Responses Directly   Another way of dealing with audience responses is to confront them directly. To those who are giving disagreement feedback, for example, you might say this:

> You may disagree with this position, but all I ask is that you hear me out and see if this new way of doing things will not simplify your accounting procedures.

Or, to those who seem impatient, you might offer this response:

> I know this has been a long day, but give me just a few more minutes and you'll be able to save hours recording your accounts.

By responding to your listeners' reactions and feedback, you acknowledge their needs. You let them know that you hear them, that you're with them, and that you're responding to their very real needs.

Communication Choice Point

Audience Knowledge

From the expressions on the faces of your audience, you immediately recognize that they're totally lost; they just don't have the knowledge needed to understand what you're saying. *What are some things you might do when faced with an audience lacking knowledge? Would you mention that you know they're lost? What might you say?*

Video Choice Point

Preparing for a Speech

Margo is excited about talking about her passion, baseball, and is planning to give a speech on it for her communication course. She feels confident about her knowledge of the topic, but she's concerned about her ability to apply that in the speaking arena. She is especially concerned that her audience may not find her a credible speaker, and she has asked her friend Vicki for help as she contemplates her communication options. See how her choices play out in the video "Preparing for a Speech", which looks at the initial steps involved in public speaking, the preparation of the speech itself, the form of its presentation, and the attitudinal approach important for public speaking effectiveness. All of these individual steps involve choices between doing one thing or another.

👁 **Watch** the **Video** "Homecoming Party" at **MyCommunicationLab**

Objectives Self-Check
- Can you explain the sociological characteristics (for example, gender, culture, age) and psychological characteristics (willingness, knowledge, and favorableness) of an audience?
- Can you use these characteristics in analyzing your own audiences?

Step 3: Research Your Topic

Throughout the process of preparing your public speeches, you'll conduct research to find examples, illustrations, and definitions to help you inform your listeners; testimony, statistics, and arguments to support your major ideas; and personal anecdotes, quotations, and stories to help you bring your topics to life. Here we consider some general research principles, some major sources of information, ways to evaluate the research you find, and suggestions for integrating research into your speech.

RESEARCH PRINCIPLES

Here are a few principles to help you research your speeches more effectively and more efficiently.

- Begin your search by examining what you already know. Write down, for example, what relevant books, articles, or websites you're familiar with or people who might know something about the topic.

For one perspective on this issue, see "Wikipedia" at **tcbdevito .blogspot.com**. How do you feel about this?

- Continue your search by getting a general overview of the topic. An encyclopedia article, book chapter, or magazine article will serve this purpose well. This general overview will help you see the topic as a whole and how its various parts fit together. If you search for material on any search engine, you'll find that Wikipedia comes up among the top search suggestions. This is a useful first step but realize that the articles in Wikipedia are not necessarily written by experts and are not fact-checked as they would be in, say, the *Encyclopaedia Britannica*. However, most articles have extensive references that you can and should check, especially for controversial issues.

- Follow up the general overview using increasingly more detailed and specialized sources. Fortunately, many of the general articles contain references or links for this very purpose.

- Gather a variety of different types of research. Although what is and what isn't appropriate research will depend partly on your topic; a variety of different types of research will generally prove more interesting and more convincing. Here are a few types:

  ○ **News sources** are especially useful for political speeches, financial news, or reports on natural disasters, congressional actions, international developments, or any of a host of other topics.

  ○ **Biographical material** will help you explain the competence and background of those you mention in your speech, present their credibility to the audience, and answer audience questions about them.

  ○ **Academic research articles** will enable you to secure the most reliable and valid research available. **MySearchLab** (a part of **MyCommunicationLab**) will help you locate the academic research articles you need to find.

- Distinguish between primary and secondary sources as you research. A primary source is original information about a topic or event—for example, an original research study in an academic journal, a corporation's annual report, and an eyewitness report of an accident. In contrast, a secondary source discusses information originally presented elsewhere—for example, a summary of research appearing in a popular magazine, a television news story on a corporation's earnings, and a report by someone who talked with an eyewitness to an accident.

RESEARCH SOURCES

Here we consider just two major research sources: the library and the interview.

Libraries   Libraries are the major storehouses of information and focus on computerized databases as well as print sources. Fortunately, you can access through your computer most of the great libraries of the world—for example, the *Library of Congress*, the largest library in the United States, which houses millions of books, maps, multimedia resources, and manuscripts. Other useful online sources are the *Virtual Library*, a collection of links to 14 subject areas and the *Internet Public Library*, a collection of links to a wide variety of materials that functions much like the reference desk at any of the world's best libraries.

Your college library will likewise prove useful. Here is probably the best place to get expert advice on databases and other resources available to you, especially nonprint resources or materials unique to your college or area. Your college library will also most likely provide you with access to databases that you might not have available on your own computer.

Interviews   One research activity that you may find helpful is to interview people who have special information that you might use in your speech. For example, you might want to interview a veterinarian for information on proper nutrition for household pets; an eyewitness for information on living through a hurricane; or average people for their opinions on politics, religion, or any of a wide variety of topics. In these interviews, a great part of your effectiveness will hinge on your ability to listen actively, for total meaning, with empathy, with an open mind, and ethically—all of the interpersonal communication skills already covered. Here are six steps you might follow:

- **Select the person you wish to interview.** You might, for example, look through your college catalog for an instructor teaching a course that involves your topic. Or visit blogs and look for people who have posted articles on your topic. If you want to contact a book author, you can always write to the author in care of the publisher or editor (listed on the

Explore the **Exercise** "Electronic Research" at **MyCommunicationLab**

copyright page), though many authors are now including their e-mail address.

- **Secure an appointment.** Phone the person or send an e-mail requesting an interview. State the purpose of your request and say that you hope to conduct a brief interview by phone or that you'd like to send this person a series of questions by e-mail.

- **Create a cheat sheet.** A cheat sheet is a list of what you want to say during the interview. If this is a phone or chat interview, you can keep the cheat sheet in front of you; if this is a face-to-face interview, review the cheat sheet immediately before the interview.

- **Ask open-ended questions.** Generally, ask questions that provide the interviewee with room to discuss the issues you want to raise. Avoid questions that can be answered with *yes* or *no*.

- **Ask for permission to tape or print the interview.** It's a good idea to keep an accurate record of the interview, so ask permission to tape the interview if it's in person or by telephone.

- **After closing the interview, follow-up with an expression of appreciation.** Even though you thank the person at the end of the interview, it's polite to follow up with a thank you note, later that day or the next day. Or perhaps you might send the person you interviewed a copy of your speech (e-mail would work well here) with a note of thanks.

> **Communication Choice Point**
>
> **Asking a Favor**
>
> You're preparing a speech on the growth of the independent film and want to ask some directors a few questions so you can integrate their most recent thoughts (and interject a more personalized note) into your speech. *What are some of your options for accomplishing this? What would you do?*

RESEARCH EVALUATION

All research materials must be evaluated. This is especially true of online materials simply because anyone can "publish" on the Internet, making it essential that you subject everything you find there to critical analysis. An article on the Internet can be written by world-renowned scientists or by elementary school students; by fair and objective reporters or by people who would spin the issues to serve their own political, religious, or social purposes. It's not always easy to tell which is which. Table 11.3 presents five criteria you'd want to use in evaluating research from the Internet or from any other place.

TABLE 11.3 Evaluating Research, Especially on the Internet

This table identifies five essential criteria that need to be examined when evaluating research of all kinds but perhaps Internet research in particular. These are some of the questions you'd want to ask and the precautions that you should take.

Criteria	Questions to Ask	Precautions to Take
Qualifications	Does the author have the necessary credentials? For example, does the author have enough of a background in science or medicine to write authoritatively on health issues?	Do an Internet search to check on the writer's expertise and credentials.
Currency	When was the information published? When were the sources that are cited in the article written?	To ensure currency check important figures in a recent almanac, in a newspaper, or at a frequently updated source, such as FedStats which lists statistics from over 100 government agencies.
Fairness	Does the author of the material present the information fairly and objectively, or is there a bias favoring one position? Some websites, although objective on the surface, are actually arms of political, religious, or social organizations.	It's often useful to go to the home page and look for information on the nature of the organization sponsoring the website. Reviewing a range of research on the subject will help you see how other experts view the issue.
Sufficiency	Is the information presented sufficient to establish the claim or conclusion? The opinion of one dietitian is insufficient to support the usefulness of a particular diet; statistics on tuition increases at five elite private colleges are insufficient to illustrate national trends in tuition costs.	The broader your conclusion, the more information you'll need to meet the requirements for sufficiency. If you claim the usefulness of a diet for all people, then you're going to need a great deal of information from different populations—men and women, old and young, healthy and sickly, and so on.
Accuracy	Is the information presented accurate? (Although accuracy is not always easy to determine, the more you learn about your topic, the more able you'll be to judge its accuracy.) Is the information primary or secondary? If it's secondary information, you may be able to locate the primary source material (often a link in the Internet article or a reference at the end).	Check to see whether the information is consistent with information found in other sources and whether the recognized authorities in the field accept this information.

Explore the **Concept**
"Avoiding Plagiarism" at
MyCommunicationLab

RESEARCH INTEGRATION AND CITATION

By integrating and acknowledging your sources of information in your speech, you'll give fair credit to those whose ideas and statements you're using; and, at the same time, you'll help establish your own reputation as a responsible researcher.

Be certain to mention your sources in your speech by citing at least author names and, if helpful, the publication titles and the dates. In your written outline, you would then give the complete bibliographical reference. Here is an example of how you might cite your source orally:

> The top careers for 2012, according to ClassesUSA, are web designer, criminal investigator, and network administrator.

Or:

> My discussion of the ways to estimate the value of the US dollar is based on the analysis by economics professor Samuel Williamson in *Measuring Worth*, published in March 2011.

Communication Choice Point

Adaptation and Plagiarism

You're really pressed to come up with a persuasive speech on a contemporary social issue, and you just don't have the time to research it. Fortunately, a friend at another school wrote a term paper for her sociology course that you could easily adapt to your required public speaking assignment. *What are some of your options for dealing with this situation? What do you feel is your ethical obligation in this case?*

Although it's possible to overdo the oral citation—giving more information than the listeners really need—it's better than leaving out useful information. Because your speeches in this course are learning experiences, it's better to err on the side of more information rather than less.

Avoid expressions such as "I have a quote here" or "I want to quote an example." Let the audience know that you're quoting by pausing before the quote, taking a step forward, or referring to your notes to read the extended quotation.

In addition to the oral citation, you'd also need a written citation, which would take the form of the references listed at the end of the typical textbook. You would then, in the reference list following the speech, identify the author, title of the article, journal title or URL, and the date. Numerous websites—for example, bibme.com and easybib.com—will help you format your sources according to the style manual your college uses.

Objectives Self-Check
- Can you identify the basic principles of and sources for researching your speech topic?
- Can you explain the criteria for evaluating research?
- Can you effectively research, evaluate research, integrate, and cite this research in your speech?

Step 4: Collect Supporting Materials

Now that you have your purpose and thesis clearly in mind and have researched your topic, you need to collect materials that will support your thesis. In the informative speech, your support primarily amplifies the concepts you discuss. Specifically, you might use these forms of support:

- Examples, illustrations, and the testimony of various authorities to breathe life into abstract or vague concepts.
- Definitions to clarify complex terms and to provide different ways of looking at some process or event.
- Numerical data to explain trends in a wide variety of topics.
- Presentation aids—charts, maps, objects, slides, films, tapes, CDs, and so on—to help clarify ideas.

These forms are covered in detail in Chapter 13.

In a persuasive speech, your support is proof—material that offers evidence, argument, and motivational appeal and that establishes your credibility and reputation. You can persuade your audience with several types of support:

COMMUNICATING ETHICALLY

Plagiarism

Because plagiarism is such an important issue in public speaking, this ethics box is a bit longer than other boxes in the text. It will cover the nature of plagiarism, the reasons why it is unacceptable, and what you can do to avoid this problem.

What Is Plagiarism?

Plagiarism is the process of passing off the work (e.g., ideas, words, or illustrations) of others as your own. Plagiarism is not the act of using another person's ideas—we all do that. Rather, it is the act of using someone else's ideas without acknowledging that they are the ideas of this other person; it is presenting the ideas as if they were your own. Plagiarism exists on a continuum, ranging from appropriating an entire term paper or speech written by someone else to using a quotation or research finding without citing the author.

Plagiarism also includes situations in which you get help from a friend without acknowledging this assistance. In some cultures—especially in collectivist cultures—teamwork is strongly encouraged. Students are encouraged to help other students with their work. But in the United States and in many individualist cultures teamwork without acknowledgment is considered plagiarism.

In U.S. institutions of higher education, plagiarism is a serious violation of the rules of academic honesty and is subject to serious penalties, sometimes even expulsion. Further, as with all crimes, ignorance of the law is not an acceptable defense against charges of plagiarism. This last point is especially important, because people often commit plagiarism through ignorance about what does and does not constitute plagiarism.

Why Plagiarism Is Unacceptable

There are three key reasons why plagiarism is unacceptable:

- Plagiarism is a violation of another person's intellectual property rights. Much as it would be wrong to take someone's watch without permission, it is wrong to take another person's ideas without giving due credit.

- You're in college to develop your own ideas and ways of expressing them; plagiarism defeats this fundamental purpose.

- Evaluations (everything from grades in school to promotions in the workplace) assume that what you present as your work is in fact your work.

Avoiding Plagiarism

Let's start with the easy part. In a speech or term paper, for example, you do not have to—and should not—cite sources for information that is readily available and not likely to be disputed. For example, the population of Thailand, the amendments to the U.S. Constitution, the actions of the United Nations, and the way the heart pumps blood are all common knowledge; and you should not cite the almanac or the book from which you got such information. On the other hand, if you were talking about the attitudes of people from Thailand or the reasons the Constitutional amendments were adopted, then you would need to cite your sources, because this information is not common knowledge and may well be disputed.

For information that is not common knowledge, you need to acknowledge your source. Here are four simple rules that will help you avoid even the suggestion of plagiarism (for more extended discussion, see Stern, 2007):

- Acknowledge the source of any ideas you present that are not your own. If you learned of an idea in your history course, cite the history instructor or history textbook. If you read an idea in an article, cite the article.

- Acknowledge the words of another person. When you're quoting someone exactly, you need to cite the person you're quoting. You should also cite the person even when you paraphrase her or his words, because you are still using another person's ideas.

- Acknowledge help from others. If your roommate gave you examples or ideas, or helped you style your speech, acknowledge the help.

- When in doubt, it's best to err on the side of over-referencing rather than under-referencing.

Take a look at some of the plagiarism websites established by different universities; these often include exercises and extended examples; those by Indiana University and Purdue University are especially helpful.

Ethical Choice Point

While listening to a classmate's impressive speech, you recognize that you've read this exact same material in an obscure online publication. You're annoyed that this student has not done the work that everyone else has done and yet will probably earn a high grade. However, you wonder if you want to or should take on being the ethical conscience of your class. What is your ethical obligation in this case? What would you do?

- Logical support includes reasoning from specific instances and from general principles, from causes and effects, and from signs.
- Motivational support includes appeals to the audience's emotions and to their desires for status, financial gain, or increased self-esteem.
- Credibility appeals involve establishing your own personal reputation or credibility, especially your competence, high moral character, and charisma.

These forms of support are covered in depth in Chapter 14.

Objectives Self-Check
- Can you explain the nature and types of supporting materials in informative and persuasive speeches?

Step 5: Develop Your Main Points

In this step, you use your thesis (which you created in Step 1) to generate your major points or ideas. Once you phrase the thesis statement, the main divisions of your speech will suggest themselves. Let's look at an example: You're giving a speech on the value of a college education to a group of people in their 30s and 40s who are considering returning to college. Your thesis is "A college education is valuable." To generate your main points, you'd then ask, "Why is it valuable?" These answers constitute your major points and might look something like this:

There are several reasons why a college education is valuable :

1. It helps you get a job.
2. It increases your potential to earn a good salary.
3. It gives you greater job mobility.
4. It helps you secure more creative work.
5. It helps you appreciate the arts more fully.
6. It helps you understand an increasingly complex world.
7. It helps you understand different cultures.
8. It helps you avoid taking a regular job for a few years.
9. It helps you meet lots of people and make friends.
10. It helps you increase personal effectiveness.

For purposes of illustration, let's stop here. You have 10 possible main points—too many to cover in a short speech. Further, not all are equally valuable or relevant to your audience. You need to make the list shorter and more relevant. Here are some suggestions.

ELIMINATE OR COMBINE POINTS

You might want to eliminate, say, number 8—it's inconsistent with the positive value of college, the thesis of your speech. Furthermore, your audience is unlikely to be able to stop working to go to college full-time.

Also notice that the first four points center on jobs. You might, therefore, consider grouping them under a general heading:

A college education will help you secure a better job.

This might be one of your major propositions, which you can develop by defining what you mean by "a better job." This main point and its elaboration might look like this:

I. A college education will help you secure a better job.

    A. College graduates earn higher salaries.

    B. College graduates enter more creative jobs.

    C. College graduates have greater job mobility.

Note that A, B, and C are all aspects or subdivisions of "a better job."

SELECT POINTS THAT ARE MOST RELEVANT

Explore the **Concept**
"Testing for Relevance of Supporting Ideas" at
MyCommunicationLab

You might drop number 5 on the assumption that your audience will be interested in more practical outcomes. And, you might eliminate number 9 on the assumption that your audience is not looking for college to help them make friends; they probably already have friends and families that occupy most of their time. Further, you might conclude that this audience cares a lot about personal effectiveness, so you might make this your second major proposition:

A college education will help you increase your personal effectiveness.

Much as you developed the subordinate points in your first proposition by defining what you meant by "a good job," you would define what you mean by "personal effectiveness":

II. A college education will help you increase your personal effectiveness.

   A. A college education will help you increase your ability to communicate.

   B. A college education will help you acquire learning skills.

   C. A college education will help you acquire coping skills.

You would then follow the same procedure used to generate these subordinate points (A, B, and C) to develop the subheadings. For example, you might divide A into two major subheads:

   A. A college education will improve your ability to communicate.

      1. A college education teaches writing skills.

      2. A college education teaches speech skills.

Remember, your aim is not to cover every aspect of a topic but to emphasize selected parts. Further, you want to have enough time to amplify and support the points you present. With too many propositions, this becomes impossible. Also, you don't want to present too much information, because your audience simply will not be able to remember it. Ideally you should use two, three, or four main points.

PHRASE PROPOSITIONS IN PARALLEL STYLE

To make it easier for listeners to follow and remember your speech, use parallel grammatical structures in wording your major propositions:

Not this:

I. Social media functions

   A. Social media entertain.

   B. The social media function to inform.

   C. Making friends and establishing relationships are major functions.

This:

I. Social media functions

   A. Social media entertain.

   B. Social media inform.

   C. Social media help establish relationships.

DEVELOP MAIN POINTS SEPARATELY AND DISTINCTLY

Don't overlap your main points. Overlapping is likely to create confusion rather than clarity.

Not This:

I. Color and style are important in clothing selection.

This:

I. Color is important in clothing selection.

II. Style is important in clothing selection.

Objectives Self-Check
- Can you generate main points by asking strategic questions of your thesis?

Explore the Concept
"Organization" at
MyCommunicationLab

Step 6: Organize Your Speech Materials

Organize your materials to help the audience understand and remember what you say. There are six ways to organize the body of a speech: (1) time pattern, (2) spatial pattern, (3) topical, (4) problem-solution pattern, (5) cause-effect and effect-cause pattern, and the motivated sequence. Additional organizational patterns are presented in Table 11.4.

TABLE 11.4 Additional Organizational Patterns

The six patterns just considered are the most common and the most useful for organizing most public speeches. But there are other patterns that might be appropriate for different topics.

ORGANIZATIONAL STRUCTURE	USES	POSSIBLE OUTLINES

In the **structure–function pattern** there are generally two main points, one for structure and one for function.	This pattern is useful in informative speeches in which you want to discuss how something is constructed (its structure) and what it does (its function). It might prove useful, for example, in a speech explaining what a business organization is and what it does, identifying the parts of a university and how they operate, or describing the nature of a living organism: its anatomy (its structures) and its physiology (its functions).	Thesis: To understand the brain you need to understand its structure and its function.
		I. The brain consists of two main parts [explanation of structures]
		  A. The cerebrum consists of . . .
		  B. The cerebellum consists of . . .
		The brain enables us to do a variety of things [explanations of functions]
		  A. The cerebrum enables us to . . .
		  B. The cerebellum enables us to . . .

In the **comparison-and-contrast pattern** your main points might be the main divisions of your topic.	This pattern is often useful in informative speeches in which you want to analyze two different theories, proposals, departments, or products in terms of their similarities and differences. In this type of speech you would be concerned not only with explaining each theory or proposal but also with clarifying how they're similar and how they're different.	Thesis: Liberal and conservative political philosophies differ in important ways.
		I. Government regulation . . .
		  A. The liberal attitude is . . .
		  B. The conservative attitude is . . .
		II. Redistribution of income . . .
		  A. Liberals view this . . .
		  B. Conservatives view this . . .

In the **pro-and-con pattern**, sometimes called the **advantages–disadvantages pattern**, the speech has two main points—the advantages of Plan A and the disadvantages of Plan A (or Plan B).	This pattern is useful in informative speeches in which you want to explain objectively the advantages (the pros) and the disadvantages (the cons) of a plan, method, or product. Or you can use this pattern in a persuasive speech in which you want to show the superiority of Plan A (identifying its advantages) over Plan B (identifying its disadvantages).	Thesis: The proposals of the two health plans differ in co-payments, hospital benefits, and sick leave.
		I. Co-payments . . .
		  A. Plan A provides . . .
		  B. Plan B provides . . .
		II. Hospital benefits . . . .
		  A. Plan A provides . . .
		  B. Plan B provides . . .
		III. Sick leave . . .
		  A. Plan A provides . . .
		  B. Plan B provides . . .

In the **claim-and-proof pattern** your thesis would essentially be your claim, and then each main point would be support for your claim.	This pattern is especially useful in a persuasive speech in which you want to prove the truth or usefulness of a particular proposition. It's the pattern that you see frequently in trials, where the claim made by the prosecution is that the defendant is guilty and the proof is the varied evidence designed to show that the defendant had a motive, opportunity, and no alibi.	Thesis/Claim: The city must become proactive in dealing with the drug addicted.
		I. Drug usage is increasing. [Proof No. 1]
		  A. A particularly vivid example . . .
		  B. Recent statistics . . .
		II. Drug related crimes are increasing. [Proof No. 2]
		  A. On-street crimes have increased . . .
		  B. Business break-ins . . .

ORGANIZATIONAL STRUCTURE	USES	POSSIBLE OUTLINES
In the **multiple-definition pattern** each of your main points would consist of a different type of definition.	This pattern is useful for informative speeches in which you want to explain the nature of a concept.	Thesis: The nature of creative thinking is often misunderstood. I. Creative thinking is not . . . [definition by negation] II. According to Webster's dictionary . . . [dictionary definition] III. Edward deBono defines . . . [a creative thinking theorist's view] IV. A good example of creative thinking . . . [definition by example]
In the **who? what? why? where? when? pattern** your main points are explanations of who, what, why, where, and/or when.	This is the pattern traditionally used by journalists and is useful when you wish to report or explain an event; for example, a robbery, political coup, war, or trial.	Thesis: Understanding the Constitution is a first step toward responsible citizenship. I. The Constitution is a document that sets forth . . . [answers the question What is the Constitution?] II. The Constitution was needed because . . . [answers the question Why was it written?] III. The Constitution was written at a time . . . [answers the question When was it written?] IV. The Constitution was written by . . . [answers the question Who wrote it?]
In the **fiction–fact pattern** your main points would be the fiction, and under these would be the facts.	This pattern may be useful in informative speeches when you wish to clarify misconceptions that people have about various things. In persuasive speeches this pattern might be used to defend or attack, whether a proposal, belief, or person.	Thesis: Three main misconceptions exist about the flu shot. I. The first misconception is that you can get the flu from the flu shot. A. Studies show . . . B. The flu shot contains . . . II. The second misconception is that antibiotics will help with the flu. A. Actually, antibiotics . . . . B. Viruses, such as the flu, however, . . . III. The third misconception is that older people spread the flu. A. Actually, children . . . B. In studies done. . . .

TIME PATTERN

When you organize your topic on the basis of a time, or temporal, relationship, you generally divide the speech into two, three, or four major parts. You might begin with the past and work up to the present or future, or begin with the present or future and work back to the past. Most historical topics lend themselves to organization by a time pattern. Topics such as events leading to the Civil War, how to plant a vegetable garden, and the history of the Internet are all candidates for temporal patterning. For example, you might organize a speech on children's development of speech and language according to a temporal pattern.

General Purpose: To inform

Specific Purpose: To inform my audience of the four stages in the child's acquisition of language

Thesis: The child goes through four stages in learning language.

I. Babbling occurs first.

II. Lallation occurs second.

III. Echolalia occurs third.

IV. Communication occurs fourth.

SPATIAL PATTERN

Organizing the main points of a speech on the basis of its spatial patterns is similar to temporal patterning. Discussions of most physical objects fit well into spatial patterns. For example, a presentation on the structure of a hospital, a school, a skyscraper, or even a dinosaur might lend itself to this pattern. Here, a speech on places to visit in Central America uses a spatial pattern.

General Purpose: To inform

Specific Purpose: To inform my audience of a great way to visit Central America

Thesis: You can have a great visit to Central America by visiting four countries.

I.   First, visit Guatemala.

II. Second, visit Honduras.

III. Third, visit Nicaragua.

IV. Fourth, visit Costa Rica.

TOPICAL PATTERN

The topical pattern divides the speech topic into subtopics or component parts. The world's major religions, great works of literature, and the problems facing the college graduate are other examples of speech topics that lend themselves to a topical organizational pattern. This pattern is an obvious choice for organizing a speech on a topic such as the branches of government:

General Purpose: To inform

Specific Purpose: To inform my audience of the ways the three branches of government work

Thesis: Three branches govern the United States.

I.   The legislative branch is controlled by Congress.

II. The executive branch is controlled by the president.

III. The judicial branch is controlled by the courts.

PROBLEM-SOLUTION PATTERN

As its name indicates, the problem-solution pattern divides the main ideas into two main parts: problems and solutions. Let's say you're trying to persuade an audience that home health aides should be given higher salaries and increased benefits. In the first part of the speech, you might discuss some of the problems confronting home health aides. In the second part, you would consider the possible solutions to these problems. The speech, in outline form, might look like this:

General Purpose: To persuade

Specific Purpose: To persuade my audience of the solutions to the three main problems of the home health care industry

Thesis: The home health care industry can be improved with three changes.

I.   Three major problems confront home health care.
   A. Industry lures away the most qualified graduates.
   B. Numerous excellent health aides leave the field after a few years.
   C. Home health care is currently a low-status occupation.

II. Three major solutions to these problems exist.
   A. Increase salaries for home health aides.
   B. Make benefits for health aides more attractive.
   C. Raise the status of the home health care profession.

CAUSE-EFFECT/EFFECT-CAUSE PATTERN

Similar to the problem-solution pattern of organization is the cause-effect, or effect-cause, pattern. Using this pattern, you divide the speech into two major sections: (1) causes and

(2) effects. Highway accidents, illnesses, or low self-esteem, for example, could be explained using a cause-effect pattern. An outline of the causes and effects of low self-esteem might look something like this:

General Purpose: To inform

Specific Purpose: To inform my audience of the causes and effects of low self-esteem

Thesis: Low self-esteem is caused by a history of criticism and unrealistic goals, which lead to depression and an unwillingness to socialize.

    I. Low self-esteem often has two main causes.

        A. A history of criticism can contribute to low self-esteem.

        B. Unrealistic goals can contribute to low self-esteem.

    II. Low self-esteem often has two main effects.

        A. Depression is one frequent effect.

        B. An unwillingness to socialize with others is another frequent effect.

You can also organize your persuasive speeches around causes and effects. For example, you might organize a persuasive speech around persuading your audience that, say, a history of criticism does in fact contribute to low self-esteem as do unrealistic goals. Here you would have two major points:

    I. A history of criticism leads to low self-esteem.

        A. Double blind studies show. . . .

        B. A recent survey . . .

        C. Psychologist, John Smith of Harvard University, has said . . .

    II. Unrealistic goals lead to low self-esteem.

        A. My own experience illustrates . . .

        B. A study conducted . . .

        C. Educational theorists have long. . . .

THE MOTIVATED SEQUENCE

The motivated sequence, useful for organizing both informative and persuasive speeches, is a pattern in which you organize your information in five steps: (1) attention, (2) need, (3) satisfaction, (4) visualization, and (5) action (German, Gronbeck, Ehninger, & Monroe, 2013).

1. Attention   Persuade the audience to give you their undivided attention. If you execute this step effectively, your audience should be eager to hear what you have to say. You can gain audience attention by, for example, asking a rhetorical question, referring to specific audience members, or using a dramatic or humorous story. These and other ways of gaining attention are discussed more fully in Chapter 13.

2. Need   Prove to the audience that they need to learn or do something. You can establish need in three ways:

- State the need or problem as it exists or will exist.
- Illustrate the need with specific examples, illustrations, statistics, testimony, and other forms of support.
- Point to how this need affects your specific listeners—for example, their financial status, career goals, or individual happiness.

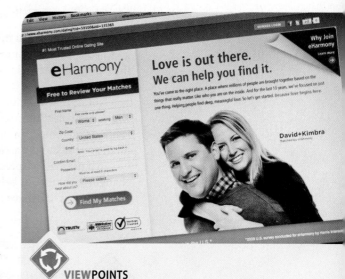

VIEWPOINTS

Organizing a Speech

Sean wants to give a speech on how to find a date on the Internet. What would be appropriate main points for such a speech? What organizational pattern would be best to use, given the main points you identified?

For example, in a speech to convince people in their 60s and 70s to purchase home computers, you might say in this step, "A survey of persons in their 60s and 70s reported that one of their greatest needs was easy and rapid access to medical information. If you are like those in this survey, then the home computer may be your answer."

3. Satisfaction

Present the "solution" that satisfies the need you demonstrated in step 2. This step should convince the audience that what you are informing them about or persuading them to do will satisfy the need. You answer the question, "How will the need be satisfied by what I am asking the audience to learn, believe, or do?" This step usually contains two types of information: (1) a clear statement (with examples and illustrations if necessary) of what you want the audience to learn, believe, or do; and (2) a statement of how or why what you are asking them to learn, believe, or do will lead to satisfying the need identified in step 2

For example, you might say, "With a home computer, you'll be able to get information on thousands of potential drug interactions in seconds." You might then show your listeners, perhaps with an actual demonstration, how this would be done.

4. Visualization

Try to intensify the audience's feelings or beliefs, to take them beyond the present place and time and to help them imagine what it would be like if the need were satisfied (with the solution suggested in step 3). You can accomplish this by (1) demonstrating the positive benefits to be derived if this advocated proposal were put into operation or (2) demonstrating the negative consequences that will occur if your plan is not followed. You could also combine the two methods and demonstrate both the positive benefits of your plan and the negative effects of the existing situation or of a competing proposal. For example, you might say, "With one simple click, you'll be able to stay at home and get valuable medical information, instead of fighting traffic and wasting time." You might then demonstrate with a specific example how they would find this information.

5. Action

Tell the audience what they should do to satisfy the need you have identified. Your goal is to move the audience in a particular direction. Here are a few ways to accomplish this step:

- State exactly what audience members should do.
- Appeal to their emotions.
- Give them guidelines for future action.

For example, you might say, "Read this pamphlet, 'Life on the Computer after 60,' and go to your nearest computer store and talk with the salespeople." Or you might suggest that they consider taking an appropriate adult education course at the local community college.

Notice that an informative speech could stop after the satisfaction step. In this example, with the satisfaction step you accomplish the goal of informing the audience about some advantages of home computers for older people. In some cases, though, you may believe it helpful to progress to the action step to emphasize your point.

In a persuasive speech, on the other hand, if you limit your purpose to strengthening or changing attitudes or beliefs, you must go at least as far as visualization. If you aim to get your listeners to behave in a certain way, you'll need to go all the way through the action step.

Objectives Self-Check
- Can you describe the major patterns of speech organization?
- Can you organize your own speeches using an appropriate organizational pattern?

PUBLIC SPEAKING SAMPLE ASSISTANT

A Poorly Constructed Informative Speech

Here is an example of a poorly constructed informative speech. As you'll see, no one really gives a speech this bad. It was constructed to illustrate clearly and briefly some of the major faults that can occur in such speeches. The PSSA box in Chapter 13 offers an example of a truly excellent speech. Together, the negative and the positive speech examples will offer you a variety of guidelines for errors you'll want to avoid and principles you'll want to follow in your own speeches. Not surprisingly researchers have found that we learn a great deal from negative examples (Hesketh & Neal, 2006).

SPEECH	PROBLEMS *AND* CORRECTIVES
Topic/Title: The Falling Dollar **Purpose:** To inform my audience about the dollar. **Thesis:** The dollar falls.	The title isn't bad; it gives listeners a general idea of the topic and arouses interest. The purpose is not specific enough—it merely repeats what's in the title. This thesis is not helpful in guiding the speech preparation process. A better phrasing might be: To inform my audience about some consequences of the dollar's decline in value. A thesis should be in statement form: *The decline in the U.S. dollar has significant consequences on our own wallets.*

INTRODUCTION

Ok, I'm here. Whew! I'm not very good at public speaking—I only took this course because it's required—and I'm really nervous. Let's see . . . [shuffles through notes, arranging them and mumbling, page 1, page 2,—ok, it's all here]. This speech is about the dollar. I'm going to explain what happens when the dollar goes down.	These comments are usually best avoided. Lead with a strong, attention-getting opener. Things like this reveal a decided lack of preparation. The speaker should have the notes arranged before getting up to speak and should have rehearsed with them in place.
This is a topic that's really important to everyone in this room, so I hope you'll listen carefully.	Although this does announce the topic, it's weak and would fail to gain the attention of most audience members. The speaker needs a strong opener to get the attention of the audience and to perhaps explain what "goes down" means. Telling the audience they should pay attention is probably not the best idea. Instead of just telling the audience that the topic is important, the speaker needs to explain why the audience should listen and why the topic is important to them—for example, it's going to cost them more when they buy something.
So, as I said, I'm going to talk about the dollar.	This is an insufficient orientation. The speaker needs to tell the audience something more, perhaps identifying the main points to be considered.

BODY

As the dollar goes down—say against the Japanese dollar or Europe's dollar—it becomes more expensive to buy stuff from Japan and Europe.	The speaker reveals a lack of knowledge and familiarity with the topic by not using the terms *yen* and *euro* for the currencies of Japan and Europe. The speaker also needs to define the relationships among these currencies and state this in the speech. A simple graph might help. Parallel wording would also have helped; the speaker might have said "Japanese dollar and European dollar" (two adjectives) or "Japan's dollar or Europe's dollar" (two nouns) instead of an adjective and a noun.

So, if you're going to buy a new Sony television—that's what I really want a big flat screen television—it's going to be more expensive.

This example does nothing to explain why merchandise from Japan or Europe become more expensive as the dollar goes down. The comment "that's what I . . ." is personal and not really related to explaining what happens when the dollar loses value compared to other world currencies. The speaker might have said, "How many of you are planning to buy a new flat-screen TV? Well, if you're planning to buy a Sony, a Samsung, a . . . you're going to be paying more. And the reason is the decline in the U.S. dollar. Let me explain how this works . . ."

And if you're going to buy stuff from Germany or Italy, it's also going to be more expensive. Like pasta—but I guess that's made in this country too. But you know what I mean.

This kind of comment shows a lack of appropriate preparation and is likely to make the audience wonder why they're wasting their time when the speaker couldn't spend the time and energy necessary to come up with a really good example. A list of popular German and Italian products that the audience uses (and the speaker would have to know something about the audience to select the most meaningful products) would have been appropriate here.

There are in fact no transitions to help the audience move with the speaker from one topic to another. A transition is needed here that leads from the first main point to the next, something like "Not only is merchandise from Europe and Japan going to cost more, you're also going to be paying more for oil."

As the dollar goes down and oil prices go up—let's see if I got this right; yes, as the value of the dollar goes down, the price of oil goes up.

Again, there is no explanation as to why oil prices go up as the dollar goes down. And the examples that follow don't help—they merely give examples of higher prices. The speaker needs to explain why the prices are higher.

Notice that there are no signposts that help the listeners follow the speech. The speaker could have helped the audience understand the speech by using signposts such as, "the *first* change when the dollar goes down is" or "the *next* change," or *another* example." Using words like the italicized ones in these examples help the audience understand your progression of ideas.

So, your gas and electric bill are going to be higher. And you know how expensive gas is. I last paid 3.29 a gallon—no, it was 3.19, no, no, 3.09. That's what it was. But that's still a lot.

Again, the speaker demonstrates a lack of preparation with the price of gas. The specific figures here and in most cases are less important than the implication of the numbers—the specific figures can be given, of course. But, the important point is the expense and that is what the speaker needs to emphasize and not go on a detour of the exact price paid the last time at the pump.

As the dollar goes down the price of merchandise made in this country goes down. So if you buy an American-made television, the price will be cheaper. And if you buy an American car—instead of a car from Japan, the car will be less expensive.

A transition would help. The audience is probably asking itself, "Why does this happen?" The speaker should answer these questions that the audience is likely to ask. Again, parallel structure would help: "Japanese car" would have paralleled "American car" and made the sentence a lot clearer.

As the dollar goes down the price of raw materials—I'm not sure what that is, but I think it's like oil and metal—increases and so the price of American merchandize increases.

On the surface, this point seems to contradict the previous examples. This speech could have profited greatly from some simple charts or graphs showing the value of the U.S. dollar versus the yen and the euro.

And here is the most important thing; all this contributes to making China's economy grow. China has almost 1 billion people and they live in an area smaller than the state of Texas.

Here the speaker brings credibility into serious question. China has *more* than 1 billion people and is almost the size of the entire United States—only about 20,000 square miles smaller. A simple glance at an Almanac or a 3-minute Internet search would have provided accurate information and would not have detracted from the speaker's credibility as these incorrect statements do. Further, the speaker needs to explain the path or logic going from the weak dollar to China's economy. Where is the connection? And what does this mean to the audience's concerns?

CONCLUSION

In summary, as I demonstrated, when the dollar goes down, lots of other things happen—like the price of oil and China's economy.

Using the word *summary* is not a bad idea; it's a clear signal that the speaker is going to recap what was just said. However, this summary is far too brief. This speech needed a more detailed summary, perhaps itemizing the three or four things that happen when the value of the dollar goes down.

I got most of my information from my Economics 101 course—it's a good course; you should take it. Oh, and from a *New York Times* article—I don't have the date.

This type of source citation is certainly not enough. And of course, we wonder, where did the other information come from? And, whether Economics 101 is or is not a good course has nothing to do with the consequences of the falling dollar. An effective informative speech must be based on several varied and reliable sources with citations to these sources interwoven throughout the speech.

 ## Messages in the Media *Wrap Up*

Watching political talk shows in terms of the principles of public speaking can be quite instructive. Inevitably you will see the use of effective and the use of ineffective techniques, arguments, and evidence. Use the principles discussed in this chapter to evaluate the speeches you hear on such shows.

 ## Summary of Concepts and Skills

 Study and **Review** materials for this chapter are at **MyCommunicationLab**

Listen to the **Audio Chapter Summary** at **MyCommunicationLab**

This chapter explained the nature of public speaking and described the first six steps involved in preparing an effective public speech.

The Nature of Public Speaking

1. In public speaking a speaker addresses a relatively large audience with a relatively continuous discourse, usually in a face-to-face situation.

2. Effective public speaking will yield a variety of personal, social, academic, and professional benefits.

3. Apprehension can be managed by gaining experience, thinking positively, being realistic, seeing public speaking as conversation, focusing on your listeners, stressing similarity, projecting confidence, preparing and practicing thoroughly, moving about and breathing deeply, and avoiding using chemicals as tension relievers (unless prescribed by a physician).

4. Public speaking takes place within a cultural context, and that context must be taken into consideration in preparing and delivering speeches.

5. Starting early is the best way to ensure adequate time for dealing with unexpected problems.

The preparation of a public speech involves 10 steps. The first six of these were discussed in this chapter; the remaining four are discussed in Chapter 12.

Step 1: Select Your Topic, Purposes, and Thesis

6. Speech topics should deal with significant issues that interest the audience. Subjects and purposes should be limited in scope. The thesis should be stated as a complete sentence.

Step 2: Analyze Your Audience

7. When analyzing the audience, consider audience members' sociology: age; sex; cultural factors; occupation, income, and status; and religion and religiousness. Also consider the psychology of the audience: that is, the degree to which the audience is willing to hear your speech, their attitudes toward the topic and thesis, and the knowledge they possess of the topic.

Step 3: Research Your Topic

8. Research your topic, beginning with general sources and gradually exploring more specific and specialized sources.
9. In evaluating research material (especially material on the Internet) consider the qualifications of the author, the currency of the information, and its fairness, sufficiency, and accuracy.

Step 4: Collect Supporting Materials

10. Support your main points with a variety of materials that amplify and provide evidence.

Step 5: Develop Your Main Points

11. Formulate the thesis of your speech. Develop your main points by asking relevant questions about this thesis.

Step 6: Organize Your Information

12. Organize your speech materials into a clear, easily identifiable pattern. Useful examples include time patterns, spatial patterns, topical patterns, problem-solution patterns, cause-effect/effect-cause patterns, and the motivated sequence (attention, need, satisfaction, visualization, and action). Other available patterns include structure–function, comparison and contrast, pro and con, claim and proof, multiple definition, the five W's (who, what, why, where, when), and fiction–fact.

These first six steps in preparing a public speech entail a variety of specific skills. Place a check mark next to those skills you most want to work on.

_____ 1. When preparing a public speech, I follow a logical progression of steps, such as the sequence outlined here.

_____ 2. I select appropriate topics, purposes, and theses and narrow them to manageable proportions.

_____ 3. I analyze my audience in terms of members' sociological and psychological characteristics, and I adapt the speech on the basis of these findings.

_____ 4. I research topics effectively and efficiently and critically evaluate the reliability of the research material.

_____ 5. I collect materials relevant to my topic, purpose, and thesis—for instance, examples, statistics, and visual aids and with logical, emotional, and ethical proofs.

_____ 6. I identify my major propositions from my thesis statement.

_____ 7. When organizing the speech's main points, I select a pattern appropriate to the subject matter, purpose, and audience.

Key Word Quiz

The Language of Public Speaking

Match the terms about public speaking with their definitions. Record the number of the definition next to the appropriate term.

_____ a. topical pattern (228)

_____ b. database (220)

_____ c. collectivist culture (222)

_____ d. thesis (216)

_____ e. motivated sequence (229)

_____ f. public speaking (208)

_____ g. logical support (224)

_____ h. visualization (230)

_____ i. plagiarism (222)

_____ j. specific purpose (215)

1. A speech pattern consisting of attention, need, satisfaction, visualization, and action.

2. The act of presenting another's material as your own.

3. A form of communication in which a speaker addresses a relatively large audience with a relatively continuous discourse.

4. One of the steps in the motivated sequence, in which the audience is shown what will happen if the speaker's plan is adopted.

5. Emphasizes cooperation among its members.

6. A statement identifying the information you want to communicate or the attitude you want to change.

7. An organized, electronic body of information contained in one place that can be easily accessed.

8. The result of reasoning from specific instances, causes and effects, and signs.

9. A pattern of speech organization in which a topic is divided into its subtopics.

10. The main idea of a speech.

These 10 terms and additional terms used in this chapter can be found in the glossary.

Answers:
a.9b.7c.5d.10e.1f.3g.8h.4i.2j.6

 Study and **Review** the **Flashcards** at **MyCommunicationLab**

MyCommunicationLab

Throughout this chapter, there are icons in the margin that highlight media content for selected topics. Go to **MyCommunicationLab** for additional materials on these initial steps in preparing your speech. Here you'll find flashcards to help you learn the jargon of communication, videos that illustrate a variety of concepts, additional exercises, and discussions to help you continue your study of public speaking.

12

Public Speaking Preparation and Delivery (Steps 7–10)

Objectives

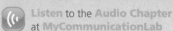
Listen to the **Audio Chapter** at **MyCommunicationLab**

After reading this chapter, you should be able to:

❶ Word your speech for clarity, vividness, appropriateness, personal style, and power.

❷ Construct effective speech conclusions, introductions, and transitions and create preparation and delivery outlines for your speeches.

❸ Explain the methods of delivery and rehearse your speech effectively.

❹ Deliver your speech using effective voice and bodily action.

❺ Evaluate the speeches of others, express constructive critical evaluations, and respond to criticism openly.

Messages in the Media

Jimmy Fallon, pictured here, and other late night talk show hosts such as Jay Leno and David Letterman, start their shows with an entertaining monologue that usually consists of humorous takes on a variety of current news items. As you've no doubt noticed, the success of these brief speeches depends largely on the language and the delivery the speaker uses—two of the topics considered in this chapter.

At this point, you're probably deep into your speech preparation. You've selected and limited your topic, defined your purpose, and stated your thesis. You've analyzed your audience and begun thinking of adaptations you can make based on the nature of your specific audience. You've researched the topic. You've identified your main points. You've organized the points and selected appropriate supporting materials. This chapter continues explaining the process of preparing a speech and offers suggestions on wording the speech (Step 7), constructing the conclusion, introduction, transitions, and outlines (Step 8), rehearsing the speech (Step 9), and finally delivering the completed public speech (Step 10).

Step 7: Word Your Speech

Explore the **Exercise** "Making Concepts Specific" at **MyCommunicationLab**

When you're reading, you can look up an unfamiliar word, reread difficult portions, or look up an unfamiliar word or check a reference. When you're listening, you don't have this luxury. Because of differences between reading and listening, and because your listeners will hear your speech only once, your talk must be instantly intelligible.

Researchers who have examined a great number of speeches and writings have found several important differences among them (DeVito, 1981; Akinnaso, 1982). Generally, **oral style,** the style of spoken language, consists of shorter, simpler, and more familiar words than does written language. For most speeches, this "oral style" is appropriate. The specific suggestions offered throughout this section will help you to style a speech that will retain the best of the oral style while maximizing comprehension and persuasion.

CLARITY

Clarity in speaking style should be your primary goal. Here are some guidelines to help you make your meanings clear:

- **Be economical.** Don't waste words. Notice the wasted words in expressions such as "at 9 a.m. *in the morning,*" "we *first* began the discussion," "I *myself personally,*" and "blue *in color.*" By withholding the italicized terms, you eliminate unnecessary words and move closer to a more economical and clearer style.

- **Use specific terms and numbers.** Be specific to create a clearer and more detailed picture. Don't say "dog" when you want your listeners to picture a St. Bernard. Don't say "car" when you want them to picture a limousine. The same is true of numbers. Don't say "earned a good salary" if you mean "earned $90,000 a year." Don't say "taxes will go up" when you mean "taxes will increase 7 percent."

- **Use short, familiar terms.** Generally, favor the short word over the long, the familiar over the unfamiliar, and the more commonly used over the rarely used term. Choose *harmless* instead of *innocuous, clarify* instead of *elucidate, use* instead of *utilize, find out* instead of *ascertain, expense* instead of *expenditure.*

- **Carefully assess idioms. Idioms** are expressions that are unique to a specific language and whose meaning cannot be deduced from the individual words used. Expressions such as "kick the bucket," and "doesn't have a leg to stand on" are idioms. Either you know the meaning of the expression or you don't; you can't figure it out from the definitions of the individual words. Idioms give your speech a casual and informal style, making your speech sound like speech and not like a written essay. But, idioms can create problems for audience members who are not native speakers of your language.

- **Vary the levels of abstraction.** Combining high abstraction (i.e., the very general) and low abstraction (i.e., the very concrete) seems to work best. Too many generalizations will be vague and difficult for your audience to comprehend, but too many specifics will leave them wondering what the big picture is.

VIVIDNESS

Select words that make your ideas vivid, that make them come alive in your listeners' minds.

Take a look at "Most Annoying Phrases" at tcbdevito.blogspot .com. What's the most annoying phrase to you?

- **Use active verbs.** Favor verbs that communicate activity. Try selecting verbs that will enable listeners to visualize an action—verbs like *dance*, *climb*, and *run*, for example.

- **Use figures of speech.** A figure of speech is a stylistic device in which words are used beyond their literal meaning. One of the best ways to achieve vividness is to use figures of speech. Table 12.1 presents a few that you may find helpful.

- **Use imagery.** Inject vividness into your speech by appealing to the audience's senses, especially their visual, auditory, and tactile senses. Using imagery can make your listeners see, hear, and feel what you're talking about. *Visual imagery* enables you to describe people or objects in images the audience can see. When appropriate, describe visual qualities such as height, weight, color, size, shape, length, and contour. Let your audience see the sweat pouring down the faces of coal miners. *Auditory imagery* helps you appeal to your listeners' sense of hearing. Let them hear the car screeching or the roar of angry protesters. *Tactile imagery* enables you to make listeners feel the temperature or texture you're talking about. Let them feel the cool water running over their bodies, the fighter's punch, or the sand beneath their feet.

APPROPRIATENESS

Appropriate language is consistent in tone with your topic, your audience, and your own self-image. It's language that does not offend anyone or make anyone feel uncomfortable; it seems natural given the situation. Here are some guidelines to help you choose appropriate language:

- **Speak at the appropriate level of formality.** Although public speaking usually takes place in a somewhat formal situation, relatively informal language seems to work best in most situations. One way to achieve a more informal style is to use contractions: *don't* instead of *do not*, *wouldn't* instead of *would not*. Contractions give a public speech the sound and rhythm of conversation—a quality listeners generally like.

- **Avoid written-style expressions.** Avoid expressions that are more familiar in writing, such as "the former" or "the latter" as well as expressions such as "the argument presented above." These make listeners feel you're reading to them rather than talking with them.

- **Avoid slang and vulgar and offensive expressions.** Be careful not to offend your audience with language that embarrasses them or makes them think you have little respect for them. Although your listeners may use such expressions, they generally resent their use by public speakers. Above all, avoid terms that might be interpreted as sexist, heterosexist, ageist, or racist (see Chapter 4).

TABLE 12.1 Figures of Speech

These are only a few of the many figures of speech you can use in your speeches. Too many are likely to make your speech sound unnatural and overly formal, so use these sparingly. On the other hand, a good figure of speech goes a long way toward making your speech memorable. Can you think of additional examples for each of the types identified here?

Figure of Speech/ Definition	Examples
Alliteration Repetition of the same initial consonant sound in two or more words close to one another	Choose from our fifty famous flavors! The basement was dirty, dingy, dark, and dank.
Hyperbole Use of extreme exaggeration	I'm so hungry I could eat a horse. They steamrolled the bill through Congress.
Metaphor Comparison of two unlike things	She's a lion when she's angry. He's a bear when it comes to his investments.
Personification Attribution of human characteristics to inanimate objects	This room cries out for color. My car needs some expert attention.
Simile Comparison of two unlike objects using the words *like* or *as*	They attacked each other like warriors. The teacher is as gentle as a lamb.
Rhetorical Question A question used to make a statement or produce some desired effect rather than to secure the answer, which is obvious	Doesn't everyone want to be popular? Who wouldn't want to get promoted?

PERSONAL STYLE

Audiences favor speakers who use a personal rather than an impersonal style—who speak *with* them rather than *at* them. A personal style makes the audience feel more involved with the speaker and the speech topic.

- **Use personal pronouns.** Choose *I, me, he, she,* and *you.* rather than expressions such as the impersonal *one* (as in, "One is led to believe that . . . "), *this speaker,* and *you, the listeners.* These expressions are overly formal and distance the audience, creating barriers rather than bridges.

- **Direct questions to the audience.** Involve the audience by asking them questions. With a small audience, you might even take brief responses. With larger audiences, you might ask the question, pause to allow the audience time to consider their responses, and then move on. When you direct questions to your listeners, you make them feel they are part of the experience.

- **Create immediacy.** Create immediacy (a closeness with your audience) by referring directly to your listeners, using *you;* say, "*You'll* enjoy reading . . ." instead of "*Everyone* will enjoy reading . . ." Refer to commonalities between you and the audience and to shared experiences and goals: for example, "*We* all need a more responsive PTA."

Communication Choice Point

Offensive Language

You want to illustrate the negative effects of racist language. *If you were addressing your class, what options would you have for making this point and yet not offending anyone?*

POWER

Public speaking, perhaps even more than interpersonal or small group communication, often requires a powerful style—a style that is certain, definite, and persuasive. The first step toward achieving a powerful style of speech is to eliminate the powerless forms that you may use now. The following weaknesses characterize powerless speech (Molloy, 1981; Kleinke, 1986; Johnson, 1987; Dillard & Marshall, 2003; Lakoff, 1975; Timmerman, 2002).

- **Hesitations** make you sound unprepared and uncertain: "I, er, want to say that, ah, this one is, er, the best, you know?"

- **Too many intensifiers** make your speech monotonous and don't allow you to stress what you do want to emphasize: "Really, this was the greatest; it was truly awesome, phenomenal."

- **Disqualifiers** signal a lack of competence and a feeling of uncertainty: "I didn't read the entire article, but . . ." "I didn't actually see the accident, but . . ."

- **Self-critical statements** signal a lack of confidence and may make public your own inadequacies: "I'm not very good at this," "This is my first public speech."

- **Slang and vulgar language** signal low social class and hence little power: "No problem!" "@*+#?$!!"

Communication Choice Point

Slang

You're preparing to speak to an audience of high school sophomores about going to Regional Community College. You wonder how you can use language to help relate to these students. For example, you wonder if you should break the general rule against using slang, thinking that slang is the language of the students and imagine that they'd be more likely to identify with you if you spoke their language. *What options do you have in choosing an appropriate style? How would you describe the style you would use?*

SENTENCE CONSTRUCTION

Effective public speaking style also requires careful attention to the construction of sentences. Here are some guidelines that will help you achieve a clear, vivid, appropriate, personal, and powerful speaking style.

- **Use short rather than long sentences.** Short sentences are more forceful and economical. They are easier to understand and to remember. Listeners don't have the time or inclination to unravel long and complex sentences. Help them to listen more efficiently by using short rather than long sentences.

- **Use direct rather than indirect sentences.** Direct sentences are easier to understand. They are also more forceful. Instead of saying, "I want to tell you the three main reasons why we should not adopt the Bennett proposal," say, "We should not adopt the Bennett proposal. Let me give you three good reasons."

VIEWPOINTS

Wording the Speech for Different Audiences

You're scheduled to give two speeches, one to a predominantly female audience of health professionals and one to a predominantly male audience of small business owners. Your topic for both groups is the same: neighborhood violence and how it must be confronted. In what major ways (identify two or three) would these speeches need to be different?

- **Use active rather than passive sentences.** Active sentences are easier to understand. They also make your speech livelier and more vivid. Instead of saying, "The lower court's original decision was reversed by the Supreme Court," say, "The Supreme Court reversed the lower court's decision." Instead of saying, "The change was favored by management," say, "Management favored the change."

- **Use positive rather than negative sentences.** Positive sentences are easier to comprehend and to remember (DeVito, 1976; Clark, 1974). Notice how sentences A and C are easier to understand than B and D.

Positive Sentences	Negative Sentences
A. The committee rejected the proposal.	B. The committee did not accept the proposal.
C. This committee works outside the normal company hierarchy.	D. This committee does not work within the normal company hierarchy.

- **Vary the type and length of sentences.** The advice to use short, direct, active, and positive sentences is valid most of the time. But too many sentences of the same type or length will make your speech sound boring. Use variety but generally follow the guidelines.

Objectives Self-Check
- Can you word your speech to achieve clarity, vividness, appropriateness, personal style, and power?
- Can you construct sentences that are short, direct, active, positive, and varied?

Step 8: Construct Your Conclusion, Introduction, Transitions, and Outlines

Your conclusion and introduction need special care, because they will determine, in large part, the effectiveness of your speech. Because you've just finished the body of the speech, and the major function of the conclusion is to summarize, it will probably be easier to work first on your conclusion and then on the introduction.

THE CONCLUSION

Watch the **Video** "Tips for an Effective Conclusion" at **MyCommunicationLab**

Devote particular attention to this brief but crucial part of your speech. In your conclusion, summarize your main points and make closing remarks.

Summarize   You may summarize your speech in a variety of ways:

- **Restate your thesis.** Present again the essential thrust of your speech—your thesis, or perhaps the purpose you hoped to achieve.
- **Restate the importance of your thesis.** Tell the audience again why your topic or thesis is so important.
- **Restate your main points.** Reiterate your two, three, or four main points.

Close   The conclusion's second function is to provide closure—to give the speech a crisp and definite end. Don't leave your audience wondering whether you've finished.

- **Summarize with a quotation.** A quotation that clearly and directly summarizes your thesis or provides an interesting perspective on your point of view often provides effective closure.

- **Pose a challenge or question.** You may wish to end your speech with a provocative question or challenge:
  - What do you intend to do about the company's refusal to increase wages?
  - Go home and clean high-cholesterol foods out of your refrigerator.
  - Sign this petition; it will help put an experienced person in office.

- **Thank the audience.** Speakers frequently thank their audience. If you do this, do it a bit more elaborately than by saying simply "Thank you." You might relate the thanks to your thesis:
  - I really appreciate your attention and hope you'll join us in Sunday's protest.

  Or you might say,
  - I want to thank you for listening and for your willingness to sign the Student Senate's petition to expand the college's online website.

- **Motivate your audience to do something.** Remind your audience of what they should do now:
  - The next time you go online, visit one of the websites I mentioned.
  - You can sign up to volunteer at the desk in the Student Union.
  - So, read the article in this handout; it could change your life.

Communication Choice Point

Conclusions

You're scheduled to give a speech on careers in computer technology to high school students who are required to attend Career Day on Saturday. You're planning to focus on the enjoyment, high salary, and employment opportunities of such careers and you're wondering about your conclusion. *What are some of the ways you might conclude your speech?*

THE INTRODUCTION

In your introduction, try to accomplish two goals: (1) gain your audience's attention and (2) orient the audience—tell them a little bit about what you'll talk about.

Gain Attention   In your introduction, focus the audience's attention on your topic. Then work to maintain that attention throughout your speech.

Communication Choice Point

Functions of Introductions

Another function of introductions often mentioned is to establish some kind of connection between your topic, your audience, and yourself. *With your next speech in mind, what are some of your choices for establishing this connection?*

- **Ask a question.** Questions are effective because they are a change from normal statements and involve the audience. They tell the audience that you're talking directly to them and care about their responses. Questions are also useful in setting the stage for what will follow.

- **Refer to specific audience members.** Involving members directly makes them perk up and pay attention. Depending on the nature of the audience and your knowledge of specific members, you might say something like this:

  Pat, you defended the NRA, whereas Chris, you argued against it. And Pablo, you argued for a pro-life position on abortion, but Sarah, you argued for a pro-choice position. Even in a small class such as this, there are wide differences in beliefs, values, and attitudes. And that's what I want to talk about today: differences in beliefs and how these can cause conflict in our relationships.

- **Refer to the specific context.** Instead of referring to specific people, you might note the relevance of the specific context. Here, for example, is how Secretary of State Hillary Clinton (1995) referred to the context of her remarks at the U.N. World Conference on Women:

  By gathering in Beijing, we are focusing world attention on issues that matter most in our lives—the lives of women and their families: access to education, health care, jobs and credit, the chance to enjoy basic legal and human rights and to participate fully in the political life of our countries.

VIEWPOINTS

Constructing an Introduction

What are some of the things you might include in your introduction to a pro-choice speech to a pro-life audience (or, if you prefer, a pro-life speech to a pro-choice audience)? Try constructing such an introduction.

Watch the **Video** "Tips for an Effective Introduction" at **MyCommunicationLab**

See "The Compliment" at **tcbdevito**.blogspot.com. to find out how comfortable you are in giving and in receiving compliments.

- **Use illustrations or dramatic or humorous stories.** We are all drawn to illustrations and stories about people—they make a speech vivid and concrete. Use them to secure audience attention in the introduction and to maintain it throughout. Here, for example, one speaker used a dramatic illustration in opening her speech on bullying (Bacon, 2011):

  A typical ninth grade female goes to her locker after a long day of classes to find a note. As she opens the note, her day goes from typical to horrendous. The note reads, "Get a new hair cut, you look like a dyke. Start wearing clothes that fit and go home and die."

Other ways to gain attention include using a visual aid; a short music or video clip; a dramatic, humorous, or interesting quotation; a startling statistic or series of little-known facts, or a sincere compliment.

Orient the Audience

Previewing what you're going to say will help listeners follow your thoughts more closely. Here are two general ways you can orient your audience:

- **Give the audience an idea about your subject.** In a speech on military suicides, one student oriented his audience and at the same time previewed his organizational pattern (McLain, 2011):

  Today we will examine the problem of an increased suicide rate among our armed forces, some of the causes behind it, and the solutions that will enable us to reduce the number of service men and women who so tragically choose to take their own lives.

- **Identify the goal you hope to achieve.** A librarian addressing my public speaking class oriented the audience by stating goals in this way: "Pay attention for the next few minutes and you'll be able to locate anything we have in the library by using the new touch-screen computer access system." In another example, President Barack Obama (2009) combined some of these purposes in his "Call to Renewal" speech:

  Today I'd like to talk about the connection between religion and politics and perhaps offer some thoughts about how we can sort through some of the often bitter arguments that we've been seeing over the last several years.

AVOIDING SOME COMMON MISTAKES

Here are a few tips for avoiding the mistakes that beginning speakers often make in introducing and concluding their speeches:

- **Engage your listeners before speaking.** Survey your audience; make eye contact and engage their attention. Stand in front of the audience with a sense of control. Pause briefly, then begin speaking.

- **Demonstrate enthusiasm and a desire to speak.** People much prefer listening to a speaker who shows that she or he enjoys speaking to them.

- **Don't apologize.** In the United States, avoid expressions such as "I am not an expert on this topic," or "I didn't do as much reading on this topic as I should have." And never start a speech with, "I'm not very good at giving public speeches." This rule, however, does not hold in all cultures; in fact, self-deprecating comments are expected in some collectivist cultures.

- **Begin with a strong introduction.** Avoid statements such as "Before I begin my talk, I want to say . . . " These make it difficult for you to open your speech with a strong attention grabber.

- **Reinforce what you have already said.** Once you reach your conclusion, it's too late to introduce new material. Instead, reinforce what you have already said, summarize your essential points, or give new expression to ideas already covered.

- **After your last statement, pause, maintain audience eye contact, and then walk (don't run) to your seat.** Show no signs of relief; focus your attention on whatever activity is taking place. If a question period follows your speech and you're in charge of this,

SKILL DEVELOPMENT EXPERIENCE

Constructing Conclusions and Introductions

Prepare a conclusion and an introduction to a hypothetical speech on one of the topics listed here, making sure that in your conclusion you (1) review the speech's main points and (2) provide closure. In your introduction, make sure that you (1) gain attention and (2) orient the audience.

1. Competitive sports programs in high schools and colleges should be abolished.
2. Same-sex marriage should be legalized.
3. Properties owned by religious institutions should be taxed.
4. Assisted suicide should be legalized.
5. Gambling should be declared illegal by all states.

Because the conclusion and the introduction are often the parts that listeners remember most, give them special attention.

pause after completing your conclusion and ask audience members in a direct manner if they have any questions. If there's a chairperson who will ask for questions, pause after your conclusion, then nonverbally signal to the chairperson that you're ready to take questions.

TRANSITIONS AND INTERNAL SUMMARIES

Transitions (sometimes called "connectives") are words, phrases, or sentences that connect the various parts of a speech. Because your audience will hear your speech only once, they may not see the connections you want them to see. By using transitions, you can help your listeners see how one point leads to another or where one argument ends and another begins. Use transitions in at least the following places:

Explore the **Concept** "Better Transitions" at **MyCommunicationLab**

- between the introduction and the body of the speech
- between the body and the conclusion
- between the main points in the body of the speech

Here are the major transitional functions and some stylistic devices that you might use:

- **To announce the start of a main point:** "First . . . ," "A second argument . . . ," "A closely related problem . . . ," "If you want further evidence, look at . . . ," "My next point . . . ," "An even more compelling argument. . . ."
- **To signal that you're drawing a conclusion:** "Thus . . . ," "Therefore . . . ," "So, as you can see . . . ," "It follows, then, that. . . ."
- **To signal a qualification or exception:** "But . . . ," "However, also consider . . . ," "On the other hand. . . ."
- **To signal a connection with another issue:** "In contrast to . . . ," "Consider also . . . ," "Not only . . . , but also . . . ," "In addition to . . . , we also need to look at. . . ."
- **To signal the next part of your speech:** "By way of introduction . . . ," "In conclusion . . . ," "Now, let's discuss why we are here today . . . ," "So, what's the solution? What should we do?"

Closely related to the transition is the **internal summary**, a statement that summarizes what you have already discussed. Usually it summarizes some major subdivision of your speech. Incorporate several internal summaries into your speech—perhaps working them into the transitions connecting, say, the major arguments or issues. An internal summary that is also a transition might look something like this:

The three arguments advanced here were (1) . . . , (2) . . . , (3) . . . Now, what can we do about them? I think we can do two things. First, . . .

PUBLIC SPEAKING SAMPLE ASSISTANT

The Preparation Outline

Here is a relatively detailed preparation outline similar to the outline you might prepare when constructing your speech. The side notes should clarify both the content and the format of a preparation outline.

Have you Ever Been Culture Shocked?

Thesis: Culture shock can be described in four stages.

Purpose: To inform my audience of the four phases of culture shock.

The title, purpose, and thesis of the speech appear before the outline.

INTRODUCTION:

I. How many of you have experienced culture shock?

  A. Many people experience culture shock, a reaction to being in a culture very different from what they were used to.

  B. By understanding culture shock, you'll be in a better position to deal with it if and when it happens.

Note that the introduction, body, and conclusion are clearly labeled and separated visually.

II. Culture shock occurs in four stages (Oberg, 1960).

  A. The Honeymoon occurs first.

  B. The Crisis occurs second.

  C. The Recovery occurs third.

  D. The Adjustment occurs fourth.

[Let's follow the order in which these four stages occur beginning with the first stage, the honeymoon.]

Notice that references are integrated throughout the outline, just as they would be in a term paper. In the actual speech, the speaker might say, "anthropologist Kalervo Oberg, who coined the term *culture shock*, said it occurs in four stages."

This introduction serves two functions: It gains attention by involving the audience and it orients the audience to what is to follow.

The transition at the end of the introduction tells the audience to expect a four-part presentation. Also, the numbers repeated throughout the outline will further aid the audience in keeping track of where you are in the speech. Most important, the transition tells the audience that the speech will follow a temporal thought pattern.

BODY

I. The Honeymoon occurs first.

  A. The Honeymoon is the period of fascination with the new people and culture.

  B. You enjoy the people and the culture.

    1. You love the people.

      a. For example, the people in Zaire spend their time very differently from the way New Yorkers do.

      b. For example, my first 18 years living on a farm was very different from life in a college dorm.

    2. You love the culture.

      a. The great number of different religions in India fascinated me.

      b. Eating was an especially great experience.

[But like many relationships, contact with a new culture is not all honeymoon; soon there comes a crisis.]

Observe the parallel structure throughout the outline. For example, note that I, II, III, and IV in the body are all phrased in exactly the same way. This will help your audience follow your speech more closely and will also help you structure your thoughts logically.

II. The Crisis occurs second.

  A. The Crisis is the period when you begin to experience problems.

    1. One-third of American workers abroad fail because of culture shock (Samovar, Porter, & McDaniel, 2008).

    2. The personal difficulties are also great.

  B. Life becomes difficult in the new culture.

    1. Communication is difficult.

    2. It's easy to offend people without realizing it.

[As you gain control over the various crises, you begin to recover.]

Notice that there are many examples in this speech. They are identified only briefly in the outline and would naturally be elaborated on in the speech.

III. The Recovery occurs third.

  A. The Recovery is the period when you learn how to cope.

  B. You begin to learn intercultural competence (Lustig & Koester, 2010).

    1. You learn how to communicate.

      a. Being able to go to the market and make my wants known was a great day for me.

      b. I was able to ask for a date.

    2. You learn the rules of the culture.

      a. The different religious ceremonies each have their own rules.

      b. Eating is a ritual experience in lots of places throughout Africa.

Note, too, the internal organization of each major point. Each main assertion in the body contains a definition of the stage (I.A, II.A, III.A, and IV.A) and examples (I.B, II.B, III.B, and IV.B) to illustrate the stage.

Notice that each statement in the outline is a complete sentence. You can easily convert this outline into a phrase or key word outline to use in delivery. The full sentences, however, will help you see relationships among items more clearly.

[handwritten note in left margin: Thesis Continue]

[Your recovery leads naturally into the next and final stage, the adjustment.]
  IV. The Adjustment occurs fourth.
     A. The adjustment is the period when you come to enjoy the new culture.
     B. You come to appreciate the people and the culture.
[Let me summarize, then, the stages you go through in experiencing culture shock.]

CONCLUSION

  I. Culture shock can be described in four stages.
    A. The Honeymoon is first.
    B. The Crisis is second.
    C. The Recovery is third.
    D. The Adjustment is fourth.
  II. By knowing the four stages, you can better understand the culture shock you may now be experiencing on the job, at school, or in your private life.

REFERENCES

Lustig, M. W., & Koester, J. (2010). *Intercultural competence: Interpersonal communication across cultures* (6th ed.). Boston: Allyn & Bacon.

Oberg, K. (1960). Culture shock: Adjustment to new cultural environments. *Practical Anthropology, 7,* 177–182.

Samovar, L. A., Porter, R. E., & McDaniel, E. R. (2008). *Communication between cultures,* 6th ed. Belmont, CA: Cengage.

Transitions are inserted between all major parts of the speech. Although they may seem too numerous in this abbreviated outline, they will be appreciated by your audience because the transitions will help them follow your speech.

Notice that these four points correspond to II.A, B, C, and D of the introduction and to I, II, III, and IV of the body. Notice how the similar wording adds clarity.

This step provides closure; it makes it clear that the speech is finished. It also serves to encourage reflection on the part of the audience as to their own experience of culture shock.

This reference list includes only those sources that appear in the completed speech.

OUTLINES

Now that you have completed your speech, it's time to put it all together in the form of an outline, something you already did, for example, when you identified your main points and amplified them with illustrations and definitions. In this connection, take a look at MyOutline on MyCommunicationLab (Figure 12.1). There are three kinds of speech outlines: (1) the preparation outline, (2) the template outline, and (3) the delivery outline.

The Preparation Outline A preparation outline like the one in the Public Speaking Sample Assistant box (as well as the template and delivery outlines that are discussed next) will help you not only to organize your thoughts more coherently but also to deliver your speech more effectively. Additional information on outlining may be found in My Outline at MyCommunicationLab, as noted in Figure 12.1.

The Template Outline The **template outline** is another useful type of organizational tool. Much as a template in PowerPoint guides you to fill in certain information in particular places, the template outline serves a similar function; it ensures that you include all the relevant material in reasonable order. At the same time, it also helps you see your speech as a whole—and may reveal gaps that need to be filled or items that are discussed at too great a length. As you become more familiar with the public speaking process, you'll soon be able to develop your speech without any template outline.

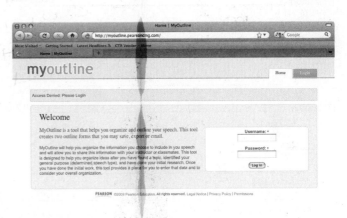

FIGURE 12.1

My Outline

This outlining tool is one of the many online resources available at MyCommunicationLab (www.mycommunicationlab.com).

PUBLIC SPEAKING SAMPLE ASSISTANT

The Template Outline

Thesis: _____ Your main assertion; the core of your speech _____

Specific Purpose: _____ What you hope to achieve from this speech _____

INTRODUCTION

I. _____ Gain attention _____

II. _____ Orient audience _____

   A. _____ First main point; same as I in body _____

   B. _____ Second main point; same as II in body _____

   C. _____ Third main point; same as III in body _____

[Transition: _____ Connect introduction to body _____]

BODY

I. _____ First main point _____

   A. _____ Support for I (first main point) _____

   B. _____ Further support for I _____

[Transition: _____ Connect first main point to second _____]

II. _____ Second main point _____

   A. _____ Support for II (second main point) _____

   B. _____ Further support for II _____

[Transition: _____ Connect second main point to third _____]

III. _____ Third main point _____

   A. _____ Support for III _____

   B. _____ Further support for III _____

[Transition: _____ Connect third main point (or all main points) to conclusion _____]

CONCLUSION

I. _____ Summary _____

   A. _____ First main point; same as I in body _____

   B. _____ Second main point; same as II in body _____

   C. _____ Third main point; same as III in body _____

II. _____ Closure _____

The sample template outline in The Public Speaking Sample Assistant included here would be appropriate for a speech using a time, spatial, or topical organization pattern. Note that in this outline there are three main points (I, II, and III in the body). These correspond to items II.A, B, and C in the introduction (where you would orient the audience) and to I.A, B, and C in the conclusion (where you would summarize your major propositions). The transitions are signaled by square brackets. As you review this outline you will see how it can be adapted for use with other organization patterns, such as problem-solution, cause-effect, or the motivated sequence. Additional template outlines for a variety of organizational patterns may be found at MyOutline on MyCommunicationLab (access code required).

The Delivery Outline

The **delivery outline** will assist you during the presentation of a speech and should be used instead of your preparation outline. Although you may feel inclined to read from your preparation outline, it is not an effective way to give a speech. Instead, write a brief delivery outline such as that presented in the next Public Speaking Sample Assistant box, which was constructed from the preparation outline on culture shock.

Some public speaking coaches and instructors recommend putting your delivery outline on a 3 × 5 or 4 × 6 index card. One advantage is that you will need to condense your delivery outline to only key words and phrases, which will prevent you from reading your speech and help you interact more freely with your audience. When notes are too extensive, speakers have a tendency to read them rather than speak to their audience. Another benefit is that the card won't bend as would an 8½ × 11 piece of paper. Additional index cards might be used for quotations or statistics that won't fit on the one card. Or you may find it helpful to use three cards, one for each of the three main parts of your speech. If you do use more than one card (but avoid using more than four), be sure to number and label them clearly; you don't want to have to fumble through the cards looking for a particular quotation or statistic.

If you're using PowerPoint (or any similar presentation software)—discussed in detail in the next chapter—then your delivery outline is going to be either the PowerPoint slides themselves or the speaker's notes that you generate along with your PowerPoint presentation (discussed in the "Using Notes" section later in this chapter). Here are some guidelines for delivery outlines.

- **Be brief.** Don't allow the outline to stand in the way of direct speaker-audience contact. Use key words to trigger in your mind the ideas you wish to discuss. Notice how brief the sample delivery outline is compared to the preparation outline, yet it's detailed enough to include all essential parts of your speech, even transitions.

- **Be delivery-minded.** Include any delivery guides you might wish to remember while you're speaking—for example, to pause or to show the visual aid.

- **Rehearse your speech with this delivery outline.** Make your rehearsal as close to the real thing as possible.

Objectives Self-Check
- Can you construct effective speech conclusions that summarize and close?
- Can you construct effective introductions that gain attention and orient your audience?
- Can you construct and integrate transitions to help your audience follow your speech?
- Can you create effective preparation and delivery outlines for your speech?

Step 9: Rehearse Your Speech

Before you begin your rehearsal, you need to decide on the methods of delivery you'll use. Generally, you'll find that the extemporaneous method will suit your needs best and is likely to be the delivery method used in your course. Nevertheless, other methods of delivery have their value as well. You can then consider the suggestions for making your rehearsals efficient and effective.

Explore the **Exercise** "Organizing a Scrambled Outline" at **MyCommunicationLab**

Explore the **Concept** "Creating a Speaking Outline" at **MyCommunicationLab**

PUBLIC SPEAKING SAMPLE ASSISTANT

The Delivery Outline

PAUSE!
LOOK OVER THE AUDIENCE!

    I. Many experience CS

        A. CS: the reaction to being in a culture very different from your own

        B. By understanding CS, you'll be better able to deal with it

PAUSE—SCAN AUDIENCE

    II. CS occurs in 4 stages (WRITE ON BOARD)

        A. Honeymoon   B. Crisis   C. Recovery   D. Adjustment

[Let's examine these stages of CS.]

PAUSE/STEP FORWARD

    I. Honeymoon

        A. Fascination w/people and culture

        B. Enjoyment of people and culture

            1. Zaire example

            2. Farm to college dorm

[But, life is not all honeymoon—the crisis.]

    II. Crisis

        A. Problems arise

            1. One-third Am workers fail abroad

            2. Personal difficulties

        B. Life becomes difficult

            1. Communication

            2. Offend others

[As you gain control over the crises, you learn how to cope.]

PAUSE

    III. Recovery

        A. Period of learning to cope

        B. You learn intercultural competence

            1. Communication becomes easier

            2. You learn the culture's rules

[As you recover, you adjust.]

    IV. Adjustment

        A. Learn to enjoy (again) the new culture

        B. Appreciate people and culture

[These then are the 4 stages; let me summarize.]

PAUSE
CONCLUSION

    I. CS occurs in 4 stages: honeymoon, crisis, recovery, and adjustment

    II. By knowing the 4 stages, you can better understand the culture shock you may now be experiencing on the job, at school, or in your private life.

PAUSE
ASK FOR QUESTIONS

METHODS OF DELIVERY

Speakers vary widely in delivery methods. Some speak off-the-cuff, with no apparent preparation. Others read their speeches from a manuscript. Others construct a detailed outline and compose the speech at the moment of delivery. These approaches represent the three general methods of delivery: (1) impromptu, (2) manuscript, and (3) extemporaneous.

Explore the **Exercise** "How Flexible Are You as a Speaker?" at **MyCommunicationLab**

The Impromptu Method   An **impromptu speech** involves speaking without preparation. On some occasions, you can't avoid impromptu speaking. In a classroom, you may be asked to comment on the speaker and speech you just heard: In effect, you give an impromptu speech of evaluation. At meetings, people are often asked for impromptu comments on various issues. Or you may have to fill in for someone who has not shown up. You can greatly improve impromptu speaking by cultivating your public speaking ability in general. The more proficient you are as a speaker, the better you will be impromptu.

Explore the **Concept** "Methods of Delivery" at **MyCommunicationLab**

The Manuscript Method   When you give a **manuscript speech,** you write out the speech and read it. This is the safest method when exact timing and wording are required. For example, it could be disastrous if a political leader did not speak from manuscript on sensitive issues. An ambiguous word, phrase, or sentence that may be insulting, belligerent, or conciliatory could cause serious problems. With a manuscript speech, you can control style, content, organization, and all other elements. A variation of the manuscript method is to write out the speech and then memorize it. You then recite the entire speech from memory, much as an actor recites a part in a play. The great disadvantages of the manuscript and memorized method are that the speech doesn't sound natural, it limits eye contact, and there is little opportunity to adjust the speech on the basis of audience feedback.

The Extemporaneous Method   The **extemporaneous speech** is useful when exact timing and wording are not required. Good lecturing by college teachers is extemporaneous. They have prepared thoroughly, know what they want to say, and have the lecture's organization clearly in mind. But they are not committed to exact wording. This method allows greater flexibility for feedback. For example, when speaking extemporaneously you can clarify a point if it needs clarification. It's also easy to be natural, because you're being yourself.

The major disadvantage of this method is that you may stumble and grope for words. You can address this disadvantage by rehearsing the speech several times. Although you won't give the precise attention to style that you would in the manuscript and memorizing methods, you can memorize certain key phrases.

The extemporaneous method is recommended for most situations, especially classroom speeches, in which the objective is to learn the art of public speaking. Overall it offers the greatest advantages with the fewest disadvantages. However, speaking impromptu and speaking from manuscript are also important skills. Fortunately, the principles of extemporaneous speaking discussed here will help you in these other kinds of speeches as well. Even when you use the extemporaneous method, however, consider the advantages of memorizing certain parts of your speech:

- Memorize your opening and closing lines—perhaps the first and last two or three sentences. This will help you focus your attention on the audience at the two most important moments of your speech.
- Memorize the main points and the order in which you will present them. After all, if you expect your audience to remember these points, they will expect you to remember them as well.

VIEWPOINTS

Announcing Your Speech

What are some of the ways in which you might announce your upcoming speech on social media sites? You might want to start by preparing a Tweet; remember you're allowed only 140 characters (though 120 would allow for comments with Retweets).

EFFECTIVE REHEARSING

Rehearsal should enable you to see how the speech will flow as a whole and to make any necessary changes and improvements. It will also allow you to time your speech so that you stay within the allotted time. The following procedures should help you use your rehearsal time most effectively:

- Rehearse the speech from beginning to end, rather than in parts. Be sure to include all the examples and illustrations (and audiovisual aids if any) in your rehearsal.

- Time the speech during each rehearsal. Adjust your speech—both what you say and your delivery rate—on the basis of this timing.

- Rehearse the speech under conditions as close as possible to those under which you'll deliver it. If possible, rehearse in the room in which you'll present the speech and in front of a few supportive listeners.

- Rehearse the speech in front of a full-length mirror to help you see how you'll appear to the audience. As you deliver your speech (aloud, of course) practice your eye contact, your movements, and your gestures in front of the mirror.

- Don't interrupt your rehearsal to make notes or changes; do these between rehearsals. If possible, record your speech (ideally, on videotape) so you can hear and see exactly what your listeners will hear and see.

- Rehearse at least three or four times, or as long as your rehearsals continue to result in improvements.

Objectives Self-Check

- Can you explain the methods of speech delivery (*impromptu, manuscript, and extemporaneous) and assess their usefulness in different situations?
- Do you know how to rehearse your speech effectively and sufficiently?

Explore the **Concept** "Speech Delivery" at **MyCommunicationLab**

Watch the **Video** "Martin Cox Discusses Tips for Speech Delivery" at **MyCommunicationLab**

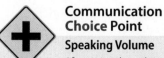

Communication Choice Point

Speaking Volume

After sitting through two rounds of speeches, you wonder if the class wouldn't be ready for a speech spoken at noticeably higher volume than normal—rather like television commercials, which are played louder than the regular broadcast. *What are some of your options concerning the use of volume?*

Step 10: Deliver Your Speech

Use your voice and body to complement and reinforce your verbal message.

VOICE

In public speaking it's especially important to give attention to **paralanguage**—the vocal but nonverbal aspect of speech. Using dimensions such as volume, rate, articulation and pronunciation, and pauses appropriately will help you use your voice to complement and reinforce your message. Chapter 5 discussed paralanguage as one of the major nonverbal communication channels (pp. 108–109).

Volume   **Volume** refers to the relative loudness or softness of your voice. When your voice is adequately controlled, you adjust its volume according to factors such as the distance between you and your listeners, the competing noise, and the emphasis you want to give an idea. Vary your volume to best reflect your ideas—perhaps increasing volume for key words or phrases, lowering volume when talking about something extremely serious. Be especially careful not to fade away at the ends of sentences.

Rate   The speed at which you speak is referred to as the **rate**—an average of about 140 words per minute for speaking as well as for reading aloud. If your rate is too

SKILL DEVELOPMENT EXPERIENCE

Checking Your Pronunciation

Here are 50 words that are often mispronounced. Consult an online audio dictionary to check on the correct pronunciations: abdomen, accessory, across, arctic, ask, asterisk, buffet, candidate, clothes, costume, diagnosis, dilate, escape, especially, espresso, et cetera, ethnicity, February, federal, film, fiscal, herb, hierarchy, jewelry, library, miniature, mischievous, nausea, nuclear, often, phenomenon, potable, prerogative, probably, prostate, realtor, relevant, remuneration, repeat, salmon, sandwich, similar, statistics, substantive, supposedly, thesaurus, ticklish, xenophobia.

Mispronouncing words may significantly lessen your credibility, and your own uncertainty about pronunciation may increase your apprehension.

fast, you deprive your listeners of the time they need to digest what you're saying. If it's too slow, your listeners' thoughts will wander. So speak at a pace that engages but doesn't bore and that allows listeners time for reflection.

Articulation and Pronunciation   **Articulation** results from physiological movements of the speech organs as they modify and interrupt the air stream from the lungs. Different movements of the tongue, lips, teeth, palate, and vocal cords produce different sounds. **Pronunciation** is the production of syllables or words according to some accepted standard, such as that of a dictionary. The most common problems associated with faulty articulation and pronunciation are these:

Communication Choice Point

Mispronunciation

In giving your speech you realize that you mispronounced a key word twice and saw that some members of the audience noticed the mistake. *What are some of your options for dealing with this?*

- **Errors of omission (articulation):** Omitting sounds or even syllables is a common articulation problem that you can easily overcome with concentration and practice. Some examples include saying *gov-a-ment, studyin,* or *comp-ny* instead of the correct *gov-ern-ment, study-ing,* and *comp-a-ny.*

- **Errors of substitution (articulation):** Substituting an incorrect sound for the correct one is also easy to fix. Among the most common substitutions are *d* for *t* and *d* for *th*—for example, *wader, dese, bedder,* and *ax* for the correct: *waiter, these, better,* and *ask.* Other common substitution errors include *ekcetera, congradulations,* and *lenth* for the correct *et cetera, congratulations,* and *length.*

- **Errors of addition (articulation):** These errors involve adding sounds where they don't belong, as in saying *acrost, athalete,* and *Americar* instead of the correct *across, athlete,* and *America.*

- **Errors of accent (pronunciation):** Every word has its own accepted **accent,** or stress pattern. Examples of words that are often accented incorrectly include *New Orleáns, ínsurance, compárable,* and *orátor* for the correct *New Órleans, insúrance, cómparable,* and *órator.*

- **Errors of adding sounds (pronunciation):** For some words, many people add sounds that are not part of the standard pronunciation, in many cases because they are part of the written word. Such errors would include pronouncing the *s* in *Illinois* or adding a syllable to *evening* instead of *Illinoi* and *evning.*

Pauses   **Pauses** are interruptions in the flow of speech. Filled pauses are gaps that you fill with vocalizations such as *er, um,* and *ah.* Even expressions such as *well* and *you know,* when used merely to fill up silence, are *filled pauses.* These pauses are ineffective and detract from the strength of your message. They will make you appear hesitant, unprepared, and unsure.

"Plunder, you idiot. We came to plunder."

Unfilled pauses, silences interjected into the stream of speech, can be especially effective if used correctly. Here are a few examples of places where unfilled pauses—silences of a second or two—can enhance your speech:

- **Pause at transitional points.** This will signal that you're moving from one part of the speech or from one idea to another. It will help listeners separate the main issues you're discussing.

- **Pause at the end of an important assertion.** This allows the audience to think about its significance.

- **Pause after asking a rhetorical question.** This will give the audience time to think about how they would answer.

- **Pause before an important idea.** This will help signal that what comes next is especially significant.

- **Pause before you begin your speech and after you finish it.** This will allow you to scan and assess the audience and gather your thoughts before your speech and then to let your ideas sink in after and to dispel any impression that you're anxious to escape).

Communication Choice Point

General Appearance

You have to give three speeches on the same topic—the school's new hate speech code of conduct—to (1) the faculty of an exclusive private school, (2) your class, and (3) the city council. You wonder how to dress for these presentations. *Assuming you have an unlimited wardrobe, what options do you have for dressing for each audience?*

Explore the **Concept**
"Speech Delivery" at
MyCommunicationLab

BODY ACTION

You speak with your body as well as your mouth, a point made clear in the discussion of the various nonverbal channels in Chapter 5. The four aspects of body action that are especially important in public speaking are (1) eye contact, (2) facial expression, (3) gestures and posture, and (4) movement. As you read about these types of action, be sure to follow the most important and general rule: Use consistent packaging; be careful that your verbal and your nonverbal messages do not contradict each other. So, if you say you're happy to be speaking today, your nonverbals (facial expression, general enthusiasm, posture and eye contact, for example) should echo that sentiment. You don't want to give your audience conflicting cues. Consistency among verbal and nonverbal messages will also communicate your self-confidence and conviction.

Eye Contact   The most important single aspect of bodily communication is eye contact. The two major problems related to this body action are not enough eye contact and eye contact that does not cover the audience fairly. If you do not maintain enough eye contact, you may appear distant, unconcerned, and less trustworthy than a speaker who looks directly at an audience. And, of course, without eye contact, you will not be able to secure that all-important audience feedback. Maintain eye contact with the entire audience. Communicate equally with the audience members on the left and on the right, in both the back and the front of the room. Keep in mind, however, that cultures differ widely on the amount and intensity of eye contact they consider appropriate. In some cultures, eye contact that is too intense may be considered offensive.

Facial Expression   Appropriate facial expressions help you express your concern for the public speaking interaction and will help you communicate your comfort and control of the public speaking situation. Nervousness and anxiety, however, can prevent you from relaxing enough for your positive emotions to come through. Time and practice will allow you to relax, and your feelings will reveal themselves appropriately and automatically.

Gestures and Posture   Spontaneous and natural gestures will help illustrate your verbal messages. If you feel relaxed and comfortable with yourself and your audience, you'll generate natural body action without conscious or studied attention. When delivering your speech, stand straight but not stiffly. Try to communicate your command of the situation rather than any nervousness you may feel. Avoid putting your hands in your pockets or leaning on the desk or chalkboard. Avoid self-manipulation (e.g., playing with your hair or touching your face) and backward leaning, which can signal an ill-at-ease feeling.

Movement   Use movement to emphasize transitions and to introduce important assertions. For example, when making a transition, you might step forward to signal that something new is coming. Similarly, use movement to signal an important assumption, bit of evidence, or closely reasoned argument. Walk slowly and deliberately (but not too slowly, of course) to and from the podium. Avoid appearing hurried, as if you want to get your speech over with as soon as possible. Walking more slowly will help you convey an air of control.

USING NOTES

Speakers who prepare their speeches around a series of slides made with one of the presentation software packages (such as PowerPoint or Corel Presentations) may use these slides as their notes. In most public speaking classes, your notes will consist of a delivery outline and your audiovisual aids. Effective delivery depends on the smooth use of notes—whether a series of slides or transparencies or an $8\frac{1}{2} \times 11$ inch piece of paper or an index card or two—during the speech. A few simple guidelines may help you avoid common errors (McCroskey, 2006).

- Use only your delivery outline when presenting your speech; never use the preparation outline. One $8\frac{1}{2} \times 11$ inch page and no more than four index cards should be sufficient for most speeches. This aid will relieve anxiety over forgetting your speech but not be extensive enough to prevent meaningful speaker—audience interaction.

- Know your notes intimately. Rehearse at least twice with the same notes you will take to the speaker's stand.

- Use your notes with "open subtlety." Don't make your notes more obvious than necessary, but don't try to hide them. Don't gesture with them, but don't turn your back on the audience to steal a glance at them, either. Watch the way television talk show personalities use notes; many of these media hosts provide models you'll find useful to imitate.

Objectives Self-Check
- Can you deliver your speech with appropriate and effective voice and bodily action (along with the use of notes)?

Communication Choice Point

Unexpected Feedback

In your last speech, you included a brief anecdote you found extremely amusing—in fact, you laughed out loud after you finished telling the story. Unfortunately, the audience just didn't get it—not one smile in the entire audience. *What can you have done to turn this negative into a positive? What might you have said?*

Critically Evaluating Speeches

Part of learning about public speaking is learning to evaluate finished, delivered speeches and to express your evaluations in a clear and constructive way. Let's look first at some of the questions you'll want to consider and then at some suggestions for expressing these evaluations.

QUESTIONS TO CONSIDER

The following questions, which come from topics covered in this chapter and Chapter 11, can serve as a beginning guide to speech evaluation. Use them to check your own speeches as well as to evaluate the speeches of others.

Subject, Purpose, and Thesis

1. Is the subject worthwhile? Relevant? Interesting to the audience and speaker?
2. Is the general purpose of the speech to inform or to persuade?
3. Is the topic narrow enough to be covered in some depth?
4. Is the specific purpose clear to the audience?
5. Is the speech's thesis clear and limited to one main idea?

Audience

6. Has the speaker considered the relevant audience variables such as culture, age, gender, occupation, income, status, and religion? How does the speaker take these factors into consideration?

7. Has the speaker considered and adapted to the willingness, favorableness, and knowledge of the audience?

Research

8. Is the speech adequately researched? Are the sources reliable and up-to-date?

9. Does the speaker seem to understand the subject thoroughly?

Supporting Materials

10. Is each major proposition adequately and appropriately supported?

11. Do the supporting materials amplify what they purport to amplify? Do they prove what they purport to prove?

Major Propositions

12. Are the speech's main points clearly related to the thesis?

13. Are there an appropriate number of main points in the speech (not too many, not too few)?

Organization

14. How is the body of the speech organized? What is the organization pattern?

15. Is the organization pattern appropriate to the speech and to the audience?

Conclusion, Introduction, and Transitions

16. Does the conclusion effectively summarize and close the speech?

17. Does the introduction gain the audience's attention and provide a clear orientation?

18. Are there adequate transitions?

Wording

19. Is the language clear, vivid, appropriate, personal, and powerful?

20. Are the sentences short, direct, active, positive, and varied?

Delivery

21. Does the speaker maintain eye contact with the audience?

22. Are the volume, rate, and pauses appropriate to the audience, occasion, and topic?

23. Are the body actions (i.e., gesture and eye, face, and body movement) appropriate to the speaker, subject, and audience?

EXPRESSING AND LISTENING TO CRITICISM

The major purpose of classroom evaluation is to improve each class member's public speaking technique. Through constructive criticism, you—will more effectively learn—as both a speaker and a listener-critic—the principles of public speaking. You will discover what you do well and what you can improve.

Despite all the benefits of evaluation, however, many people resist this process, often perceiving evaluations and suggestions for improvement as personal attacks. Before reading the specific suggestions for expressing criticism, take the self-test, "What's Wrong with These Comments?" Then consider the suggestions for offering criticism more effectively that follow the test.

PUBLIC SPEAKING SAMPLE ASSISTANT

A Poorly Constructed Persuasive Speech

This speech illustrates some really broad as well as some more subtle errors that a beginning speaker might make when constructing a persuasive speech. First, read the entire speech without reading any of the "Problems/Correctives." As you read the speech, consider what errors are being demonstrated and how you might correct them. Then, after you've read the entire speech, reread each paragraph and combine your own analysis with the "Problems/Correctives" annotations.

SPEECH	PROBLEMS AND CORRECTIVES
Title: Prenups	This title sounds like an informative speech title and doesn't give the idea that a position will be argued. In addition, the topic, purpose, and thesis are not clearly focused or appropriately worded. A more appropriate title might be something like "Prenups Have Got to Go" or "The Dangers of Prenups." The topic would need to be narrowed by some qualification such as *The negative aspects of prenuptial agreements*. The purpose should be stated as an infinitive phrase: *To persuade my audience that prenuptial agreements should be declared illegal*. The thesis needs to be stated as a declarative sentence: *Prenuptial agreements should be declared illegal*.
Topic: Prenuptial agreements	
Purpose: Prenuptials are bad.	
Thesis: Why do we need prenuptial agreements?	

INTRODUCTION

You're probably not worried about prenuptial agreements yet. But maybe you will be. At any rate, that's what my speech is on. I mean that prenuptial agreements should be made illegal.

This opening is weak and can easily turn off the audience. After all, if they're not worried about it now, why listen? The speaker could have made a case for the importance of this topic in the near future, however. It appears as if the speaker knows the topic's not important but will speak on it anyway. A more effective introduction would have (1) captured the audience's attention—perhaps by citing some widely reported celebrity prenup; (2) provided a connection among the speaker-audience-topic—perhaps by noting the consequences individuals might suffer with or without a prenup; and (3) oriented the audience as to what is to follow.

BODY

Here, a transition would help. In fact, transitions should be inserted between the introduction and the body and between the body and the conclusion. Using transitions between the main points and signposts when introducing each main point would help. The speaker might have said something like: "There are three main reasons why prenups should be banned."

Prenuptial agreements make marriage a temporary arrangement. If you have a prenuptial agreement, you can get out of a marriage real fast—and we know that's not a good thing. So if we didn't have prenups—that's short for prenuptial agreements—marriages would last longer.

This is the speaker's first argument but it isn't introduced in a way the audience will find easy to understand. Abbreviations should be introduced more smoothly. A simple signpost like, "My first argument against prenups is . . . ." would make the audience see where the speaker is and get a visual of the outline. To introduce the abbreviation that will be used throughout the speech, the speaker might have incorporated it into the first sentence—"Prenuptial agreements—for short, prenups—make a marriage . . . ."

Right now, most people don't have prenups and yet somewhere around 50 percent of marriages last. That would be equivalent to a baseball player batting 500. If we had prenups that number would go up—I mean down—I mean the number of marriages that last will go up if we had prenups, I mean if we didn't.

Poor people are going to be discriminated against. Poor people won't be able to marry rich people because rich people will want a prenup and if a poor person doesn't want a prenup they wouldn't get married.

These agreements are difficult to discuss. I mean, how do you tell someone you've told you love that you now want a prenup just in case the marriage gets screwed up? I guess you can say something like, "By the way, how about signing a prenup?"

And they're expensive. I mean you need a lawyer and all. I don't know what a lawyer charges but I'd guess it's a lot. So it's expensive and a young couple could use the money on other things.

I had a prenup two years ago. And when we got divorced, I got nothing. If we didn't have a prenup I'd be rich and I'd be at some private college instead of here.

The fact that 50 percent of the marriages fail seems to be the more telling statistic, yet the speaker treats a 50 percent success rate as good—something the audience is likely to see very differently. And the baseball analogy seems weak at best. The speaker also betrays a lack of preparation in confusing *up* with *down*.

This argument just doesn't seem logical and the speaker would have been better served by omitting this entirely. For this argument to be useful in advancing the speaker's purpose, the speaker would have had to show that in fact poor people suffer in, say, divorce proceedings *because of* prenups.

This argument too doesn't seem important or logical. The fact that something is difficult to discuss doesn't mean you shouldn't discuss it; it merely means it's difficult to discuss. The speaker seems to be implying that if something is difficult to discuss it should be abandoned—clearly a poor communication strategy.

This argument also seems weak simply because if there is enough money involved to warrant a prenup, there's probably enough money to hire a lawyer. If the speaker wanted to make this argument, specific costs should have been cited.

Here the audience is likely thinking that there was a personal and emotional reason for arguing against prenups and not any logical reasons. And yet, the audience is probably asking itself, what were the specifics of the prenup and how much money was involved. The speaker probably should have disclosed this earlier in the speech and assured the audience that this personal experience led to a thorough study of the subject. And if a personal experience is going to be used—and there's no reason it shouldn't—then it needs to be discussed more fully and, at the least, answer the audience's obvious questions.

CONCLUSION

My conclusions. So you can see that prenups are not a good thing. Like they're unfair to poor people. And it creates a lot of stress for the couple, especially for the one who didn't want the prenup in the first place, like myself.

Any questions?

Using the word "conclusion" is not a bad idea but it stands out like a heading in a textbook. This speech also needed a more detailed conclusion, reiterating the main points in the speech. This speaker also commits one of the common faults of conclusions—that is, to introduce new material. Notice that we hadn't heard of the stress factor before. The speaker might have said something like: "In conclusion, we can see there are three main arguments against prenups. First, . . . "

This seems too abrupt. A good pause should preface this request for questions and perhaps a more inviting request could be offered— something like, "If anyone has any questions, I'd be happy to respond."

TEST YOURSELF

What's Wrong with These Comments?

Examine each of the following critical comments. For the purposes of this exercise, assume that each comment represents the critic's complete criticism. What's wrong with each?

_____ **1** I loved the speech. It was great. Really great.

_____ **2** The introduction didn't gain my attention.

_____ **3** You weren't interested in your own topic. How do you expect us to be interested?

_____ **4** Nobody was able to understand you.

_____ **5** The speech was weak.

_____ **6** The speech didn't do anything for me.

_____ **7** Your position was unfair to those of us on athletic scholarships; we earned those scholarships.

_____ **8** I found four things wrong with your speech. First, . . .

_____ **9** You needed better research.

_____ **10** I liked the speech; we need more police on campus.

HOW DID YOU DO? Before reading the discussion that follows, try to explain why each of these statements is ineffective.

WHAT WILL YOU DO? To help improve your criticism, try to restate the basic meaning of each of these comments in a more constructive manner.

Expressing Criticism Here are a few suggestions for expressing your evaluations and criticisms.

- **Say something positive.** Start any criticism with something positive. So, instead of saying—as in the self-test—"The speech didn't do anything for me," tell the speaker what you liked first and then bring up a weakness and suggest how it might be corrected: "Your introduction really made me realize that many colleges have problems with campus violence, but I wasn't convinced early on that we have one here at Andrews. I would have preferred to hear the examples that you gave near the end of the speech—which were excellent, by the way—in the introduction."

- **Be specific.** Criticism is most effective when it's specific. Statements such as "I thought your delivery was bad" or "I thought your examples were good" (or, as in the self-test, "I loved the speech. . . . Really great" and "The speech was weak") don't specify what the speaker might do to improve delivery or to capitalize on the examples used. Refer to specifics such as the evidence used, the language choices, the delivery style, or whatever else is of consequence.

"To answer your question, we may or may not be trying to have it both ways."

Communication Choice Point

Giving Criticism

You've been asked to serve as a guest judge for students in a sixth-grade class who are giving their first public speeches. The audience will consist of elementary school students, a few teachers, and the parents of the students. *What are some of your choices for giving criticism in this situation? Put differently, what guidelines would you seek to follow?*

Communication Choice Point

Criticizing a Speech

After listening to a speech on the glory of bullfighting, you decide that bullfighting condones cruelty to animals; to the speaker, however, this traditional spectacle is an important part of his culture. As you bristle inside, the instructor asks you to critique the speech. *What are your choices in this situation?*

- **Be culturally sensitive.** There are vast cultural differences in what is considered proper when it comes to criticism. People in cultures that are highly individualistic and competitive (the United States, Germany, and Sweden are examples) may see public criticism as a normal part of the learning process. Thus, they may readily criticize others and are likely to expect the same "courtesy" from other listeners. People from cultures that are more collectivist and that emphasize the group rather than the individual (Japan, Mexico, and Korea are examples) are likely to find giving and receiving public criticism uncomfortable. They may feel that it's more important to be polite and courteous than to help someone learn a skill.

- **Limit criticism.** Cataloging a speaker's weak points, as in "I found four things wrong with your speech," will overwhelm, not help, the speaker. Mentioning one or two items that you found especially good or that might have been improved is likely to be more effective in helping the speaker.

- **Be constructive.** Give the speaker the insight that you feel will help in future public speaking situations. For example, "The introduction didn't gain my attention" doesn't tell the speaker how he or she might have gained your attention. Instead, you might say, "The example about the computer crash would have more effectively gained my attention in the introduction."

- **Focus criticism on behavior.** Look at what the speaker said and did during the actual speech. Avoid mind-reading the speaker and assuming that you know *why* the speaker did one thing rather than another. Instead of saying, "You weren't interested in your topic" (a comment that attacks the speaker), say, "I would have liked to see greater variety in your delivery. It would have made me feel you were more involved."

Listening to Criticism

At the same time that you are expressing criticism effectively, you'll also want to listen to criticism. Here are some suggestions for making listening to criticism a less difficult and more productive experience. These guidelines are appropriate in a learning environment such as a public speaking class, where criticism is used as a learning tool. In business and professional public speaking, in contrast, listeners don't offer suggestions for improvement; rather, they focus on the issues you raised.

- **Listen with an open mind.** If you've already given your first speech, you know that public speaking is highly ego-involving. Because of this it may be tempting to block out criticism. After all, it's not easy to listen to criticism, especially in a fairly public place like a classroom filled with your peers. But if you do block out such criticism, you'll likely lose out on some useful suggestions for improvement. Encourage critics to share their insights by demonstrating your willingness to listen with an open mind. Don't take criticism too personally; view criticism as objectively as you can.

- **Accept the critic's viewpoint.** If the critic says your evidence wasn't convincing, it doesn't help to identify the 12 references that you used in your speech; this critic simply was not convinced. Instead, think about why your evidence was not convincing to this person.

- **Seek clarification.** If you don't understand the criticism, ask for clarification. If you're told that your specific purpose was too broad but it's unclear to you how you might improve it, ask the critic how you might narrow the specific purpose.

VIEWPOINTS

Noting an Error

In listening to a speech, you note that the speaker misstated an important statistic. What are some of the things you might say? What would be inappropriate to say?

COMMUNICATING ETHICALLY

The Ethical Critic

Just as the speaker and the listener have ethical obligations, so does the critic. As you reflect on the suggestions that follow, consider any additional guidelines that you would like to see critics of public speaking follow (especially in the classroom).

- The ethical critic separates personal feelings about the speaker from his or her evaluation of the speech. A liking for the speaker should not lead the critic to give positive evaluations of the speech, nor should disliking the speaker lead to negative evaluations. Similarly, attitudes toward the speaker's thesis should not get in the way of fair and objective evaluation. The ethical critic recognizes the validity of an argument even if it contradicts a deeply held belief and, at the same time, recognizes the fallaciousness of an argument even if it supports a deeply held belief.

- The ethical critic takes responsibility for his or her own thoughts. The best way to express this ownership is to use I-messages rather than you-messages. Instead of saying, "You needed better research," say, "I would have been more persuaded if you had used more recent research."

- The ethical critic rejects any ethnocentric orientation and doesn't negatively evaluate customs and beliefs simply because they differ from her or his own. The ethical critic doesn't discriminate against or favor speakers simply because they're of a particular gender, race, affectional orientation, nationality, religion, or age group.

Ethical Choice Point

You and your best friend are taking a communications course together. Your friend just gave a terrible speech, and unfortunately, the instructor has asked you to offer a critique. The wrinkle here is that the instructor's grades seem to be heavily influenced by what student critics say. So in effect your critique will largely determine your friend's grade. You'd like to give your friend a positive critique so he can earn a good grade—which he badly needs—and you figure you can always tell him the truth later and even help him to improve. What is your ethical obligation in this situation? What would you do?

Video Choice Point
Speaking on the Arts

Sue works on the public relations staff of a large art museum and has been asked to speak to a local women's group about special programs and classes the museum is offering this season. She wants to prepare and deliver a speech that will hold the attention of this group of highly educated women whom the museum sees as potential patrons and to give them a good feeling for the museum. She has shared her speech with her coworker, Stephanie, who has offered to help Sue refine her words. Sue knows a lot is riding on her speech to these potential patrons, and she wants to be sure her style and delivery are on target. She considers the topics covered in this chapter as she contemplates her communication choices.

👁 **Watch** the **video** "Speaking on the Arts" at **MyCommunicationLab.com**

Objectives Self-Check
- Can you evaluate the speeches of others, express constructive critical evaluations, and respond to criticism openly and with a view toward improvement?

⚠ Messages in the Media *Wrap Up*

As you watch talk show hosts, consider their choice of language and the delivery techniques they use. Ask yourself why they are effective or ineffective and what you might take from these professionals to make your own speeches more effective.

Summary of Concepts and Skills

Study and Review materials for this chapter are at **MyCommunicationLab**

 Listen to the **Audio Chapter Summary** at **MyCommunicationLab**

This chapter looked at the last four steps in the public speaking process: wording the speech; constructing the conclusion, introduction, transitions, and outlines; and rehearsing and delivering the speech.

Step 7: Word Your Speech

1. Compared with written style, oral style contains shorter, simpler, and more familiar words; greater qualification; and more self-referential terms.

2. Effective public speaking style is clear (economical and specific; uses transitions, and short, familiar, and commonly used terms); vivid (uses active verbs, strong verbs, figures of speech, and imagery); appropriate to your audience (is on a suitable level of formality; avoids written-style expressions; avoids slang, vulgar, and offensive terms); personal (uses personal pronouns, asks questions, and creates immediacy); and powerful (avoids hesitations, intensifiers, disqualifiers, self-critical statements, and slang and vulgar language).

3. Effective sentences for public speeches are generally short, direct, active, positively phrased, and varied in type and length.

Step 8: Construct Your Conclusion, Introduction, Transitions, and Outlines

4. Conclusions summarize and close the speech.

5. Introductions gain the attention of the audience and orient them about what is to follow.

6. Transitions and internal summaries connect the parts of a speech and help listeners better remember the speech.

7. Preparation, template, and delivery outlines all serve different functions and will help any speaker, but especially the beginning speaker, in preparing and presenting effective public speeches.

Step 9: Rehearse Your Speech

8. There are three basic methods of delivering a public speech: (1) the impromptu method, which involves speaking without any specific preparation; (2) the manuscript method, which involves writing out the entire speech and reading it to the audience; and (3) the extemporaneous method, which involves thorough preparation and memorizing the main ideas and their order of appearance, but not a commitment to exact wording.

9. Use rehearsal to time and perfect your speech from beginning to end; rehearse under realistic conditions and with listeners if possible.

Step 10: Deliver Your Speech

10. When you deliver your speech, regulate your voice for greatest effectiveness. For example, adjust your volume on the basis of the distance between you and your audience and the emphasis you wish to give certain ideas. Adjust your rate on the basis of time constraints, the speech's content, and the listening conditions.

11. Avoid the major problems of articulation and pronunciation; errors of omission, substitution, addition, and accent.

12. Use unfilled pauses to signal a transition between the major parts of the speech, to allow the audience time to think, to allow the audience to ponder a rhetorical question, and to signal the approach of a particularly important idea. Avoid filled pauses; they weaken your message.

13. Effective body action involves maintaining eye contact with your entire audience, allowing facial expressions to convey your feelings, using your posture to communicate command of the public speaking interaction, gesturing naturally, moving around a bit, and using notes effectively.

Critically Evaluating Speeches

14. When expressing critical evaluations, try to say something positive, be specific, be culturally sensitive, limit criticism, be constructive, and focus on behavior. When receiving criticism, listen with an open mind, accept the critic's point of view, and seek clarification as needed.

This chapter stressed several significant skills for style and delivery. Place a check mark next to those skills you most want to work on.

_____ 1. I word my speech so it's clear, vivid, appropriate, and personal.

_____ 2. I construct sentences that are short, direct, active, and positive, and I vary the type and length of sentences.

_____ 3. I construct conclusions that summarize the major ideas of the speech and bring the speech to a crisp close.

_____ 4. I construct introductions that gain attention and preview what is to follow.

_____ 5. I use transitions and internal summaries to connect the parts of the speech and to help listeners remember what I say.

_____ 6. In general, I use the extemporaneous method of delivery.

_____ 7. I rehearse my speech from beginning to end, time it, rehearse under similar conditions to the actual delivery, rehearse in front of a mirror, and rehearse often.

_____ 8. I vary my vocal volume and rate to best reflect and reinforce my verbal messages and avoid the common problems with volume and rate.

_____ 9. I avoid the articulation and pronunciation errors of omission, substitution, addition, accent, and pronouncing sounds that should be silent.

_____ 10. I use pauses to signal transitions, to allow listeners time to think, and to signal the approach of a significant idea.

_____ 11. During my delivery of a speech, I maintain eye contact with the entire audience, allow my facial expressions to convey my feelings, gesture naturally, and incorporate purposeful body movements.

_____ 12. When expressing critical evaluations of the speeches of others, I try to say something positive, be specific, be culturally sensitive, limit criticism, be constructive, and focus my criticism on behavior.

Key Word Quiz

The Language of Public Speaking Preparation and Delivery

Match the terms about public speaking preparation with their definitions. Record the number of the definition next to the appropriate term.

_____ a. impromptu speech (249)

_____ b. powerless forms of language (239)

_____ c. internal summary (243)

_____ d. extemporaneous speech (249)

_____ e. oral style (237)

_____ f. transitions (243)

_____ g. rhetorical question (238)

_____ h. idiom (237)

_____ i. articulation (251)

_____ j. simile (238)

1. An expression that is unique to specific language and whose meaning cannot be deduced from the individual words.

2. Words, phrases, or sentences that connect the various parts of speech and guide listeners to focus on the next argument or idea.

3. A question whose answer is obvious and is used to make a statement.

4. Speech made off-the-cuff, without preparation.

5. The production of words resulting from movements of the speech organs.

6. Faults such as hesitations, disqualifiers, and self-critical statements.

7. A statement that recaps what you've discussed so far.

8. A speech that is thoroughly prepared and organized in detail but in which only certain aspects of style are predetermined.

9. A figure of speech that compares two unlike objects, using words such as *like* or *as*.

10. Language that sounds like someone is speaking rather than writing.

These ten terms and additional terms used in this chapter can be found in the glossary and on flashcards.

Answers: a. 4; b. 6; c. 7; d. 8; e. 10; f. 2; g. 3; h. 1; i. 5; j. 9

 Study and **Review** the **Flashcards** at **MyCommunicationLab**

MyCommunicationLab

Throughout this chapter, there are icons in the margin that highlight media content for selected topics. Go to **MyCommunicationLab** for additional information on public speaking preparation. Here you'll find flashcards to help you learn the jargon of communication, videos that illustrate a variety of concepts, additional exercises, and discussions to help you continue your study of public speaking. This site also contains a variety of template outlines for different types of informative and persuasive speeches and additional guidance in preparing your introductions and conclusions.

13

The Informative Speech

Objectives

 Listen to the **Audio Chapter** at **MyCommunicationLab**

After reading this chapter, you should be able to:

❶ Identify the suggested guidelines for informative speaking and apply these in your own speeches.

❷ Define *examples, illustrations,* and *narratives* as well as *testimony, numerical data,* and *definitions* as supporting materials in informative speeches and use these successfully in your own speeches.

❸ Use effectively varied types of presentation aids, including those that are computer-assisted.

❹ Define, give examples of, construct, and deliver effective *speeches of description, definition,* and *demonstration.*

Messages in the Media ⚠

Televised cooking shows are perfect examples of speeches of demonstration, one of the three types of informative speeches discussed in this chapter. Cooking show host and chef Bobby Flay, demonstrates in words and action how to prepare certain recipes, and in the process illustrates a variety of techniques that make informative speaking interesting to an audience.

This chapter covers speeches of information, through which a speaker tells listeners something they didn't already know. The next chapter covers speeches of persuasion, through which a speaker changes listeners' attitudes or beliefs or gets them to do something.

Guidelines for Informative Speaking

When you communicate information in a speech, you tell your listeners something they don't know, something new. You can inform them about a new way of looking at old things or an old way of looking at new things. You may discuss a theory not previously heard of or a familiar concept not fully understood. You may talk about events that the audience may be unaware of or explain happenings they may have misconceptions about. Regardless of what type of informative speech you intend to give, the following guidelines should help.

Explore the **Concept** "Informative Speeches" at **MyCommunicationLab**

CENTER INFORMATION ON THE AUDIENCE

The information you communicate in your informative speech should center around and focus on the audience's needs and interests. The audience should want to hear what you have to say. Somewhere early in your speech, answer the audience's unspoken questions: Why should I listen? Why should I care about this information? In your speech, for example, you might stress that what you have to say will save the audience money or time, will help them understand the current financial market, or will enable them to make themselves more attractive. In this way you'll capture and hold your audience's attention by showing them that the information you have is relevant and useful to their goals and interests.

Watch the **Video** "Eat Right" at **MyCommunicationLab**

LIMIT THE INFORMATION

There's a limit to the amount of information that your listeners can take in at one time. Resist the temptation to overload them. Instead of enlarging the breadth of information you communicate, expand its depth. It's better to present two new items of information and explain these in depth, with examples, illustrations, and descriptions, than to present five items without this needed amplification. The speaker who attempts to discuss the physiological,

COMMUNICATING ETHICALLY

Speaking Ethically

One interesting approach to ethics that has particular relevance to public speaking is Karl Wallace's "An Ethical Basis of Communication" (1955; see also Johannesen, Valde, & Whedbee, 2007). Wallace suggested four principles or guidelines. As you reflect on these principles, consider if there are other guidelines about speaking ethics that should be considered.

- The ethical speaker has a thorough knowledge of the topic, an ability to answer relevant questions, and an awareness of the significant facts and opinions bearing on the topic.
- The ethical speaker presents both facts and opinions fairly, without bending or spinning them to personal advantage; the listener makes the final decision.
- The ethical speaker reveals the sources of cited facts and opinions and helps listeners evaluate any biases and prejudices in the sources.
- The ethical speaker acknowledges and respects opposing arguments and evidence and avoids hiding valid opposing arguments from the audience.

Ethical Choice Point

You're giving an informative speech to explain the new initiative for more healthy food on campus. Among the important items that should logically be covered is the cost of this change, which is going to come from an increase in student fees. Since you are in favor of this initiative, you'd like to omit discussing cost largely because the students may vote against this plan if they find out that their fees will be raised. You decide that you don't have time to include all issues, that it's really the responsibility of the audience to ask where the money is coming from, and that this initiative is really for everyone's benefit. What is your ethical obligation in this situation? What will you do?

psychological, social, and linguistic differences between men and women, for example, is clearly trying to cover too much and is going to be forced to cover each area only superficially. Instead, select one subdivision of one area—say, language development or differences in language problems—and develop that in depth. Use the techniques for limiting a topic covered in Chapter 11.

ADJUST THE LEVEL OF COMPLEXITY

As you know from attending college classes, information can be presented in very simple or very complex forms. The level of complexity of the information you communicate should depend on the wide variety of factors considered throughout this book: the level of knowledge your audience has, the time you have available, the purpose you hope to achieve, the topic on which you're speaking, and so on. If you simplify a topic too much, you risk boring or, even worse, insulting your audience; if your talk is too complex, you risk confusing your audience and failing to communicate your message. In your beginning speeches at least, try to keep it simple. Make sure the words you use are familiar to your audience and that you explain clearly any unfamiliar terms.

In many ways the holiday letter is similar to an informative speech. Take a look at an example of this type of letter at **tcbdevito** .blogspot.com. In what ways is the holiday letter similar to an informative speech?

RELATE NEW INFORMATION TO OLD

Listeners will learn information more easily and retain it longer when you relate it to what they already know. Relate the new to the old, the unfamiliar to the familiar, the unseen to the seen, the untasted to the tasted. Here, for example, Teresa Jacob, a student from Ohio State University (Schnoor, 1997, p. 97), relates the problems of drug interactions (i.e., the new) to the dangers of mixing chemicals in the school lab (i.e., the old or familiar).

> During our high school years, most of us learned in a chemistry class the danger of mixing harmless chemicals in lab. Add one drop of the wrong compound, and suddenly you've created a stink bomb, or worse, an explosion. Millions of Americans run the same risk inside their bodies each day by combining drugs that are supposed to help restore or maintain good health.

VIEWPOINTS

Informative Speaking Guides

Thinking back to all the informative speeches you have heard (especially those at school and at work), what guidelines do you see violated especially often? What additional guidelines would you like to see speakers follow?

MAKE THE INFORMATION EASY TO REMEMBER

The principles of public speaking (of language, delivery, and supporting materials, for example) will all help your listeners remember your speech. Here are a few additional suggestions:

- **Repeat or restate important points.** Help your audience to remember what you want them to remember.

- **Use guide phrases.** Direct your audience's attention to your most important points by saying, for example, "The first point to remember is that . . ."

- **Use internal summary transitions.** These will remind the audience of what you have said and how it relates to what is to follow, for example, "Now that we've seen the problem, let's look at the solution."

- **Pattern your messages.** If the audience can see the logic of the organization of your speech, they'll be better able to organize (and remember) what you say in their own minds.

- **Focus audience attention.** The best way to focus listeners' attention is to tell them to focus their attention. Simply say, "I want you to focus on three points that I'll make in this speech. First, . . ." or "What I want you to remember is this: . . ."

Video Choice Point

Interfaith Meeting

Chigoze, a Nigerian student at an American university, is one of the few Africans and Muslims on campus. A friend of his who is active in the school's Interfaith Club has asked him to come to their next meeting and talk a little bit about his culture. Chigoze has agreed to speak at the campus interfaith meeting whose members know very little about Muslims. He considers the topics covered in this chapter as he contemplates his communication choices.

Watch the **video** "Interfaith Meeting" at **MyCommunicationLab.com**

Objectives Self-Test

- Can you identify and apply the suggested guidelines for information speaking (center information on the audience, limit the amount of information, adjust the level of complexity, relate new information to old, and make the information easy to remember) in your own speeches?

Supporting Materials

In constructing your speech you'll want to use a variety of what are called supporting materials—numerical data and illustrations, for example. These supporting materials serve a variety of functions and will help you clarify and explain ideas; make ideas vivid, interesting, and attention getting; and reinforce your ideas so that they are remembered.

In selecting appropriate supporting materials, keep in mind the nature of your audience. Select materials that are appropriate to their educational and age levels and their interests, for example. Also, select materials with cultural sensitivity. Using examples from only one religion (say, your own) when a variety of religious beliefs would be more appropriate and relevant is likely to distance your audience rather than draw them to you.

Here we look at four major material types in detail: (1) examples, illustrations, and narratives; (2) testimony; (3) numerical data; and (4) definitions). We'll also look at some additional forms in brief.

EXAMPLES, ILLUSTRATIONS, AND NARRATIVES

Examples, illustrations, and narratives are specific instances that help you explain your ideas. An **example** is a relatively brief specific instance:

Pat's on the varsity and has a 4.0.

SKILL DEVELOPMENT EXPERIENCE

Supporting Statements

Select one of the following overly broad statements and support it, using at least three different types of supporting material. Because the purpose of this exercise is to provide greater insight into supporting materials, in this case you may invent facts, figures, illustrations, examples, and the like.

- Immigrants contribute significantly to the U.S. economy.
- The author of this essay is a real authority.
- People in their 80s and older have contributed greatly to society.
- Candidate Williams cares for people.

Often it's the vivid example or alarming statistic that your listeners will remember most; give your supporting materials concentrated attention.

An **illustration** is a longer and more detailed example:

> Pat has always been an athlete but at the same time has always maintained an outstanding academic record, and there are many others on the varsity that have been both athletes and scholars, effectively destroying the stereotype of the dumb jock.

A **narrative** is longer still and presented in the form of an anecdote or brief story. The parables in many religious works are good examples of narratives used to illustrate a general principle.

Examples, illustrations, and narratives may be factual or imaginary. Thus, in explaining friendship, you might tell about an actual friend's behavior, or you might formulate a composite, ideal friend and describe how this person would act in a particular situation. In using these forms of support, be sure to include only those details that are needed to help your audience understand the point you're making. Don't clutter up an otherwise pointed example with unnecessary details. Also, because it is the example, illustration, or narrative that listeners will remember most clearly, be sure to connect this very explicitly to the proposition in your speech.

Communication Choice Point

Testimony

You want to present the testimony of a retired judge to explain the problems that probation causes. *For your purposes, what would be the ideal qualifications of this judge? How might you weave these qualifications into your speech? What are some of the things you might say?*

TESTIMONY

Testimony is a form of supporting material consisting of experts' opinions or of witnesses' accounts. Testimony supports your ideas by adding a note of authority. So, for example, if one of your main points was that the deficit is increasing, you might cite an economist's predictions concerning the increasing size of the deficit. Or if one of your main points was that today's prisons are inhumane, you might cite the eyewitness testimony of a former inmate or prison guard.

In presenting the testimony, stress the person's credibility. When you cite an authority, make sure the person is in fact an authority. Tell the audience who the authority is, and state the basis for the individual's expertise. The testimony will be much more effective when your audience is convinced that this person is worth listening to.

NUMERICAL DATA

Numerical data are useful for supporting a wide variety of statements. For example, if you want to show that significant numbers of people now get their news from the Internet, you could give the total number of online users for each of the last 10 years and compare that with the numbers of newspaper readers and television news viewers in those same years. These data would then allow you to show that the number of people who get their news from the Internet is increasing while the number of those getting the news from papers and television is declining. Or, you might compare the percentage of a tuition increase at your school with the national average or with the rate of inflation. To illustrate the growth of instant messaging or social networking as a means of communication, you might note the percentage that usage has grown in each of the last five years.

Information about phone interviews and cheat sheets can be found at tcbdevito.blogspot.com.

SKILL DEVELOPMENT EXPERIENCE

Evaluating Testimony

If you were presenting someone's testimony on one of the following issues, how would you establish the person's qualifications so that your audience would accept what he or she said?

Testimony is likely to be more effective if you establish the person's qualifications to the audience's satisfaction.

- Nutritionist, on proper diet
- Real estate agent, on the advantages and disadvantages of condos and co-ops
- Psychiatrist, on the nature of bipolar disorder
- Biologist, on how to feed your pet
- Drama teacher, on how to write a play

When using numerical data of any kind, consider these suggestions:

- **Make the numbers easy to remember.** Your audience will hear the figures only once. For most purposes it's best to round off any figures so that they are more easily processed and remembered. For example, if you're trying to make the point that the population of China dwarfs many European nations, you are probably better off rounding China's population to "over 1 billion people" or perhaps "1.3 billion people" than saying China's population is 1,336,718,015.

- **Clarify your meaning for using numbers.** For example, if you state that the average home health aide makes less than $30,000 a year, you need to compare this figure to the salaries of other workers and to your proposition that these salaries need to be increased.

- **Connect numbers to something familiar.** Comparisons and analogies will prove useful in making your numbers relevant and meaningful to your specific audience. Instead of saying the new exhibition hall will be 750 × 350 feet—hard in itself to visualize—elaborate on the figures with something like, *it will be twice the size of a professional football field, forty times the size of our cafeteria.*

- **Reinforce your numerical data.** Use a presentation aid—perhaps a graph or a chart—with numbers presented as visual reinforcement.

- **Use numbers in moderation.** Most listeners' capacity for numerical data presented in a speech is limited.

- **Stress reliability.** If you want your audience to accept your figures, you need to show that they come from a trusted source.

- **Stress currency.** Most things that are described with numbers change rapidly. So, use the most recent figures you can find and stress their currency to the audience.

Take a look at "Making Numbers Real" for an example of how to present numbers to an audience at tcbdevito.blogspot.com.

DEFINITIONS

Definitions, essentially explanations of terms and concepts that may not be familiar to your listeners, may be useful as a form of support in many types of speeches. Here are several ways to incorporate definitions in a speech.

- **Define by etymology or linguistic development.** For example, in defining *communication* you might note that it comes from the Latin *communis* meaning "common"; in "communicating" you seek to establish a commonness, a sameness, a similarity with another individual.

- **Define by authority.** For example, you might define "inflation" by citing the definition of a noted economist or define "metal fatigue" in the words of a respected engineer.

- **Define by negation.** For example, you might say that "A teacher isn't someone who teaches you what to learn but rather one who teaches you how to learn."

- **Define by the actual object or by a picture or model of it.** For example, a speech on magazine layout or types of fabrics might include actual layout pages or fabric samples.

- **Define by operations.** An **operational definition** describes how you would construct the object. For example, in defining a chocolate cake, you could give instructions about how to bake a cake.

ADDITIONAL FORMS OF SUPPORT

There are several other useful forms of support you might consider:

- **Quotations:** Quote the exact words of an expert or of an interesting or notable person to add spice and wit as well as authority to your speeches. Quotations work best when they're short and easily comprehended and remembered. Most important, connect the quotations directly to the point you're making and do so as smoothly as possible (avoid the too-often-used "I have a quote . . .").

Communication Choice Point

Unexpected Events

You're going to speak on the new version of Microsoft Windows, which you've used for the past few weeks. Unfortunately, the speaker before you turns out to be a Microsoft program designer and gives a speech on exactly your topic. *If you feel it would be necessary to say something, what are some of your options? What would you say?*

VIEWPOINTS

Supporting Materials

What types of supporting materials would you use in an informative speech in which your purpose is to explain the way in which a particular sport or game is played to an audience who never heard of the sport or game?

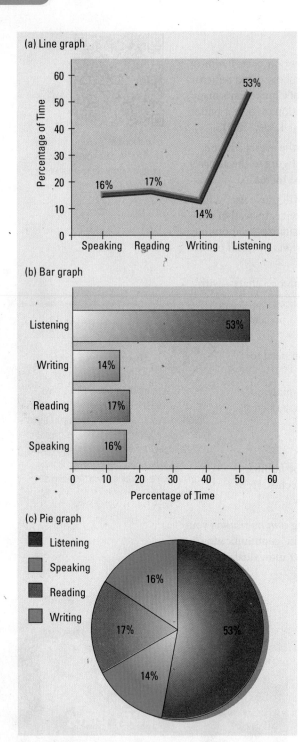

(a) Line graph

(b) Bar graph

(c) Pie graph

FIGURE 13.1

Three Graphs

Three graphs illustrating data from a study on the amount of time people spend on each of the four communication activities (Barker, Edwards, Gaines, Gladney, & Holley, 1980). All of these graphs are useful for illustrating comparisons. Many additional types of graphs can be easily constructed using the graphics software integrated with most word processing packages or, of course, with the more sophisticated graphics programs.

- **Comparisons and contrasts:** Focus on the major similarities and differences between two ideas, events, or concepts but avoid itemizing every possibility. Consider using a presentation aid that visualizes the most crucial information.
- **Statements of fact or a series of facts:** Illustrate and support a statement for your position by linking the facts to your main points. State the connections when introducing the facts and perhaps again after you've finished identifying the list of facts.
- **Repetition and restatement:** Repeat ideas in the same words at strategic places during the speech) or *restate* ideas in different words to add clarity and emphasis and to also help compensate for the audience's inevitable lapses in attention.

Objectives Self-Test
- Can you define *examples, illustrations,* and *narratives; testimony; numerical data;* and *definitions* as supporting materials in informative speeches?
- Can you use these forms of supporting materials to effectively support your assertions?

Presentation Aids

Presentation aids—visual or auditory means for clarifying ideas—can also be considered a form of supporting material. But because they're so important in public speaking today, because they're so numerous and varied, and because technology has provided a wealth of alternatives and some pretty sophisticated techniques, we'll look at presentation aids separately here and will consider them in detail.

As you plan any type of speech, consider using some kind of presentation aid. Ask yourself how you can visually present what you want your audience to remember. For example, if you want your audience to see the growing impact of the sales tax, consider showing them a chart of rising sales taxes over the last 10 years. Of course, you can deliver your entire speech supplemented by projected slides—using PowerPoint or Prezi, for example.

TYPES OF PRESENTATION AIDS

Be sure to consider the many types of presentation aids you can choose from when preparing an informative speech:

- **Object being discussed:** If it's feasible, bring the object itself to your speech. Notice that infomercials sell their products not only by talking about them but by showing them to potential buyers.
- **Models:** Replicas of the actual object are useful if you want to explain complex structures such as the human hearing or vocal mechanisms, the brain, or the structure of DNA. Models can clarify relative size and position and how the parts interact.
- **Graphs:** Graphs are useful for illustrating differences over time, how a whole is divided into parts, and different amounts or sizes. Figure 13.1 shows three types of graphs. Keep your

graphs as simple as possible, limiting the number of items to five or fewer and be sure you add the legend, the labels, and the numerical values you wish to emphasize.

- **Word chart:** You can use a word chart (which also can contain numbers and graphics) to identify the key points of one of your propositions or of your entire speech. Figure 13.2 is an example of a simple word chart that identifies the major topics discussed in a speech on culture shock. The word chart in Figure 13.3, an organizational chart, clarifies relationships among roles in an organization, and Figure 13.4, a flowchart, identifies the steps in a process.

- **Maps:** You can use maps to illustrate the locations of geographic features, population densities, immigration patterns, world literacy rates, varied economic conditions, the spread of diseases, and hundreds of other issues you may wish to examine in your speeches.

- **People:** If you want to demonstrate the muscles of the body, different voice patterns or hairstyles, consider using people as your aids. Their presence also helps to secure and maintain the attention and interest of the audience.

- **Photographs and illustrations.** Types of trees, styles of art, kinds of exercise machines, and the horrors of war—all of these can be made more meaningful with photographs and illustrations. Be sure to project the image in a format large enough for everyone to see clearly.

Once you've decided on the type of presentation aid to use, you need to decide on the medium you'll use to present it. Acquire skill in using both low-tech (the whiteboard or flip chart) and high-tech (presentation software such as PowerPoint or Prezi) resources. A variety of media, with their major uses, and some suggestions for using them effectively are presented in Table 13.1.

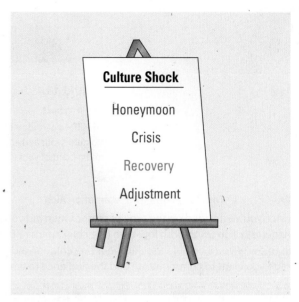

FIGURE 13.2

A Word Chart

The word chart is helpful when your main ideas can be clearly explained in key words or when you wish to emphasize certain concepts.

Explore the **Exercise** "Analyzing Presentation Aids" at **MyCommunicationLab**

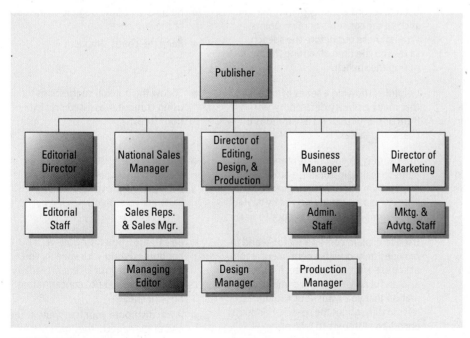

FIGURE 13.3

An Organizational Chart

Organizational charts can easily be constructed using the table function on most word processors and then enlarged for an entire audience to see. This figure was constructed in Illustrator.

FIGURE 13.4

A Flowchart

This flowchart identifies the stages a child goes through in learning language. You can use such charts to guide your audience through an entire speech—where each section of the chart might represent a main point of your speech.

TABLE 13.1 The Many Forms of Presentation Aids

Once you've decided on the type of presentation aid you'll use, you need to decide on the medium you'll use to present it. Acquire skill in using both low-tech (the chalkboard or flip chart) and high-tech (the computerized slide show) resources. In this way you'll be able to select your presentation aids from the wide array available, choosing on the basis of the message you want to communicate and the audience to whom you'll be speaking.

Type of Aid	Uses	Suggestions
Whiteboards	Used to record key terms or names, important numerical data, or even the main points of your speech (in very abbreviated form).	● Don't use whiteboards when you can present the same information with a preplanned chart or model. ● Keep what you write brief; don't lose audience eye contact.
Chartboards Large semirigid boards that come in a variety of colors and sizes.	Used to present one or two relatively simple graphs, a few word charts, or diagrams that you want to display during your speech.	● Be sure you have a way of holding the boards up—for example, with masking tape or with the aid of an audience member. ● Black lettering on a white background generally works best; it's easiest for people to read.
Flip Charts Large pads of paper (usually about 24 × 24 inches) mounted on a stand or easel.	Used to record a variety of information, such as key concepts or main points. Writing these out before the speech saves you the time of writing them during the speech.	● Be sure the print is legible to the back of the audience. ● Keep the charts simple.
Slides and Transparencies Visuals created with many of the popular computer programs (see "Computer-Assisted Presentations," p. 371.)	Helpful in showing a series of visuals that may be of very different types—from photographs and illustrations to charts and tables.	● Follow the general suggestions for using computer-assisted presentations (p. 371).
Audios and Videos Basically, you have two options with videos or audios: record a scene from a film or television show or create your own.	Adds variety to your presentation and helps to maintain audience attention. A speech on advertising jingles or music styles would be greatly helped by having actual samples for the audience to hear.	● Videos are best used in small doses; in many instances just 20- or 30-second excerpts will prove sufficient to illustrate your point.
Handouts Printed materials that are distributed to the audience A variety of handouts can be easily prepared with many of the computer presentation packages that we'll consider later in this chapter.	Used to explain complex material and to provide listeners with a permanent record of some aspect of your speech. They are also useful for presenting complex information that you want your audience to refer to throughout the speech. Handouts encourage listeners to take notes—especially if you leave enough white space on each page or even provide a specific place for notes—which keeps them actively involved in your presentation.	● Be careful: if you distribute your handouts during your speech, you run the risk of your listeners reading the handout and not concentrating on your speech. ● If you distribute your handouts at the end of the speech, they may never be read. Encourage your audience to read them by including additional material (and giving your audience an idea of what you've included).

Watch the **Video** "Informative Speech: Transcranial Magnetic Stimulation" at **MyCommunicationLab**

USING PRESENTATION AIDS

Your presentation aids will be more effective if you follow a few simple guidelines.

- **Know your presentation aids intimately.** Be sure you know in what order your aids are to be presented and how you plan to introduce them.

- **Pretest the presentation aids.** Verify that your aids can be seen easily from all parts of the room.

- **Rehearse your speech with the presentation aids.** Do all your rehearsals with your presentation aids so that you'll be able to use them smoothly and effectively.

- **Integrate presentation aids into your speech seamlessly.** Just as a verbal example should flow naturally into the text so should a presentation aid. The aid should appear to be an essential part of the speech.

- **Avoid talking to your aids.** Know your aids so well that you can point to what you want without breaking eye contact with your audience.

- **Use your aids only when they're relevant.** Present each aid when you want the audience to concentrate on it; then remove it. If you don't, the audience's attention may remain focused on the visual when you want them to focus on your next assertion.

COMPUTER-ASSISTED PRESENTATIONS

Before reading about computer assisted presentations, take the self-test included here to see what you already know about PowerPoint and similar presentation packages.

TEST YOURSELF

Using Presentation Software

Indicate whether you think each of the following statements is **T** (true) or **F** (false).

_____ ❶ A good size font to use is about 16 or 18 points with about 8 or 9 lines per slide.

_____ ❷ Use italics for emphasis.

_____ ❸ Read your slides word for word.

_____ ❹ Use lots of color and sound effects; these will keep the audience awake.

_____ ❺ Blue and green or red and green are almost always appropriate colors for slides.

_____ ❻ As in a preparation outline, use full sentences for the slides.

_____ ❼ Your slides should be your main attraction.

_____ ❽ When you have few words on a slide, add a photo or graphic.

_____ ❾ A 10-minute informative speech can easily have 30 or 40 slides.

_____ ❿ Liven up your slides by including images from websites.

HOW DID YOU DO? This test was designed to point out some of the misconceptions people have about computer-assisted presentations; all are false. Briefly, here's why:

1. Sixteen or 18 is too small; use at least 24 point font, although 30 point font would be even better. Four lines is best though six is generally fine. Any more than this will work against you.

2. Italics are difficult to read and don't give real emphasis.

3. Never do this.

4. Too much color and too many sounds will be distracting.

5. These colors do not provide sufficient contrast—as would, say, red and black. Also, many people have difficulty distinguishing red and green.

6. Use phrases for the slides; sentences take too much time to read.

7. No, you should be the main attraction. Your slides are simply aids to your presentation.

8. Only add photos or graphics when they are integral to your slide's message.

9. Any more than 10 slides is probably too much.

10. Images from websites don't translate well to slides; instead, use clip art images if you need graphics.

WHAT WILL YOU DO? Presentation software is a fact of life for public speakers. Resolve to learn to use it as effectively as you can and keep up with the new developments. For starters, take a look at the humorous but most helpful *Life After Death by PowerPoint* by Don McMillan.

Computer-assisted presentations possess all of the advantages of aids already noted (from maintaining interest and attention to adding clarity and reinforcing your message). In addition, however, they have advantages all their own—so many, in fact, that you'll want to seriously consider using this technology in your speeches. They give your speech a professional, up-to-date look, and in the process add to your credibility. They show that you're prepared and that you care about your topic and audience.

Various presentation software packages are available. Figure 13.5 illustrates how a set of slides might look. The slides are built around the "culture shock" speech outline discussed in Chapter 12 and were constructed in PowerPoint. As you review this figure, try to visualize how you'd use a slide show to present your next speech.

Ways of Using Presentation Software   Presentation software enables you to produce a variety of aids. The easiest is to create your slides and then show them on your computer screen. If you're speaking to a very small group and you have a large monitor, it may be possible to have your listeners gather around your computer as you speak. With larger audiences, you'll need a computer projector.

Computer presentation software also enables you to print out a variety of materials to use as handouts: slides, slides with speaker's notes, slides with room for listener notes, and outlines of your speech. You can print out your complete set of slides to distribute to your listeners, or you can print out a selection of slides from the talk or even slides that you didn't have time to cover in your speech but would like your audience to look at later.

Another useful option is to print out your slides with speaker's notes for your own use (as illustrated in Figure 13.6). That way you'll have your slides and any notes you may find useful—examples you want to use, numerical data that would be difficult to memorize, quotations that you want to read to your audience, or delivery notes. Still another option is to print out your slides with room for listeners to write their own notes (as illustrated in Figure 13.7).

Rehearsing with Presentation Programs   Presentation programs are especially helpful in enabling you to rehearse your speech and time it precisely. As you rehearse, the computer program records the time you spend on each slide and will display it under the slide; it will also record the

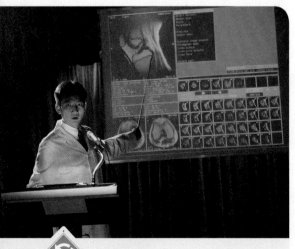

VIEWPOINTS

Presentation Aids
Although presentation aids are extremely useful, speakers often use them ineffectively. What are some of the major mistakes people make in using presentation aids?

Slide 1

Speech title

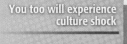

Have You Ever Been Culture Shocked?

This first slide introduces the topic with the title of the speech. Follow the general rules for titling your speech: Keep it short, provocative, and focused on your audience. If you put a graphic on this page, make sure that it doesn't detract from your title. What other graphics might work well here?

Slide 2

The thesis of the speech

Culture shock can be described in 4 stages
- The honeymoon
- The crisis
- The recovery
- The adjustment

You may or may not want to identify your thesis directly right at the beginning of your speech. Consider the arguments for and against identifying your thesis—both cultural and strategic—and the suggestions for when and how to state the thesis. As a listener, do you prefer it when speakers state their thesis right at the beginning or do you prefer it when the thesis is only implied and left for you to figure out?

Slide 3

Attention-getting device; corresponds to the introduction's "I A–B"

You too will experience culture shock
- Near universal experience
- With understanding comes control

This slide gains attention by relating the topic directly to the audience; it answers the listener's obvious question, "Why should I listen to this speech?"

Slide 4

Orientation; corresponds to the introduction's "II A–D"

Culture Shock
- The honeymoon
- The crisis
- The recovery
- The adjustment

In this slide you give your orientation by identifying your main points. These four bullets will become your four main points.

Slide 5

First main point; corresponds to the body's "I A–B"

The Honeymoon
- Fascination
- Enjoyment of people and culture

This is your first main point. You'd introduce it, perhaps, by saying, "The honeymoon occurs first." If you wanted your audience to keep track of the stage numbers, you could use numbers in your slides; for example, "1. The Honeymoon" or "Stage 1, The Honeymoon." The graphic of the heart is meant to associate culture shock with good times and a romancelike experience. As a listener, would you prefer that the speaker explain this graphic or say nothing about it?

FIGURE 13.5

A Slide Show Speech

presentation's total time. You can see these times at the bottom of each slide in a variety of views, but they won't appear in the slides the audience sees or in a printed handout such as the one in Figure 13.5. You can use these times to program each slide to run automatically or to see if you're devoting the desired amount of time to each of your ideas. If you find in your rehearsal that your speech is too long, these times can help you see which parts could be shortened.

Communication Choice Point

Technical Problems

You've prepared a great Prezi show for your informative speech. Unfortunately, the equipment that you need in order to show the slides never arrives. But you have to give your speech and you have to explain what happened (or do you?). *What are your options for dealing with this unexpected technical problem?*

Slide 6

Second main point; corresponds to the body's "II A–B"

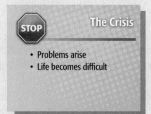

This is your second point and follows in format the previous slide. Again, a graphic is used. Can you think of a better graphic?

Slide 7

Third main point; corresponds to the body's "III A–B"

This is your third main point and again follows the format of the previous two slides.

Slide 8

Fourth main point; corresponds to the body's "IV A–B"

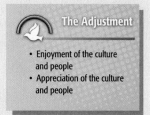

This is your fourth main point; the sound of applause is programmed to come on with this slide, reinforcing the idea that we do adjust to culture shock. Examine the sound effects you have available; what other sound effects would you use in this speech?

Slide 9

Summary; corresponds to the conclusion's "I A–D"

This is your summary of your four points; notice that it's the same as your orientation (Slide 4). This slide violates the general rule to use graphics in moderation. What do you think of the repetition of graphics? Do you think they add reinforcement? Do they detract from the verbal message?

Slide 10

Closure; corresponds to the conclusion's "II"

This slide is intended to wrap up the speech—it contains the title and two graphics that will support the speaker's concluding statement: "By knowing about culture shock you'll be in a better position to deal with it at school and on the job." Notice that the conclusion is tied to the introduction by a similarity in font and text color; it helps signal that this is the last slide and the end of the speech.

FIGURE 13.5

A Slide Show Speech *(continued)*

Another aspect of rehearsal is checking out the equipment available in the room you'll speak in and its compatibility with the presentation software you're using. If possible, rehearse with the actual equipment you'll have available on the day you're speaking. In this way you can adjust to or remedy any incompatibilities or idiosyncrasies that you come across.

PUBLIC SPEAKING SAMPLE ASSISTANT

Special Occasion Speeches *Largely Informative*

In addition to the speeches of description, definition, and demonstration, there are special occasion speeches. These speeches are dominated by the context and occasion for the speech. Here are a few such speeches that are largely (though not exclusively) informative. For specific examples of these and other types of special occasion speeches, search YouTube or any search engine's videos. Chapter-length coverage of the "special occasion speech," may be found at MyCommunicationLab.

The Speech of Presentation or Acceptance

In a **presentation speech** you seek to (1) place an award or honor in some kind of context and (2) give the award an extra air of dignity or status. A speech of presentation may focus on rewarding a colleague for an important accomplishment (being named Teacher of the Year) or on recognizing a particularly impressive performance (winning an Academy Award). It may honor an employee's service to a company or a student's outstanding grades or athletic abilities.

The **acceptance speech** is the other side of this honoring ceremony. Here the recipient accepts the award and attempts to place the award in some kind of context.

In your speeches of presentation, follow these three principles:

- State the reason for the presentation. Make clear why this particular award is being given to this particular person.
- State the importance of the award.
- Be brief.

Follow these guidelines when preparing and presenting your speech of acceptance:

- Thank the people responsible for giving you the award.
- Acknowledge those who helped you achieve the award.
- Put the award into personal perspective.

The Eulogy

The **eulogy,** a speech of tribute to praise someone who has died, puts a person's life and contributions in a positive light. This type of speech is often given at a funeral or at the anniversary of the person's birth or death. This is not the time for a balanced appraisal of the individual's life. Rather, it's a time for praise. In developing the eulogy, consider the following:

- Relate the person whose life you're celebrating to yourself and to those in the audience.
- Be specific; show that you really knew the person or know a great deal about the person.
- Make the audience see this person as deserving of the praise you're bestowing.
- Show the audience what they can learn from this individual's life.

Watch the **Video** "Elegy for a Special Person" at **MyCommunicationLab**

"We are gathered here today to bid farewell to the best assistant any magician could ask for."

The Toast

The **toast** is a brief speech designed to celebrate a person or an occasion. You might, for example, toast the next CEO of your company, a friend who just got admitted to a prestigious graduate program, or a colleague on the occasion of a promotion. Often toasts are given at weddings or at the start of a new venture. The toast is designed to say "congratulations" or "good luck" in a relatively formal sense. In developing your toast consider the following:

- Be brief; realize that people want to get on with the festivities.
- Focus attention on the person or persons you're toasting, not on yourself.
- Avoid inside jokes that only you and the person you're toasting understand.
- When you raise your glass in the toast—an almost obligatory part of toasting—make the audience realize that they should drink and that your speech is at an end.

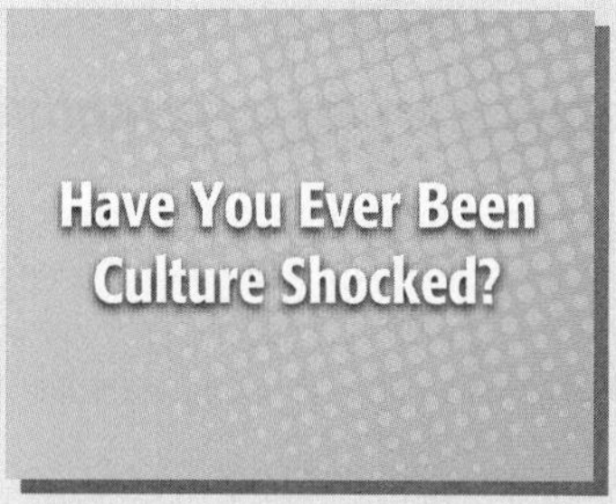

PAUSE!
Scan audience.
Slide #1
Have you ever been culture shocked?
PAUSE!
I have.
And many of you have too.
If you haven't, you will be.
People all over the world (and especially bright college graduates like ourselves) are becoming increasingly mobile.
We'll all spend time in different cultures.
Understanding culture shock → better to deal with it.
Preventive medicine.

FIGURE 13.6
Slide with Speaker's Notes

Objectives Self-Check

- Can you effectively use a variety of presentation aids, including computer-assisted aids?

Three Types of Informative Speeches

Now that you have considered the principles of informative speaking, types of supporting materials, and presentation aids, it's time to consider the three types of informative speeches: speeches of description, definition, and demonstration. In addition, see the accompanying Public Speaking Sample Assistant on special occasion speeches (p. 375).

SPEECHES OF DESCRIPTION

Watch the **Video** "Tall Girls" at **MyCommunicationLab**

In a speech of *description*, you're concerned with explaining an object, person, event, or process. You would describe an object or person in a speech about, for example, the structure of the brain, the contributions of Thomas Edison, the parts of a telephone, the layout of Philadelphia, the hierarchy of a corporation, or the components of a computer system.

You would be describing an event or process in a speech about, for example, the process of organizing a bodybuilding contest; how to create a blog; how a child acquires language; how people purchase stocks online; or the events leading to the Arab Spring.

Have You Ever Been Culture Shocked?

_____
_____
_____
_____

Culture shock can be described in 4 stages

- The honeymoon
- The crisis
- The recovery
- The adjustment

_____
_____
_____
_____

You too will experience culture shock

- Near universal experience
- With understanding comes control

_____
_____
_____
_____
_____

FIGURE 13.7
Slides with Space for Listener's Notes

Thesis and Main Points   The thesis of a speech, as explained in Chapter 11, is your single most important concept, your main or central idea. The thesis of a speech of description simply states what you'll describe in your speech:

The child acquires language in four stages.

There are three steps to purchasing stock online.

Four major events led to the Arab Spring.

The main points of a speech of description are the major subdivisions of the thesis. You derive your main points from your thesis by asking strategic questions:

What are the four stages in child language acquisition?

What are the three steps to purchasing stock online?

What events led to the Arab Spring?

For an excellent special occasion speech take a look at "A Speech of Dedication" at tcbdevito.blogspot.com.

PUBLIC SPEAKING SAMPLE ASSISTANT

An Excellent Informative Speech

This speech was delivered by Marty Wiebe, a student at Centralia College, in Washington, in an introductory communication course taught by Jeff McQuarrie that used the previous edition of this textbook. You can watch a video of this speech at **MyCommunicationLab**. Here is a transcript of that speech with annotations to help guide your reading/viewing and questions to help guide your analysis. Some of the key terms we used throughout the section on public speaking appear in the annotations in boldface.

Communication in an Ever-Changing World
Marty Wiebe

 Watch the **Video** "Communication in an Ever-Changing World" at **MyCommunicationLab**

SPEECH	ANNOTATIONS AND QUESTIONS
Good morning. Drumming [the sound of drumming on the desk]. That's one of the things we just did today. My name is Marty Wiebe, and drumming, we just did, is one form of communication. Talking to you like I am doing right now is another form of communication.	This speech is appropriately titled Communication in a Changing World. It gives you a very clear idea of what the speech will be about. What other titles might be appropriate if you were giving this speech to your class? [Read or view the speech before creating a title.]
	Notice that the speaker not only gained **attention** by drumming but she related this attention-getter to the topic of the speech. **In what other ways might she have introduced the speech?**
My speech is going to be about how communication is changing and how the media is changing and how we as communicators have got to become better and more acquainted with the new modes of communication and some of the new rules that we're going to have to learn.	Here the speaker gives a very direct **orientation,** telling her audience what her speech will be about. **How would you define the purpose and thesis of this speech? How appropriate would this speech be if delivered in your class? Why?**
There are two main forms of communication: verbal, which is what I'm doing right now, and nonverbal, like our drums. They're nonverbal. Music is nonverbal. When I smile at you, it's nonverbal. So verbal and nonverbal go hand in hand, and it's really, really important that we use both, verbal and nonverbal communication, when we are doing presentations.	You'll notice that the speaker effectively uses lots of specific **examples** as **supporting materials** throughout this speech. **What other types of supporting materials would be useful in this speech? For example, if this were a longer speech, in what way might the speaker have used illustrations, testimony, numerical data, and definitions?**
We live in a shrinking world. When I grew up back in the stone age, face-to-face was the normal type of communication that we did. We met somebody. We talked to them face to face. We sat down, and we wrote a letter, and we sent them, but which is now considered by snail mail. We had newspapers and televisions and probably in the 70's when I was just graduating from high school, we did phone conferencing, which was a really, really big deal.	Here the speaker describes communication as it was in the 70s. **How effectively did the speaker describe communication in the "stone age"? What else might the speaker have said?**
Because up to that point, our world was just what was around us. We weren't global at this point. Computers were just getting developed. My first computer was a Commodore 64, and we had little 5 and a half inch floppy disks that we used, but there was no Internet. Bill Gates was still in the baby stage of developing Microsoft.	Here the speaker describes the state of computing in the 70s. **If this were a longer speech, what else might she have mentioned to emphasize this contrast between then and now?**
But today we've got tons and tons of communication. Lots of us have Facebook accounts. We can now communicate with people around the world. We have a classmate in here, name is CJ, he lives in Africa, and we can actually communicate with him after he gets back to Africa. We can also use Skype.	Referring to specific audience members is often a useful technique to maintain interest and attention. **If you were giving this speech in your class, what specific references might you make?**

SPEECH

We have cell phones. When I was growing up, we were just still using landlines and long distance charges applied, which don't anymore. Now cell phones, we can talk internationally. We couldn't even talk internationally on our landlines many, many years ago. We now have something called teleconferencing. In other words, you can be sitting here in this classroom, studying, and someone from Australia could be in the same classroom with you, and you can be discussing things and learning together.

Our communicating world is shrinking, but with new communications, we also have to realize that there are cultural differences.

We have to learn whether it is proper to speak or not to speak. In this culture, speaking is fine. In Asian cultures, you need to listen first. In our culture, we're more individualism. In other words, if you make a mistake, you're responsible for it. But on the other hand, if you live in a collective culture, such as our Asian counterparts, their thinking is different. They work as a group. If you make a mistake, the whole group makes a mistake. So it's really important that we learn that cultural differences can make the difference between communication skills that you're learning are going to be effective or not.

You have to realize that just because we're allowed to speak in our culture doesn't necessarily mean that you can speak in another. Remember, once the words are out there, you can't go stop, come back. They're out there for the whole world, and it isn't just our little world or the neighborhood that I grew up in. It's the world. We're talking Sweden, Australia, the Congo, South America. Those words that you spoke that you thought were just for you to hear are no longer your words. They're out there. You can't say come back. I made a mistake.

Before you press that send button on your Facebook page, or before you press any send button or even talk in teleconferencing, you have to make sure that what you're saying is not going to be offensive to someone else. Again, once it's said, there are no do overs. And what you can say may be very offensive to someone else. So, again, in our culture, in our communication, those are the things that we have to remember. There are no do overs. There are no stop, come back moments

And in conclusion, we have different forms of communication. It isn't just me talking to you face to face. It's Facebook. It's Skype. It's mass media. There are different platforms. We've got Facebook. I've got a general account. I can Skype. I can talk to someone on a cell phone. I can e-mail them on my computer. Those weren't available several years ago, and I suspect as time progresses that our platforms are going to be changing.

Technology's going to allow us to even further communicate with those people that we were unable to do so even ten years ago. We live in a shrinking world, and because the world is shrinking, it is important to realize that what we here in the United States may think is normal, someone in Asia may find very offensive. So the bottom line is communication is really important, but it's also an awareness.

It's a challenge to each student every day that when we learn to communicate, we communicate on a level that is both effective and not offensive, and with that, I thank you.

ANNOTATIONS AND QUESTIONS

If the speaker had chosen to use **visual aids,** what types would have been useful? This particular speech assignment did not call for citing **research.**

If it had, what types of research might the speaker have used? Here the speaker introduces the element of cultural differences in a neat transition from the discussion of changing communication technology to culture.

The distinction between individualist and collectivist cultures is made clear with a simple example contrasting the cultures of the United States and Asia. If this were a longer speech what other examples might have been used to emphasize this distinction?

How would you describe the speaker's delivery style? Would this be effective in your class? What can you learn from this model?

How would you describe the speaker's adherence to the suggestions for informative speaking: Focus on the audience? Limiting the amount of information? Adjustment of the level of complexity? Relating new information to old?

The speaker uses **repetition** in making the point that communication is irreversible and unerasable in this technological world. In what other ways might this point have been made?

Lots of speakers announce their **conclusion** with the word "conclusion". What other ways might be used to signal that you're going into your conclusion?

Here the speaker provides a kind of **motivation**—to learn more about communication and especially the cultural implications. If this speech were given in your class, what would you say in motivating your classmates to learn more about communication and culture?

Here it's clear that the speaker is providing crisp **closure** to her speech. What would you say in closing?

Support   Instead of simply listing your main points, you should instead flesh them out and make them memorable, interesting, and, most of all, clear. In a speech of description you do this by using a variety of materials that amplify and support your main ideas. Because you are giving a speech of description, give extra consideration to the variety of description you might use in your supporting materials: examples, illustrations, testimony, numerical data, and presentation aids.

SKILL DEVELOPMENT EXPERIENCE

Preparing an Informative Speech

Select a topic in which you're interested (or consult the Dictionary of Topics at **MyCommunicationLab** for ideas) and then follow these steps:

1. Formulate a thesis and a specific purpose suitable for an informative speech of approximately 10 minutes.
2. Analyze this class as your potential audience and identify ways in which you can relate this topic to their interests and needs.
3. Generate at least two main points from your thesis.
4. Support these main points with examples, illustrations, definitions, testimony, and so on.
5. Construct a conclusion that summarizes your main ideas and brings the speech to a definite close.
6. Construct an introduction that gains attention and orients your audience.

Working repeatedly with the process of preparing a speech will ultimately make the process easier, more efficient, and more effective.

Discuss these outlines in small groups or with the class as a whole. Try to secure feedback from other members on how you can improve your outline.

Communication Choice Point

Speech of Description

As you approach the lectern to give a speech of description on how a child acquires language, you notice a woman with a one-year-old child in the audience. *What are your options in this situation? Would you depart from your plans and comment on the woman and child? If you do decide to comment, what are your options? What would you say (if anything)?*

Organization   Consider using a *spatial* or a *topical organization* when describing objects and people. For example, if you were to describe the layout of the center of Philadelphia, you might start from the north and work down to the south (using a spatial pattern). If you were to describe the contributions of Steve Jobs, you might select the three or four major contributions and discuss each of these equally (using a topical pattern).

Consider using a *temporal pattern* when describing events and processes. If you were to describe the events leading up to the Arab Spring, for example, you might start with the earliest and work up to the latest. A temporal pattern would also be appropriate for describing how a hurricane develops or how a parade is put together. The "who, what, where, when, and why" pattern of organization can also be useful to describe an event or a process. For example, if you're going to describe how to purchase a house, you might want to consider the people involved (who?), the steps you have to go through (what?), the places you'll have to go (where?), the timing or sequence of the steps (when?), and the advantages and disadvantages of buying the house (why?).

Here is an example of how the bare bones of a descriptive speech might look. Notice that the speaker derives the main points from asking a question about the thesis.

General purpose:	To inform
Specific purpose:	To describe the way fear works in intercultural communication
Thesis:	Fear influences intercultural communication. (How does fear influence intercultural communication?)

   I. We fear disapproval.

  II. We fear embarrassing ourselves.

 III. We fear being harmed.

In delivering such a speech, the speaker might begin with this information:

Three major fears interfere with intercultural communication. First, we fear disapproval—from members of our own group as well as from members of the other person's group. Second, we fear embarrassing ourselves, even making fools of ourselves, by saying the wrong thing or appearing insensitive. And third, we may fear being harmed—our stereotypes of the other group may lead us to see its members as dangerous or potentially harmful to us.

Let's look at each of these fears in more detail. We'll be able to see clearly how they influence our own intercultural communication behavior.

Consider, first, the fear of disapproval.

The speaker would then amplify and support this fear of disapproval, giving examples of disapproval seen in his or her own experience, the testimony of communication theorists on the importance of such fear, research findings on the effects that such fear might have on intercultural communication, and so on.

SPEECHES OF DEFINITION

Watch the **Video** "Sweat" at **MyCommunicationLab**

What is leadership? What is a born-again Christian? What is the difference between sociology and psychology? What is a cultural anthropologist? What is safe sex? These are all topics for informative speeches of definition.

In giving a speech of definition, you may focus on defining a term, defining a system or theory, or pinpointing the similarities and/or differences among terms or systems. For example, a speech in which you define a term might cover an endless range of topics: What is a smart card? What is machismo? What is political correctness?

A speech may also define a system or theory: What are the major beliefs in Confucianism? What is expressionism? What is the "play theory" of mass communication?

Some speech topics may involve your defining similar and dissimilar terms or systems: Football and soccer—what's the difference? What do Christians and Muslims have in common? How does Facebook differ from Twitter?

Thesis and Main Points   The thesis in a speech of definition is a statement identifying a term or system and stating your intention to define it or to contrast it with other terms:

> Christianity and Islam have much in common
>
> Text and online dictionaries are similar and different.

You derive the main points from asking questions of your thesis: What do Christianity and Islam have in common? How are text and online dictionaries similar and different?

Support   Once you have each of the main points for your speech of definition, support them with examples, testimony, and the like. For example, one of your main points in the Christianity-Islam example might be that both religions believe in the value of good works. You might then quote from the New Testament and from the Quran to illustrate this belief, you might give examples of noted Christians and Muslims who exemplify this characteristic, or you might cite the testimony of religious leaders who have talked about the importance of good works.

Because this is a speech of definition, you'll want to give special attention to all your definitions, as discussed earlier.

Organization   For a speech of definition, an obvious organizational pattern is the pattern of multiple definitions (see Chapter 11). Alternatively, you might consider using a topical order, in which each main idea is treated equally. In either case, however, proceed from the known to the unknown. Start with what your audience knows and work up to what is new or unfamiliar.

Here is an example of how you might go about constructing a speech of definition. In this particular example, the speaker selects three major types of lying for discussion and arranges these in a topical pattern.

General purpose:	To inform
Specific purpose:	To define lying by explaining the major types of lying
Thesis:	There are three major kinds of lying. (What are the three major kinds of lying?)

   I. Concealment is the process of hiding the truth.

  II. Falsification is the process of presenting false information as if it were true.

 III. Misdirection is the process of acknowledging a feeling but misidentifying its cause.

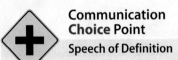

Communication Choice Point

Speech of Definition

You want to give a speech defining the basic tenets of your religion. Most members of your audience, you suspect, have a negative view of your religion; a few may hold neutral or slightly positive views. You want to acknowledge your understanding of these attitudes. *What are some things you can say to help you get this point across? What would you say?*

Speeches at the Academy Awards span the range from absolutely terrible to great. Take a look at "Academy Speeches" at **tcbdevito .blogspot.com**. Select a speech and explain why you think it's one of the best (or one of the worst).

Watch the **Video** "How to Unlock Your Car if You Lock Your Keys Inside" at **MyCommunicationLab**

In delivering such a speech, the speaker might begin with this:

> A lie is a lie is a lie. True? Well, not exactly. Actually, there are a number of different ways we can lie. We can lie by concealing the truth. We can lie by falsification, by presenting false information as if it were true. And we can lie by misdirection, by acknowledging a feeling but misidentifying its cause.
> Let's look at the first type of lie—the lie of concealment. . . .

SPEECHES OF DEMONSTRATION

In a speech of *demonstration*, you show the audience how to do something or how something operates Examples of speeches in which you demonstrate how to do something might include how to give mouth-to-mouth resuscitation, how to drive defensively, how to mix colors, how to ask for a raise, how to burglarproof your house, or how to use Prezi in business meetings. Examples of speeches in which you demonstrate how something operates might include how the body maintains homeostasis, how perception works, how divorce laws work, how e-mail works, how a hurricane develops, or how a heart bypass operation is performed.

Thesis and Main Points　　The thesis for a speech of demonstration identifies what you will show the audience how to do or how something operates:

> E-mail works through a series of electronic connections from one computer to a server to another computer.
>
> You can burglarproof your house in three different ways.
>
> These guidelines will help you get that raise.

You derive the main points by asking a simple *how* or *what* question related to your thesis:

> How do these electronic connections work?
>
> What are the things you can do to burglarproof your house?
>
> What are the guidelines for asking for a raise?

VIEWPOINTS

Description, Definition, Demonstration

Speeches often have three general purposes—description, definition, and demonstration. Can you identify these elements of informative speeches in class lectures, home shopping network shows, cooking shows, or social media sites?

Support　　To support each of the main ideas in a speech of demonstration, you can use a variety of materials. For example, you might show diagrams of houses with different burglarproofing arrangements, demonstrate how various locks work, or show how different security systems are installed.

Presentation aids are especially helpful in speeches of demonstration. Signs in restaurants demonstrating the Heimlich maneuver, for example, demonstrate the sequence of steps with both words and pictures. The combination of verbal and graphic information makes it easy to understand this important process. In a speech on this topic, however, it would be best to use only the pictures as aids so that written words would not distract your audience from your oral explanation.

Organization　　In most cases, a temporal pattern will work best in speeches of demonstration. Demonstrate each step in the sequence in which it is to be performed. In this way, you'll avoid one of the major difficulties in demonstrating a process—backtracking. Don't skip steps even if you think they're familiar to the audience; they may not be. Connect each step to the next with appropriate transitions. For example, in explaining the Heimlich maneuver, you might say, "Now that you have your arms around the choking victim's chest, your next step is to . . ." Assist your listeners by labeling the steps clearly: for example, say, "The first step," "The second step," and so on.

Begin with an overview. It's often helpful when demonstrating to give a broad general picture and then present each step in turn. For example, suppose your talk were about how to prepare a wall for painting. You might begin with a general overview to give your listeners a general idea of the process, saying something like this:

> In preparing the wall for painting, you want to make sure that the wall is smoothly sanded, free of dust, and dry. Sanding a wall isn't like sanding a block of wood. So let's look first at the proper way to sand a wall.

Here is an example of a speech of demonstration using a temporal organization. In this example, the speaker identifies and demonstrates the steps of listening actively.

General purpose:	To inform
Specific purpose:	To demonstrate three techniques of active listening
Thesis:	We can engage in active listening. (How can we engage in active listening?)

   I. Paraphrase the speaker's meaning

  II. Express understanding of the speaker's feelings

 III. Ask questions

In delivering the speech, the speaker might begin with this:

> Active listening is a special kind of listening. It's listening with total involvement, with a concern for the speaker. It's probably the most important type of listening you can engage in. Active listening consists of three steps: paraphrasing the speaker's meaning, expressing understanding of the speaker's feelings, and asking questions.
>
>   Your first step in active listening is to paraphrase the speaker's meaning. . . .

Communication Choice Point

Speech of Demonstration

  You want to demonstrate to your audience how to construct bumper stickers on Facebook. Your audience is probably mixed in terms of their knowledge and use of social networking sites—some know a great deal and others know very little. *What are some things you can do to gain the attention of your entire audience early in your speech? What specifically, might you say?*

Objectives Self-Check

- Can you define and distinguish between informative speeches of description, definition, and demonstration?
- Can you prepare and present such speeches with appropriate theses and main points, supporting materials, and organization?

⚠ Messages in the Media *Wrap Up*

Watch a sampling of cooking shows, and analyze how chefs use the principles for communicating information and the ways in which they integrate verbal with nonverbal description.

Summary of Concepts and Skills

 **Study** and **Review** materials for this chapter are at **MyCommunicationLab**

 **Listen** to the **Audio Chapter Summary** at **MyCommunicationLab**

This chapter covered the nature of the informative speech and the ways you can most effectively communicate information.

Guidelines for Informative Speaking

1. When preparing informative speeches, observe the guidelines for informative speaking: center the information on the audience, limit the amount of information, adjust the level of complexity, stress the information's relevance and usefulness, relate new information to information the audience already knows, and make the information easy to remember.

Supporting Materials

2. To make your ideas clear to your audience, use amplifying materials such as examples, illustrations, and narratives; testimony; numerical data; definitions; and presentation aids.

Presentation Aids

3. Presentation aids include a wide variety of audio and visual means to help you communicate your ideas. Especially important are computer assisted aids such as PowerPoint and Prezi.

Three Types of Informative Speeches

4. Speeches of description focus on or explain an object, person, event, or process.

5. Speeches of definition define important concepts and perhaps similarities and differences between concepts.

6. Speeches of demonstration explain how something operates or how to do something.

Effective public speakers need to master a variety of informing skills. Place a check mark next to those skills you most want to work on.

_____ 1. In my informative speeches I follow the principles of informative speaking: I stress the information's usefulness, relate new information to information the audience already knows, present information through several senses, adjust the level of complexity, limit the amount of information I present, and recognize cultural variations.

_____ 2. For my informative speeches I select a variety of amplifying materials; examples, illustrations, and narratives; testimony; definitions; numerical data; and visual aids.

_____ 3. When developing a speech of information, I follow the suggestions for constructing speeches of description, definition, and demonstration.

Key Word Quiz

The Language of Informative Speaking

Match the terms about informative speaking with their definitions. Record the number of the definition next to the appropriate term.

_____ a. speech of description (276)
_____ b. guide phrases (264)
_____ c. operational definition (267)
_____ d. speech of demonstration (282)
_____ e. example (265)
_____ f. etymology (267)
_____ g. testimony (266)
_____ h. restatement (268)
_____ i. narrative (265)
_____ j. illustration (265)

1. An expert's opinion or a witness's account.
2. A relatively brief specific instance.
3. A means of defining a term by tracing its historical or linguistic development.
4. A speech in which you explain an object, person, event, or process.

5. Repetition in different words for emphasis and clarity.
6. A relatively long illustration presented as an anecdote or story.
7. Repetition of an idea in different words.
8. A speech in which you show listeners how to do something or how something works.

9. A longer and more detailed example.
10. A description of how something would be produced.

These ten terms and additional terms used in this chapter can be found in the glossary.

Answers: a. 4 b. 10 c. 7 d. 8 e. 2 f. 3 g. 1 h. 5 i. 6 j. 9

 Study and **Review** the **Flashcards** at **MyCommunicationLab**

MyCommunicationLab

Throughout this chapter, there are icons in the margin that highlight media content for selected topics. Go to **MyCommunicationLab** for additional information on informative speech. Here you'll find flashcards to help you learn the jargon of communication, videos that illustrate a variety of concepts, additional exercises, and discussions to help you continue your study of preparing information and presenting it to an audience.

14

The Persuasive Speech

Objectives

 Listen to the **Audio Chapter** at **MyCommunicationLab**

After reading this chapter, you should be able to:

❶ Explain the goals of persuasive speaking.

❷ Explain the suggestions for persuasive speaking and apply these in your own persuasive speeches.

❸ Explain the types of and the fallacies of logical, emotional, and credibility appeals.

❹ Define, give examples of, construct, and deliver effective persuasive speeches on questions of fact, value, and policy.

Messages in the Media

Baseball player Derek Jeter, seen here in an advertisement for Ford, is in effect giving a brief persuasive speech on the advantages of buying a particular automobile. All advertisements are persuasive speeches, the subject of this chapter.

You'll no doubt find yourself in a wide variety of situations in which you'll have to persuade others—to urge them to accept or reject a union proposal, redesign a company's website, negotiate a business deal, or donate blood or money or time, to give only a few examples. As with having to provide information, the higher up you go in your organization's hierarchy, the more you'll find yourself having to persuade others.

Goals of Persuasion

Explore the **Concept** "Persuasion" at **MyCommunicationLab**

It's useful to view persuasion along a continuum. Let's say, to take a current example from the news, that you want to give a persuasive speech on same-sex marriage. You might visualize your audience as existing on a continuum ranging from strongly in favor to strongly opposed, as shown in Figure 14.1. Your task is to move your audience along this continuum in the direction of your persuasive purpose, which you can do in any of three ways (corresponding to the goals of persuasion):

- **Strengthen or weaken attitudes, beliefs, or values.** Persuasion often aims to strengthen audience views. For example, religious sermons and public service announcements usually seek to strengthen the existing beliefs of the listeners. At times, however, you may want to weaken the existing beliefs of the audience—to suggest that what they currently believe may not be entirely true.

- **Change attitudes, beliefs, or values.** Sometimes you'll want to change how your audience feels. You may want to change their attitudes toward the college's no-smoking rules, their beliefs about television's influence on viewer violence, or their values about the efficacy of war.

- **Motivate your audience to take action.** Ultimately, your goal is to get people to do something—for example, to vote for one person rather than another, to donate money to a fund for the homeless, or to take a course in personal finance.

If your purpose is to persuade the audience to *oppose* same-sex marriage, then any movement toward the right of the continuum in Figure 14.1 will be successful persuasion; if your purpose is to persuade listeners to *support* same-sex marriage, then any movement toward the left of the continuum will be successful persuasion. Notice, however, that it's quite possible to give a speech in which you attempt to move your listeners in one direction but actually succeed in moving them in the other direction. This "negative persuasion" could occur, for example, if the audience perceives you as dishonest or self-promoting or feels that you presented biased evidence or faulty reasoning.

Strongly in favor of same-sex marriage ____ : ____ : ____ : ____ : ____ : ____ : ____ Strongly opposed to same-sex marriage

FIGURE 14.1

The Persuasion Continuum
Any movement along the continuum would be considered a result of persuasion.

Objectives Self-Check
- Can you explain the three major goals of persuasive speaking (to strengthen or weaken attitudes, to change attitudes, to motivate action)?

Guidelines for Persuasive Speaking

You can become more successful in strengthening or changing attitudes or beliefs and in moving your listeners to action by following these guidelines for persuasive speaking.

FOCUS ON YOUR AUDIENCE

Begin constructing your persuasive speech with knowledge about your specific audience. What will work with one audience will not work with another; appeals to increase salaries for teaching will probably prove effective with teachers but may not do so well with homeowners who feel overtaxed.

If you show your audience that you share with them important attitudes, beliefs, and values, you'll clearly advance your persuasive goal. For example, if you know your listeners are concerned with helping the homeless, you might share your own experiences in working at a homeless shelter. Similarities of cultural, educational, or social background may also help you identify yourself with your audience. But beware of insincere or dishonest attempts at identification: These are likely to backfire and create problems, so avoid even implying similarities between you and your audience that don't exist.

ASK FOR REASONABLE AMOUNTS OF CHANGE

Persuasion is most effective when it strives for small changes and works over a period of time. Put in terms of the continuum of persuasion shown in Figure 14.1, this guideline suggests that you'll be more successful if you ask for small (rather than large) movements. The greater and more important the change you want your audience to make, the more difficult your task will be. The reason is simple: Listeners demand a greater number of reasons and a lot more evidence before making big changes such as changing careers, moving to another state, or committing to an investment strategy.

When you're addressing an audience that is opposed to your position and your goal is to change their attitudes, beliefs, or values, it is especially important that you focus on small changes. Let's say, for example, that your ultimate goal is to get a pro-life group to favor abortion on demand. Obviously, this goal is too great to achieve in one speech. Therefore, you need to strive for small changes. Here, for example, is an excerpt in which the speaker tries to get a pro-life audience to agree that at least some abortions should be legal. Notice that the speaker does not state a pro-choice position but instead focuses on one situation involving abortion and attempts to get the audience to agree that in some cases abortion should be legal.

One of the great lessons I learned in college was that most extreme positions are wrong. Most of the important truths lie somewhere between the extreme opposites. And today I want to talk with you about one of these truths. I want to talk with you about rape and the problems faced by the mother carrying a child conceived in this most violent of all violent crimes.

VIEWPOINTS

Gender and Persuasion

You're planning to give a speech urging more conscientious recycling to two separate audiences. One audience will be composed solely of women and the other of men. Otherwise the audience members will be similar: college-educated professionals about 30 years old. In what ways would you make the two speeches differ? What general principles or assumptions about gender are you making as you differentiate these two speeches?

Take a look at "Communication Strategies: Foot-in-the-Door and Door-in-the-Face" at **tcbdevito** .blogspot.com. How useful do you think these techniques are?

ANTICIPATE SELECTIVE EXPOSURE

As discussed in Chapter 2, perception follows the principle of **selective exposure,** which states that (1) listeners actively seek out information that supports their opinions, beliefs, values, decisions, and behaviors; and (2) listeners actively avoid information that contradicts their existing opinions, beliefs, attitudes, values, decisions, and behaviors.

Let's say you're giving a speech on the need to reduce spending on college athletic programs. If your audience consists largely of people who agree with you, you can lead with your thesis and show them that you're on the same side. Your introduction might go something like this:

Our college athletic program is absorbing money that we can more profitably use for the library and computer labs. Let me explain how the excessive money now going to athletic programs could be better spent in these other areas.

But if you want to persuade an audience that holds attitudes different from those you're advocating, you'll need to anticipate selective exposure and proceed inductively; that is, hold back on your thesis until you've given your evidence and argument, then relate this evidence and argument to your thesis. If you present your listeners with your thesis first, they may tune you out without giving your position a fair hearing.

Communication Choice Point

Countering Selective Exposure

You're planning to give a persuasive speech advocating a position you know your audience is opposed to and you know that selective exposure will be operating. *What are some of the things you might say to counteract this tendency?*

ADAPT TO THE CULTURE OF YOUR AUDIENCE

Cultural distinctions become especially important in persuasion; the appeals you would use to influence one cultural group would not be the same you would use for a different group (Singh & Pereira, 2005; Hofstede, Hofstede, & Minkov, 2010). Here are a few examples of the kinds of cultural adaptations you'll find useful to consider.

- If addressing members of a *collectivist* culture (such as Guatemala, Panama, Venezuela, Pakistan, and China, where the group is more important than the individual), you'll need to emphasize the importance of family, loyalty (to brand names or local organizations), and national identity and pride. On the other hand, if addressing members of individualistic cultures (such as the United States, Canada, New Zealand, Italy, and Sweden, where the individual is more important than the group), you'd emphasize such themes as independence, nonconformity, and uniqueness.

- With audience members from *high-power-distance* cultures (such as Malaysia, the Philippines, Russia, Suriname, and Mexico, where there are great differences in power among groups of the population), references to important and prominent people and to what they believe and advocate will prove effective. In contrast, in a low-power-distance culture (such as Austria, Denmark, Ireland, Norway, and Great Britain, where there is little distance in power between people), these appeals will prove less effective than would, say, references to or testimonials from people much like the people you want to influence.

- With audience members from cultures high in *uncertainty avoidance* (such as Greece, Portugal, Russia, Poland, and Japan, where they're uncomfortable with ambiguity and uncertainty), you would present information from experts (or supported by experts) that would explain very clearly where everyone can go for information and guidance. Because these audiences also value tradition, appeals to the past will prove effective. Audiences low in uncertainty avoidance (from countries such as Singapore, Jamaica, Denmark, Hong Kong, and India) can tolerate more ambiguity, and appeals to the new and different will be more effective.

- With audience members from cultures teaching a *long-term orientation* (such as South Korea, China, Ukraine, Germany, and Russia, where the importance of future rewards is stressed), appeals to delayed rewards (for example, the values of working hard to get a promotion) will prove more effective than they would to short-term oriented cultures (such as Puerto Rico, Ghana, Egypt, Dominican Republic, and Iran, where immediate rewards are valued).

"Mimicry, Persuasion, and Pro-social Behavior" at tcbdevito.blogspot .com discusses the persuasive value of mimicry.

FOLLOW A MOTIVATED SEQUENCE

One time-honored principle of persuasion is the **motivated sequence,** an organizational pattern in which the persuasive speaker must do five things: (1) gain attention, (2) establish a need for a change, (3) advance a proposal to satisfy the need, (4) visualize for the audience what things would be like were they to do what you suggest, and (5) move them to action (German, Gronbeck, Ehninger, & Monroe, 2013).

Let's say you want to persuade your audience to boycott a local restaurant because of its discriminatory policy toward immigrants. You might develop a speech something like this:

Watch the **Video** "Courting Responsibility" at **MyCommunicationLab**

- **Attention:** How would you like it if you earned only 50 percent of what other people earn for the exact same work? . . .

- **Need:** Discrimination infects the entire community; it needs to be stopped. . . .

TABLE 14.1 **The Motivated Sequence as a Persuasive Strategy**
This table summarizes the motivated sequence as used in persuasive speeches.

Step and Purpose	Audience Question Speaker Should Answer	Ideal Audience Response	Cautions to Observe
Attention: Focus listeners' attention on you and your message	Why should I listen? Is this worth my time?	• This sounds interesting. • Tell me more.	Make attention relevant to speech topic.
Need: Demonstrate that there is a problem that affects them	Why do I need to know or do anything?	• Ok, I understand; there's a problem. • Something needs to be done.	Don't overdramatize the need.
Satisfaction: Show listeners how they can satisfy the need	How can I do anything about this?	• I can change things. • I know what I can do. • I'm empowered.	Answer any objections listeners might have to your plan.
Visualization: Show listeners what the situation will be like with the need satisfied.	How would anything be different or improved?	• *Wow!* Things look a lot better this way. • That change was really needed.	Be realistic; don't visualize the situation as perfect .
Action: Urge listeners to act.	What can I do to effect this change?	• Let me sign up. • Here's my contribution. • I'll participate.	Be specific. Ask for small changes and behaviors.

- **Satisfaction:** We *can* force management to stop these policies. . . .
- **Visualization:** If this policy were ended we'd all experience a wealth of rewards. . . .
- **Action:** Boycott the XYZ Restaurant.

Table 14.1 provides a way of looking at the motivated sequence in terms of audience responses and some cautions to observe in using the motivated sequence.

Objectives Self-Check
- Can you explain the suggestions for persuasive speaking (focus on your audience, ask for reasonable amounts of change, anticipate selective exposure, adapt to the culture of your audience, and follow a motivated sequence)?
- Can you apply these principles in your own persuasive speeches?

Supporting Materials

In addition to the supporting materials described in Chapter 13—examples, testimony, numerical data, and definitions, for example—three forms of support are of special importance in persuasive speeches: logical appeals, emotional appeals, and credibility appeals. These forms of support have been an essential part of public speaking for over 2000 years and were known in the rhetoric of Greece and Rome as *logos, pathos,* and *ethos*. Each of these, unfortunately, can also be misused; such fallacies are noted for each of these three forms of support.

LOGICAL APPEALS

When you use logical appeals—when you argue on the basis of **logic** supported by reliable facts and evidence—your listeners are more likely to remain persuaded over time and to resist counterarguments that may come up in the future (Petty & Wegener, 1998). There are three main ways of using logical appeals: (1) specific instances, (2) causes and effects, and (3) sign.

Explore the **Exercise** "Evaluating the Adequacy of Reasoning" at **MyCommunicationLab**

Watch the **Video** "Interstate Commerce Commission" at **MyCommunicationLab**

Reasoning from Specific Instances and Generalizations

When reasoning from **specific instances** (or examples), you examine several specific instances and then conclude something about the whole. This form of reasoning, known as *induction*, is useful when you want to develop a general principle or conclusion but cannot examine the whole. For example, you sample a few communication courses and conclude something about communication courses in general; you visit several Scandinavian cities and conclude something about the whole of Scandinavia. In reasoning from specific instances, be sure to examine a sufficient number of instances. Three general guidelines will help you determine how much is enough.

"In the Interest of streamlining the judicial process, we'll skip the evidence and go directly to sentncing."

@ J.B. Handelsman/Condé Nast Publications/www.cartoonbank.com

- The larger the group you want your conclusion to cover, the greater the number of specific instances you should examine. If you wish to draw conclusions about members of an entire country or culture, you'll have to examine a considerable number of people before drawing even tentative conclusions.

- The greater the diversity of items in the class, the more specific instances you will have to examine. Pieces of pasta in boiling water are all about the same; thus, sampling one usually tells you something about all the others. On the other hand, college courses are probably very different from one another, so valid conclusions about the entire range of college courses will require a much larger sample.

- Beware of anecdotal evidence. Often you'll hear people use anecdotes to "prove" a point: "Women are like that; I have three sisters." "That's the way Japanese managers are; I've seen plenty of them." One reason this type of "evidence" is inadequate is that it overgeneralizes on the basis of too few observations. A second reason is that one person's observations may be unduly clouded by his or her own attitudes and beliefs.

Reasoning from Causes and Effects   When reasoning from **causes and effects,** you may go in either of two directions: (1) You may reason from cause to effect—for example, *Smoking* (the cause) *contributes to lung cancer* (the effect)—or (2) you may reason from effect to cause: for example, *Low reading scores among elementary school children* (the effect) *are due to poverty* (the cause). In order to establish a cause-effect connection, you need to prove that possible causes other than the one you're postulating are not producing the effect. And so you'd need to determine whether causes other than smoking may contribute to lung cancer, or whether factors other than poverty contribute to low reading scores. Usually you won't be able to rule out *all* other factors, but it's important to demonstrate that the factors you are identifying are the main contributors. Scientific studies on the effects of smoking on cancer rates and the effects of poverty on reading scores would enable you to establish these cause-effect relationships.

You'd also want to demonstrate that the causation is in the direction you say it is. If two things occur together, it's often difficult to determine which is the cause and which is the effect. For example, a lack of interpersonal intimacy and a lack of self-confidence often occur in the same person but it's not clear which is the cause and which is the effect or even if a causal relationship exists.

Reasoning from Sign   When reasoning from **sign,** you may draw a conclusion on the basis of the presence of clues or symptoms that frequently occur together. Medical diagnosis is a good example of reasoning by sign. The general procedure is simple: If a sign and an object, event, or condition are frequently paired, the presence of the sign is taken as proof of the presence of the object, event, or condition. For example, fatigue, extreme thirst, and overeating serve as signs of hyperthyroidism, because they frequently accompany the condition.

You'd also want to show that other signs cannot logically point to the same conclusion. In the thyroid example, extreme thirst could be brought on by any number of factors. Similarly, the fatigue and the overeating could be attributed to other causes. Yet, taken together, the three signs seem to point to thyroid problems as a reasonable diagnosis. Generally, the more signs that point toward the conclusion, the more confidence you can have that it's valid.

Listening to the Fallacies of Logical Appeals   At the same time that you'll want to reason logically from specific instances, causes and effects, and sign, you'll want to avoid the fallacies of argument: persuasive tactics that have the feel of real arguments and seem to involve logical reasoning but are actually logically unsound and misleading. These fallacies appear to address the issues but really don't. Here are a few such fallacies that you'll want to avoid as a speaker and recognize as a listener (Lee & Lee 1972, 1995; Pratkanis & Aronson, 1991; Herrick, 2004).

- **Appealing to authority as proof** often takes the form of passing someone off as an authority when the person actually has little authority, expertise, or knowledge in the subject under discussion. Sometimes this fallacy takes the form of "experts say . . ." —without telling you who the experts are. In still another form, it consists of using an authority's opinion instead of or as a substitute for facts and evidence. In listening to appeals to authority, ask yourself: Does the authority offer proof or reliable evidence? If so, then this is not fallacious reasoning. Is this pure opinion? If so, then ask whether this person is a recognized authority in the pertinent field? If yes, then the argument is worth listening to. If not, then the argument may be logically suspect.

- **Appealing to numbers as truth** (in Latin *ad numerum*—literally, *to the numbers*—also referred to as *ad populum*, literally *to the people*), known as the bandwagon fallacy, argues that truth is determined by an idea's popularity. The best example is what was a near-universal belief before Columbus and at the time of Galileo, that the world was flat and that the sun revolved around the earth. A majority does not make a belief true. People (even all people) can be and have been wrong. In listening to argument by the numbers, ask yourself: Do these people have evidence for thinking as they do? If they have, then examine the evidence. If they have good reasons instead, then examine the logic of their reasoning and ask yourself if it makes sense.

- **Sliding down the slippery slope** involves the assumption that one event (i.e., the one the person is arguing against) will lead to another event that everyone agrees would be undesirable. In some cases, the connection between one event and another event is *assumed* to be direct (e.g., smoking pot will lead to smoking crack). In other cases, the connection between the original event and the unpleasant ultimate event is made through a series of linkages (e.g., smoking pot will lead to smoking crack, which will lead to more robberies, which will lead to general lawlessness). In listening to arguments implying a slippery slope, ask yourself: What evidence is there for the influence of one event on another event? How likely is it that the original event will cause the disastrous final event? As the chain of events gets longer, the connection becomes more suspect.

Watch the **Video** *"Tree Hugger"* at **MyCommunicationLab**

EMOTIONAL APPEALS

Emotional appeals, often called **motivational appeals,** are appeals to your listeners' feelings, needs, desires, and wants, and are extremely powerful in persuasion. When you use emotional appeals, you appeal to those forces that motivate people to develop, change, or strengthen attitudes or ways of behaving. Developed more than 30 years ago, one of the most useful analyses of human motives remains Abraham Maslow's fivefold hierarchy of needs, reproduced in Figure 14.2 (Maslow, 1970; Benson & Dundis, 2003; Hanley & Abell, 2002; Kiel, 1999). If you can appeal to the needs the audience wants to fulfill, then you're likely to be persuasive.

- **Physiological needs:** In many parts of the world, and even parts of the United States, people's basic physiological needs are not fully met, and thus are powerful motivating forces. In such circumstances the speaker who promises to meet fundamental physiological needs is the one the people will follow.

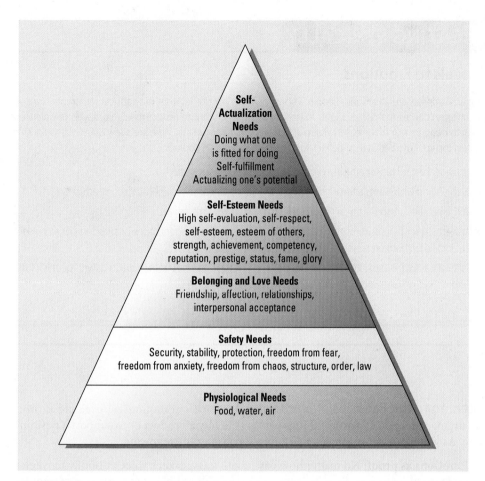

FIGURE 14.2

Maslow's Hierarchy of Needs

From which of these motives would your class members be convinced that campus violence is a real problem? Which might move them to donate their used books to students who can't afford them?

Source: From Abraham Maslow, *Motivation and Personality*, 3rd ed., edited by Robert D. Frager and James Fadiman. Copyright © 1987. Printed and Electronically reproduced by permission of Pearson Education, Inc., Upper Saddle River, New Jersey.

- **Safety needs:** People who do not have their basic safety and freedom-from-fear needs met will be motivated by appeals to security, protection, and freedom from physical and psychological harm. You see this need addressed in advertisements for burglar protection devices for home and car and in political speeches promising greater police protection in schools.

- **Belonging and love needs:** For most people, friendship and love relationships occupy a considerable amount of time and energy, especially, perhaps, among college students. If you can teach your audience how to be loved, how to find a partner, or how to be more popular they'll be not only attentive but also grateful.

- **Self-esteem needs:** We all want to see ourselves as self-confident, worthy, and contributing human beings. Speeches of the "you're the greatest" type, never seem to lack receptive and suggestible audiences. Self-esteem is raised by success (for example, a good grade or a promotion at work) and if your speech can tell people how to succeed in what they set out to do, you'll probably have an active and receptive audience.

- **Self-Actualization Needs:** Each of us has a desire to self-actualize, to become what we feel we're fit for. If you see yourself as a poet, you must write poetry. If you see yourself as a teacher, you must teach. Appeals to self-actualization needs—to people's yearning "to be the best they can be"—encourage listeners to strive for their highest ideals and are welcomed by many audiences.

Communication Choice Point

Fear Appeals

You're a parent of two young teenagers, and you want to dissuade them from engaging in sex. Would it be ethical for you to use fear appeals to get them to avoid sexual relationships? Similarly, would it be ethical to use fear appeals in a public campaign to help prevent sexually transmitted diseases? Would it be ethical to use fear appeals if your motive was to sell SUVs? *What are your choices for dealing with these situations persuasively and ethically?*

COMMUNICATING ETHICALLY

Appeals to Emotions

Ethical Choice Point

You've been asked by the PTA to address the students at your old elementary school on the values of delaying sexual relationships. Would it be ethical to use emotional appeals to scare them so that they'll avoid sexual relationships? Would it be ethical to use the same appeals to get them to avoid associating with teens of other races? What ethical obligations do you have in using emotional appeals in these situations? What would you do?

Emotional appeals are all around. People who want to censor the Internet may appeal to parents' fears about their children's accessing pornographic materials. Those who want to restrict media portrayals of violence may appeal to people's fear of increased violence in their own communities. Here are a few questions to consider as you develop your own ethical guidelines for the use of emotional appeals:

- Is the real estate broker ethical in appealing to your desire for status?
- Is the friend who wants a favor and appeals to your desire for social approval acting ethically?
- Is the car salesperson's appeal to your desire for sexual rewards ethical?
- Is it ethical for parents to use fear appeals to exaggerate the dangers of sex or smoking pot to prevent their children from engaging in these behaviors?
- Is it ethical for parents to use fear appeals to prevent their children from interacting with people of different races or nationalities or affectional orientation?

Take a look at "Credibility Argument" at **tcbdevito.blogspot.com**. What do you think about this type of "argument"?

Listening to the Fallacies of Emotional Appeals   Emotional appeals are all around you, urging you to do all sorts of things—usually to buy a product or to support a position or cause. As you listen to these inevitable appeals, consider the following:

- **Emotions as proof:** No matter how passionate the speaker's voice or bodily movement, no matter how compelling the language, passion does not prove the case a speaker is presenting.
- **Emotional appeals as diversion:** If emotional appeals are being used as a diversion, to the exclusion of argument and evidence, or if you suspect that the speaker seeks to arouse your emotions so you forget that there's no evidence, ask yourself why.
- **Appeals to pity:** Be especially on the lookout for the appeal to pity. This is what logicians call *argumentum ad misericordiam*, as in "I really need your help; I tried to do the work, but I've been having terrible depression and can't concentrate."

CREDIBILITY APPEALS

Your **credibility** is the degree to which your audience regards you as a believable spokesperson. Your credibility is in the minds of your audience; if your listeners see you as competent and knowledgeable, of good character, and charismatic or dynamic, they'll find you credible (i.e., believable). As a result, you'll be more effective in changing their attitudes or in moving them to do something.

What makes a speaker credible will vary from one culture to another. In some cultures people see competence as the most important factor in, say, their choice of a teacher for their preschool children. In other cultures the most important factor might be the goodness or moral tone of the teacher or perhaps the reputation of the teacher's family. At the same time, every culture may define each of the factors of credibility differently. For example, "character" may mean following the rules of a specific religion in some cultures but following your individual conscience in others. The Quran, the Torah, and the New

VIEWPOINTS

The Persuasiveness of Blogs

Visit a few blogs and analyze them in terms of their use of logical versus emotional support. Which mode of support dominates? Or, do different types of blogs use different types of support? How are blogs like persuasive speeches? How are they different?

Testament will be ascribed very different levels of credibility depending on the religious beliefs of the audience. And this will be true even when all three books say essentially the same thing.

Before reading any more about the ways to establish your credibility, you may wish to take the self-test "How Credible Are You?"

TEST YOURSELF

How Credible Are You?

Respond to each of the following phrases to indicate how you think members of your class see you when you deliver a speech. Use the following scale:

5 = definitely true; **4** = probably true; **3** = neither true nor untrue; **2** = probably untrue; and **1** = definitely untrue

The audience/class generally sees me as someone who is:

_____ ❶ knowledgeable

_____ ❷ a thorough researcher

_____ ❸ informed about the subject matter

_____ ❹ fair in the presentation of material (i.e., evidence and argument)

_____ ❺ concerned with the audience's needs

_____ ❻ honest; unlikely to bend the truth

_____ ❼ assertive in personal style

_____ ❽ enthusiastic about the topic and in general

_____ ❾ active rather than passive

"I've never actually stormed a castle, but I've taken a bunch of siege-management courses."

@ Danny Shanahan/Condé Nast Publication/www.cartoonbank.com

HOW DID YOU DO? This test focuses on the three qualities of credibility—competence, character, and charisma—and is based on a large body of research (see McCroskey, 2006; Riggio, 1987). Items 1 to 3 refer to perceived competence: How capable do you seem to the audience? Items 4 to 6 refer to character: Does the audience see you as a good and moral person? Items 7 to 9 refer to charisma: Does the audience see you as dynamic and active? Total scores will range from a high of 45 to a low of 9. If you scored relatively high (around 32 or higher), then you feel your audience sees you as credible. If you scored relatively low (below 27), then you feel your audience sees you as lacking in credibility.

WHAT WILL YOU DO? Think about how you might go about increasing your credibility. What specific steps can you take to change undesirable audience perceptions of your credibility? As you read the discussion that follows, consider how you might strengthen your competence, character, and/or charisma.

Competence   To demonstrate your **competence,** show your listeners that you are knowledgeable and thoroughly familiar with your topic. The more knowledge and expertise the audience attributes to you, the more likely the audience will believe you, just as you are more likely to believe a teacher or doctor if you think he or she is knowledgeable about the subject at hand.

One way to demonstrate your competence is simply to tell listeners about it. Let the audience know of any special experience or training that qualifies you to speak on your topic. Another way is to cite a variety of research sources. Make it clear to your audience that you've thoroughly researched your topic. Do this by mentioning some of the books you've read, the people you've interviewed, and/or the articles you've consulted.

Communication Choice Point

Establishing Credibility

You're planning a speech against free agency in professional sports. The problem is that you're a woman and you suspect that the men in your audience will not perceive you as credible, despite your knowing more about professional sports than any other person in the room. *What are some options you have to establishing your credibility? What are some of the things you might say?*

Video Choice Point
Planning for Success

Margo has been volunteering as a Big Sister for the past year and has made excellent progress with her mentee. The organization is planning a service day for at-risk high school girls on the importance of planning for college, and Margo has been asked to give a speech to the entire group of volunteers and mentees. Because she has only dealt with this topic on a one-to-one basis, Margo is concerned about how to be persuasive while speaking to a fairly large group. She considers the topics covered in this chapter as she contemplates her communication choices.

Watch the **video** "Planning for Success" at **MyCommunicationLab.com**

Explore the **Exercise** "Comparative Credibility Judgments" at **MyCommunicationLab**

Watch the **Video** "The Special Olympics" at **MyCommunicationLab**

Character   An audience will judge your credibility in terms of what they perceive is your **character**—whether they see you as someone who is honest and whom they can trust. One way to establish your moral character is to stress fairness. For example, stress that you've examined both sides of the issue (if indeed you have). Also, make it clear to the audience that you're interested in their welfare rather than seeking self-gain. If the audience feels that you're "out for yourself," they'll justifiably question your credibility. Tell your audience how the new legislation will reduce *their* taxes, how recycling will improve *their* community, how a knowledge of sexual harassment will make *their* workplace more comfortable.

Charisma   Another quality that establishes credibility is **charisma,** a combination of your personality and dynamism as seen by the audience. An audience will perceive you as credible if they like you and see you as friendly and pleasant rather than aloof and reserved. Similarly, audiences favor the dynamic speaker over the hesitant, nonassertive speaker.

One way to stress charisma is to demonstrate a positive outlook. Show the audience that you have a positive orientation to the public speaking situation and to the entire speaker–audience encounter. Stress your pleasure at addressing the audience. Stress hope rather than despair, happiness rather than sadness. Demonstrate enthusiasm. Be emphatic. Use language that's vivid and concrete rather than colorless and vague. Use gestures that are clear and decisive rather than random and hesitant. Demonstrate a firm commitment to the position you're advocating.

Listening to the Fallacies of Credibility Appeals and Character Attacks

As with logical or emotional appeals, become conscious of fallacious strategies that focus on attacking the person. Be alert for the following fallacies in the speeches of others, and eliminate them from your own reasoning:

- **Personal interest attacks** may attempt to disqualify someone from having a legitimate point of view because he or she isn't directly affected by an issue or proposal or doesn't have firsthand knowledge; for example, a speaker might dismiss an argument on abortion merely because it was made by a man. This type of fallacy may also attempt to disqualify someone because he or she will benefit in some way from a proposal. For example, arguing that someone is rich, middle class, or poor and thus will benefit greatly from a proposed tax cut does not mean that the argument for the tax cut is invalid. The legitimacy of an argument can be judged only on the basis of the evidence and reasoning presented.

- **Character attacks,** often referred to as *ad hominem* arguments, involve accusing another person (usually an opponent) of some wrongdoing or of some character flaw. The purpose is to discredit the person or to divert attention from the issue under discussion. Arguments such as "How can we support a candidate who has smoked pot [or avoided the military]?" or "Do you want to believe someone who has been unfaithful on more than one occasion?" are often heard in political discussions but probably have little to do with the logic of the argument.

- **Name-calling** occurs when the speaker gives an idea, a group of people, or a political philosophy a bad name ("bigoted," "soft on terrorism,") to try to get listeners to condemn an idea without analyzing the argument and evidence. The opposite of name-calling is the use of "glittering generalities," in which the speaker tries to make you accept some idea by associating it with things you value highly ("democracy," "free speech," "academic freedom"). By using these "virtue words," the speaker tries to get you to ignore the evidence and simply approve of the idea.

Objectives Self-Check
- Can you explain the types of logical, emotional, and credibility appeals in persuasion?
- Can you effectively use these supporting materials and at the same time avoid the fallacies for each type of proof?
- Can you identify the common logical, emotional, and credibility fallacies?

Communication Choice Point

Introducing Credibility
You are going to speak to an audience about Internet censorship, and you've been asked to provide a brief bio note (about one minute in length or about 150 words) about yourself for another speaker to use to introduce you. *What are some of the things you might want to include to establish your competence, character, and charisma? What would you say?*

Explore the **Exercise** "The Persuasive Speech on Questions of Fact, Value, and Policy" at **MyCommunicationLab**

For a really excellent special occasion speech (this one a commencement address), see the one given by Steve Jobs at Stanford University at tcbdevito.blogspot.com.

Three Types of Persuasive Speeches

Here we examine persuasive speeches on questions of fact, value, and policy and look at how you can develop appropriate theses and main points, supporting materials, and organizational pattern for such speeches. In addition see the accompanying PSSA: Special Occasion Speeches (Largely Persuasive) on page 298.

PERSUASIVE SPEECHES ON QUESTIONS OF FACT

Questions of fact concern what is or is not true, what does or does not exist, what did or did not happen. Some questions of fact are easily answered. These include many academic questions you're familiar with: Who was Nostradamus? When was the first satellite launched? Questions of fact also include more mundane questions: What's on television? What's Jenny's e-mail address? You can easily find answers to these questions by finding the information online or in a book or asking someone who knows the answer.

The questions of fact that persuasive speeches deal with are a bit different. Although these questions also have answers, the answers are not that easy to find and in fact may never be found. The questions concern controversial issues for which different people have different answers. Daily news reports abound in questions of fact. For example, on May 18, 2012, Google News dealt with questions of fact that included issues such as these: Is Facebook worth $38 a share? Who is at fault in the Trayvon Martin killing? Is John Edwards guilty of campaign fraud? Does sugar make you stupid? Is J. P. Morgan's chief guilty of fraud? Is obesity a risk factor in liver disease?

Thesis and Main Points   For a persuasive speech on a question of fact, you'll formulate a thesis based on a factual statement:

- This company has a glass ceiling for women.
- The plaintiff was slandered [or libeled or defamed].
- The death was a case of physician-assisted suicide.
- Gay men and lesbians make competent military personnel.
- Television violence leads to violent behavior in viewers.

If you were preparing a persuasive speech on, say, the first example given above, you might phrase your thesis as "This company discriminates against women." Whether or not the company does discriminate is a question of fact; clearly the company either does or does

VIEWPOINTS

Persuasive Messages at Work
Consider the places you've worked or observed in some way. In what ways was persuasion used? What form did the persuasive message take? Who used it? What effect did the messages have?

PUBLIC SPEAKING SAMPLE ASSISTANT

Special Occasion Speeches *Largely Persuasive*

Sometimes a special occasion presents an opportunity for a speaker to give a speech with a persuasive message. Here are three types of special occasion speeches, with ideas to help you make them effective. For specific examples of these and other types of special occasion speeches, search YouTube or any search engine's videos. Chapter-length coverage of the "special occasion speech" may be found at **MyCommunicationLab**

The Speech to Secure Goodwill

The *goodwill speech* is part information and part persuasion. On the surface, the speech informs the audience about a product, company, profession, institution, or person. Beneath this surface, however, lies a more persuasive purpose: to heighten the image of a person, product, or company—to create a more positive attitude toward this person or thing. Many speeches of goodwill have a further persuasive purpose: to get the audience ultimately to change their behavior toward the person, product, or company.

A special type of goodwill speech is the speech of self-justification, in which the speaker seeks to justify his or her actions to the audience. In securing goodwill, whether for another person or for yourself, consider the following suggestions:

- Demonstrate the contributions that deserve goodwill.
- Establish credibility.
- Don't be obvious. The effective goodwill speech looks, on the surface, very much like an objective informative speech. It will not appear to ask for goodwill, except on close analysis.

The Commencement Speech

The *commencement speech* is designed to congratulate and inspire recent graduates and is often intended to mark the transition from school to the next stage in life. When giving a commencement speech, consider the following:

- Organize the speech in a temporal pattern, beginning with the past, commenting on the present, and projecting into the future.
- Do your research. Learn something about the school, the student body, the goals and ambitions of the graduates, and integrate these into your speech.
- Be brief. Recognize that your audience has other things on their minds.
- Congratulate the graduates, parents, and instructors.
- Offer the graduates some kind of motivational message, some guidance.
- Offer your own good wishes to the graduates.

The Speech of Inspiration

A great many special occasion speeches are designed to inspire, to raise the spirits of an audience. Many religious speeches are of this type. Similarly, speeches that corporate leaders give to stockholders when introducing a new product or a new CEO, for example, would be designed to inspire investors. In speaking to inspire, follow these guidelines:

- Demonstrate your oneness with the audience. Try to show in some way that you and your listeners have significant similarities.
- Demonstrate your own intense involvement, the kind of intensity you want your audience to show.
- Stress emotional appeals. Inspiring an audience has to do more with emotions than with logic.
- Stress the positive—especially at the end of your speech, which should conclude on a positive note. Inspirational speeches are always positive.

SKILL DEVELOPMENT EXPERIENCE

Developing Persuasive Speeches

Select one of the following thesis statements and (1) identify the type of persuasive speech it is—fact, value, or policy; (2) from this thesis, generate two, three, or four main points for a persuasive speech; (3) identify a few forms of supporting material that might prove useful; and (4) select a suitable organizational pattern.

1. Condoms should be distributed to students in junior and senior high school.
2. Sports involving cruelty to animals, such as bullfighting, cockfighting, and foxhunting, should be universally condemned and declared illegal.
3. All states should recognize same-sex marriage.

Practicing the art of persuasion will prove useful in a wide variety of communication situations.

not discriminate. Whether you can prove either option, however, is another issue and the subject of your speech.

Once you've formulated your thesis, you can generate your main points by asking the simple question "How do you know this?" or "Why would you believe this is true [or factual]?" The answers to one of these questions will enable you to develop your main points. The bare bones of your speech might then look something like this:

General purpose:	To persuade
Specific purpose:	To persuade my listeners that this company discriminates against women
Thesis:	This company discriminates against women. (How can we tell that this company discriminates against women?)

   I. Women earn less than men.

   II. Women are hired less often than men.

   III. Women occupy fewer managerial positions than men.

Make sure that you clearly connect your main points to your thesis in your introduction, when introducing each of the points, and again in your summary. Don't allow the audience to forget that when women earn lower salaries than men, it directly supports the thesis that this company discriminates against women.

Support   Once you've identified your main points you can then use the supporting materials you've collected to flesh out and develop the main points. Taking the first point, you might develop it something like this:

   I. Women earn less than men.

      A. Over the past five years, the average salary for editorial assistants was $6,000 less for women than it was for men.

      B. Over the past five years, the entry-level salaries for women averaged $4,500 less than the entry-level salaries for men.

      C. Over the past five years, the bonuses earned by women were 20 percent below the bonuses earned by men.

In a speech on questions of fact, you'd want to emphasize logical support. Facts are your best support. The more facts you have, the more persuasive you'll be in dealing with questions of fact. For example, the more evidence you can find that women earn less than men, the more convincing you will be in proving that women do in fact earn less and, ultimately, that women are discriminated against.

Use the most recent materials possible. The more recent your materials, the more relevant they will be to the present time and the more persuasive they're likely to be. Note that, in this example, if you were to say that in 1980 women earned on average $13,000 less than men, it would be meaningless in proving that the company discriminates against women *now*.

SKILL DEVELOPMENT EXPERIENCE

Preparing a Persuasive Speech

Discussing rough outlines of speeches in small groups is an excellent way to see your speech from the perspective of your audience.

Consult the online dictionary of topics at **MyCommunicationLab** for suggestions for persuasive speech topics. Select a topic and then create a rough outline in which you follow these guidelines:

1. Identify a specific purpose and thesis.
2. Analyze your classroom audience and note adaptations you'd make.
3. Generate at least two main points with persuasive supporting materials.
4. Construct a conclusion and an introduction.

Organization   Speeches on questions of fact fit clearly into a topical organizational pattern, in which each reason for your thesis is given approximately equal weight. Notice, for example, that the outline for this "discrimination" example uses a topical order: All three facts (women earn less, women are hired less often, women occupy fewer managerial positions) pointing to discrimination are treated as equal main points (I, II, and III).

PERSUASIVE SPEECHES ON QUESTIONS OF VALUE

Questions of value concern what people consider good or bad, moral or immoral, just or unjust. The May 18, 2012, issue of Bing News dealt with questions of value such as these: What is the value of Greece remaining in the European Union? What value do the UN monitors in Syria serve? What's the economic value of Hewlett-Packard's planned layoffs? What's the relative value of Windows Phone and the iPhone? What's the value of an at-home HIV test? How valuable is breastfeeding?

Speeches on questions of value will usually seek to strengthen audiences' existing attitudes, beliefs, or values. This is true of much religious and political speaking: People who listen to religious speeches, for example, usually are already believers and are willing to listen; these speeches strive to strengthen the beliefs and values the people already hold. Speeches that seek to change audience values are much more difficult to construct, because most people resist change. When you try to get people to change their values or beliefs, you're fighting an uphill (though not necessarily impossible) battle.

Be sure that you define clearly the specific value on which you're focusing. For example, let's say that you're developing a speech to persuade high school students to attend college. You want to stress that college is of value, but what type of value do you focus on? The financial value (e.g., that college graduates earn more money than high school graduates)? The social value (e.g., that college is a lot of fun and a great place to make friends)? The intellectual value (e.g., that college will broaden your view of the world and make you a more critical and creative thinker)? Once you clarify the type of value on which you'll focus, you'll find it easier to develop the relevant points. You'll also find it easier to locate appropriate supporting materials.

Communication Choice Point

Persuasive Appeals

You want to give a speech urging your listeners (students and instructors at your college) to vote in favor of establishing a hate speech code at the college. *What are some persuasive appeals you might use to get students to vote for a hate speech code?*

Thesis and Main Points   Theses devoted to questions of value might look something like this:

- The death penalty is unjustifiable.
- Bullfighting is inhumane.
- Discrimination on the basis of affectional orientation is wrong.
- Human cloning is morally justified.
- College athletics minimize the importance of academics.

As with speeches on questions of fact, you can generate the main points for a speech on a question of value by asking a strategic question of your thesis, such as "Why is this good?" or "Why is this immoral?" For example, you can take the first thesis given above and ask, "Why is the death penalty unjustifiable?" The answers to this question will give you the speech's main points. The body of your speech might then look something like this:

General purpose: To persuade

Specific purpose: To persuade my listeners that the death penalty is unjustifiable

Thesis: The death penalty is unjustifiable. (Why is the death penalty unjustifiable?)

    I. The criminal justice system can make mistakes.

    II. The death penalty constitutes cruel and unusual punishment.

    III. No one has the moral right to take another's life.

Support   Once you've identified your main points, you can then use the supporting materials you've collected to develop the main points. For example, to show that mistakes have been made (your first main point), you might itemize three or four high-profile cases in which people were put to death and later, through DNA, found to have been innocent.

At times, and with certain topics, it may be useful to identify the standards you would use to judge something moral, justified, fair, or good. For example, in the "bullfighting is inhumane" speech, you might devote your first main point to defining when an action can be considered inhumane. In this case, your main points and subpoints might look like this:

    I. An inhumane act has two qualities.

        A. It is cruel and painful.

        B. It serves no human necessity.

    II. Bullfighting is inhumane.

        A. It is cruel and painful.

        B. It serves no necessary function.

Notice that in the example of capital punishment the speaker aims to strengthen or change the listeners' beliefs about the death penalty. The speaker is not asking the audience to do anything about capital punishment, but merely to believe that it's not justified. However, you might also follow up your goal of changing their beliefs by persuading them to take some action—for example, to support an anti–death-penalty politician, to vote for or against a particular proposition, or to join an organization fighting against the death penalty.

Organization   Like speeches on questions of fact, speeches on questions of value often lend themselves to topical organization. For example, the speech on capital punishment outlined earlier uses a topical order. But within this topical order there is another level of organization that begins with those items on which there is least disagreement or opposition and moves on to the items that your listeners are likely to see very differently. It's likely that even those in favor of the death penalty would agree that mistakes can be made; in fact, they probably would be willing to accept evidence that mistakes have been made, especially if you cite reliable statistical evidence and expert testimony. By starting with this issue, you secure initial agreement and can use that as a basis for approaching aspects on which you and the audience are more likely to disagree.

Communication Choice Point

Value Strategies
You want to give a persuasive speech on a question of value, specifically arguing that violent computer games should be banned for children under 16 years of age. You know your audience of software developers will be against your position and so you wonder how you might win them over to your side. *What are some of your options for stimulating positive responses in your listeners?*

PUBLIC SPEAKING SAMPLE ASSISTANT

An Excellent Persuasive Speech

This speech, which won first place in the 2011 Interstate Oratorical Association contest, was delivered by Patrick Martin from the University of Wisconsin Eau Claire; the speaker was coached by Karen Morris. The speech is reprinted from *Winning Orations of the Interstate Oratorical Association 2011*. Mankato, MN: Interstate Oratorical Association.

　　　This is a truly excellent example of a persuasive speech. The annotations will help guide your reading and the questions will help guide your analysis. Some of the key terms used throughout the section on public speaking appear in the annotations in boldface.

The Energy Cure that Kills: Hydraulic Fracturing for Natural Gas

Patrick Martin

SPEECH

ANNOTATIONS AND QUESTIONS

The **title** makes the subject and the position taken very clear to the audience. It tells you the **thesis** of the speech: Hydraulic fracturing kills. After reading the entire speech, what other choices would you suggest for a title if this speech were to be given to your class? In what other ways does the speaker identify his thesis? The **general purpose** is "to persuade" and the more **specific purpose**—as you'll see when you read the speech—is to persuade the audience to support the FRAC act.

First came a report out of Alabama. The McMillan family found their tap water black, oily, and bubbling. Soon after came Texas. Three ranchers said their water smelled foul, and two days later, seven of their animals were dead. Ohio. A gas buildup in the Payne family's basement well caused the house to explode, and testing found similar levels in the wells of 22 neighbors. Even now, across the country, folks are realizing that with just a match, they can light their tap water on fire. As reports mount, a shocking revelation is taking shape. For years, the drinking water of tens of millions of Americans has been systematically poisoned with chemicals like arsenic, formaldehyde, and sulfuric acid. But far from acts of terrorism, this sabotage is not only allowed by our government, but subsidized. It's called hydraulic fracturing, a drilling technique which harnesses incredible amounts of natural gas, but at the cost of destroying our most precious resource, our drinking water. Tragically, to a federal government desperate for domestic energy, and awash in industry money, this price has been deemed acceptable. The *New York Times* of April 1, 2011, notes the Obama administration is calling fracturing the key to our energy future.

The **introduction** contains extremely dramatic examples and makes listeners feel that wherever they are, this problem will affect them. These examples gain the attention of the listeners and make the topic relevant to them. In what other ways might this speech have been introduced?

　　　In order to understand the fundamental threat fracturing poses, we must first understand the dangers at each step of the process, second, expose the corrupt legal maneuvering which protects it, and finally, champion the simple solution that will save American lives. For too long, hydraulic fracturing has made a threat out of something we should never have to fear, our next glass of water.

The **orientation** is especially clear; you know that the major parts of the speech are (1) the dangers, (2) the corrupt maneuvering, and (3) the solution. This is clearly a **problem-solution organizational pattern.** The speaker identifies two related problems—the dangers and the corruption—and the solution (which the speaker holds back until he's convinced that the audience can appreciate the dangers). Would you have identified the solution here?

　　　Thanks to hydraulic fracturing, natural gas has become one of our nation's fastest growing industries. The Department of Energy predicts that America's 450,000 wells will, this year alone, pump over 100 billion gallons of toxins into U.S. soil. To understand the scope of this destruction, we must examine its two major steps, the drilling itself, and the waste water disposal. *ProPublica* of December 31, 2009, reports the first step on hydraulic fracturing is to pump up to seven million gallons of toxic chemicals at high pressure into the ground. These fluids at such pressure crack the subterranean rock and free the gases to flow to the surface. However, there are countless problems with this. Often, those cracks can extend miles into the groundwater supplies, allowing millions of gallons of toxic sludge and misdirected gas to flow right

Here the speaker elaborates on the first problem—the dangers posed by hydraulic fracturing to our own drinking water and to the air we breathe and that this presents "significant risks for cancer." Has what the speaker said convinced you that there's a problem? If not, what else might the speaker have said that would have convinced you?

into the source of our drinking water. Or worse, the companies drill right into the ground water itself, and pump the chemicals directly in. Alarming, considering that a leaked gas industry study admitted that drinking contaminated water posed "significant risks for cancer." The gas industry's mouthpiece, NaturalGas.org (copyright 2010) contends that any harm posed in the first step is more than countered in the second, which they euphemistically term "wastewater disposal." The industry will tell you that the vast majority of the fluid is simply recovered and treated. In reality, this is a joke. Only about half of the fluid ever leaves the ground, and the "treatment" follows one of two options. First option, and I'm not kidding, the toxic mix is put into a massive open pit and sprayed into the air, hoping the sun evaporates it, a procedure which conveniently coincided with a tripling in the number of children with severe asthma in Texas, and left one county in Wyoming with worse air quality than Los Angeles. Or second option, it's dumped into rivers. The *Wall Street Journal* of March 13, 2011, reports that last year, in Pennsylvania alone, over 3.6 million gallons of toxic fluids were dumped into rivers, rivers supplying drinking water to 27 million Americans. Hydraulic fracturing in the smallest amount is a public health nightmare. What our waters face today is nothing less than a torrent of these poisons.

So, how has hydraulic fracturing so successfully dodged the Clean Air Act, Clean Water Act, and the EPA?

The answer lies in two bits of legal maneuvering which shield the industry. The Halliburton Loophole, and the abuse of Proprietary Secrets. The 2009 documentary *Gasland* describes how, beginning in 2005, Vice-President Dick Cheney began a series of meetings with 40 of the top drilling companies. The product of these meetings was the Halliburton Loophole (named after the beneficiary at whom Cheney had just been CEO). The loophole exempted hydraulic fracturing from all federal regulation, with no stated reason for doing so. This theoretically shifts authority to states. But according to the previously cited *ProPublica* of the 31 major drilling states, only four have any regulation on the books. Of those four, West Virginia has 17 inspectors for over 55,000 wells, New York State allowed a 700% increase in drilling while cutting regulators 20%, and Texas has completely given up, promising a 72-hour turnaround on drilling applications. With the federal government willfully looking the other way, and the states simply unable to keep up, the only option left to families is to take legal action themselves, which brings us to our second legal maneuver, the abuse of proprietary secrets. When a gas driller involves proprietary secrets, it means they are not required to reveal what's in their toxic sludge, like a restaurant with a secret sauce. Even when scientists have found lethal chemicals in a family's water, the companies respond "we don't use that one," and that's the end of the legal story. The *Christian Science Monitor* of July 22, 2010, reports that these families can't leave; their property is worthless. Their only clean water is trucked in by the drilling company, and not until they sign a gag order swearing they'll never tell a soul what happened to their family. Our government turns its back on devastated families, and assures them the drilling company knows best.

It is clear the situation is desperate.

But while the mounting evidence of environmental catastrophe may seem, well, insurmountable, there is a simple solution at hand that will save American lives: the 2011 Fracturing Responsibility and Awareness of Chemicals Act. We'll explore the incredible reach of this paragraph-long legislation by looking at its two clauses, and how we can help. First clause: Regulated activities "shall include the underground injection of fluids . . . pursuant to hydraulic fracturing." This closes the Halliburton Loophole and puts fracturing back where it should have been all along, under federal supervision. No longer will we have to wonder if a well has seen an inspection in the last ten years. No longer will gas drillers be able to run circles around state regulators. Second clause: "Any person using hydraulic fracturing [shall] disclose to the

State . . . and public . . . the chemical constituents used in the fracturing process." Gas companies will finally be forced to disclose what they dump into our soil by the billions of gallons a year. Devastated families will finally be able to bring legal action against the companies which have ignored their cries. Tragically, according to the websites of the House and Senate sponsors Diane DeGette and Robert Casey, the previous three FRAC Acts were all killed by industry lobbying in committee. It is more critical now than ever before we lend our support. After the round, I'll have a handout available with a link to an online petition I created that you can sign in support of the FRAC Act.

I further urge any of you who visit the petition to use the built-in feature to share it with your friends on Facebook and Twitter. Further, with just one click, a letter with your signature will be sent to every member of the House and Senate Energy Committee, as well as all party leadership. Beyond this, we need to get loud. Tell your family, your friends, tell your co-workers about the Faustian bargain our government has made for cheap gas. Students, send editorials to local and national papers and send letters to major news programs, like I've done. The FRAC Act has given Congress every tool for justice; all they need is the courage to use them. And we can lend it. We're the nation that put a man on the moon, signed the Civil Rights Act, and for over 200 years has stood as the most successful democracy in human history. Getting our government to realize we can hit that light switch without poisoning our neighbor should not be this hard.

COMTEX News of September 21, 2010, reports fracturing is set to double in the next five years. We can't wait any longer. Beginning today, we stand together with one voice for our health, with one voice of our future, with one voice for our next glass of water.

Note that the speaker asks the audience to do something—not a requirement in a persuasive speech but definitely an option—in this case, sign a petition in support of the FRAC Act and to disseminate it through social media. Here the speaker goes beyond his immediate audience and attempts to also reach his remote audience. What else might the speaker have asked the audience to do?

Here the speaker makes a further **appeal to action** by stressing the importance of this issue. How successful was the speaker is gaining your agreement? If you were a member of the audience, would you sign the petition? Would you share it on Facebook or Twitter?

With the last phrase—"our next glass of water"—the speaker clearly signals that the speech is finished and achieves **closure**. How would you have ended this speech?

Watch the **Video**
"Same Sex Marriage" at
MyCommunicationLab

VIEWPOINTS

Fact, Value, and Policy in the News

Examine one issue of an online news page for the city in which you live. What are the questions of fact, value, and policy that this news outlet features? Now, examine an online news page from a foreign country—Google will translate for you—for the same types of questions? Do they differ? If so, in what ways?

PERSUASIVE SPEECHES ON QUESTIONS OF POLICY

When you move beyond focusing on values to urging your audience to do something about an issue, you've broached a question of policy. For example, in a speech designed to convince your listeners that bullfighting is inhumane, you'd be focusing on a question of value. But, if you were to urge that bullfighting should therefore be declared illegal, you'd be focusing on a question of policy. Items that focused on questions of policy in the May 18, 2012, issue of Yahoo News included the following: Should Greece remain in the European Union? What should be the nation's policy on same-sex marriage? What should be the policy on negative campaign ads? Should municipalities tax colleges and universities? What action should New York take to combat the mosquito invasion?

Questions of policy concern what should be done, what procedures should be adopted, what laws should be changed—in short, what policy should be followed. In some speeches you may want to defend a specific policy; in others you may wish to argue that a current policy should be discontinued.

Thesis and Main Points   Persuasive speeches frequently revolve around questions of policy and may use theses such as the following:

- Smoking in municipal parks should be banned.
- Facebook's privacy settings should be changed.
- Colleges should not allow guns on campus.
- Abortion should be available on demand.
- Medical marijuana should be legalized.

As you can tell from these examples, questions of policy almost invariably involve questions of values. For example, the argument that hate speech should be banned at colleges is based on the value judgment that hate speech is wrong. To argue for a zero tolerance policy on guns in schools implies that you think it's wrong for students or faculty to carry guns to school.

You can develop your main points on a question of policy by asking a strategic question of your thesis. With policy issues, the question will be "Why should this policy be adopted?" or "Why should this policy be discontinued?" or "Why is this policy better than what we now have?" Taking our first example, we might ask, "Why should smoking be banned from municipal parks?" From the answers to this question, you would develop your main points, which might look something like this:

I. Smoking creates dangers for park land.

II. Smoking creates health hazards for park users.

III. Smoking creates litter problems.

Support   Once you've identified your main points, you're ready to incorporate the supporting materials you've collected to develop these points. For example, you would further develop each main point with supporting materials that would convince your audience that smoking should be banned from municipal parks. Taking the first main point as an illustration, you might develop it something like this:

I. Smoking creates dangers for park land.

    A. The forest fire in Montana was caused by a cigarette.

    B. Japanese cherry trees in Wisconsin were destroyed by careless smokers.

    C. Animals in numerous parks lost their homes.

In some speeches on questions of policy, you might simply want your listeners to agree that the policy you're advocating is a good one. In other cases you might want them to do something about the policy—to vote for a particular candidate, to take vitamin C, to write to their elected officials, to participate in a walkathon, to wear an AIDS awareness ribbon, or to vote against smoking in parks in the upcoming referendum.

Organization   Speeches on questions of policy may be organized in a variety of ways. For example, if you're comparing two policies, consider the comparison-and-contrast method. If the existing policy is doing harm, consider using a cause-to-effect pattern. If your proposed policy is designed to solve a problem, consider the problem-solution pattern. In the smoking in parks example, a simple topical pattern was used. Table 14.2 presents a brief summary of these questions of fact, value, and policy.

Communication Choice Point

Changing Behavior
As the supervisor of a team of 6 co-workers, you've just been informed that computer parts are being stolen by one or more of the workers. You've been assigned the task of stopping the theft, and you decide to tackle this in your weekly meeting with the workers and to apply the principles of persuasion. *What types of appeals (logical, emotional, or ethical) would you use? What are some of the things you might say?*

Communication Choice Point

Selecting Arguments
You want to prepare a persuasive speech on a question of policy, arguing that owners of psychic services should be prosecuted for fraud. *What are some of your options for persuading your audience to accept your thesis?*

TABLE 14.2 Questions of Fact, Value, and Policy

This table summarizes the three types of persuasive speeches in terms of their purposes, examples of the types of questions such speeches deal with, and the questions the audience is likely to ask and that you will likely want to have answers for somewhere in your speech.

Questions and Purposes	Examples	Questions Audience May Want Answered
Questions of Fact To persuade listeners that something is true or false	• Higgins is guilty (not guilty). • What he did was criminal (legal). • The stock market will go much higher (much lower).	• Is this the most likely interpretation of the issue? • Are other, more likely, explanations possible? • How do we know that this is true or that this is false?
Questions of Value To persuade listeners in the value of something, that something is good, moral, or just	• Higgins deserves the chair (to go free). • Universal health care is essential (not essential). • The war is just (unjust)	• Why is this good or just or the right thing to do? Are there alternatives that would be more just or fairer?
Questions of Policy To persuade listeners that this is the policy to adopt or not adopt	• The verdict must be guilty (not guilty). • Plan B needs to be enacted (discarded). • The war needs to be continued (discontinued).	• Might there be better courses of action to follow? • Are there downsides to this course of action?

Objectives Self-Check
- Can you define and give examples of persuasive speeches of fact, value, and policy?
- Can you prepare and present such speeches with appropriate theses and main points, supporting materials, and organization?

 Messages in the Media *Wrap Up*

As you watch advertisements, notice the persuasive techniques being used. How do they establish credibility? How do they appeal to your emotions? How do they present evidence and argument to persuade you to change toothpastes or to buy the new designer tote?

 Summary of Concepts and Skills

Study and **Review** materials for this chapter are at **MyCommunicationLab**

 Listen to the **Audio Chapter Summary** at **MyCommunicationLab**

This chapter looked at the persuasive speech, first covering guidelines and types of supporting materials for persuasion and then discussing three main types of persuasive speeches.

Goals of Persuasion

1. Persuasion has three main goals: (1) to strengthen or weaken attitudes, beliefs, or values, (2) to change attitudes, beliefs, or values, and (3) to motivate to action.

Guidelines for Persuasive Speaking

2. Among the important guidelines for persuasive speaking are (1) focus on your audience, (2) ask for reasonable amounts of change, (3) anticipate selective exposure, (4) adapt to the culture of your audience, and (5) follow a motivated sequence.

Supporting Materials

3. Three major types of support have special importance in speeches of persuasion: logical appeals, emotional appeals, and credibility appeals.

Three Types of Persuasive Speeches

4. Persuasive speeches on questions of fact focus on what is or is not true.

5. Persuasive speeches on questions of value focus on issues of good and bad, justice and injustice.

6. Persuasive speeches on questions of policy focus on what should or should not be done, what procedures should or should not be adopted.

To be an effective public speaker, you need to master a variety of persuading skills. Place a check mark next to those skills you want to work on most.

_____ 1. In my persuasive speeches I apply (where relevant) the principles of persuasion: selective exposure, amounts of change, and identification.

_____ 2. In my persuasive speeches I critically analyze reasoning from specific instances to generalizations, causes and effects, and sign.

_____ 3. When listening to persuasive attempts, I detect fallacies such as personal attacks, appeals to authority, appeal to numbers, and the slippery slope.

_____ 4. To motivate my audience I use motivational appeals—for example, appeals to desires for power, control, and influence; self-esteem and approval; safety; achievement; and financial gain.

_____ 5. In my speeches I seek to establish my credibility by displaying competence, high moral character, and dynamism, as well as charisma.

Key Word Quiz

The Language of Persuasive Speaking

Match the terms about the persuasive speech with their definitions. Record the number of the definition next to the appropriate term.

_____ a. attitude (287)

_____ b. credibility (294)

_____ c. selective exposure (288)

_____ d. belief (287)

_____ e. questions of value (300)

_____ f. self-actualization (293)

_____ g. charisma (296)

_____ h. reasoning from sign (291)

_____ i. questions of policy (304)

_____ j. questions of fact (297)

1. Drawing conclusions from clues (or symptoms) that often occur together.

2. A motive that influences people only after all other needs are satisfied.

3. Issues that concern what should be done or what procedures should be followed.

4. The tendency to respond in a certain way.

5. Issues that concern what is or is not true or what does or does not exist.

6. The degree to which your audience regards you as believable.

7. The principle stating that listeners will actively seek out information that supports their beliefs and will actively avoid information that contradicts their existing beliefs.

8. The conviction of the existence or reality of something or of the truth of some assertion.

9. A quality of personal attractiveness, dynamism, and forcefulness that enhances credibility.

10. Issues that concern what people consider good or bad, just or unjust.

These ten terms and additional terms used in this chapter can be found in the glossary.

Answers: a. 4 b. 6 c. 7 d. 8 e. 10 f. 2 g. 9 h. 1 i. 3 j. 5

 Study and **Review** the **Flashcards** at **MyCommunicationLab**

MyCommunicationLab

Throughout this chapter, there are icons in the margin that highlight media content for selected topics. Go to **MyCommunicationLab** for additional materials on persuasion. Here you'll find flashcards to help you learn the jargon of communication, videos that illustrate a variety of concepts, additional exercises, and discussions to help you continue your study of persuasive speaking.

Glossary

Definitions of the technical terms of human communication—the words that are peculiar or unique to this discipline—are presented here along with relevant skills where applicable (in *italic*). These definitions and skill statements should make new or difficult terms a bit easier to understand and should serve as reminders of the skills discussed throughout this text. All boldface terms within the definitions appear as separate entries in the glossary.

ableism. Discrimination against people with disabilities. *Use person-first language; put the person first and the disability second, not "the blind boy" but "the boy who is blind . . ."*

abstraction. A general concept derived from a class of objects; a part representation of some whole. Also, the quality of being abstract. *Use both abstract and specific terms when describing or explaining.*

abstraction process. The process by which a general concept is derived from specifics; the process by which some (never all) characteristics of an object, person, or event are perceived by the senses or included in some term, phrase, or sentence.

accent. The stress or emphasis placed on a syllable when it is pronounced.

accommodation. The process of adjusting your communication patterns to those with whom you're interacting. *Accommodate to the speaking style of your listeners in moderation; too much mirroring of the other's style may appear manipulative.*

acculturation. The processes by which a person's culture is modified or changed through contact with or exposure to another culture.

active listening. The process of putting together into some meaningful whole an understanding of a speaker's total message—the verbal and the nonverbal, the content and the feelings. *If you wish to listen actively, paraphrase the speaker's meaning, express understanding of the speaker's feelings, and ask questions when you need something clarified.*

adaptors. Nonverbal behaviors that satisfy some personal need and usually occur without awareness, such as scratching to relieve an itch or moistening your lips to relieve dryness. Three types of adaptors are often distinguished: **self-adaptors, alter-adaptors,** and **object-adaptors.**

adjustment (principle of). The principle of verbal interaction claiming that communication takes place only to the extent that the parties communicating share the same system of signals.

advice. Messages that tell another person what he or she should do.

affect displays. Movements of the facial area that convey emotional meaning—for example, anger, fear, or surprise.

affinity-seeking strategies. Behaviors designed to increase interpersonal attractiveness. *Use in moderation.*

affirmation. The communication of support and approval.

agapic love. One of Lee's (1976) six types of love; compassionate and selfless love offered without concern for personal reward and without any expectation of reciprocation.

ageism. Discrimination based on age. *Avoid it.*

agenda. A list of the items that a small group must deal with in the order in which they should be covered. *As a leader or member, keep focused on the agenda.*

aggressiveness. *See* **verbal aggressiveness.**

allness. The assumption that all can be known or is known about a given person, issue, object, or event. *Avoid allness statements (for example, statements containing such words as all, never, or always); they invariably misstate the reality and will often offend the other person.*

alter-adaptors. Body movements you make in response to your current interactions, such as crossing your arms over your chest when someone unpleasant approaches or moving closer to someone you like.

altercasting. Placing a listener in a specific role for a specific purpose and asking that person to approach the question or problem from the perspective of this specific role.

ambiguity. The condition in which a message can be interpreted as having more than one meaning. *Recognize that all messages are potentially ambiguous, so clarify as necessary.*

amount of change principle. A principle of persuasion stating that the greater and more important the change desired by the speaker, the more difficult its achievement will be.

amplification. *See* **supporting materials.**

analogy (reasoning from). A type of reasoning in which you compare similar things and conclude that, because they are alike in so many respects, they also must be alike in some other respect.

anger management. The methods and techniques by which anger is controlled and managed. *Calm down as best you can; then consider your communication options and the relevant communication skills for expressing your feelings.*

apology. Expressions of regret or sorrow for having done what you did or for what happened.

appeals to authority. A fallacy of reasoning in which someone is passed off as an authority when the person logically has little authority, expertise, or knowledge in the subject under discussion. *Ask for evidence.*

appeals to numbers. An appeal in which the speaker argues that truth is determined by popularity.

apprehension. *See* **communication apprehension.**

arbitrariness. A feature of human language; the absence of a real or inherent relationship between the form of a word and its meaning.

argument. The presentation of evidence (for example, facts or statistics) and a conclusion drawn from the evidence.

argumentativeness. A willingness to speak your mind, to argue for a point of view. *In conflict, avoid attacking the other person's self-concept. Instead, focus logically on the issues, emphasize finding solutions, and work to ensure that what is* *said will result in positive self-feelings for both individuals.* Contrast **verbal aggressiveness.**

articulation. The physiological movements of the speech organs as they modify and interrupt the air stream emitted from the lungs.

artifactual messages. Messages conveyed through the wearing and arrangement of various artifacts—for example, clothing, jewelry, buttons, or the furniture in your house and its arrangement. *Use artifacts (e.g., color, clothing, body adornment, space decoration) to communicate your desired messages. But check to find out whether others are in fact receiving the messages you think you are communicating.*

assertiveness. A willingness to stand up for your rights while maintaining respect for the rights of others. *Increase your own assertiveness by analyzing the assertive messages of others, rehearsing assertive messages, and communicating assertively by describing the problem, saying how the problem affects you, proposing solutions, confirming your understanding, and reflecting on your own assertiveness.*

assertiveness training group. A type of group that aims to increase the willingness of its members to stand up for their rights and to act more assertively in a wide variety of situations.

assimilation. A process of distortion in which we reconstruct messages to make them conform to our own attitudes, prejudices, needs, and values.

asynchronous. Communication in which sending and receiving of a message takes place at different times. Contrast **synchronous.**

attack. A persuasive technique that involves accusing another person (usually an opponent) of some serious wrongdoing so that the issue under discussion never gets examined. *Avoid this as a speaker and recognize it for what it is as a listener.*

attention. The process of responding to a stimulus or stimuli; usually involves some consciousness of responding.

attitude. A predisposition to respond for or against an object, person, or position.

attraction. The state or process by which one individual is drawn to another, forming a highly positive evaluation of that other person.

attraction theory. A theory holding that we form relationships on the basis of our attraction for another person.

attractiveness. The degree to which a person is perceived to be physically attractive and to possess a pleasing personality.

attribution. A process through which we attempt to understand the behaviors of others (as well as our own), particularly the reasons or motivations for these behaviors.

attribution theory. A theory concerned with the processes involved in attributing causation or motivation to a person's behavior.

audience analysis. The process of analyzing a speaker's intended listeners. *Analyze the audience in terms of its sociological and psychological characteristics and adapt your speech based on these findings.*

audience participation principle. A principle of persuasion stating that persuasion is achieved more effectively when the audience participates actively.

authoritarian leader. A group leader who determines the group policies or makes decisions without consulting or securing agreement from group members.

avoidance. An unproductive conflict strategy in which a person takes mental or physical flight from the actual conflict. *Do not practice avoidance; engaging in conflict actively is generally the more effective management strategy.*

backchanneling cues. Listener responses to a speaker that do not ask for the speaking role.

bandwagon. A persuasive technique in which the speaker tries to gain compliance by saying that "everyone is doing it" and urging audience members to jump on the bandwagon.

barriers to communication. Physical or psychological factors that prevent or hinder effective communication.

behavioral synchrony. The similarity in the behavior, usually nonverbal, of two persons; generally taken as an index of mutual liking.

belief. Confidence in the existence or truth of something; conviction.

beltlining. An unproductive conflict strategy in which one person hits at the emotional level at which the other person cannot withstand the blow. *Avoid it; beltlining is likely to cause resentment that may extend well beyond the argument itself.*

blame. An unproductive conflict strategy in which we attribute the cause of the conflict to the other person or devote our energies to discovering who is the cause and avoid talking about the issues causing the conflict. *Focus on resolving the conflict rather than affixing blame.*

boundary marker. A marker dividing one person's territory from another's—for example, a fence.

brainstorming. A technique for generating ideas either alone or, more usually, in a small group. *Follow these general rules: Avoid negative criticism, strive for quantity, combine and extend the contributions of others, and contribute as many wild ideas as possible. Appropriately restimulate a brainstorming group that has lost its steam by asking for additional contributions or for further extensions of previously contributed ideas.*

breadth. The number of topics about which individuals in a relationship communicate.

bullying. A pattern of abusive behavior (verbal or nonverbal) repeatedly committed by one person (or group) against another.

causes and effects (reasoning from). A form of reasoning in which you conclude that certain effects are due to specific causes or that specific causes produce certain effects. *Be careful that you don't fall into the trap of assuming that, because things occur in sequence, one necessarily causes the other.*

censorship. Legal restriction imposed on the right to produce, distribute, or receive various communications.

central marker. An item that is placed in a territory to reserve it for a specific person—for example, a sweater thrown over a library chair to signal that the chair is taken.

certainty. An attitude of closed-mindedness that creates a defensiveness among communication participants. *Contrast* **provisionalism.**

channel. The vehicle or medium through which signals are sent. *Assess your channel options (e.g., speaking face-to-face, sending e-mail, or leaving a voicemail when you know the person won't be home) before communicating important messages.*

character. One of the qualities of **credibility;** the individual's honesty and basic nature; moral qualities.

charisma. One of the qualities of **credibility;** the individual's dynamism or forcefulness.

cherishing behaviors. Small behaviors we enjoy receiving from others, especially from our relational partner—for example, a kiss, a smile, or a gift of flowers. *Exchanging such behaviors is one way of increasing relationship satisfaction.*

chronemics. The study of the communicative nature of time—the way we treat time and use it to communicate. Two general areas of chronemics are **cultural time** and **psychological time.**

civil inattention. A polite ignoring of others so as not to invade their privacy.

cliché. An overused expression that has lost its novelty and part of its meaning and that calls attention to itself because of its overuse, such as "tall, dark, and handsome" as a description of a man.

closed-mindedness. An unwillingness to receive certain communication messages. *Listen openly even to messages that may contradict existing attitudes and beliefs.*

code. A set of symbols used to translate a message from one form to another.

coercive power. Power based on a person's ability to punish or to remove rewards from another person. *Exerting coercive power often creates resistance and defensiveness.*

cognitive restructuring. A process aimed at substituting logical and realistic beliefs for unrealistic ones; used in reducing communication apprehension and in raising self-esteem.

cohesiveness. A quality of togetherness; in group communication situations, the mutual attraction among members and the extent to which members work together as a group.

collaboration. A win-win conflict style in which you address both your own and another person's needs.

collective orientation. A cultural orientation that stresses the group's rather than the individual's goals and preferences. Contrast **individual orientation.**

collectivist culture. A culture that emphasizes the group's rather than the individual's goals; a culture that values, for example, benevolence, tradition, and conformity. Contrast **individualistic culture.**

color communication. The meanings that different cultures communicate via color. *Use color to reinforce your meanings and recognize the cultural differences in the way colors are given meaning.*

communication. (1) The process or act of communicating; (2) the actual message or messages sent and received; (3) the study of the processes involved in the sending and receiving of messages.

communication accommodation theory. A theory holding that speakers adjust their speaking styles to their listeners to gain social approval and achieve greater communication effectiveness.

communication apprehension. Fear or anxiety over communicating; may be "trait apprehension" (i.e., fear of communication generally, regardless of the specific situation) or "state apprehension" (i.e., fear that is specific to a given communication situation). *Acquire communication skills and experiences, focus on your prior successes, reduce unpredictability, and put apprehension in perspective.*

communication competence. Knowledge of the rules and skills of communication; the qualities that make for effectiveness in communication.

communication network. The pathways of messages; the organizational structure through which messages are sent and received.

competence. One of the dimensions of **credibility;** consists of a person's perceived levels of ability and knowledge.

complementarity. A principle of **attraction** stating that we are attracted by qualities that we do not possess or that we wish to possess and to people who are opposite or different from ourselves. *Contrast* **similarity.**

complementary relationship. A relationship in which the behavior of one person serves as the stimulus for the complementary behavior of the other; in such relationships behavioral differences are maximized.

compliance-gaining strategies. Behaviors directed toward gaining the agreement of others; behaviors designed to persuade others to do as we wish.

compliance-resisting strategies. Behaviors directed at resisting the persuasive attempts of others.

compliment. A message of praise, flattery, or congratulations.

computer-mediated communication. A general term denoting all forms of communication between people that take place through some computer, electronic, or Internet connection.

confidence. A quality of interpersonal effectiveness; a comfortable, at-ease feeling in interpersonal communication situations.

confirmation. A communication pattern that acknowledges another person's presence and also indicates an acceptance of this person and his or her definition of self, and the relationship as defined or viewed by this person. *When you wish to be confirming, acknowledge (verbally and/or nonverbally) others in your group and their contributions. Contrast* **disconfirmation.**

conflict. *See* **interpersonal conflict.**

congruence. A condition in which verbal and nonverbal behaviors reinforce each other.

connotation. The feeling or emotional aspect of meaning, generally viewed as consisting of evaluative (e.g., good/bad), potency (i.e., strong/weak), and activity (i.e., fast/slow) dimensions; the associations of a term. *As a speaker, clarify your connotative meanings if you have any doubts that your listeners might misunderstand you; as a listener, ask questions if you have doubts about the speaker's connotations. Contrast* **denotation.**

consciousness-raising group. A type of group that aims to help people cope with the problems society confronts them with.

consensus. A process of reaching agreement (not necessarily unanimous) among group members.

consistency. A perceptual process that influences us to maintain balance among our perceptions; a process that makes us tend to see what we expect to see and to be uncomfortable when our perceptions run contrary to our expectations.

contact. The first stage of an interpersonal relationship, in which perceptual and interactional contact occurs.

contamination. A form of territorial encroachment that renders another's territory impure.

content and relationship dimensions. Two simultaneous aspects of any given communication: the aspect that pertains to the world external to both speaker and listener (i.e., content) and the aspect having to do with the relationship between the individuals (i.e., relationship). *Listen to both the content and the relationship aspects of messages, distinguish between them, and respond to both.*

content conflict. A type of conflict that centers on objects, events, and persons that are usually, though not always, external to the parties involved in the conflict. Contrast **relationship conflict.**

context of communication. The physical, psychological, social, and temporal environment in which communication takes place.

contrast (principle of). Often-followed rule of perception: messages or people who are very different from each other probably don't belong together, and do not constitute a set or group.

controllability. One of the factors we consider in judging whether a person is responsible for his or her behavior. If the person was in control, then we judge that he or she was responsible. *See also* **attribution theory.**

conversation. Two-person communication that usually includes an opening, feedforward, a business stage, feedback, and a closing.

conversational management. The ways in which a conversation is conducted.

conversational turns. The process of exchanging speaking and listening turns during a conversation.

conversational maxims. The principles that people follow in conversation to ensure that the goal of the conversation is achieved. *Follow (generally) the basic maxims of conversation, such as the maxims of quantity, quality, relations, manner, and politeness.*

conversational turns. The process of exchanging the speaker and listener roles during conversation. *Maintain relatively short conversational turns and then pass the speaker's turn to another person nonverbally or verbally.*

cooperation. An interpersonal process by which individuals work together for a common end; the pooling of efforts to produce a mutually desired outcome.

cooperation (principle of). A cultural principle stating that speaker and listener will cooperate in trying to communicate effectively and to understand each other.

credibility. The believability of a speaker; **competence, character,** and **charisma** (dynamism) are its major dimensions. *Seek to establish credibility by displaying competence, high moral character, and dynamism, or charisma.*

critical thinking. The process of logically evaluating reasons and evidence and reaching a judgment on the basis of this analysis.

critical-thinking-hats technique. A technique developed by Edward deBono (1976) in which a problem or issue is viewed from six distinct perspectives.

criticism. The reasoned judgment of some work; although often equated with fault finding, criticism can involve both positive or negative evaluations.

cultural display. Signs that communicate cultural identification—for example, group-specific clothing or religious jewelry.

cultural rules. Rules that are specific to a given cultural group. *Increase your sensitivity to these rules by learning about different cultures, recognizing and facing your own fears of intercultural interaction, recognizing differences between yourself and others, and becoming conscious of the cultural rules and customs of other cultures.*

cultural time. The meanings given to time communication by a particular culture.

culture. The relatively specialized lifestyle of a group of people—consisting of values, beliefs, artifacts, ways of behaving, and ways of communicating—that is passed on from one generation to the next.

culture shock. The psychological reaction we experience when we find ourselves in a culture very different from our own or from what we are used to.

date. An **extensional device** used to emphasize the notion of constant change and symbolized by a subscript; for example, John Smith$_{2008}$ is not John Smith$_{2011}$. *Use the date (verbally or mentally) to guard against static evaluation.*

deception cues. Verbal or nonverbal cues that reveal that a person is lying.

decoder. Something that takes a message in one form (e.g., sound waves) and translates it into another form (e.g., nerve impulses) from which meaning can be formulated (e.g., in vocal–auditory communication). In human communication the decoder is the auditory mechanism; in electronic communication the decoder is, for example, the telephone earpiece. *See also* **encoder.**

decoding. The process of extracting a message from a code—for example, translating speech sounds into nerve impulses. *See also* **encoding.**

defensiveness. The self-protective attitude of an individual or an atmosphere in a group characterized by threats, fear, and domination. Messages evidencing evaluation, control, strategy, neutrality, superiority, and certainty are assumed to lead to defensiveness. *Contrast* **supportiveness.**

delivery outline. The outline a speaker brings to a public speaking situation and refers to during the speech.

Delphi method. A type of group whose members are experts but there's no interaction among them; instead, they communicate by repeatedly responding to questionnaires.

democratic leader. A group leader who stimulates self-direction and self-actualization of the group members.

denial. One of the obstacles to the expression of emotion; the process by which we deny our emotions to ourselves or to others. *Become mindful of the reasons for denial and the negative impact this generally has on communication.*

denotation. The objective or descriptive meaning of a word; its referential meaning. *Contrast* **connotation.**

depenetration. A reversal of penetration; a condition in which the **breadth** and **depth** of a relationship decrease. *See also* **social penetration theory.**

depth. The degree to which the inner personality—the inner core of an individual—is penetrated in interpersonal interaction.

deterioration. A stage in an interpersonal relationship in which the bonds holding the individuals together are weakened and the partners begin drifting apart.

determinism (principle of). The principle of verbal interaction holding that all verbalizations are to some extent purposeful—that there is a reason for every verbalization.

dialogue. A form of **communication** in which each person is both speaker and listener; communication characterized by involvement, concern, and respect for the other person. *Treat conversation as a dialogue rather than a monologue; show concern for the other person, and for the relationship between you, with other-orientation. Contrast* **monologue.**

direct speech. Speech in which the speaker's intentions are stated clearly and directly.

disclaimer. A statement that asks the listener to receive what the speaker says as intended without its reflecting negatively on the image of the speaker. *Preface your comments with disclaimers if you feel you might be misunderstood. But avoid disclaimers when they aren't necessary; too many disclaimers can make you appear unprepared or unwilling to state an opinion.*

disclaiming. A form of feedforward in which you ask listeners to hear you favorably and without bias.

disconfirmation. A communication pattern in which someone ignores a person or that person's messages, even denying the right of the individual to define himself or herself. *Avoid sexist, heterosexist, racist, and ageist language; such language is disconfirming and insulting and invariably contributes to communication barriers. Contrast* **confirmation.**

dissolution. The breaking of the bonds holding an interpersonal relationship together.

downward communication. Communication sent from the higher levels of a hierarchy to the lower levels—for example, messages sent by managers to workers or from deans to faculty members.

dyadic communication. Two-person communication.

dyadic consciousness. An awareness of the interpersonal relationship in a pairing or between two individuals; distinguished from situations in which two individuals are together but do not perceive themselves as being a unit or twosome.

dyadic effect. The process by which one person in a dyad, or two-person group, imitates the behavior of the other person. Usually refers to the tendency of one person's self-disclosures to prompt the other also to self-disclose. *Pay attention to the dyadic effect; it may indicate the other person's degree of involvement in the conversation.*

earmarker. A marker that identifies an item as belonging to a specific person—for example, a nameplate on a desk or initials on an attaché case. *Use earmarkers with a consideration for the rights of others as well as your own.*

effect. The outcome or consequence of an action or behavior; communication is assumed always to have some effect.

emblems. Nonverbal behaviors that directly translate words or phrases—for example, the signs for "OK" and "peace." *Use these with an awareness of the great cultural differences in the meanings given to various emblems.*

emergent leader. A leader who is not appointed and instead "emerges" during the group process.

emoticon. A visual symbol to indicate an emotion.

emotions. The feelings you have—for example, joy, guilt, anger, or sorrow. *Express your emotions and interpret the emotions of others in light of the cultural rules dictating what is and is not appropriate emotional expression.*

empathy. The ability to feel what another person feels; feeling or perceiving something from another person's point of view. A key component of interpersonal effectiveness. *Communicate empathy when appropriate: resist evaluating another person's behaviors, focus concentration on the person, express active involvement through facial expressions and gestures, reflect back the feelings you think are being expressed, self-disclose, and address any mixed messages.*

encoder. Something that takes a message in one form (for example, nerve impulses) and translates it into another form (for example, sound waves). In human communication, the encoder is the speaking mechanism; in electronic communication, the encoder is, for example, the telephone mouthpiece. *See also* **decoder.**

encoding. The process of putting a message into a code—for example, translating nerve impulses into speech sounds. *See also* **decoding.**

encounter group. Often referred to as a *sensitivity* or *T [Training]-group*, this type of group constitutes a form of psychotherapy; these groups try to facilitate members' personal growth and to foster their ability to deal effectively with other people.

enculturation. The process by which culture is transmitted from one generation to another.

e-prime. A form of the language that omits the verb "to be" except as an auxiliary or in statements of existence. E-prime is designed to eliminate the tendency toward **projection.** *When you feel that you may be overgeneralizing or making assumptions about all from only a few instances, try thinking in e-prime by eliminating the verb* to be.

equality. An attitude that recognizes that each individual in a communication interaction is equal, that no one is superior to any other; encourages **supportiveness.**

equilibrium theory. A theory of **proxemics** holding that intimacy and physical closeness are positively related; as a relationship becomes more intimate, the distances between the individuals will diminish.

equity theory. A theory claiming that you experience relational satisfaction when there is an equal distribution of rewards and costs between the two persons in the relationship.

eros love. One of Lee's (1976) six types of love; seeks beauty and sensuality and focuses on physical attractiveness.

et cetera or etc. An **extensional device** used to emphasize the notion of infinite complexity; because we can never know all about anything, any statement about the world or an event must end with an explicit or implicit "etc." *Finish your thoughts with etc.—that is, be mindful that there is always more to say, see, hear, etc.*

ethics. The branch of philosophy that deals with the rightness or wrongness of actions; the study of moral values.

ethnic identity. Commitment to the beliefs and customs of a culture.

ethnocentrism. The tendency to see others and their behaviors through our own cultural filters, often as distortions of our own behaviors; the tendency to evaluate the values and beliefs of our own culture more positively than those of another culture. *Recognizing our own ethnocentrism may help to prevent evaluating different cultural practices negatively.*

etymology. The historical or linguistic development of a word or phrase and often a useful way to help define a word.

euphemism. A polite word or phrase used to substitute for some **taboo** or otherwise offensive term.

example. A relatively brief specific instance.

excluding talk. Speaking about a subject or in a vocabulary that only certain people understand, often in the presence of someone who does not belong to this group and therefore does not understand; use of terms unique to a specific culture as if they were universal.

excuse. An explanation designed to lessen the negative consequences of something done or said. *When using excuses—for example, to repair a misunderstood conversation—remember to do five things: (1) demonstrate that you understand the problem, (2) acknowledge your responsibility,* (3) acknowledge your regret for what you did, (4) request forgiveness, and (5) make it clear that this will never happen again.

expectancy violations theory. A theory of **proxemics** holding that people have certain expectations for spatial relationships. If those expectations are violated (e.g., if a stranger stands too close to you or a romantic partner maintains an abnormally large distance from you), the relationship comes into clearer focus and you wonder why this "normal distance" is being violated.

experiential limitation. The limit of an individual's ability to communicate, as set by the nature and extent of that individual's experiences.

expert power. Personal power derived from expertise or knowledge.

expressiveness. Genuine involvement in speaking and listening, conveyed verbally and nonverbally; a component of interpersonal effectiveness. *Communicate active involvement in the interaction: Use active listening, address mixed messages, use I-messages, and use appropriate variations in paralanguage and gesture.*

extemporaneous speech. A speech that is thoroughly prepared and organized in detail and in which certain aspects of style are predetermined.

extensional device. A linguistic device proposed by Alfred Korzybski to make language a more accurate means for talking about the world. The extensional devices include **et cetera, date,** and **index** (i.e., the working devices) and the **hyphen** and **quotes** (i.e., the safety devices). *Think mindfully with these devices.*

extensional orientation. A tendency to give primary consideration to the world of experience and only secondary consideration to labels. *Look first to the event, the person, or the situation and only then to the way it's talked about.* Contrast **intensional orientation.**

face-attacking conflict strategies. Strategies that attack a person's positive face or self-esteem or a person's negative face or need for autonomy and independence. *Avoid these.*

face-enhancing conflict strategies. Strategies that support and confirm a person's positive face or self-esteem or a person's negative face or need for autonomy. *Use these when appropriate.*

face-saving. Maintaining a positive public self-image in the minds of others. *During a conflict, use face-saving strategies to allow your opponent to save face; avoid beltlining, or hitting your opponent with attacks that he or she will have difficulty absorbing and will resent.*

facial feedback hypothesis. The theory that a person's facial expressions can produce physiological and emotional effects in the person.

facial management techniques. Techniques used to mask certain emotions and to emphasize others: for example, intensifying your expression of happiness to make a friend feel good about a promotion. *Use these ethically as well as effectively. Use facial expressions to communicate that you're involved in the interaction. As a listener, look to the emotional facial expressions of others as additional cues to their meaning.*

fact–inference confusion. A misevaluation in which someone makes an inference, regards it as a fact, and acts on it as if it were a fact. *Distinguish facts (i.e., verifiably true past events) from inferences (i.e., guesses, hypotheses, hunches), and act on inferences with tentativeness and with mindfulness that they may turn out to be incorrect.*

factual statement. A statement made by an observer after an observation and limited to what is observed. *Contrast* **inferential statement.**

family. A group of people who consider themselves related and connected to one another and among whom the actions of one person have consequences for others.

fear appeal. An effort to exploit or create fear in an individual or group of individuals in order to persuade them to believe or act in a certain way.

feedback. Information that is given back to the source. Feedback may come from the source's own messages (as when we hear what we are saying) or from the receiver(s)—in forms such as applause, yawning, puzzled looks, questions, pokes, retweets, increased followers, and so forth. *Listen to both verbal and nonverbal feedback—from yourself and from others—and use these cues to help you adjust your messages for greatest effectiveness. See also* **negative feedback; positive feedback.**

feedforward. Information that is sent before a regular message telling the listener something about what is to follow. *Preface your messages with some kind of feedforward when you feel your listener needs some background or when you want to ease into a particular topic, such as bad news.*

flexibility. The ability to adjust communication strategies on the basis of the unique situation. *Because no two communication situations are identical, because everything is in a state of flux, and because everyone is different, cultivate flexibility and adjust your communication to the unique situation.*

flirting. A type of communication that signals romantic interest.

focus group. A group designed to explore the feelings and attitudes of its members; usually follows a question-and-answer format.

force. An unproductive conflict strategy in which someone attempts to win an argument by physical force, threats of force, or some type of psychological bullying.

forum. A small group format in which members of the group answer questions from the audience; often follows a **symposium.**

friendship. An interpersonal relationship between two people that is mutually productive, established and maintained through perceived mutual free choice, and characterized by mutual positive regard. *Establish friendships to help serve such needs as utility, ego support, stimulation, and*

security. *At the same time, seek to serve similar needs that your friends have.*

fundamental attribution error. The tendency to attribute a person's behavior to the kind of person he or she is (to internal factors such as the person's personality) and not to give sufficient importance to the situation the person is in. *Avoid the fundamental attribution error by mindfully focusing on the possible influence of situational forces.*

game. A simulation of some situation with rules governing the behaviors of the participants and with some payoff for winning. In transactional analysis, a "game" is a series of ulterior transactions that lead to a payoff; the term also refers to a basically dishonest kind of transaction in which participants hide their true feelings.

general purpose. The major aim or objective of a public speech; usually identified as *to inform* and *to persuade*.

general semantics. The study of the relationships among language, thought, and behavior.

glittering generality. The opposite of **name calling;** a speaker's effort to gain your acceptance of an idea by associating it with things you value highly.

gobbledygook. Overly complex language that overwhelms the listener instead of communicating meaning. *Simplify your own language and ask for clarification when in doubt.*

gossip. Communication about someone who is not present, usually about matters that are private to this third party.

grapevine. Informal routes by which messages in an organization may travel; these informal lines resemble the physical grapevine, with its unpredictable pattern of branches.

group. A collection of individuals who are related to one another by some common purpose and in which some structure exists.

group norm. Rules or expectations for appropriate behavior for a member of a group. *Actively seek to discover the norms of a group, and take these norms into consideration when interacting in the group.*

groupthink. A tendency observed in some groups in which agreement among members becomes more important than the exploration of the issues at hand. *Recognize and actively counter any groupthink tendencies evidenced in a group.*

gunnysacking. An unproductive conflict strategy of storing up grievances—as if in a gunnysack—and holding them in readiness to dump on the other person in a conflict.

halo effect. The tendency to generalize an individual's virtue or expertise from one area to another.

haptics. The study of touch communication.

heterosexist language. Language that assumes all people are heterosexual and that thereby denigrates lesbians and gay men.

high-context culture. A culture in which much of the information in communication is in the context or in the person rather than explicitly coded in the verbal messages. **Collectivist cultures** are generally high context. *Adjust your messages and your listening in light of the differences between high- and low-context cultures.* *Contrast* **low-context culture**.

high-power-distance cultures. Cultures in which power is concentrated in the hands of a few, and there is a great difference between the power held by these people and the power held by the ordinary citizen. *Contrast* **low-power-distance cultures.**

home field advantage. The increased power that comes from being in your own territory.

home territories. Territories about which individuals have a sense of intimacy and over which they exercise control—for example, a person's home.

human communication. The sending and receiving of verbal and nonverbal messages between two or more people.

hyphen. An **extensional device** used to illustrate that what may be separated verbally may not be separable on the event level or on the nonverbal level; for example, although body and mind are often discussed as if they were separable, in reality they are better referred to as body–mind.

idea-generation group. A group whose purpose is to generate ideas. *See also* **brainstorming.**

idioms. Expressions that are unique to a specific language and whose meaning cannot be deduced from the individual words used.

illustration. A relatively long and detailed example.

illustrators. Nonverbal behaviors that accompany and literally illustrate verbal messages—for example, upward hand movements that accompany the verbalization "It's up there."

image-confirming strategies. Techniques used to communicate or to confirm your self-image, the image you want others to see.

I-messages. Messages in which the speaker accepts responsibility for personal thoughts and behaviors; messages in which the speaker's point of view is stated explicitly. *Use I-messages when communicating your feelings; take responsibility for your own feelings (as in "I get angry when you . . .") rather than attributing them to others (as in "you make me angry"). Contrast* **you-messages.**

immediacy. A sense of contact and togetherness; a feeling of interest in and liking for the other person in an interchange. A quality of interpersonal effectiveness. *Maintain nonverbal immediacy through close physical distances, eye contact, and smiling; maintain verbal immediacy by using the other person's name and focusing on his or her remarks.*

Impostor phenomenon. The tendency to disregard outward signs of success and to consider yourself an "impostor," a fake, a fraud, one who doesn't really deserve to be considered successful.

impression formation. The processes you go through in forming an impression of another person.

impression management. The processes you go through to create the impression you want the other person to have of you.

impromptu speech. A speech delivered off-the-cuff, without preparation.

inclusion principle. In verbal interaction, the principle stating that all members should be a part of (i.e., included in) the interaction.

inclusive talk. Communication that includes all people; communication that does not exclude certain groups, such as women, lesbians and gays, or members of certain races or nationalities.

index. An **extensional device** used to emphasize the notion of nonidentity (i.e., that no two things are the same) and symbolized by a subscript—for example, $politician_1$ is not $politician_2$.

indirect speech. Speech that may hide the speaker's true intentions or that may be used to make requests and observations indirectly. *Make judicious use of indirect messages when a more direct style might prove insulting or offensive. But be aware that indirect messages can create communication problems, because they are easier to misunderstand than direct messages.*

indiscrimination. A misevaluation caused when we categorize people, events, or objects into a particular class and respond to them only as members of the class; a failure to recognize that each individual is unique; a failure to apply the **index.** *Avoid indiscrimination by treating each situation and each person as unique (when possible) even when they're covered by the same label or name. Index your key concepts.*

individual orientation. A cultural orientation that stresses the individual's rather than the group's goals and preferences. *Adjust your messages and your listening on the basis of differences between individualistic and collectivist cultures. Contrast* **collective orientation.**

individual roles (in groups). Behavior in groups that is usually dysfunctional and works against a sense of groupness. *In a group avoid playing the popular but dysfunctional individual roles—those of the aggressor, blocker, recognition seeker, self-confessor, and dominator.*

individualistic culture. A culture that emphasizes the individual's rather than the group's goals and preferences. *Contrast* **collectivist culture.**

inevitability. In communication, the fact that communication cannot be avoided—that all behavior in an interactional setting is communication.

inferential statement. A statement that can be made by anyone, is not limited to what is observed, and can be made at any time. *Contrast* **factual statement.**

influencing strategies. Strategies designed to influence the attitudes or behaviors of others.

informal time terms. Expressions that denote approximate rather than exact time intervals—for example, "soon," "early," and "in a while."

information. Knowledge that reduces uncertainty.

information overload. A condition in which the amount of information is too great to be dealt with effectively or the number or complexity of messages is so great that the individual or organization is not able to deal with them.

information power. Power derived from the possession of information and the ability to communicate logically and persuasively. Also called "persuasion power."

informative interview. A type of **interviewing** in which the interviewer asks the interviewee, usually a person of some reputation and accomplishment, questions designed to elicit his or her views, predictions, and perspectives on specific topics.

informative speech. A public speech in which the speaker describes, demonstrates, or defines something. *Follow the principles of informative speaking: Stress the information's usefulness, relate new information to information the audience already knows, present information through several senses, adjust the level of complexity, vary the levels of abstraction, avoid information overload, and recognize cultural variations.*

inoculation principle. A principle stating that persuasion will be more difficult to achieve when the would-be persuader attacks beliefs and attitudes that have already been challenged previously, because the listener has built up defenses (i.e., has been "inoculated") against such attacks.

insulation. A reaction to territorial encroachment in which you erect some sort of barrier between yourself and the invaders.

intensional orientation. A tendency to give primary consideration to the way things are labeled and only secondary consideration (if any) to the world of experience. *Contrast* **extensional orientation.** *Avoid intensional orientation by responding to things first and to labels second; the way a person is talked about is not the best measure of who that person really is.*

interaction management. The control of interpersonal interaction to the satisfaction of both parties; management of conversational turns, fluency, and message consistency. A component of interpersonal effectiveness. *Speak in relatively short conversational turns, avoid long and frequent pauses, and use verbal and nonverbal messages that are consistent.*

interaction process analysis. A content analysis method that classifies messages into four general categories: social emotional positive, social emotional negative, attempted answers, and questions.

intercultural communication. Communication that takes place between persons of different cultures or persons who have different cultural beliefs, values, or ways of behaving. *When communicating interculturally, become mindful of (1) the differences between yourself and culturally different individuals, (2) the differences within the other cultural group, (3) cultural differences in meanings for both verbal and nonverbal signals, and (4) different cultural rules and customs. Communicate interculturally with appropriate openness, empathy, positiveness, immediacy, interaction management, expressiveness, and other orientation.*

internal summary. A statement that summarizes what you have already discussed in the speech, usually some major

subdivision of your speech. *Use such summaries to help your audience follow your speech*

interpersonal communication. Communication between two persons or among a small group of persons, as distinguished from public or mass communication; communication of a personal nature, as distinguished from impersonal communication; communication between or among intimates or those involved in a close relationship; often, intrapersonal, dyadic, and small group communication in general.

interpersonal conflict. A conflict or disagreement between two persons. *Prepare for a conflict by arranging to fight in private, knowing what you're fighting about, and fighting about problems that can be solved. After the conflict, profit from it by learning what worked and what didn't, by keeping the conflict in perspective, and by increasing the exchange of rewards. Avoid the common causes of online conflicts—such as sending out unsolicited commercial messages, spamming, and flaming.*

interpersonal perception. The perception of people; the processes through which we interpret and evaluate people and their behavior.

interruptions In conversation, attempts to take over the role of the speaker.

intervention group. A type of group in which participants gather to help one of their members confront and overcome some problem.

interviewing. A particular form of interpersonal communication in which two persons interact largely through questions and answers for the purpose of achieving specific goals.

intimacy. The closest interpersonal relationship; usually involves a close primary relationship such as the relationship between spouses or partners.

intimacy claims. Obligations that a person incurs by virtue of being in a close and intimate relationship.

intimate distance. The closest proxemic distance, ranging from touching to 18 inches away. *See also* **proxemics.**

intrapersonal communication. Communication with the self.

invasion. Unwarranted entrance into another's territory that changes the meaning of the territory; territorial encroachment.

involvement. The stage in an interpersonal relationship that normally follows contact, in which the individuals get to know each other better and explore the potential for greater intimacy.

irreversibility. The impossibility of reversing communication; a principle stating that once something has been communicated it cannot be uncommunicated.

jargon. The technical language of any specialized group, often a professional class, that is unintelligible to individuals not belonging to the group; "shop talk."

Johari window. A diagram of the four selves (i.e., open, blind, hidden, and unknown) that illustrates the different kinds of information in each self.

kinesics. The study of the communicative dimensions of facial and bodily movements.

laissez-faire leader. A group leader who allows the group to develop and progress or make mistakes on its own.

lateral communication. Communication among equals—for example, manager to manager, worker to worker.

leadership. The quality by which one individual directs or influences the thoughts and/or the behaviors of others. *See also* **laissez-faire leader, democratic leader,** and **authoritarian leader.**

leave-taking cues. Verbal and nonverbal cues that indicate a desire to terminate a conversation.

legitimate power. Power derived from people's belief that a person has a right, by virtue of position, to influence or control the behavior of others.

leveling. A process of message distortion in which a message is repeated but the number of details is reduced, some details are omitted entirely, and some details lose their complexity.

level of abstraction. The relative distance of a term or statement from an actual perception; a low-order abstraction would be a description of the perception, whereas a high-order abstraction would consist of inferences about descriptions of the perception.

listening. An active process of receiving messages sent orally; this process consists of five stages: receiving, understanding, remembering, evaluating, and responding.

logic. The science of reasoning; the principles governing the analysis of inference making.

long-term memory. Memory that is (theoretically) unlimited in storage capacity and that holds information for long periods of time. *Contrast* **short-term memory.**

looking-glass self. The self-concept that results from the image of yourself that others reveal to you.

loving. An interpersonal process in which one person feels a closeness, a caring, a warmth, and an excitement in relation to another person.

low-context culture. A culture in which most of the information in communication is explicitly stated in the verbal messages. An **individualistic culture** is usually a low-context culture. *Contrast* **high-context culture.**

low-power-distance cultures. Cultures in which power is more evenly distributed throughout the citizenry. *Contrast* **high-power-distance cultures.**

ludic love. One of Lee's (1976) six types of love; based on entertainment and excitement, it is love as a game, not to be taken too seriously and with emotions held in check.

lying. The act of sending messages with the intention of giving another person information you believe to be false.

maintenance. A stage of relationship stability at which the relationship does not progress or deteriorate significantly; a continuation as opposed to a dissolution of a relationship.

maintenance strategies. Specific behaviors designed to preserve an interpersonal relationship.

manic love. One of Lee's (1976) six types of love; obsessive love, it is marked by a need for constant attention and affection, which when withheld leads to depression, jealousy, and self-doubt.

manipulation. An unproductive conflict strategy in which a person avoids open conflict but attempts to divert the conflict by being especially charming and getting the other person into a noncombative frame of mind.

manuscript speech. A speech designed to be read verbatim from a script.

markers. Devices that signify that a certain territory belongs to a particular person. *Become sensitive to the (central, boundary, and ear) markers of others, and learn to use these markers to define your own territories and to communicate the desired impression.* See also **boundary marker, central marker,** and **earmarker.**

mass communication. Communication that is addressed to an extremely large audience, mediated by audio and/or visual transmitters, and processed by gatekeepers before transmission.

matching hypothesis. The theory that we tend to date and mate with people who are similar to us—who match us—in physical attractiveness.

meaningfulness. As a principle of perception, our assumption that people's behavior is sensible, stems from some logical antecedent, and is consequently meaningful rather than meaningless.

mentoring. Guidance and support given by an experienced individual to a less-experienced person.

mere exposure hypothesis. The theory that repeated or prolonged exposure to a stimulus may result in a change in attitude toward the stimulus object, generally in the direction of increased positiveness.

message. Any signal or combination of signals that serves as a stimulus for a receiver.

meta-advice. Advice about advice—for example, when asked for advice, suggesting that the asker seek more expert advice.

metacommunication. Communication about communication. *Metacommunicate when you want to clarify the way you're talking or what you're talking about; for example, give clear feedforward and paraphrase your own complex messages.*

metalanguage. Language used to talk about language.

metamessage. A message that makes reference to another message—for example, remarks such as "Did I make myself clear?" or "That's a lie."

metaskills. Skills for regulating more specific skills. For example, skills of interpersonal communication such as openness and empathy must be regulated by the metaskills of flexibility, mindfulness, and metacommunication.

mindfulness and mindlessness. States of relative awareness. In a mindful state, we are aware of the logic and rationality of our behaviors and the logical connections existing among elements. In a mindless state, we are unaware of this logic and rationality. *Increase your mindfulness by creating and recreating categories, being open to new information and points of view, and avoiding excessive reliance on first impressions.*

mixed message. A message that contradicts itself; a message that asks for two different (often incompatible) responses. *Avoid encoding mixed messages by focusing clearly on your purposes when communicating and by increasing conscious control over your verbal and nonverbal behaviors.*

model. A representation of an object or process.

monochronic time orientation. A view of time in which things are done sequentially, with one thing being scheduled at a time. *Contrast* **polychronic time orientation.**

monologue. A form of communication in which one person speaks and the other listens; there is no real interaction among participants. *Contrast* **dialogue.**

motivated sequence. An organizational pattern in which a speaker arranges the information in a discourse to motivate an audience to respond positively to the speaker's purpose. *In using the motivated sequence, gain attention, establish a need, satisfy the need, visualize the need satisfied, and move to action.*

motivational appeal. Appeals to an audience's motives and emotions rather than to their logic. *Use motivational appeals (i.e., appeals to motives such as fear; power, control, and influence; safety; achievement; or financial gain) as appropriate to the speech and audience.*

name calling. A persuasive technique in which the speaker gives an idea or a person a derogatory name.

narrative. A long example presented in the form of an anecdote, short story, or report, for example, Aesop's fables.

negative face. The need and desire to be autonomous, to have the right to do as one wishes.

negative feedback. Feedback that serves a corrective function by informing the source that his or her message is not being received in the way intended; serves to redirect the source's behavior. Examples include looks of boredom, shouts of disagreement, letters critical of newspaper policy, and a teacher's instructions on how better to approach a problem. Contrast **positive feedback.**

netiquette. The rules for polite communication over the Internet. *Learn what these are and follow them.*

networking. A broad process of enlisting the aid of other people to help you solve a problem or offer insight that bears on your problem. *Establish a network of relationships to provide insights into issues relevant to your personal and professional life, and be willing to lend your expertise to the networks of others.*

neutrality. A response pattern lacking in personal involvement; encourages defensiveness. *Contrast* **empathy.**

noise. Anything that interferes with a person's receiving a message as the source intended the message to be received. Noise is present in a communication system to the extent that the message received is not the message sent. *Reduce the influence of physical, physiological, psychological, and semantic noise to the extent that you can; use repetition and restatement and, when in doubt, ask if you're being clear.*

nominal group. A collection of individuals who record their thoughts and opinions, which are then distributed to others. Without direct interaction, the thoughts and opinions are gradually pared down until a manageable list of solutions or decisions is produced. When this occurs, the nominal group (a group in name only) may restructure itself into a problem-solving group that analyzes the final list. *Use the nominal group technique to solve problems when anonymity in suggesting ideas may be desirable.*

non-allness. An attitude or point of view recognizing that we can never know all about anything; that what we know, say, or hear is only a part of what there is to know, say, or hear.

nondirective language. Language that does not direct or focus our attention on certain aspects of a topic; neutral language.

nonnegotiation. An unproductive conflict strategy in which an individual refuses to discuss the conflict or to listen to the other person in the encounter.

nonverbal communication. Communication without words; for example, communication by means of space, gestures, facial expressions, touching, vocal variation, or silence.

nonverbal dominance. Nonverbal behavior through which one person psychologically dominates another.

norm. *See* **group norm.**

object-adaptors. Movements that involve manipulation of some object, such as punching holes in or drawing on a Styrofoam coffee cup, clicking a ballpoint pen, or chewing on a pencil.

object language. Language used to communicate about objects, events, and relations in the world; the structure of the object language is described in a metalanguage; the display of physical objects—for example, flower arranging and the colors of the clothes we wear.

oculesis. A technical term for the study of eye movements.

olfactics. The study of communication by smell.

olfactory communication. Communication by smell.

onymous messages. Messages that are signed; messages whose author is identified.

openness. A quality of interpersonal effectiveness encompassing (1) a willingness to interact openly with others, to self-disclose as appropriate; (2) a willingness to react honestly to incoming stimuli; and (3) a willingness to own your feelings and thoughts.

operational definition. A type of definition in which the steps to construct the object are identified.

oral style. The style of spoken discourse that, when compared with written style, consists of shorter, simpler, and more familiar words; more qualification, self-reference terms, allness terms, verbs and adverbs; and more concrete terms and terms indicative of consciousness of projection, such as "as I see it."

other-orientation. A quality of interpersonal effectiveness involving attentiveness, interest, and concern for the other person. *Acknowledge the importance of the other person; use focused eye contact and appropriate facial expressions; smile, nod, and lean toward the other person; express agreement when appropriate.*

other talk. Talk about the listener or about some third party.

overattribution. The tendency to attribute a great deal of what a person does or believes to one or two obvious characteristics of the person. *Avoid overattribution; rarely is any one factor an accurate explanation of complex human behavior.*

panel. A small group format in which "experts" meet to discuss a topic or solve a problem; participants often speak without any set pattern.

paralanguage. The vocal but nonverbal aspect of speech. Paralanguage consists of voice qualities (e.g., pitch range, resonance, tempo), vocal characterizers (e.g., laughing or crying, yelling or whispering), vocal qualifiers (e.g., intensity, pitch height), and vocal segregates (e.g., "uh-uh" meaning "no" or "sh" meaning "silence"). *Vary paralinguistic features such as rate, pausing, pitch, and volume to communicate your meanings and to add interest and color to your messages.*

paraphrase. A restatement of another's message in your own words.

parasocial relationship. Relationship between a person and an imagined or fictional character; usually refers to a relationship between a viewer and a fictional character in a television show.

pauses. Silent periods in the normally fluent stream of speech. Pauses are of two major types: filled pauses (i.e., interruptions in speech that are filled with such vocalizations as "er" or "um") and unfilled pauses (i.e., silences of unusually long duration). *Use pauses to signal transitions to allow listeners time to think or respond, and to signal the approach of a significant idea.*

perception. The process of becoming aware of objects and events via the senses. *Increase accuracy in interpersonal perception by (1) identifying the influence of your physical and emotional state; (2) making sure that you're not drawing conclusions from too little information; and (3) identifying any perceptions that may be the result of mind reading. See also* **interpersonal perception.**

perception checking. The process of verifying your understanding of some message or situation or feeling to reduce uncertainty.

perceptual accentuation. A process that leads you to see what you expect to see and what you want to see—for example, seeing people you like as better looking and smarter than people you do not like.

personal attack. A fallacy of argument in which the speaker attacks the person instead of the person's arguments. *Avoid this in your own reasoning and reject these when used by others.*

personal distance. The second closest **proxemic distance,** ranging from 18 inches to four feet. *See also* **proxemics.**

personal growth group. Often referred to as *support group,* this type of group aims to help members cope with particular difficulties—such as drug addiction, not being assertive enough, or dealing with a relationship breakup.

personality theory. A theory or set of assumptions about personality, complete with rules or systems, that each individual maintains and through which the individual perceives others. *In order to subject your perceptions and conclusions about people to logical analysis, bring to your mindful state your personality theory.*

personal rejection. An unproductive conflict strategy in which one person withholds love and affection and seeks to win the argument by getting the other person to break down under this withdrawal.

persuasion. The process of influencing attitudes, beliefs, values, and/or behavior.

persuasive speech. In public speaking, a speech designed to change an audience's attitudes or behaviors. *Apply (where relevant) the principles of persuasion: selective exposure, audience participation, identification, and amounts of change.*

phatic communication. Communication that is primarily social; "small talk" designed to open the channels of communication rather than to communicate something about the external world. "Hello" and "How are you?" in everyday interaction are examples.

pitch. The highness or lowness of the vocal tone.

plagiarism. The process of claiming authorship for the work of another and can apply to ideas as well as specific words. *Avoid even the suggestion of plagiarism.*

plain folks. A persuasive strategy that identifies the speaker and his or her proposal with the audience.

polarization. A form of fallacious reasoning by which only the two extremes are considered; also referred to as "black-and-white" or "either/or" thinking or as two-valued orientation. *Avoid thinking and talking in extremes by using middle terms and qualifiers. At the same time, remember that too many qualifiers may make you appear unsure of yourself.*

politeness. Civility, consideration, refinement, respect, and regard for others as expressed verbally and nonverbally; interaction that follows the socially accepted rules for interpersonal interaction.

politeness strategies. Strategies that support another's face needs and may be used as a strategy to appear likeable.

polychronic time orientation. A view of time in which several things may be scheduled or engaged in at the same time. *Contrast* **monochronic time orientation.**

positive face. The need and desire to be viewed positively by others, to be thought of favorably.

positive feedback. Feedback that supports or reinforces the continuation of behavior along the same lines in which it is already proceeding—for example, applause during a speech. *Contrast* **negative feedback.**

positiveness. A characteristic of effective communication involving positive attitudes toward the self and toward the interpersonal interaction. *Communicate positiveness by expressing your own satisfaction with the interaction, compliment others by expressing your positive thoughts and feelings about and to the other person, and express acceptance and approval.*

power. The ability to control the behaviors of others. *Communicate power by avoiding such powerless message forms as hesitations, too many intensifiers, disqualifiers, tag questions, one-word answers, self-critical statements, overly polite statements, and vulgar and slang expressions.*

power distance. A cultural dimension referring to the degree of distance between those with power and those without power. *Adjust your messages and listening based on the power distance orientation of the culture in which you find yourself.*

power play. A consistent pattern of behavior in which one person tries to control the behavior of another. *Use cooperative strategies to deal with power plays: (1) express your feelings, (2) describe the behavior to which you object, and (3) state a cooperative response.*

pragma love. One of Lee's (1976) six types of love; traditional approach to love, valuing social qualifications and family background and emphasizing logic and practicality over feelings.

pragmatic implication. An assumption that seems logical but is not necessarily true.

premature self-disclosures. Disclosures that are made before a relationship has developed sufficiently.

presentation aids. Visual or auditory means for clarifying ideas.

primacy effect. The condition by which what comes first exerts greater influence than what comes later. *Contrast* **recency effect.**

primacy–recency. A principle of **perception** stating that we generally use early information to get a general impression of a person and use later information to add specificity to this impression.

primary relationship. The relationship between two people who both consider it to be their most (or one of their most) important relationship; the relationship between spouses or domestic partners would be an example.

primary source. Original information about a topic or event—for example, an original research study. *See* **secondary source.**

primary territory. An area that you can consider your exclusive preserve—for example, your room or office.

problem-solving group. A group whose primary task is to solve a problem or, more often, to reach a decision.

problem-solving sequence. A logical step-by-step process for solving a problem that is frequently used by groups; consists of defining and analyzing the problem, establishing criteria for evaluating solutions, identifying possible solutions, evaluating solutions, selecting the best solution, and testing the selected solutions.

process. Ongoing activity; communication is referred to as a process to emphasize that it is always changing, always in motion.

projection. A psychological process whereby we attribute characteristics or feelings of our own to others; often refers to the process whereby we attribute our own faults to others.

pronunciation. The production of syllables or words according to some accepted standard—for example, as presented in a dictionary. Avoid the common pronunciation errors of omission, substitution, addition, and pronouncing sounds that should be silent.

protection theory. A theory of proxemics referring to the fact that people establish a body-buffer zone to protect themselves from unwanted closeness, touching, or attack.

provisionalism. An attitude of open-mindedness that leads to the creation of supportiveness. *Contrast* **certainty.**

proxemic distances. The spatial distances that people maintain in communication and social interaction. *Use spatial distance to signal the type of relationship you are in: intimate, personal, social, or public. Let your spatial relationships reflect your interpersonal relationships. Maintain spatial distances that are comfortable (i.e., neither too close nor too far apart) and that are appropriate to the situation and to your relationship with the other person.*

proxemics. The study of the communicative function of space and of how people unconsciously structure their space—the distances between people in their interactions, the organization of space in homes and offices, and even the design of cities.

proximity. As a principle of **perception,** the tendency to perceive people or events that are physically close as belonging together or representing some kind of a unit. Also, physical closeness; one of the factors influencing interpersonal attraction.

psychological time. The importance placed on past, present, or future time.

public communication. Communication in which the source is one person and the receiver is an audience of many persons.

public distance. The longest **proxemic distance,** ranging from 12 to more than 25 feet.

public territory. Area that is open to all people—for example, a restaurant or park.

punctuation of communication. The breaking up of continuous communication sequences into short sequences with identifiable beginnings and endings or stimuli and responses.

punishment. Noxious or aversive stimulation.

pupillometrics. The study of communication through changes in the size of the pupils of the eyes.

purr words. Highly positive words that express the speaker's feelings rather than any objective reality. *Contrast* **snarl words.**

Pygmalion effect. Condition in which we make a prediction of success, act as if it were true, and thereby make it come true; a type of **self-fulfilling prophecy.**

quality circles. Groups of workers (usually 6 to 12) whose task it is to investigate and make recommendations for improving the quality of some organizational function.

questions of fact. Questions concerned with what is or is not true, what does or does not exist, what did or did not happen.

questions of policy. Questions concerning what should be or should not be done (or what policy should be adopted).

quotes. An **extensional device** to emphasize that a word or phrase is being used in a special sense and should therefore be given special attention.

racist language. Language that denigrates or is derogatory toward members of a particular race.

rate. The speed with which a person speaks, generally measured in words per minute.

receiver. Any person or thing that takes in messages. Receivers may be individuals listening to or reading a message, a group of persons hearing a speech, a scattered television audience, or machines that store information.

recency effect. The condition in which what comes last (i.e., happened most recently) exerts greater influence than what comes first. *Contrast* **primacy effect.**

redundancy. The quality of a message that makes it totally predictable and therefore lacking in information. A message of zero redundancy would be completely unpredictable; a message of 100 percent redundancy would be completely predictable. All human languages contain some degree of built-in redundancy, generally estimated to be about 50 percent.

referent power. Personal power derived from others' desire to identify with or be like the individual.

reflexiveness. The feature of human language that makes it possible for that language to be used to refer to itself; that is, reflexiveness lets us talk about our talk and create a **metalanguage**—a language for talking about language.

regulators. Nonverbal behaviors that regulate, monitor, or control the communications of another person.

rehearsal. The process of fixing in mind the delivery of your public speech. *Rehearse your speech often, perfect your delivery, rehearse the speech as a whole, time the speech at each rehearsal, approximate the specific speech situation as much as possible, see and think of yourself as a public speaker, and incorporate any delivery notes that may be of value during the actual speech presentation.*

rejection. A response to an individual that disagrees with or denies the validity of something the individual says or does.

relational communication. Communication between or among intimates or people in close relationships; used by some theorists as synonymous with **interpersonal communication.**

relationship conflict. A type of conflict that centers on the nature and meaning of a particular relationship. *Contrast* **content conflict.**

relationship deterioration. The process whereby the bonds holding an interpersonal relationship together lessen. *To cope with the ending of a relationship, break the loneliness–depression cycle, take time out, bolster your self-esteem, seek the support of nourishing others, and avoid repeating negative patterns.*

relationship development. The stages of relationships during which you move closer to intimacy; in the model of relationships presented here, relationship development includes the stages of **contact** and **involvement** .

relationship dialectics theory. A theory that describes relationships as defined by competing, opposite desires or motivations, such as the desire for autonomy and the desire to belong to someone, desires for novelty and predictability, and desires for closedness and openness.

relationship maintenance. The processes by which you attempt to keep a relationship stable.

relationship messages. Messages that comment on the relationship between the speakers rather than on matters external to them. *Formulate messages that are appropriate to the stage of the relationship, and listen for messages from relationship partners that may reveal differences in perception about your relationship stage.*

relationship rules. Principles that relationship partners establish to help define their relationship. *Follow the rules for maintaining relationships when you do in fact wish to maintain and even strengthen them.*

repair. Attempts to reverse the process of relationship **deterioration.** *Recognize the problem, engage in productive conflict resolution, pose possible solutions, affirm each other, integrate solutions into normal behavior, and take risks as appropriate.*

response. Any overt or covert behavior.

restatement. A message that repeats an idea in different words, often used to achieve emphasis or clarity.

reward power. Power based on a person's ability to reward another person.

rigid complementarity. Inability to break away from a complementary type of relationship that was once appropriate but is no longer.

role. The part an individual plays in a group; an individual's function or expected behavior.

roundtable. A small group format in which group members arrange themselves in a circular or semicircular pattern; participants meet to share information or solve problems without any set pattern as to who speaks when.

rules theory. A theory that describes relationships as interactions governed by a series of rules that the members agree to follow. When the rules are followed, the relationship is maintained; when they are broken, the relationship experiences difficulty.

schemata. (Singular: *schema*) Mental templates or structures that help us organize items of sensory information and information in memory.

script. A template or organizational structure describing the sequence of events in a given action, procedure, or occurrence.

secondary source. A summary or interpretation of information—for example, a newspaper's summary of a research study. See **primary source**.

secondary territory. An area that does not belong to a particular person but that has been occupied by that person and is therefore associated with her or him—for example, the seat a person normally takes in class.

selective attention. The tendency to attend to those things that you want to see or that you expect to see.

selective exposure. The tendency of listeners to actively seek out information that supports their existing opinions, beliefs, attitudes, and values and to actively avoid information that contradicts them.

selective perception. The tendency to perceive certain things and not others; includes **selective attention** and **selective exposure**.

self-acceptance. Satisfaction with yourself, your virtues and vices, and your abilities and limitations.

self-actualization needs. A basic need to become and do what you feel you must do; a need that is only satisfied, in Maslow's theory, after all other needs are satisfied.

self-adaptors. Movements that satisfy a physical need, especially to make you more comfortable; for example, scratching your head to relieve an itch, moistening your lips because they feel dry, or pushing your hair out of your eyes.

self-attribution. A process through which you seek to account for and understand the reasons and motivations for your own behaviors.

self-awareness. The degree to which you know yourself. *Increase self-awareness by listening to others, increasing your open self as appropriate, and seeking out information (discreetly) to reduce any blind spots.*

self-concept. An individual's self-evaluation or self-appraisal. *Learn who you are: See yourself through the eyes of others; compare yourself to similar (and admired) others; examine the influences of culture; and observe, interpret, and evaluate your own message behaviors.*

self-deprecating strategies. Techniques used to signal your inability to do some task or your incompetence to encourage another to help you out. *Avoid these or use in moderation; such strategies can easily backfire and simply make you seem incompetent.*

self-disclosure. The process of revealing something about yourself to another person. Usually refers to information that would normally be kept hidden. *In considering self-disclosure, consider the legitimacy of your motives for disclosing, the appropriateness of the disclosure, the listener's responses (is the dyadic effect operating?), and the potential burdens self-disclosures might impose.*

self-esteem. The value you place on yourself; your self-evaluation. Usually refers to a positive self-evaluation. *Raise your self-esteem: Increase your communication effectiveness, challenge self-destructive beliefs, seek out nourishing people with whom to interact, work on projects that will result in success, and engage in self-affirmation.*

self-fulfilling prophecy. The situation in which you make a prediction or prophecy that comes true because you act on it as if it were true. *Take a second look at your perceptions when they correspond very closely to your initial expectations; the self-fulfilling prophecy may be at work.*

self-handicapping strategies. Techniques used to excuse possible failure—for example, setting up barriers or obstacles to make a task impossible so that when you fail, you won't be blamed or thought ineffective.

self-monitoring. The manipulation of the image presented to others in interpersonal interactions so as to create a favorable impression.

self-serving bias. A bias in the self-attribution process that leads us to take credit for positive consequences and to deny responsibility for negative outcomes of our behaviors. *Become mindful of any self-serving bias—that is, of giving too much weight to internal factors (when explaining your positives) and too little weight to external factors (when explaining your negatives).*

self-talk. Talk about the self.

semantics. The area of language study concerned with meaning.

sexist language. Language derogatory to one gender, usually women. *Avoid it.*

sexual harassment. Unsolicited and unwanted sexual messages.

short-term memory. Memory that is very limited in capacity; contains information that is quickly lost if it is not passed on to **long-term memory**.

shyness. The condition of discomfort and uneasiness in interpersonal situations.

sign (reasoning from). A form of reasoning in which the presence of certain signs (clues) is interpreted as leading to a particular conclusion.

signal reaction. A conditioned response to a signal; a response to some signal that is immediate rather than delayed.

signal-to-noise ratio. In verbal interaction, the relationship between what is signal (i.e., meaningful) and what is noise (i.e., interference). This ratio also is relative to the communication analyst, the participants, and the context.

silence. The absence of vocal communication; often misunderstood to refer to the absence of any and all communication. Silence often communicates feelings or prevents communication about certain topics. *Because silence can communicate many different meanings (e.g., your anger or your need for time to think), examine your use of silence just as you would eye movements or body gestures.*

similarity. As a principle of **perception,** the tendency to see things that are physically similar as belonging together and/or constituting a unit. As a principle of **attraction,**

your tendency to be attracted to people with qualities similar to your own and to people who are similar to you. *Contrast* **complementarity.**

simile. A figure of speech in which two unlike objects are compared using the words *like* or *as.*

situational listening. A view of listening holding that effective listening needs to be adjusted to the specific situation; one style of listening does not fit all forms of communication.

slang. Language used by special groups that is not considered proper by the general society.

slippery slope. A reasoning fallacy involving the assumption that one event (the one the person is arguing against) will inevitably or most likely lead to another event that everyone agrees would be undesirable. *Seek proof of causality*

small group. A collection of individuals who are connected to one another by some common purpose, are interdependent, have some degree of organization among them, and see themselves as a group.

small group communication. Communication among a collection of individuals small enough in number that all members may interact with relative ease as both senders and receivers, the members being related to one another by some common purpose and with some degree of organization or structure.

small talk. Noncontroversial talk that is usually short in duration and often serves as a polite way of introducing oneself or a topic.

snarl words. Highly negative words that express the feelings of the speaker rather than any objective reality. *Contrast* **purr words.**

social comparison. The processes by which you compare aspects of yourself (e.g., your abilities, opinions, and values) with those of others and then assess and evaluate yourself; one of the sources of **self-concept.**

social distance. The third **proxemic distance,** ranging from 4 to 12 feet; the distance at which business is usually conducted.

social exchange theory. A theory hypothesizing that people develop relationships in which their rewards, or profits, will be greater than their costs and that people avoid or terminate relationships in which the costs exceed the rewards.

social loafing. A theory holding that you exert less effort when you're part of a group than when alone; people have a tendency to loaf.

social network. An organizational structure that allows people to communicate, popularly used to refer to the online sites such as Facebook and Twitter that enable people to communicate with others who share a common interest.

social penetration theory. A theory describing how relationships develop from the superficial to the intimate levels and from few to many areas of interpersonal interaction.

source. Any person or thing that creates messages. A source may be an individual speaking, writing, or gesturing or a computer sending an error message.

specific instances (reasoning from). A form of reasoning in which a speaker examines several specific instances and forms a conclusion about the whole on the basis of those instances.

specific purpose. The information you want to communicate (in an informative speech) or the attitude or behavior you want to change (in a persuasive speech).

speech. Messages utilizing a vocal–auditory channel.

speech of demonstration. A speech devoted to showing how to do something or how something operates.

speech of description. A speech devoted to describing an object or person.

spontaneity. The communication pattern in which a person verbalizes what he or she is thinking without attempting to develop strategies for control; encourages **supportiveness.**

stability. A principle of perception stating that our perceptions of things and of people are relatively consistent with our previous perceptions.

static evaluation. An orientation that fails to recognize that the world is characterized by constant change; an attitude that sees people and events as fixed rather than as constantly changing. *Mentally date your statements to avoid thinking and communicating that the world is static and unchanging. In your messages, reflect the inevitability of change.*

status. The relative level a person occupies in a hierarchy; status always involves a comparison, and thus one person's status is only relative to the status of another.

stereotype. In communication, a fixed impression of a group of people through which we then perceive specific individuals; stereotypes are most often negative but may also be positive. *Be careful of thinking and talking in stereotypes; recognize that members of all groups are different, and focus on the individual rather than on the individual's membership in one group or another.*

stimulus. Any external or internal change that impinges on or arouses an organism.

storge love. One of Lee's (1976) six types of love; a gradually unfolding, peaceful and tranquil love marked by companionability and shared interests and activities, sometimes difficult to distinguish from friendship.

subjectivity. A principle of perception stating that our perceptions are not objective but are influenced by our wants and needs and our expectations and predictions.

supporting materials. Usually used in reference to public speaking, enlarging a concept or principle through the use of examples, illustrations, and narratives; testimony; definitions; statistics; and visual aids. *Use supporting materials that will prove interesting to your audience, that are consistent in style with the rest of the speech, and that clearly relate to the concept and principle that they are designed to explain.*

supportiveness. An attitude of an individual or an atmosphere in a group that is characterized by openness, absence of fear, and a genuine feeling of equality. *Try to respond supportively by expressing your empathy, being open even to opposing viewpoints, and acting as an equal in the interaction.*

symmetrical relationship. A relation between two or more persons in which one person's behavior serves as a stimulus for the same type of behavior in the other person(s). Examples of such relationships include those in which anger in one person encourages or serves as a stimulus for anger in another person or in which a critical comment by the person leads the other person to respond in like manner.

symposium. A small group format in which each member of the group delivers a relatively prepared talk on some aspect of the topic. Often combined with a **forum.**

synchronous communication. Communication that takes place in real time; sending and receiving take place at the same time (as in face-to-face communication). Contrast asynchronous communication.

systematic desensitization. A theory and technique for dealing with a variety of fears (such as communication apprehension) in which you gradually expose yourself to an anxiety-producing stimulus so as to become hardened to it.

taboo. Forbidden; culturally censored. Taboo language is language that is frowned on by "polite society." Topics and specific words may be considered taboo—for example, death, sex, certain forms of illness, and various words denoting sexual activities and excretory functions. *Generally, avoid violating any cultural taboo; the more formal the situation, the more important it is to avoid such taboos.*

tag questions. Questions that ask for another's agreement and often signal weakness or uncertainty—for example, "That dinner was fine, don't you think?" *Avoid these when you want your speech to have power.*

team. A particular kind of small group that is constructed for a specific task and whose members have clearly defined roles, are committed to achieving the same goal, and are content focused.

template outline. A type of outline that contains the essential categories of a speech to be filled in during speech preparation.

temporal communication. The messages communicated by a person's time orientation and treatment of time.

territoriality. A possessive or ownership reaction to an area of space or to particular objects.

testimonial. A persuasive technique in which the speaker uses the authority or image of some positively evaluated person to gain an audience's approval or of some negatively evaluated person to gain listeners' rejection.

testimony. A form of supporting material consisting of an experts' opinions or witnesses' accounts and may add an authoritative tone to your arguments.

theory. A general statement or principle applicable to related phenomena.

thesis. The main assertion of a message—for example, the theme of a public speech.

topical pattern. An organizational pattern for a public speech in which the topic is organized into its subtopics or component parts.

touch avoidance. The tendency to avoid touching and being touched by others. *Respect the touch-avoidance tendencies of others; pay special attention to cultural and gender differences in touch preferences and in touch avoidance.*

touch communication. Communication through tactile means.

transactional. A view of human communication characterized by mutual influence and interdependence; communication is a transactional process because no element is independent of any other element.

transfer. A persuasive technique in which a speaker associates an idea with something the audience respects in order to gain approval or with something the audience dislikes in order to be rejected.

transitions. Words or statements that connect what was said to what will be said. *Use transitions and internal summaries to connect the parts of a speech and to help listeners remember the speech.*

truth bias. The assumption that most people operate under that the messages they hear are truthful.

turn-denying cues. Verbal or nonverbal cues indicating that the listener does not want to assume the role of speaker.

turn-maintaining cues. Verbal or nonverbal signals that communicate the wish to maintain the role of speaker.

turn-requesting cues. Verbal or nonverbal behaviors that let the speaker know that you would like to say something and take a turn as speaker.

turn-taking cues. Verbal or nonverbal signals that speakers and listeners use to comment on their roles in a conversation; behaviors that help regulate and structure conversation. *Respond to both the verbal and the nonverbal conversational turn-taking cues given to you by others, and make your own cues clear to them.*

turn-yielding cues. Verbal or nonverbal signals indicating the speaker's desire to give up the speaker's role.

uncertainty reduction strategies. Passive, active, and interactive ways of increasing accuracy in interpersonal perception.

uncertainty reduction theory. A theory holding that as relationships develop, uncertainty is reduced; relationship development is seen as a process of reducing uncertainty about one another.

universal of interpersonal communication. A feature of communication common to all interpersonal communication acts.

unknown self. A part of the self that is unknown to the self as well as to others, but that is inferred to exist on the basis of various projective tests, slips of the tongue, dream analyses, and the like.

upward communication. Communication in which the messages are sent from lower levels to upper levels of an organization or hierarchy—for example, from line worker to management.

value. The relative worth of an object; a quality that makes something desirable or undesirable; an ideal or custom about which we have emotional responses, whether positive or negative.

verbal aggressiveness. A method of winning an argument by attacking the other person's **self-concept.** *Contrast* **argumentativeness.**

violation. The unwarranted use of another's territory.

visual dominance. The use of your eyes to maintain a superior or dominant position; for example, when making an especially important point, you might look intently at the other person.

voice qualities. Aspects of **paralanguage**—specifically, pitch range, vocal lip control, glottis control, pitch control, articulation control, rhythm control, resonance, and tempo.

volume. The relative loudness of the voice. *Use volume to reinforce the meanings you want to communicate.*

weasel words. Words whose meanings are slippery and difficult to pin down. *Ask for specifics when confronted with weasel words.*

win–win solutions. Solutions that benefit both parties in a conflict. *Consider the possibility of solutions in which both parties gain from the conflict. Focus on these rather than solutions in which one person wins and the other loses.*

withdrawal. A reaction to territorial encroachment that involves leaving the territory; the tendency to become closed off from conflicts rather than confronting the issues.

you-messages. Messages in which the speaker denies responsibility for his or her own thoughts and behaviors; messages that attribute the speaker's perception to another person; messages of blame. *Contrast* **I-messages.**

References

Abel, G. G., & Harlow, N. (2001). *The stop child molestation book.* Philadelphia: Xlibris.

Acor, A. A. (2001). Employers' perceptions of persons with body art and an experimental test regarding eyebrow piercing. *Dissertation Abstracts International: Section B. The Sciences and Engineering, 61,* 3885.

Adams-Price, C. E., Dalton, W. T., & Sumrall, R. (2004, October). Victim blaming in young, middle-aged, and older adults: Variations on the severity effect. *Journal of Adult Development, 11,* 289–295.

Adrianson, L. (2001). Gender and computer-mediated communication: Group processes in problem solving. *Computers in Human Behavior, 17,* 71–94.

Afifi, W. A. (2007). Nonverbal communication. In B. B. Whaley & W. Samter (Eds.), *Explaining communication: Contemporary theories and exemplars* (pp. 39–60). Mahwah, NJ: Lawrence Erlbaum.

Afifi, W. A., & Johnson, M. L. (2005). The nature and function of tie-signs. In V. Manusov (Ed.), *The sourcebook of nonverbal measures: Going beyond words* (pp. 189–198). Mahwah, NJ: Lawrence Erlbaum.

Akinnaso, F. N. (1982). On the differences between spoken and written language. *Language and Speech, 25*(Part 2), 97–125.

Alessandra, T. (1986). How to listen effectively. *Speaking of success* [Videotape series]. San Diego, CA: Levitz Sommer Productions.

Altman, I. (1975). *The environment and social behavior.* Monterey, CA: Brooks/Cole.

Altman, I., & Taylor, D. (1973). *Social penetration: The development of interpersonal relationships.* New York: Holt, Rinehart & Winston.

Amato, P. R. (1994). The impact of divorce on men and women in India and the United States. *Journal of Comparative Family Studies, 25,* 207–221.

Andersen, J. F., Andersen, P. A., & Lustig, M. W. (1987). Opposite sex touch avoidance: A national replication and extension. *Journal of Nonverbal Behavior, 11,* 89–109.

Andersen, P. A. (1991). Explaining intercultural differences in nonverbal communication. In L. A. Samovar & R. E. Porter (Eds.), *Intercultural communication: A reader* (6th ed., pp. 286–296). Belmont, CA: Wadsworth.

Andersen, P. A. (2004). *The complete idiot's guide to body language.* New York: Penguin Group.

Andersen, P. A., & Leibowitz, K. (1978). The development and nature of the construct of touch avoidance. *Environmental Psychology and Nonverbal Behavior, 3,* 89–106.

Anderson, K. J. et al. (1998, August). Meta-analysis of gender effects on conversational interruption: Who, what, when, where, and how. *Sex Roles, 39,* 225–252.

Angier, N. (1995, May 9). Scientists mull role of empathy in man and beast. *New York Times,* C1, C6.

Angier, N. (2010, August 29). Just don't call me. . . . . *New York Times,* Weekend, p. 3.

Argyle, M. (1986). Rules for social relationships in four cultures. *Australian Journal of Psychology, 38,* 309–318.

Argyle, M. (1988). *Bodily communication* (2nd ed.). New York: Methuen.

Argyle, M., & Henderson, M. (1984). *The anatomy of relationships: And the rules and skills needed to manage them successfully.* London: Heinemann.

Argyle, M., & Ingham, R. (1972). Gaze, mutual gaze and distance. *Semiotica, 1,* 32–49.

Arnold, L. B. (2008). *Family communication: Theory and research.* Boston, MA: Allyn & Bacon.

Aronson, E., Wilson, T. D., & Akert, R. M. (2013). *Social psychology: The heart and the mind* (7th ed.). New York: Longman.

Aronson, J., Cohen, J., & Nail, P. (1998). Self-affirmation theory: An update and appraisal. In E. Harmon-Jones & J. S. Mills (Eds.), *Cognitive dissonance theory: Revival with revisions and controversies* (pp. 127–147). Washington, DC: American Psychological Association.

Asch, S. (1946). Forming impressions of personality. *Journal of Abnormal and Social Psychology, 41,* 258–290.

Ashcraft, M. H. (1998). *Fundamentals of cognition.* New York: Longman.

Atkinson, C. (2010). *The backchannel: How audiences are using Twitter and social media and changing presentations forever.* Berkeley, CA: New Riders.

Avtgis, T., & Rancer, A. S. (Eds.) (2010). *Arguments, aggression, and conflict: New directions in theory and research.* Clifton, NJ: Routledge.

Axtell, R. E. (1990). *Do's and taboos of hosting international visitors.* New York: Wiley.

Axtell, R. E. (1993). *Do's and taboos around the world* (3rd ed.). New York: Wiley.

Axtell, R. E. (2007). *Essential do's and taboos: The complete guide to international business and leisure travel.* Hoboken, NJ: Wiley.

Ayres, J. (1986). Perceptions of speaking ability: An explanation for stage fright. *Communication Education, 35,* 275–287.

Bach, G. R., & Wyden, P. (1968). *The intimate enemy.* New York: Avon.

Bacon, K. (2011). More deadly than sticks and stones. In Larry Schnoor (Ed.), *Winning Orations* (pp. 104–106). Mankato, MN: Interstate Oratorical Association.

Balsam, K. F., Beauchaine, T. P., Rothblum, E. D., & Solomon, S. E. (2008). Three-year follow-up of same-sex couples who had civil unions in Vermont, same-sex couples not in civil unions, and heterosexual married couples. *Developmental Psychology, 44,* 102–116.

Barker, L. L. (1990). *Communication* (5th ed.). Englewood Cliffs, NJ: Prentice-Hall.

Barker, L., Edwards, R., Gaines, C., Gladney, K., & Holley, F. (1980). An investigation of proportional time spent in various communication activities by college students. *Journal of Applied Communication Research, 8,* 101–109.

Barnlund, D. C. (1970). A transactional model of communication. In J. Akin, A. Goldberg, G. Myers, & J. Stewart (Eds.), *Language behavior: A book of readings in communication.* The Hague: Mouton.

Barnlund, D. C. (1975). Communicative styles in two cultures: Japan and the United States. In A. Kendon, R. M. Harris, & M. R. Key (Eds.), *Organization of behavior in face-to-face interaction.* The Hague: Mouton.

Barnlund, D. C. (1989). *Communicative styles of Japanese and Americans: Images and realities.* Belmont, CA: Wadsworth.

Baron, R. A., Branscombe, N. R., & Byrne, D. R. (2009). *Social psychology,* 11th ed. Boston: Allyn & Bacon.

Baron, R. A., & Byrne, D. (1984). *Social psychology: Understanding human interaction* (4th ed.). Boston: Allyn & Bacon.

Barrett, L., & Godfrey, T. (1988). Listening. *Person Centered Review, 3,* 410–425.

Barry, D. T. (2003). Cultural and demographic correlates of self-reported guardedness among East Asian immigrants in the U.S. *International Journal of Psychology, 38,* 150–159.

Basso, K. H. (1972). To give up on words: Silence in Apache culture. In P. P. Giglioli (Ed.), *Language and social context.* New York: Penguin.

Baumeister, R. F., Bushman, B. J., & Campbell, W. K. (2000, February). Self-esteem, narcissism, and aggression: Does violence result from low self-esteem or from threatened egotism? *Current Directions in Psychological Science, 9,* 26–29.

Bavelas, J. B. (1990). Can one not communicate? Behaving and communicating: A reply to Motley. *Western Journal of Speech Communication, 54,* 593–602.

Baxter, L. A. (1983). Relationship disengagement: An examination of the reversal hypothesis. *Western Journal of Speech Communication, 47,* 85–98.

Baxter, L. A. (1984). An investigation of compliance-gaining as politeness. *Human Communication Research, 10,* 427–456.

Baxter, L. A. (1986). Gender differences in the heterosexual relationship rules embedded in break-up accounts. *Journal of Social and Personal Relationships, 3,* 289–306.

Beatty, M. J. (1988). Situational and predispositional correlates of public speaking anxiety. *Communication Education, 37,* 28–39.

Beatty, M. J., Rudd, J. E., & Valencic, K. M. (1999). A re-evaluation of the verbal aggressiveness scale: One factor or two? *Communication Research Reports, 16,* 10–17.

Bechler, C., & Johnson, S. D. (1995). Leadership and listening: A study of member perceptions. *Small Group Research, 26,* 77–85.

Beck, A. T. (1988). *Love is never enough.* New York: Harper & Row.

Bedford, V. H. (1996). Relationships between adult siblings. In A. E. Auhagen & M. von Salisch (Eds.), *The diversity of human relationships* (pp. 120–140). New York: Cambridge University Press.

Beebe, S. A., & Masterson, J. T. (2012). *Communicating in small groups: Principles and practices* (10th ed.). Boston, MA: Allyn & Bacon.

Bell, R. A., & Daly, J. A. (1984). The affinity-seeking function of communication. *Communication Monographs, 51,* 91–115.

Bellafiore, D. (2005). Interpersonal conflict and effective communication. Retrieved May 7, 2006, from www.drbalternatives.com/articles/cc2.html

Benne, K. D., & Sheats, P. (1948). Functional roles of group members. *Journal of Social Issues, 4,* 41–49.

Bennis, W., & Nanus, B. (2003). *Leaders: The strategies for taking charge.* New York: Harper & Row.

Benoit, W. L., & Benoit, P. J. (1990). Memory for conversational behavior, *Southern Communication Journal, 55,* 17–23.

Benson, S. G., & Dundis, S. P. (2003). Understanding and motivating health care employees: Integrating Maslow's hierarchy of needs, training and technology. *Journal of Nursing Management, 11,* 315–320.

Berg, J. H., & Archer, R. L. (1983). The disclosure-liking relationship. *Human Communication Research, 10,* 269–281.

Berger, C. R., & Bradac, J. J. (1982). *Language and social knowledge: Uncertainty in interpersonal relations.* London: Edward Arnold.

Bernstein, W. M., Stephan, W. G., & Davis, M. H. (1979). Explaining attributions for achievement: A path analytic approach. *Journal of Personality and Social Psychology, 37,* 1810–1821.

Berry, J. N. III (2004). Can I quote you on that? *Library Journal, 129,* 10.

Berscheid, E., & Reis, H. T. (1998). Attraction and close relationships. In D. Gilbert, S. Fiske, & G. Lindzey (Eds.), *The Handbook of Social Psychology,* 4th ed. (Vol. 2, pp. 193–281).

Blake, R. R., & Mouton, J. S. (1984). *The managerial grid III* (3rd ed.). Houston, TX: Gulf.

Blieszner, R., & Adams, R. G. (1992). *Adult friendship.* Newbury Park, CA: Sage.

Bochner, S., & Hesketh, B. (1994). Power distance, individualism/collectivism, and job-related attitudes in a culturally diverse work group. *Journal of Cross-Cultural Psychology, 25,* 233–257.

Bok, S. (1978). *Lying: Moral choice in public and private life.* New York: Pantheon.

Bok, S. (1983). *Secrets.* New York: Vintage.

Borden, G. A. (1991). *Cultural orientation: An approach to understanding intercultural communication.* Englewood Cliffs, NJ: Prentice-Hall.

Bower, B. (2001). Self-illusions come back to bite students. *Science News, 159,* 148.

Bower, S. A., & Bower, G. A. (2005). *Asserting yourself: A practical guide for positive change.* Cambridge, MA: DaCapo Press.

Brashers, D. E. (2007). A theory of communication and uncertainty management. In B. B. Whaley & W. Samter (Eds.), *Explaining communication: Contemporary theories and exemplars* (pp. 201–218). Mahwah, NJ: Lawrence Erlbaum.

Bridges, C. R. (1996). The characteristics of career achievement perceived by African American college administrators. *Journal of Black Studies, 26,* 748–767.

Brilhart, J., & Galanes, G. (1992). *Effective group discussion* (7th ed.). Dubuque, IA: Brown & Benchmark.

Brown, P. (1980). How and why are women more polite: Some evidence from a Mayan community. In S. McConnell-Ginet, R. Borker, & M. Furman (Eds.), *Women and language in literature and society* (pp. 111–136). New York: Praeger.

Brown, P., & Levinson, S. C. (1987). *Politeness: Some universals of language usage.* Cambridge, England: Cambridge University Press.

Brownell, J. (1987). Listening: The toughest management skill. *Cornell Hotel and Restaurant Administration Quarterly, 27,* 64–71.

Brownell, J. (2010). *Listening: Attitudes, principles, and skills* (5th ed.). Boston: Allyn & Bacon.

Brownell, J. (2008). Exploring the strategic ground for listening and organizational effectiveness. *Scandinavian Journal of Hospitality and Tourism, 8,* 211–229.

Brownell, J. (2010). *Listening: Attitudes, principles, and skills* (4th ed.). Boston, MA: Allyn & Bacon.

Bruneau, T. (1985). The time dimension in intercultural communication. In L. A. Samovar & R. E. Porter (Eds.), *Intercultural communication: A reader* (4th ed., pp. 280–289). Belmont, CA: Wadsworth.

Bruneau, T. (1990). Chronemics: The study of time in human interaction. In J. A. DeVito & M. L. Hecht (Eds.), *The nonverbal communication reader* (pp. 301–311). Prospect Heights, IL: Waveland Press.

Bruneau, T. (2009/2010). Chronemics: Time-binding and the construction of personal time. *General Semantics Bulletin, 76,* 82–94.

Buber, M. (1958). *I and thou* (2nd ed.). New York: Scribner's.

Buller, D. B., LePoire, B. A., Aune, K., & Eloy, S. (1992). Social perceptions as mediators of the effect of speech rate similarity on compliance. *Human Communication Research, 19,* 286–311.

Burgoon, J. K., & Bacue, A. E. (2003). Nonverbal communication skills. In J. O. Greene & B. R. Burleson (Eds.), *Handbook of communication and social interaction skills* (pp. 179–220). Mahwah, NJ: Erlbaum.

Burgoon, J. K., & Hale, J. L. (1988). Nonverbal expectancy violations: Model elaboration and application to immediacy behaviors. *Communication Monographs, 55,* 58–79.

Burgoon, J. K., & Hoobler, G. D. (2002). Nonverbal signals. In M. L. Knapp & J. A. Daly (Eds.), *Handbook of interpersonal communication* (3rd ed., pp. 240–299). Thousand Oaks, CA: Sage.

Burgoon, J. K., Berger, C. R., & Waldron, V. R. (2000). Mindfulness and interpersonal communication. *Journal of Social Issues, 56,* 105–127.

Burgoon, J. K., Buller, D. B., & Woodall, W. G. (1996). *Nonverbal communication: The unspoken dialogue* (2nd ed.). New York: McGraw-Hill.

Burgoon, J. K., Guerrero, L. K., & Manusov, V. (2011). In Knapp, M. L., & Daly, J. A. (Eds.), *The sage handbook of interpersonal communication,* (4th ed., pp. 239–282). Los Angeles, CA: Sage.

Burgoon, J., Guerrero, L., & Floyd, K. (2010). *Nonverbal communication.* Boston, MA: Allyn & Bacon.

Burgstahler, S. (2007, July). Managing an e-mentoring community to support students with disabilities: A case study. *Distance Education Report 11,* 7–15.

Burleson, B. R., Holmstrom, A. J., & Gilstrap, C. M. (2005). "Guys can't say *that* to guys": Four experiments assessing the normative motivation account for deficiencies in the emotional support provided by men. *Communication Monographs, 72,* 468–501.

Burleson, B. R., Kunkel, A. W., & Birch, J. D. (1994). Thoughts about talk in romantic relationships: Similarity makes for attraction (and happiness, too). *Communication Quarterly, 42,* 259–273.

Burleson, B. R., Samter, W., & Luccetti, A. E. (1992). Similarity in communication values as a predictor of friendship choices: Studies of friends and best friends. *Southern Communication Journal, 57,* 260–276.

Burnard, P. (2003). Ordinary chat and therapeutic conversation: Phatic communication and mental health nursing. *Journal of Psychiatric and Mental Health Nursing, 10,* 678–682.

Butler, J., Pryor, B., & Grieder, M. (1998). Impression formation as a function of male baldness. *Perceptual and Motor Skills, 86,* 347–350.

Butler, P. E. (1981). *Talking to yourself: Learning the language of self-support.* New York: Harper & Row.

Byers, E. S., & Demmons, S. (1999). Sexual satisfaction and sexual self-disclosure within dating relationships. *Journal of Sex Research, 36,* 180–189.

Cahn, D. D., & Abigail, R. A. (2007). *Managing conflict through communication* (3rd ed.). Boston: Allyn & Bacon.

Cai, D. A., & Fink, E. L. (2002). Conflict style differences between individualists and collectivists. *Communication Monographs, 69,* 67–87.

Canary, D. J. (2003). Managing interpersonal conflict: A model of events related to strategic choices. In J. O. Greene & B. R. Burleson (Eds.), *Handbook of communication and social interaction skills* (pp. 515–550). Mahwah, NJ: Lawrence Erlbaum.

Canary, D. J., & Hause, K. (1993). Is there any reason to research sex differences in communication? *Communication Quarterly, 41,* 129–144.

Canary, D. J., Cupach, W. R., & Messman, S. J. (1995). *Relationship conflict: Conflict in parent-child, friendship, and romantic relationships.* Thousand Oaks, CA: Sage.

Cappella, J. N. (1993). The facial feedback hypothesis in human interaction: Review and speculation. *Journal of Language and Social Psychology, 12,* 13–29.

Caproni, P. J. (2012). *Management skills for everyday life* (3rd ed.). Boston, MA: Prentice-Hall.

Carroll, D. W. (1994). *Psychology of language* (2nd ed.). Pacific Grove, CA: Brooks/Cole.

Cate, R. J., Henton, J., Koval, R., Christopher, F., & Lloyd, S. (1982). Premarital abuse: A social psychological perspective. *Journal of Family Issues, 3,* 79–90.

Caughlin, J. P., Koerner, A. F., Schrodt, P., & Fitzpatrick, M. A. (2011). Interpersonal communication in family relationships.

In Knapp, M. L., & Daly, J. A. (Eds.), *The Sage handbook of interpersonal communication*, 4th ed. (pp. 679–714). Los Angeles, CA: Sage.

Cawthon, S. W. (2001). Teaching strategies in inclusive classrooms with deaf students. *Journal of Deaf Studies and Deaf Education, 6,* 212–225.

Chadwick-Jones, J. K. (1976). *Social exchange theory: Its structure and influence in social psychology.* New York: Academic Press.

Chang, H., & Holt, G. R. (1996). The changing Chinese interpersonal world: Popular themes in interpersonal communication books in modern Taiwan. *Communication Quarterly, 44,* 85–106.

Chanowitz, B., & Langer, E. (1981). Premature cognitive commitment. *Journal of Personality and Social Psychology, 41,* 1051–1063.

Cheney, G., & Tompkins, P. K. (1987). Coming to terms with organizational identification and commitment. *Central States Speech Journal, 38,* 1–15.

Childress, H. (2004). Teenagers, territory and the appropriation of space. *Childhood: A Global Journal of Child Research, 11,* 195–205.

Chung, L. C., & Ting-Toomey, S. (1999). Ethnic identity and relational expectations among Asian Americans. *Communication Research Reports, 16,* 157–166.

Clance, P. R. (1985) *The impostor phenomenon: Overcoming the fear that haunts your success.* New York: Peachtree, 1985.

Clark, H. (1974). The power of positive speaking. *Psychology Today, 8,* 102, 108–111.

Clinton, H. (1995). Remarks to the U.N. 4th World Conference on Women Plenary Session. Retrieved May 9, 2012, from http://www.americanrhetoric.com/speeches/hillaryclintonbeijingspeech.htm.

Cody, M. J., & Dunn, D. (2007). Accounts. In B. B. Whaley and W. Samter (Eds.), *Explaining communication: Contemporary theories and exemplars* (pp. 237–256). Mahwah, NJ: Lawrence Erlbaum.

Coleman, P. (2002). *How to say it for couples: Communicating with tenderness, openness, and honesty.* Paramus, NJ: Prentice-Hall.

Collins, J. E., & Clark, L. F. (1989). Responsibility and rumination: The trouble with understanding the dissolution of a relationship. *Social Cognition, 7,* 152–173.

Comer, L. B., & Drollinger, T. (1999). Active emphatic listening and selling success: A conceptual framework. *Journal of Personal Selling and Sales Management, 19,* 15–29.

Cooley, C. H. (1922). *Human nature and the social order* (Rev. ed.). New York: Scribner's.

Cooper, A., & Sportolari, L. (1997). Romance in cyberspace: Understanding online attraction. *Journal of Sex Education and Therapy, 22,* 7–14.

Coover, G. E., & Murphy, S. T. (2000). The communicated self: Exploring the interaction between self and social context. *Human Communication Research 26,* 125–147.

Cornwell, B., & Lundgren, D. C. (2001). Love on the Internet: Involvement and misrepresentation in romantic relationships in cyberspace vs. realspace. *Computers in Human Behavior, 17,* 197–211.

Crawford, M. (1994). Rethinking the romance: Teaching the content and function of gender stereotypes in the Psychology of Women course. *Teaching of Psychology, 21,* 151–153.

Crowley, A. (1999, August 30). Project leaders wanted. *PC Week,* 76.

Crown, C. L., & Cummins, D. A. (1998). Objective versus perceived vocal interruptions in the dialogues of unacquainted pairs, friends, and couples. *Journal of Language and Social Psychology, 17,* 372–389.

Dahle. C. (2004, July 25). Choosing a mentor? Cast a wide net. *New York Times,* BU 9.

Davis, F. (1973). *Inside intuition.* New York: New American Library.

Davitz, J. R. (Ed.). (1964). *The communication of emotional meaning.* New York: McGraw-Hill.

Deal, J. E., & Wampler, K. S. (1986). Dating violence: The primacy of previous experience. *Journal of Social and Personal Relationships, 3,* 457–471.

deBono, E. (1976). *Teaching thinking.* New York: Penguin.

Dell, K. (2005, February 14). Just for dudes. *Time,* B22.

DePaulo, B. M., Lindsay, J. J., Malone, B. E., Muhlenbruck, L., Charlton, K., & Cooper, H. (2003). Cues to deception. *Psychological Bulletin, 129,* 74–118.

Derlega, V. J., Winstead, B. A., & Wong, P. T. P., & Greenspan, M. (1987). Self-disclosure and relationship development: An attributional analysis. In M. E. Roloff & G. R. Miller (Eds.), *Interpersonal processes: New directions in communication research* (pp. 172–187). Thousand Oaks, CA: Sage.

DeTurck, M. A. (1987). When communication fails: Physical aggression as a compliance-gaining strategy. *Communication Monographs, 54,* 106–112.

DeVito, J. A. (1965). Comprehension factors in oral and written discourse of skilled communicators. *Communication Monographs, 32,* 124–128.

DeVito, J. A. (1976). Relative ease in comprehending yes/no questions. In J. Blankenship & H. G. Stelzner (Eds.), *Rhetoric and communication* (pp. 143–154). Urbana: University of Illinois Press.

DeVito, J. A. (1981). *The psychology of speech and language: An introduction to psycholinguistics.* Washington, DC: University Press of America.

DeVito, J. A. (1996). *Brainstorms: How to think more creatively about communication (or about anything else).* New York: Longman.

DeVito, J. A. (2003). SCREAM before you scream. *ETC: A Review of General Semantics* 60 (Spring), 42–45.

Dewey, J. (1910). *How we think.* Boston, MA: Heath.

Dillard, J. P., & Marshall, L. J. (2003). Persuasion as a social skill. In J. O. Greene & B. R. Burleson (Eds.), *Handbook of communication and social interaction skills* (pp. 479–514). Mahwah, NJ: Erlbaum.

Dindia, K., & Canary, D. J. (2006). (Eds). *Sex differences and similarities in communication* (2nd ed.). Mahwah, NJ: Lawrence Erlbaum.

Donahue, W. A., with Kolt, R. (1992). *Managing interpersonal conflict.* Thousand Oaks, CA: Sage.

Donaldson, S. (1992). Gender and discourse: The case of interruptions. *Carleton Papers in Applied Language Studies, 9,* 47–66.

Dovidio, J. F., Gaertner, S. E., Kawakami, K., & Hodson, G. (2002). Why can't we just get along? Interpersonal biases and interracial distrust. *Cultural Diversity and Ethnic Minority Psychology, 8,* 88–102.

Drass, K. A. (1986). The effect of gender identity on conversation. *Social Psychology Quarterly, 49,* 294–301.

Dresser, N. (1996). *Multicultural manners: New rules of etiquette for a changing society.* New York: Wiley.

Drews, D. R., Allison, C. K., & Probst, J. R. (2000). Behavioral and self-concept differences in tattooed and nontattooed college students. *Psychological Reports, 86,* 475–481.

Dreyfuss, H. (1971). *Symbol sourcebook.* New York: McGraw-Hill.

Drummond, K., & Hopper, R. (1993). Acknowledgment tokens in series. *Communication Reports, 6,* 47–53.

Dsilva, M., & Whyte, L. O. (1998). Cultural differences in conflict styles: Vietnamese refugees and established residents. *The Howard Journal of Communication, 9,* 57–68.

Dunbar, N. E., & Burgoon, J. K. (2005). Measuring nonverbal dominance. In V. Manusov (Ed.), *The sourcebook of nonverbal measures: Going beyond words* (pp. 361–374). Mahwah, NJ: Lawrence Erlbaum.

Dunbar, R. I. M. (2004). Gossip in evolutionary perspective. *Review of General Psychology 8,* 100–110.

Duncan, S. D., Jr. (1972). Some signals and rules for taking speaking turns in conversation. *Journal of Personality and Social Psychology, 23,* 283–292.

Dunn, D., & Cody, M. J. (2000). Account credibility and public image: Excuses, justifications, denials, and sexual harassment. *Communication Monographs, 67,* 372–391.

Duval, T. S., & Silva, P. J. (2002). Self-awareness, probability of improvement, and the self-serving bias. *Journal of Personality and Social Psychology, 82,* 49–61.

Eastwick, P. W., & Finkel, E. J. (2009). Reciprocity of Liking. In H. T. Reis & S. Sprecher (Eds.), *Encyclopedia of human relationships* (pp. 1333–1336). Thousand Oaks, CA: Sage.

Eden, D. (1992). Leadership and expectations: Pygmalion effects and other self-fulfilling prophecies in organizations. *Leadership Quarterly, 3,* 271–305.

Eder, D., & Enke, J. L. (1991). The structure of gossip: Opportunities and constraints on collective expression among adolescents. *American Sociological Review, 56,* 494–508.

Egan, K. G., & Moreno, M. A. (2011). Alcohol references on undergraduate male's Facebook profiles. *American Journal of Men's Health 5,* 413–420.

Ehrenhaus, P. (1988). Silence and symbolic expression. *Communication Monographs, 55,* 41–57.

Einhorn, L. (2006). Using e-prime and English minus absolutisms to provide self-empathy. *ETC: A Review of General Semantics, 63,* 180–186.

Einstein, E. (1995). Success or sabotage: Which self-fulfilling prophecy will the stepfamily create? In D. K. Huntley (Ed.), *Understanding stepfamilies: Implications for assessment and treatment.* Alexandria, VA: American Counseling Association.

Ekman, P. (2009). *Telling lies: Clues to deceit in the marketplace, politics, and marriage* (3rd ed.). New York: Norton.

Ekman, P., & Friesen, W. V. (1969). The repertoire of nonverbal behavior: Categories, origins, usage, and coding. *Semiotica, 1,* 49–98.

Ekman, P., Friesen, W. V., & Ellsworth, P. (1972). *Emotion in the human face: Guidelines for research and an integration of findings.* New York: Pergamon Press.

Elfenbein, H. A., & Ambady, N. (2002). Is there an in-group advantage in emotion recognition? *Psychological Bulletin, 128,* 243–249.

Ellis, A. (1988). *How to stubbornly refuse to make yourself miserable about anything, yes anything.* Secaucus, NJ: Lyle Stuart.

Ellis, A., & Dryden, W. (2007). *The practice of rational emotive therapy* (2nd ed.). New York: Springer.

Elmes, M. B., & Gemmill, G. (1990). The psychodynamics of mindlessness and dissent in small groups. *Small Group Research, 21,* 28–44.

Emmers-Sommer, T. M. (2004). The effect of communication quality and quantity indicators on intimacy and relational satisfaction. *Journal of Social and Personal Relationships, 21,* 99–411.

Exline, R. V., Ellyson, S. L., & Long, B. (1975). Visual behavior as an aspect of power role relationships. In P. Pliner, L. Krames, & T. Alloway (Eds.), *Nonverbal communication of aggression.* New York: Plenum Press.

Faigley, L. (2009). *The Penguin handbook* (3rd ed.). New York: Longman.

Fengler, A. P. (1974). Romantic love in courtship: Divergent paths of male and female students. *Journal of Comparative Family Studies,* 134–139.

Festinger, L. (1954). A theory of social comparison processes. *Human Relations, 7,* 117–140.

Fielder, F. E. (1967). *A theory of leadership effectiveness.* New York: McGraw-Hill.

Fitzpatrick, M. A. (1983). Predicting couples' communication from couples' self-reports. In R. N. Bostrom (Ed.), *Communication Yearbook 7* (pp. 49–82). Thousand Oaks, CA: Sage.

Fitzpatrick, M. A. (1988). *Between husbands and wives: Communication in marriage.* Thousand Oaks, CA: Sage.

Fitzpatrick, M. A. (1991). Sex differences in marital conflict: Social psychophysiological versus cognitive explanations. *Text, 11,* 341–364.

Fitzpatrick, M. A., Jandt, F. E., Myrick, F. L., & Edgar, T. (1994). Gay and lesbian couple relationships. In R. J. Ringer (Ed.), *Queer words, queer images: Communication and the construction of homosexuality* (pp. 265–285). New York: New York University Press.

Floyd, K., & Mikkelson, A. C. (2005). In V. Manusov (Ed.), *The sourcebook of nonverbal measures: Going beyond words* (pp. 47–56). Mahwah, NJ: Lawrence Erlbaum.

Folger, J. P., Poole, M. S., & Stutman, R. K. (2013). *Working through conflict: A communication perspective* (7th ed.). New York: Longman.

Folger, J. P., Poole, M. S., & Stutman, R. K. (2013). *Working through conflict: A communication perspective* (7th ed.). Boston, MA: Allyn & Bacon.

Forbes, G. B. (2001). College students with tattoos and piercings: Motives, family experiences, personality factors, and perception by others. *Psychological Reports, 89,* 774–786.

Freedman, J. (1978). *Happy people: What happiness is, who has it, and why.* New York: Ballantine.

French, J. R. P., Jr., & Raven, B. (1968). The bases of social power. In D. Cartwright & A. Zander (Eds.), *Group dynamics: Research and theory* (3rd ed., pp. 259–269). New York: Harper & Row.

Frentz, T. (1976). A general approach to episodic structure. Paper presented at the Western Speech Association Convention, San Francisco, CA. Cited in Reardon (1987).

Fridlund, A. J., & Russell, J. A. (2006). The functions of facial expressions. What's in a face? In V. Manusov & M. L. Patterson (Eds.), *The Sage handbook of nonverbal communication* (pp. 299–320). Newbury Park, CA: Sage.

Fukushima, S. (2004). *Requests and culture: Politeness in British English and Japanese.* New York: Peter Lang.

Fuller, D. (2004). Electronic manners and netiquette. *Athletic Therapy Today, 9,* 40–41.

Furlow, F. B. (1996). The smell of love. *Psychology Today,* 38–45.

Galvin, K. M., Bylund, C. L., & Brommel, B. J. (2012). *Family communication: Cohesion and change,* 8th ed. Boston: Allyn & Bacon.

Gamble, T. K., & Gamble, M. W. (2003). *The gender communication connection.* Boston: Houghton Mifflin.

Gamson, J. (1998). Publicity traps: Television talk shows and lesbian, gay, bisexual, and transgender visibility. *Sexualities* 1 (February), 11–41.

Gao, G., & Gudykunst, W. B. (1995). Attributional confidence, perceived similarity, and network involvement in Chinese and American romantic relationships. *Communication Quarterly, 43,* 431–445.

Gelfand, M. J., Nishii, L. H., Holcombe, K. M., Dyer, N., Ohbuchi, K., & Fukuno, M. (2001). Cultural influences on cognitive representations of conflict: Interpretations of conflict episodes in the United States and Japan. *Journal of Applied Psychology, 86,* 1059–1074.

Georgas, J., et al. (2001). Functional relationships in the nuclear and extended family: A 16-culture study. *International Journal of Psychology, 36,* 289–300.

Gergen, K. J., Greenberg, M. S., & Willis, R. H. (1980). *Social exchange: Advances in theory and research.* New York: Plenum Press.

German, K., Gronbeck, B., Ehninger, D., & Monroe, A. H. (2013). *Principles of public speaking* (18th ed.). Boston, MA: Free Press.

Gibb, J. (1961). Defensive communication. *Journal of Communication, 11,* 141–148.

Giles, D. C. (2001). Parasocial interaction: A review of the literature and a model for future research. *Media Psychology, 4,* 279–305.

Giles, D. C., & Maltby, J. (2004, March). The role of media figures in adolescent development: Relations between autonomy, attachment, and interest in celebrities. *Personality and Individual Differences, 36,* 813–822.

Giles, H. (2008). Communication accommodation theory. In L. A. Baxter & D. O. Braithwaite (Eds.), *Engaging theories in interpersonal communication: Multiple perspectives* (pp. 161–173). Los Angeles, CA: Sage.

Giles, H., Mulac, A., Bradac, J. J., & Johnson, P. (1987). Speech accommodation theory: The first decade and beyond. In M. L. McLaughlin (Ed.), *Communication yearbook 10* (pp. 13–48). Thousand Oaks, CA: Sage.

Goffman, E. (1967). *Interaction ritual: Essays on face-to-face behavior.* New York: Pantheon.

Goffman, E. (1971). *Relations in public: Microstudies of the public order.* New York: HarperCollins.

Goldin-Meadow, S., Nusbaum, H., Kelly, S. D., & Wagner, S. (2001). Gesture—psychological aspects. *Psychological Science, 12,* 516–522.

Goldsmith, D. J. (2007). Brown and Levinson's politeness theory. In B. B. Whaley & W. Samter (Eds.), *Explaining communication: Contemporary theories and exemplars* (pp. 219–236). Mahwah, NJ: Lawrence Erlbaum.

Goldsmith, D. J., & Fulfs, P. A. (1999). "You just don't have the evidence": An analysis of claims and evidence. In M. E. Roloff (Ed.), *Communication yearbook 22* (pp. 1–49). Thousand Oaks, CA: Sage.

Goleman, D. (1995). *Emotional intelligence.* New York: Bantam.

Gonzalez, A., & Zimbardo, P. G. (1985). Time in perspective. *Psychology Today, 19,* 20–26.

Goodwin, R., & Lee, I. (1994). Taboo topics among Chinese and English friends: A cross-cultural comparison. *Journal of Cross-Cultural Psychology, 25,* 325–338.

Gorden, W. I., & Nevins, R. J. (1993). *We mean business: Building communication competence in business and professions.* New York: HarperCollins.

Gordon, T. (1975). *P.E.T.: Parent effectiveness training.* New York: New American Library.

Gottman, J. M., & Carrere, S. (1994). Why can't men and women get along? Developmental roots and marital inequities. In D. J. Canary and Laura Stafford (Eds.), *Communication and relational maintenance* (pp. 203–229). San Diego, CA: Academic Press.

Gottman, J. M., & Levenson, R. W. (1999). Dysfunctional marital conflict: Women are being unfairly blamed. *Journal of Divorce and Remarriage, 31,* 1–17.

Graham, J. A., & Argyle, M. (1975). The effects of different patterns of gaze combined with different facial expressions on impression formation. *Journal of Movement Studies, 1,* 178–182.

Graham, J. A., Bitti, P. R., & Argyle, M. (1975). A cross-cultural study of the communication of emotion by facial and gestural cues. *Journal of Human Movement Studies, 1,* 68–77.

Greene, J. O. (2003). Models of adult communication skill acquisition: Practice and the course of performance improvement. In J. O. Greene & B. R. Burleson (Eds.), *Handbook of communication and social interaction skills* (pp. 51–92). Mahwah, NJ: Lawrence Erlbaum.

Greengard, S. (2001). Gossip poisons business. HR can stop it. *Workforce, 80,* 24–28.

Greif, E. B. (1980). Sex differences in parent-child conversations. *Women's Studies International Quarterly, 3,* 253–258.

Grice, H. P. (1975). Logic and conversation. In P. Cole & J. L. Morgan (Eds.), *Syntax and semantics,* Vol. 3, *Speech acts* (pp. 41–58). New York: Seminar Press.

Gross, L. (1991). The contested closet: The ethics and politics of outing. *Critical Studies in Mass Communication, 8,* 352–388.

Gross, T., Turner, E., & Cederholm, L. (1987, June). Building teams for global operation. *Management Review,* 32–36.

Grossin, W. (1987). Monochronic time, polychronic time and policies for development. *Studi di Sociologia, 25,* 18–25.

Gu, Y. (1997). Polite phenomena in modern Chinese. *Journal of Pragmatics, 14,* 237–257.

Gudykunst, W. (1993). Toward a theory of effective interpersonal and intergroup communication: An anxiety/uncertainty management (AUM) perspective. In R. L. Wiseman, (Ed.), *Intercultural communication competence.* Thousand Oaks, CA: Sage.

Gudykunst, W. B. (1994). *Bridging differences: Effective intergroup communication* (2nd ed.). Newbury Park, CA: Sage.

Gudykunst, W. B., & Kim, Y. Y. (Eds.). (1992). *Readings on communication with strangers: An approach to intercultural communication.* New York: McGraw-Hill.

Guerrero, L. K., & Andersen, P. A. (1991). The waxing and waning of relational intimacy: Touch as a function of relational stage, gender and touch avoidance. *Journal of Social and Personal Relationships, 8,* 147–165.

Guerrero, L. K., & Andersen, P. A. (1994). Patterns of matching and initiation: Touch behavior and touch avoidance across romantic relationship stages. *Journal of Nonverbal Behavior 18,* 137–153.

Guerrero, L. K., Andersen, P. A., & Afifi, W. A. (2007). *Close encounters: Communication in relationships* (2nd ed.). Thousand Oaks, CA: Sage.

Guerrero, L. K., & Hecht, M. L. (Eds.). (2006). *The nonverbal communication reader: Class and contemporary readings* (3rd ed.). Prospect Heights, IL: Waveland Press.

Haar, B. F., & Krabe, B. (1999). Strategies for resolving interpersonal conflicts in adolescence: A German-Indonesian comparison. *Journal of Cross-Cultural Psychology, 30,* 667–683.

Hackman, M. Z., & Johnson, C. E. (1991). *Leadership: A communication perspective.* Prospect Heights, IL: Waveland Press.

Hafen, S. (2004). Organizational gossip: A revolving door of regulation and resistance, *Southern Communication Journal, 69* (Spring), 223–240.

Haga, Y. (1988). Traits de langage et caractère Japonais. *Cahiers de Sociologie Economique et Culturelle, 9,* 105–109.

Hall, E. T. (1959). *The silent language.* Garden City, NY: Doubleday.

Hall, E. T. (1963). A system for the notation of proxemic behavior. *American Anthropologist, 65,* 1003–1026.

Hall, E. T. (1966). *The hidden dimension.* Garden City, NY: Doubleday.

Hall, E. T. (1976). *Beyond culture.* Garden City, NY: Doubleday.

Hall, E. T. (1983). *The dance of life: The other dimension of time.* New York: Anchor Books/Doubleday.

Hall, E. T., & Hall, M. R. (1987). *Hidden differences: Doing business with the Japanese.* Garden City, NY: Doubleday.

Hall, J. A. (1998). How big are nonverbal sex differences? The case of smiling and sensitivity to nonverbal cues. In D. J. Canary & K. Dindia (Eds.), *Sex differences and similarities in communication: Critical essays and empirical investigations of sex and gender in interaction* (pp. 155–178). Mahwah, NJ: Erlbaum.

Haney, W. (1973). *Communication and organizational behavior: Text and cases* (3rd ed.). Homewood, IL: Irwin.

Hanley, S. J., & Abell, S. C. (2002, Fall). Maslow and relatedness: Creating an interpersonal model of self-actualization. *Journal of Humanistic Psychology, 42,* 37–56.

Hart, F. (1990). The construction of masculinity in men's friendships: Misogyny, heterosexuality, and homophobia. *Resources for Feminist Research, 19,* 60–67.

Harvey, J. C., & Katz, C. (1985). If I'm so successful why do I feel like a fake: The Impostor Phenomenon. New York: St. Martin's Press.

Hastings, S. O. (2000). "Egocasting" in the avoidance of disclosure: An intercultural perspective. In S. Petronio (Ed.), *Balancing the secrets of private disclosures* (pp. 235–248). Mahwah, NJ: Erlbaum.

Hatfield, E., & Rapson, R. L. (1996). *Love and sex: Cross-cultural perspectives.* Boston: Allyn & Bacon.

Hayakawa, S. I., & Hayakawa, A. R. (1989). *Language in thought and action* (5th ed.). New York: Harcourt Brace Jovanovich.

Hays, R. B. (1989). The day-to-day functioning of close versus casual friendships. *Journal of Social and Personal Relationships, 6,* 21–37.

Heap, J. L. (1992). Seeing snubs: An introduction to sequential analysis of classroom interaction. *Journal of Classroom Interaction, 27,* 23–28.

Heasley, J. B., Babbitt, C. E., & Burbach, H. J. (1995a). Gender differences in college students' perceptions of "fighting words." *Sociological Viewpoints, 11* (Fall), 30–40.

Heasley, J. B., Babbitt, C. E., & Burbach, H. J. (1995b). The role of social context in students' anticipatory reaction to a "fighting word." *Sociological Focus 27,* 281–283.

Heath, W. P., Stone, J., Darley, J. M., & Grannemann, B. D. (2003). Yes, I did it, but don't blame me: Perceptions of excuse defenses. *Journal of Psychiatry and Law, 31,* 187–226.

Hecht, M. L. (1978). The conceptualization and measurement of interpersonal communication satisfaction. *Human Communication Research, 4,* 253–264.

Hecht, M. L., Jackson, R. L., & Ribeau, S. (2003). *African American communication: Exploring identify and culture* (2nd ed.). Mahwah, NJ: Erlbaum.

Helgeson, V. S. (2009). *Psychology of gender* (3rd ed.). Upper Saddle River, NJ: Prentice-Hall.

Hendrick, C., & Hendrick, S. (1990). A relationship-specific version of the love attitudes scale. In J. W. Heulip (Ed.), *Handbook of replication research in the behavioral and social sciences* [Special issue]. *Journal of Social Behavior and Personality,* 5, 239–254.

Hendrick, C., Hendrick, S., Foote, F. H., & Slapion-Foote, M. J. (1984). Do men and women love differently? *Journal of Social and Personal Relationships, 1,* 177–195.

Herrick, J. A. (2004). *Argumentation: Understanding and shaping arguments.* State College, PA: Strata.

Hersey, P., Blanchard, K. H., & Johnson, D. E. (2001). *Management of organizational behavior: Leading human resources* (8th ed.). Upper Saddle River, NJ: Prentice-Hall.

Hesketh, B., & Neal, A. (2006). Using "war stories" to train for adaptive performance: Is it better to learn from error or success? *Applied Psychology: An International Review, 55,* 282–302.

Hewitt, J. P. (1998). The myth of self-esteem: Finding happiness and solving problems in America. New York: St. Martin's Press.

Hewitt, J., & Stokes, R. (1975). Disclaimers. *American Sociological Review, 40,* 1–11.

Himle, J. A., Abelson, J. L., & Haghightgou, H. (1999). Effect of alcohol on social phobic anxiety. *American Journal of Psychiatry, 156,* 1237–1243.

Hinduja, S., & Patchin, J. W. (2008). *Bullying: Beyond the schoolyard.* Thousand Oaks, CA: Corwin Press/Sage.

Hocker, J. L., & Wilmot, W. W. (1985). *Interpersonal conflict* (2nd ed.). Dubuque, IA: William C. Brown.

Hocker, J. L., & Wilmot, W. W. (2007). *Interpersonal conflict* (7th ed.). New York: McGraw Hill.

Hofstede, G. (1997). *Cultures and organizations: Software of the mind.* New York: McGraw-Hill.

Hofstede, G., Hofstede, G., & Minkov, M. (2010). *Cultures and organizations: Software of the mind* (3rd ed.). New York, NY: McGraw-Hill.

Hofstrand, D. (2006). Retrieved from http://www.extension.iastate.edu

Hoft, N. L. (1995). *International technical communication: How to export information about high technology.* New York: Wiley.

Holmes, J. (1995). *Women, men and politeness.* New York: Longman.

Hunt, M. O. (2000). Status, religion, and the "belief in a just world": Comparing African Americans, Latinos, and whites. *Social Science Quarterly, 81,* 325–343.

Huston, M., & Schwartz, P. (1995). The relationships of lesbians and gay men. In J. T. Wood, & S. Duck (Eds.), *Under-studied relationships: Off the beaten track* (pp. 89–121).. Thousand Oaks, CA: Sage.

Iizuka, Y. (1993). Regulators in Japanese conversation. *Psychological Reports, 72,* 203–209.

Infante, D. A. (1988). *Arguing constructively.* Prospect Heights, IL: Waveland Press.

Infante, D. A., & Rancer, A. (1982). A conceptualization and measure of argumentativeness. *Journal of Personality Assessment, 46,* 72–80.

Infante, D. A., & Rancer, A. S. (1995). Argumentativeness and verbal aggressiveness: A review of recent theory and research. In B. R. Burleson (Ed.), *Communication yearbook, 19* (pp. 319–351). Thousand Oaks, CA: Sage.

Infante, D. A., Rancer, A. S., & Womack, D. F. (2003). Building communication theory (4th ed.). Prospect Heights, IL: Waveland Press.

Infante, D. A., & Wigley, C. J. (1986). Verbal aggressiveness: An interpersonal model and measure. *Communication Monographs, 53,* 61–69.

Jacobson, D. (1999). Impression formation in cyberspace: Online expectations and offline experiences in text-based virtual communities. *Journal of Computer Mediated Communication, 5.*

Jambor, E., & Elliott, M. (2005, Winter). Self-esteem and coping strategies among deaf students. *Journal of Deaf Studies and Deaf Education, 10,* 63–81.

Jandt, F. E. (2010). *Intercultural communication* (6th ed.). Thousand Oaks, CA: Sage.

Janis, I. (1983). *Victims of group thinking: A psychological study of foreign policy decisions and fiascoes* (2nd ed.). Boston: Houghton Mifflin.

Jaworski, A. (1993). *The power of silence: Social and pragmatic perspectives.* Newbury Park, CA: Sage.

Jecker, J., & Landy, D. (1969). Liking a person as a function of doing him a favor. *Human Relations, 22,* 371–378.

Johannesen, R. L. (2001). *Ethics in human communication* (6th ed.). Prospect Heights, IL: Waveland Press.

Johannesen, R. L., Valde, K. S., & Whedbee, K. E. (2007). *Ethics in human communication* (6th ed.). Prospect Heights, IL: Waveland.

Johansson, W., & Percy, W. A. (1994). *Outing: Shattering the conspiracy of silence.* New York: Harrington Park Press.

Johnson, C. E. (1987). An introduction to powerful and powerless talk in the classroom. *Communication Education, 36,* 167–172.

Johnson, S. D., & Bechler, C. (1998). Examining the relationship between listening effectiveness and leadership emergence: Perceptions, behaviors, and recall. *Small Group Research, 29,* 452–471.

Johnson, S. M., & O'Connor, E. (2002). *The gay baby boom: The psychology of gay parenthood.* New York: New York University Press.

Joinson, A. N. (2001). Self-disclosure in computer-mediated communication: The role of self-awareness and visual anonymity. *European Journal of Social Psychology, 31,* 177–192.

Jones, B. C., DeBruine, L. M., Little, A. C., Burriss, R. P., & Feinberg, D. R. (2007). Social transmission of face preferences among humans. *Proceedings of the Royal Society* 274 (March 22): 899–903.

Jones, C., Berry, L., & Stevens, C. (2007). Synthesized speech intelligibility and persuasion: Speech rate and non-native listeners. *Computer Speech and Language, 21,* 641–651.

Jones, S. (2005). The touch-log record: A behavioral communication measure. In V. Manusov (Ed.), *The sourcebook of nonverbal measures: Going beyond words* (pp. 67–81). Mahwah, NJ: Lawrence Erlbaum.

Jones, S., & Yarbrough, A. E. (1985). A naturalistic study of the meanings of touch. *Communication Monographs, 52,* 19–56.

Jourard, S. M. (1968). *Disclosing man to himself.* New York: Van Nostrand Reinhold.

Jourard, S. M. (1971a). *Self-disclosure.* New York: Wiley.

Jourard, S. M. (1971b). *The transparent self* (Rev. ed.). New York: Van Nostrand Reinhold.

Judge, T. A., & Cable, D. M. (2004). The effect of physical height on workplace success and income. *Journal of Applied Psychology, 89,* 428–441.

Kallos, J. (2005). *Because netiquette matters! Your comprehensive reference guide to e-mail etiquette and proper technology use.* Philadelphia: Xlibris.

Kanner, B. (1989, April 3). Color schemes. *New York Magazine,* pp. 22–23.

Kapoor, S., Hughes, P. C., Baldwin, J. R., & Blue, J. (2003). The relationship of individualism-collectivism and self-construals to communication styles in India and the United States. *International Journal of Intercultural Relations, 27,* 683–700.

Katz, S. (2007). The importance of being beautiful. In *Down to earth sociology: Introductory readings* (14th ed., pp. 341–348). Henslin, J. W. (Ed.). New York: Free Press.

Kelley, H. H., & Thibaut, J. W. (1978). *Interpersonal relations: A theory of interdependence.* New York: Wiley/Interscience.

Kelly, P. K. (1994). *Team decision-making techniques.* Irvine, CA: Richard Chang Associates.

Kennedy, C. W., & Camden, C. T. (1988). A new look at interruptions. *Western Journal of Speech Communication, 47,* 45–58.

Kenrick, D. T., Neuberg, S. L., and Cialdini, R. B. (2007). *Social psychology: Goals in interaction* (4th ed.). Boston: Allyn & Bacon.

Ketcham, H. (1958). *Color planning for business and industry.* New York: Harper.

Keyes, R. (1980). *The height of your life.* New York: Warner.

Kiel, J. M. (1999). Reshaping Maslow's hierarchy of needs to reflect today's education and managerial philosophies. *Journal of Instructional Psychology, 26,* 167–168.

Kindred, J., & Roper, S. L. (2004). Making connections via instant messenger (IM): Student use of IM to maintain personal relationships. *Qualitative Research Reports in Communication, 5,* 48–54.

Kleinfeld, N. R. (1992, October 25). The smell of money. *New York Times* (Section 9), pp. 1, 8.

Kleinke, C. L. (1986). *Meeting and understanding people.* New York: W. H. Freeman.

Knapp, M. L. (1984). *Interpersonal communication and human relationships.* Boston: Allyn & Bacon.

Knapp, M. L. (2008). *Lying and deception in human interaction.* Boston: Pearson.

Knapp, M. L., & Hall, J. (2010). *Nonverbal communication in human interaction* (7th ed.). Thousand Oaks, CA: Wadsworth.

Knapp, M. L., & Vangelisti, A. (2000). *Interpersonal communication and human relationships* (4th ed.). Boston: Allyn & Bacon.

Knapp, M. L., Hart, R. P., Friedrich, G. W., & Shulman, G. M. (1973). The rhetoric of goodbye: Verbal and nonverbal correlates of human leave-taking. *Communication Monographs, 40,* 182–198.

Knobloch, L. K., & Solomon, D. H. (1999). Measuring the sources and content of relational uncertainty. *Communication Studies, 50,* 261–278.

Knobloch, L. K., Haunani, D., & Theiss, J. A. (2006). The role of intimacy in the production and perception of relationship talk within courtship. *Communication Research, 33,* 211–241.

Koerner, A. F., & Fitzpatrick, M. A. (2002, Fall). You never leave your family in a fight: The impact of family of origin of conflict behavior in romantic relationships. *Communication Studies 53,* 234–252.

Komarovsky, M. (1964). *Blue collar marriage.* New York: Random House.

Koppelman, K. L., with Goodhart, R. L. (2005). *Understanding human differences: Multicultural education for a diverse America.* Boston: Allyn & Bacon.

Koscriski, K. (2007). Facial attractiveness: General patterns of facial preferences. *Anthropological Review 70,* 45–79.

Krebs, G. L. (1989). *Organizational communication* (2nd ed.). Boston: Allyn & Bacon.

Krivonos, P. D., & Knapp, M. L. (1975). Initiating communication: What do you say when you say hello? *Central States Speech Journal, 26,* 115–125.

Kurdek, L. A. (1994). Areas of conflict for gay, lesbian, and heterosexual couples: What couples argue about influences relationship satisfaction. *Journal of Marriage and the Family, 56,* 923–934.

Lakoff, R. (1975). *Language and women's place.* New York: Harper & Row.

Lamm, K., & Lamm, K. (1999). *10,000 ideas for term papers, projects, reports, and speeches* (5th ed.). New York: Arco.

Langer, E. J. (1989). *Mindfulness.* Reading, MA: Addison-Wesley.

Lanzetta, J. T., Cartwright-Smith, J., & Kleck, R. E. (1976). Effects of nonverbal dissimulations on emotional experience and autonomic arousal. *Journal of Personality and Social Psychology, 33,* 354–370.

Laroche, C., & deGrace, G. R. (1997). Factors of satisfaction associated with happiness in adults. *Canadian Journal of Counselling, 31,* 275–286.

Larsen, R. J., Kasimatis, M., & Frey, K. (1992). Facilitating the furrowed brow: An unobtrusive test of the facial feedback hypothesis applied to unpleasant affect. *Cognition and Emotion, 6,* 321–338.

Latané, B., Williams, K., & Harkins, S. (2006). Many hands make the light work: The causes and consequences of social loafing. In J. M. Levine & R. L. Moreland (Eds.), *Small groups* (pp. 297–308). New York: Psychology Press.

Lauer, C. S. (2003, February 10). Listen to this. *Modern Healthcare, 33,* 34.

Leathers, D., & Eaves, M. H. (2008). *Successful nonverbal communication: Principles and applications* (4th ed.). Boston: Allyn & Bacon.

Lederer, W. J. (1984). *Creating a good relationship.* New York: Norton.

Lee, A. M., & Lee, E. B. (1972). *The fine art of propaganda.* San Francisco: International Society for General Semantics.

Lee, A. M., & Lee, E. B. (1995). The iconography of propaganda analysis. *ETC: A Review of General Semantics, 52,* 13–17.

Lee, C. M., & Gudykunst, W. B. (2001). Attraction in initial interethnic interactions. *Journal of Intercultural Relations, 25,* 373–387.

Lee, H. O., & Boster, F. J. (1992). Collectivism–individualism in perceptions of speech rate: A cross-cultural comparison. *Journal of Cross-Cultural Psychology, 23,* 377–388.

Lee, J. A. (1976). *The colors of love.* New York: Bantam.

Lee, K., Cameron, C. A., Xu, F., Fu, G., & Board, J. (2011, June). Chinese and Canadian children's evaluations of lying and truth telling: Similarities and differences in the context of pro- and antisocial behaviors. Article published online: doi:10.1111/j.1467-8624.1997.tb01971.x.

Lee, R. L. M. (1984). Malaysian queue culture: An ethnography of urban public behavior. *Southeast Asian Journal of Social Science, 12,* 36–50.

Leech, G. (1983). *Principles of pragmatics.* London: Longman.

Lenhart, A. (2009). Social networks grow: Friending Mom and Dad. Retrieved January 27, 2009, from http://www.Pewresearch.org/.../social-networks

Lenhart, A., Madden, M., Smith, A., Purcell, K., Zickuhr, K., & Rainie, L. (2011). Teens, kindness and cruelty on social network sites. Retrieved fromhttp://pewinterest.org/Reports/2011/Teens-and-social-media.aspx.

Leung, K. (1988, March). Some determinants of conflict avoidance. *Journal of Cross-Cultural Psychology, 19,* 125–136.

Leung, S. A. (2001). Editor's introduction. *Asian Journal of Counseling, 8,* 107–109.

Lever, J. (1995). The 1995 Advocate survey of sexuality and relationships: The women, lesbian sex survey. *The Advocate, 687/688,* 22–30.

Levine, D. (2000). Virtual attraction: What rocks your boat. *Cyber Psychology and Behavior, 3,* 565–573.

Levine, M. (2004, June 1). Tell the doctor all your problems, but keep it to less than a minute. *New York Times,* p. F6.

LeVine, R., & Bartlett, K. (1984). Pace of life, punctuality, and coronary heart disease in six countries. *Journal of Cross-Cultural Psychology, 15,* 233–255.

Lindeman, M., Harakka, T., & Keltikangas-Jarvinen, L. (1997). Age and gender differences in adolescents' reactions to conflict situations: Aggression, prosociality, and withdrawal. *Journal of Youth and Adolescence, 26,* 339–351.

Lu, L., & Shih, J. B. (1997). Sources of happiness: A qualitative approach. *Journal of Social Psychology, 137,* 181–188.

Luft, J. (1984). *Group process: An introduction of group dynamics* (3rd ed.). Palo Alto, CA: Mayfield.

Lukens, J. (1978). Ethnocentric speech. *Ethnic Groups, 2,* 35–53.

Lumsden, G., & Lumsden, D. (1996). *Communicating in groups and teams* (2nd ed.). Belmont, CA: Wadsworth.

Lustig, M. W., & Koester, J. (2013). *Intercultural competence: Interpersonal communication across cultures,* 7th ed. Boston, MA: Allyn & Bacon.

Ma, K. (1996). *The modern Madame Butterfly: Fantasy and reality in Japanese cross-cultural relationships.* Rutland, VT: Charles E. Tuttle.

Mackey, R. A., Diemer, M. A., & O'Brien, B. A. (2000). Psychological intimacy in the lasting relationships of heterosexual and same-gender couples. *Sex Roles, 43,* 201–227.

MacLachlan, J. (1979). What people really think of fast talkers. *Psychology Today, 13,* 113–117.

MacMillan, D., & Lehman, P. (2007, November 15). Social networking with the elite. *Business Week.* Retrieved from www.businessweek.com.

Madon, S., Guyll, M., & Spoth, R. L. (2004). The Self-fulfilling prophecy as an intrafamily dynamic. *Journal of Family Psychology, 18,* 459–469.

Mahaffey, A. L., Bryan, A., & Hutchison, K. E. (2005, March). Using startle eye blink to measure the affective component of antigay bias. *Basic and Applied Social Psychology, 27,* 37–45.

Malandro, L. A., Barker, L., & Barker, D. A. (1989). *Nonverbal communication* (2nd ed.). New York: Random House.

Marano, H. E. (2003). Procrastination: Ten things to know. *Psychology Today.* Retrieved September 12, 2009, from http://www.psychologytoday.com/articles/200308/procrastination-ten-things-know

Marsh, P. (1988). *Eye to eye: How people interact.* Topside, MA: Salem House.

Marshall, L. L., & Rose, P. (1987). Gender, stress and violence in the adult relationships of a sample of college students. *Journal of Social and Personal Relationships, 4,* 299–316.

Martin, G. N. (1998). Human electroencephalographic (EEG) response to olfactory stimulation: Two experiments using the aroma of food. *International Journal of Psychophysiology, 30,* 287–302.

Martin, M. M., & Anderson, C. M. (1993). Psychological and biological differences in touch avoidance. *Communication Research Reports, 10,* 141–147.

Martin, M. M., & Anderson, C. M. (1995). Roommate similarity: Are roommates who are similar in their communication traits more satisfied? *Communication Research Reports, 12,* 46–52.

Martin, M. M., & Rubin, R. B. (1998). Affinity-seeking in initial interactions. *Southern Communication Journal, 63,* 131–143.

Maslow, A. (1970). *Motivation and personality.* New York: HarperCollins.

Matsumoto, D. (1991). Cultural influences on facial expressions of emotion. *Southern Communication Journal, 56,* 128–137.

Matsumoto, D., & Kudoh, T. (1993). American-Japanese cultural differences in attributions of personality based on smiles. *Journal of Nonverbal Behavior, 17,* 231–243.

McBroom, W. H., & Reed, F. W. (1992). Toward a reconceptualization of attitude-behavior consistency. Special Issue. Theoretical advances in social psychology. *Social Psychology Quarterly, 55,* 205–216.

McCarthy, M. (2003, January). Talking back: "Small" interactional response tokens in everyday conversation. *Research on Language and Social Interaction, 36,* 33–63.

McCroskey, J. C. (2006). *An introduction to rhetorical communication* (9th ed.). Boston, MA: Allyn & Bacon.

McCroskey, J. C., & Wheeless, L. (1976). *Introduction to human communication.* Boston: Allyn & Bacon.

McDevitt, M., Kiousis, S., & Wahl-Jorgensen, K. (2003). Spiral of moderation: Opinion expression in computer-mediated discussion. *International Journal of Public Opinion Research, 15,* 454–470.

McDonald, E. J., McCabe, K., Yeh, M., Lau, A., Garland, A., & Hough, R. L. (2005). Cultural affiliation and self-esteem as predictors of internalizing symptoms among Mexican American adolescents. *Journal of Clinical Child and Adolescent Psychology, 34,* 163–171.

McGill, M. E. (1985). *The McGill report on male intimacy.* New York: Harper & Row.

McGinley, S. (2000). Children and lying. Retreived from http://www.ag.arizona.edu/pubs/general/resrpt2000/childrenlying.pdf.

McGlone, M. S., & Giles, H. (2011). Language and interpersonal communication. In M. L. Knapp & J. A. Daly (Eds.), *The Sage handbook of interpersonal communication,* 4th ed. (pp. 201–238). Los Angeles, CA: Sage.

McKerrow, R. E., Gronbeck, B. E., Ehninger, D., & Monroe, A. H. (2000). *Principles and types of speech communication* (14th ed.). Boston: Allyn & Bacon.

McLain, G. (2011). Deadlier than war: Combating military suicides. In Larry Schnoor (Ed.), *Winning Orations* (pp. 21–23). Mankato, MN: Interstate Oratorical Association.

McNamee, S., & Gergen, K. J. (Eds.). (1999). *Relational responsibility: Resources for sustainable dialogue.* Thousand Oaks, CA: Sage.

McNatt, D. B. (2001). Ancient Pygmalion joins contemporary management: A meta-analysis of the result. *Journal of Applied Psychology, 85,* 314–322.

Mealy, M., Stephan, W., & Urritia, C. (2007). The acceptability of lies: A comparison of Ecuadorians and Euro-Americans. *International Journal of Intercultural Relations, 31,* 689–702.

Mehl, M. R., Vazire, S., Ramirez-Esparza, N., Slatcher, R. B., & Pennebaker, J. W. (2007, July). Are women really more talkative than men? *Science 6,* 82.

Merton, R. K. (1957). *Social theory and social structure.* New York: Free Press.

Messick, R. M., & Cook, K. S. (Eds.). (1983). *Equity theory: Psychological and sociological perspectives.* New York: Praeger.

Metts, S., & Planalp, S. (2002). Emotional communication. In M. L. Knapp & J. A. Daly (Eds.), *Handbook of interpersonal communication* (3rd ed., pp. 339–373). Thousand Oaks, CA: Sage.

Midooka, K. (1990). Characteristics of Japanese style communication. *Media Culture and Society, 12,* 47–49.

Miller, G. R. (1978). The current state of theory and research in interpersonal communication. *Human Communication Research, 4,* 164–178.

Miller, G. R. (1990). Interpersonal communication. In G. L. Dahnke & G. W. Clatterbuck (Eds.), *Human communication: Theory and research* (pp. 91–122). Belmont, CA: Wadsworth.

Miller, G. R., & Parks, M. R. (1982). Communication in dissolving relationships. In S. Duck (Ed.), *Personal relationships: Vol. 4. Dissolving personal relationships.* New York: Academic Press.

Miller, L. R. (1997, December). Better ways to think and communicate. *Association Management, 49,* 71–73.

Moghaddam, F. M., Taylor, D. M., & Wright, S. C. (1993). *Social psychology in cross-cultural perspective.* New York: W. H. Freeman.

Molloy, J. (1981). *Molloy's live for success.* New York: Bantam.

Monin, B. (2003, December). The warm glow heuristic: When liking leads to familiarity. *Journal of Personality and Social Psychology, 85,* 1035–1048.

Montagu, A. (1971). *Touching: The human significance of the skin.* New York: Harper & Row.

Moon, D. G. (1996). Concepts of "culture": Implications for intercultural communication research. *Communication Quarterly, 44,* 70–84.

Morreale, S. P., & Pearson, J. C. (2008, April). Why communication education is important: The centrality of the discipline in the 21st century. *Communication Education, 57,* 224–240.

Morrill, C. (1992). Vengeance among executives. *Virginia Review of Sociology, 1,* 51–76.

Morris, D. (1977). *Manwatching: A field guide to human behavior.* New York: Abrams.

Motley, M. T. (1990a). On whether one can(not) not communicate: An examination via traditional communication postulates. *Western Journal of Speech Communication, 54,* 1–20.

Motley, M. T. (1990b). Communication as interaction: A reply to Beach and Bavelas. *Western Journal of Speech Communication, 54,* 613–623.

Mottet, T., & Richmond, V. P. (1998). Verbal approach and avoidance items. *Communication Quarterly, 46,* 25–40.

Mullen, B., Salas, E., & Driskell, J. (1989). Salience, motivation, and artifact as contributions to the relation between participation rate and leadership. *Journal of Experimental Social Psychology, 25,* 545–559.

Mullen, B., Tara, A., Salas, E., & Driskell, J. E. (1994). Group cohesiveness and quality of decision making: An interaction of tests of the groupthink hypothesis. *Small Group Research, 25,* 189–204.

Mullen, C. A. (2005). *Mentorship primer.* New York: Peter Lang.

Myers, K. K., Siebold, D. R., & Park, H. S. (2011). Interpersonal communication in the workplace. In Knapp, M. L., & Daly, J. A. (Eds.), *The Sage handbook of interpersonal communication,* 4th ed. (pp. 527–562). Los Angeles, CA: Sage.

Myers, S. A., & Zhong, M. (2004). Perceived Chinese instructor use of affinity-seeking strategies and Chinese college student motivation. *Journal of Intercultural Communication Research 33* (September–December), 119–130.

Napier, R. W., & Gershenfeld, M. K. (1989). *Groups: Theory and experience* (4th ed.). Boston: Houghton Mifflin.

Neher, W. W., & Sandin, P. (2007). *Communicating ethically.* Boston: Allyn & Bacon.

Neher, W. W., & Sandin, P. (2007). *Communicating ethically.* Boston, MA: Allyn & Bacon.

Nelson, P. E., Pearson, J. C., & Kurylo, A. (2008). Developing an intellectual communication. In S. Morreale & P. Arneson (Eds.), *Getting the most from your graduate education in communication: A student's handbook,*. Washington, DC: National Communication Association.

Neugarten, B. (1979). Time, age, and the life cycle. *American Journal of Psychiatry, 136,* 887–894.

Neuliep, J. W., & Grohskopf, E. L. (2000). Uncertainty reduction and communication satisfaction during initial interaction: An initial test and replication of a new axiom. *Communication Reports, 13,* 67–77.

Neuliep, J. W., Chaudoir, M., & McCroskey, J. C. (2001). A cross-cultural comparison of ethnocentrism among Japanese and United States college students. *Communication Research Reports, 18,* 137–146.

Newport, F. (2007). Black or African American. Retrieved May 5, 2012, from www.gallup.com/poll/28816/Black-African-American.aspx?

Ng, S. H., Loong, C. S. F., He, A. P., Liu, J. H., & Weatherall, A. (2000). Communication correlates of individualism and collectivism: Talk directed at one or more addressees in family conversations. *Journal of Language and Social Psychology, 19,* 26–45.

Noble, B. P. (1994, August 14). The gender wars: Talking peace. *New York Times,* p. 21.

Noelle-Neumann, E. (1973). Return to the concept of powerful mass media. In H. Eguchi & K. Sata (Eds.), *Studies in broadcasting: An international annual of broadcasting science* (pp. 67–112). Tokyo: Nippon Hoso Kyokai.

Noelle-Neumann, E. (1980). Mass media and social change in developed societies. In G. C. Wilhoit & H. de Bock (Eds.), *Mass communication review yearbook* (Vol. 1, pp. 657–678). Thousand Oaks, CA: Sage.

Noelle-Neumann, E. (1991). The theory of public opinion: The concept of the spiral of silence. In J. A. Anderson (Ed.), *Communication yearbook* 14 (pp. 256–287). Thousand Oaks, CA: Sage.

Noller, P. (1993). Gender and emotional communication in marriage: Different cultures or differential social power? [Special issue: Emotional Communication, Culture, and Power.] *Journal of Language and Social Psychology, 12,* 132–152.

Noller, P., & Fitzpatrick, M. A. (1993). *Communication in family relationships.* Englewood Cliffs, NJ: Prentice-Hall.

Northouse, P. G. (1997). *Leadership: Theory and practice.* Thousand Oaks, CA: Sage.

O'Hair, D., Cody, M. J., & McLaughlin, M. L. (1981). Prepared lies, spontaneous lies, Machiavellianism, and nonverbal communication. *Human Communication Research, 7,* 325–339.

Obama, B. (2009). www.obamaspeeches.com.

Osborn, A. (1957). *Applied imagination* (Rev. ed.). New York: Scribner's.

Park, H. S., Levine, T. R., McCornack, S. A., Morrison, K., & Ferrara, M. (2002). How people really detect lies. *Communication Monographs, 69,* 144–157.

Parks, M. R. (2011). Social networks and the life of relationships. In M. L. Knapp & J. A. Daly (Eds.), *The Sage handbook of interpersonal communication* (4th ed., pp. 355–388). Los Angeles, CA: Sage.

Paul, A. M. (2001). Self-help: Shattering the myths. *Psychology Today, 34,* 60ff.

Pearson, J. C. (1993). *Communication in the family* (2nd ed.). Boston: Allyn & Bacon.

Pearson, J. C., & Spitzberg, B. H. (1990). *Interpersonal communication: Concepts, components, and contexts* (2nd ed.). Dubuque, IA: William C. Brown.

Pearson, J. C., West, R., & Turner, L. H. (1995). *Gender and communication* (3rd ed.). Dubuque, IA: William C. Brown.

Pei, M. (1978). *Weasel words: the art of saying what you don't mean.* New York: Harper & Row.

Pelham, A. M., & Kravitz, P. (2008). An exploratory study of the influence of sales training content and salesperson evaluation on salesperson adaptive selling, customer orientation, listening and consulting behaviors. *Journal of Strategic Marketing, 16,* 413–435.

Penfield, J. (Ed.). (1987). *Women and language in transition.* Albany, NY: State University of New York Press.

Pennebacker, J. W. (1991). *Opening up: The healing power of confiding in others.* New York: Morrow.

Peterson, C. C. (1996). The ticking of the social clock: Adults' beliefs about the timing of transition events. *International Journal of Aging and Human Development, 42,* 189–203.

Petty, R. E., & Wegener, D. T. (1998). Attitude change: Multiple roles for persuasion variables. In D. T. Gilbert, S. T. Fiske, & G. Lindzey (Eds.), *The handbook of social psychology* (4th ed., Vol. 1, pp. 323–390). New York: McGraw-Hill.

Pittenger, R. E., Hockett, C. F., & Danehy, J. J. (1960). *The first five minutes.* Ithaca, NY: Paul Martineau.

Place, K. S., & Becker, J. A. (1991). The influence of pragmatic competence on the likeability of grade school children. *Discourse Processes, 14,* 227–241.

Placencia, M. E. (2004). The online disinhibition effect. *Journal of Sociolinguistics, 8,* 215–245.

Plaks, J. E., Grant, H., & Dweck, C. S. (2005). Violations of implicit theories and the sense of prediction and control: Implications for motivated person perception. *Journal of Personality and Social Psychology, 88,* 245–262.

Pornpitakpan, C. (2003). The effect of personality traits and perceived cultural similarity on attraction. *Journal of International Consumer Marketing, 15,* 5–30.

Porter, R. H., & Moore, J. D. (1981). Human kin recognition by olfactory cues. *Physiology and Behavior, 27,* 493–495.

Pratkanis, A., & Aronson, E. (1991). *Age of propaganda: The everyday use and abuse of persuasion.* New York: W. H. Freeman.

Psychometrics (2010). Warring egos, toxic individuals, feeble leadership. Retrieved May 11, 2012 from http://www.psychometrics.com/docs/conflictstudy_09.pdf

Rainie, L., Purcell, K., Goulet, L. S., & Hampton, K. N. (2011). Social networking sites in our lives. Pew Research Center Publications (www.pewresearch.org).

Rancer, A. S. (1998). Argumentativeness. In J. C. McCroskey, J. A. Daly, M. M. Martin, & M. J. Beatty (Eds.), *Communication and Personality: Trait Perspectives* (pp. 149–170). Cresskill, NJ: Hampton Press.

Rancer, A. S., & Avtgis, T. A. (2006). *Argumentative and aggressive communication: Theory, research, and application.* Thousand Oaks, CA: Sage.

Rapsa, R., & Cusack, J. (1990). Psychiatric implications of tattoos. *American Family Physician, 41,* 1481–1486.

Raven, R., Centers, C., & Rodrigues, A. (1975). The bases of conjugal power. In R. E. Cromwell & D. H. Olson (Eds.), *Power in families* (pp. 217–234). New York: Halsted Press.

Read, A. W. (2004). Language revision by deletion of absolutisms. *ETC: A Review of General Semantics, 61,* 456–462.

Reardon, K. K. (1987). *Where minds meet: Interpersonal communication.* Belmont, CA: Wadsworth.

Reisman, J. M. (1979). *Anatomy of friendship.* Lexington, MA: Lewis.

Reisman, J. M. (1981). Adult friendships. In S. Duck & R. Gilmour (Eds.), *Personal relationships. 2: Developing personal relationships* (pp. 205–230). New York: Academic Press.

Richards, I. A. (1951). Communication between men: The meaning of language. In Heinz von Foerster (Ed.), *Cybernetics: Transactions of the Eighth Conference.* NY: Josiah Macy, Jr. Foundation.

Richmond, V. P., & McCroskey, J. C. (1998). *Communication: Apprehension, avoidance, and effectiveness* (5th ed.). Needham Heights, MA: Allyn & Bacon.

Richmond, V. P., Davis, L. M., Saylor, K., & McCroskey, J. C. (1984). Power strategies in organizations: Communication techniques and messages. *Human Communication Research, 11,* 85–108.

Richmond, V. P., McCroskey, J. C., & Hickson, M. L. (2012). *Nonverbal behavior in interpersonal relations* (7th ed.). Boston: Allyn & Bacon.

Richmond, V. P., McCroskey, J. C., & McCroskey, L. L. (2005). *Organizational communication for survival: Making work, work.* Boston: Allyn & Bacon.

Richmond, V. P., Smith, R., Heisel, A., & McCroskey, J. C. (2001). Nonverbal immediacy in the physician/patient relationship. *Communication Research Reports, 18,* 211–216.

Riggio, R. E. (1987). *The charisma quotient.* New York: Dodd, Mead.

Riggio, R. E., & Feldman, R. S. (Eds.). (2005). *Applications of nonverbal communication.* Mahwah, NJ: Lawrence Erlbaum.

Robbins, S. P., & Hunsaker, P. L. (2009). *Training in interpersonal skills* (5th ed.). Boston: Allyn & Bacon.

Rogers, C. (1970). *Carl Rogers on encounter groups.* New York: Harrow Books.

Rogers, C., & Farson, R. (1981). Active listening. In J. DeVito (Ed.), *Communication: Concepts and processes* (3rd ed., pp. 137–147). Upper Saddle River, NJ: Prentice-Hall.

Roisman, G. I., Clausell, E., Holland, A., Fortuna, K., & Elieff, C. (2008). Adult romantic relationships as contexts of human development: A multimethod comparison of same-sex couples with opposite-sex dating, engaged, and married dyads. *Developmental Psychology, 44,* 91–101.

Rokach, A. (1998). The relation of cultural background to the causes of loneliness. *Journal of Social and Clinical Psychology, 17,* 75–88.

Rokach, A., & Brock, H. (1995). The effects of gender, marital status, and the chronicity and immediacy of loneliness. *Journal of Social Behavior and Personality, 19,* 833–848.

Rollman, J. B., Krug, K., & Parente, F. (2000, April). The chat room phenomenon: Reciprocal communication in cyberspace. *Cyber-Psychology and Behavior, 3,* 161–166.

Roloff, M. E., and Chiles, B. W. (2011). Interpersonal conflict: Recent trends. In M. L. Knapp & J. A. Daly (Eds.), *The Sage handbook of interpersonal communication,* 4th ed. (pp. 423–442). Los Angeles, CA: Sage.

Rose, A. J., & Asher, S. R. (1999, January). Children's goals and strategies in response to conflicts within a friendship. *Developmental Psychology, 35,* 69–79.

Rosen, E. (1998, October). Think like a shrink. *Psychology Today,* 54–69.

Rosengren, A., Orth-Gomér, K., Wedel, H., & Wilhelmsen, L. (1993). Stressful life events, social support, and mortality in men born in 1933. *British Medical Journal* (October 1993), 1102. doi:10.1136/bmj.307.6912.1102.

Rosenthal, R. (2002). Covert communication in classrooms, clinics, courtroom, and cubicles. *American Psychologist, 57,* 839–849.

Rosenthal, R. (2002). The Pygmalion effect and its mediating mechanism. In J. Aronson (Ed.), *Improving academic achievement: Impact of psychological factors on education* (pp. 25–36). San Diego, CA: Academic Press.

Rosenthal, R., & Jacobson, L. (1992). *Pygmalion in the classroom: Teacher expectations and pupils' intellectual development* (Rev. ed.). Norwalk, CT: Crown House.

Roth, P. L., Schleifer, L. L. F., & Switzer, F. S. (1995). Nominal group technique—An aid in implementing TQM. *The CPA Journal, 65,* 68–69.

Rubin, R. B., & McHugh, M. (1987). Development of parasocial interaction relationships. *Journal of Broadcasting and Electronic Media, 31,* 279–292.

Rubin, R. B., Fernandez-Collado, C., & Hernandez-Sampieri, R. (1992). A cross-cultural examination of interpersonal communication motives in Mexico and the United States. *International Journal of Intercultural Relations, 16,* 145–157.

Rubin, Z. (1973). *Liking and loving: An invitation to social psychology.* New York: Holt, Rinehart & Winston.

Sagrestano, L. M., Heavey, C. L., & Christensen, A. (2006). Individual differences versus social structural approaches to explaining demand-withdrawal and social influence behaviors. In K. Dindia & D. J. Canary (Eds.), *Sex differences and similarities in communication* (2nd ed., pp. 379–395). Mahwah, NJ: Lawrence Erlbaum.

Samovar, L. A., & Porter, R. E. (Eds.). (1991). *Communication between cultures.* Belmont, CA: Wadsworth.

Samter, W., & Cupach, W. R. (1998). Friendly fire: Topics variations in conflict among same- and cross-sex friends. *Communication Studies, 49,* 121–138.

Sanders, J. A., Wiseman, R. L., & Matz, S. I. (1991). Uncertainty reduction in acquaintance relationships in Ghana and the

United States. In S. Ting-Toomey & F. Korzenny (Eds.), *Cross-cultural interpersonal communication* (pp. 79–98). Thousand Oaks, CA: Sage.

Satir, V. (1983). *Conjoint family therapy* (3rd ed.). Palo Alto, CA: Science and Behavior Books.

Scandura, T. (1992). Mentorship and career mobility: An empirical investigation. *Journal of Organizational Behavior, 13,* 169–174.

Schaap, C., Buunk, B., & Kerkstra, A. (1988). Marital conflict resolution. In P. Noller & M. A. Fitzpatrick (Eds.), *Perspectives on marital interaction* (pp. 203–244). Philadelphia: Multilingual Matters.

Schafer, M., & Crichlow, S. (1996). Antecedents of groupthink. *Journal of Conflict Resolution, 40,* 415–435.

Schegloff, E. (1982). Discourses as an interactional achievement: Some uses of "uh huh" and other things that come between sentences. In Deborah Tannen (Ed.), *Georgetown University roundtable on language and linguistics* (pp. 71–93). Washington, DC: Georgetown University Press.

Scherer, K. R. (1986). Vocal affect expression. *Psychological Bulletin, 99,* 143–165.

Scheufele, D. A., & Moy, P. (2000). Twenty-five years of the spiral of silence: A conceptual review and empirical outlook. *International Journal of Public Opinion Research, 12,* 3–28.

Schnoor, L. G. (Ed.). (1997). *Winning orations of the interstate oratorical association.* Mankato, MN: Interstate Oratorical Association.

Schnoor, L. G. (Ed.). (1999). *Winning orations of the interstate oratorical association.* Mankato, MN: Interstate Oratorical Association.

Schnoor, L. G. (Ed.). (2000). *Winning orations of the interstate oratorical association.* Mankato, MN: Interstate Oratorical Association.

Schultz, B. G. (1996). *Communicating in the small group: Theory and practice* (2nd ed.). New York: HarperCollins.

Schwartz, E. (2005, February 28). Watch what you say. *InfoWorld 27,* 8.

Schwartz, M., & Task Force on Bias-Free Language of the Association of American University Presses. (1995). *Guidelines for bias-free writing.* Bloomington: Indiana University Press.

Scott, M. L., & Lyman, S. M. (1968). Accounts. *American Sociological Review, 33,* 46–62.

Seiter, J. S. (2007, March). Ingratiation and gratuity: The effect of complimenting customers on tipping behavior in restaurants. *Journal of Applied Social Psychology 37,* 478–485.

Seiter, J. S., & Sandry, A. (2003). Pierced for success? The effects of ear and nose piercing on perceptions of job candidates' credibility, attractiveness, and hirability. *Communication Research Reports, 20,* 287–298.

Sethna, B., Barnes, C. C., Brust, M., & Kay, L. (1999). E-mail communications in colleges and universities: Are they private? *Journal of Education for Business, 74,* 347–350.

Severin, W. J. & Tankard, J. W., Jr. (2001). *Communication theories: Origins, methods, and uses in the mass media.* Boston: Allyn & Bacon.

Shaw, M. E., & Gouran, D. S. (1990). Group dynamics and communication. In G. Dahnke & G. W. Clatterbuck (Eds.), *Human communication: Theory and research.* Belmont, CA: Wadsworth.

Shechtman, Z., Hiradin, A., & Zina, S. (2003). The impact of culture on group behavior: A comparison of three ethnic groups. *Journal of Counseling and Development, 81,* 208–216.

Shimanoff, S. (1980). *Communication rules: Theory and research.* Thousand Oaks, CA: Sage.

Shuter, R. (1990). The centrality of culture. *Southern Communication Journal, 55,* 237–249.

Siavelis, R. L., & Lamke, L. K. (1992). Instrumentalness and expressiveness: Predictors of heterosexual relationship satisfaction. *Sex Roles, 26,* 149–159.

Signorile, M. (1993). *Queer in America: Sex, the media, and the closets of power.* New York: Random House.

Singelis, T. M. (1994). The measurement of independent and interdependent self-construals. *Personality and Social Psychology Bulletin, 20,* 580–591.

Singh, N., & Pereira, A. (2005). *The culturally customized web site.* Oxford, England: Elsevier Butterworth-Heinemann.

Slade, M. (1995, February 19). We forgot to write a headline. But it's not our fault. *New York Times,* p. 5.

Smith, A. (2011). Why Americans use social media. Pew Research Center Publications (www.pewresearch.org).

Smith, M. H. (2003). Body adornment: Know the limits. *Nursing Management, 34,* 22–23.

Smith-Lovin, L., & Brody, C. (1989). Interruptions in group discussions: The effects of gender and group composition. *American Sociological Review, 54,* 424–435.

Smoreda, Z., & Licoppe, C. (2000). Gender-specific use of the domestic telephone. *Social Psychology Quarterly, 63,* 238–252.

Snyder, C. R. (1984). Excuses, excuses. *Psychology Today, 18,* 50–55.

Snyder, C. R., Higgins, R. L., & Stucky, R. J. (1983). *Excuses: Masquerades in search of grace.* New York: Wiley.

Snyder, M. (1992). A gender-informed model of couple and family therapy: Relationship enhancement therapy. *Contemporary Family Therapy: An International Journal, 14,* 15–31.

Solomon, G. B., Striegel, D. A., Eliot, J. F., Heon, S. N., et al. (1996). The self-fulfilling prophecy in college basketball: Implications for effective coaching. *Journal of Applied Sport Psychology, 8,* 44–59.

Song, I, LaRose, R., Eastin, M. S., & Lin, C. A. (2004, August). Internet gratifications Internet addiction: On the uses and abuses of new media. *CyberPsychology & Behavior 7,* 384–394.

Sorenson, P. S., Hawkins, K., & Sorenson, R. L. (1995). Gender, psychological type and conflict style preferences. *Management Communication Quarterly, 9,* 115–126.

Spence, C. (2008). Sensing the future. www.aqr.org.uk/inbrief/document.shtml?doc=charles.spence.28-02-2008.fut.

Spitzberg, B. H., & Cupach, W. R. (1989). *Handbook of interpersonal competence research.* New York: Springer.

Spitzberg, B. H., & Cupach, W. R. (2011). Interpersonal skills. In M. L. Knapp & J. A. Daly(Eds.), *The Sage handbook of interpersonal communication,* 4th ed. (pp. 481–526). Los Angeles, CA: Sage.

Spitzberg, B. H., & Hecht, M. L. (1984). A component model of relational competence. *Human Communication Research, 10,* 575–599.

Sprecher, S. (1987). The effects of self-disclosure given and received on affection for an intimate partner and stability of the relationship. *Journal of Social and Personal Relationships, 4*, 115–127.

Sprecher, S., & Metts, S. (1989). Development of the "romantic beliefs scale" and examination of the effects of gender and gender-role orientation. *Journal of Social and Personal Relationships, 6*, 387–411.

Stafford, L. (2008). Social exchange theories. In L. A. Baxter & D. O. Braithwaite (Eds.), *Engaging theories in interpersonal communication: Multiple perspectives* (pp. 377–389). Los Angeles, CA: Sage.

Steil, L. K., Barker, L. L., & Watson, K. W. (1983). *Effective listening: Key to your success*. Reading, MA: Addison-Wesley.

Stein, M. M., & Bowen, M. (2003). Building a customer satisfaction system: Effective listening when the customer speaks. *Journal of Organizational Excellence, 22* (Summer), 23–34.

Stern, L. (2007). *What every student should know about avoiding plagiarism*. Boston: Pearson Education.

Stewart, L. P., Cooper, P. J., & Stewart, A. D., with Friedley, S. A. (2003). *Communication and gender* (4th ed.). Boston: Allyn & Bacon.

Stewart, S. (2006, October). A pilot study of email in an e-mentoring relationship. *Journal of Telemedicine and Telecare 12*, 83–85.

Stratford, J. (1998). Women and men in conversation: A consideration of therapists' interruptions in therapeutic discourse. *Journal of Family Therapy, 20*, 383–394.

Strom, D. (2006, April 5). I.M. generation is changing the way business talks. *New York Times*, p. D4.

Suler, J. (2004). The online disinhibition effect. *CyberPsychology and Behavior, 7*, 321–326.

Sunnafrank, M., & Ramirez, A. (2004). At first sight: Persistent relational effects of get-acquainted conversations. *Journal of Social and Personal Relationships, 21*, 361–379.

Tang, T. L., & Butler, E. A. (1997). Attributions of quality circles' problem-solving failure: Differences among management, supporting staff, and quality circle members. *Public Personnel Management, 26*, 203–225.

Tannen, D. (1990). *You just don't understand: Women and men in conversation*. New York: Morrow.

Tannen, D. (1994a). *Gender and discourse*. New York: Oxford University Press.

Tannen, D. (1994b). *Talking from 9 to 5: How women's and men's conversational styles affect who gets heard, who gets credit, and what gets done at work*. New York: Morrow.

Tannen, D. (2006). *You're wearing that? Understanding mothers and daughters in conversation*. New York: Random House.

Tardiff, T. (2001). Learning to say "no" in Chinese. *Early Education and Development, 12*, 303–323.

Tata, J. (2000). Toward a theoretical framework of intercultural account-giving and account evaluation. *International Journal of Organizational Analysis, 8*, 155–178.

Tersine, R. J., & Riggs, W. E. (1980). The Delphi technique: A long-range planning tool. In S. Ferguson & S. D. Ferguson (Eds.), *Intercom: Readings in organizational communication* (pp. 366–373). Rochelle Park, NJ: Hayden Books.

Thibaut, J. W., & Kelley, H. H. (1986). *The social psychology of groups*. New Brunswick, NJ: Transaction.

Thompson, C. A., & Klopf, D. W. (1991). An analysis of social style among disparate cultures. *Communication Research Reports, 8*, 65–72.

Thompson, C. A., Klopf, D. W., & Ishii, S. (1991). A comparison of social style between Japanese and Americans. *Communication Research Reports, 8*, 165–172.

Thorne, B., Kramarae, C., & Henley, N. (eds.). (1983). *Language, gender and society*. Rowley, MA: Newbury House.

Tierney, P., & Farmer, S. M. (2004). The Pygmalion process and employee creativity. *Journal of Management, 30*, 413–432.

Timmerman, L. J. (2002). Comparing the production of power in language on the basis of sex. In M. Allen & R. W. Preiss (Eds.), *Interpersonal communication research: Advances through meta-analysis* (pp. 73–88). Mahwah, NJ: Lawrence Erlbaum.

Ting-Toomey, S. (1981). Ethnic identity and close friendship in Chinese-American college students. *International Journal of Intercultural Relations, 5*, 383–406.

Ting-Toomey, S. (1985). Toward a theory of conflict and culture. *International and Intercultural Communication Annual, 9*, 71–86.

Tolhuizen, J. H. (1989). Communication strategies for intensifying dating relationships: Identification, use, and structure. *Journal of Social and Personal Relationships, 6*, 413–434.

Trager, G. L. (1958). Paralanguage: A first approximation. *Studies in Linguistics, 13*, 1–12.

Trager, G. L. (1961). The typology of paralanguage. *Anthropological Linguistics, 3*, 17–21.

Trower, P. (1981). Social skill disorder. In S. Duck & R. Gilmour (Eds.), *Personal relationships, Vol. 3* (pp. 97–110). New York: Academic Press.

Tyler, J. J., Feldman, R. S., & Reichert, A. (2006). The price of deceptive behavior: Disliking and lying to people who lie to us. *Journal of Experimental Social Psychology, 42*, 69–77.

Vainiomaki, T. (2004). Silence as a cultural sign. *Semiotica, 150*, 347–361.

Vangelisti, A. L. (2011). Interpersonal processes in romantic relationships. In M. L.Knapp, & J. A. Daly (Eds.), *The Sage handbook of interpersonal communication*, 4th ed. (pp. 597–622). Los Angeles, CA: Sage.

Varma, A., Toh, S. M, Pichler, S. (2006). Ingratiation in job applications: Impact on selection decisions. *Journal of Managerial Psychology, 21*, 200–210.

Veenendall, T. L., & Feinstein, M. C. (1995). *Let's talk about relationships: Cases in study* (2nd ed.). Prospect Heights, IL: Waveland Press.

Velting, D. M. (1999). Personality and negative expectations: Trait structure of the Beck Hopelessness Scale. *Personality and Individual Differences, 26*, 913–921.

Victor, D. (1992). *International business communication*. New York: HarperCollins.

Vonk, R. (2002). Self-serving interpretations of flattery: Why ingratiation works. *Journal of Personality and Social Psychology, 82,* 515–526.

Wallace, K. (1955). An ethical basis of communication. *Communication Education, 4,* 1–9.

Walster, E., Walster, G. W., & Berscheid, E. (1978). *Equity: Theory and research.* Boston: Allyn & Bacon.

Walther, J. B. (2011). Theories of computer-mediated communication and interpersonal relations. In M. L. Knapp & J. A. Daly (Eds.), *The Sage handbook of interpersonal communication,* 4th ed. (pp. 443–480). Los Angeles, CA: Sage.

Watkins, K. (2007). How much time do you spend listening? Retrieved August 9, 2009, from http://articles/webraydian.com/article4793-How_much_time_do_you_spend_listening.html

Watzlawick, P. (1977). *How real is real? Confusion, disinformation, communication: An anecdotal introduction to communications theory.* New York: Vintage.

Watzlawick, P. (1978). *The language of change: Elements of therapeutic communication.* New York: Basic Books.

Watzlawick, P., Beavin, J., & Jackson, D. D. (1967). *Pragmatics of human communication: A study of interactional patterns, pathologies, and paradoxes.* New York: Norton.

Weathers, M. D., Frank, E. M., & Spell, L. A. (2002). Differences in the communication of affect: Members of the same race versus members of a different race. *Journal of Black Psychology, 28,* 66–77.

Weinberg, H. L. (1959). *Levels of knowing and existence.* New York: Harper & Row.

Wennerstrom, A., & Siegel, A. F. (2003). Keeping the floor in multiparty conversation: Intonation, syntax, and pause. *Discourse Processes, 36,* 77–107.

Wert, S. R., & Salovey, P. (2004). Introduction to the special issue on gossip. *Review of General Psychology, 8,* 76–77.

Westwood, R. I., Tang, F. F., & Kirkbride, P. S. (1992). Chinese conflict behavior: Cultural antecedents and behavioral consequences. *Organizational Development Journal, 10,* 13–19.

Wetzel, P. J. (1988). Are "powerless" communication strategies the Japanese norm? *Language in Society, 17,* 555–564.

Wheeless, L. R., & Grotz, J. (1977). The measurement of trust and its relationship to self-disclosure. *Human Communication Research, 3,* 250–257.

Whitty, M., & Gavin, J. (2001). Age/sex/location: Uncovering the social cues in the development of online relationships. *Cyber-Psychology and Behavior, 4,* 623–630.

Wigley, C. J., III. (1998). Verbal aggressiveness. In J. C. McCroskey, J. A. Daly, M. M. Martin, & M. J. Beatty (Eds.), *Communication and personality: Trait perspectives* (pp. 191–214). Cresskill, NJ: Hampton Press.

Wilkins, B. M., & Andersen, P. A. (1991). Gender differences and similarities in management communication: A meta-analysis. *Management Communication Quarterly, 5,* 6–35.

Willis, J., & Todorov, A. (2006). First impressions: Making up your mind after a 100-Ms Exposure to a Face. *Psychological Science, 17,* 592–598.

Windy, D., & Constantinou, D. (2005). *Assertiveness step by step.* London: Sheldon Press.

Winquist, L. A., Mohr, C. D., & Kenny, D. A. (1998). The female positivity effect in the perception of others. *Journal of Research in Personality 32,* 370–388.

Winters, J. (2009). Olfactory communication and mate choice. Retrieved from www.replicatedtypo.wordpress.com/2009/09/01/olfaction

Witcher, S. K. (1999, August 9–15). Chief executives in Asia find listening difficult. *Asian Wall Street Journal Weekly,* p. 11.

Won-Doornink, M. (1985). Self-disclosure and reciprocity in conversation: A cross-national study. *Social Psychology Quarterly, 48,* 97–107.

Won-Doornink, M. (1991). Self-disclosure and reciprocity in South Korean and U.S. male dyads. In S. Ting-Toomey & F. Korzenny (Eds.), *Cross-cultural interpersonal communication* (pp. 116–131). Newbury Park, CA: Sage.

Wood, J. T. (1994). *Gendered lives: Communication, gender, and culture.* Belmont, CA: Wadsworth.

Worthington, D. L., & Fitch-Hauser, M. E. (2012). *Listening: Processes, functions, and competency.* Boston: Allyn & Bacon.

Wrench, J. S., & McCroskey, J. C. (2003). A communibiological examination of ethnocentrism and homophobia. *Communication Research Reports, 20,* 24–33.

Wrench, J. S., McCroskey, J. C., & Richmond, V. P. (2008). *Human communication in everyday life: Explanations and applications.* Boston: Allyn & Bacon.

Yau-fair Ho, D., Chan, S. F., Peng, S., & Ng, A. K. (2001). The dialogical self: Converging East–West constructions. *Culture and Psychology, 7,* 393–408.

Zaleski, Z., Cycon, A., & Kurc, A. (2001). Future time perspective and subjective well-being in adolescent samples. In P. Schmuck & K. M. Sheldon (Eds.), *Life goals and wellbeing: Towards a positive psychology of human striving* (pp. 58–67). Cambridge, MA: Hogrefe & Huber.

Zornoza, A., Ripoll, P., & Peiró, J. M. (2002, October). Conflict management in groups that work in two different communication contexts: Face-to-face and computer-mediated communication. *Small Group Research 33,* 481–508.

Zuckerman, M., Klorman, R., Larrance, D. T., & Spiegel, N. H. (1981). Facial, autonomic, and subjective components of emotion: The facial feedback hypothesis versus the externalizer–internalizer distinction. *Journal of Personality and Social Psychology, 41,* 929–944.

Zunin, L. M., & Zunin, N. B. (1972). *Contact: The first four minutes.* Los Angeles, CA: Nash.

Index

Note: Italicized letters *f* and *t* following page numbers indicate figures and tables, respectively.